616.895 BEU

GUIDELINES FOR THE SYSTEMATIC TREATMENT OF THE DEPRESSED PATIENT

GUIDEBOOKS IN CLINICAL PSYCHOLOGY

Series Editors
Larry E. Beutler
John F. Clarkin

Guidelines for the Systematic Treatment of the Depressed Patient
Larry E. Beutler, John F. Clarkin, and Bruce Bongar

Guidelines FOR THE SYSTEMATIC TREATMENT OF THE DEPRESSED PATIENT

Larry E. Beutler, Ph.D.

John F. Clarkin, Ph.D.

Bruce Bongar, Ph.D.

New York   Oxford

Oxford University Press

2000

Oxford University Press

Oxford   New York
Athens   Auckland   Bangkok   Bogotá   Buenos Aires   Calcutta
Cape Town   Chennai   Dar es Salaam   Delhi   Florence   Hong Kong   Istanbul
Karachi   Kuala Lumpur   Madrid   Melbourne   Mexico City   Mumbai
Nairobi   Paris   São Paulo   Singapore   Taipei   Tokyo   Toronto   Warsaw

and associated companies in
Berlin   Ibadan

Published by Oxford University Press, Inc.
198 Madison Avenue, New York, New York 10016

Oxford is a registered trademark of Oxford University Press

Library of Congress Cataloging-in-Publication Data
Beutler, Larry E.
    Guidelines for the systematic treatment of the
depressed patient / by Larry E. Beutler, John F. Clarkin,
Bruce Bongar.
        p.   cm. — (Guidebooks in clinical psychology)
    Includes bibliographical references and index.
    ISBN 0-19-510530-3
    1. Depression, Mental—Treatment.   I. Clarkin, John F.
II. Bongar, Bruce Michael,   III. Title.   IV. Series.
RC537.B485   1999
616.85'2706—DC21   99-019377

9 8 7 6 5 4 3 2 1

Printed in the United States of America
on acid-free paper

Preface

This is the first in a series of guidebooks designed to provide practitioners with some structure in the development of treatment programs. These guidelines are designed to be different, in several respects, from the ones that have been previously developed. Previous guidelines have been based either on consensus panels of experts or on the opinions of membership groups. Such guidelines are often quite distant from the findings of empirical research and sometimes are very closely tied to the preferred treatments of certain groups. The current guidelines begin with a set of hypotheses that are well founded in available research. These hypotheses are then subjected to an independent validational study. The result are guidelines that are formulated in terms of treatment principles rather than in terms of specific treatment models or theories. The guidelines presented do not advocate one theory of psychopathology or psychotherapy over another but define strategies and considerations that can be incorporated into comprehensive treatment programs that cut across narrow theoretical and parochial concerns.

This first book is devoted to the treatment of depression. Depression is a pervasive condition that cuts across most other mental health conditions. Thus, it is suitable that this first volume be devoted to this problem. The other guidebooks will follow suit in presenting both the results of extant empirical research and new results that provide independent verification of findings from contemporary literature. These guidebooks will cover a variety of topics, including anxiety disorders, drug abuse, alcohol abuse, and treatment of serious mental disorders.

The volumes are organized in order to provide practitioners with both basic and optimal guidelines. Basic guidelines are distinguished from optimal ones by their generality. Basic guidelines can be applied independent of the therapist and can be constructed as routine decisions managed by health care managers. However, optimal guidelines are usually more detailed and may involve the need for special training, monitoring, or oversight of the clinician who applies them.

We are obliged to observe that these guidelines are not intended to be used to restrict treatment to certain forms or procedures. They are suggestions that can be superimposed on many different treatment models and used to guide treatment. When they are used in that way, we believe they will improve treatment efficiency.

This volume is organized into six major parts. We have purposely placed the guidelines themselves in the early part of this book, believing that these are our most important contributions. Later parts are reserved for presenting more controversial issues that may or may not have general appeal. Part I introduces the problems and criteria that form the bases for the development of treatment guidelines. Part II identifies what we consider, from our understanding of extant research, to be the trait-like dimensions that seem most promising for planning and selecting treatments, and then presents suggestions and guidelines for the measurement and assessment of these dimensions.

Part III presents the basic and optimal treatment guidelines that evolved from our efforts to cross-validate the dimensions revealed in our literature review. The material contained in Parts IV, V, and VI is offered in the form of background material and is subject to debate and controversy. These parts present general issues related to the nature of depression, issues in treatment research, the nature of contemporary treatments, and implications for education and training. This material is important, however, as background for both understanding the treatment guidelines that we suggest and using this volume as a textbook on treatment of non-bipolar depressive disorders.

Many people have contributed to this volume and to the thoughts that we have expressed here. First and foremost, we want to thank Oxford University Press and Joan Bossert for the commitment and support that allowed this series to see the light of day. Much of the research that supported this work was also supported by New Standards Inc., under the presidential leadership of Rick Kaplan, and we thank them for their contributions as well. The task of writing and reviewing literature for this book was partially supported by grant no. DA-09394 from the National Institute for Drug Abuse. Many students have assisted in the literature reviews, in summarizing and organizing material, and in helping us clarify our thoughts. Some of these students have been acknowledged as coauthors of various chapters or acknowledged in other ways, but the contributions of still others have been more invisible. We thank them, nonetheless, and appreciate the opportunity that they have afforded us to express and organize our ideas.

We also want to thank our board of consultants, whose members have provided feedback and assistance in the completion of this book. These individuals include James Coyne, Kenneth I. Howard, and Edward Watkins.

Santa Barbara   L. E. B.
White Plains   J. F. C.
Palo Alto   B. B.
December 1998

Contents

PART I

Introduction to Treatment Guidelines

1 _Essentials of Treatment Guidelines_

With the advent of managed health care have come guidelines by which to standardize and direct treatment. Although a recent development in mental health, guidelines have been available in most areas of medical treatment for many years. In this introductory chapter, we present some of the definitions and uses of treatment guidelines and outline our own intentions in writing this set of guidelines for systematic treatment selection.

General treatment guidelines are designed to assist physicians, mental health professionals, and other primary-care providers in the diagnosis and treatment of behavioral disorders (Rush et al., 1993a). In the area of mood disorders, guidelines are intended to aid in the diagnosis and treatment of major depression and are based on the assumption that mental health professionals who use the guidelines will be aware of emerging scientific knowledge and new research findings and will use this information to modify and refine the guidelines to make them applicable to individual cases. These assumptions are exemplified in the American Psychiatric Association's (1993) consensual guidelines for the treatment of major depressive disorder. This document states that the articulated principles are intended to be used as guidelines only, not as dictums, and urges that cases be evaluated on an individual basis, with clinicians making changes that take into consideration all available clinical data.

This admonition captures the strengths and identifies the problems of treatment guidelines. They offer the hope of improving the quality and consistency of treatment given to patients, but their focus has traditionally been too broad to be responsive to the needs of individual patients. At the same time, they are easily adopted by managed-care systems as standards of care and by attorneys who use them to lead expert witnesses to identify lists of clinician behaviors that ostensibly have been accepted by peers and that can then be used to prove a defendant innocent or guilty of negligence or malpractice in individual cases (Frances, Kahn, Carpenter, Ross, & Docherty, 1996). The emergence of practice guidelines for mental health professionals must be understood within the broader context of guidelines for general medical practice, taking into account the well-known fact that a depressed individual within the community is most likely to be seen initially by a nonpsychiatrically trained primary-care physician (Coyne & Schwenk, 1997; Coyne, personal communication, September 1998).

Another part of the problem resides in the fact that the way guidelines are presented is inconsistent. Some guidelines are presented as specific and rigid rules that are easily interpreted as being standards of care, while others are overly cautious, offering only a general list of suggestions whose non-specificity provides little assistance to the practitioner. Another and more hidden aspect of the problem is that guidelines are being developed by an increasing variety of groups, each with different agendas, philosophies, and objectives. These groups include national organizations, such as the American Psychiatric Association, that seek to make practitioners aware of the state of knowledge regarding clinical care, and independent organizations or individual researchers whose agendas sometimes include efforts simply to legitimize their own unvalidated programs by proclaiming the nature of their services to be beyond the purview of scientific inquiry.

While it is an unjustified leap of logic to transform what are by necessity generalizations based on mean tendencies into dictates or standards by which the treatment of an individual patient is judged, it is equally problematic to assert the need for individuality of treatment to a degree that ignores nomethetic evidence of what works with whom. There is a natural tension between the nomethetic bases of knowledge and the idiographic nature of treatment. These competing forces invariably introduce a logical paradox into the nature and use of guidelines that persuasively allows the valid objective of improving the consistency of service provided to be translated into efforts to establish enforceable standards of care. The fact that all guidelines claim some access to a body of knowledge that is not readily available to practitioners renders impotent the disclaimer that is intended to limit the liability associated with their use as standards of care.

The fact that different guidelines often derive from different assumptions about what constitutes legitimate evidence of treatment effectiveness seriously limits the viability of guidelines as either standards of care or guide rules for practice. Some guidelines are advanced purely on the basis of the clinical experience of one group or another; others arise from majority opinions or consensual agreement among panels of experts (so-called consensus panels); still others are developed by one or another specialist group to advance the agenda of its members. These approaches vary in how they treat scientific evidence, some are even inconsistent with the state of scientific knowledge, and most rest their claims to validity on their popularity among one interest group or another.

The most often touted guidelines were developed to reflect the majority opinions of those who practice in a particular specialty. For example, the National Institute of Mental Health (NIMH, 1985) used a consensus conference format to construct guidelines that reflected the usual and best-rationalized practices of a panel of clinical practitioners. A second approach to developing guidelines is the use of a panel made up of scholarly experts in the field. This approach was used in the construction of the *Diagnostic and Statistical Manual of Mental Disorders, 4th Edition* (American Psychiatric Association, 1994). While the clinical panel may be insensitive to concerns with empirical validity, the scholar-expert panel may remain insensitive to issues of clinical utility. Recently, another approach has been utilized at the Delphi/RAND Corporation by Frances and colleagues (1996). However, these guidelines, too, are subject to error because they focus on the use of discrete interventions for specific psychiatric disorders such as schizophrenia, bipolar disorder, and major Depression. Researchers who have attempted to create guidelines to deal with complicated, multidimensional problem such as suicide and comorbidity have typically been criticized because such guidelines are deemed to be clinically unrepresentative and insensitive.

In truth, validity and clinical utility, as approaches to developing guidelines, are not equally ensured by these several foundational methods of defining the status of knowledge. Since it is likely and perhaps inevitable that guidelines will be used in ways for which they were not intended, it is imperative that their limitations be specified and that they themselves be developed in ways that ensure maximal utility and scientific validity. Thus, as we embark on the task of providing still another set of guidelines, it is imperative to define the considerations that underwrite the particular method that we have selected and to define the limits and limitations of this effort.

HISTORICAL DEVELOPMENT OF GUIDELINES AND STANDARDS OF CARE

The American Psychiatric Association and the Agency for Health Care and Policy Research (AHCPR) published practice guidelines for the diagnosis and treatment of Major Depression in 1993 (American Psychiatric Association, 1993; Rush et al., 1993a). These two groups created compatible sets of guidelines that made diagnosis and treatment recommendations that were based on reviews of the literature and clinical judgment (New Federal Guidelines, 1993). The American Psychiatric Association's guidelines were developed by a committee of medical doctors and the AHCPR guidelines were developed by a committee composed of a number of medical doctors, one nurse, one social worker, one psychologist, and one consumer representative (American Psychiatric Association, 1993; Rush et al., 1993a, 1993b).

The AHCPR, functioning within the U.S. Department of Health and Human Services, under Public Law 101-239, was charged with establishing guidelines for promoting the goal of "enhancing quality, appropriateness and effectiveness of health care services" in the diagnosis and treatment of depression (Rush et al., 1993a, p. I). Depression was chosen as the first psychiatric guideline to be published because of its high prevalence rates, the success of available treatments at the time, and the high cost of the illness to society. Significantly, the AHCPR guidelines were intended for primary-care physicians and other nonpsychiatric practitioners (general practitioners, family practitioners, internists, nurse practitioners, registered nurses, mental health nurse specialists, physicians assistants) who provide services for depressed patients in nonpsychiatric settings. Using this framework, primary-care physicians would diagnose and provide treatment, while psychologists would function as case consultants on a relatively few complex cases (Schulberg & Rush, 1994).

The goals of each of these guidelines are intended for two diverse groups of professionals: generalists, such as primary-care providers, and specialists, such as psychiatrists.

A review analysis by a team of psychologists (Munoz, Hollon, McGrath, Rehm, & VandenBos, 1994) found the AHCPR literature review to be the most accurate available. However, the AHCPR committee implemented separate guidelines that do not adequately reflect the literature on the efficacy of psychotherapy and that overstate the efficacy of pharmacotherapy for treating less severe depressions (Munoz et al., 1994).

Some of the inconsistencies, ambiguities, and problems with treatment guidelines (e.g., Nathan, 1998) can be understood within the context of the history of guidelines in modern mental health treatment. Many, citing historical precedent, have strongly negative opinions about the advisability of developing and employing specific treatment guidelines within a field that is defined by the current state of knowledge about mental health (e.g., Garfield, 1998; Persons & Silberschatz, 1998).

These concerns are well taken, given that there has been such a disparity between the intended and the actual use of guidelines in the health care and legal sectors. For example, while the American Psychiatric Association's guidelines state that they are "not intended to be construed as representing a standard of medical care" (American Psychiatric Association, 1993, p. v), they have been seen by some not only as a standard but as the gold standard for defining the efficacy of treatment in the field. Controversy over the guideline's generalized validity arose when it became apparent that some groups intended to use them to guide decisions in malpractice cases (see Pearlman, 1994). Accordingly, the American Psychiatric Association work group that had developed the guidelines quickly pointed out that it had never been their intention to have the guidelines used in this way (Karasu, Merriam, Glassman, Gelenberg, & Kupfer, 1994).

Pearlman (1994) has addressed the disparity between intention and practice, arguing that guidelines do not have the flexibility to respond to variability among patients. This is the same argument constructed against using the guidelines as a gold standard but does nothing to address how the professions might avoid this tendency.

The AHCPR's guidelines are similar to those of the American Psychiatric Association and have similarly been viewed as a standard by which one can judge the quality of care received by a patient. However, like the other guidelines, they were not intended to be mandatory requirements for practitioners (Rush et al., 1993, p. 486). The panel that developed the AHCPR guidelines recognized the possible negative impact of clinical guidelines and tried (unsuccessfully) to avoid the problem by citing and predicting the tendency to place political and economic agendas above the needs of patients.

Attorneys also inappropriately use the guidelines as standards of care. They sometimes emphasize the concrete application of guidelines without concern for individual patient differences or provide little protection against misinterpretations of guidelines by inexperienced or untrained individuals who use them in ways that cause the quality of care to decrease as a result of cost-containment efforts (Rush, 1993).

Objections to Guidelines among Mental Health Professionals

When the American Psychiatric Association and the Agency for Health Care Policy Research guidelines were published in 1993, psychologists became concerned about their role as envisioned in the medically influenced treatment guidelines (Rush et al., 1993). Psychologists and the American Psychological Association were asked to endorse guidelines that embodied philosophies and conclusions with which they did not agree. For example, the guidelines advocated pharmacotherapy as a first-line treatment, a position that American psychology did not accept and that threatened to devalue the services provided by psychological practitioners in the health-care enterprise.

The American Psychological Association voiced its opposition to the new federal guidelines and refused to endorse them (Moses-Zirkes, 1993). The American Psychological Association expressed similar reservations regarding the AHCPR's positive stance toward the use of electroconvulsive therapy (ECT) and questioned the assumed generalizability of these treatments to primary-care settings (Rush et al., 1993). Wiggins (1992), a former president of the American Psychological Association, and Newman (1993), the organization's acting executive director for practice, urged psychologists to take an active role in response to the American Psychiatric Association and the AHCPR guidelines. Some observers suggested that psychologists begin developing their own guidelines, a step that was considered necessary to represent the philosophies that would preserve the autonomy of psychologists and to protect the mental health profession from overly rigid guidelines. In all of these developments, however, it is apparent that philosophy and guild issues may have played as much of a role as science in the determination of guidelines.

That is not to say that the guidelines were not valuable or useful, however. Munoz, Hollon, McGrath, Rehm, and VandenBos (1994) reviewed the meta-analytic literature review (Rush et al., 1993) that was used by the AHCPR in formulating federal guidelines. They found it to be of the highest quality available. Munoz et al. (1994, p. 43) strongly supported many of the conclusions and recommendations of the AHCPR (Rush et al., 1993), including:

1. The Depression Guideline Panel's (DGP) call for better detection of depression by primary-care personnel
2. The DGP's conclusion that virtually all patients will respond to some form of treatment
3. The recommendation that, because there are multiple effective treatments for depression, including pharmacotherapy and psychotherapy, no patient be kept for too long on an ineffective treatment
4. The recommendation that, because multiple agents appear to have comparable efficacy, medication selection be based largely on side-effect profiles when drugs are indicated
5. The clear statement that at least once-a-week-visits on a regular basis are recommended for formal psychotherapy
6. The recommendation that patients who are psychotic, seriously suicidal, or otherwise in need of hospitalization be referred to a mental health specialist
7. The suggestion that third-party coverage for the diagnosis and treatment of depression be equal to that available for other medical disorders.

However, concerns emerged regarding the method by which the literature review was translated and interpreted to create guidelines for primary-care providers and patients. For example, Munoz et al. (1994) concluded that the AHCPR (Rush et al., 1993) guidelines overstated the efficacy of pharmacotherapy for less severe depressions and understated the efficacy of psychotherapy for more severe depressions. They expressed other concerns about the contents of the guidelines, including their deemphasis of the difficulty of detection and diagnosis of depression in primary care; the lack of attention given in the literature review to the low generalizability of clinical trials to a primary-care population; the biomedical biases evident in the brief educational pamphlets for patients and clinicians; the neglect of significant ethnic, gender, and age differences in the diagnosis and treatment of depression; and the failure to mention prevention as a treatment with patients at risk.

Because of these omissions and biases, it was feared that primary-care physicians would become the preferred source of treatment without empirical validation of this treatment assumption and that pharmacotherapy would be relied on as a first-line treatment without patients and physicians knowing all of the available treatment options. In addition, some feared that primary-care providers insufficiently trained in the diagnosis and treatment of mental disorders might not adequately monitor pharmacotherapy and that as a result patients might be maintained on medication for long periods, which might not be in their best interest (Munoz et al., 1994).

Other responses were even less optimistic. Some have claimed that Munoz and colleagues' (1994) examination of the AHCPR's (Rush et al., 1993) guidelines gave too little attention to the underrepresentation of psychotherapy research (Antonuccio, 1995; Karon & Teixeira, 1995). It was suggested that the acceptance of antidepressant medication by Munoz, and especially by the guidelines themselves, was mainly a result of marketing by pharmaceutical companies and that the conclusions did not represent the state of science. Critics argued that psychologists needed to be aggressive in highlighting the effectiveness of psychotherapy in treating depression (Antonuccio, 1995). Katon et al. (1992) also looked at the impact of a collaborative management protocol and its effect on adherence to treatment, patient satisfaction, and the reduction of depressive symptomatology. Katon et al. (1995) found that the intervention improved outcome for only one group of patients with major depressive disorder (those patients who required an adjustment of medication regimens); their secondary analysis of patients who received either "adequate" or "inadequate" antidepressant treatments found similar rates of improvements for both groups of patients, measured either by the use of symptom scales or by the proportion of patients meeting the diagnostic criteria at four-month follow-up (Simon et al., 1995).

Coyne and Schwenk (1997) have been especially concerned with the over-generalized research behind the AHCPR (Rush et al., 1993) guidelines and by Munoz et al.'s application of the literature to primary-care settings. Pointing to research indicating that there is widespread underdiagnosis and mismanagement of depression by primary-care physicians, Coyne and Schwenk (1997) indicated a need for surveys of psychologists' attitudes and practices to ensure that many patients do not receive unneeded long-term therapy without considering the option of psychotropic medications.

Stance of the Legal System toward Guidelines

It is likely that part of the reason for the confounding of guidelines and standards of care is the excessive number of goals embodied in these guidelines. Treatment guidelines were developed to assist mental health practitioners in diagnosis and treatment of patients, to improve the quality of health care, to reduce unnecessary health practices, to help patients become more informed about health care, to reduce costs, and to provide feedback to researchers (Clinton, McCormick, and Besteman, 1994). With a mission so broad, it is no wonder that they also took on the burden of serving as a standard of care.

However, standards of care have come to have legal implications that go beyond the role of guidelines as a map or list of suggestions. In fact, a variety of judicial rulings have reinforced the view that guidelines establish standards of care. Standards of care are applicable primarily to malpractice actions in which the care provided by a defendant is compared to that offered by other reasonable and prudent practitioners with the same level of training to establish whether misconduct occurred. This is not a burden that can be assumed by any guideline, given the current and still uncertain state of research.

Yet, there is a need for some standard within the legal community by which to assess the degree to which an individual practitioner may have engaged in malpractice. The rub, of course, is that treatment recommendations and preferences vary widely. Thus, the advent of guidelines has appeared to offer a significant way for nonclinicians to define what constitutes good practice. Few in the court and legal system would question the fact that, at present, psychiatric diagnosis and treatment are imprecise arts. Considering that there are more than 450 schools of psychotherapy and that the number is constantly increasing (Simon, 1987), there is little doubt that most mental health professionals contend with a considerable lack of consensus. Within the mental health fields, disagreements abound regarding appropriate theoretical models, problem etiologies, appropriate diagnostic criteria and terminologies, treatment indications, goals, and modalities, curative factors in treatment, and assessment of treatment progress and outcome (Klerman, 1990; Malcolm, 1986; Simon, 1987; Stone, 1990). Many believe that this diversity is healthy and even necessary for continued advancement of the field (King, 1987; Robertson, 1988; Simon, 1987; Stone, 1990). While such variety may foster the evolution of the field and the development of new diagnostic and treatment modalities (Harris, 1973), progress is not without a cost. And, in this case, the cost often has legal implications.

Some authorities have argued for the creation of national standards of treatment (King, 1986; Klerman, 1983, 1990). Such standards would be designed to protect patients from dangerous, ineffective, and abusive treatments (Klerman, 1983, 1990). These standards could also enhance the reputation of the mental health profession in a variety of ways (Klerman, 1983, 1990). For example, clear standards would improve treatment consistency and quality, while demystifying the profession for the general public (Klerman, 1983). Adjudication of malpractice would be greatly simplified, since the courts would be provided with an instrument for straightforward, cost-effective, legal decision making. National standards of treatment could be available to all legal and mental health training programs, allowing for more efficient education and general agreement over malpractice standards, and would make student assessment and licensing more reliable and efficient.

While various attempts have been made by a number of professional organizations to establish diagnostic and treatment standards, none of these efforts has enjoyed widespread acceptance within the mental health profession or the courts (see Klerman, 1983, 1990). As a result, the courts have taken on the task of setting these standards, a task that involves two primary challenges. The standard must be applicable to approaches as disparate as psychoanalysis, behaviorism, and psychopharmacology, while balancing the right of practitioners to develop new treatments with the rights of patients to receive responsible care. The courts have accepted the fact that mental health experts often disagree, and they have responded by developing the respectable minority rule (Hampton, 1984; *Hood v. Phillips*, 1976; Keeton et al., 1984; King, 1987; Klerman, 1990; *Leach v. Braillar*, 1967; Robertson, 1988; Simon, 1987; Stone, 1990).

The Respectable Minority Rule

The respectable minority rule holds that where there are disputes based on differences among theoretical approaches and methods of practice that cannot be settled by the law, the clinician is entitled to be judged according to the school he or she professes to follow (Keeton et al., 1984). This "school" must be "one with definite principles, and it must be the line of thought of a 'respectable minority' of the profession" (p. 187). However, at this time, the courts have not adequately defined what constitutes a respectable minority (King, 1986). For example, in *Hood v. Phillips* (1976), a malpractice action against a surgeon was not upheld even though his highly controversial procedure was used by only six other physicians in the world (Malcolm, 1986). The court accepted the respectable minority defense "despite the fact that the medical community considered the procedure (1) to be below minimum standards of medical treatment of emphysema; (2) to have no medical justification; (3) to be useless at best and potentially quite dangerous" (p. 60).

In *Leach v. Braillar* (1967), the court upheld a malpractice action against a physician because his procedure varied from that of the school of sixty-five physicians he claimed to follow. Had he followed the school's procedure properly, he could have successfully defended himself through the respectable minority rule.

Although no explicit definitions of this rule have been offered, in general, the courts have considered several factors when determining the respectable minority support of a therapeutic approach (Robertson, 1988): First, is there a clearly identifiable professional association that follows the approach? Second, are there specific standards of practice associated with the approach? Third, are there articulated ethical guidelines that are followed by the practitioners of the approach?

Osheroff Case

Under the rather loose standards discussed previously, it appears that almost any "school" of therapy might well meet the respectable minority test unless it espouses techniques that blatantly harm patients (Malcolm, 1986). The Osheroff lawsuit provides an enlightening example of the specific limitations of this rule. This case has been described in detail elsewhere (see Klerman, 1990; Malcolm, 1986; Stone, 1990). To summarize, Raphael Osheroff, a physician, sought inpatient treatment for depression at the Chestnut Lodge, a highly respected, psychoanalytically oriented private psychiatric hospital. He was diagnosed as suffering "primarily from major narcissistic injuries due to an underlying narcissistic personality disorder and secondarily from a manic-depressive illness, depressed type" (Malcolm, 1986, p. 16). Long-term psychoanalytic psychotherapy was prescribed, but, after seven months, Dr. Osheroff showed signs of psychotic deterioration (Stone, 1990). At the encouragement of his mother and his stepfather, the patient elected to terminate treatment at the Chestnut Lodge and to transfer to Silver Hill, another private psychiatric hospital. Upon admittance, he was diagnosed as suffering primarily from a psychotic depressive reaction, agitated type, and immediately prescribed psychotropic medication and supportive psychotherapy (Malcolm, 1986). According to the staff at Silver Hill, the patient showed improvement after only two weeks, and, after three months, he discharged himself (Malcolm, 1986).

Dr. Osheroff instituted a malpractice suit against Chestnut Lodge, alleging that the Lodge negligently failed to diagnose and treat the biological depression and failed to obtain informed consent by neglecting to disclose and discuss alternative treatments and the costs and benefits of each with the patient (Malcolm, 1986).

While space precludes a lengthy discussion of the differing diagnostic and treatment opinions offered by each hospital, it is important to note that the defense based its case primarily on the respectable minority rule (Klerman, 1990; Malcolm, 1986). Considering the application of previous court definitions of this rule, it would be difficult to argue that psychoanalytically based diagnosis and treatment of depression would not be supported by a respectable minority of the profession (Malcolm, 1986; Stone, 1990).

While the Osheroff case was settled out of court and thus set no legal precedent, a number of legal and mental health authorities have discussed the ramifications of this case at length and have made specific suggestions regarding the future of the respectable minority rule (see Klerman, 1990; Malcolm, 1986; Stone, 1990). On one side are those who believe that the rule must remain in place in order to protect innovative therapies from being litigated out of existence, an outcome that would effectively quash the search for new, more effective treatments (Malcolm, 1986; Simon, 1987; Stone, 1990). These authorities assert that if "biological psychiatrists had gone to court or to any other official authority to impose efficacious dose standards on all their colleagues, it would have been a disaster for our patients and for biological psychiatry" (Stone, 1990, p. 424). They maintain that efficacy research on treatment approaches is of varying quality and that the leap from research to clinical practice often produces unexpected results (Stone, 1990).

On the other side are those who argue that the respectable minority rule should no longer hold if "there is a body of evidence supporting a particular treatment and if there is agreement within the profession that this is the proper treatment of a given condition" (Klerman, 1990, p. 415). This view holds that patients have a right to effective treatment (ie., treatment for which there is substantial evidence derived from controlled, clinical trials) (Klerman, 1983, 1990). But, the question remains how best to determine at what point agreement among professionals is sufficient to constitute a consensus on which one treatment can serve as a useful standard of care. Of course, there is also still an uncertain link between the popularity of a course of treatment and its effectiveness.

The importance of these questions can be illustrated with regard to the respectable minority rule. They reduce to a concern with whether this rule clearly protects the patient's interests and safety and whether the rule allows broad but enforceable standards for the profession, while still allowing for the development of new and innovative therapies.

Let us imagine for a moment that the courts were to put forth exacting definitions of "respectable" and "minority" and that practitioners were held to this standard. One might imagine that a "minority" could constitute at least 10 percent of the profession and that "respectable" might apply to those schools that have articulated ethical standards, formed professional associations, and specified treatment standards (Robertson, 1988). The dynamic, ever-changing nature of the field would make it very difficult for practitioners or the courts to ascertain whether a given treatment approach was supported by 10 percent of the profession. What would be the consequences if the percentage of professional support for a treatment dropped below 10 percent, either after a practitioner had initiated treatment or at some time after the treatment had been terminated and before the lawsuit was filed? Finally, innovative therapies are often the product of the work of one or a handful of charismatic individuals. If minorities of one were not allowed, many of the most important clinicians in the field could have been found guilty of malpractice under the conditions we have posited.

It is apparent that clients would not be protected even if the definition of "minority" were set at 49 percent of the profession, since even treatments followed by majorities can harm certain patients (Malcolm, 1986). Also, nothing in the significant minority doctrine enlists patient participation in the decision-making process, since the delineation of appropriate treatment is still left to the profession and to the courts.

However, there are also difficulties with the solutions posed by those who are in favor of eliminating the respectable minority rule altogether and establishing scientifically validated standards of treatment. First, scientific validation is often threatened by the varying quality of efficacy studies and the inconsistent generalizability of experimental results to the clinical setting (Stone, 1990). Also, it is important to note that a strict empirical standard would place practical limitations on the use or development of innovative treatments (Hampton, 1984; Stone, 1990).

Other issues that a scientifically based standard must address are these: (1) How much scientific support is sufficient for a treatment approach to meet a scientifically based standard, and is "scientific support" reliably quantifiable? (2) How is a standard set when efficacy studies provide equivocal support for a treatment? (3) Who will decide which methodologies are "scientific" and appropriate for consideration? (4) Would practitioners have to conduct a thorough, scientific literature review before initiating a treatment, or would this information be available elsewhere? If the former, who would pay for the time and effort this review would require? If the latter, who would provide this information, and how would it be kept up to date? (5) Some treatments may be effective for certain populations and not for others. Must a scientific standard include an exhaustive description of the population to be treated by each approach? (6) How would a clinician proceed if the scientific evidence supported a treatment or treatments that did not work with a particular patient? We will return to some of these questions from time to time throughout this discussion of guidelines.

In an ideal world, the questions posed would be easy to answer, and mental health practitioners and the courts would be provided with a scientifically supported "cookbook" of treatment options. A clinician would simply look up the type of person being treated, cross-reference that information with the presenting complaint, and find the proper specific treatment plan(s). Malpractice would be avoided by following the cookbook. However, in this fictional world, innovation might well be considered a form of malpractice.

Malpractice, Standards of Care, and the Law

The term "standards of care" is of legal origin and falls under the rubric of torts and malpractice. A tort implies that one person has caused harm to another. Malpractice is a subclassification of a tort action in which it is alleged that a civil wrong has been committed by one person that has caused harm to a second person (Black, 1990; Bongar, 1991).

Thus, malpractice is a tort defined as any misconduct, negligence, or lack of skill on the part of a professional that results in harm to a patient or client (Black, 1990; Bongar, 1991). In mental health malpractice cases, negligence is commonly alleged. Negligence is defined as the failure to use the same amount of care that a "reasonably prudent and careful" person would use under the same circumstances (Black, 1990).

The standard of care is directly concerned with what a "reasonably prudent person" with the same credentials and level of training would have done in the same or similar circumstances (Black, 1990, p. 1405). To prove negligent malpractice in a court of law, there are four elements that must be demonstrated (Black, 1990, p. 959):

1. The existence of the physician-patient relationship
2. The applicable standard of care and its violation
3. The existence of a compensable injury
4. A causal connection between the violation of the standard of care and the alleged harm.

The first concern in a malpractice action is the establishment of a relationship that indicates that a duty is owed by the defendant (doctor) to the injured party (client or patient) (Simon, 1992). Actions by therapists that may create a doctor-patient relationship include (Bongar, 1991; Simon, 1992, p. 9):

1. Giving advice to prospective patients, friends, and neighbors
2. Making psychological interpretations of the patient's behavior
3. Writing a prescription or providing sample medications

4. Supervising treatment given by others
5. Conducting lengthy phone conversations with an identified or prospective patient
6. Treating an unseen patient by mail
7. Giving a patient an appointment for consultation or other service
8. Telling walk-in patients that they will be seen
9. Acting as a substitute therapist
10. Providing treatment during an evaluation.

Once a doctor-patient relationship is established, a duty of care is owed to the patient, and the treating clinician can be held liable for damages that are caused by any breach of this duty (Simon, 1992).

In the second phase of a malpractice suit, the plaintiff must establish that the clinician breached his or her duty by an act not in accord with professional standards. This standard of care is normally established by the use of expert witnesses who document the defendant's deviation from the standard (Furrow, 1993). In some states, articles from professional journals and treatises may be used in lieu of expert testimony (Simon, 1992) to characterize the expertise of another.

Historically, the trends in establishing standards of care have relied on the locality rule, implying that a local standard of care is the most relevant (Black, 1990; Furrow, Johnson, Jost, & Schwartz, 1985). However, in reality, the locality rule has been usurped occasionally in favor of a national test or standard of care (Black, 1990; Furrow et al., 1985; Simon, 1992). Some protection is provided for less traditional treatments by the doctrine of the respectable minority, as noted earlier. By protecting a psychologist or psychiatrist who follows a method approved by at least a respectable minority of the profession, this doctrine shelters practitioners in those instances in which a clearer standard of effective and safe treatment is not present. However, it is likely that this doctrine will be reconsidered in the courts within the next decade (Simon, 1992).

Critical to establishing a breach of duty is a consideration of the performance of the alleged offending clinician compared to that of a reasonable and prudent practitioner with the same or equivalent level of training under the same or similar circumstances. This principle was exemplified in *Lundgren v. Eusterman* (1984), in which a Minnesota Court of Appeals held that a licensed psychologist was competent to give expert testimony in a medical malpractice case involving the prescribing practices of a physician. The Minnesota Supreme Court overturned this case, proclaiming that a licensed psychologist was not qualified to give an opinion in a medical malpractice case on the standard of care provided by a medical doctor, since the licensed psychologist was not a medical doctor and therefore was not familiar with the actual day-to-day practice of general medicine (*Lundgren v. Eusterman,* 1985; Simon, 1992).

In addition to establishing a standard based on the performance of one who has training that is demonstrably equivalent to that of the alleged mal-practicing clinician, some courts have distinguished between a minimal level of competence and the average level of competence as represented by the hypothetical reasonable and prudent practitioner. In *Hall v. Hilbun* (1985), the defendant was judged on the basis of a minimal level of competence, not an average level of competence (Furrow, 1993).

In the legal arena, a higher standard of care is demanded of mental health specialists than is required of family physicians and other generalists (Simon, 1992). Furthermore, legislation has been passed in Maine that protects physicians from malpractice suits if they comply with treatment standards (Furrow, 1993). The extension of this legislation to other states could impose many limitations on psychologists, especially when psychologists have been underrepresented among those responsible for the development of treatment guidelines (American Psychiatric Association, 1993; Rush et al., 1993). Further complicating the matter, individual practitioners can be held to standards of care established by drug manufacturers, governmental agencies, managed-care firms, and third-party payers (Simon, 1992).

The third phase of a malpractice case is concerned with whether or not the patient has been harmed by the clinician's actions. The defense must show that the patient has been harmed as the result of the practitioner's deviation from the standard of care (Simon, 1992). If a practitioner has provided substandard treatment but there was no harm, there is no malpractice case (Simon, 1992). Simon (1992, p. 545) has stated his concern regarding the federal government's efforts to control medical payments and to monitor the quality of care to recipients in federal health care programs, thus "defining and funding appropriate" care. The danger of this practice lies in the fact that specific agendas are often placed above the quality of patient care, and the use of politically driven standards of care sets a dangerous precedent for a quasi-judicial treatment.

The final phase of a malpractice case is the establishment of a causal connection between the violation of the standard of care and the harm suffered by the patient (Black, 1990). Causation is divided into two categories: (1) cause-in-fact or actual cause, and (2) proximate or legal cause (Simon, 1992). Cause-in-fact is expressed as the "but for" rule and states that, but for A's actions, B's injuries would not have occurred (Simon, 1992, p. 549). This rule implies that A's actions were absolutely essential for B's injuries to have occurred. In other words, no causation would exist if B would not have been injured without the intervening force of A.

Proximate cause is present when an "uninterrupted chain of events occurs from the time of the defendant's negligent conduct to the time of the plaintiff's injury" (Simon, 1992, p. 550). Proximate cause implies the exacerbation of a secondary source that combines with the negligent act to cause injury to the plaintiff. Thus, if an action occurs that is foreseeable by the defendant, he or she may be held liable.

Simon (1992, p. 550) describes a proximate-cause scenario this way: "A physician who is initially negligent in harming a patient is usually liable for aggravation of the patient's condition caused by the negligent conduct of the subsequent treating physician."

Problems are inherent in this judicial model, as the definition of a "reasonable and prudent" practitioner is established through the testimony of relatively few expert witnesses regarding typical practice behavior (Greaney, 1995, p. 5; VandeCreek, Knapp, & Herzog, 1987).

GUIDELINES TO SYSTEMATIC TREATMENT SELECTION

We believe that the development and use of guidelines continues to be beneficial, since guidelines often reflect new research developments. In addition, they influence all standards of practice. Intrinsic in the development of guidelines is an increase in the required standard of care for practitioners. A beneficial outcome of the guidelines is the universal availability of all treatment options (Rush et al., 1993).

In hindsight, it probably was a mistake from the outset to assume that treatment guidelines would not have an inevitable impact on the legal system and that they would not be used as if they were standards of care. A malpractice suit may develop if a contemporary clinician is not familiar with recent changes in accepted practice (Furrow, 1993). On the other hand, guidelines can be used defensively by a physician or psychologist who is attempting to demonstrate adherence to accepted practice, regardless of the fact that the guidelines were not intended to be used for this purpose (Furrow, 1993; Rush et al., 1993).

Currently, the adequacy of care is determined by that care's accordance with a standard that is assumed to characterize the efforts of a reasonable and prudent practitioner and that is defined or determined by expert witness testimony (Simon, 1992). Basing a standard of care on a "mythical" person known as a reasonable and prudent practitioner is less beneficial than relying on treatment guidelines that may become a part of expert testimony (Greaney, 1995, p. 7). Often, the consensus of the practicing behaviors of a larger, more representative sample of practitioners is more helpful than the reports of a singular "expert" practitioner.

As long as treatment guidelines are developed with the intent of providing immediate help to practitioners in clinical work, they will inevitably be used as standards against which to assess an individual practitioner's behavior. If they cease to be important or usable in this way, even if such use is deemed inappropriate, they also cease to be effective in their primary mission of providing expert guidance and external validation of clinical experience (Frances et al., 1996).

Thus, to be effective, guidelines must be both consistent with scientific knowledge and sensitive to the needs of individual patients. Developers of expert consensus guidelines have remarked on the need to pay close attention to individual case situations in conjunction with implementation of treatment guidelines. Historically, the balance between these two requirements has not been well served by guidelines that are completely dependent on patient diagnosis or that sacrifice scientific validity in order to accommodate clinician ignorance. Some of these mistakes have been underlined by the conflict stirred among members of the various mental health professions by existing guidelines.

In an attempt to provide suggestions for practice, treatment guidelines may explicitly or implicitly be taken as representing standards of care. Standards of care are primarily concerned with jurisprudence and malpractice and are used in malpractice cases where comparisons with others of similar training are compared. In contrast to standards of care, the treatment guidelines that we will present in this volume accept the principle articulated by the Committee to Advise the Public Health Service on Clinical Practice Guidelines, a committee within the National Institute of Medicine, that guidelines are "systematically developed statements to assist practitioners and patients to make decisions about appropriate health care for specific clinical circumstances" (Field & Lohr, 1990, p. 8).

The current guidelines, however, were not developed to comply with the political agenda or the dictating philosophies of any specific group, though we have found them to be compatible with the value systems of several professional groups, including the American Psychological Association. Instead, the guidelines were developed from our personal collective efforts to extract principles from the literature that would best direct and lead practice and that are organized around a philosophy of empirically based practice as articulated by Beutler and Clarkin (1990). They are unique in four respects: (1) They are explicitly based in the current body of scientific research, rather than on theoretical formulations; (2) principles extracted from extant literature were systematically cross-validated, using a variety of primary databases of patients who present with complicated and uncomplicated depressive symptoms; (3) they are focused primarily on questions of differential treatment selection and planning, the effort to match patients to particular varieties, classes, and dimensions of treatment; and (4) they differentiate between basic guidelines that can be applied by a large number of clinicians, quite independently of specialized training or expertise, and optimal guidelines that require special monitoring and training to implement. The conclusions we reach have passed, in our judgment, the test both of deriving from the current scientific literature and of surviving direct, cross-validating, scientific tests.

2 *Nature of Current Treatment Guidelines*

Chapter 1 has made clear how various forces have contributed to an environment that has spawned different treatment guidelines. The generation of an operationalized diagnostic system since DSM-III and the dominance of this system has led mental health professionals to communicate about patients in terms of these categories and driven researchers assessing both pharmacological and psychosocial treatments to use its terminology. In addition, treatment research has flourished. Clinical trials of psychosocial treatments defined in previously unheard-of detail in treatment manuals have led to a movement by American Psychological Association (APA) Division 12 to emphasize treatments that have empirical support. Furthermore, there has been a growing awareness in medical circles in general that there is tremendous variability in the treatment of a given disorder, raising questions about the common practices of health care providers. How can quite diverse treatments for the same condition all be supported by scientific logic? With the operationalized diagnostic system of DSM and the empirically validated psychosocial treatments in psychology and psychiatry, the same question has also been raised about variability in treatment for psychiatric disorders. Finally, the issue of variability in treatment leading to variable costs has captured the intense attention of the managed-care companies that have moved in to police the delivery of all reimbursable health and mental health services. These forces have been in operation for some time, and it appears that treatment guidelines will be with us for the foreseeable future. It remains to be seen how qualitatively adequate the treatment guidelines will be, how useful they will be to the clinician in caring for the individual patient, how the guidelines will be used by third-party payors in apportioning health care dollars, and how the guidelines will inform the education of mental health professionals.

Treatment guidelines are not simply and straightforwardly scientific statements about the leading-edge treatments of various disorders. They are responses by various groups to the pressures on the delivery of health care in the United States at the present time. Thus, the ultimate contribution of treatment guidelines in the education and service delivery of mental health professionals remains to be seen. Use of such guidelines by managed-care organizations, organizers of mental health services, and the legal system will also evolve. From an optimistic point of view, treatment guidelines may be a useful tool in training mental health professionals to combine clinical experience with current research information in a format that enables the practitioner to narrow treatment variance to the benefit of the patient. On the other hand, treatment guidelines have the potential to narrow the range of available services and to stifle clinician creativity.

In this chapter, we use as a template for comparing treatment guidelines those prepared by the American Psychological Association (APA). These guidelines for the generation of guidelines highlight the process and the political context of treatment guidelines. We also examine the existing treatment guidelines for depression in some detail. The examination of existing guidelines provides the background for the generation of more extensive guidelines by the authors later in this volume.

TEMPLATE FOR DEVELOPING TREATMENT GUIDELINES

The American Psychological Association recognizes the need for treatment guidelines and views the generation of guidelines as a process that involves articulation and periodic update, rather than a once-and-for-all product. In order for the resulting guidelines to have quality and usefulness, they must be interdisciplinary and based on research and must consider clinical utility in local settings. The APA views the guidelines as an educational tool, not as a weapon with which to "blame" clinicians. Above all, the resulting guidelines are intended for the welfare of the patient, with the implication that they should not be tools to foster the limited interests of various provider professions or managed-care agencies. These guidelines for guidelines are summarized in table 2.1.

AMERICAN PSYCHIATRIC GUIDELINES
FOR TREATING DEPRESSION

Content of the Guidelines

The guidelines of the American Psychiatric Association emphasize that each patient with major depression should have an individually tailored therapeutic program, since comorbidity of alcohol and substance abuse, medical morbidities, and suicidal ideation may or may not be present. Treatments considered effective for major depression are psychotherapy, antidepressants, and electroconvulsive therapy (ECT). In general, the guidelines state that the majority of patients are best treated with antidepressant medication combined with psychotherapeutic management or psychotherapy. Patients with mild to moderate impairment may be treated with psychotherapy alone before a trial of antidepressants is initiated.

In the acute phase of treatment, psychosocial interventions may range from psychotherapeutic management to a number of systematic psychotherapies, including interpersonal psychotherapy (IPT), cognitive therapy, psychodynamic therapy, and marital, family and group therapies. Somatic treatments include antidepressant medications or ECT.

In the continuation phase of therapy, ongoing use of an antidepressant agent is recommended. In the maintenance phase, medication should be used, sometimes indefinitely. Psychological factors often play a substantive role in increasing the risk of recurrence; therefore, psychotherapy may be very effective during the maintenance phase.

Evaluation of the Guidelines

Using the APA template for generating guidelines, one can evaluate the American Psychiatric Association Guidelines for depression. All the "experts" in the panel were physicians except for one, who holds a Ph.D.; the criteria used to select the experts are not explained. The empirical data used to gen-

Table 2.1 APA Template for the Generation of Guidelines

Foci of Evaluation

1. Subject interventions to empirical confirmation.
2. Subject each intervention subject to increasingly stringent methodology.
3. Seek consensus across interdisciplinary groups.
4. Evaluate acceptability of the treatment to the patient.
5. Evaluate the ease of dissemination of the treatment.
6. Consider the breadth of patient variables.
7. Evaluate efficacy of treatment as delivered by different therapists.
8. Evaluate data on treatment robustness.
9. Consider costs and benefits of treatments, and costs of withholding treatments.

Characteristics of the Panel

10. Panel should include those with broad expertise.
11. Panelists should seek to prevent interprofession conflict.
12. Panel should encourage a free exchange of views.
13. Panelists should define their process and methods.
14. Panel should agree on goals (e.g., intended audience, appropriate use of guidelines).
15. Panel should agree on methods and strategies for reviewing the evidence.
16. Panel should provide full report.
17. Panel should specify method for evaluating its guidelines.

erate the guidelines go up to 1991, and there is no indication of when the guidelines will be updated. The audience for the guidelines seems to be only psychiatrists, as they refer to actions by physicians. Treatment is conceptualized in terms of the acute, continuation, and maintenance phases of the depressive symptoms, and the guidelines are most extensive for the acute phase.

The APA template for guidelines suggest that not only efficacy studies but effectiveness data (data on the use of the treatments in sites outside highly controlled randomized studies) must show that the treatments are feasible and have desired outcomes. Both the AHCPR and American Psychiatric Association guidelines utilize efficacy studies but pay little attention to the issue of local clinical utility. (In contrast, to generate our guidelines, presented in chapters 6 and 7, we have used data from multiple sites in studies that tackle effectiveness research.)

AGENCY FOR HEALTH CARE POLICY AND RESEARCH GUIDELINES

The Agency for Health Care Policy and Research (AHCPR) of the U.S. Department of Health and Human Services was established to enhance the quality, appropriateness, and effectiveness of health care services and to improve access to these services. The AHCPR organized a twelve-member panel that included several psychiatrists, along with representatives of family and general medicine, social work, nursing, and psychology. The panelists developed a guide set for the treatment of depression in the primary-care setting (Depression Guideline Panel, 1993).

Content of the Guidelines

Table 2.2 summarizes the AHCPR guidelines, which focused on planning and providing treatment in the acute, continuation, and maintenance phases of depression.

Comparison of AHCPR and American Psychiatric Association Guidelines

It is instructive to compare the process and content of the AHCPR guidelines with those of the American Psychiatric Association. The former are intended for primary-care physicians and the latter for psychiatric physicians. The documentation of data reviewed and the process of review (i.e., metaanalysis) are much more thoroughly documented in the AHCPR report. The AHCPR panel was smaller and more interdisciplinary. Both sets of guidelines conceptualize treatment in the acute, continuation, and maintenance phases of depression and heavily emphasize the use of medication, although psy-

Table 2.2 Summary of AHCPR Guidelines

Aims of Treatment

1. The objective of treatment is to reduce and remove symptoms of depression, restore occupational and psychosocial functioning, and reduce the likelihood of relapse and recurrence.
2. Patients' adherence to treatment is improved by education for patients and their families.
3. If the patient shows only a partial response to treatment (whether medication or psychotherapy) by twelve weeks, other treatment options should be considered.

Planning for Acute-Phase Treatment

4. Treatment is indicated for those with major depression but not for those with normal sadness or distress.
5. Patients with moderate to severe major depressive disorder are appropriately treated with medication.
6. Patients with mild to moderate major depression who prefer psychotherapy without medication as the initial acute treatment may be treated with this option.
7. Combined treatment may have an advantage for patients with partial responses to either treatment alone, and for those with a chronic history or poor interepisode recovery.

Acute-Phase Management with Medication

8. Medications are first-line treatments for major depression when depression is moderate to severe; psychotic, or melancholic or shows atypical symptoms; when the patient requests medication; when psychotherapy not available; when the patient has a history of positive responses to medication; or when maintenance treatment is planned.
9. By six weeks, those patients with continued impairment may find psychotherapy beneficial.

Acute-Phase Management with Psychotherapy

10. Psychotherapy alone as a first-line treatment may be considered if the major depressive episode is mild to moderate, the depression is not chronic, psychotic, or melancholic, and the patient desires psychotherapy.
11. Medication is recommended as the first-line treatment in patients with melancholic (endogenous) symptom features.
12. If psychotherapy alone is ineffective by six weeks or does not result in nearly a full symptomatic remission within twelve weeks, a switch to medication may be appropriate.
13. Psychotherapies that target depressive symptoms, such as cognitive or behavioral therapy, or specific interpersonal problems, such as interpersonal psychotherapy, are more similar than different in efficacy. Long-term therapies are not indicated as first-line acute-phase treatments.

Acute-Phase Management with Medication and Psychotherapy

14. Combined treatment is reasonable if the depression has been chronic or characterized by poor interepisode recovery, if either treatment alone has been only partially effective, or if the patient has a history of chronic psychosocial problems or of treatment adherence difficulties.
15. Psychotherapy can be combined with medication to address problems related to depression, such as pessimism, low self-esteem, or marital difficulties.

(*continued*)

Table 2.2 (*Continued*)

Acute-Phase Management with ECT

16. Indications for ECT for acute phase depression include severe depression associated with severe vegetative symptoms and/or marked functional impairment, presence of psychotic symptoms, or failure to respond full to several adequate trials of medications.

Special Situations

17. When major depressive disorder is comorbid with another psychiatric disorder, there are three options: (1) treat the major depression first, (2) treat the associated condition as the initial focus, or (3) decide which condition is primary, and select it as the initial treatment target.

Continuation and Maintenance Phases

18. The objective of continuation treatment is to decrease the likelihood of relapse. If the patient responds to acute-phase medication, it is usually continued.
19. Continuation-phase psychotherapy is advisable if there are residual symptoms, psychosocial problems, or a history of psychological functioning between episodes.
20. Patients with a history of three or more episodes of major depression are potential candidates for long-term maintenance medication.
21. Maintenance psychotherapy does not appear to be effective in preventing recurrence, although it may delay the onset of the next episode.

chotherapy is not totally ignored. The AHCPR guidelines are more sharply delineated and therefore more readily lend themselves to evaluation at the clinical level (e.g., do physicians use them? Do patients treated according to the guidelines improve more than those who are not?). While there is extensive reference to and use of empirical data in the AHCPR panel, the group's conclusions are not always consistent with the data surveyed (e.g., Barlow, 1994).

It is unfortunate that both sets of guidelines focus exclusively on the course of the symptoms of depression alone across what are called the acute, continuation, and maintenance phases. It would be equally plausible to assess the course over time of the resumption of work and social functioning. In fact, managed-care companies and those who pay for worker insurance are much more interested in the course of functional recovery than in simple symptom removal. Furthermore, in the whole treatment-planning algorithm, the only patient variable used is the presence or absence of major depression, and, within that subset, the minor, moderate, or severe levels of symptoms. This results in a set of treatment guidelines that are totally deficient for the clinician who must treat distinct individuals with a number of salient treatments.

EXPERT CONSENSUS GUIDELINES

In yet another attempt to generate treatment guidelines for various disorders (not yet including depression), Frances, Docherty, and Kahn (1996), using interesting statistical procedures, have used a standardized questionnaire completed by a large group of experts to generate guidelines. Since this group has not produced guidelines for depression, we focus here on their method, not on content. The first step in this group's process is to construct an extensive questionnaire that asks very specific questions (see figure 2.1). The sample question is drawn from the questionnaire for those working with bipolar disorder.

The obvious limitation here is the coverage of the questions in the questionnaire. For the mixed bipolar guidelines set, psychosocial treatments are barely referred to.

The researchers' second step was to select a group of experts, who were requested to fill out the questionnaire. For the bipolar disorder data set, sixty-eight leading experts in the field, including authors named in recent research publications, recipients of funded grants, DSM-IV advisers on mood disorders, members of the task force for the American Psychiatric Association's Practice Guidelines for Bipolar Disorder, and those who work on other mood disorder guidelines, were identified. Of these sixty-eight experts, 88 percent responded to an initial survey.

A mean standard deviation and confidence interval were calculated for each question. The authors designated a rating of first-, second-, or third-line treatment for each item on which there was consensus; this rating was determined by the category into which the 95 percent confidence interval of the mean score fell. The results are presented graphically. The results for the question in figure 2.1 indicate that these experts consider lithium and valproates to be first-line treatments, and the rest second-line treatments.

Figure 2.1 Sample Question from Study on Treatment Efficacy

Please rate each of the following treatments for a patient who has acute mania with "classic" (euphoric) features:

a. carbamazepine	1	2	3	4	5	6	7	8	9
b. lithium	1	2	3	4	5	6	7	8	9
c. valproate	1	2	3	4	5	6	7	8	9
d. carbamazepine + valproate	1	2	3	4	5	6	7	8	9
e. lithium + carbamazepine	1	2	3	4	5	6	7	8	9
f. lithium + valproate	1	2	3	4	5	6	7	8	9
g. electroconvulsive therapy	1	2	3	4	5	6	7	8	9

Source: Francas, Doherty, and Kahn (1996).

STRATEGIC POLICY REVIEW OF
PSYCHOTHERAPY SERVICES

On the basis of a report commissioned by the National Health Service Executive of the English (UK) Department of Health, which formed a part of the Department's Strategic Policy Review of Psychotherapy Services, Roth and Fonagy (1996) reviewed the literature on a number of disorders, including depression, and formulated service recommendations. While not guidelines in the way that term is used in the United States, these recommendations provide another perspective on services for depressed individuals. The recommendations are focused on the important aspects one would incorporate in devising a system of care for depressed individuals. This emphasis on the system of care seems different from the focus of the two sets of guidelines generated in the United States. The British report is also openly skeptical about the overuse of brief psychotherapy, in contrast to the emphasis on brief treatment in the United States treatment guidelines. We now summarize the major points made in this report.

Content

Depression is a common disorder that must be addressed in any system of care. A distinction should be made between those with acute episodes of depression and those with a chronic course of depression. In terms of severity, those with more severe depression are less likely to respond to psychological therapy. Depression is a chronic disorder in many patients, and there is a danger when the balance of service is skewed too far in the direction of brief interventions. Research data suggests that cognitive behavior therapy (CBT), IPT, and dynamic therapies are efficacious. The impact of brief treatment is relatively short lived. Long-term pharmacological treatment is, to date, the only method that has been shown to be effective in the prevention of relapse. However, IPT may be a useful adjunct in the prevention of relapse. Evidence for the superiority of combination treatments over psychological intervention alone is weak. The superiority of psychotherapeutic treatment over medical treatment is small, and the evidence for it across studies is unreliable. The absence of long-term, controlled follow-up studies in the majority of trials undermines conclusions concerning long-term effectiveness and generalizability of treatments. In terms of dysthymic or chronic-course patients, the prevalence of double depression should be considered. There is some indication that the quality of therapy correlates with long-term outcome, and this suggests that the maintenance of high-quality therapy is important for service providers. Given the poor long-term effects and the chronicity of many cases, a stepwise mode of service provision in which patients who fail to respond to brief treatments are offered longer-term therapy is appropriate. It is clear that very brief treatments are not adequate for more severely depressed patients, and this underscores the importance of regular follow-ups for this patient group.

SUMMARY

This review of the template for generating guidelines and the two existing U.S. guideline sets is helpful in a number of ways:

1. The two existing guideline sets are limited in their intended audience. One is targeted for primary-care physicians, and the other for psychiatrists. Many, if not the majority, of mental health professionals who treat depressed individuals are not included in these intended audiences. There is a clear need for treatment guidelines for a wider audience, an audience not preoccupied with medication treatment.

2. The existing treatment guideline sets review some of the same research data but use the data in different ways. In our approach we not only use single studies, patterns from separate studies considered in aggregate, and meta-analyses but also highlight those studies that search for patient-therapy matches.

3. The existing guideline sets focus on medication treatment and fail to articulate a complete treatment plan, especially one including psychotherapy.

4. The guidelines themselves must be articulated specifically so that their value can be empirically determined. The American Psychiatric Association guidelines are so vague as to preclude such examination. The AHCPR guidelines, with their limited extent, could be evaluated in primary-care settings. We articulate our guidelines later in this volume with tools that allow them to be assessed on an ongoing basis.

5. A review of both a template for evaluating treatment guidelines and the existing guidelines for the treatment of depression sets the stage for any possible improvement on what exists. Since we find the existing guidelines inadequate, we are now in a position to generate yet another set of guidelines for treatment planning with those who present with the symptoms of depression. We invite the reader to examine our guidelines (see chapters 6 and 7) and to compare them to the template and the existing guidelines.

HOW (AND BY WHOM) TREATMENT
GUIDELINES SHOULD BE USED

Treatment guidelines can be used by different classes of individuals for quite different purposes. We consider here the use of guidelines by those providing care to depressed individuals (e.g., primary-care doctors and nurses, psychiatrists, psychologists, social workers, and nurses), by training programs, by managed-care companies, and by the courts. They can also be used by mental health administrators to organize care in clinic settings.

The existing data sets are inadequate for training mental health professionals. In teaching basic and optimal clinical care to psychology graduate students and interns and to psychiatry residents, one needs to include much more detail than is provided in the existing treatment guidelines. The existing data sets are inadequate for use in clinical care, for the same reason. While the fear was that managed-care companies would use the guidelines to limit what services they pay for, this has not been the case. Rather, managed-care providers in most cases have not attended to guidelines but simply arbitrarily limit the duration and the frequency of visits for treatment of depression. It is the responsibility of professional groups to articulate guidelines of treatment that protect the patients and to intervene with managed-care providers, rather than to let managed care rule. We have already discussed, in chapter 1, how the courts view treatment guidelines.

PART II

Guidelines for Treatment-Relevant Assessment

3 *Identifying Treatment-Relevant Dimensions*

Arguably the most important function of a diagnosis is its contribution to decisions about distinctive and specific treatments. Identifying clusters of symptoms that classify patients into groups makes sense only to the degree that these classifications predict the prognostic course of a given patient's condition and provide information that allows the clinician to select one treatment or intervention over another. While current diagnostic nomenclature bears some relatiohship to prognosis, it has proven to be only inconsistently related to the effectiveness of differential treatments. Because contemporary diagnostic groups are neither exclusive nor specific, the identification of specific treatment indicators and contraindicators based on them is very problematic.

Diagnostic criteria for defining ostensibly different disorders frequently overlap, diagnoses within similar classes (e.g., affective disorder, anxiety disorder) are sometimes contradictory, and diagnostic criteria are frequently only loosely associated with the course of any available treatment (Carson, 1997; Follette & Houts, 1996). Similar treatment effects are often associated with widely different treatments; by the same token, ostensibly different conditions frequently seem to be affected by the same or similar treatments. For example, even such widely disparate conditions as schizophrenia and transient situational disturbance can be positively affected by similar interventions (e.g., behavioral exchange and structure). The similarity of effect is probably most apparent in conditions, such as anxiety and depression, where there are shared symptoms. There is some indication that the problem of common effects of different treatments is not restricted to psychosocial interventions. Even anxiolytic and antidepressant medications seem able to affect both depressive symptoms and anxiety (Beutler, 1998b; Kirsch & Saperstein, 1998). Thus, efforts to identify and catalogue patients and treatments and to match

Ms. Roslyn Caldwell was a coauthor for chapter 3 and did the preponderance of the work in organizing the tables and reviewing the research studies.

dimensions that might be implicated in enhancing or retarding treatment effects invariably result in a large and cumbersome list of overlapping constructs (Beutler, 1991). An organizing system is needed by which to collapse and cluster similar variables and to prioritize the relevance to treatment of the resultant variable classes and types.

Responding to the need for an organizing system, in recent years, many authors have attempted to identify those patient qualities that are implicated in moderating treatment, independent of any specific theory of psychotherapy. While some of these efforts have attended to patient states, most have focused on trait-like qualities, since these are more easily used as the basis for planning differential treatment. In either case, the objectives of these efforts have been to identify how various treatments might selectively "fit" different patients (Beutler et al., 1996; Frances, Clarkin, & Perry, 1984; Lazarus, 1976; Norcross, 1986, 1994). Some of these organizing systems have generated important research. Aptitude Treatment Interaction (ATI) research models (Shoham-Salomon, 1991; Snow, 1991) provide a methodology for defining the relevance and meaningfulness of patient traits and aspects of treatment. Decision-making models have been developed to help clinicians plan effective treatments and tailor them to the particular needs, problems, and personalities of patients. These models offer means of predicting, with some precision, what collection of treatment procedures is most likely to be beneficial for a given patient.

Research from this ATI perspective (e.g., Beutler & Clarkin, 1990; Frances, Clarkin, & Perry, 1984; Norcross & Goldfried, 1992; Orlinsky, Grawe, & Parks, 1994; Prochaska, 1984; Striker & Gold, 1993) has provided a workable list of patient trait-like dimensions and qualities that may exert a mediating effect on therapeutic change. To translate these dimensions into a workable set of guidelines, however, it is necessary to understand both the relative support available for each dimension individually and the collective importance of various combinations. This chapter is designed to accomplish the first of these purposes and summarizes the level of empirical support available for the mediating role of some of the more promising patient predictors.

The identification of patient characteristics and the corresponding aspects of treatment that are indicated for each has been a multidimensional and multifaceted task (Beutler, Engle, Shoham-Salomon, Mohr, Dean, & Bernat, 1991). Its genesis was a comprehensive review (Beutler, 1979) of the then available studies that had compared the effects of one type of psychotherapy against another. It was found that independent raters could reliably identify a number of patient qualities that were present in those instances where one model of psychotherapy proved to be more effective than another. The potential list of patient variables and corresponding qualities of treatment was subsequently expanded (Beutler & Clarkin, 1990) by a conventional review of literature that was organized, in part, around the dimensions identified in the earlier review as providing patient-therapy patterns associated with improvement. Through this and subsequent reviews, the list of patient variables that can be identified as mediators of treatment has been modified by a process of combining variables that, on their face, appeared to be similar constructs or that demonstrate a similar pattern of prediction in controlled research studies. At the same time, new variables and new descriptive names have been developed as research has accumulated to indicate the nature of the constructs being considered (Beutler & Berren, 1995; Beutler, Consoli, & Williams, 1995; Beutler, Goodrich, Fisher, & Williams, 1999; Beutler, Wakefield, & Williams, 1994; Gaw & Beutler, 1995).

For the purposes of this book, we initiated a much more extensive process that both extended the literature review and applied a process of cross-validation. The procedures used to identify relevant indicators and contraindicators for various treatments involved six basic steps:

1. A comprehensive review of all treatment studies of non-bipolar depression that we could find
2. Extraction and paring of this list to include studies on which a trait-like quality of the patient's condition was studied as a mediator of one or more treatments
3. A reiterative reading of these studies to create a consensually defined and relatively small list of the most promising variables that appear to differentially affect some aspect of treatment context, model, or method
4. A selective review of the literature regarding these patient constructs to determine their generality to nondepressive conditions that are frequently coexistent with non-bipolar depression (primarily anxiety and substance abuse disorders)
5. The development of a method of measuring these constructs across samples of archival and prospectively selected patients
6. The conducting of a predictive validity study of these constructs to determine their individual and joint contributions to the treatment of depression and depression-related conditions.

In these steps, we largely restricted our efforts to the identification of relatively stable or trait-like qualities, rather than including transitory states. We reasoned that transitory anxiety and other states that change from day to day may be difficult to employ as variables on which to predict treatment response and to plan differential treatments. Variables that are stable at least over a period of a few weeks were the objects of our focus because they were thought to be useful in developing treatment plans that extend beyond the moment. However, it should be said that a variety of state variables, such as anxiety and resistance to interventions, may be related to similar trait-like ones and may serve as indicators of how effective a treatment may be.

The first four of the foregoing tasks are described in this chapter. Chapter 4 describes the current status of measurements that assess the qualities that emerge from our review, and chapter 5 describes our efforts to develop a measurement device that could be applied to archival and prospective data for the subsequent predictive validity test. Chapter 6 describes and draws on the findings of this predictive validity effort to present our findings regarding basic guidelines for selective application of treatments, and chapter 7 presents the more stringent guidelines that we consider to be helpful in optimizing treatment effects, again based on our cross-validating study.

The initial steps of reviewing the literature were intended to be hypothesis generating rather than confirmatory. Nonetheless, we draw on these findings in the presentation of what we call basic guidelines to treatment (chapter 6). The distinction between these basic guidelines and the more intensive optimal guidelines for systematic treatment selection is the special expertise, training, and monitoring that are required in the latter. Basic guidelines are those that the literature suggests can be applied by a variety of clinicians and through a variety of interventions models. One need not be trained in any one specific approach or be able to mix models to apply most of these guidelines. In contrast, optimal guidelines require special training, treatment mixes, and monitoring of actual clinician activities during the process of planning and implementing interventions.

The first step of the literature search focused on identifying the nature of effective treatments. It did not favor any specific type of treatment or any particular outcome. From key words and reference works, we identified and subsequently reviewed more than two thousand studies that purported to study one or more treatments for non-bipolar depression. These studies included those that included specifically diagnosed samples of individuals with major depressive disorder, dysthymic disorder, minor depression, and adjustment disorder with depression, as well as mixed samples of patients whose primary or associated symptoms included depression. This review was intentionally overinclusive in order to consider the possibility that treatments were differentially effective for major and minor depressive conditions. We intended to open as many avenues as possible to the subsequent exploration of differential treatment effects.

The second step in this review involved selecting, from the larger list, studies that specifically studied or reached some conclusion about the role of a patient-based mediator of treatment effects. Because our focus was specifically on differential indicators and predictors, this meant excluding a great many good studies of treatment effectiveness that compared treatments of various types but did not measure or postulate the presence of mediating variables or that did not include post hoc efforts to disaggregate the findings around a differential patient indicator. Some but certainly not all of this excluded literature is reviewed selectively and summarized in chapter 11. The summaries of what treatments work rely less heavily on specific studies than did our effort to define differential treatment indicators; it relies instead on secondary reviews and especially on meta-analyses that have addressed questions of efficacy and effectiveness. The more intensive and comprehensive step that underwrites the basic and optimal guidelines to systematic treatment planning was heavily dependent on the ability to reliably identify some stable aspect of the patient's condition, beyond the general diagnostic label, that is associated with variability and selectivity of outcomes. We continued, in the intensive literature review described in the current chapter, to include studies that cut across a spectrum of depressive conditions. We focused on studies on the treatment of depression that included both a well-defined treatment and a reliable assessment of one or more patient dimensions. Through this process, we extracted 325 studies as potentially valuable.

The third step of the review process was to extract a consolidated list of the most promising patient constructs. This entailed reiterative reading of articles and a review of the measures used to identify various patient mediators in order to seek some consensual agreement among raters on the nature of the constructs and the methods of measuring them. Consensual agreement was used as the criterion from which to identify both the specificity and the level of abstraction that would be useful for identifying constructs that could be used in treatment planning. At this point, we did not worry about the findings presented by any particular study but concentrated on the description of the patient qualities that were used either prospectively or post hoc as potential mediators and moderators of treatment effects. These selected studies are presented in this chapter in tabular form. Some of these studies included a single sample of individuals that was quite homogeneous on a readily identifiable dimension (e.g., high functional impairment, high distress). Other studies bifurcated or trifurcated the samples into subsets (e.g., high and low impairment). Including both single, homogeneous samples and stratified samples allowed us to look at the effects of various patient variables both across and within studies. The same was true when we identified aspects of treatment that might be more or less effective with individuals who represented variations on patient variables. In some studies, the treatment studied was of a single type, and our focus was on which patients obtained good and less good results. In other cases, two or more distinctive treatments were investigated. Except for problems that occasionally arose in reaching agreement on the relationship of the patient dimension represented to those studied in other investigations, we found that this made our task easier in that the components of treatment that differentially affected patients were more easily identified.

Thus, we identified, through standard library searches and computerized databases, more than one thousand studies that (1) compared two or more well-controlled or well-defined treatments that were tested on one or more reliably defined populations of patients (e.g., randomized clinical trials); (2) compared the effects of one well-defined therapy among two or more stratified or contrasting groups of depressed patients; or (3) systematically inspected the differential influence of a continuous, patient moderator within the context of one or more well-defined treatments.

Throughout this review, we considered treatment variables to be adequately defined if the components of treatment were described and if the treatment models themselves were applied by use of a manual. We elected not to focus on the general model of treatment used (e.g., cognitive, psychodynamic, experiential) for fear that such distinctions were too broad to capture the nature of treatment procedures and differences among therapists. Thus, our focus was on the components of treatments and on defining dimensions of treatment at a level of abstraction that was not model specific. Following the system and results of previous work (Beutler, 1979, 1981; Beutler & Clarkin, 1990; Prochaska, 1984), we began with general descriptors of therapy focus (e.g., behavioral versus internal), level of therapist directiveness, level of intervention (e.g., individual versus interpersonal), and locus of intended change (e.g., insight versus symptoms). This list was expanded and contracted as two or more raters were able to reach maximal agreement on the nature of the variables that distinguished the treatments being studied.

We elected not to use either a box score tabulation or a meta-analysis to analyze these data for fear that the importance of individual findings would be occluded by these processes. Meta-analysis is rather insensitive to such differences (e.g., Capelleri et al., 1996), especially when, as in our case, the nature of variables and methods were often not reducible to a single type of metric (e.g., nominal and interval scales). Rather, we initiated a qualitative review designed to generate hypotheses. We considered but did not weigh studies that didn't support the hypotheses as strongly as we weighed studies that produced some positive findings to give us guidance for the later predictive validity study. This process of review and extrapolation generated some suggestive relationships that are described later in this chapter. These relationships were then tested with a selective review of the related literature, as we searched terms related to the various constructs defined.

The fourth step of the review yielded information about the potential relationship between the designated construct(s) and treatment variations as applied to conditions other than depression per se. We found that most of the related work involved patients with substance abuse or anxiety disorders of various kinds. We extracted the most important and interesting studies that we came upon. (These studies are reported both in tabular form and in the narrative in this chapter). They were generally consistent with the findings of research on depression.

This process of identifying qualities of treatment paralleled that initially used to define patient dimensions that were independent of diagnostic labels. The latter process was expanded to define a final list of patient qualities, as well. The final list of patient qualities was not as extensive as that used to define variations of treatment. It included patient demographic factors, levels of functional impairment, level of subjective distress, level of impulsivity versus constraint (i.e., coping style), level of objective and subjectively experienced social support, problem complexity/comorbidity, chronicity, and level of trait-like resistance to external influence.

Once the dimensions of treatment and patient solidified in our ratings, each study was subjected to a final set of ratings that developed profiles of cross-tabulations between the patient and treatment variables that we had identified. Both patient and treatment variations were profiled using independent ratings on a final list of variables. We used these cross-tabulations to guide the development of selective reviews of research on nondepressed conditions and ultimately for developing hypotheses about what patient and treatment matches constituted good fits in the body of studies. For example, one of the treatment qualities that we identified as contributing differentially to outcome among selective patient groups was treatment intensity. We identified the level of intensity of treatments in each study by ordering them along a continuum representing this level, taking into account both their length and their spacing (the amount of treatment per unit of time). Similarly, on the patient side, we identified level of impulsivity as a potentially important patient variable and subsequently placed patient groups in each study along a bifurcated dimension of high and low impulsivity. Samples of spouse abusers, incarcerated felons, substance abusers, and those with problems of aggression were classified as being impulsive. Similarly, we judged the patients in samples from university counseling centers as being distinguishable from mental health center patients by the chronicity of the majority of their problems. For most studies, we were able to derive a reliable, consensual indication of patient and treatment qualities. When we were not able to reach a consensus on either the nature of the treatment or the nature of the patient moderator, the study was not included in the analysis.

A careful inspection of the resulting literature resulted in the extraction of six patient variables that appear to serve as moderators of treatment outcomes. In the following section, we summarize the literature pertaining to these variables. Both supportive and nonsupportive findings are reported, largely in tabular form, with the narrative summarizing the findings with respect to which treatment dimension(s) is indicated or contraindicated by the presence of a given patient quality.

PATIENT PREDISPOSING AND TREATMENT-MODERATING VARIABLES

Patient Functional Impairment

The severity of the patient's problem has long been thought to be an indicator of the patient's needed level of care and the advisability of providing medical interventions. However, research on this dimension has yielded inconsistent results, probably because it has been conventional until recently to confound, in measures of problem severity, measures of patient distress with observed or rated levels of impairment in daily functioning. Strupp, Horowitz, and Lambert (1997) have suggested bringing some order to these studies by distinguishing between these two concepts. Thus, "functional impairment" was the category used in our analyses (see Table 3.1) when the patient measure reflected changes in the broadly defined roles within which a patient functioned. Assessment of functional impairment was usually measured by some external observer, while subjective distress usually was measured via patient self-reports. The person making the ratings was not the

Table 3.1. Functional Impairment

Study	N	Sample (InP vs. OutP)	Age (Median/ Mean)	Sex	Diagnosis (Formal vs. Not Formal)	Functional Impairment Measure	Type of Treatment	Outcome Differential Effects
Studies of Depressed Samples								
Beutler, Frank Schieber et al., 1984	176	InP	32.4	F=108, M=68	Psychiatric diagnosis	Psychological disturbance, all high impairment	Three group therapy formats: interactive, process-oriented group format, and behaviorally oriented group format, no treatment control group.	After artifactual and milieu effects were accounted for, a systematic deterioration effect occurred among patients exposed to expressive experience versus group process, who tended to produce best results, which were maintained 13 months later.
Beutler, Kim, Davison et al., 1996	63	OutP	46.76	F=63%, M=37%	Major Depression	Global Severity Index (GSI) subscale of Brief Symptom Inventory (BSI)	Focused expressive psychotherapy (FEP) and cognitive therapy (CT), 90-min. sessions/week; supportive/ self-directed therapy (S/SD) 20 min./week on phone.	FEP not significantly more effective than CT as determined by patient's initial distress; efficacies of CT and FEP are negatively related to patient initial distress by self report. When rated by clinician, CT was most effective among those w/ initially low levels of distress.
Billings, Cronkite, & Moos, 1985	424	OutP/ InP	18+	F=56.5%, M=43.5%	Major or Minor Unipolar Depressive Disorder	Based on assessments using HDLF Manual	Treatment at inpatient or outpatient facilities was not specified.	Poor functioning at treatment intake was not predictive of later difficulty at follow-up.

Study	N	Setting	Age	Gender	Diagnosis	Measures	Treatment	Results/Comments
Blackburn et al., 1981	64	OutP	43.3	F = 50, M = 14	Major Depression	Beck Depression Inventory (BDI), Hamilton Rating Scale for Depression (HRSD)	Cognitive therapy, pharmacotherapy, or both treatments combined. Treatments consisted of 1 weekly appointment for 20 weeks.	The combination of drug and psychotherapy was superior to either treatment alone. Little difference was observed between the drug treatment alone and the cognitive therapy alone groups.
Burvil et al., 1991	103	InP	71.4	F = 66, M = 37	Major Depressive Illness	Hamilton Rating Scale for Depression (HRSD) (Severity); Mini Mental State Exam	Psychiatric treatment in a clinic for one year. Electro-convulsive treatment and tricyclid antidepressant.	Not able to draw a conclusion on the role of possible risk factors in the prognosis of depressed elderly. Poor prognosis linked to severity of the initial depression.
DiMascio et al., 1979	81	OutP	18–65	F = 69, M = 12	Acute Unipolar Depression	Raskin Three-Area Depression Scale (score of 7 or more) and Hamilton Rating Scale for Depression	Psychotherapy (12 weeks of 50-min. sessions 1 time per week); pharmacotherapy alone (HCL 100–200 mg); psychotherapy plus pharmacotherapy; nonscheduled treatment (as-needed) control (16-wk treatment).	Both psychotherapy and pharmacotherapy had significant effects for symptom reduction; both treatments combined had an additive effect; psychotherapy had greater effect on mood, suicidal ideation, etc., while pharmacotherapy had greatest effects on vegetative symptoms.

(continued)

39

Table 3.1. (Continued)

Study	N	Sample (InP vs. OutP)	Age (Median/ Mean)	Sex	Diagnosis (Formal vs. Not Formal)	Functional Impairment Measure	Type of Treatment	Outcome Differential Effects
Elkin et al., 1989 (NIMH)	239	OutP	35	F = 70%, M = 30%	Major Depressive Disorder	Global Assessment Scale (GAS): moderate > 50 severe < 50	Interpersonal psychotherapy (IPT), cognitive behavior therapy (CBT); imipramine (IMI-average 185 mg, >150 mg), placebo (pla) control.	Moderate severity IMI = IPT, CBT, Pla (both HRSD & GAS) high severity (HRSD) IMI, IPT > CBT > Pla (GAS), IMI > IPT, CBT > Pla.
Fremouw & Zitter, 1978	46	under-graduates	NA	F=27, M=19	Informal diagnosis: speech anxiety	Social Avoidance and Distress Scale (SAD), Anxiety Differential	Skills training (ST); cognitive restructuring-relaxation training (CRRT).	CRRT more effective for high social anxiety; ST equally effective for both high and low anxiety.
Friedman, 1975	196	OutP	21–67	F = 79%	Depression	DiMascio Global Severity of Illness Scale; Psychiatric Rating Scale	12-week course of treatment in either drug-marital therapy, drug-minimal contact, placebo-marital therapy, or placebo-minimal contact.	Therapy had significant effect on symptom relief and clinical improvement. Both drug and marital therapy had significant effects over the control conditions.
Garvey, Hollon, & DeRubeis, 1994	64	OutP	34	NA	Major Depressive Disorder	Hamilton Rating Scale for Depression (HRSD), St. Paul Ramsey Life Experience Scale (measures current distress from 5 areas of life events)	Cognitive therapy (CT), pharmacotherapy imipramine (IMI) with continuation treatment, IMI w/o continuation treatment, combo CT and IMI.	No significant correlation for percentage of improvement on HRSD. Longitudinal Interval Follow-up Evaluation (LIFE) at week 6 for IMI; trend for same at week 12.

Study	N	Setting	Age	Gender	Disorder	Measures	Design	Results
Gitlin et al., 1995	82	OutP	37	F = 45, M = 37	Bipolar Disorder	Global Assessment Scale (severity); 3 scales: job status, social functioning, family support	Patients seen varying every week—3 patient groups seen varying from every week to every 3 months; psychosocial status evaluated at each session on a 5-point scale; meds prescribed in an uncontrolled manner.	Five-year risk of relapse into mania or depression was 73%. Poor psychosocial functioning predicts shorter time to relapse and outcome results parallel poor syndromal course.
Gonzales, Lewinsohn, & Clarke, 1985	113	OutP	35.3	F = 33, M = 80	Unipolar depressives	Schedule for Affective Disorders and Schizophrenia (SADS); Longitudinal Interval Follow-up Evaluation (LIFE); Psychiatric Epidemiology Research Interview (PERI)	Cognitive behavior therapy (12 2-hr. sessions over 2 months w/ 1- to 6-month follow-up)	Recovery rate for major depressives (75%) was significantly higher than for intermittent or double depressives. Cognitive-behavioral interventions less effective for intermittents.

41

Table 3.1. (*Continued*)

Study	N	Sample (InP vs. OutP)	Age (Median/ Mean)	Sex	Diagnosis (Formal vs. Not Formal)	Functional Impairment Measure	Type of Treatment	Outcome Differential Effects
Grove et al., 1987	512	InP/ OutP	39.28	F = 298, M = 214	Unipolar Major Depressive Disorder	Social Avoidance & Distress Scale (SADS), Eysenck Personality Inventory (EPI), MMPI	Treatment as usual. Two groups: nuclear (endogenous) and nonnuclear (less neurotic) depression.	Nuclear group shows poor prognosis on 2-yr. prospective follow-up, > disturbance on personality inventories and increased heritability of depression in siblings.
Joyce & Piper, 1996	60	OutP	32	F = 47%, M = 53%	Low and high quality of object relations patients	QOR (quality of object relations)	Short-term individual therapy, Hierarchical Linear Modeling procedure, antidepression medication, immediate therapy, delayed therapy (control).	High functional impairment was negatively correlated to outcomes with dynamic and insight-oriented treatment. The amount of transference focus-work relationship was found to be inversely related to outcome.
Kocsis et al., 1988	76	OutP	40	2.1 female to 1 male	Dysthymic Disorder and Dysthymic with Major Depression Disorder	Hamilton Depression Scale (HAM-D), Global Assessment Scale (GAS), self-rated Social Adjustment Scale (SAS-SR)	IMI, Pla pills.	IMI produced significant advantage for depressive symptoms, global severity of illness and self-rated social and vocational function.

Study	N	Setting	Age	Gender	Diagnosis	Measures	Treatment	Results
Krantz & — Moos, 1988	395	InP/OutP	18 or older	F = 223, M = 172	Major or Minor Depression	Depressive Symptoms Severity Index (DSSI: depression symptoms w/ score of 36 or greater)	Treatment at different facilities not specified. Inventories given to patients, and 12-month follow-up occurred.	Risk factors assessed at intake were used to predict remission, partial remission, or nonremission 1 year later. When risk factors were considered together, nonremission increased. Depressive severity score at intake was a strong risk factor.
Mazure, Nelson, & Jatlow, 1990	52	InP	45	F = 37, M = 15	DSM III-R Unipolar Major Depression	Hamilton Rating Scale for Depression (HRSD)	Treatment as usual.	Five variables: DSM III melancholia, panic disorder, DSM III-R absence of personality disorder, admission severity, and age were correlated w/ lack of hospital response.
McLean & Taylor, 1992	151	OutP	20–60	NA	Unipolar Depression	Beck Depression Inventory (BDI). Self-report of coping behavior, personal activity, social functioning, somatic indicators, general life satisfaction.	Nondirective pyschotherapy (PT), behavior therapy (BT), pharmacotherapy amitriptyline (AMI), relaxation training (RT) control.	On BDI moderator group BT = AMI > PT = RT; severe group BT > PT = RT = AMI; subjective distress: severe group somatic complaints PT >AMI = RT = BT.
Ogles, Sawyer, & Lambert, 1995	162	OutP	35	Both (not specified)	Major Depressive Disorder	Hamilton Rating Scale for Depression (HRSD)	Cognitive-behavioral therapy (CBT), interpersonal psychotherapy (IPT), imipramine—clinical management (IMI-CM), placebo–clinical management (PLA-CM).	No difference in clinical significance rates among treatment groups for measures of depressive symptoms.

(continued)

Table 3.1. (*Continued*)

Study	N	Sample (InP vs. OutP)	Age (Median/ Mean)	Sex	Diagnosis (Formal vs. Not Formal)	Functional Impairment Measure	Type of Treatment	Outcome Differential Effects
Prudic, Sackheim et al., 1993	100	OutP	57.38	F = 56, M = 44	Major Depression and Double Depression	Decreased score in Hamilton Rating Scale for Depression (HRSD) of at least 60% and maintained for 1 week	Right unilateral or bilateral electroconvulsive treatment (ECT) therapy.	Patients responded to ECT regardless of depression diagnosis and showed the same change in symptomatology. Symptom severity was unrelated to ECT outcome for MD.
Rush, Beck, Kovacs et al., 1982	35	OutP	NA	NA	Unipolar Depression	Beck Depression Inventory (20 or higher); Hamilton Rating Scale for Depression (14 or higher).	Random assignment into cognitive therapy or imipramine group; approx. 11-week treatment.	Both treatments were associated with significant reductions in hopelessness and some improvements in self-concept. Changes in self-concept were unrelated to overall depressive condition, while hopelessness was significantly related. Cognitive therapy exceeded imipramine treatment in both dimensions.
Sargent, 1990	423	OutP /InP	18 or older	F = 77.1%, M = 22.9%	DSM III— Major Depression	DSM-III criteria, 1-yr. follow-up: depression/no depression	Treatment as usual.	Confirmed high rate of non-recovery among DSM III diagnosed.

Study	N	Setting	Age	Gender	Diagnosis	Measures	Treatment	Results
Scogin, Bowman, Wamison et al., 1994	133	InP/OutP	51.7	F = 107, M = 26	Mild, moderate, and major depression	Dysfunctional Attitudinal Scale (DAS), Hamilton Rating Scale for Depression (HRSD) >9 or >17 and mean score results to 16.8 at pretreatment.	Group cognitive therapy (CT), cognitive bibliotherapy (CB).	Results failed to replicate previous findings of a poorer response to treatment for participants higher in dysfunctional thinking. CT may not be contraindicated for persons evidencing higher levels of dysfunctional thinking.
Shapiro, Barkham, Rees et al., 1994	117	OutP	40.5	F = 61, M = 56	Depression stratified low, moderate, and high severity	Global severity index (GSI), Beck's Depression Inventory (BDI)	8 or 16 sessions of either manualized treatment (CB) or psychodynamic interpersonal psychotherapy.	Those subjects presenting w/ severe depression improved more after 16 than after 8 sessions irrespective of treatment.
Shapiro, Rees, Barkham et al., 1995	117	OutP	40.5	F = 61, M = 56	Depression (3 ranges—low, moderate, and high severity)	Global Severity Index (GSI), Beck Depression Inventory (BDI) —Low severity 10 to 20; Moderate 21 to 26; High 27+	Cognitive-behavioral therapy (CBT) and psychodynamic-interpersonal psychotherapy. 8 or 16 1-hr. weekly sessions.	No measurable benefits between 16 over 8 sessions of CBT, irrespective of initial severity of depression.

(continued)

45

Table 3.1. (Continued)

Study	N	Sample (InP vs. OutP)	Age (Median/Mean)	Sex	Diagnosis (Formal vs. Not Formal)	Functional Impairment Measure	Type of Treatment	Outcome Differential Effects
Shea, Elkin, Imber et al., 1990	239	OutP	35	F = 70%, M = 30%	Major Depressive Disorder	Hamilton Rating Scale for Depression (HRSD), Social Adjustment Scale (SAS), General Life Functioning Scale (GLFS), Hopkins Symptom Checklist-90-R (HSCL-90), Hamilton Depression Scale (HAM-D)	Cognitive-behavior therapy, interpersonal therapy, imipramine w/ clinical management, and placebo w/ clinical management (16-week treatment conditions).	Patients w/ Personality Disorders (PD) had worse outcome in social functioning than those w/o PD and were more likely to have residual symptoms of depression. No significant treatment differences in work functioning or in mean depression scores at treatment termination.
Simons et al., 1984	87	OutP	18–60	NA	Nonbipolar Affective Disorder	Hopelessness Scale (HS), Beck Depression Inventory (BDI; 20 or above), and Hamilton Rating Scale for Depression (HRSD; 14 or above)	Assignment into 1 of 4 treatments: cognitive therapy (CT), pharmacotherapy, CT plus pharmacotherapy, or CT plus active placebo.	Patients receiving medication alone have a lower probability of completing therapy than those in any other treatment group.

Study	N	Setting	Age	Gender	Diagnosis	Measures	Treatment	Findings
Sotsky et al. 1991 (NIMH)	239	OutP	35	F = 70.3%, M = 29.7%	Major Depressive Disorder	Dysfunctional Attitudinal Scale (DAS), Social Adjustment Scale (SAS)	Interpersonal psychotherapy (IPT), cognitive-behavioral (CBT), imipramine w/ clinical management (IMI-CM), placebo w/ clinical man. (Pla-CM).	High severity, high work dysfunction IMI-CM > other low cognitive dysfunction CBT; IMI-CM > others low severity, low social dysfunction; IPT > other low severity CBT; IPT > IMI-CM, Pla-CM.
Thase, Simons et al. 1991	59	OutP	37.7	F = 44, M = 15	Major Depression w/ endogenous features	Hamilton Rating Scale for Depression (HRSD), Global Assessment Scale (GAS), Beck Depression Inventory (BDI).	16-week, 20-session CBT.	More severe group had significantly lower response rate on BDI. Groups showed comparable rates of symptomatic improvement. More severely depressed tended to remit less completely.
Vallejo et al., 1991	116	OutP	45.7	F = 84, M = 32	Major Depression w/ Melancholia	Eysenck Personality Inventory (EPI-B), Neuroticism (N), Extraversion (E), Hamilton Depression Scale (HDS—severity)	Phenelzine; imipramine; diazepam. 6-week and 6-month follow-up.	Severity of depression is not a good response predictor.

(*continued*)

47

Table 3.1. (*Continued*)

Study	N	Sample (InP vs. OutP)	Age (Median/ Mean)	Sex	Diagnosis (Formal vs. Not Formal)	Functional Impairment Measure	Type of Treatment	Outcome Differential Effects
Wells, Burman, & Rogers, 1992	626	OutP	18–40	M = 24–34%	Major Depression, Dysthymia, and either double depression or depressive symptoms w/ no current depression disorder	Course of Depression Interview (COD)	No treatment comparison.	Higher baseline severity in double depressed. Patients w/ dysthymia have worst outcomes. Patients w/ depression symptoms have best outcomes. Severity and level of functional status explained variance in outcomes more than did type of depression disorder.
Zuckerman, Prusoff, & Weissman, 1980	96	OutP	34	F = 85%, M = 15%	Unipolar Major Depression	Hamilton Depression Scale (HDS — severity), Global Illness Scale (GIS — severity of mental illness), Social Adjustment Self-Report (SASR — role performance in various areas of functioning).	Psychotherapy (psy.), pharmacotherapy (pharm.), combined psy. and pharm., and nonscheduled control treatment.	Significant main effect for treatment for HDS, RDS, and GIS (for each, $p < .01$). Scores on 4 personality scales not significantly related to outcome scores on HDS, RDS, GIS, or SASR at end of treatment, either as main effect or as interaction w/ treatment groups.

Selected Studies Related to Depression

Study	N	Setting	Age	Sex	Disorder	Measures	Treatment	Results
Ackerman et al., 1994	520	OutP	12–62	NA	Obsessive-Compulsive Disorder	Hamilton Rating Scale for Depression (HRSD), Hamilton Depression Scale (HAM-D).	Two- to 4-week drugfree washout interval followed by 10 weeks of active treatment, placebo, or clomipramine treatment (CMI).	Baseline depression is associated w/ response, but the association appears to be nonlinear. Significant relationship between response and baseline HAM-D. Higher initial scores were more predictive of good response.
Basoglu et al., 1994	144	OutP	35	NA	Panic disorder and Agoraphobia	PQ-Agoraphobia: fear and avoidance, family and social adjustment, work and social disability; Hamilton Depression Scale (HAM-D).	Four treatments: medication (anxiolytic) and exposure; placebo and exposure; medication and relaxation; placebo and relaxation. Individual treatment 8 weeks; medication from 8 to 16 weeks; follow-up week 43.	Predictors of poorer outcome at 6-month follow-up were older age, past history of depression, severity of phobia targets, and longer duration of illness. Severity of functioning impairment was a strong predictor of outcome.
Beutler, Frank, Scheiber et al., 1984	176	InP	32.4	F = 68, M = 108	Substance abuse, schizophrenia, bipolar, personality, anxiety, major depression disorders	PPI (initial impairment)	Four groups, each paired w/ at least two other groups for: behavioral/task (BT), expressive-experiential (EE), interactive/patient (IP).	IP groups received less individual therapy than other groups, but tended to produce the best results. Systematic deterioration effect occurred w/EE group. PPI showed significant relationship to group membership.

(*continued*)

Table 3.1. (*Continued*)

Study	N	Sample (InP vs. OutP)	Age (Median/ Mean)	Sex	Diagnosis (Formal vs. Not Formal)	Functional Impairment Measure	Type of Treatment	Outcome Differential Effects
Brown & Barlow, 1995	63	OutP	33.33	F = 65.1%, M = 34.9%	Panic Disorder	ADIS-R	CB, pain control treatment (PCT). 4 treatment conditions: cognitive restructuring (CR), CR and breathing retraining, CR and interoceptive exposure, or a combination of all 3 components. Follow-ups to 24 months.	Pretreatment severity of panic disorder was associated w/ poor outcome at 24-month follow-up. Use of psychotropic medication was associated w/ poor outcome.
Fahy & Russell, 1993	39	NA	23.8	F = 100%	Bulimia Nervosa	Bulimic Inventory Test (BITE), Eating Attitude Test (EAT), Montgomery-Asberg Depression Scale (MADRS), Eating Disorder Exam (EDE), Maudsley Compulsive/Obsessive Inventory (MOCI)	Cognitive-behavioral therapy (CBT). 8 weeks w/ 1 yr. follow-up.	High severity, lower body mass, and personality disorders result in poor clinical response at end of treatment.

Study	N	Setting	Age	Gender	Diagnosis	Measures	Treatment	Results
Jones, Cummings, & Horowitz, 1988	40	OutP	40	F = 100%	DSM III PTSD, adjustment anxiety or affective disorders	Global Severity Index (GSI); Stress Response Rating Scale (SRRS); Experience of Stress Scale (ESS).	Psychodynamic psychotherapy (12 sessions).	Improvement for patients w/ high pretreatment disturbance levels; stress-specific scales (ESS) showed greater amounts of change than did trait scales.
Keijsers et al., 1994	40	OutP	34.8	F = 22, M = 18	Obsessive Compulsive Disorder (OCD)	Maudsley Obsessive/Compulsive Inventory (MOCI), Anxiety Discomfort Scale (ADS)	Standardized treatment of 18 sessions behavioral in vivo exposure and response prevention.	High severity and depression predicted poor outcome for OCD.
Luborsky, Mintz, Auerbach et al., 1980	73	OutP	26.33	F = 44, M = 29	Nonpsychotic patients	Adequacy of functioning	Psychotherapy (mean results to 44 sessions).	Adequacy of functioning results in low level of prediction success.
Lueger, 1996	243	OutP	18–35	F = 65%, M = 35%	Distress, anxiety, depression, anger, problems w/ romantic partner or spouse, reacting too emotionally to events	Self-report scales (Subjective Well-being, Current Symptoms, and Current Life-functioning)—MHI at intake mean T-score of 61.5 and Global Assessment Scale (GAS) at intake mean T-score of 50	Psychotherapy (8 to 57 sessions).	Specific feedback on problem severity, early response to therapy, symptom remediation, and improvement in life functioning predicted treatment success. Higher severity results in more improvement on average.

(continued)

51

Table 3.1. (*Continued*)

Study	N	Sample (InP vs. OutP)	Age (Median/ Mean)	Sex	Diagnosis (Formal vs. Not Formal)	Functional Impairment Measure	Type of Treatment	Outcome Differential Effects
McLellan et al., 1983	476 veterans	InP/ OutP	NA	M = 100%	Alcoholics and drug addicts	Addiction Severity Index (ASI)	Average of 26 individual and 24 group therapy sessions. Follow-up through ASI interviews (6 months).	Patients w/ low severity improved in all phases; patients w/ high severity showed no improvement; patients w/ mid-range severity showed outcome differences from different treatments.
Mersch, Emmel, Krup, & Lips, 1991	74	OutP	32	F = 41, M = 33	Social Phobia	SSIT (a behavioral test) and RBI (a cognitive questionnaire)	Social skills training (SST), and rational emotive therapy (RET), 8 weekly sessions for 2.5 hrs. each.	No difference in effectiveness of SST or RET. Explorative analysis indicated the potential predictive power at treatment outcome, of confederate ratings of overt behavior on the SSIT. Patients needing additional treatment performed significantly worse on this measure at pretest.
Project MATCH research group, 1997	952	OutP	NA	F = 28%, M = 72%	Alcoholics	Severity (drinks per drinking day) during the 1-year posttreatment period	Twelve-week treatments: cog-beh. coping skills therapy, motivational enhancement therapy, or 12-step facilitation therapy (1-year posttreatment period).	Severity predicted outcome.

52

Study	N	Setting	Age	Gender	Diagnosis	Measures	Control/Comparison	Findings
Rounsaville, Chevron, Prassoff et al., 1987	321	InP	NA	Both	Alcohol Dependence or Abuse	Minnesota Multiphasic Personality Inventory (MMPI) for depression and antisocial personality	Treatment as usual.	Patients with antisocial personality disorder had poorer outcomes than those without.
Woody et al., 1984	110	OutP	18–55	M = 100%	Nonpsychotic opiate addicts	Addiction Severity Index (ASI), Social Avoidance and Distress Scales (SADS-L and SADS-C)	Paraprofessional drug counseling, counseling w/ cog beh. therapy, or counseling w/ supportive-expressive psychotherapy.	Low-severity patients made equal progress w/ added psychotherapy or w/ counseling alone. Moderate patients had better outcomes with added psychotherapy. High-severity patients showed poorer response than did mid- or low-severity patients.

This and subsequent tables are presented in two sections, one summarizing the studies that are specific to depressive conditions and disorders and the other summarizing the selective review of depression-related conditions. The narrative draws attention to some of the more interesting studies, not necessarily the most important or well-conducted ones, and tends to emphasize positive rather than representative findings.

defining characteristic of this distinction, however. We reasoned that self-reports should not be excluded from the definition of functional impairment if they specifically required ratings of performance in a variety of settings. Likewise, subjective distress could conceivably be obtained from clinician ratings if the questions were framed in a way that drew the clinician to judge how the patient felt or how the patient would describe his or her emotional state. As a result, estimates of functional impairment included patient reports and reports by external observers, or scores from standardized tests, if they reflected specifically on reduced levels of functioning in such areas as self-care, social responsibility, interpersonal relationships, work activity, and intimacy (Sperry et al., 1996).

Relying on this distinction, our literature review revealed modest but relatively consistent direct evidence that level of functional impairment is negatively correlated with prognosis generally. It also produced indirect evidence that impairment level may be an indicator both for the application of long-term and intensive treatment and for the use of pharmacological or combined psychosocial and pharmacological interventions.

In regard to the first point, our review produced direct evidence that depressed patients who have experienced reduced functioning and performance have a correspondingly low general rate of improvement in a variety of brief treatments (e.g., Gitlin, Swendsen, & Heller, 1995; Kocsis et al., 1988; Sotsky et al., 1991). Specifically, studies that included a range of impairment levels and treatments revealed a negative relationship between level of impairment and both speed and magnitude of improvement, virtually independent of treatment types (e.g., Beutler, Kim, Davison, Karno, & Fisher, 1996). The higher the level of impairment, the lower the rate of improvement, the greater the number of functional areas associated with evidence of disturbance, the poorer the patient's prognosis.

The poor prognosis associated with functional impairment was also observed in our review of studies outside the area of major depression. For example, bulimia nervosa (Fahy & Russell, 1993), obsessive-compulsive disorder (Keijsers, Hoogduin, & Schaap, 1994), and chemical dependency (McLellan, Woody, Luborsky, O'Brien, & Druley, 1983) have all been found to have a retarded response to treatment as a function of the level of patient initial impairment. Indeed, McLellan et al. concluded that high functional impairment was the single worst prognostic sign among patients with chemical abuse disorders.

The problem is more complex when we look at differential responses among various forms and models of treatment. For example, different methods of analyses, applied to data from the NIMH Treatment of Depression Collaborative Research Program have produced contradictory and mixed findings on the issue of whether functional impairment is a differential predictor for the application of interpersonal psychotherapy (IPT), imipramine, and cognitive therapy (CT). On one hand, the original report by Elkin et al. (1989) stated that patients with moderate and mild impairment (Global

Assessment Scores [GAS] scores higher than 50) responded equivalently to imipramine (plus clinical management), interpersonal psychotherapy, and cognitive therapy, while more seriously impaired patients (GAS scores less than 50) were more effectively treated with either imipramine or IPT than with CT.

In a later analysis in which functional impairment was assessed by formal assessment of cognitive dysfunction and self-reports of role impairment, Sotsky et al. (1991) reported that IPT exhibited a superiority over imipramine as well as over CT when cognitive and social impairment were low, rather than high. Apparently, relatively high levels of functional impairment are indicators for the use of IPT and antidepressants (in this case, imipramine), while relatively low levels of social impairment in cognitive functioning and social roles are either indicators for IPT or, more probably, given the rates and levels of change, contraindicators for the use of tricyclic antidepressants.

Within the domain of psychosocial treatment models, there is both direct and indirect evidence that functional impairment may be a mediator of the differential effects that can be attributed to various treatment models (e.g., Fremouw & Zitter, 1978; Joyce & Piper, 1996; McLellan et al., 1983; Shoham-Salomon & Rosenthal, 1987; Woody et al., 1984). Of special note, disturbed object relations (high functional impairment) among depressed patients (Joyce & Piper, 1996) and the presence of comorbid personality disorders among substance abusers (Woody et al., 1984) have been strongly and negatively related to outcomes with dynamically oriented and insight treatments, especially compared to other psychosocial interventions.

More direct evidence of the role of functional impairment was obtained by Beutler, Frank, et al. (1984), among a diagnostically mixed group of acute, socially impaired, psychiatric inpatients. They found that, in this population, experiential-expressive interventions are not as effective as interactive, process-oriented, or behaviorally oriented therapies. Patients treated with experiential-expressive therapies showed increased symptoms and deterioration at the end of treatment, while these negative effects were not found among those treated with the other interventions.

Aside from modality (pharmacotherapy versus psychosocial therapy) and model of therapy (specific drug or type of psychotherapy), clinical wisdom has typically led to the assumption that functional impairment is an indicator for increasing the intensity of treatment (Gaw & Beutler, 1995; Keijsers et al., 1994). However, we found only one controlled study of depression that directly bears on the issue of treatment intensity. Shapiro et al. (1994) compared behavioral and psychodynamic-interpersonal therapies, all of which were applied at two levels of intensity—either eight or sixteen weekly sessions. The more intensive and lengthy treatment showed the most positive effects among those with high levels of impairment, regardless of the model or type of treatment implemented. Those with low levels of impairment were not benefited by intensified treatment.

Of course, sixteen sessions of treatment is hardly what most clinicians consider to be intensive treatment. In the absence of more frequent and long-term treatment, one might expect that the effects of treatment applied in this way would dissipate. Even the relatively good results found by Shapiro et al. (1994) largely disappeared after one year (Shapiro et al., 1995).

But Shapiro et al.'s definition of high and low intensity should not be rejected prematurely. There is indirect evidence, largely garnered from work with other mental health conditions, that severity of impairment may be a contraindication for short-term treatment. For example, Brown and Barlow (1995) demonstrated that even when treatment of severely panic-disordered patients produced an immediate benefit, this benefit disappeared without continued treatment. Relapse rates among the most impaired patients were reduced by treatment that continued beyond the point of initial improvement. Continued treatment did not have such advantages for those with lesser levels of initial impairment.

Contrary to clinical lore, there is little and only inconsistent evidence in our review that functional impairment serves as a useful clinical indicator for the use of pharmacotherapy or for different types of psychotherapy. Several meta-analyses have confirmed the general equivalence of pharmacotherapeutic and psychotherapeutic approaches, even among relatively impaired but ambulatory individuals. Missing in these analyses are studies of inpatient populations and of subjects with truly severe functional impairments, for whom it is most likely that psychosocial approaches to treatment will be ineffective. Nonetheless, the available results of several meta-analyses raise serious questions about the validity of the clinical impression that pharmacotherapy is indicated over psychotherapy among moderately impaired patients (Antonuccio, Danton, & DeNelsky, 1995; Nietzel, Russell, Hemmings, & Gretter, 1987; Robinson, Berman, & Neimeyer, 1990).

Some studies have found a general difference in favor of pharmacotherapy over psychotherapy for functionally impaired but still ambulatory patients, but it is uncertain how much faith to place in these findings. Some findings point to the decade in which the studies were conducted as a variable that influences the results. The treatment provided in older studies may not be representative of how the same treatment type is practiced today (e.g., imipramine may not yield the same effect as the selective serotonin reuptake inhibitors (SSRIs) and the CT of the 1980s may not be the same as the CT of the 1990s (e.g., Antonuccio, Danton, & DeNelsky, 1995). This observation may explain why the findings of recent studies (e.g., Garvey, Hollon, & DeRubeis, 1994) do not support those of older studies, which suggest that moderately and mildly severe patients respond somewhat better to psychosocial treatments (cognitive therapy in particular) than to antidepressant medications. Nonetheless, the available evidence does suggest that high level of impairment is an indicator for pharmacotherapy, but this conclusion may not generalize to the differential prescription of pharmacotherapy and psychotherapy.

In summary, our review suggests the following general hypotheses:

1. Level of functional impairment is negatively correlated with prognosis generally.
2. Impairment level may be an indicator for the application of a long-term and intensive treatment, particularly one that focuses on interpersonal relationships.
3. Impairment level may be a potentiator for the effects of pharmacological treatment.

Intensive treatments may be needed in order to offset the poor prognosis associated with high impairment and to stabilize initial gains or to maintain initially good effects of treatment. Moderate and severe impairment of functioning may lead the clinician to explore medical and psychopharmacological options, to take an active role in teaching social skills, and to seek out opportunities in the patient's environment where the patient can practice social skills. It appears, however, that high levels of impairment do not contraindicate the use of psychosocial interventions but may suggest the coupling of pharmacological and psychosocial interventions (e.g., Dobson, 1989; Hollon, 1990).

Subjective Distress

While they have frequently been confounded, subjective distress and level of impairment are distinctly different concepts and, at least in theory, have distinctly different implications for treatment. Patient distress represents a patient's internal state rather than objective performance and, from a theoretical and clinical perspective, is assumed to have motivational properties (Frank & Frank, 1991). That is, some distress and discomfort is assumed to be a necessary or important factor in keeping a patient engaged in treatment.

Patient distress is ordinarily assessed through patient self-reports. In our review of clinical research, a variety of symptom checklists and mood scales (e.g., Beck Depression Inventory [BDI], Beck et al., 1961; SCL-90R, Derogatis, 1994; State Trait Anxiety Inventory [STAI], Spielberger, Gorsuch, & Lushene, 1970) were used to assess patient distress. Measured in these ways, subjective distress is relatively independent of specific diagnoses and represents transient states of well-being. That is, subjective distress is a changeable state that may correlate with symptom intensity but that is a poor reflection of impairment and an inconsistent correlate of specific symptomotology (Lambert, 1994; Strupp, Horowitz, & Lambert, 1997).

Our review suggests at least modest support (See table 3.2) for the assumption that distress is motivational, and this cuts across types of disorder. For example, our review uncovered evidence that moderate amounts of subjective distress may be a positive correlate of subsequent improvment (Lambert, 1994). Psychosocial treatments achieve their greatest effects among those with moderate to high initial levels of subjective distress (e.g., Klerman,

Table 3.2. Subjective Distress

Study	N	Sample (InP vs. OutP)	Age (Median/Mean)	Sex	Diagnosis (Formal vs. Not Formal)	Subjective Distress Measure	Type of Treatment	Outcome Differential Effects
Studies of Depressed Samples								
Beutler, Kim, Davison et al., 1996	63	OutP	46.76	F = 63%, M = 37%	Major Depression	Brief Symptom Inventory (BSI)	Focused expressive psychotherapy (FEP) and cognitive therapy (CT), both 90-min. sessions/week; supportive/self-directed therapy (S/SD), 20 min./week on phone.	Efficacies of CT and FEP were negatively related to patient initial distress, but clinicians rate CT most effective among those w/ initially low levels of distress.
Elkin et al., 1996	239	OutP	NA	NA	Major Depression	Beck Depresssion Inventory (BDI)	Cognitive behavior therapy (CBT), interpersonal psychotherapy (IPT), imipramine plus clinical management (IMI-CT), or placebo plus clinical management (Pla-CM), 16-wk. program, 16–20 sessions	IMI-CM was more effective with severe and more functionally impaired patients; IPT was better than CBT or Pla-CM for patients who were more severely depressed but not functionally impaired.
Hoencamp et al., 1994	119	OutP	39.8	F = 56.3%, M = 43.7%	Major Depressive Disorder	Newcastle Scales I and II (differentiated between endogenous versus neurotic and reactive types of depression).	Phase I—6-week trial w/ matropotiline; Phase II—6-week trial w/ lithium and matropotiline; Phase III—crossover trial.	Patients w/ somatization/passive-aggressive personality showed reduced chance of recovery. Psychiatric premorbid history or symptomatology was not significantly related to outcome; endogenous/nonendogenous distinction was not a predictor of response.

Study	N	Setting	Age	Gender	Diagnosis	Measure	Treatment	Results
Imber et al., 1990	239	OutP	35	F = 70%, M = 30%	Major Depressive Disorder (formal diagnosis)	Dysfunctional Attitudinal Scale (DAS—need for social approval)	Interpersonal therapy (IPT), cognitive-behavioral therapy (CBT), imipramine w/ clinical management (IMI-CM), placebo w/ clinical management (Pla-CM).	Improved need for social approval CBT>IPT, IMI-CM, placebo.
Klerman et al., 1974	150	OutP	Late 30s	F = 100%	Neurotic, depressed, ambulatory, and nonpsychotic	Hopkins Symptom Checklist (HSCL)	Preliminary phase: moderate dosages of amitriptyline therapy 4–6 weeks; experimental phase: 6–8 months of drug therapy or psychotherapy or both; follow-up phase.	Amitriptyline had greater immediate effect on symptoms and relapse prevention. Effectiveness of psychotherapy was cumulative and evident in interpersonal relations and social adjustment.
Lafferty, Beutler, & Crago, 1989	60	OutP	30.88	F = 49, M = 11	Anxiety or affective disorders and transitory disturbances	Symptom Checklist-90-R (SCL-90-R)	General individual therapy.	Benefits related to patient's anxiety and neuroticism.

(continued)

Table 3.2. (*Continued*)

Study	N	Sample (InP vs. OutP)	Age (Median/Mean)	Sex	Diagnosis (Formal vs. Not Formal)	Subjective Distress Measure	Type of Treatment	Outcome Differential Effects
McLean & Taylor, 1992	151	OutP	20–60	Not given	Unipolar Depression (formal diagnosis)	Beck Depression Inventory (BDI—self-report of coping behavior, social functioning), Depression Adjective Check List	Nondirective psychotherapy (PT), behavior therapy (BT), pharmacotherapy amitriptyline (AMI), relaxation training (RT), placebo control.	On subjective distress severe group somatic complaints PT>AMI=RT=BT.
Mohr et al., 1990	62	OutP	46.93	F = 32, M = 30	Major Depression	SCL-90 GSI subscales	Focus expressive psychotherapy (FEP), gestalt-based group therapy, cognitive therapy (CT), supportive/self-directed therapy (S/SD), 30-min. sessions weekly.	Negative responders had high levels of interpersonal difficulty/low levels of subjective distress. Nonrespondents had moderate levels of interpersonal difficulties/subjective distress. Positive responders had high levels of interpersonal difficulties/subjective distress.
Parker et. al., 1986	109	OutP/ InP	37.98	F=76, M = 33	Depression	Beck Depression Inventory (BDI—self-report coping questionnaire)	General psychotherapy—assessments at 6-week and 20-week follow-up.	Patients using more self-consolation coping behaviors at baseline assessment were highly unlikely to improve at 6 and 20 weeks. Higher scores on affect reduction were weakly linked w/ greater improvement at 6 and 20 weeks.

Selected Studies Related to Depression

Study	N	Setting	Mean age	Gender	Diagnosis	Measures	Treatment	Results
Blanchard et al., 1988	45	OutP	40.6	F=33, M=12	Irritable bowel syndrome (IBS)	Psychosomatic Symptom Checklist, State-Trait Affect Inventory (STAI), Beck Depression Inventory (BDI)	Muscle relaxation, thermal biofeedback, and training in cognitive stress coping, 12 sessions over 8 weeks.	Anxiety levels pretreatment were inversely related to clinical improvement and length of treatment.
Jacob et al., 1983	17	OutP	34	F=14, M=3	DSM III Diagnosis with tension or mixed headache ratings	Beck Depression Inventory (BDI), baseline headache activity ratings	8-session relaxation therapy program. After treatment program, biofeedback relaxation for 2 months followed by amitriptyline.	Significant negative correlation between improvement of headaches and scores on the BDI: > 8 predicted poor prognosis, < 3 predicted favorable prognosis.

1986; Klerman, DiMascio, Weissman, Prusoff, & Paykel, 1974; Lambert & Bergin, 1983), especially among those with ambulatory depressions, general anxiety, and diffuse somatic symptoms (e.g., McLean & Taylor, 1992).

For example, Parker, Holmes, and Manicavasager (1986) found that initial depression levels were positively correlated with treatment response among general medical patients. Similarly, Mohr et al. (1990) observed that the likelihood (though not the magnitude) of treatment response among moderately depressed patients was positively related to initial intensity of self-reported distress.

While some distress does seem to be important to sustain commitment and participation in treatment, the relationship is not always linear and continuous. Very high initial distress may even impede the speed and magnitude of therapeutic progress among patients whose depression is accompanied either by a personality disorder or by a somatic disorder (e.g., Hoencamp, Haffmans, Duivenvooden, Knegtering, & Dijken, 1994).

For example, Blanchard, Schwarz, Neff, and Gerardi (1988) determined that high initial distress was negatively, rather than positively, associated with improvement among patients with irritable bowel syndrome. Somatic patients who initially presented with low levels of subjective anxiety were the ones who were most likely able to benefit from behavioral and self-regulatory treatment. A similar pattern has been found among patients who present with chronic headaches (Jacob, Turner, Szekely, & Eidelman, 1983). Headache patients with relatively low initial distress levels may be more likely than those with high initial levels to benefit from self-monitored relaxation. In these studies, patients with moderate and high levels of subjective distress, perhaps because they could not sustain commitment and motivation, failed to benefit from behavioral and psychotherapeutic treatments.

Beutler, Kim, Davison, Karno, and Fisher (1996) tested the hypothesis that the type of treatment, as well as the type of symptomatic presentation, may help account for the variations of response observed in the foregoing studies. They demonstrated that high initial distress was a positive predictor of positive effects among those seen in supportive and self-directed therapy but was not related to the potency of more active and therapist-guided cognitive and experiential treatments. Similarly, McLean and Taylor (1992) found that high subjective discomfort, when accompanied by somatic symptoms of distress, disposed the patient to respond to nondirective psychotherapy. In this study, when distress level was high but did not activate somatic symptoms, behavior therapy generated more improvement than psychotherapy.

The role of subjective distress as a differential predictor was also reported in the NIMH collaborative study of depression (Imber et al., 1990). In this study, patients with the most severe distress were most effectively treated by IPT, while both IPT and CT worked reasonably well among those with mild and moderate distress levels. This finding has been repeated through a number of reiterations of the analysis of severity (e.g., Elkin, 1994; Elkin, Gibbons, Shea, & Shaw, 1996).

Collectively, the foregoing research suggests three hypotheses, reflecting differences in the nature of the treatments offered as a function of patient distress:

1. Moderate distress may be be important to sustain commitment and participation in treatment.
2. High initial distress may be an indicator for the use of supportive and self-directed therapy but bears no relationship to the effectiveness of active and therapist-guided interventions.
3. High distress may be an indicator for interpersonally focused interventions, perhaps including group or family formats.

Social Support

Social support derives from one's family, friends, and work relationships. It can be assumed that dysfunction in these relationships may be correlated with one's level of objective impairment of functioning. Nonetheless, social support in its own right has received a good deal of attention both from theoreticians and from outcome researchers. It has been widely postulated as a predictor of therapeutic outcome and as a buffer against relapse.

Accordingly, our review uncovered many research studies whose results indicated that high levels of social support both improved outcomes in psychotherapy and decreased the likelihood of relapse (e.g., Sherbourne, Hays, & Wells, 1995; Vallejo, Gasto, Catalan, Bulbena, & Menchon, 1991). However, the self-evident nature of this conclusion belies the degree of complexity in the nature and definition of social support.

Specifically, social support may be measured as an objective aspect of one's relationships, for example, by identifying the number of people available with whom one relates each day, specifying the number of individuals in the extended family, assessing the geographic proximity of family members, counting the number of people in a household, or identifying marital and relationship status. However, an objective count of this type identifies only the *availability* of social support systems, not the degree of support sought or experienced. There is a difference between *subjective* (e.g., Moos & Moos, 1981) elements of experienced support and the *objective* presence of others (e.g., Ellicott, Hammen, Gitlin, Brown, & Jamison, 1990). It is one thing to have others available and quite another either to access these resources during times of stress or to feel supported by other people when comfort is offered.

It has been widely demonstrated that social support, especially subjective support, may provide a buffer against relapse and improve prognosis (see table 3.3). For example, Moos (1990) found that the proximal availability of an objectively identified confidant and the level of satisfaction derived from relationships each significantly and independently increased the likelihood of improvement among depressed patients. Likewise, Zlotknick, Shea, & Pilkonis (1996) found that a large number of support objects improved patients' abilities to retain gains made in treatment. Such findings have been

Table 3.3 Social Support

Studies of Depressed Samples

Study	N	Sample (InP vs. OutP)	Age (Median/Mean)	Sex	Diagnosis (Formal vs. Not Formal)	Social Support Measure	Type of Treatment	Outcome Differential Effects
Andrew et al., 1993	59	InP	48.4	F = 100%	Major Depressive Disorder (MDD)	Index of social support on the Parental Bonding Inventory; Maudsley Marital Questionnaire; Brow's measure of social support (confidant)	Electroconvulsive therapy (ECT), tricyclic antidepressants, MAO inhibitors, lithium, dynamic psychotherapy, marital therapy, anxiety managment.	There were no associations between outcome and presence of a close confidant or the degree of either close or diffuse social support.
Avery & Winokur, 1977	609	InP	NA	F = 360, M = 249	Depression	No social support measured	Antidepressants or electroconclusive therapy (ECT) or no treatment.	Nonsignificant results were found for social support.
Beach et al., 1983	145	InP	NA	Couples	Major Depression, Bipolar, Schizophrenia	Marital Adjustment Test—I and II	No treatment (follow-up at discharge and at 3–4 years).	Only the depressives differed from the normal group in having significantly worse course of marital relationship (84% of depressive couples resulted in negative course of marital change over time). MAT scores successfully predicted course of marital relationship.
Beutler & Mitchell, 1981	40	OutP	31.5	F = 23, M = 17	Patients seeking psychotherapy at a psychiatric clinic	Minnesota Multiphasic Personality Inventory (MMPI)—scale clusters	Analytic and experiential (defined by ratings of treatment techniques/ behaviors).	Impulsive externalizers benefited more from experiential than analytic; analytic treatments achieved greatest effect among depressive anxious patients/less than effective among impulsive, externalizing patients.

Study	N	Setting	Age	Gender	Diagnosis	Measures	Treatment/Follow-up	Findings
Billings, Cronkite, & Moos, 1985	424	OutP/InP	40.7	F = 56.5%, M = 43.5%	Major or Minor Unipolar Depressive Disorder	Social activities w/ friends and family examined on scale of 0–12, occupational functioning (employed or nonemployed)	Treatment at inpatient or outpatient facilities was not specified. Follow-up after 12 months of entry.	Poor social functioning at treatment intake was not predictive of later difficulty at follow-up; patients w/ less support (single and with low occupational level) were more difficult to follow up.
Billings & Moos, 1984	424	InP/OutP	39.9	F = 54.7%, M = 45.3%	Chronic, non-chronic depressed patients	Social networks were assessed: number of friends, number of networks, number of close relationships, family support (FRI), work support (WRI)	Treatment as usual.	Correlations were found between stressors and social resources and functioning among nondepressed and non-chronic depressed patients, but not among chronic patients.
Billings & Moos, 1985	424	OutP/InP	49.8	F = 43.5%, M = 56.5%	Unipolar Depression	HDLF (social resources), Family Environment Scale (FES), Work Environment Scale (WES)	Treatment as usual.	Improvements in patients' functioning at follow-up were associated w/ increases in patients' social resources but no overall decrease in stressors. Both were related to patient's functioning at follow-up. Quality of support was more related to functioning than was amount.

(continued)

Table 3.3 (*Continued*)

Study	N	Sample (InP vs. OutP)	Age (Median/Mean)	Sex	Diagnosis (Formal vs. Not Formal)	Social Support Measure	Type of Treatment	Outcome Differential Effects
Corney, 1987	80	OutP	29.8	F = 100%	Acute or chronic depression	Social Maladjustment Schedule rated on four items: shared interests/activities, sources of conflict, responsibilities/decision making, and sexual compatibility	Experimental group for referral to attached social workers, or control group for routine treatment by GPs (w/ 6–12-month follow-up).	Women w/ major marital problems had more depression at follow-up. Patients w/ marital difficulties in the experimental group made more improvements than the control group. Women w/ acute or chronic depression, major marital difficulties, and poor social contact improved more w/social weekly intervention.
DiMascio et al., 1979	81	OutP	18–65	F = 69, M = 12	Acute Depression	History	Interpersonal psychotherapy (12 weeks of 50-min. sessions 1 time per week); pharmacotherapy alone (HCL); psychotherapy plus pharmacotherapy; nonscheduled treatment (as-needed treatment).	Nonsignificant results for social support.
Ellicott et al., 1990	61	OutP	39.6	F = 33, M = 28	Bipolar Disorder	Life stress assessment, which entailed a face-to-face interview.	Maintenance treatment over a 2-yr. period (included lithium carbonate as a medication regimen, as well as carbazepine, valproate, and neuroleptics).	Significant relationship between the highest levels of stress and the likelihood of relapse was found. Subjects with low or average stress did not show a greater risk of relapse than those who stayed well. No differences between levels of medication or compliance.

Study	N	Setting	Age	Gender	Diagnosis	Measure	Treatment/Design	Findings
Gangadhar et al., 1982	32	NA	44	F = 18, M = 14	Major Depression	KAS measured various aspects of social functioning (social dysfunction)	Electroconvulsive therapy (ECT): thiopentone, succinylcholine, and atropine; or imipramine (IMI).	Both treatments produced improvement; ECT produced effects quicker w/ less subjective side effects to the patient. Both groups showed equal/significant improvement in social functioning at the end of 3 months/maintained the same to end of 6 months.
George et al., 1989	150	InP	35–50 and 60+	F = 60%, M = 40%	Major Depression	Duke Social Support Index (four dimensions: size of social network, amount of social interaction, instrumental support, and subjective social support)	No treatment; general interviews used and assessments administered at 6–32 months after intake.	Social support affects the outcome of depressive illness. Subjective social support measure exhibited the strongest and most complex relationship with the outcome scores. Other dimensions of social support were not significant.
Hoencamp et al., 1994	119	OutP	39.8	F = 56.3%, M = 43.7%	Major Depressive Disorder	Social Adjustment Scale (SAS)	Phase I–6-week trial w/ matropotiline; Phase II–6-week trial w/ lithium augmentation of matropotiline; Phase III—crossover trial.	Patients w/ somatization/passive-aggressive personality had less of a chance to recovery; perceived social support from the family was negatively related to outcome.

(continued)

Table 3.3 (Continued)

Study	Sample (InP vs. OutP)	N	Age (Median/ Mean)	Sex	Diagnosis (Formal vs. Not Formal)	Social Support Measure	Type of Treatment	Outcome Differential Effects
Hooley & Teasdale, 1989	InP	39	47.6	F = 23, M = 16	Unipolar patients, married and nonpsychotic	Dyadic adjustment scale—assess marital satisfaction; Camberwell Family Interviews—assess expressed emotion (EE)	Antidepressants, electroconvulsive therapy (ECT), occupational therapy, group therapy; follow-up at 3 and 9 months (length of treatment not stated).	Levels of spouse criticism were strongly associated w/ clinical relapse; patients with high EE spouses were more likely to relapse than those with low EE spouses. Marital stress also predicted outcome.
Hooley et al., 1986	InP	39	47.6	F = 23, M = 16	Major Depressive Disorder (MDD)	Expressed emotion (EE), family interview (CFI), Dyadic Adjustment Scale, perceived criticism from spouse.	No treatment.	Expressed emotion and marital distress have predictive validity in both schizo and depressed populations. Perceived level of spouse criticism was most strongly associated with relapse.
Imber et al., 1990	OutP	239	35	F = 70%, M = 30%	Major Depressive Disorder (formal diagnosis)	Need for social approval (DAS), Social Adjustment Scale	Interpersonal psychotherapy (IPT), cognitive-behavioral (CBT), imipramine w/ clinical management (IMI-CM), placebo w/ clinical management (Pla-CM).	Improved need for social approval, CBT>IPT, IMI-CM, Pla-CM. No differences were found for social adjustment or interpersonal sensitivity.
Kupfer & Spiker, 1981	InP	76	38.6	F = 51, M = 25	Major Depressive Syndrome	History	Pharmacotherapy; evaluations 2 times per week for 24 days.	Nonsignificant results for social support were found.

Study	N	Setting	Age	Gender	Diagnosis	Measures	Control	Results
Maling et al., 1995	307	OutP	NA	F=74%, M=26%	Axis I or II diagnosis, interpersonal distress	Abbreviated version of Inventory of Interpersonal Problems (IIP)	Treatment as usual.	Self-effacing patients did not respond as much to treatment as did detached patients, and in turn these were slower than controlling patients.
McLean & Taylor, 1992	151	OutP	20–60	NA	Unipolar Depression (formal diagnosis)	Self-report of coping behavior, social functioning, life satisfaction, and mood (DACL); Beck Depression Inventory (BDI)	Nondirective psychotherapy (PT), behavior therapy (BT), pharmacotherapy amitriptyline (AMI), relaxation training (RT) control.	No significant results were related to social functioning or social support.
Moos, 1990	265	OutP	38	F=65%, M=35%	Unipolar Depression (formal diagnosis) major=57% minor=43%	Health and Daily Living Form (HDL), family conflict (0–14), quality of confidant and family support from Family Environment Scale (FES)	Treatment as usual (range from 0 to 30 sessions).	High quality of support (close confidant and less family conflict) had better outcome with brief treatment. Low quality of support did better with long treatment. More social resources predicted better outcome.

(*continued*)

69

Table 3.3 (*Continued*)

Study	N	Sample (InP vs. OutP)	Age (Median/Mean)	Sex	Diagnosis (Formal vs. Not Formal)	Social Support Measure	Type of Treatment	Outcome Differential Effects
Paivio & Greenberg, 1995	34	OutP	41	F = 22, M = 12	Unresolved feelings related to a significant other	Structured analysis of social behavior; Inventory of Interpersonal Problems; Unfinished Business Resolution Scale	Experiential therapy (ECH) or psychoeducational group (PED) (group treatment of 8–12 members for 3 months 1 time per week).	Experiential therapy achieved meaningful gains for most clients and was significantly greater than improvement over the psychoeducational group on all measures. Treatment gains for experiential group were maintained at follow-up.
Pfohl et al., 1984	78	InP	18 or older	NA	Major Depression Disorder (formal diagnosis) w/ or w/o Personality Disorder	Brown's measure of social support	Electroconvulsive therapy (ECT), antidepressants.	Patients w/ depression and personality disorders (PD) differed from patients w/ depression alone on many measures. The PD group was significantly more likely to have poor social support.
Sotsky et al., 1991	239	OutP	35	F = 70.3%, M = 29.7%	Major Depressive Disorder (formal diagnosis)	Social Adjustment Scale (SAS), social satisfaction	Interpersonal psychotherapy (IPT), cognitive-behavioral (CBT), imipramine w/ clinical management (IMI-CM), placebo w/ clinical management (Pla-CM).	Low social dysfunction predicted better outcome for IPT. Low cognitive dysfunction had better outcome w/ CBT and IMI-CM.
Spangler, Simons, Monroe, & Thase, 1997	59	OutP	37.71	F = 44, M = 15	Major Depression	Psychiatric Epidemiology Research Interview (PERI)—occurrences and undesirability of life events, Bedford's life events and difficulties scale	Sixteen weeks of individual cognitive-behavioral therapy (CBT).	Significant reductions in level of depression from pre- to posttreatment; patients w/ interpersonal stressors responded less well to CBT.

Study	N	Setting	Age	Gender	Diagnosis	Measures	Treatment	Findings
Steinmetz et al., 1983	75	OutP	36	F = 69.3%, M = 30.7%	Major Depressive Disorder (MDD), minor or intermittent depression	Social adjustment assessed by interviewer ratings on social adjustment scale; Perceived Social Support Inventory; Social Reaction Inventory	Skills training.	Severity improved and prior social adjustment and perceived social support were good predictors of outcome and posttreatment; clients' perception of being more in control was associated w/ the greatest reduction in symptomatology.
Swindle et al., 1989	370	OutP/ InP	39.4	F = 209, M = 161	Unipolar Depressive Disorder	Self-esteem, social activities w/ family, employment, life stressors, social resources, coping responses	38% of sample received psychiatric treatment, either individual, marital, or group; entire sample assessed at treatment intake and at 1-yr. and 4-yr. follow-up.	Patients improved in symptom outcomes, quality of social resources, and coping responses. There were some declines in life stressors. Life stressors, social resources, and coping were positively related to patient functioning.
Teri & Lawrhsohn, 1986	66	OutP	34.7	F = 40, M = 26	Major or Minor Depressive Disorder	Social Adjustment Scale; social support measured by Perceived Social Support Inventory	Coping with Depression course (12-session group treatment based on social learning view of depression) or individual behavior therapy (12-session structured training program designed to increase pleasant activities and decrease negative activities).	Patients were more likely to improve in symptoms if they were more socially self-confident, more socially adjusted, more emotionally reliant on others, and with less stressful life events. No differences between treatments were found.
Vallejo et al., 1991	116	OutP	45.7	F = 72.4%, M = 27.6%	Major Depression with Melancholia	Lowenthal-Haven-Kaplan Questionnaire (social support); Medalie-Goldbourt Scale (marital difficulties)	6 months of treatment with medication, either imipramine or phenelzine	Social support during follow-up treatment influenced outcome and predicted therapeutic response.

(continued)

Table 3.3 (Continued)

Study	N	Sample (InP vs. OutP)	Age (Median/ Mean)	Sex	Diagnosis (Formal vs. Not Formal)	Social Support Measure	Type of Treatment	Outcome Differential Effects
Veiel et al., 1992	190	InP	41.76	F=65%, M=35%	Discharged depressed patients	Manhattan interview on social support to assess social network	Unspecified psychiatric treatment (methodological issues and baseline differences assessed between recovered and nonrecovered patients).	Few differences between recovered and nonrecovered w/ respect to stable personality traits; recovered patients less likely to have had severe long-term life difficulties, and their coping style differed, having a lesser inclination to solicit social support.
Zlotnick et al., 1996	188	OutP	21–60	F = 134, M = 54	Major Depressive Disorder (formal diagnosis)	Social Network Form interview that measured the number of persons in several domains of relationships and degree of satisfaction of these relationships	Interpersonal therapy, cognitive behavior therapy, and imipramine plus clinical management.	6-month follow-up showed number of satisfying supports was significant predictor of depressive symptoms. Positive social support leads to decreased severity of depression.

Selected Studies Related to Depression

Azrin et al., 1982	43	OutP	33.9	F = 17%, M = 83%	Alcohol dependence	Married versus single	Traditional disulfiram only (DO); Disulfiram Assurance (DA) including monitoring/encouragement from significant other; behavior therapy including DA (BDA).	DO was least successful, DA was more effective, and BDA was the most effective. Marital status was associated w/ outcome, though in BDA condition good results were also found w/ clients who were single.

72

Study	N	Setting	Age	Gender	Population	Measure	Intervention	Results
Dadds & McHugh, 1992	22	OutP	32.8	F = 21, M = 1	Single parents of children w/ conduct or oppositional disorder	Perceived social support from both family and friends (PSS—Fa/Fr); Inventory of Socially Supportive Behaviors	6-week parent training (CMT), plus social support intervention only for ally social treatment group (AST)	Responders from either group were more likely than nonresponders to report high levels of social support from friends. Having an ally revealed no significant results.
Harrison et al., 1988	319	InP/OutP	36	F = 30%, M = 70%	Alcoholics w/ or w/o drug-use disorders	Marital status	InP treatment, OutP treatment, and combination InP/OutP treatment for alcoholism	Successful 6-month follow-up of 73% of the patients revealed a 67% abstinence rate w/ no significant differences by treatment setting. Marital status did not predict outcome.
Longabaugh, Beattie, Noel et al., 1993	229	OutP	38	F = 31%, M = 69%	Alcohol dependence or alcohol abuse (formal diagnosis)	Important People and Activities, self-report measures of social investment (not specified)	Individual cognitive-behavioral therapy (CBT) or relationship enhancement therapy (RE) followed for 12 months.	Social support was associated w/ better response to treatment. High support did equally well, while low support benefited more from CBT than RE.
Maisto et al., 1988	23	OutP	NA	M = 100%	Alcoholic males (who had relapsed) and their wives	Husbands and wives independently interviewed	Behavioral marital therapy w/ 2-yrs. follow-up.	Both the alcoholics and their spouses reported intrapsychic and situational determinants of the relapses, but showed poor agreement. For situational attributions, patients tended to see their spouses as causes of relapse more than did the spouses.

(continued)

Table 3.3 (Continued)

Study	N	Sample (InP vs. OutP)	Age (Median/Mean)	Sex	Diagnosis (Formal vs. Not Formal)	Social Support Measure	Type of Treatment	Outcome Differential Effects
Sherbourne, Hays, & Wells, 1995	604	OutP	46	F = 74%, M = 26%	Depressive Disorder	Self-report questionnaire that measured support, coping style, lifestyle factors, and beliefs.	Treatment as usual	Decreased depression was associated with patients who had high levels of social support and who had more active and less avoidant coping styles.
Vaughn & Leff, 1976	67	InP	35.6	F = 42, M = 25	Schizophrenic and depressed patients	Family interview schedule; rating of expressed emotion, number of criticisms, hostility, and overinvolvement.	No treatment (assessment upon relapse)	The expressed emotion of the relative was associated w/ relapse independently of all other social, background, and clinical factors investigated. Social support was a good predictor of outcome.

cross-validated by many others (e.g., Billings & Moos, 1984; George, Blazer, & Hughes, 1989). Indeed, George et al. (1989) found that felt support was the best predictor among a variety of patient and symptom characteristics of treatment benefit among patients with major depression. These effects also appear, in our review, to be consistent across various problems. For example, the availability of a critical mass of supportive people has been found to be a factor in the effectiveness of alcohol treatment (Longabaugh, Beattie, Noel, Stout, & Malloy, 1993).

In exploring the roles of subjective versus objective support, Hooley and Teasdale (1989) found that the quality of the marital relationship, rather than the mere presence of a marital partner, was more closely related to reductions in relapse. The importance of the subjective quality of social support as a predictor of treatment outcome was also supported by Hoencamp et al. (1994). In this case, the absence of perceived or subjectively experienced family support had a significant negative impact on treatment outcome among moderately depressed outpatients.

Billings and Moos (1984) found that both chronic and nonchronic patients reported having fewer available social resources than did nondepressed controls. However, only among patients with nonchronic depression was the severity of the problem related to the lack of available social support systems. Compared to support availability, the felt level of support was the more consistent predictor of benefit. These findings raise some interesting questions about the possibility that acute depression is an indicator for using procedures that activate and strengthen available support systems, for example, through the use of group therapy methods and other methods that encourage social participation.

One of the most interesting roles of social support may be in the moderating influence it exerts on planned treatment intensity. Moos (1990) found that accessibility of social support systems was quite strongly indicative of the optimal duration of treatment. Not only did low levels of social support availability serve as an indicator for long-term treatment, but also high experienced social support was a contraindicator for long-term treatment. Depressed patients who lacked social support resources improved as a linear function of the length and intensity of treatment, but those who experienced satisfaction with their level of support achieved maximal treatment benefit quite quickly and, thereafter, continued treatment produced little benefit. In fact, these supported patients were at risk for deterioration if they were provided with long-term therapy.

Contemporary literature also suggests that a modest amount of social support is necessary, or at least very important, for potentiating the effects of psychosocial interventions. When aspects of social support or availability are moderate or high, the effects of a variety of behavioral and supportive interventions are enhanced relative to various antidepressant drug regimens (e.g., McLean & Taylor, 1992; Sotsky et al., 1991). To some degree, the absence of support may also serve as an indicator for pharmacotherapy.

As an aside, it is notable that this pattern has also been observed among alcoholics (Azrin, et al., 1982). Moreover, indirect evidence from alcohol treatment studies sheds further light on the probable guidelines that may be indicated by social support levels. This literature suggests that social investment, a concept that combines aspects of social support availability and experienced support, has considerable power in the prediction of treatment benefits. Longabaugh and his colleagues (Longabaugh et al., 1993) defined social investment as the amount of effort expended in maintaining involvement with others, an aspect of objective support, combined with the experienced support from these contacts. They compared the independent roles of observed social resources and the combined measure of social investment in predicting both prognosis and differential response to two different psychotherapies. Both objective support and social investment predicted differential response to relationship-enhancement and cognitive-behavioral therapies. Social investment, however, had a more central and pervasive mediating role in this process.

Specifically, among those who experienced little satisfying support from others, cognitive-behavioral therapy was more effective than relationship-enhancement therapy. However, among individuals who had high levels of social investment, relationship-enhancement therapy was both more effective and had lower relapse rates than cognitive therapy, regardless of the level of social support available or experienced. This pattern of relationships was also observed in other studies of treatment for depressed patients. Those with low levels of experienced or observed support have tended to respond better to cognitive and behavioral therapies than to interpersonal therapies (e.g., Sotsky et al., 1991). A certain level of experienced or felt support, but not necessarily the availability of significant others, may be necessary to activate the power of interpersonal and relationship therapies.

Collectively, though complex, extensive studies on social support suggest the hypothesis that:

1. High levels of experienced social support may both improve outcomes in treatment and decrease the likelihood of relapse.
2. Low levels of social support seems to be an indicator for long-term treatment and, conversely, high experienced social support appears to be a contraindicator for long-term treatment.
3. A certain level of experienced or felt support may be necessary to activate the power of interpersonal and relationship therapies.

Whether the third conclusion suggests the need for group and multiperson therapies to establish this level of support is a critical but still unanswered question.

Problem Complexity/Chronicity

It is readily observed that there are many variations in the breadth of the objectives valued by different treatment models. These objectives range from symptomatic goals to thematic and conflictual change. Specific goals vary in breadth of impact or intended impact and conceivably may be suited to patients whose problems correspond to the intended impact on a dimension of problem complexity. For example, behavioral and medical/pharmacological interventions, as a rule, are aimed at making some change in narrow symptom presentations, while relationship, psychodynamic, systems-oriented, and interpersonal therapies focus on changing themes and conflicts (DeRubeis et al., 1990; Simons, Garfield, & Murphy, 1984), many of which may be associated with the presence of comorbid Axis I and Axis II conditions. That is, treatments that are oriented toward insight and awareness focus on broader themes than do treatments that are oriented toward behavioral and cognitive change (e.g., Caspar, 1995; Luborsky, 1996; Strupp & Binder, 1984).

The apparent and often obvious correspondence between problem complexity and treatment focus suggests that a beneficial treatment match might be one that entails a fit between problem complexity and the breadth of the objectives inherent in the treatment applied. If this is true, high problem complexity should favor the effects of a broad-band treatment. Within psychosocial domains, for example, high complexity should favor systemic and dynamic treatments over symptom-focused ones (Gaw & Beutler, 1995), while among medical interventions, ECT should be favored over pharmacotherapies.

The complexity of patient problems might, for clarity, be indexed in a number of ways. Complexity may be related to such factors as comorbidity, enduring personality disturbance, and chronicity or recurrence of the depressed condition. Indeed, variations on the dimension of complexity may be conceptually and roughly similar to the distinction between endogenous and nonendogenous conditions. Depressed patients who present with comorbid disorders, long-standing personality disturbances, and recurrent or comorbid conditions present special treatment needs. That is, the most effective treatment for depression may be determined in part by how complex, chronic, and multifaceted the presenting problem is judged to be. Patterns of recurrence, persistence/chronicity, comorbidity, and broadly generalized disturbances in interpersonal relationships have all been identified as indicators of the presence of a complex disorder.

Clinical lore holds that pharmacological and medical interventions are indicated for very complex, recurrent conditions and that psychosocial and behavioral interventions are relatively more effective than medical ones for conditions that are acute and relatively noncomplex and that represent situational adjustment. Specifically, it is conventionally assumed in clinical literature that complex problems require medical or pharmacological intervention while psychosocial interventions may work only for those whose problems are relatively less complex in nature.

Several studies of depression (e.g., Corbishley et al., 1990; Last, Thase, Hersen, Bellack, & Himmelhoch, 1985; Rush et al., 1989; Simons, Gordon, Monroe, & Thase, 1995) have explored the relative advantages of psychosocial and medical interventions attendant on levels of problem complexity (see table 3.4). These studies have adopted the hypothesis that patients with biological markers indicating a complex and endogenous depressive disorder are more likely to respond to pharmacotherapy than psychotherapy and that the opposite is true for those with nonendogenous depression. These studies also have explored the role of endogenous indicators as indicators for the use of medication.

Virtually all of the studies to date confirm the hypothesis that pharmacotherapy achieves its greatest efficacy among patients with endogenous depressive symptoms, as compared to those with nonendogenous, acute, or nonmelancholic depressions. Surprisingly, however, with only a couple of exceptions, these studies have failed to find the difference that has been hypothesized to exist between various forms of psychosocial (largely cognitive) therapy and pharmacotherapy among either type of depressed patient. Last et al. (1985) determined that endogenous (i.e., melancholic) patients were more responsive to amitriptyline than to a behavioral skills training regime but that non-melancholic depressed patients did better in the behavioral treatment than they did when assigned to the drug treatment condition.

With this and a few early studies as exceptions, studies on this topic (e.g., Corbishley et al., 1990; Rush et al., 1989; Simons, Gordon, Thase, & Monroe, 1995) have found that psychotherapy produces effects that are surprisingly equivalent to those obtained by pharmacotherapy when melancholic or endogenous depression is studied. The advantages noted by the other investigators for psychotherapy over pharmacotherapy among patients with nonendogenous conditions continued to hold. At least one difference among these various studies is that those that produced the latter effects relied on biological markers (e.g., sleep parameters) for defining endogeneity, while those of the first type relied on clinical ratings of vegetative signs. Thus, the nature of the assessment may be a factor in differential treatment.

The assumption that it is desirable to match the breadth of the treatment with the breadth or complexity of the problem has received some support from several quarters. One line of evidence has come from comparisons of ECT and pharmacotherapeutic treatments among patients who have complex and chronic conditions. For example, several studies in our review (e.g., Gangadhar, Kapur, & Kalyanasundara, 1982; Lykours et al., 1986) found that ECT outperformed pharmacotherapy among patients with complex and chronic depressions, suggesting some advantage to fitting the breadth of treatment to the breadth of the presenting problem. Looking at comparisons of pharmacological and broad-band psychotherapies, studies in our review found that pharmacotherapy outperformed various interpersonal psychotherapies among complex patients (Weissman et al., 1979).

Research in our review also supported the advantages of narrow-band behavioral and cognitive-behavioral treatments among depressed patients whose problems were non-endogenous. For example, Knight-Law, Sugerman, and Pettinati (1988) found that the effectiveness of behavioral-symptom-

Table 3.4 Complexity

Study	N	Sample (InP vs. OutP)	Age (Median/ Mean)	Sex	Diagnosis (Formal vs. Not Formal)	Complexity Measure	Type of Treatment	Outcome Differential Effects
Studies of Depressed Samples								
Beutler, Frank, Sheiber et al., 1984	176	InP	32.4	F = 108, M = 68	Substance abuse, schizophrenia, bipolar, personality, anxiety, major depression, and transient disorders	Minnesota Multiphasic Personality Inventory (MMPI) (initial disturbance)	4 groups: total of 8 months, paired w/ at least two other groups. Behavioral/task (BT), expressive-experiential (EE), interactive/ patient (IP) therapies.	IP groups received less individual therapy than other groups. Systematic deterioration effect occurred w/ EE group. IP group tended to produce the best results. PPI showed significant relationship to membership in the treatment groups.
Corbishley et al., 1990	56	OutP	70	F = 31, M = 25	Major depression	Dexamethasone Suppression Test; Rapid Eye Movement latency and density test	Cognitive-behavioral therapy (CBT) or pharmacotherapy (alprazolam). CBT consisted of 20 weeks of group therapy; pharmacotherapy consisted of 8 mg/day w/ management meetings 1 time per week. Placebo group also used.	Depression not characterized by biologic abnormalities/sleep variables not predictive of response to either treatment; low baseline DST levels associated w/ good response to psychotherapy.

(continued)

79

Table 3.4 (*Continued*)

Study	N	Sample (InP vs. OutP)	Age (Median/ Mean)	Sex	Diagnosis (Formal vs. Not Formal)	Complexity Measure	Type of Treatment	Outcome Differential Effects
DeRubies et al., 1990	112	OutP	33	F = 80%, M = 20%	Major Depressive Disorder	Automatic Thoughts Questionnaire; HS (to measure respondent's general pessimism); Dysfunctional Attitudinal Scale	One of four types of treatment, randomly assigned: cognitive therapy (CT) alone, imipramine pharmacotherapy alone, combination of CT w/ imipramine, and imipramine plus maintenance. All treatments were 16–20 sessions over 12-week period.	Cognitive constructs play a role in cognitive therapy (not causally sufficient) rather than in pharmacotherapy.
Gangadhar et al., 1982	32	NA	44	F = 18, M = 14	Major Depression	Severity measured by Hamilton Rating Scale of Depression (HRSD); social dysfunction assessed by the modified version of KAS (version 2); organic brain dysfunction also measured	Electroconvulsive therapy (ECT): thipentone, succinylcholine, and atropine or imipramine.	Both treatments produced significant improvement; ECT achieved its effects quicker w/ lesser subjective side effects to the patient. Both groups showed equal/significant improvement in social functioning at end of 3 months/ maintained the same to end of 6 months.

Study	N	Setting	Mean Age	Gender	Diagnosis	Measures	Design/Treatment	Results
Hoencamp et al., 1994	119	OutP	39.8	F = 56.3, M = 43.7	Major Depressive Disorder	Newcastle Scales I and II (differentiated between endogenous versus neurotic and reactive types of depression)	Phase I—6-week trial w/ matropotiline; Phase II—6-week w/ lithium augmentation of matropotiline; Phase III—crossover trial.	Patients w/ somatization/passive-aggressive personality had less of a chance to recovery; psychiatric/premorbid history or symptomatology was not significantly related to outcome; endogenous/nonendogenous distinction was not a predictor of response.
Knight-Law et al., 1988	113	InP	41	F = 38, M = 75	Alcoholics	Rudie-McGaughran Reactive-Essential Alcoholism Scale to assess reactive/essential alcoholism; MMPI	No treatment—structured interview and assessments administered.	The classified "essential" group derived by MMPI types was rated as drinking significantly more than the reactive group; females in this group had significantly poorer adjustment.
Kupfer & Spiker, 1981	76	InP	38.6	F = 51, M = 25	Major Depressive Disorder	KDS self-rating scale (used for anxious and depressed patients), part 1—psychological symptoms and part 2—somatic symptoms; MMPI	Drug treatment of amitriptyline for 14 days. Pharmacotherapy evaluations 2 times per week.	Anxiety, rated by patients, was a predictor of nonresponse; agitation also contributed to nonresponse; agitation and delusional status contributed independently to nonresponse.

(continued)

Table 3.4 (Continued)

Study	N	Sample (InP vs. OutP)	Age (Median/Mean)	Sex	Diagnosis (Formal vs. Not Formal)	Complexity Measure	Type of Treatment	Outcome Differential Effects
Last et al., 1985	125	OutP	NA	F=100%	Non-bipolar depression	Neuroticism, extroversion, and lie subscales of the Eysenck Personality Inventory; Hamilton Depression Scale (HAM-D); RGSD	12 weeks in either social skills training w/ placebo, short-term psychotherapy w/ placebo, amitriptyline alone, or social skills w/ amitriptyline.	Premature termination of pharmacotherapy tended to be mildly related to depressed/intolerant of medication side effects. Dropouts from psychosocial treatment were more severely depressed/dissatisfied w/ lack of early response.
Lykouras et al., 1986	58	InP	18–65	NA	Delusional and nondelusional depressed patients	History, co-morbidity	Electroconvulsive therapy (ECT), tricyclic antidepressants, or antidepressants including neuroleptics.	Delusional patients had a significantly higher depression score on HRSD. Outcome of current episodes in delusional depressives did not vary w/ treatment received.
Rush et al., 1989	42	OutP	40.7	F = 57%, M = 43%	Major Depressive Disorder	Schedule for Affective Disorders and Schizophrenia—Lifetime Version, sleep structure	Amitriptyline (AMI) or desipramine (DMI) treatments; patients were seen weekly for 6–8 weeks.	Reduced REM predicted a positive response to tricyclic antidepressants. REM latency did not differentiate between AMI and DMI responders. 80% of REM latency responders responded to treatment, compared w/ 50% of patients w/ nonreduced REM latency.
Simons et al., 1984	87	OutP	NA	NA	Nonbipolar Affective Disorder	Dysfunctional Attitudinal Scale (DAS), Hopelessness Scale (HS), sleep structure	Assignment into one of four treatments: cognitive psychotherapy (CT, 20 sessions), pharmacotherapy (maximum 12 sessions), CT plus pharmacotherapy, or CT plus placebo.	Patients receiving medication alone had a lower probability of completing therapy than those in any other treatment group.

Study	N	Setting	Age	Gender	Diagnosis	Measures	Treatment	Results
Simons et al., 1995	53	OutP	37.71	F = 41, M = 12	Major Depression	Dysfunctional Attitudinal Scale (DAS) to measure cognitive abilities; Life Events and Difficulties Schedule (LEDS); EEG sleep recording	16-week, 20-session protocol of cognitive-behavioral therapy.	High levels of dysfunctional attitudes were found to be associated w/ poorer response to treatment (except those who had experienced a severe negative life event).
Veiel et al., 1992	190	InP	41.76	F = 65%, M = 35%	Discharged depressed patients	Inventory to Diagnose Depression; long term vs. acute problems	Treatment as usual (differences between recovered and nonrecovered patients).	Few differences found between recovered and nonrecovered w/ respect to stable personality traits; recovered patients were less likely to have had severe long-term life difficulties.
Vlissides & Jenner, 1982	104	InP	48.8	F = 65, M = 39	Major Depression	Newcastle and Hamilton rating scales, endogenous vs. reactive depression	Electroconvulsive therapy (ECT).	Use of ECT was productive in the treatment of depression; age and severity of depression were predictive in the classification of endogenous or reactive depression according to the scale; psychological stress was not predictive of outcome to treatment.

(continued)

Table 3.4 (*Continued*)

Study	N	Sample (InP vs. OutP)	Age (Median/Mean)	Sex	Diagnosis (Formal vs. Not Formal)	Complexity Measure	Type of Treatment	Outcome Differential Effects
Weissman et al., 1979	96	OutP	NA	NA	Acutely depressed patients, Axis I or II	Raskin Three-Area Depression Scale	Psychotherapy alone (once weekly session) or pharmacotherapy (amitriptyline), or psychotherapy w/ pharmacotherapy over 16 weeks.	Combination of pharmacotherapy and psychotherapy was more effective than either treatment alone. Combination of treatment delayed onset of symptomatic failure.

Selected Studies Related to Depression

Study	N	Sample (InP vs. OutP)	Age (Median/Mean)	Sex	Diagnosis (Formal vs. Not Formal)	Complexity Measure	Type of Treatment	Outcome Differential Effects
Edwin, Andersen, & Rosell, 1988	68	InP	20.7	NA	Anorexia nervosa	Minnesota Multiphasic Personality Inventory (MMPI)	Treatment as usual. Two classifications of groups— Anorexia Nervosa Restrictor (ANR) and Anorexia Nervosa Bulimia (ANB).	39% maintained treatment gains while 61% relapsed; ANR showed greater improvement and were found to be more distressed/ dramatic; greater distress/ impulsivity predicted failure among ANB.
Fahy & Russell, 1993	39	NA	23.8	F=100%	Bulimia nervosa	Bulimic Inventory Test (BITE), Eating Attitude Test (EAT), Montgomery-Asberg Depression Scale (MADRS), Eating Disorder Exam (EDE), Maudsley Obsessive-Compulsive Inventory (MOCI)	Cognitive-behavioral therapy (CBT) (8 weeks w/1-yr. follow-up).	High severity, lower body mass, and personality disorders were associated with poor clinical response at end of treatment.

Study	N	Setting	Age	Sex	Diagnosis	Measure	Treatment	Results
Fairburn et al., 1983	75	OutP	24.2	F = 100%	Bulimia nervosa	Eating disorder examination assessed range of psychopathologic features of eating disorders	19 sessions of either cognitive-behavioral therapy (CBT) or behavioral therapy (BT) or interpersonal therapy (IPT).	Personality disorders were predictors of poorer outcomes.
Gangadhar et al., 1982	32	NA	44	F = 18, M = 14	Major Depression	Social dysfunction assessed by the modified version of KAS (version 2); organic brain dysfunction also measured	Electroconvulsive therapy (ECT): thipentone, succinylcholine and atropine or imipramine.	Both treatments produced significant improvement; ECT achieved its effects quicker w/ lesser subjective side effects to the patient. Both groups showed equal/significant improvement in social functioning at the end of 3 months/ maintained the same to end of 6 months.
Kadden et al., 1989	96	InP	39.1	F = 34%, M = 66%	Alcohol dependence and alcohol abuse	California Psychological Inventory Socialization Scale (CPI-So), sociopathy	Coping Skills Training (CS) or Interactional Group Therapy (IG)	High in sociopathy, CS>IG. Low in sociopathy, IG>CS.
La Croix et al., 1986	45	InP	40.6	NA	Patients suffering from back injury leading to chronic pain	MMPI	Treatment consisted of either biofeedback or relaxation strategies, or a combination of both. 3 habituation, 16 training, and 2 posttraining generalization sessions over a 2½-week period.	No differences were found between treatment groups with respect either to treatment or to physiological changes. Complexity was unrelated to outcome.

(continued)

Table 3.4 (*Continued*)

Study	N	Sample (InP vs. OutP)	Age (Median/ Mean)	Sex	Diagnosis (Formal vs. Not Formal)	Complexity Measure	Type of Treatment	Outcome Differential Effects
Sheppard et al., 1988	86	InP	32	M=100%	Alcoholics admitted to residential detoxification treatment program	MacAndrew Scale (assesses propensity toward general substance abuse); Minnesota Multiphasic Personality Inventory (MMPI)	Detoxification 30-day treatment. MMPI administered 3–5 days after admission and again 14–16 days after end of treatment.	The profile types from the MMPI obtained early in treatment related significantly to treatment outcome.
Trief and Yuan, 1983	132	InP	Varying ranges depending on outcome groups	M = 51%, F = 49%	Chronic low back pain	Patients' level of physical function and global evaluations through self-report.	No treatment	MMPI can predict successful outcome but is not a valid tool for predicting outcome with chronic back pain populations.

focused interventions was highest among those patients whose scores on the Minnesota Multiphasic Personality Inventory (MMPI) indicated that their problems were relatively acute, compared to those whose problems were less complex. Similar evidence that situation-specific problems are more responsive to behavioral treatments than are chronic and recurrent problems has accrued among individuals who seek treatment for mixed somatic symptoms (LaCroix, Clarke, Bock, & Doxey, 1986), those who abuse alcohol (Sheppard, Smith, & Rosenbaum, 1988), those with eating disorders (Edwin, Anderson, & Rosell, 1988), and those with chronic back pain (Trief & Yuan, 1983).

Conversely, evidence of the superiority of theme- or conflict-focused interventions among more complex patients is quite sparse. A direct test of the hypotheses would involve both samples of patients who vary in problem breadth and treatments whose foci are correspondingly broad and varied. Such complex studies are not available in the area of depression. However, Kadden, Cooney, Getter, & Litt (1989) have provided some promising indirect evidence of the role of complexity of the problem in differential selection of psychotherapies as applied to substance abusers. They studied alcohol-dependent patients and discovered that the more seriously mpaired individuals, as indicated by the presence of sociopathic personality patterns, responded better to cognitive-behavioral coping skills training than to an insight-oriented interpersonal interactional group therapy.

Moreover, there are several sources of indirect support for the foregoing hypotheses. In these studies, either samples or treatments were varied. One line of research has studied a selectively homogeneous patient sample, looking at the effect of variations in the breadth and focus of the psychotherapy. This research indicates that pursuing a single pervasive theme in psychotherapy facilitates the power of the interventions. For example, in a randomized clinical trial of 176 psychiatric inpatients, all of whom were characterized by complex and recurrent problems and acute depression or dysphoria, Beutler, Frank, et al. (1984) found that supportive-insight group therapy produced better results than either cognitive-behavioral therapy or experiential therapy. In this study of complex patients, the experiential therapy was actually associated with increased risk for deterioration.

Even more indirect evidence of this hypothetical interaction was obtained by Crits-Christoph, Cooper, and Luborsky (1988). These authors demonstrated that treatment outcomes were enhanced in those psychodynamic treatments where the therapists offered interpretations that were consistent with the most pervasive, independently determined theme drawn from the patient's history of relationships.

Still another line of research has explored the effects of a relatively homogeneous treatment among patients who vary in problem complexity. This line of research reveals that problem complexity is inversely related to the impact of narrow band treatments. Using comorbidity (coexisting personality or somatic disorder) as an index of complexity, several studies (e.g., Fahy &

Russell, 1993; Fairburn, Peveler, Jones, et al., 1993; Hoencamp et al., 1994) have found that, in treating patients with cognitive-behavioral therapy (a symptom-focused treatment), complexity was a negative indicator of improvement. Wilson (1996) concedes that cognitive-behavioral treatment has been observed to have poor effects on such patients, but he points out that such complexity is a negative prognostic factor for all interventions. This point is well taken and indicates the need to study this phenomenon in more complex studies.

Collectively, the foregoing results suggest several hypotheses of relevance to the development of treatment guidelines:

1. High problem complexity should favor the effects of a broad-band treatment, both of a psychosocial and a medical type.
2. Pharmacotherapy, though not necessarily psychotherapy, achieves its greatest efficacy among patients with complex and chronic depressive symptoms.

Reactant/Resistance Tendencies

Patient resistance has always been identified as comprising behaviors that affect how and what subsequent interventions are implemented. Accordingly, most models of psychotherapy and most of the clinical lore that guides treatment suggest strategies for dealing with resistance to and noncompliance with treatment recommendations. These models have largely addressed the therapy-induced examples of resistance, or the states of resistance that are observed within the psychotherapy session. Only recently has the possibility been considered seriously that a patient's resistance can be identified as a trait-like dimension. Viewing it in this way would allow the clinician to anticipate problems and to plan a set of strategies to prevent resistance from impeding progress. Seeing resistance as a trait-like quality, rather than as a state that is aroused by therapist interventions, is not to diminish the importance of resistance states. However, it does acknowledge that it may be the trait-like aspects of resistance (i.e., resistance-proneness) that require attention in treatment planning. Thus, in our review, we focused on these trait-like dimensions as possessing sufficient stability to be advantageous for treatment planning.

The empirical evidence for using patient resistance-proneness to plan for the implementation of specific procedures suggests that similar guidelines apply to a variety of diagnostic groups. Based on this assumption, we review the literature available on depressed populations and on those whose problems are related to depression.

It should be noted that it is often difficult to disentangle state and trait aspects of defensiveness. These two manifestations of defensiveness are probably interrelated, and both must be understood to optimize treatment effects. Nonetheless, some very exciting research on treatment planning has focused on the trait-like aspects of patient defensive behaviors. Most notable among those who have explored this area are S. S. Brehm (1976) and J. W. Brehm (1966; Brehm & Brehm, 1981), who coined the term "reactance" to describe instances in which individuals respond in oppositional ways to perceived loss of choice. Within this framework, "reactance" is considered to be an extreme example of the more general phenomenon of therapeutic resistance. While reactance, by definition, entails responses that are directly and actively contrary to those being advocated by an authority such as a therapist, resistance includes a variety of more passive behaviors, such as simple noncompliance and delayed compliance (Beutler, 1983; Beutler & Clarkin, 1990).

Studies of individuals who are prone to reactant behaviors in psychotherapy (e.g., Dowd, Wallbrown, Sanders, & Yesenosky, 1994) have revealed that these individuals are more unconcerned about "impression management" and more likely to resist rules and social norms in a variety of contexts than are individuals whose resistant traits are assessed to be low. Individuals who are characterized by high scores on measures of reactance-proneness tend to reject structure and to prefer work settings that allow them to exercise personal freedom and initiative. Less reactant/resistance-prone people tend to do best with some degree of external structure and guidance.

As one might expect from such descriptions, studies of individual dispositions to resist mental health treatment have yielded interesting and promising relationships with treatment outcomes, especially as mediated by the degree of direction and structure provided by treatment (see table 3.5).

A review of the studies presented in table 3.5 suggests that one of the most clearly established findings may be that resistance (e.g., Bischoff & Tracey, 1995; Miller, Benefield, & Tonigan, 1993; Stodmiller, Duncan, Bank, & Patterson, 1993) is a poor prognostic indicator. Patients who resist either a recommended treatment or the clinician who provides it tend to do more poorly than those who are cooperative and compliant.

From the standpoint of planning and tailoring treatment to individual patient needs, the implication that the degree of structure and directiveness embodied in the treatment provided should and can be adjusted to fit with the patient's level of resistance-proneness is even more important than knowing that resistance-proneness is a poor prognostic sign. With respect to the development of differential treatment guidelines, the presence of measurable resistance traits allows a clinician to selectively plan treatment programs that vary in level of therapist control, structure, and directiveness (Beutler & Mitchell, 1981, 1991; Dowd, Wallbrown, Sanders, & Yesenosky, 1994; Horvath & Goheen, 1990; Hunsley, 1993; Shoham-Salomon & Hannah, 1991; Tracey, Ellickson, & Sherry, 1989).

A prospective test of the hypothesis that depressed patients will respond in an opposite way to directive/authoratative and to nondirective/egalitarian therapies as a function of whether they have low or high resistance-prone traits was undertaken by Beutler, Engle, Mohr, et al. (1991). They demonstrated that manualized therapies that differed in level of therapist directiveness were differentially effective for reducing depressive symptoms. Among

Table 3.5 Resistance Traits

Study	N	Sample (InP vs. OutP)	Age (Median/ Mean)	Sex	Diagnosis (Formal vs. Not Formal)	Resistance Measure	Type of Treatment	Outcome Differential Effects
Studies of Depressed Samples								
Beutler, Dunbar, & Baer, 1980	51	OutP	27	F = 58%, M = 42%	Adjustment reactions, neuroticism, personality disturbances, borderline conditions, psychotic disorders	Therapy Process scale	Therapy as usual.	Relatively effective therapists perceived more resistance and competitiveness, engagement, and progress and provided more direction and support for their patients than did less effective therapists.
Beutler & Mitchell, 1981	40	OutP	F = 30.7, M = 32.6	F = 23, M = 17	Impulsive-externalizers and depressive-internalizers	Locus of Control Index	Experientially oriented therapy and analytically oriented therapy.	Experientially oriented therapy was the more powerful treatment procedure than analytically oriented therapy among both depressed and impulsive patients. However, analytic treatments had least effect on impulsive-externalizing patients and greatest effect on depressive-anxious patients.
Beutler, Engle, Mohr, Daldrup, Bergan, Meredith, & Merry, 1991	63	OutP	46.76	F = 63%, M = 37%	Major Depressive Disorder	Minnesota Multiphasic Personality Inventory (MMPI), anxiety and social defensiveness subscales	Group cognitive behavior therapy (CT), focused expressive psychotherapy (FEP), supportive/self-directed therapy (S/SD).	Low-resistance potential CT; FEP (authoritative) greater than S/SD (nondirective). High-resistance S/SD greater than CT or FEP.

Study	N	Setting	Age	Sex	Diagnosis	Measures	Treatment	Results
Beutler, Machado, & Engle, 1993	49	OutP	46.44	F = 32, M = 17	Major Depressive Disorder	Minnesota Multiphasic Personality Inventory (MMPI)	20-week group cognitive behavior therapy (CT), focused expressive psychotherapy (FEP), supportive/self-directed therapy (S/SD). Follow-up study of treatment.	Externalizers in CT had lower relapse rates than nonexternalizers in S/SD and FEP, high resistance-prone Ss in S/SD and low resistance-prone Ss in CT and FEP.
Beutler, Mohr, Grave et al., 1991	60	OutP	20–70	NA	Moderate and Major Depression, nonpsychotic	Defensive anxiety scale based on manifest and social anxiety subscales of MMPI	Cognitive therapy (CT), focused expressive therapy (FEP), supportive/self-directed therapy (S/SD).	For CT and FEP, high reactance potential was negatively related to treatment benefit; for nonauthoritative S/SD, positive relationships were shown.
Blatt et al., 1996	162	OutP	NA	NA	Major Depressive Disorder (MDD), nonbipolar	Measures of Anactitic Depression, Social Adjustment Scale (SAS)	NIMH data; 4 conditions: CBT, IPT, IMI-CM, and Pla-CM. 12 treatment sessions over 15 weeks.	Ss preoccupied w/ self-definition, self-control, self-worth may be more resistive to change.
Greenberg & Watson, 1996	34	OutP	NA	NA	Major Depression	Inventory of Interpersonal Problems	Individual psychotherapy, either client centered (CC) or process experiential (PE) treatment, or relational plus active intervention process experiential therapy.	PE group responded more rapidly initially but no different from CC at 6-month follow-up. All treatment groups effective in treating depression.

(continued)

Table 3.5 (*Continued*)

Study	N	Sample (InP vs. OutP)	Age (Median/ Mean)	Sex	Diagnosis (Formal vs. Not Formal)	Resistance Measure	Type of Treatment	Outcome Differential Effects
Hersen et al., 1984	120	OutP	30.4	F = 120	Unipolar Depressed	Social skill measure	Cognitive therapy (CT), social skills, placebo, amitriptyline	Patients in each group showed improvements in depressive symptoms, but no differential effectiveness among the four approaches.
Joyce & Piper, 1994	60	OutP	32	F = 47%, M = 53%	93% Axis I diagnosis; 28% Axis II diagnosis	Quality of Object Relations (QOR)	Short-term Individual Therapy (STI), Hierarchical Linear Modeling procedure, antidepression medication, immediate therapy, delayed therapy (control).	Significant variation in work/ resistance responses to therapist's use of transference interpretation; high QOR patients distinctly reactive to STI. Pretreatment anxiety/ symptom distress was related to work performance.
Last et al., 1985	125	OutP	Unknown	F = 100%	Nonbipolar depression	Hopkins Symptom Checklist-90 (HSCL-90), Wolpe-Lazarus Assertiveness Scale (WLAS)	12 weeks in either social skills training w/ placebo, short-term psychotherapy w/ placebo, amitriptyline alone, social skills w/ amitriptyline. Social skills training 1 hr./wk.	Premature terminators from psychopharmacotherapy mildly depressed/intolerant of medication side effects. Dropouts from psychosocial treatment more severely depressed/dissatisfied w/ lack of early response.

Study	N	Setting	Age	Gender	Diagnosis	Measure	Treatment	Findings
Lykouras et al., 1986	58	InP	18–65	NA	Delusional and nondelusional major depression	Hamilton Rating Scale for Depression (HRSD)	3 treatment regimes: electroconvulsive therapy (ECT), tricyclic antidepressants, antidepressants including neuroleptics	Type of treatment was unrelated to outcome at discharge. Six of seven delusional depressives who did not respond to tricyclic antidepressants had a full recovery w/ ECT.
Persons et al., 1988	70	OutP	37.5	F = 41.4%, M = 58.6%	Major Depression, dysthymia, bipolar, cyclothymia	Drop out	Individual cognitive therapy (CT) involving both technical and empathic interventions. Sessions 1 to 2 times per week.	50% of sample dropped out of treatment—possible expression of resistance; patients who did not complete homework were more likely to terminate treatment prematurely.
Sherbourne et al., 1995	604	OutP	46	F = 74%, M = 26%	Major Depression, dysthymia	Course of Depression Interview (COD)	General psychotherapy.	Improvements were shown in measures of functioning and well-being associated with patients who were employed, drank less, and had active coping styles.
Swoboda et al., 1990	74	OutP	NA	NA	Primary diagnosis of depression	Therapeutic Reactance Scale	Paradoxical restraining directive, paradoxical reframing directive, and pseudotherapy control group; sessions consisted of 1-hour counseling sessions over a 5-week period w/ follow-up session.	All three treatments showed significant decrease in depression w/ framing showing the greatest decrease; reactance level may be an important variable in mild degrees of disturbance.

(*continued*)

93

Table 3.5 (*Continued*)

Study	N	Sample (InP vs. OutP)	Age (Median/Mean)	Sex	Diagnosis (Formal vs. Not Formal)	Resistance Measure	Type of Treatment	Outcome Differential Effects
Tracey et al., 1989	78	OutP	27	M = 32, F = 46	Practicum counselors under supervision	Therapeutic Reactance Scale	Four treatment conditions: suicidal content w/ high supervisor structure; suicidal content w/ low supervisor structure; relationship content w/ high supervisor structure; and relationship content w/ low supervisor structure.	Trainees' reactions to supervision were related to a variety of dimensions: content and structure of supervision, experience and developmental level of the supervisee, and reactance potential level of the supervisee. Inverse relationship between supervisee reactance levels and level of structure preferred.

Selected Studies Related to Depression

Study	N	Sample (InP vs. OutP)	Age (Median/Mean)	Sex	Diagnosis (Formal vs. Not Formal)	Resistance Measure	Type of Treatment	Outcome Differential Effects
Calvert et al., 1988	108	InP	32	F = 71, M = 37	DSM III psychiatric diagnoses	Minnesota Multiphasic Personality Inventory (MMPI), Fundamental Interpersonal Relations Orientation Scale (FIRO-B).	Varied on amount of directiveness obtained from treatment of quality (TOQ) and internal (insight/awareness) (INT) versus external behavioral therapy (BT).	No results on resistance level.
Conners et al., 1997	698 OutP, 498 aftercare	OutP	Aftercare = 39.2	M = 71%, M = 80%, respectively	Alcohol abuse or dependence	Working Alliance Inventory (WAI) used to assess therapeutic alliance	12 weeks of treatment; 3 types of treatment: twelve-step facilitation view that alcoholism is a spiritual and medical disease; cognitive-behavioral therapy; and motivational enhancement therapy based on internally motivated change.	Site effects prominent.

Study	N	Population	Age	Gender	Diagnosis	Measure	Treatment	Findings
Dowd et al., 1994	326	Grad and undergrad students	19	F = 261, M = 65	No diagnosis	Therapeutic Reactance Scale (TRS); questionnaire for the measure of psychological resistance (QMPR)	Treatment as usual.	Reactant individuals were less likely to be engaged in impression management than were nonreactant individuals, although this difference did not appear for the subsample of women only. Reactant women were more decisive/action-oriented and sociable than less reactive women.
Edelman & Chambless, 1993	54	OutP	Unknown	F = 45, M = 9	Agoraphobia	Behavioral Avoidance Test, Expectancy and Treatment credibility scale, and compliance	10 sessions of individual cognitive behavioral in vivo exposure and anxiety management training (90-min. sessions) 1, 2, or 5 times per week.	Clients who spent more time doing homework reported significantly greater decrements in fear than less compliant patients; more self-confident therapists experienced more compliance.
Endicott et al., 1979	175	OutP/InP	More than half were under 35	F = 50%, M = 50%	Psychiatric illness (schizophrenia, etc.)	Psychiatric Status Schedule, Family Evaluation Form	Standard InP care, brief hospitalization followed by day care, and standard InP care followed by day care.	For overtly angry patients, brief hospitalization w/ day care was contraindicated.
Horvath & Goheen, 1990	41	OutP	31.3	F = 25, M = 16	Sleeping disorders (e.g., insomnia)	Therapeutic Reactance Scale	Treatment manuals and paradoxical treatments for symptom prescription (SP) and stimulus control (SC) groups.	SP group: more reactant clients improved w/ paradoxical intervention. Less reactant lost some initial gains. Opposite interaction observed w/ SC group.
Lantz et al., 1983	3,396	InP/OutP	NA	F = 1,877, M = 1,519	DSM-III criteria of various disorders	Level of Functioning Scale (LOF)	General psychotherapy.	Clients w/ transient, situational, and maladjustment diagnoses treated at CMHCs were rated as better functioning than were hospitalized clients.

(continued)

Table 3.5 (*Continued*)

Study	N	Sample (InP vs. OutP)	Age (Median/ Mean)	Sex	Diagnosis (Formal vs. Not Formal)	Resistance Measure	Type of Treatment	Outcome Differential Effects
Leung & Heimberg, 1996	154	OutP	34.96	F=71, M=83	Anxiety disorder or social phobia	Locus of Control Index (LOC)	Cognitive-behavioral therapy (CBT) met in groups of 6 for 12 2.5-hour weekly sessions; comparison sample completed the LOCS/other questionnaires at home.	Neither internal nor external locus of control was related to homework compliance.
McCullough et al., 1991	16	OutP	38	F=13, M=3	DSM III long-standing Axis II personality disorders	Target Complaints Inventory, Symptoms Checklist 90 (SCL-90), and Social Adjustment Scale (SAS)	Brief psychotherapy—Short-Term Dynamic Psychotherapy (STDP) and Brief Adaptation Psychotherapy (BAP). Treatment ranged from 27 to 53 sessions with a mean of 40 sessions.	Patient/therapist interpretations followed by defense were negatively related to outcome.
McLellan et al., 1983	476 veterans	InP/ OutP	NA	M=100%	Alcoholics and drug addicts	Axis II diagnosis	Substance-abuse programs and individual therapy. Matched (M) patient/program and mismatched (MM) groups in average of 26 individual and 24 group therapy sessions.	M patients were significantly more motivated for treatment, stayed in treatment longer, had fewer irregular discharges than MM patients. Possible that MM patients were less compliant and less motivated than M patients.
Miller, Benefield, Tonigon et al., 1993	42	OutP	40	F=18, M=24	Problem drinkers (no formal diagnosis)	Simple correlations between in-session processes and drinking outcomes	Three groups: Immediate check-up w/ directive confrontational counseling; immediate check-up w/ client-centered counseling; and delayed check-up wait list control.	Therapist style was not significant in overall impact on drinking. Directive confrontational style yielded most resistance.

96

Morgan et al., 1982	20	OutP	26	F = 13, M = 7	NA	Patient Resistance Scale	Psychoanalytically oriented psychotherapy.	Predictive outcome was associated with alliance in treatment; other measures were not significantly related.
Patterson & Forgatch, 1985	7 families w/ 7 children	OutP	C = 7.8	C: F = 4, M = 3	Child management problems— social aggression, child abuse (no formal diagnosis)	Client Noncompliance Code (studies noncompliant behavior in therapy sessions); Therapist Behavior Code (describes therapist verbal behavior).	Parent training sessions, 5 weeks minimum, role play.	Results revealed that therapist efforts to teach and confront produced increases in client noncompliance; therapist efforts to support and facilitate reduced noncompliance.
Shoham-Salomon, Avner, & Neeman, 1989	49	OutP	24	F = 33, M = 16	Procrastinating undergraduate students	20 questions related to procrastination and estimation of personal control.	Two 30-min. individual sessions of either paradoxical or self-control interventions.	Paradoxical intervention seemed to reduce procrastination through the mechanism of reactance in some clients and lead others to cognitive change with a possible mediation of behavior change.

(continued)

Table 3.5 (*Continued*)

Study	N	Sample (InP vs. OutP)	Age (Median/ Mean)	Sex	Diagnosis (Formal vs. Not Formal)	Resistance Measure	Type of Treatment	Outcome Differential Effects
Shoham-Salomon & Jancourt, 1985	43	OutP	18	F = 23, M = 20	Undergraduate volunteers. No diagnosis	Resistance (self-report questionnaire)	Stress inductions, followed by paradoxical, stress management, or self-help treatment.	Stress-prone subjects performed better and expressed more resistance. Stress management and self-help groups equally beneficial for less stress-prone subjects. Stress proneness, continuous stress, and resistance facilitated performance in paradoxical group.
Skinner, 1981	296	OutP/ InP	33.7	F = 24%, M = 76%	Alcohol and drug-abuse patients	Basic Personality Inventory	General psychotherapy.	InP clients experienced greater withdrawal symptoms, greater defensiveness, and minimization of problems. OutP higher on social desirability and stability.

very resistance-prone depressed subjects, a self-directed therapy regimen surpassed directive ones in effecting change in depressive symptoms. The test also demonstrated that the opposite pattern held among high resistant-prone patients. This result was cross-validated at a one-year follow-up of depression severity and relapse (Beutler, Machado, Engle, & Mohr, 1993) and also was extended to a cross-cultural sample of depressed patients (Beutler, Mohr, Grawe, Engle, & MacDonald, 1991).

Some researchers have also suggested that, among patients with especially high levels of trait-like resistance potential, paradoxical interventions may be effective because they capitalize on the patient's tendency to respond in oppositional ways (e.g., Shoham-Salomon, Avner, & Neeman, 1989; Swoboda, Dowd, & Wise, 1990). Horvath and Goheen (1990) supported this hypothesis, finding that patients with high levels of trait-like resistance responded well to a paradoxical intervention and maintained their improvements beyond the period of active treatments. Less resistance-prone patients exposed to the same treatment deteriorated after active treatment stopped. The reverse pattern was found among those treated with a nonparadoxical, stimulus control intervention.

The foregoing evidence suggests the vitality of a hypothesis, similar to one originally posed as a working guideline by Beutler, Sandowicz, Fisher, and Albanese (1996):

1. Minimally structured, self-directed interventions, nondirective procedures, or paradoxical directives are effective among patients who are highly prone to interpersonal resistance.
2. Directive treatment interventions and clinician guidance are advantageous to patients who have low resistance tendencies.

These may be among the strongest hypotheses reviewed thus far in this chapter.

Coping Styles

People use a variety of strategies to minimize the negative effects of anxiety. They select and come to favor, however, certain methods that become habitually employed and individually characteristic of a person's interactions with others, especially when these interactions take place within the context of anxiety-evoking events. These stylistic preferences seem to be reasonably captured within the general framework of a "coping style." Unlike with the concept of defensive style, in our extrapolation of this construct we did not assume underlying motives or processes, and designations were not tied to a specific model of human functioning. In our use, style of coping is largely descriptive and does not imply the presence of psychopathology. Coping styles embody both conscious and nonconscious acts that transcend situations and times and that are designed to enhance one's ability to adapt to the environments in which one functions. This framework is consistent with that suggested and described by empirical approaches to personality description (e.g., Butcher, 1990; Widiger & Trull, 1991).

There is not a single body of literature on coping style, partly because this is not a term that is universally accepted in the psychotherapy or psychopathology literature. However, research literature has measured a variety of patient characteristics that have similar descriptions, and it is this similarity on which we relied as we reviewed the literature. Thus, within the concept of what we identified as "externalized coping style" are measures of extroversion, impulsivity, sociopathy, and projection. Within the concept of what we identified as "internalized coping style" are measures of introversion, obsessiveness, inhibition, inner directedness, and restraint or control. If one can accept these several related constructs as reflections of the more general construct of coping style and can acknowledge that this dimension can be bifurcated into internal and external types, then it appears clear that there are some well-defined and consistent patterns of patient by treatment interactions.

The bifurcation of coping style into extreme groups, similar to those proposed here, is quite conventional. The bifurcated dimensions have been referred to in such terms as extroversion-introversion, sociotrophic-autotrophic, and active-passive (see Anderson, 1998; Goldberg, 1992). On one end of each of these dimensions, behaviors are described as impulsive, action- or task-oriented, gregarious, aggressive, hedonistic, stimulation-seeking, and/or lacking in insight. These are the individuals and traits that we identified as representing "externalizers" (Beutler, 1983; Beutler & Clarkin, 1990; Gaw & Beutler, 1995).

Behaviors at the other end of these several dimensions are described as, introverted, self-critical, withdrawn, constrained, over-controlled, self-reflective, worried, and inhibited (Costa & Widiger, 1994; Eysenck & Eysenck, 1969). These are the traits that we identified, in our review, as "internalizers" (Beutler, 1983; Gaw & Beutler, 1995).

A variety of studies (see table 3.6) have undertaken the task of assessing how individuals who vary in their balance of externalizing and internalizing traits respond differentially to treatments that emphasize direct and those that emphasize indirect changes in behaviors and symptoms. This research reveals that the effects of behavioral interventions, which emphasize direct symptom change methods, and insight-oriented psychotherapy, which emphasizes indirect symptomatic change, are differentially moderated by patient coping style. These studies included samples of patients with a variety of conditions, in addition to major depression. For example, in a well-controlled series of studies of interpersonal and behavior therapies, Kadden, Cooney, Litt, and colleagues (Kadden, Getter, & Litt, 1990; Litt, Babor, DelBoca, Kadden, & Cooney, 1992) determined that, for alcoholic subjects, high and low scores on the California Personality Inventory socialization subscale, a measure of externalization/impulsivity, were predictive of distinctive and differential responses to behavioral and interpersonal treatments. Impulsive patients did best when treated with behavioral treatments, while more introspective and

Table 3.6 Coping Style

Study	N	Sample (InP vs. OutP)	Age (Median/ Mean)	Sex	Diagnosis (Formal vs. Not Formal)	Coping Style Measure	Type of Treatment	Outcome Differential Effects
Studies of Depressed Samples								
Barber & Muenz, 1996	250	OutP	NA	NA	Major depressive disorder (MDD)	Personality Assessment Form, an index of external coping strategies	Cognitive therapy (CT); interpersonal psychotherapy treatment (IPT); imipramine w/ clinical management; placebo w/ clinical management.	Significant interaction between type of treatment/dimensions of personality: CT had better results w/ avoidant clients, while IPT had better results w/ obsessive coping clients.
Beutler, Engle, Mohr, Daldrup, Bergan, Meredith, & Merry, 1991	63	OutP	46.76	F = 40, M = 23	Major Depressive Disorder (MDD)	MMPI Index (externalization-internalization defensiveness	Cognitive therapy (CT), 20 weeks; focused expressive psychotherapy (FEP), 20 weeks; and supportive/ self-directed (S/SD), nonindirective support, 20 weeks; 20–30 min. phone calls	Externally oriented procedures of CT showed strongest effects for externalizing patients; less impulsive and less externalizing depressed patients did best in S/SD therapy and FEP.

(continued)

Table 3.6 (*Continued*)

Study	N	Sample (InP vs. OutP)	Age (Median/ Mean)	Sex	Diagnosis (Formal vs. Not Formal)	Coping Style Measure	Type of Treatment	Outcome Differential Effects
Beutler, Machado, Engle, & Mohr, 1993	49	OutP	46.44	F = 32, M = 17	Major Depressive Disorder (MDD)	MMPI Index (externalization-internalization defensiveness)	Over 20 weeks, group behavioral therapy (CBT), focused expressive psychotherapy (FEP), supportive/ self-directed therapy (S/SD)	Externalizing coping was associated w/ better results w/ CT, whereas internalizing coping was related to better results with S/SD.
Beutler, Mohr, Grawe, Engle, & MacDonald, 1991	68	OutP	20–70	NA	Moderate depression	Certain combinations of the MMPI (scales 6 and 4)	Random assignment into one of three treatments: cognitive therapy (CT), focused expressive psychotherapy (FEP), or supportive/self-directed (S/SD). CT and FEP treatment consisted of 20 weeks of treatment and S/SD consisted of 20–30 min. phone calls over 20-week period.	CT showed strongest effects among patients whose externalizing patterns were poorly controlled. Less impulsive and less externalizing patients did best in S/SD therapy and to a lesser extent in FEP.
Beutler & Mitchell, 1981	40	OutP	31.5	F = 23, M = 17	Patients seeking psychotherapy at a psychiatric clinic	MMPI Index (externalizers and internalizers)	Analytic and experiential (defined by ratings of treatment techniques and behaviors).	Impulsive externalizers benefited more from experiential than analytic treatments; analytic treatments achieved greatest effect among depressive anxious patients and less effectiveness among impulsive externalizing patients.

Study	n	Setting	Age	Gender	Diagnosis	Measure	Treatment	Results
Burns, Shaw, & Croker, 1987	25	OutP/InP	39.2	F = 100%	Major Depressive Disorder (formal diagnosis) and controls	Self-Help Inventory (SHI)	No treatment (correlational study)	Cognitive distortion and willingness to cope had significant correlation w/ diagnosis/severity of depression. The most depressed individuals were less willing to try active coping and had lower expectations about coping.
Calvert et al., 1988	108	InP	32	F = 71, M = 37	Schizophrenia, Bipolar Affective Disorder, Major Depressive Disorder, Dysthymic Disorder, Anxiety Disorder, Personality Disorder, Substance Abuse, and Adjustment Reaction	Minnesota Multiphasic Personality Inventory (MMPI) subscale composite results into patient internalization ratio	General psychotherapy provided by interns, varied on amount of directiveness obtained from TOQ and internal insight/awareness (INT) vs. external behavioral (BT).	With internalizing patients, INT led to better results (behavior and feelings); with externalizing clients, BT led to their feeling better but behaving worse.
Coyne, Lazarus, & Aldwin, 1981	87	OutP	54.2	F = 41, M = 52	Depressed and nondepressed (not formal diagnosis)	Ways of Coping Checklist	Treatment as usual (assessment of thoughts and actions used in coping in specific stressful situations over a 1-yr. period).	Depressed persons sought more emotional and informational support from others and engaged in more wishful thinking.

(continued)

Table 3.6 (*Continued*)

Study	N	Sample (InP vs. OutP)	Age (Median/ Mean)	Sex	Diagnosis (Formal vs. Not Formal)	Coping Style Measure	Type of Treatment	Outcome Differential Effects
Hoffart & Martinsen, 1991	117	InP	40.1	F = 65, M = 52	Anxiety Disorder and Unipolar Depressive Disorder (formal diagnosis)	Multidimensional Health Locus of Control, Attributional Style Questionnaire, Ways of Coping Checklist	Treatment as usual.	Agoraphobia: correlation to chance, externality to powerful others, problem-focused coping, wishful thinking. Depression: correlation to internality of good events, internality of bad events, stability of bad events, importance and globality of bad events.
Karno, 1997	74	OutP	NA	F = 12, M = 62	Problem drinkers	Welsch internalization Ratio from the MMPI-2	Treatments of either cognitive-behavioral therapy or family systems therapy. Both treatments delivered in a 20-session format that included the problem drinker's spouse or partner.	Coping style did not significantly interact with the behavior or insight focus of treatment in predicting changes in alcohol consumption. Patients with an internalizing coping style had greater decrease in drinking during course of treatment than did externalizers.
Kiethly et al., 1980	18	OutP volunteers	NA	M = 100%	Depression, psychoastenia, and social introversion	Cooke Maladjustment Index	Up to 25 sessions of treatment as usual.	Motivation was a good predictor of process measures by the third session. Patient's motivation was negatively related to negative therapist attitude/patient hostility. Patient participation was positively correlated w/ motivation. Patient self-rating had positive but nonsignificant relationship w/ outcome.

Study	N	Setting	Age	Gender	Diagnosis	Measure	Treatment	Results
Koscis et al., 1988	76	OutP	38.9	F = 53, M = 23	Major Depressive Disorder and Dysthymic Disorder (formal diagnosis)	Social Adjustment Scale	Treatment w/ imipramine hydrochloride or placebo for 6 weeks.	Nonsignificant results were found relative to coping style.
Parker, Brown, & Blignault, 1986	128	InP/ OutP	37.9	F = 89, M = 39	Nonmelancholic, depressed patients and volunteers	Questionnaire developed by authors.	No treatment was specified.	Those using more self-consolation coping behavior at baseline were unlikely to have improved at 6 and 20 weeks. Displacement of attention and affect reduction were also poorly related to improvement.
Rehm et al., 1979	24	OutP	18–60	F = 100%	Major Depression	Wolpe-Lazarus Assertion Scale	Assertion skills or self-control programs (6 weekly group sessions).	Self-control subjects improved more on measures of self-control; assertion skill subjects improved on assertion skill measures; and self-control subjects improved more on both self-report and behavioral measures of depression.

(continued)

Table 3.6 (Continued)

Study	N	Sample (InP vs. OutP)	Age (Median/ Mean)	Sex	Diagnosis (Formal vs. Not Formal)	Coping Style Measure	Type of Treatment	Outcome Differential Effects
Tasca et al., 1994	20	OutP	32	F = 15, M = 5	Major Depression, Schizophrenia, Bipolar Disorder, Personality Disorder	Defense Mechanisms Inventory	Psychodynamic or experiential, activity-oriented group therapy (2 weekly sessions over 12 weeks).	Patients who chose a verbal and process-oriented psychotherapy tended to have externalizing defenses. Patients who chose a structured/activity-oriented group therapy tended to have internalizing defenses.

Selected Studies Related to Depression

Study	N	Sample (InP vs. OutP)	Age (Median/ Mean)	Sex	Diagnosis (Formal vs. Not Formal)	Coping Style Measure	Type of Treatment	Outcome Differential Effects
Arntz et al., 1996	36	OutP	34.1	F = 14, M = 22	Panic disorder w/ secondary diagnosis of either social or mood disorder	Fear Questionnaire, diary	Cognitive therapy (CT), or applied relaxation (AR), both w/ 12 weekly 1-hr. sessions and 6-mo. follow-up.	CT was superior to AR in reducing frequency of panic attacks; CT > AR > wait-list.
Bruder-Mattson & Hovanitz, 1990	176	OutP (college students)	18.4	F = 86, M = 90	Dysphoric	Ways of Coping Checklist; Attributional Style Questionnaire	No treatment (correlational study).	Escape/avoidance is associated w/ depression as measured by the Beck Depression Inventory (BDI), especially for females. Problem focus is associated with low BDI. Coping had more predicted value than did attribution style.
Carroll,, Rounswale, Gordon et al., 1994	110	OutP	28.8	F = 27%, M = 73%	Cocaine dependency	Defined by problem	Manualized cognitive-behavioral therapy (CBT) plus desipramine; clinical management plus desipramine; CBT plus placebo; or clinical management plus placebo.	Significant main effects for medication or psychotherapy not found for treatment retention and reduction of cocaine use; severe cocaine users at baseline had better outcomes w/ CBT.

106

Study	N	Setting	Age	Gender	Diagnosis	Measure	Treatment	Results
Cooney et. al., 1991	96	InP	39.1	F=34%, M=66%	Alcohol dependence and alcohol abuse (formal diagnosis)	California Psychological Inventory Socialization Scale (CPI-So) (sociopathy)	Coping skills training (CS) or interactional group therapy (IG), w/ 2-yrs. follow-up.	Among patients high on sociopathy or global psychopathology CS>IG; among patients low on sociopathy or psychopathology IG>CS.
Cramer et al., 1988	90	InP	21	F=45, M=45	Anaclitic or introjective personality configuration diagnosis (not formal)	Interpersonal Weather Ward Behavior Rating Scale; responses to 3 TAT cards.	No treatment (correlational study).	Analytic and introjective didn't differ in use of denial, projection, and identification. For analytic only, psychopathology was positively related to denial and negatively related to identification; lower level of dysfunction was related to lower level of defense use.
Folkman et al, 1980	85 married couples	OutP	F=39.6; M=41.4	F=50%, M=50%	Not formal	Ways of Coping Measure	No treatment (interview 1 time per month for 6 months).	When threat on self-esteem was high, confrontative coping, self-control, and avoidance were used. Satisfactory outcomes were related to use of problem-solving and positive reappraisal.
Ford, Fisher, & Larson, 1997	74	InP	48	M=100%	Posttraumatic Stress Disorder (PTSD)	Internalized/externalized anger subscales of the STAI Multidimensional Anger Inventory; Object Relations Clinician Rating	Individual therapy focusing on more successful here-and-now coping skills and life plans (3 months of treatment).	Participants w/ moderate levels of object relations showed reliable gains on perceived symptoms/self-control and resumed community living.

(continued)

Table 3.6 (*Continued*)

Study	N	Sample (InP vs. OutP)	Age (Median/ Mean)	Sex	Diagnosis (Formal vs. Not Formal)	Coping Style Measure	Type of Treatment	Outcome Differential Effects
Fromme & Rivet, 1994	113	OutP (college students)	NA	F = 46%, M = 54%	Not formal— two measures of drinking behavior	COPE question-naire (list)	No treatment (correlational study).	Young adults' coping styles were related to their use of alcohol. Deficits in emotion-focused and avoidant coping were related to heavier drinking.
Hovanitz, 1986	150	OutP (college students)	19.7	F = 76, M = 74	Not formal	Coping Strategies Inventory	No treatment (correlational study).	Certain coping styles (avoidant, emotional, and self-denigration) were related to elevations on psychopathology (MMPI scores). Coping styles contributed more than negative life events to psychopathology.
Kadden et al., 1989	96	InP	39.1	F = 34%, M = 66%	Alcohol dependence and alcohol abuse (formal diagnosis)	California Psychological Inventory Socialization Scale (CPI-SO) (sociopathy)	Coping skills training (CS) or interactional group therapy (IG).	High in sociopathy CS>IG. Low in sociopathy IG>CS.
Litt et al., 1992	79	InP	39	M = 100%	Alcoholics	California Psychological Inventory Socialization Scale (CPI-SO) (sociopathy)	Coping skills training (CS) or interactional group therapy (IG).	Type B alcoholics (early onset and more familial alcoholism) had better outcomes with coping skills treatment and worse outcomes with interactional therapy than type A alcoholics (more symptoms of antisocial personality characteristics).

Study	Setting	N		Gender	Diagnosis	Measure	Treatment	Results
Longabaugh et al., 1994	OutP	149	38	F = 31%, M = 69%	Substance abuse or dependence; alcohol dependence w/ or w/o Antisocial Personality Disorder (ASP) (formal diagnosis)	Important People and Activities Scale (ASP)	Individually focused extended cognitive-behavioral therapy (20 sessions) or group relationship enhanced cognitive behavior therapy (16 sessions)	ASP status mediated the relationship between overall consumption and alcohol-specific support. For non-ASPs, the greater their post-treatment support, the lower their subsequent consumption; the greater the support, the greater the abstinence.
Lyons et al., 1990	InP	1,340	NA	NA	Behaviorally impaired drinkers and alcoholics	Client Topology Scale	Medical, peer group, rehabilitation orientation; treatment length varied.	Behaviorally impaired males had significantly higher abstinence rate when treatment in dominant medical; matching of treatment orientation to client type results in significant positive change in abstinence rates for both males and females.
Miller & Joyce, 1979	OutP	141	40.6 abstinent; 41.5 controlled; 43.5 uncontrolled	F = 11.1% (Abs.) F = 39.6% (Contr.) F = 15.8% (Uncontr.)	Problem drinkers	Defined by problem, Rotters Internal-External Locus of Control Scale	Behavioral self-control training w/ the goal of controlled drinking.	Those who controlled drinking had less severe drinking problems; no results on differential coping or locus of control.
Project Match Research Group, 1997	InP/ OutP	952 OutP; 774 InP	NA	OutP: F = 28%, M = 72% InP: F = 20%, M = 80%	Alcohol dependency	Defined by diagnosis and CPI-50	Three 12-week, manual-guided, individual treatments: cognitive behavioral coping skills therapy, motivational enhancement therapy, or 12-step facilitation therapy (follow-up over a 1-year posttreatment period).	Nonsignificant results in regard to coping style.

socially sensitive patients did best with an interpersonal therapy. Continued improvement over a two-year follow-up period was also found to be greatest among compatibly matched client-therapy dyads (Cooney, Kadden, Litt, & Getter, 1991).

Similarly, Longabaugh et al. (1994) found that alcoholics who were characterized as being impulsive and aggressive (externalizing behaviors) drank less frequently and with less intensity after receiving cognitive-behavioral treatment than after receiving relationship-enhancement therapy. The reverse was found with alcoholic clients who did not have these traits. These findings have been further confirmed by Karno (1997) among alcoholic couples in a large-scale project that compared cognitive and family systems therapies (Beutler, Patterson, et al., 1994).

It is notable and curious, given the consistency of these findings among alcoholics, that these results were not replicated in the large-scale Project Match (Project Match Research Group, 1997). Variations in the severity of the pathology of the subjects and the treatments used have not yet been investigated as explanations for these discrepancies.

In the domain of depression, several related studies have confirmed this general relationship and have expanded the role of patient coping style as a differential predictor of patient response to various psychotherapies. For example, Beutler and his colleagues (e.g., Beutler, Engle, Mohr, et al., 1991) have found that depressed patients who scored high on MMPI indicators of externalization/impulsivity responded better to a cognitive-behavioral treatment than to an insight-oriented therapy, and the reverse was observed among patients who were judged to represent introverted/internalizing coping styles. Beutler and Mitchell (1981), Beutler, Mohr, et al. (1991), and Calvert, Beutler, and Crago (1988) found similar patterns among mixed psychiatric in- and outpatients who complained of depressive symptoms.

Similarly, among a mixed sample of outpatients, Barber and Muenz (1996) found cognitive therapy to be more effective than interpersonal therapy among patients who employed direct behavioral avoidance (externalization) as a coping mechanism, while interpersonal therapy was most effective among obsessively organized (internalizing) patients. The authors note the similarity to the findings of Beutler, Engle, Mohr, et al. (1991) and advance an interpretation based on the theory of opposites—individuals respond to interventions that are counter to and that thereby undermine their own customary styles. Specifically, among avoidant or externalizing clients, cognitive therapy was successful because it pushed clients to confront anxiety-provoking situations through homework and specific instructions. Likewise, among obsessive or internalizing clients, who tended to be rigid and intellectualized, interpersonal therapy encouraged them to give up their defenses and to become more flexible by removing external structure and fostering internal inspection and insight. Thus, the authors propose that exposure is a central feature of effective therapy. Expanding on the authors' suggestions, we suggest that differential response may hinge on the selection of procedures that encourage patients to confront the feared event (for externalizers) or internal process (for internalizers).

This interpretation has received some indirect support in studies of patient preferences for treatment type. Tasca, Russell, and Busby (1994) found that externalizers preferred a process-oriented psychodynamic group over a structured, activity-oriented group when allowed to make a choice, while internalizers preferred a cognitive-behavioral intervention. In each case, the therapy that is suggested as least effective by other research was preferred, perhaps because it posed less threat to the clients' normal defenses. Further research is called for on this interesting paradox, however.

The foregoing findings suggest two general hypotheses pertaining to patient coping style:

1. Extroverted/externalizing/impulsive coping styles indicate the use of interventions designed to directly affect symptoms or build skills.
2. Introverted/internalizing/restricted coping styles indicate the use of interventions designed to enhance insight and awareness.

SUMMARY AND CONCLUSIONS

From our literature review, six patient qualites emerged. Some of these variables are indicative of general prognosis, but all carry implications for selecting and fitting treatments. Within some limits, the six dimensions can be related to corresponding aspects of treatment. These aspects of treatment are not well represented as specific models (e.g., cognitive therapy, psychodynamic therapy, interpersonal therapy, antidepressant medication) but can be identified as families of related interventions. These are qualities or dimensions of treatment. Thus, at least six rough pairs of patient-treatment dimensions can be identified that appear to have some significance for treatment planning. In each case, a particular pattern or "fit" between a patient variable and one or more corresponding aspects of treatment was identified in our review that was associated with good outcomes, whereas the absence of this pattern was not associated with positive outcomes and in some cases was negatively correlated with treatment benefits. The consistency of the findings that characterized each pair of variables across studies was surprisingly high, suggesting that the patient and treatment dimensions are relatively robust and are readily subject to methods of measurement.

The patient qualities that relate to treatment include: (1) functional impairment, (2) subjective distress, (3) experienced social support, (4) problem complexity/chronicity, (5) level of resistance, and (6) coping style.

Specifically, our literature review suggests the following relationships:

1. Level of functional impairment is negatively correlated with prognosis generally.
2. Impairment level may be an indicator for the application of a long-term

and intensive treatment, particularly one that focuses on interpersonal relationships.

3. Impairment level may be a potentiator for the effects of pharmacological treatment.

4. Moderate distress may be be important to sustain commitment and participation in treatment.

5. High initial distress may be an indicator for the use of supportive and self-directed therapy but bears no relationship to the effectiveness of active and therapist-guided interventions.

6. High distress may be an indicator for interpersonally focused interventions, perhaps including group or family formats.

7. High levels of experienced social support may both improve outcomes in treatment and decrease the likelihood of relapse.

8. Low levels of social support seem to be an indicator for long-term treatment, and, conversely, high experienced social support appears to be a contraindicator for long-term treatment.

9. A certain level of experienced or felt support may be necessary to activate the power of interpersonal and relationship therapies.

10. High problem complexity should favor the effects of a broad-band treatment, of both a psychosocial and a medical type.

11. Pharmacotherapy, but not necessarily psychotherapy, achieves its greatest efficacy among patients with complex and chronic depressive symptoms.

12. Minimally structured, self-directed interventions, nondirective procedures, or paradoxical directives are effective among patients who are highly prone to interpersonal resistance.

13. Directive treatment interventions and clinician guidance are advantageous to patients who have low resistance tendencies.

14. Extroverted/externalizing/impulsive coping styles indicate the use of interventions designed to directly affect symptoms or build skills.

15. Introverted/internalizing/restricted coping styles indicate the use of interventions designed to directly affect insight and awareness.

To summarize, the six patient dimensions have been associated with the following ten general classes of intervention types and features: (1) intensity and length of treatment, (2) psychopharmacological interventions, (3) supportive interventions, (4) interpersonally focused interventions, (5) relationship/insight-focused interventions, (6) breadth of treatment focus, (7) nondirective and self-directed interventions, (8) paradoxical interventions, (9) directive interventions, (10) symptom-oriented interventions.

Stated another way, the principles suggest that general prognosis is a function of level of the patient's impairment, initial distress, and social support. Moreover, decisions about the use of medication for depression and related conditions reflect on the patient's level of impairment and on the complexity/chronicity of the patient's problems. The intensity (frequency and duration) of treatment may best be based on levels of impairment and experienced social support. The use of supportive and low therapist-directed treatments seem to be a function of initial distress and resistance level. Adopting an interpersonal focus for therapy may be most important among those who have high distress and at least a modest level of experienced social support. Broadly focused treatments may be indicated for those with complex or chronic problems. Paradoxical interventions may be indicated for those with high levels of trait-like resistance. Therapist directiveness may be indicated for those with low levels of trait-like resistance. Symptom-oriented treatments may be indicated for those with externalized coping styles. Finally, relationship/insight-oriented approaches may be indicated for those with at least a modest level of social support, who have chronic or complex problems, and who use internalized coping styles.

These relationships cannot automatically be taken as the final word on guidelines, but they suggest ways to adapt and apply interventions among varying depressed patients. We will revisit this list on the basis of our efforts to cross-valididate these principles, as reported in chapters 6 and 7.

4 *Issues in Treatment-Relevant Assessment*

The complexity of problems related to defining and identifying depression, as well as to formulating and implementing its treatment, can be illustrated by some clinical examples. The cases of Alice and Harold illustrate the variety of symptoms and provoking events with which depression is associated and the diversity of what constitutes effective treatment. These two cases are presented here for illustration and will be revisited throughout this book in order to illustrate various aspects of depression and its treatment. The cases are modified in several nonessential ways from actual cases in our experience.

Alice

Suicide is the sincerest form of self-criticism.
—Benjamin Franklin

Alice is a forty-one-year-old white female. She has been divorced for three years; her former husband retains custody of their three children (ages 12, 15, and 17). She first noted her current depression shortly after her marriage; it persisted over the twelve years since. She also reports an unhappy childhood and probable depressive episodes throughout her adolescence and early adulthood. She came to the authors' attention after she made a serious suicide attempt—her second—following the loss of her second job in less than a year.

Alice was raised within a very fundamental Christian tradition, one that did not accept the value or the necessity of either medical or mental health treatment. Her family considered faith to be sufficient to ensure that God's will would be served during medical crises. She was the youngest of two children and always felt protective of her older brother, but they were never close. Her mother was described as ineffective and helpless, being largely controlled

114

by the patient's dominating father and the mandates of a very stringent religious and male-oriented religious code.

Alice's father, a very strong and dogmatic man, was described as an alcoholic. When she was an early adolescent, he developed lung cancer. The disease was slow and progressive, and during its later stages he was confined to his bed most of the time. As she was emerging into puberty, he was a source of significant fright to Alice. She recalls that he insisted that she leave the door open to the bathroom when she needed either to relieve herself or to take a bath, ostensibly so that he could keep an eye on her and prevent her from sin. He watched from his bedroom, leaving Alice feeling violated and threatened. Alice's mother excused her father and went along with his suggestion that she needed to be carefully watched to prevent her from lapsing into some unforgivable but unspecified sin. When he finally died shortly after she turned seventeen, she was both relieved and anxious.

Alice describes herself as a rebel during the last months of her father's life, and this pattern continued through young adulthood. She frequently sneaked out of the house, most of the time undetected despite her father's intrusive presence. She had numerous relationships with men older than herself, although she resisted most of their sexual approaches. Shortly after her father's death, after she did finally succumb both to social pressures for sexual intercourse and to her own impulses, she was overcome with fear and guilt. She became depressed and suicidal but did not share this information with anyone, and the feelings gradually passed. She continued to take pleasure in the attentions of men and in the excitement of every new relationship. These interests earned criticism and anger from her family, most notably her grandmother, who frequently berated her and predicted the direst of consequences for her after life.

Despite these struggles, Alice was a good student and became a modestly accomplished pianist. She began college but returned home on a regular schedule. On one of these trips home, she met Ralph. Ralph was also a fundamental Christian, but from a different religious tradition. His religious background was even more severe and rigid than hers in the rules that dictated what roles and behaviors were acceptable. Ralph began visiting Alice at school. When the couple began engaging in premarital sex, it produced tremendous turmoil for both of them. They regularly criticized themselves following these episodes, and each time they agreed that it would not happen again. But, predictably, it did, almost always on Ralph's very next visit. Finally, feeling compelled to preserve her relationship with God and to rescue her lost sense of salvation, Alice initiated a discussion about marriage. Ralph reluctantly agreed to marry her, also feeling guilty, although he asserted that he neither loved nor liked her. Shocked by this news but not knowing what else to do, she consented to an agreement that ensured the marriage. The conditions of his commitment included Alice's promise that she would convert to Ralph's religion prior to their marriage, which she did. For more than five years, Alice committed herself to being a good wife and Christian. Three children were born during this time. As the family grew, so did Ralph's restlessness. He began staying at work longer and traveling more. He sometimes didn't return home at night and then began accusing Alice of having affairs, an accusation that she denies. Alice finally talked Ralph into taking their problems to their clergy for consultation. The church convened a meeting of the Council of Elders.

By Alice's report, this meeting resulted in this group of older men berating her for not being a good enough wife. They reminded her that her husband's happiness was her primary responsibility. It was at this time that her depression deepened, and, shortly thereafter, she attempted to kill herself for the first time. She took an overdose of medication, clearing out most of what had accumulated in her medicine cabinet over the years. She was admitted to a psychiatric hospital. After two weeks, she was sent home with a recommendation that she and Ralph get marital therapy. He refused, ostensibly for religious reasons, but Alice arranged to enter individual therapy, to her husband's chagrin. Ralph subsequently used this fact as evidence against her when he appealed to the church council for permission to divorce her, declaring her in violation of church doctrine, and asserted that she was inadequate as a mother.

The Council of Elders moved to have her excommunicated, and Ralph obtained a psychologist who tendered a report that identified her depression as "moderately impairing" and recommended that Ralph be given custody of their three children. This report also referred to Alice as "overly anxious" and "borderline." When the divorce became final, Alice's family cut off all contact; Alice moved away to find a new job and to learn to support herself.

Three years later, Alice was still struggling; she had gained forty pounds, was drinking too much, and had been unable to make or keep friends. She continued to be quite impulsive and more than occasionally had difficulty with supervisors at work and with acquaintances. She had terminated her contact with the church and had no source of emotional or social support with which to replace it. She had many medical complaints, including those arising from an injury to her leg that she had sustained in an automobile accident, a gradual loss of hearing from an undiagnosed condition, irritable bowel syndrome, and recurrent tension headaches.

Alice watched her children enter adolescence from a distance, and when they began to have problems with their father and stepmother, she agreed to have them stay with her. She found it difficult to be a single mother on a minimum wage, with no support from her former husband and estranged from her family. Within a year, one and then two of her children moved back to live with Alice's former husband, on two occasions, both following violent arguments with their mother. Moreover, she frequently had to move to smaller quarters, usually following some conflict and argument with her landlord. She lost her job because of similar conflicts and because she was unable to coordinate the children's school schedules with her own in a way that allowed her to keep scheduled work hours. The children finally had to return to live with their father because she was unable to provide them with sufficient support.

Alice moved in with a roommate. She was drinking too much, overmedicating herself with the minor tranquilizers prescribed by her primary-care physician, and remained very depressed. Then she lost her second job. She went home—her roommate was out of town for the week—and took all of the benzodiazapines that she had on hand, along with a bottle of aspirin and three beers. Then she stepped into the bathtub and cut her wrists.

Harold

Harold is a forty-year-old businessman. He presented himself for treatment after his company was forced into foreclosure by the Federal Trade Commission's Consumer Fraud Division. Harold had been enticed into the business of selling business opportunities. He recruited salespersons to market information software and was paid a commission on the sales of those salespersons as well as of those they recruited. He advanced to the position of senior vice president. Unfortunately, the salespersons only recruited other salespersons and sold merchandise only to one another. The FTC ruled that the business constituted a pyramid scheme. Harold's good friend and supervisor disappeared with all of the personal assets that Harold been able to accumulate from a lien on his home, loans on his life insurance policies, and sale of his personal property. He had lent these assets to the company to fight the FTC action.

Harold was able to negotiate a settlement of the charges pending against him, but it cost him the remainder of his assets. Within a month, Harold was forced to move from his fourteen-room mansion to his parents' small farm. He was suddenly unemployed and embarrassed. For the first time in his life, he was doubting his worth and his ability. He was ashamed to face his wife and children and had withdrawn from his social circles for fear of ridicule and questions.

Harold was the fourth of seven children, and the second oldest son. There were four boys and three girls. He grew up on the family farm and was always popular and successful at school and church. He earned a reputation as a model son, brother, and friend. He was always close to his parents and siblings, although he grew up in the shadow of his older brother. The older brother died in an automobile accident when Harold was fourteen, leaving him with the responsibility for maintaining the family name and for being the role model for his younger siblings. Harold was the third to leave home, after his two older sisters had married. Unlike his siblings, however, Harold moved far away from the family, pursuing, finding, and then losing his fortune in a distant state. During the good times, he was the object of family pride and was held out as the proof of the validity of the American dream. While he had many friends, he never approved of loud parties and was always very sensitive to things that might cause conflict among his friends. He was seen as the peacemaker, pacifying and consoling others when conflicts arose.

When the problems with his job came, Harold returned to his parents' home, not by choice but by necessity founded in sudden poverty. His father had retired and lived a simple and inexpensive life. Harold was embarrassed to face his siblings, his parents, and his former friends.

Harold denies prior episodes of depression. He has never been in treatment before and has never felt the need for it. He was raised in a conventional, conservative, and traditional family and continues to hold these values. He has never smoked, has never tasted alcohol, has never used illegal drugs. His health has always been good, but now he is experiencing some disturbances of sleep and mild hypertension; he has lost fifteen pounds over the past three months and complains about loss of libido. He married a hometown girl two years after graduating from college and the couple has four children. Harold and his wife are committed to each other, and, although they have been arguing more lately, she seems accepting of the hand they have been dealt. They view it as one of God's trials, designed to prove them worthy of his grace. There is no history of legal or emotional problems on either side of the family.

At the time he entered treatment, Harold was feeling suicidal for the first time in his life. He had begun to think a great deal about his older brother, recalling "strange" things that his brother said in the weeks prior to his death. Harold was reassessing the circumstances of his brother's early death and asking himself if it is possible that his brother actually suicided. Harold doesn't trust his ability to drive, for fear that he may not be able to resist the impulse to drive into a bridge embankment, as did his brother. He is skeptical of mental health professionals and is concerned that his family will see him as weak if they know he is entering treatment. He finally sought treatment after confessing his problem to his oldest sister, who found therapy helpful during a brief bout with postpartum depression. She was successfully treated by a counselor who was referred by her obstetrician. He does not want his family to know about his decision, and, like his sister, he believes that he can get help quickly and get out before anyone finds out about his therapy. He expresses a desire for Prozac and is reluctant to consider psychotherapy.

SYSTEMATIC TREATMENT SELECTION (STS): A MODEL OF TREATMENT PLANNING

Many believe, and we've been forced to agree (see chapters 8 and 9), that at least non-bipolar depressions, such as those presented by Alice and Harold, are parsimoniously considered to occur along a nonspecific continuous dimension that varies in severity and impairment and that reflects a multitude of causes and developmental pathways, rather than a collection of several specific disease entities or disorders. This is a controversial point, we know, but it is supported by a good deal of data and helps clinicians plan discriminating treatment plans.

Because of this assumed dimensionality, the assessment of the individual who presents with any of the multitude of symptoms of depression must include but go beyond an assessment of symptoms to try to understand the proximal and often distal causes and mediating factors that relate to depressed mood. Theory and past research can guide the selective attention of the assessor in this process. In addition, with the advent and impact of managed systems of care, the assessment must take place in the first session and cannot consume much time. Thus, there is now even greater need for a template or guidelines to direct and focus the assessment of the individual presenting with depression. Most important, we recommend focusing the assessment on the patient variables that we have identified and summarized in chapter 3, which have been shown by prior research to be essential in shaping the intervention on both a basic and an optimal level.

To guide our efforts to develop these guidelines, we initially relied on and then subjected to testing the phase model of treatment planning that was initially proposed by Beutler and Clarkin (1990). This model provided a general framework through which to view the process of patient assessment and subsequent treatment decision making. Although the review of literature described in chapter 3, from which we distilled potential patient mediators of treatment effect, was more extensive and current than that offered in the 1990 book, those reviews are overlapping, and it should therefore be no surprise that the systematic treatment selection (STS) model hypothesizes predictive dimensions that are consistent with the literature reviewed here. In chapters 5, 6, and 7, however, we present a prospective effort to validate the hyothesized dimensions and to seek methods of combining the dimensions and economizing their assessment within the general model. Before doing so, we review the basic model as it has been modified through selective reviews of the literature. Then we present formal methods of assessing the identified dimensions and a system for using decision-tree logic to derive treatment plans.

Overview of the Systematic Treatment Selection Model

Systematic treatment selection (STS) is a general model for identifying patient dimensions that may contribute to predictions of treatment outcome and hence to treatment planning. It is useful to compare this model to several others that are frequently used to plan or predict treatment in conventional treatment literature.

The STS model proposes four levels of intervention, the first of which is patient and problem assessment, the primary focus of this and the following chapter. These levels or phases are summarized in table 4.1. The first level is defined as the process of selecting *predisposing patient qualities*. This level is defined by decisions about what dimensions of patient functioning to assess. In the STS model, these are dictated by research that demonstrates a relationship between patient and treatment outcome characteristics. On the basis of our current review of literature, three general areas are included in the

Table 4.1 Systematic Treatment Selection: Phase Model of Treatment Plan

Patient Predisposing Qualities
   Problem—symptoms, intensity/severity, complexity/chronicity
   Personality—coping style, trait defensiveness, subjective distress,readiness/motivation for
   change, self-esteem
   Environment—functional impairment, social support, breadth of positive functioning

Context of Treatment
   Setting—restrictiveness of care
   Intensity—frequency, spacing
   Mode—pharmacological, psychosocial, or both
   Format—drug class, group/individual/family therapy

Therapist Activity and Relationship
   Personal fit—therapist–patient matching
   Therapeutic actions—directiveness, insight vs. symptom focus, cathartic vs. affect reduction,
   skill of therapist
   Alliance/relationship factors

Match of Levels #1 and #3
   Functional impairment and complexity with setting and treatment intensity
   Social support with interpersonally-focused treatment
   Coping style with symptom change vs. insight goals
   Resistance traits with directiveness
   Subjective distress with abreactive vs. supportive therapies

assessment of these qualities: (1) patient problem, including diagnosis; (2) patient personality or response dispositions; and (3) aspects of the patient's living environment, including level of social support, strengths and positive functioning, and level of impairment in daily functioning.

The second level of decision entails selecting the *context of treatment*. There are four domains in which decisions are typically made at this level: (1) setting or level of restriction; (2) intensity, including some combination of frequency and length of treatment; (3) mode of treatment, meaning the balance of pharmacological, other medical interventions, and psychosocial interventions of one type or another; and (4) format, or whether the treatment is delivered within the context of a family or other group versus individual administration of treatment to the patient alone.

The third level of decision making is that of *relationship facilitation* and *clinician interventions* that are designed to enhance and facilitate that relationship. This level of decision involves three types of factors: (1) the fit of patient and therapist backgrounds and perspective, a serendipitous or at best an indirectly controlled variable in most treatment; (2) the interventions on which the clinician typically relies, including the use of insight procedures, level of activity and directiveness, and general therapeutic or clinical skill; and (3) the evolution of the therapeutic alliance or working relationship itself.

The fourth decision level is the attempt to match or fit the intervention to the patient. On the basis of the literature reviewed in chapter 3, for example, good potential matches between patient predisposing qualities and treatment dimensions would be expected to include the following areas of fit: (1) functional impairment with treatment intensity; (2) subjective distress with abreactive versus affect reduction; (3) social support with multiperson versus individual treatment and with treatment intensity (long- versus short-term treatment); (4) problem complexity with restrictiveness of setting or multiplicity of treatment modalities; (5) resistance traits with clinician level of activity and directiveness; and (6) coping style with the use of symptom change versus insight-oriented goals.

Alternative Treatment Planning Models

The distinguishing feature of the STS model is that it asserts the importance of seeing all these levels of intervention as interdependent and interactive. Thus, its power of prediction might be compared to five frequently used alternative models that employ linear logic to the tasks of treatment planning.

The *prognostic* model is one of the most used models in treatment research and has been translated to treatment planning and in effectiveness research as the search for patient identifiers that include or exclude one from receiving treatment. With reference to the STS model, it uses a host of *patient predisposing qualities* to directly predict or anticipate treatment outcomes. Alice and Harold, for example, may have different prognoses and courses of symptom development, regardless of the type of treatment they receive. These differences may be attributed to differences in chronicity/complexity and in history.

The *health care* model (or what may be called the *service delivery* model) inserts another systematic level into the equation of treatment decision making, making decisions about the context (intensity, mode, format) of treatment as an effort to improve outcome. This model usually employs a more restricted list of patient predisposing qualities than the prognostic model, often relying completely on patient diagnostic dimensions. In this or in some more expanded forms, it parallels the usual effort to find a fit between the patient problem and context, or level of care, and likely outcomes. For example, Alice and Harold may be differentially responsive to the various levels of care that could be provided (e.g., intensity, setting).

The *common factors* model is frequently used in psychotherapy research and has explored the roles of common relationship elements to account for the observed relationship and outcomes. In most renditions, this model does not attend to any specific aspects of patient factors but concentrates on the psychotherapist's contributions to outcome. Its predictive focus is on identifying common qualities that account for change across treatments. In the case of psychotherapy, and even in much of medical treatment, these factors are similar to the therapeutic actions or relationship factors in the STS model; less frequently, they include similarity between patient and therapist on such dimensions as sex, race, belief systems, and culture. Patient expectations and therapist skill are still emerging as factors being considered in such research as variables that may contribute to developing a satisfactory treatment relationship or alliance.

This model would propose that both Alice and Harold would benefit from the same type of supportive and caring treatment relationship. No differential effects would be expected from the common factors model.

The *psychotherapy procedures* model attempts to fit the specific nature of the therapist's or clinician's activities, the third level of the STS model, to specific outcomes. This model represents the pure treatment model. It assumes that the effects of treatment are the direct result of the procedures used by the therapist. Research comparisons of different treatment models are based on this assumption. As applied to the STS model, this method of treatment matching concentrates on bridging the relationship between therapist activity (a relationship/activity quality) and outcomes.

Thus, Alice and Harold would be expected to require different therapeutic techniques to fit with the unique and distinguishing aspects of their problems.

It is also useful to compare the STS model to a more restrictive *technical-eclectic therapy matching* model. Unlike the psychotherapy procedures model, which identifies the most compatible therapist from a cadre of similarly trained individuals, technical-eclectic models focus on ways for each therapist to fit the treatment to some aspect of patient responsivity and problems. In our comparative analysis, we tested the predictive power of an earlier treatment planning model proposed by Beutler (1983), one that lacked the comprehensive quality of the STS model.

The STS model, like the more restrictive technical-eclectic model, proposes moderating variables as causal, but in the technical-eclectic formulation, focus is largely restricted to how these moderators work within the restricted treatment dimensions of psychotherapy. The STS model looks more broadly to the nature of the patient's interpersonal environment and the context in which any specific treatment is offered. For example, the Beutler (1983) model of technical eclecticism proposes a link primarily between the STS first level, patient predisposing qualities, and the selection of treatment procedures across theoretical models, an aspect of therapist activity. It ignores the specific selection and variation of relationship and contextual qualities that might be implicated in treatment planning.

MEASURING PATIENT PREDISPOSING QUALITIES

We recommend that the clinician utilize a structured or semistructured clinical interview and a set of standardized assessment instruments during the assessment phase to identify patient characteristics. In chapter 5, we report some promising efforts to integrate several sources of information, including external observations and self-report measures, through the use of clinician ratings. The most reliable and valid primary data, however, combine various sources of information and include both the impressions of the treating clinician and the patient's own self-reports. We are well aware, however, that most clinicians, even psychologists, do not routinely use patient self-report instruments in the process of initial assessment. They rely heavily, and often solely, on an unstructured clinical interview to obtain information on which they plan treatment. We think this is a mistake, as unguided clinical interviews are notoriously unreliable and seldom offer strong evidence of criterion validity across clinicians. We also think that structuring the assessment with some direct queries relevant to depression, combined with patient report obtained through the use of instruments with normative data, help position the clinician to make judgments about the extent and relative severity of depression that are central to treatment decisions such as choice of treatment setting (e.g., whether to hospitalize the patient), referral for medication (severity of depression), and risk to the safety of the patient (signs of suicidal ideation and impulses). Another possibility is the targeted use of formally derived assessment instruments based on initial data derived from the clinical interview and any other assessment materials used. This is the method applied in the use of the STS Clinician Rating Form, which we describe in chapter 5.

Ecology of Seeking Treatment

Individuals are variable in the degree of upset or discomfort that motivates them to seek help from others. Thus, a good initial assessment is shaped, in part, by the timing of the patient's help-seeking behavior. In turn, a patient's help-seeking behavior is probably directly related to his or her coping strategies, levels of resistance or reactance, and other patient predisposing variables, described in chapter 3.

For example, individuals vary in the amount of social support available to them and in their accepted avenues of help. Depression is an interpersonal process (Klerman, Weissman, Rounsaville, & Chevron, 1984) and cannot be understood or, probably, treated outside the social network in which it exists. Thus, the level and nature of social support and the nature of the interpersonal impacts and forces in depression must be assessed.

Some individuals who are distressed confide in a spouse or other trusted family members. Others seek help through a family physician or a religious leader, such as a priest, minister, or rabbi. This was the case in our example of Alice, who initially sought the comfort of religious leaders until she found them to be unresponsive and critical.

Even as individuals seek help, the way they attribute or articulate their distress to themselves and to others will vary. Drug-company-sponsored depression screening days attest to the fact that many, if not most, sufferers probably see their distress not as "depression" but as the result of overwhelming circumstances within which they are beginning to lose hope. This may be especially true of those living in poverty (Miranda, 1996).

Treatment Guidelines and Patient Assessment

If treatment guidelines are successful in indicating crucial patient issues that are intimately related to treatment planning, they will be useful to the clinician in focusing the assessment process. Our review of the existing treatment guidelines in chapter 2 reveals that they are heavily dependent on establishing a formal diagnosis of one or another depressive disorder. After an extensive review of the literature, we believe that the evidence is weak for the assumption that there exist the varieties and types of discrete depressive conditions that are presented in the current diagnostic framework. Nonetheless, given both the conventional use of this framework as means of determining payment and its possible utility as a means of assessing changes and, relatedly, the effectiveness of treatment, we adopt the convention of including a diagnostic determination among the procedures to be employed in the initial assessment. Indeed, we suggest that the clinician examine the following issues in this initial assessment process:

1. The diagnosis of major depression and comorbid conditions
2. The functional severity (mild, moderate, or severe) of the depressive symptoms
3. The history of the patient's depression
4. The history of the patient's response to medication for depression
5. The presence or absence of comorbid symptoms or diagnoses such as bipolar disorder, substance abuse, or medical disorders
6. The presence and severity of psychosocial stressors
7. The nature of interpersonal interactions and support systems that may foster or exacerbate the depression.

Our own expanded treatment guidelines indicate that one may cull from this list information about some important organizational variables that permits them to go even further to define aspects of all six of the patient predisposing qualities (functional impairment, subjective distress, social support, problem complexity, coping style, and resistance level) that the research we reviewed in chapter 3 suggests may be implicated in selecting an optimal treatment for a given patient.

While we report in chapters 6 and 7, on our efforts to streamline this list of differential considerations, the strength of the research in each of these areas make them good points from which to consider differential treatment planning.

Focus of Assessment

Roth and Fonagy (1996) identify the assessment and hypothesis phase of treatment planning as crucial, and we agree. This essential step precedes the use of treatment guidelines, which presuppose that the patient has been properly assessed and "categorized." We think most people are better served by discussing them as possessing dimensional rather than categorical qualities, but categorical thinking among health care providers and, perhaps more important, among third-party payers is a fact with which we must contend. This fact alone argues for the use of clearly reliable and consensually valid instruments that give at least some meaning to classification. Without adequate assessment procedures, the correct set of treatment guidelines cannot be determined. Most relevant to this volume, treatment guidelines presuppose that the patient has been subject to a reliable and valid assessment procedure, that depressive symptoms are prominent, and that depression is a primary (not necessarily the only) target of intervention.

The simplest part of the assessment is a review of the depressive symptoms. The complex task, as pointed out by Roth and Fonagy (1996), is in proceeding beyond the diagnostic criteria to the step of making a set of working clinical hypotheses about what has led to the patient's particular configuration of symptom states. This is the step that demands clinical experience, sound measurement procedures, and clinical judgment. Since depression is such a nonspecific end state, there are multiple possible pathways to identifying the depression, and the treatment should be focused on the paths that are most relevant to the patient being evaluated.

Patients typically do not come in for an evaluation complaining of specific symptoms. Rather, they come in with a complex story of demoralization, conflicts with other people in their lives, and stressors in the environment. The symptoms they present are general ones (e.g., "I'm depressed," "my life is messed up," "I can't get along with my wife/husband"). Out of this complex mosaic, the clinician must focus on relevant and specific targets that will index and constitute a pattern of change. In addition, the clinician must share this somewhat reduced yet more precise focus with the patient and elicit the patient's active cooperation with the beginning outline of a treatment plan. In situations where depression is prominent, often the patient has been depressed for six months before coming to treatment, so it is also wise to assess what trials at "treatment" and self-help the patient has tried (and failed), so as not to blindly prescribe more of what has not worked in the past.

Symptoms and Diagnosis of Depression

The most helpful aspect of DSM for the clinician is not the diagnosis per se; it is the attention that the diagnostic process gives to exploring a range of symptoms, the history of their development and manifestation, and the severity of impairment with which they are associated. Specific symptoms, regardless of category, are often thought to be helpful in determining the need for medication as one part of the treatment process, and there is at least some evidence that this may be true (see chapter 11), although this may have more to do with setting the limits of medication effects than with setting the limits of psychosocial treatment effects. It is also clear from this research, that beyond the decision for initiating a treatment that includes or doesn't include medication, the DSM categorical designations, at least as applied to non-bipolar depression, are limited in their usefulness for treatment planning. However, when the DSM information is more at the criterion level than at the "diagnosis" level and is combined with the assessment information based on empirical research and clinical practice, a treatment plan can be formulated using the guidelines for basic (see chapter 6) and optimal care (see chapter 7).

The DSM-IV branching logic (see chapter 8 for a critical review) allows an individual complaining of depressive mood to be placed in one or another of the diagnostic categories, depending on (1) duration of symptoms, (2) relation of symptoms to identifiable stress, and (3) breadth of depressive symptoms.

The decision tree is useful in directing the process of placing the individual patient in a depression-related category, and these decision branches may be important for differential treatment decisions relating to aspects of patient prognosis and assigning level of care (basic treatment guidelines). The logic of these decision points is more important than the resulting categorization or diagnosis itself.

Branch 1

The first branch of the decision tree is concerned with potential causes of the current depression. Out of a plethora of potential stressors or causes of depression, the branching logic isolates only two: depression in the context of a general medical condition and depression related to substance abuse. We suggest that one should also assess for other stressors or causes of depression. Among the variables identified in the STS model, compiling a complete list of problem areas and symptoms, participants and consequences, rather than just those factors traditionally associated with the diagnosis of a specific depression, will facilitate this step.

Branch 2

The second branch of the decision tree is the presence or absence of manic symptoms, either currently or in the patient's past. Since bipolar disorder is the one depression-related condition on which there is relatively good agreement that it is a distinct entity with some specific treatment planning implications, this branch is important in the clinician's assessment. Note that because it is a unique disorder, in many ways quite unrelated to other expressions of depression in psychiatric populations, we have not addressed the treatment of bipolar disorder in this volume. However, within the STS model, once again, compiling a complete list of symptoms rather than considering only those related to depression will help the clinician make a determination on the presence or absence of this type of comorbidity.

Branch 3

The third branch of the decision tree is based on the extent and duration of the current depressive symptoms. These factors, with arbitrary cutoffs, result in classifications of major depressive disorder, depressive disorder NOS, dysthymic disorder, or adjustment disorder with depressed mood. These fine distinctions may not be as relevant to planning treatment as the severity, subjective experience of dysphoria itself, or the similar concepts of chronicity and complexity that are identified as potential treatment planning variables in the STS model. We return to this issue in later sections of this book, as we consider additional branching decisions that might guide the clinician.

Additional Branches Needed for Treatment Planning

Since a DSM diagnosis does not directly translate into a comprehensive treatment plan, we suggest that branches be added to the conventional three-branch decision tree in order to arrive at a treatment plan that takes into account the entire range of characteristics of the individual patient. We review here the necessary background needed to isolate futher branches to enable treatment planning in accordance with the STS model.

The assessing clinician must have in his or her mind some model of how the symptoms and experience of depression develops and is maintained in order to guide the evaluation process in fruitful directions. Models of depression by Gotlib (1993), Hammann et al. (1985), and Clarkin, Pilkonis, and Magruder (1996) such as those outlined in table 4.2 provide illustrations of models based on current research. Important for the assessor are the constructs in these models that are worthy of assessment of the individual presenting with depression. The constructs that appear in such models include stressors, both severe and minor, social support, personality features, cognitive style and characteristics, and living environments, many of which have

Table 4.2 Treatment Planning Models

Model	Relationship
Prognosis Model	Between patient predisposing variables and outcomes
Health Care Model	Between treatment context (intensity, mode, format) and outcomes
Common Factors Model	Between therapist (actions, skill, alliance) and outcomes
Psychotherapy Procedures Model	Among patient predisposing variables, activity/relationship variables, and outcomes
Technical-Eclectic Therapy Matching Model	Between matching variables and outcomes, drawn from Beutler (1983)
Systematic Treatment Selection (STS) Model	Joint and interactive, among all levels (excluding context for lack of variability) and outcomes

been included in one way or another and under one or another label in the STS model and in the review provided in the previous chapter.

Indeed, in chapter 3, we posited the importance of six crucial clusters of patient variables, most of which are unrelated directly to diagnosis, that we have identified as organizing constructs for planning treatment. These clusters or consolidating constructs are essential in assisting the clinician to plan optimal treatment. They are theoretically sound and reliably identifiable, and we report later on efforts to test their interrelationships and collective utility for planning treatment and predicting outcome. Here, however, we merely define their composition and clustering within the context of three additional branching decisions that are designed to refine treatment decision processes beyond the point of relying solely on diagnostic labeling. We revisit each of these decisional branches as we discuss basic and optimal guidelines for systematic treatment selection.

Branch 4

How far has the problem of depression spread to the rest of the patient's life, and how serious are its implications for the patient's ability to adapt to current or anticipated environments? This decisional branch hinges on the determination of a composite construct to which we have come to refer as *functional impairment,* and another that reflects *complexity/chronicity,* within the STS model. Collectively, these constructs are a reflection of (1) the number of problem areas reported, (2) the level of social impairment (the inverse of social support), and (3) the persistence and recurrence of the problem. They may also be related to aspects of Axis II pathology (Hilsenroth, Holdwick, Castlebury, & Blais, 1998). In turn, they are expected to be indicators for altering the setting, the intensity, the modality, and the focus of treatment from individual behaviors to interpersonal supports and interdependencies, respectively.

Branch 5

As a second additional branch, we address the resources that the patient has available to deal with the depression and related problems. This branch includes assessment of patient predisposing variables, with a heavy focus on the level of social support systems, the nature of interpersonal facilitators and inhibitors of behavior, and social resources—that is, the degree of felt social support in the patient's life and the patient's available resources for coping. These variables address the general question of whether the patient is likely to seek and use information and advice from others.

Branch 6

Finally, we ask the question, "What is the patient's unique pattern of response, of which depression is a part?" The answer to this question is defined in a cluster of three variables that include the general constructs of *coping style,* *resistance traits,* and *level of distress.* The first of these represents a composite balance or ratio of separate measures of internalizing (self-reflective) and externalizing (action-oriented) patterns of interaction when problems in life occur. It is derived from both clinician ratings and self-report measures and often is a composite descriptor that reflects a variety of sources. The second construct (variable #4), *resistance traits,* indicates the level of resistance or negativism to treatment and, in an extreme form, includes tendencies to behave in ways opposite to those suggested by an authority. The *level of distress* is drawn from the interplay of separate indices of three dimensions: level of self-esteem (negative loading), self-reported dysphoria and distress, and observed manifestation of clinical distress.

The remainder of this chapter focuses on the use of formal, established methods, both interview and self-report, that can be useful to the clinician, since they provide information on each of these six treatment planning branches and thus help in the formulation of a treatment plan.

METHODS OF DATA COLLECTION

The advantages of the clinical interview include its flexibility, its reliance on the clinical judgment and acumen of the interviewer, and the opportunity it affords for the interviewer to initiate a positive alliance with the patient for treatment adherence. Clinicians usually place more faith than is warranted in the validity of the impressions they form with such procedures. They find it hard to accept that the advantages of the free-flowing clinical interview are far outweighed by those of the structured clinical interview and the judicious use of formal measurement instruments. The disadvantage of the inflexibility of formally developed assessment procedures is offset by the increased validity and precision they provide. It is at the assessment stage of treatment that the wide variations in treatment noted by the critics and abhorred by managed-care companies arise. We suggest that both flexibility and validity can be preserved during the initial assessment by combining the use of structured assessment tools and a semistructured clinical interview (Beutler & Berren, 1995). A general suggested structure is provided in table 4.3. Clinicians must be advised, however, to resolve discrepancies by relying on the more formal, structured procedures, a process that often flies in the face of their general inclinations.

It is difficult, if not impossible, to set down the exact parameters by which to combine the use of formal and semistructured formal methods, because each individual who is seen for assessment is different and because treatment settings vary tremendously. Despite these uncertainties and difficulties, it is clear that the assessment phase is crucial to the construction of a treatment that put the patient on the road to some recovery.

Formal assessment procedures are helpful to the degree to which they provide the clinician with (1) a comparison of the individual patient with nor-

Table 4.3 Semi-Structured Interview Outline

Chief Complaint

This is usually presented in the client's words and is very brief (one or two sentences).

History of Problem

Solicit information about how long the problem has been occurring, what initiated it, how severe it is, and what pattern of change has been noted over time (e.g., is it cyclic or periodic).

Determine the history of prior treatment, including how successful or unsuccessful it has been.

Social and Family History

Explore client's developmental social history, structure of the early family, and the nature of early environmental factors, and identify important family relationships and how they've changed over time. Experiences of early abuse or deprivation should be elicited.

Inquire about friendships, including past relationships with peers in school, problems with the law or with authorities, educational achievements, work history, and the demonstrated ability to develop close relationships. Solicit information regarding Include an assessment of how disruptions to social relationships have been handled. Current and past attachment levels should be compared.

Explore current and past sexual experiences, including a history of sexual abuse, marriages and pattern of sexual difficulties.

Medical History

Review past and current medical problems, their associated treatments, and the drugs that have and are currently being taken.

Solicit a description of alcohol use and illicit drug use, including historical and current use patterns, frequency, pattern, and mode of use.

Observations and Organizing Summary/Mental Status

Note the patient's appearance.

Estimate level of cognitive functioning, language fluency and speed, memory, and coherence.

Note patient's observed affect (level of dysphoria, control, and appropriateness), mood (e.g., reported anger, depression, sadness, fear) and patient's estimate of how severely this affects daily functioning. This can be translated into a Global Severity Rating (GAF in DSM terms).

Personality and Interpersonal Behaviors

Attempt to organize the patient's description and integrate your impressions into a formulation or description of what initiates problems, how they are maintained, and how they cease or are resolved. This ordinarily should be framed in interpersonal terms to identify the interaction qualities that relate to needs, expectations from others, response to others, and resolution efforts.

Noted special needs and considerations; especially considerations for special treatment settings, special consultations, and other special arrangements for treatment.

---

mative data, and (2) a standardized method of assessment that reduces variability in communication about the patient to others who are increasing in the accountability chain in present-day managed care. We discuss here a selected group of instruments that we recommend to the individual practitioner and to the organizers or managers of systems of mental health care for the initial assessment, as well as for, in some cases, the assessment of change over time of patients who present with depressive symptoms.

Branch 1: Causes of Depression

DSM-IV suggests that substance abuse should be explored as potential cause, or at least correlate, of depression. This is of course a limited view, but at the initial levels of the decision tree, we will comply with these general suggestions.

Psychological distress and dysfunction associated with the abuse of a wide variety of chemical substances is perhaps the chief reason for seeking psychological or psychiatric treatment. The treatment of alcoholism, drug abuse, and eating disorders, combined with the income lost, probably consumes more health dollars than does any other group of disorders. Thus, the identification of these disorders deserves careful attention. The risk in relying on self-report screening instruments to detect substance abuse is sufficient that these instruments should be buttressed by urine screens and interviews (Greene & Banken, 1995). However, it is helpful to review the instruments that have been used for this purpose.

The prominent instruments used to assess substance abuse are the MacAndrew Alcoholism Scale, the Addiction Potential Scale from the Minnesota Multiphasic Personality Inventory-2 (MMPI-2) (Weed, Butcher, McKenna, & Ben-Porath, 1992), and scales B and T from the Millon Clinical Multiaxial Inventory, MCMI-II and MCMI-III, all of which are omnibus symptom or personality inventories.

The MacAndrew Alcoholism Scale (MacAndrew, 1965) quite accurately identifies patients who have histories of alcohol abuse or who have the potential to develop problems with alcohol (Hoffmann et al., 1974). A more thorough instrument, the Alcohol Use Inventory (AUI) (Horn et al., 1986), is a self-administered test standardized on more than 1,200 admissions to an alcoholism treatment program. It contains twenty-four scales that measure alcohol-related problems and considers subjects' responses in four separate domains: benefits from drinking, style of drinking, consequences of drinking, and concerns associated with drinking.

Branches 2 and 3: Extent and Duration
of Depressive and Manic Symptoms

As psychiatric nomenclature has undergone revision, relatively pure psychometric methods have been developed that rely on structured interviews and self-reports. providing data that are immediately relevant to diagnosis (see table 4.4).

Spitzer and his associates (1986) developed the Structured Clinical Interview for diagnosis. It has subsequently been adopted to the DSM-IV (SCID) (First et al., 1995) and directly orients the diagnostic process to the Axis I and Axis II categories of the DSM-IV system. It allows one to rule out or distinguish the bipolar and non-unipolar depression and structures efforts to determine the duration and seriousness of current and past episodes. However, with its explicit focus on psychiatric classification, the SCID has ac-

Table 4.4 Assessment Domains and Methods

Domain	Instrument
Depressive symptoms	Beck Depression Inventory (BDI); Hamilton Rating Scale for Depression (HRSD); Structured Clinical Interview for Diagnosis IV, Axis I and II (SCID), SCL90R; Brief Psychiatric Rating Scale (BPRS); Hopkins Psychiatric Rating Scale (HPRS)
Depressive diagnosis	HRSD; SCID-IV; Personality Assessment Inventory (PAI); BPRS
Drug abuse	MacAndrews (MMPI); Addiction Potential Scale (APS); Millon Clinical MultiAxial Inventory II or III (MCMI); Alcohol Use Inventory
Suicidal factors	Suicide Probability Scale (SPS); Index of Potential Suicide (IPS); Beck Hopeless Scale (BHS); Beck Suicide Intent Scale (BSIS); HRSD
Functional impairment	GAF, MMPI, HRSD
Subjective distress	MMPI (PT); MCMI II or III; 16-Personality Factors (16PF); Eysenck Personality Inventory (EPI); State-Trait Anxiety Inventory (STAI); Endler Self-Report Inventory of Anxiousness (ES-R IA); Anxiety Status Inventory, Zung Self-Report Anxiety Scale (SRAS)
Social support	Sarason Social Support Questionnaire (SSQ)
Coping style	MMPI; MCMI II or III; Buss-Durkee Hostility Inventory (B-DHI); Over Controlled Hostility Scale (MMPI, O-H); State-Trait Anger Inventory
Reactance level	MMPI; Therapeutic Reactance Scale
Problem complexity	MMPI; Clinical History, Brief Symptom Inventory

quired all of the problems inherent in adopting the present psychiatric nomenclature as the reference point for assessment. For example, differentiation among subcategories of non-bipolar depression and among the Axis II disorders remains unreliable, reflecting the difficulty of imposing a categorical system on phenomena that are dimensional in nature. While the relative lack of validation of the diagnostic subcategories themselves is significant, as tools for investigating the range, severity, frequency, and duration of symptomatic disturbance and for training in the formal interview assessment of psychopathology, these instruments are an important part of the assessment armamentarium.

Omnibus Measures of Symptoms

There are a number of instruments that have been developed for the assessment of a wide variety of symptoms (see table 4.4). These measures depend on either self-report or interview methods for data collection.

Minnesota Multiphasic Personality Inventory

The Minnesota Multiphasic Personality Inventory (MMPI) (Hathaway & McKinley, 1943), and its successor, the MMPI-2, is probably the most widely used assessment instrument in existence. There are a number of reasons for its extensive use, including its efficiency (the patient spends one to two hours taking the test, which can then be computer scored), the extensive data accumulated with the test, its normative base, and the use of validity scales that indicate the patient's test-taking attitude. Although labeled as a personality test, the MMPI was constructed to assess what are now categorized as Axis I conditions and, to a lesser extent, a few dimensions of personality that are not represented on Axis II.

The MMPI has been revised and restandardized as the MMPI-2 (Butcher, Dahlstrom, Graham, Tellegen, & Kaemmer, 1989). Revisions include the deletion of objectionable items and the rewording of other items to reflect more modern language usage, as well as the addition of several new items focusing on suicide, drug and alcohol abuse, Type A behavior, interpersonal relations, and treatment compliance. Restandardization of the norms was based on a randomly solicited national sample of 1,138 males and 1,462 females.

Personality Assessment Inventory

A relatively new instrument, the Personality Assessment Inventory (PAI) (Morey, 1991), focuses on clinical syndromes that have been staples of psychopathological nosology and have retained their importance in contemporary diagnostic practice. Items were written with careful attention to their content validity, which was designed to reflect the phenomenology of the clinical construct across a broad range of severity. An initial pool of 2,200 items was generated from the research literature, classic texts, the DSM and other diagnostic manuals, and the clinical experience of practitioners who participated in the project. This pool of items was finally reduced to 344 items covering four validity scales, eleven clinical syndromes, five treatment planning areas, and the two major dimensions of the interpersonal complex. All items are rated based on a four-point Likert-type response format. For example, on the borderline scale is the following item: "I'm too impulsive for my own good." Final clinical validation was carried out on the data from 235 subjects from ten clinical sites and two community and two college student samples.

Hopkins Symptom Checklist-90

The Hopkins Symptom Checklist-90 (SCL-90) (Derogatis, 1977) is another example of a self-report instrument designed to provide information about a broad range of complaints typical of individuals with psychological symptomatic distress. Briefer than the MMPI-2 and the PAI, the SCL-90 contains only ninety items and can be administered in thirty minutes and scored by computer. These items are combined into nine symptom scales: (1) somatization, (2) obsessive-compulsive behavior, (3) interpersonal sensitivity, (4) depression, (5) anxiety, (6) hostility, (7) phobic anxiety, (8) paranoid ideation, and (9) psychoticism. In addition, three global indices are compiled: (1) general severity, (2) positive symptom distress index, and (3) total positive symptoms. The criterion group method was not used in the development of this test. Rather, the content validity and internal consistency of the items guided the construction of the scales.

A companion instrument, the Hopkins Psychiatric Rating Scale (HPRS) (Derogatis et al., 1974), can be used to rate material obtained through direct interview of the patient on each of the nine symptom dimensions of the SCL-90. No structured interview procedure is associated with the HPRS, so formal training in the interview assessment of psychopathology is essential to the accuracy of the assessment. Eight additional dimensions are covered in the interview.

Brief Psychiatric Rating Scale

Another widely used rating scale for a range of psychiatric symptoms is the Brief Psychiatric Rating Scale (BPRS) (Overall & Gorham, 1962), which was developed mainly for the assessment of symptoms with an inpatient population. Areas rated include somatic concern, anxiety, emotional withdrawal, conceptional disorganization, guilt, tension, mannerisms and posturing, grandiosity, depressive mood, hostility, suspiciousness, hallucinatory behavior, motor retardation, uncooperativeness, unusual thought content, blunted affect, excitement, and disorientation.

The MMPI-2, PAI, SCL-90, HPRS, and BPRS represent efforts to develop procedures for the general assessment of psychopathology that meet standards of test construction. These procedures provide coverage of symptomatically distressing areas that are independent of psychiatric classifications. However, through the extensive use of these procedures in psychiatric settings, a large body of literature has developed that relates the findings of these tests to diagnostic categories favored in such settings.

Specific Areas of Symptomatology

In addition to the omnibus measures of symptomatology, there are a number of instruments that assess one area of symptomatology in depth (table 4.4). Relevant to the theme of this volume is the assessment of depression, anxiety, anger/hostility, and suicidal behavior.

Depression

Instruments are most helpful in assessing the relative severity (mild, moderate, or severe, in the parlance of the American Psychiatric Association and the AHCPR guidelines) of depression for treatment planning decisions. Scores on instruments such as the Beck Depression Inventory (BDI) (Beck, Ward, Mendelson, Mock, & Erbaugh, 1961) and the Hamilton Rating Scale for Depression (HRSD) (Endicott, Cohen, Nee, Fleiss, & Sarantakos, 1981; Hamilton, 1967) are most helpful in communicating the level of severity to colleagues. We think the focus on severity of symptoms alone is misguided and that global clinician ratings such as the Global Assessment Survey (GAS) (DSM-IV), which are helpful in assessing the relative degree of impaired functioning, are useful and central in treatment planning. Indeed, Strupp, Horowitz, and Lambert (1997) have observed that patient reports are sufficiently infused with distress to minimize the distinctiveness and validity of ratings of actual impairment in functioning.

The BDI is probably the most widely used self-report inventory of depression. The original scale was administered in an interviewer-assisted manner, but a later version is completely self-administered. The twenty-one items of the inventory were selected to represent symptoms commonly associated with a depressive disorder. The rating of each item relies on the endorsement of one or more of four statements, listed in order of symptom severity. Item categories include mood, pessimism, crying spells, guilt, self-hate and accusations, irritability, social withdrawal, work inhibition, sleep and appetite disturbance, and loss of libido. The content of the BDI emphasizes pessimism, a sense of failure, and self-punitive wishes. This emphasis is consistent with Beck's cognitive view of depression and its causes.

This self-report instrument is frequently used in conjunction with the Hamilton Rating Scale for Depression (HRSD) (Hamilton, 1967), which allows a clinician to rate the severity of depressive symptoms during an interview with the patient. In comparison to the BDI, the HRSD is more systematic in assessing neurovegetative signs. There are only rough interview guidelines for using the HRSD, but interrater reliability is generally good (Endicott, Cohen, Nee, Fleiss, & Sarantakos, 1981).

Anxiety

As one factor in the larger context of the total personality, anxiety can be assessed with the 16-Personality Factor Inventory (16-PF) (Cattell et al., 1970), the Eysenck Personality Inventory (EPI) (Eysenck & Eysenck, 1969), and the Taylor Manifest Anxiety Scale (TMAS) (Taylor, 1953), a scale that is part of the MMPI.

Compared to these omnibus personality measures, most instruments assess only anxiety or other forms of fearfulness and thus may be clinically useful as focused, dimensional measures of the severity of anxiety or in the identification of specific situational anxiety that will become the focus of intervention. The Anxiety Status Inventory (ASI) is a rating scale for anxiety developed for clinical use following an interview guide, and the Self-Rating Anxiety Scale (SRAS) is a companion self-report instrument, both developed by Zung (1971). Both scales assess a wide range of anxiety-related behaviors: fear, panic, physical symptoms of fear, nightmares, and cognitive effects. These scales are recommended for the serial measurement of the effects of therapy on anxiety states. Hamilton (1959) has devised an anxiety rating scale that is parallel to the Ham-D but is less frequently utilized.

The State-Trait Anxiety Inventory (STAI) (Spielberger et al., 1970, 1983) is a self-report instrument in which the patient is asked to report on anxiety in general (i.e., trait) and at particular points in time (i.e., state). The Endler S-R Inventory of Anxiousness (Endler et al., 1962) is a self-report measure of the interaction between the patient's anxiety and environmental situations such as interpersonal, physically dangerous, and ambiguous situations. This instrument has been widely used as a therapy outcome measure and is recommended as an instrument that may be helpful in tailoring treatment to the specific circumstances of the patient's anxiety.

Aggression

Aggressive behavior, including aggressive imagery and hostile affect, is an important area in treatment planning both for the individual patient and for the general concepts that the inventory assesses. The Buss-Durkee Hostility Inventory (Buss & Durkee, 1957) is a seventy-five-item self-report questionnaire that measures different aspects of hostility and aggression. There are eight subscales: assault, indirect hostility, irritability, negativism, resentment, suspicion, verbal hostility, and guilt. Some norms exist for clinical populations. Megargee et al. (1967) developed an overcontrolled hostility scale using MMPI items. A review of the number of studies involving this scale (Greene, 1991) suggests that it can be used to screen for patients who display excessive control of their hostile impulses and are socially alienated. Spielberger has developed a State-Trait Anger Expression Inventory (STAXI) (Spielberger, 1988) that takes about fifteen minutes to complete. This forty-four-item scale divides behavior into state anger (i.e., current feelings) and trait anger (i.e., disposition toward angry reactions); the latter area has subscales for angry temperament and angry reaction (sample items: "How I feel right now: I feel irritated"; "How I generally feel: I fly off the handle").

Suicidal Behavior

Instruments may be useful in assessing and documenting the potential suicidal ideation and impulses of depressed patients. Suicidal threats, suicidal planning and/or preparation, suicidal ideation, and recent parasuicidal behavior are all direct indicators of current risk and should be assessed thoroughly and specifically in the clinical interview. In addition, self-report instruments that focus specific and detailed attention on known predictors of suicidal behavior are sometimes clinically useful. Thus, it is recommended that the assessment of suicidal behavior be embedded in an assessment package that involves interview and use of instruments (Bongar, 1991).

Suicidal assessment instruments that are frequently used include the Beck Hopelessness Scale, the Beck Suicide Intent Scale, and the Suicide Intent Scale (Jobes, Eyman, & Yufit, 1990). In addition, it should be noted that the Koss-Butcher critical item set revised on the MMPI is a list of twenty-two-items that are related specifically to depressed, suicidal ideation. These critical items should be seen not as scales but rather as markers of particular item content that might be significant in assessing the individual patient (Butcher et al., 1989).

The Suicide Intent Scale (SIS) (Beck et al., 1974), the Index of Potential Suicide (Zung, 1974), and the Suicide Probability Scale (SPS) (Cull & Gill, 1982) are three widely used instruments. A complementary approach has been taken, culminating in the development of the Reasons for Living Inventory (RFL) (Linehan et al., 1983). Of practical interest is that the fear-of-suicide subscale in the RFL differentiates between those who have only considered suicide and those who have made previous suicide attempts. Individuals who scored high on reasons for living and on subscales measuring survival and coping skills, responsibility to family, and child-related concerns were less likely to attempt suicide.

Branch 4: Functional Impairment and Problem Complexity

Functional Impairment

Symptoms (e.g., depression) and personality traits and disorder vary in the degree to which they invade and corrode the functional success, both social and vocational, of the individual. An individual may be depressed, for example, but get up and go to work and perform at top levels. An individual who is avoidant may combat the anxiety and relate to people in successful ways. The distinction between symptoms and functioning is heuristically important, but for purposes of assessing individuals who come for assistance, the degree to which symptoms invade functioning may be the most important factor in prognosis and treatment planning.

Other than the GAF rating from the DSM-IV, there are few direct measures of functional impairment that don't rely on patient self-report (see table 4.4). Indirect evidence of global impairment can be obtained by inspecting the general elevations of most omnibus symptom or personality tests (e.g., MMPI, MCMI, SCL-90R). Particular MMPI elevations on the Sc and Si scales may be suggestive of high levels of impairment, as well (Butcher, 1995).

Problem Complexity

Like functional impairment, few direct measures of problem complexity are available. The best evidence derives from information gathered during the semistructured interview about the patient's history. These considerations include some aspect of recurrence or persistence, including (1) whether there are pervasive patterns or symptoms across different environments, (2) whether the patient has a variety of symptoms or symptoms in only one domain, (3) whether symptoms are chronic or recurrent in the patient's history, and (4) whether patterns seem to be stimulated by conflicts that are internal to the individual or whether they are part of an individual's response to an outside event.

Consider, for example, Mr. A, who is an achieving individual who has been laid off because his employer has just merged with another company. He is depressed, confused, and temporarily deskilled. Mr. B, on the other hand, has had many jobs, and in each job situation he has run into difficulty with his immediate supervisor and one way or another has been let go. The personnel reports indicate that over and over again he has gotten "inappropriately" angry when supervisors pointed out his shortcomings and that he has followed each angry interchange with deficient performance. Mr. A has a situation specific difficulty, and Mr. B has a problem that is complex, that is, pervasive, across environments, and repetitive in his personal history.

One can think of problem complexity as the degree to which the problem spreads across multiple symptom domains. Thus, a BSI can indicate symptoms across a multitude of symptom areas.

Another indication of problem complexity is the duration or chronicity of the problem. Another aspect of problem complexity is whether the presenting problem reflects a recurring internal conflict or is a simple response to externally evoking events.

Branch 5: Social Support

In most models of depression, social support and interpersonal patterns of interaction are important predictors of longitudinal course and outcome. In a real sense, supportive interpersonal interactions facilitate positive change, while interactions that are infused with negative affect foster depression and relapse. Most interpersonal facilitators are captured in most measures of social support, a concept that transcends most theoretical models.

Whether cause or effect, the presence of social support in an individual's life is antithetical to the presence of depression. Ironically, the use of therapy itself is the utilization of social support and resources by the individual who is suffering from depression. Successful psychotherapy will probably initiate and help the patient expand his or her social support system. Some patients with depression have social skills but isolate themselves from supportive social interactions during the depression, while others are poor in social skills and have chronic difficulties relating to others.

Social support cannot be represented simply by the number of people in one's life but must include the positive nature of interactions with those people. Thus, measurement of social support is invariably dependent on patient report. For example, the Social Support Questionnaire (SSQ) (Sarason, Levine,

Basham, & Sarason, 1983) provides information about the number of available sources of support (i.e., quantity) and also provides a rating of a patient's satisfaction with this support system (i.e., quality). As noted in chapter 3, one's satisfaction with one's social support may be a more important indicator of the adequacy of that support than merely the availability of people in one's life.

While social support measures capture the positive nature of interpersonal relationships, there are also pathognomic interactions, or those whose negativity actually fosters depression. We are not aware of any good, formal measures of these negative interactions, although they can frequently be inferred from interviews and observations with significant others. These factors must be considered in juxtaposition with evidences of social support.

Branch 6: Unique Patterns of Patient Response

Resistance Traits

Interpersonal resistance reflects patients' receptivity to external influence. Reactance is an extreme form of resistance, characterized by oppositional behavior. Reactance is conceived as an individual's tendency to respond by rejecting suggestions, information, advice, or demands that come from others (Beutler & Consoli, 1992). In reference to treatment planning, reactance level can be seen as the level of the patient's potential resistance to the therapist's interventions, without specifying the form that this resistance might take. Probably the best instrument for assessing reactance (see table 4.4) is the Therapeutic Reactance Scale (TRS) (Dowd, Milne, & Wise, 1991). This is a twenty-eight-item self-report instrument that produces a single score. A score above the mean of 68 suggests that the subject will be likely to resist the therapist's direction and control.

In addition, several measures from the MCMI, MMPI, and MMPI-2 have been explored as indicators of resistance (Beutler & Berren, 1995), but there is currently no consensus as to their validity. Most such measures emphasize a patient's lack of receptivity to treatment, hostility, dominance, need for control, or problems with authority. In this, they all have face validity, but they unfortunately have not been found to have consistently high intercorrelations with one another, raising questions about their construct validity.

Motivational Distress

Self-reports of some type are required to assess the level of internal distress, particularly if one attempts to distinguish this concept from functional impairment. The GSI from the BSI is the single best indicator of overall distress level (Derogatis, 1992). When the GSI value exceeds a T-score of 63, a treatment that is designed to reduce subjective distress levels is indicated.

The Pt subscale or scale 7 on the MMPI represents an index of psychological discomfort (Graham, 1993). Also, scores above 70 on the F subscale may suggest motivation for treatment. However, those with high scores on the F scale accompanied by high elevations on L and K tend to disown their discomfort and to be resistant to and reactant to authority figures.

Coping Style

Coping style can be indexed both from independent observers and from patient reports. General, omnibus personality/symptom inventories provide relatively good indices of the components of this dimension. Scales that emphasize impulsivity, stimulation seeking, poor socialization, lack of foresight, and extroversion all seem to contribute to a common factor that can be conceptualized as one end of a continuum that ranges from externalization to internalization. Grossly speaking, externalizing individuals blame others for their problems, and internalizing individuals blame themselves for their difficulties.

The MMPI is among the most used measures of coping style. The MMPI scales that indicate an externaling pattern are the Hy, Pd, Pa, and Ma scales. In contrast, scales that indicate internalizing coping styles are Hs, D, Pt, Si. These patterns appear to be quite stable, and a relatively high level of correlation exists between these scales and other test measures of similar dimensions.

IMPLICATIONS FOR TREATMENT PLANNING

At the conclusion of chapter 5, we illustrate the use of the branching logic outlined here in the assessment process of Alice and Harold.

It is likely that several of the dimensions identified in our review are intercorrelated. Thus, there may be patterns of interest and even of significance to the task of defining categorical or diagnostic groups that are related to treatment assignments. For example, at least conceptually, individuals who are judged to be externalizers are also likely to be resistant. Together with indices of chronicity/complexity, these elevations may identify patients with characterological disturbances. The treatment implications suggest that a collaborative (patient-led) focus on symptoms may be indicated and that insight-oriented and authoritative interventions may be contraindicated.

In contrast, those with high functional impairment, low social support, and high internalization tendencies may impress one as characteristically withdrawn and alienated. These individuals require long-term, multiperson, or socially focused treatments that work to change recurrent and generalized interpersonal patterns.

To say that there may be clusters or patterns among the dimensions that are correlated with diagnostic groupings is not to say that conventional diagnoses can be reconstructed to become treatment relevant. Many of the dimensions vary widely within diagnostic groups. It is likely, for example, that those diagnosed as depressive or as having an anxiety disorder will present with high levels of distress, and patients with either of these designations may draw from the clinician and reject efforts to reduce discomfort and to provide structure or support. Patients so diagnosed vary widely in other treatment-relevant dimensions, however. For example, not unless one also knows the relative level of externalization and internalization, the level of symptom specificity versus generality, and the level of resistance can one define a treatment program that will be responsive and meaningful.

The advantage of using a dimensional description rather than a categorical, diagnostic distinction is that dimensions may better capture individual differences and are likely to be more representative and inclusive of relevant patient variations than are nominal classifications. Moreover, dimensions do not convey or necessarily indicate the pejorative judgments associated with diagnoses. Instead, they reflect normal patterns of behavior as well as pathologies and thereby provide a less bias-driven picture of the people involved.

Diagnostic classifications also draw on a wide variety of other dimensions, only some of which have been empirically associated with treatment benefit. By restricting our consideration to a few, empirically identified dimensions, it may be possible to clarify and specify needed treatments.

In a later chapter, as we explore the results of our analysis of treatment matching variables, we return to this analysis in order to define its implications for optimal treatment matching. At this point, it bears emphasizing that treatment plans based on dimensions and principles have some distinct advantages over treatment plans that emphasize diagnostic groups and technical procedures or techniques. Treatment guidelines based on defined principles of change can be more easily translated into strategies of intervention and tailored to individuals than can recipes that presume the existence of rigid patient-to-technique relationships. Guidelines that emphasize principles and strategies rather than techniques acknowledge that techniques are flexible and vary widely from therapist to therapist. Principles and strategies are more likely to lead to the development of interventions that are responsive to patient variations and sensitive to patient needs. Guidelines based on general principles, moreover, allow the clinician to integrate clinical experience with empirical observation and scientific knowledge without sacrificing the advantages of creativity and flexibility.

ASSESSMENT OF CHANGE

The existing treatment guidelines are excellent in their recommendation for continuing assessment as treatment progresses. If the patient does not make sufficient progress as the initial treatment plan unfolds, the treatment plan should be altered, say these treatment guidelines. This is an excellent principle, but, unfortunately, the existing treatment guidelines use as the marker of change only the symptoms of depression. While agreeing with the need for in-therapy assessment of change, we emphasize the need for multiple-focused assessment of patient change. To make the case starkly, the reassessment of Harold and Alice as they progress in the early stage of treatment would be quite different. As his depression lifts, Harold is capable of structuring and guiding his life. In contrast, as Alice's depression lifts, she continues to be faced with multiple areas of dysfunction and the need for evaluation and change.

An informed therapist knows not only what can change and what cannot but the relative time trajectories of different types of changes. Howard (ref) has captured in large numbers of patients the type of trajectory of change that makes clinical sense. Hope comes before significant symptom change. Symptom change predates change in functioning. Character change is slow and not huge. Life is like that. Given the reality of change and its trajectory, the therapist can judge where the individual patient is compared to the patient group as a whole. This comparison enables the therapist to assess and change intervention strategies as time goes on.

5

Integrating and Economizing
Treatment-Relevant Assessment

COMPUTER-ASSISTED ASSESSMENT

To implement optimally tailored treatment plans, instruments are needed that both combine sources of information (clinician and patient report) and efficiently measure patient states and traits that have been found to specifically indicate or contraindicate the use of various treatments in a way that minimizes the measurement of superfluous or noncontributory dimensions. As we have seen, however, no single instrument in common use includes all of the dimensions that are important; in fact, they frequently include information that is superfluous to the processes of treatment planning. Multiple instruments must be used or new instruments developed. Developing instruments for special purposes is no mean task and involves a number of complex processes (Reckase, 1996).

In developing treatment plans, the clinician must look at multiple dimensions, but the variety and complexity of the interrelationships among these promising dimensions is so great that integrating these measures and extracting a consistent meaning may be beyond the clinician's ability in the absence of assistance. Computer technology offers the possibility of economizing the effort necessary to combine and balance variables by constructing complex algorithms that can be self-correcting and efficient, especially if attached to an interactive and dynamic database. Such objective technology could significantly improve the efficiency of treatment planning and provide valuable guidance to clinicians who attempt to tailor their treatments to patient needs.

However, computers can respond only to those variables that are entered, and it is critical that the patient dimensions selected for assessment and the methods of rating be relevant to predicting treatment outcome, psychometri-

We thank Daniel Fisher, Ph.D., who assisted with the analysis of these data and served as a coauthor of this chapter.

cally sound, and based on sound research. Concepts that are of value to only one specific theory, those that have little demonstrated relationship to outcomes, and those that are not reliably measured are of little use to clinician practitioners. It is also important to include in the predictive equation aspects of patients beyond their particular symptoms, both as predictors of treatment effects and as measures of outcome.

The advent of the computer, coupled with the demands for speed and efficiency from the managed health care movement, has stimulated innovative applications of new assessment procedures that assist in anticipating the course of treatment and in tracking patient changes. Kenneth I. Howard and his colleagues at Northwestern University (e.g., Howard et al., 1996; Sperry, Brill, Howard, & Grissom, 1996) have led the way in these applications, both in developing a research methodology and in translating research findings into clinical practice. Their Compass system is a brief, self-report procedure that identifies both general and specific areas of patient functioning and, because of the researchers' commitment to making research tools that are clinically useful, has now been applied to more than fifty thousand patients being treated in more than one hundred hospitals and health care systems. Compass has recently been revived with an expanded marketing strategy and is offered widely to both primary-care and psychiatric providers. Integra, Inc., publishes and distributes the Compass program to mental health programs, and Bristol-Myers Squibb distributes the system to primary-care providers.

The contributions of Compass, developed by Howard and colleagues, have been manifest and extensive in the area of research methodology. Using large samples, drawn from both private and public clinics, representing a variety of payment options and relationships with indemnity and managed health care agencies, the researchers have made valuable suggestions to the scientific community on methods for demonstrating comparison group equivalence (Rogers, Howard, & Vessey, 1993), when to disaggregate groups to look for treatment indicators (Howard, Krause, & Lyons, 1993), and the nature of changes induced by long- and short-term treatments (Howard, Kopta, Krause, & Orlinsky, 1986; Sperry et al., 1996). These suggestions are working their way into the methodology of treatment research at somewhat less than warp speed, but in our opinions they will prove to be of immense value in helping scientists clarify the nature of treatment processes and outcome patterns.

The contributions of this work to clinical practice are equally valuable and can be distilled into three salient and critical points: (1) Treatment outcomes occur in predictable phases, (2) there is a decreasing but positive growth function between amount of treatment and total benefit, and (3) it is possible to identify a criterion that is usable for determining when to cease treatment.

A phase theory of change is not new, but Howard and his colleagues (Howard et al., 1986; Kopta, Howard, Lowry, & Beutler, 1994) have been the most successful in identifying the sequential nature of the stages and in demonstrating their interrelationships as well as their relationship to formats and modes of treatment (Sperry et al., 1996). They demonstrate, for example, that the first experience to change for the typical mental health outpatient, regardless of specific diagnosis, is a sense of hope and optimism. A change in this dimension is generally expected for the majority of patients, if it is to occur, within a period of approximately six sessions conventionally offered at a rate of one session per week. Moreover, change in hope or optimism precipitates and seems to be necessary to activate the second phase of change, symptomatic relief. Symptoms of depression and anxiety, the usual accompaniments of the problems that lead people to seek help, change within a period of about six months of treatment, or approximately twenty-five treatment sessions for the majority of patients. Nearly 80 percent of patients experience a significant reduction of symptoms over the course of a year's treatment (fifty-four sessions).

The third phase of change, enduring personality changes, appears most relevant for only a relatively small portion of patients who initially seek assistance. These individuals change in the third phase only if they have first experienced changes in the earlier phases, and those most likely to benefit or require the long-term treatment required for the third phase of change are those who have endemic and chronic disturbances associated with persistent interpersonal and personality disturbances. Personality changes, including enduring changes in interpersonal patterns of behavior, coping styles, and affiliational attitudes, require long-term interventions. Thus, identifying those whose problems are associated with these enduring behavioral patterns and personality styles becomes an important aspect of treatment planning.

The second major implication of Howard et al.'s work is related to the first. It is a demonstration that outcomes are highly correlated, albeit at a decreasing rate over time, with the amount of treatment one receives. This "dose-response" demonstration flies in the face of many managed health care policies but, coupled with the demonstration of stages, introduces the possibility of making discriminating assignments of treatment length. Those for whom symptom relief is the objective can be treated within the context of a six-month to one-year regimen, depending on the complexity of the problem, while those whose problem complexity is further compounded by serious personality difficulties would be selectively retained for long-term treatment.

Predictably, those who are treated and released after initiating change in only optimism and hope may be expected to be at high risk for relapse. Thus, the researchers' third contribution, not to diminish its importance by any means, has been the introduction of a criterion for helping clinicians determine when to terminate or cease treatment (Sperry et al., 1996). Observing that, as a general rule, clinicians seek to continue treatment for a longer period than is needed and third-party payers seek to end it sooner than desirable, Howard and colleagues have taken the innovative step of establishing a criterion point on the Compass scale that identifies when the patient resembles a nonpathological population sufficiently to suggest that he or she no longer warrants treatment for symptoms (Sperry et al., 1996). Thus, an objective indicator is defined that can be used to inform practitioners and third-party payers alike not only when clinically meaningful changes have occurred but when the patient has returned to a level of "normal" functioning.

Other clinician researchers have extended the ideas initiated by Howard and colleagues and further expanded the applicability of patient self-report measures as a means of predicting and tracking treatment response (e.g., Lambert, Okiishi, Finch, & Johnson, 1998). Each new idea adds its own unique twist to the assessment of change, but all such methods have some common weaknesses. For example, they tend to rely on one source of information about patient change, self-reports. While we have emphasized the importance of this source of data, there are aspects of patient functioning that probably cannot be distinctively or reliably measured through self-report alone. Patients may function well externally but rate themselves as doing poorly because they feel very distressed. Other patients may report low distress but do very poorly in their interpersonal behaviors in work settings and relationships. This has important implications for assessing outcomes, as well as for determining characteristics of patients that are predictive and useful in assigning treatment.

Additionally, the methods used in these procedures often are restricted to measurement of symptoms that are closely akin to diagnostic criteria or at least have strong links to a diagnostic philosophy. As we've seen, diagnostically relevant symptoms and the categorical descriptions that arise from them do not fit well with the nature of what most people experience as depression. More important, neither are they the most efficient predictors of what treatment will work, although they are important for assessing the effects and effectiveness of these treatments (e.g., Beutler & Clarkin, 1990).

Moreover, in the search for efficiency, most indications of the nature of treatment employed in studies that use these time-efficient instruments have relied on simple determinations of the type, mode, format, frequency, and location or setting in which treatment takes place. To the degree that specific treatment procedures are studied in most research of this type, the research relies on clinician or patient reports to describe what treatment is offered. While clinician and patient reports should not be discounted, and while at least the direct observation of treatment is not automatically antagonistic to the use of such instruments, the time-intensive effort required to actually inspect the nature of treatment is seldom afforded in this research. Direct observations of what is done often provide a view of the process very different from the subjective experiences of those who are participating in it.

As a result, measures like Compass and its derivatives have limited use for planning specific treatment responses. They are problem centered and brief, and because they often lack clinician perspectives, they also may slow the recognition or minimize the importance of specific indicators for specific interventions.

At the same time, computer-based procedures have the ability and the power to identify the pattern of empirically identified patient characteristics that best fits with available treatments and treaters to enhance the likelihood of a satisfactory outcome. Computers have the ability to combine more variables in more complex and systematic ways than is possible for individual clinicians. Thus, if one could identify and measure differential predictors and apply predictive algorithms from an interactive database to effectively identify and progressively refine the prediction of what treatments would be most likely to help, therapeutic interventions could become more rational, faster, and more effective than they currently are (Beutler, Kim et al., 1996; Beutler, & Baker, 1998; Korchin & Schuldberg, 1981).

The advent of managed health care systems has, unfortunately, effectively eliminated the use of standard psychological assessment. Third-party payers discouraged the use of screening and even diagnostic batteries of tests by denying coverage and substituting less objective and less valid clinical impressions and unstructured clinical interviews as the basis for treatment decisions. In truth, the way that psychological tests and test batteries have been used invited this exclusion. The primary focus of psychological test batteries has been to describe levels and patterns of deficit, with the objectives of assigning a diagnosis or making a statement of prognosis. We have noted in earlier sections of this book that diagnostic and prognostic statements are not usually the same as statements that are useful for identifying treatments that are likely to be effective (Hayes, Nelson, & Jarrett, 1987).

Unfortunately, by abandoning the use of standardized and validated assessment procedures, the always inefficient process of planning treatment has become even less reliable and more dependent on the individual proclivities and skills of the clinician who conducts the initial evaluation. The level of any given clinician's skill is seldom known. However, psychological assessment procedures that are focused and time-efficient could be important tools for the task of efficiently identifying the patient qualities that have been empirically related to treatment characteristics. This is precisely the objectives of *systematic treatment selection* (STS) (Beutler & Clarkin, 1990; Beutler & Berren, 1995).

All of the foregoing considerations led the first author and his research group at the University of California to embark on the task of developing a measurement procedure that integrates both patient self-report and clinician judgment into a computerized, user-friendly environment that can provide direction to selective and empirically sound treatment planning. The result was the development of the systematic treatment selection treatment planner, based on clinician consolidation of patient intake, self-report test, and historical data (Beutler & Williams, 1995).

The STS Clinician Rating Form is the hard-copy version of this software program. In the test development and the predictive validity research that we will describe here as the basis for our ultimate development and test of basic and optimal treatment guidelines for systematic treatment selection, it was this form that we used for data capturing and recording. The computer version has the advantage over the hard-copy form of employing a branching mechanism that circumvents unnecessary questions. This luxury is not permitted during the process of instrument development and testing, where all questions must be asked and all dimensions must be rated.

STS provides a template for measuring the dimensions reviewed previously in this volume, as well as for using the resulting patterns to make decisions about treatment selection. The STS model offered a relatively easy translation to a computerized version (Beutler & Williams, 1995). The development of the computerized version of the STS assessment procedure has evolved hand in hand with efforts to develop efficient assessment procedures and to conduct prospective tests of the patterns observed in our reviews of literature. All of these aspects of the procedure are described in the following pages in as much detail as necessary to help us achieve the more important task of identifying guidelines for intervening among those who experience significant depression.

STS: DESCRIPTION OF INTEGRATED COMPUTER-ASSISTED ASSESSMENT

While standardized instruments are available for assessing most of the dimensions that we identified for potential inclusion in the development of treatment guidelines in the previous chapter, most of these are long and cumbersome, contain superfluous information, and have inconsistent value for identifying compatible treatments. Moreover, there are no conventionally accepted methods for measuring some of the dimensions. For example, there is no specific test for problem complexity, and measurement is poor on patient resistance traits. A single multidimensional instrument whose subscales are specifically designed to identify treatment-relevant variables promises to be more time efficient and valuable in contemporary managed health care systems than those that have traditionally been used in diagnosis-focused assessment. In the prototypic computerized version of STS that we have developed, however, clinicians are given the option of using many of the standardized psychological tests that we described as useful in chapter 4 to the extent that these instruments identify one or more of the variables that research has suggested may be relevant for treatment planning. Alternatively, they can use a computer-assisted and shortened assessment procedure that is specifically focused on identifying these dimensions. The software allows initial treatment planning as well as patient tracking and clinician profiling and offers a variety of diagnostic and decisional aids to facilitate treatment planning. However, for our purposes, it is not important that the reader know the specifics of the computerized STS. It is important, however, that potential users understand how we developed the questions that make up the subscales and how we incorporated the general principles and dimensions that emerged in our review of the empirical literature as described in chapter 3. It is also useful to know the process of independently cross-validating these dimensions as predictors of differential treatment plans and bases for guidelines in the application of systematic treatment selection.

In the remaining pages of this chapter, we describe more of the details about the development of the STS measurement procedure and the procedures used in our research program to test the predictive validity of the matching relationships. The descriptions and psychometric properties summarized in this presentation represent an inclusive extension of previous analyses that are reported elsewhere (Fisher, Beutler, & Williams, in press). Because some of the psychometric findings have been previously reported, this presentation is confined to summarizing the instrument and its development and describing the procedures used to validate the dimensions of treatment compatibility extracted from the previous literature review.

In chapters 6 and 7 we report the results of our efforts to use the concepts measured by the STS Clinician Rating Form as a basis for predicting patient response to different qualities and types of treatment. This research summarizes the nature of the treatment algorithms that predict level of care (basic guidelines) and specific type of intervention (optimal guidelines) as a means of providing a set of aids to clinicians for planning and conducting treatment.

Validational Assessment of the
STS Clinician Rating Form

The STS Clinician Rating Form is a multidimensional assessment procedure that forms the basis of the STS computer software and that is designed to overcome the shortcomings of existing omnibus personality and single-source (i.e., self-report) assessment procedures. It was designed to assess the patient dimensions identified in our literature review as potential mediators of differential treatment effects. These variables, it will be recalled, include the following: level of functional impairment, subjective patient distress, level of social support, problem complexity, level of trait-like resistance to external influence, and coping style.

Each of these dimensions has suggested the use of some treatment quality or method that may represent a particularly good fit for a patient who has a matching correspondent characteristic. Thus, it was important to also identify and tabulate qualities of treatment, given the observation that these may be useful to the clinician who has a knowledge of these patient dimensions. Some of the qualities and parameters of treatment could be identified objectively, external to the therapy process (e.g., group, family, individual therapy, use and type of medication, intensity of treatment, therapist demographic characteristics). A cursory review of the proposed relationships extracted from our literature review reveals that other dimensions could be defined only by viewing and rating in-session behaviors, activities, and procedures (e.g., therapist directiveness, focus of treatment, breadth of treatment goals).

Identifying the presence of these dimensions requires special measures of therapy processes that in turn, allow a determination of the relationship between the patient-treatment fit and treatment outcome.

Patient Participants

Three archival samples and one prospective patient sample were utilized at various steps in the joint processes of developing the STS Clinician Rating Form and validating its predictive power. Sample 1 was a prospective sample of minimally disturbed individuals who initiated mental health treatment, while samples 2, 3, and 4 were archival groups that were extracted from three separate research programs. To enhance generalizability of our findings, these samples were selected to ensure the geographic diversity of the subjects, as well as to provide for substantial variation in patient ages, sex, and problem severity. These samples were collectively used to test aspects of the psychometric properties of the STS Clinician Rating Form and to evaluate the predictive power of combining therapy, patient, and matching dimensions. Varying types and sources of information available on study participants occasionally limited the purposes for which each sample could be used in the development of the rating form (e.g., reliability, convergent validity). This was less of a problem for analyzing the predictive validity of the study, which forms the basis for the basic and optimal guidelines chapters, than it was for determining the reliability and clarity of the STS Clinician Rating Form.

For both the psychometric and the predictive validity analyses, available intake information provided the basis on which experienced clinicians completed the STS Clinician Rating Form for all subjects in the four samples. The STS Clinician Rating Form was a method of reducing the disparate measures used in different research programs or clinical settings to a common set of scores, each of which assesses treatment-relevant measures and scores and applies them to all patients across settings and samples. Likewise, for the development of basic and optimal treatment guidelines, a procedure was applied to cataloguing the objective qualities of treatment (e.g., intensity, modality, treatment format) and for observing actual within-treatment activities of the treating clinicians. This assessment procedure is the STS Therapy Rating Scale, which allowed the translation of procedures from a variety of treatment models into a set of continuous measures reflecting a common set of both treatment dimensions. These dimensions served as the basis for the emergence of treatment guidelines.

Sample 1

This sample comprised essentially consecutively admitted patients ($N = 54$) who were seeking services at the Ray E. Hosford Clinic (a university-affiliated outpatient mental health training clinic at the University of California at Santa Barbara). All included patients were ambulatory outpatients who presented with nonsubstance-abuse primary diagnoses and at least average intellectual ability and who had the ability to read at a sixth-grade level or more. Patients were diagnosed as having major depression (37 percent), dysthymia (37 percent), anxiety disorders (8 percent), or transient situational disturbances with depression and personality disorders (18 percent). These diagnoses were established by an independent clinical interview, supplemented by a computer-assisted structured clinical interview for the DSM-III-R (SCID).

Although they were offered no incentives, more than 90 percent of the qualified individuals who were approached within the period of screening agreed to participate. For various analyses, and in order to preserve generalization, we included the maximum number of participants on whom data were available for each analysis.

Clinician-rated outcomes were available on all patients, but only forty-six of the individuals provided self-report assessment of intake and end-of-treatment status. Among these individuals, the final outcomes were based on composite scores. Only when self-report was not available did we rely solely on clinician report of treatment-induced changes. The sample of forty-six participants were largely Anglo (84 percent) or Latino (11 percent), young adults (age = 34.55 years, SD = 11.71), and female (31 females, 15 males). The sample was indistinguishable from the larger pool of those who were screened by telephone on all demographic variables.

In this sample, no effort was made to structure or control the therapy outside of providing the usual supervision that was required for each therapist and that was offered by independent, professional psychologists from the local community who remained blind to the nature of the study. As was conventional in this setting, all treatment sessions were videorecorded, and two sessions were randomly selected from the initial and subsequent series of five sessions for assessing both treatment-related changes and evaluating treatment processes. The interrater time was between eight and ten sessions, with a follow-up initiated one month later.

Sample 2

One hundred and five individuals who entered a federally funded study on the treatment of alcoholism (Beutler, Patterson, et al., 1994) constituted the second sample. The sample was recruited from a variety of substance abuse treatment programs in the Santa Barbara community. Participants underwent initial telephone screening, followed by a structured diagnostic interview and psychological measures of drinking patterns, personality, and personal history to establish the diagnoses and substance use patterns.

The participants in this sample included those who were identified as having substance abuse or substance-dependent diagnoses and who successfully entered one of two manualized, couples-oriented treatments. Of the 105 identified alcohol abusers, the ninety males averaged 37.78 (SD = 8.81) and the fifteen females averaged 40.00 (SD = 7.06) years of age. Eighty-eight percent of the sample were Caucasian. As a group, these individuals presented with mild depression (Mean BDI = 13.14; SD = 7.24), but the range of depression represented in the sample was relatively broad, with initial BDI scores ranging from 8 to 26.

The manualized treatments were provided in a couples format, and participants were randomly assigned to treatment condition. Cognitive therapy for alcoholic couples (Wakefield, Williams, Yost, & Patterson, 1996) was based on standard cognitive therapy principles and emphasized the role of personal responsibility and change. The manualized family systems therapy (Rohrbaugh, Shoham, Spungen, & Steinglass, 1995), on the other hand, emphasized the role of systemic roles and dynamics in maintaining alcohol problems and in initiating change. Participants were tracked through twenty sessions of active treatment followed by a one-year follow-up period. All sessions were videotaped, and two sessions were randomly selected from the first and last third of the treatment. The 105 individuals on whom outcome data were available (seventy-nine had completed the BDI at pre- and posttreatment; all were rated by independent clinician raters on the STS Clinician Rating Form, depression subscale. Participants were included if they were assigned to treatment, and all those who attended at least one assigned treatment session were used in the predictive validity portion of this study.

Sample 3

This sample consisted of sixty-three individuals who were reliably diagnosed as presenting with a major depressive disorder (Beutler, Engle, et al., 1991). The sample consisted of twenty-two males and forty-one females, ranging in age from 22 to 76 years. They averaged 48.77 (SD = 14.95) and 45.41 (SD = 13.15) years of age, respectively. The sample was predominantly Caucasian (92 percent) and lived in southern Arizona. These individuals were recruited and treated as part of a federally funded, randomized clinical trial study of cognitive, experiential, and self-directed therapies. Referred individuals were screened by telephone and then assessed by an independent clinician and subjected to a variety of standardized interviews and tests to ensure compliance with depressive diagnostic and severity criteria. Those who initially were on psychoactive medication were withdrawn ($n = 15$) prior to completing the intake materials that were used in the current study.

Individuals in this study were randomly assigned to one of two group therapies (CT or FEP) or to an individually conducted self-directed therapy (S/SD). The group therapies consisted of cognitive therapy (CT) (Yost, Beutler, Corbishley, & Allender, 1986) and an experiential therapy fashioned on the principles of gestalt therapy, or focused expressive psychotherapy (FEP) (Daldrup, Beutler, Engle, & Greenberg, 1988). The therapies were all manualized and monitored for therapist compliance with process criteria, and the treatments were designed to vary systematically in level of directiveness and symptomatic versus conflictual focus. All group sessions were videotaped, and two sessions were randomly selected from early and late sessions to provide information on the treatment process for this project.

Sample 4

This sample comprised sixty-two depressed adults over age 60 and was extracted from two separate research studies performed by the Palo Alto Veterans Administration Geropsychiatry program (Thompson, Gallagher-Thompson, Hanser, Gantz, & Steffen, 1991; Thompson, Gallagher, & Breckenridge, 1987). Sixty-three percent of the sample was female, and the sample ranged in age from 60 to 81 years. The samples for the two separate studies were drawn from the same geographic area, were selected on the basis of identical selection criteria, and were all randomly assigned to the various treatments under study. Because the sizes of the samples differed for the different studies, we elected to simplify comparisons by randomly selecting patients on whom both outcome data and audio- or videotapes of two treatment sessions were available. The participants represented three treatment conditions: desiprimine therapy ($n = 20$), cognitive therapy ($n = 22$), and psychodynamic therapy ($n = 20$), all of which were monitored and conducted according to a manual.

All treatment sessions were audiorecorded, and two sessions were randomly selected to represent early and late sessions in the sixteen- to twenty-week treatment protocol.

Patient-Matching Variables

For purposes of developing the STS Clinician Rating Form, a clinician-based measure derived from numerous sources of information, we compared composite clinician ratings to scores for each separate dimension, using established psychological tests. Because the different samples underwent different evaluations as part of the research protocol in which they were embedded, the particular psychological tests available for assessing the various dimensions varied from sample to sample. In the case of some samples, not all dimensions of interest were identifiable with the instruments available. Thus, for purposes of the development of the STS Clinician Rating Form, the number of data points available for analysis varied from dimension to dimension. Experienced and trained clinicians rated the dimensions of the STS Clinician Rating Form after, at the least, viewing or listening to an audio- or videotape of the patient's intake, reviewing a sociodemographic background form, inspecting a wide variety of psychological tests, and reviewing the diagnostic criteria with which the patient was in compliance at intake.

The content of the dimensions assessed in the STS Clinician Rating Form was extracted from the evolving literature review reported in chapter 3. The dimensions were identified as promising for assigning particular aspects or types of treatment. They included functional impairment, social support level, problem complexity, subjective distress, coping style (separate measures of internal and external coping), and trait resistance level. Some dimensions were separated into subscales to reflect different aspects of the particular patient quality. These were largely face-valid measures, and their ultimate utility was assessed by their contribution to a common dimension and a demonstration that these dimensions, in turn, were predictive of the patient's response to the targeted aspect of treatment. Reliability estimates were obtained on all of these dimensions, but because of the inconsistent availability of relevant and valid psychological tests generally or for the four samples specifically, tests of convergent and discriminant validity were possible on only some of the dimensions assessed in the STS Clinician Rating Form.

The psychometric analysis reported here applied to the dimensions of functional impairment, social support, subjective distress, coping style, and resistance level, dimensions on which validated external tests are available. Each of these dimensions was assessed both through ratings by experienced and trained clinicians and through the use standardized tests (criterion measures). Our psychometric analysis included an assessment of interrater reliability, criterion validity, and construct (convergent and discriminant) validity. The validity assessments were based on a comparison of the STS with standardized, self-report tests.

Psychological Test Measures

The selection of criteria scores for the patient dimensions was constrained by the need to use instruments that had been used in the various research samples at the time of intake. The following dimensions were measured by formal psychological tests, and relevant scores on these dimensions were used to validate the summarizing STS ratings of clinicians.

Functional impairment was assessed by independent clinicians in all four samples, using a version of the Global Assessment of Functioning (GAF) extracted from the Diagnostic and Statistical Manual (American Psychiatric Association, 1994). This measure provides a general estimate of adequacy of functioning on a 100-point scale. Low scores, especially those below 70, indicate that impairment is present. The scale is reversed so that high scores mean low impairment.

Subjective distress was indexed by three different measures, reflecting, respectively, state-like and trait-like qualities. The Eysenck Personality Inventory (EPI) (Eysenck & Eysenck, 1969) and the MMPI-2 (Butcher, 1990; Graham, 1993) are both widely used omnibus self-report measures of personality. Each yields a variety of trait-like dimensions that are thought to be related to the patient's status and treatment planning. The standardized Pt subscale (MMPI) was used as one index of subjective distress (samples 1, 2, and 3), and the EPI Neuroticism subscale was used as another (sample 4). The state-like aspects of distress were assessed in all samples, using the Beck Depression Inventory (BDI) (Beck, Ward, et al., 1961). The three scales were analyzed separately as reflecting different aspects of subjective distress.

Social support was assessed by the Sarason Social Support Scale (SSQ) (Sarason, Levine, Basham, & Sarason, 1983) in sample 1 and by the Social Adjustment Scale (SAS) (Weissman & Bothwell, 1976) in sample 4. The other samples did not include a formal, standardized measure of social support. Each of the instruments assessed both the availability of and the satisfaction with existing support systems.

Coping style was represented by two separate indicators in each sample, and these domains were obtained from somewhat different tests in the various samples. In each case, coping style comprised the separate dimensions of *externalization* and *internalization*. The test measures of these dimensions were based either on the MMPI and MMPI-2 (Graham, 1993), for samples 1, 2, and 3, or on the Millon Clinical Multiaxial Inventory (Millon & Davis, 1995), for sample 4. The two components of coping were used to assess separately the construct validity of comparable STS scales, and then both were combined as a ratio to index a relative measure of externalization, as originally suggested by Welsh (1952).

In the case of the MMPI, combinations of four subscales had been identified in prior research (Beutler & Mitchell, 1981; Beutler, Engle, et al., 1991; Calvert, Beutler, & Crago, 1988; Welsh, 1952) as indicating externalizing or internalizing tendencies. In this study, coping styles were identified by indexing the mean elevations of these scales, and the mean elevations of these scales were used to index each dimension, on the basis of prior research with this instrument. Externalization was indexed by a combination of scales 3 (Hy), 4 (Pd), 6 (Pa), and 9 (Ma). Internalization was indexed by a combination of scales 1 (Hs), 2 (D), 7 (Pt), and 0 (Si). A single measure of coping style was constructed, following the rationale of Welsh (1952), by developing a ratio of externalization-to-internalization scores. Scores above 1.0 reflected relative degree of externalization, while scores below this value indicated a balance favoring internalizing tendencies.

In the case of sample 4, the criteria used were scales from the MCMI-II. The specific subscales used to index externalization were drawn from the Axis II categories of Hystrionic and Narcissistic personality. The internalization scores included the Avoidant, Dysthymic, and Self-Defeating personality scores. The BR scores were treated as standard-score equivalents, with the ratio of mean BR scores serving as an index of the relative external-to-internal coping style scores.

Resistance traits have been the most difficult of the dimensions to measure (Beutler, Sandowicz, et al., 1996). To reflect this complex dimension in samples 1, 2, and 3, we constructed a composite scale from the MMPI/MMPI-2. Through consultation with experts in the field and reviews of prior research, we identified scales that conceptually reflected aspects of patient resistance. An intercorrelation of many of these scales, using the MMPI-2 normative sample,[1] allowed us to identify several that conceptually reflected a common dimension. To confirm our impressions, we cross-validated the separate subscales selected against the Dowd Therapeutic Reactance Scale (TRS) (Dowd, Milne, & Wise, 1991), a scale that was available only for sample 1. In this sample, we found that the TRS was moderately correlated (from .31 to .64; $M = .53$; all ps $< .05$) with various of the STS Clinician Rating Form subscales.

We next subjected the resulting scales to a factor analysis, using the combined samples, and obtained a composite factor that included the following scales: Cn (Control), Do (Dominance, weighted inversely), and Pa (Paranoia). The mean of these scales was then used as a final measure of resistance traits in the analysis of construct validity.

Resistance in sample 4 was based on the mean elevations of Passive-Aggressive personality, Antisocial Personality, and Aggressive-Sadistic personality scores drawn from the MCMI-II.

STS Clinician Rating Form

Dimensions assessed by the rating form included the various areas of functioning described earlier (functional impairment, subjective distress, social support, problem complexity, resistance level, and coping style), as well as some specific problem areas. The specific problem areas included depression, suicidal risk, self-esteem, various diagnostic disorders, and areas of social impairment (e.g., family, partner, work, legal).

The items on these scales require clinician ratings based on all information available to them at the time of intake. Four (three female and one male) experienced psychologists were recruited and paid to review each of the 384 patients' intake material, including an intake audio- or videotape, and to complete the STS Clinician Rating Form. One clinician-rater was Asian-American and one was African American; three were licensed as psychologists; two were self-employed in full-time clinical or consultive practice; one was a consultant to educational institutions; one was engaged in full-time clinical research training; and one directed the outpatient clinic from which sample 1 was obtained. All but one of the clinician-raters had more than five years of clinical experience, and their average level of experience exceeded ten years.

A series of training sessions was provided to the clinician-raters prior to their making the ratings in order to ensure a common level of familiarity with the various procedures that served as the basis for rating patient variables. Training included a review of patient assessment procedures, including the MMPI and the MCMI, the nature of the dimensions being assessed, and a description of the materials that raters would have available to them as they completed the intake patient ratings.

---

1. The authors wish to thank Dr. James Butcher, Ph.D., for his consultation and assistance.

To parallel how such judgments are made in clinical practice, clinicians were provided with a videotape of an intake or first session with the patient, clinical notes from the intake clinician, and whatever intake tests were available at the time the patient entered treatment.[2] For those portions of the criteria validity assessment that did not include the use of standardized psychological tests, all four samples were used (maximal $N = 289$).

The STS items were presented in a checklist format, and clinicians were required to provide a dichotomous rating (present-not present) on each of the 226 initial items. Raters who were quite certain that a symptom or attribute was present were asked to mark the item box with a check. If there was no evidence of the symptom or attribute being present, they left the box blank.

Interrater Reliability of the STS Clinician Rating Form

For sample 1, two raters assessed each patient using the STS Clinician Rating Form. This sample entailed the most complete data, and, in order to hold amount and type of intake information constant, the other samples were not used in this analysis. Interrater reliability assessment took place in two stages. In the first stage, raters were compared to a sample of cases on which a performance criterion had been established by "criterion judges." In the second stage, clinician-raters were paired randomly and asked to complete independent ratings. Interrater reliabilities were computed for all pairs of clinician-judges. Both the overall reliability of the STS Clinician Rating Form subscales and the reliabilities of the various subscales were analyzed.

To indicate level of reliability, three types of concordance agreements were calculated: (1) overall agreement of each possible rater pair, (2) agreement of each rater with the sum of all other raters, and (3) specific levels of interrater agreement for each of the three specific dimensions for which psychological tests were available.

Overall interrater agreement was computed on all subscales of the STS Clinician Rating Form, using sample 1 data. The calculations reflected the mean degree of agreement across all rater pairs. The mean interrater concordance (kappa) coefficients ranged from .77 (functional impairment) to .99 (presence of eating disorder), with an average coefficient of concordance of .84.

Rater-level agreement was computed for each of the five individual raters, averaging their pairings with those for each of the other raters. With a sample of fifteen pairings for each rater, the mean coefficients of concordance ranged from .80 to .89.

Specific levels of agreement were assessed by comparing raters to one another, again relying on sample 1 data. The mean levels of interrater agreement

2. In samples 1 and 2, intake interviews were available. For sample 3, videotapes of the intake interviews were not available; instead, the first videotaped session of psychotherapy was used.

were .82 (subjective distress), .86 (internalization), .86 (externalization), and .80 (resistance).

Validity of the STS Clinician Rating Form

To assess discriminant and convergent validity, samples 1 and 2 were collapsed because they used similar tests (sample 4 was assessed separately). STS Clinician Rating Forms were completed on all patients after the clinicians reviewed the intake materials described in the previous paragraphs. The material supplied to the raters for assessing sample 2 data was the same types of material supplied to the clinicians before rating sample 1 data. The intake material included a history of the patient and problem, a battery of intake tests used in the original research protocol, and a videotape of the patient's intake evaluation.

The summary scores from the STS Clinician Rating Form, representing subjective distress, internalization, externalization, and resistance traits, were compared against one another (discriminant validity) and against the same constructs as measured by standardized self-report tests (convergent validity). In samples 2, 3, and 4, individual clinicians rated each patient, with a randomly selected 20 percent of cases being double-rated to check reliability levels. When test-wise reliabilities dropped below a mean kappa of .70, criterion tapes were inserted and raters were retrained to protect against rater drift.

Criterion validity of the entire STS Clinician Rating Form was assessed in sample 1 by comparing clinicians' ratings to an "expert" standard. In addition, three other comparisons were initiated in order to determine the construct validity of seven STS-based dimensions (functional impairment, social support, coping style, subjective distress, externalization, internalization, resistance traits): (1) agreement with expert criteria-based ratings, (2) convergent validity with measures of similar constructs, and (3) discriminant validity with measures of dissimilar constructs.

Expert Criterion Validity

Overall expert criterion agreement was calculated by averaging the concordance estimate of each rater with two randomly selected "expert-rated" cases from sample 1. Twelve cases were used as criterion samples for checking rater accuracy. The criteria of accuracy were consensual ratings from two expert raters who had the greatest familiarity with the cases. The mean individual concordance estimates (kappa) with these criteria ranged from .69 to .80. The overall mean concordance coefficient across 260 STS Clinician Rating Form items was .77, indicating a satisfactory level of criterion agreement across clinician raters.

When these criteria-based ratings were applied to the seven focal scales, the following mean kappa values were obtained: .75 (functional impairment; .84 (subjective distress); .85 (social support); .83 (complexity/chronicity); .85 (internalization), .86 (externalization), and .83 (resistance traits).

Convergent Validity

The test of convergent validity consisted of a comparison between the refined STS Clinician Rating Form scales and the psychological test criteria for similar constructs. Sample 3 lacked some important psychological test dimensions and was excluded from this analysis. We computed a series of Pearson product-moment correlations between the STS Clinician Rating Form dimensions and the independently derived scores for each dimension, excluding problem complexity for lack of a consistent alternative measure of this dimension.

The STS Clinician Rating Form measure of patient subjective distress correlated at the highest levels with the external criteria ($rs = .63$ and $.65$ with Pt and BDI, respectively; $p < .001$) in samples 2 and 3 and correlated with EPI Neuroticism (sample 4) at a somewhat lower level ($r = .32; p < .001$). The correspondence of STS and GAF measures of functional impairment failed to correlate at a significant level ($r = .04$; ns). MMPI measures (samples 1 and 2) of externalization ($r = .35; p < .001$) and internalization ($r = .42; p < .001$) were significant but modest. Corresponding measures based on the MCMI-II (sample 4) were much higher, however. The MCMI composite measures correlated at moderate levels with the clinician ratings of externalization ($r = .75; p < .001$) and internalization ($r = .54; p < .001$).

As a further check on coping style, ratios of external to internal coping styles were constructed and then correlated for the measures extracted from the STS and the standardized tests. Using the MMPI measures (samples 2 and 3), these two summary measures of relative coping style correlated at level of $.46$ ($p < .001$). Using MCMI data (sample 4), the correlation was $.31; p < .001$).

The convergence between MMPI and STS Clinician Rating Form measures of patient resistance levels were moderate ($r = .43; p < .001$) while the MCMI-II measure correlated somewhat better with the STS Clinician Rating Form measure of this construct ($r = .63; p < .001$).

Discriminant Validity

Another aspect of construct validity is the determination of how the various subscales and measures related to one another. Discriminant validity requires that various constructs be relatively independent and reveal a prescribed pattern of relationship with one another. Specifically, it was expected that (1) the two coping-style dimensions (internalization and externalization) would be significantly and negatively correlated; (2) subjective distress would be moderately correlated with internalization but not with externalization coping-style dimensions; and (3) resistance traits would be moderately correlated with externalization but not with either internalization or subjective distress.

Using only the first three samples to capitalize on the most consistent data sets, the expected patterns of relationships were obtained consistently. Internalization and externalization were negatively correlated at a moderate level ($r = -.44$; $p < .001$); subjective distress was correlated with internalization ($r = .48$; $p < .001$) but not with externalization ($r = -.03$); and resistance traits were highly correlated with externalization ($r = .70$) but only modestly with the other patient dimensions (rs of $.21$ and $-.26$). Thus, the pattern of intercorrelations supported the discriminant validity of the three dimensions (collapsing internalization and externalization).

Discussion

The STS Clinician Rating Form appears to be a promising method of assessing treatment-relevant patient traits. Overall agreement among raters, as well as criterion and scale-specific agreement, was high. Clinicians agreed with externally derived "expert criteria" of accuracy at just slightly lower levels than they agreed with one another. With relatively little training, clinician-raters reached agreement on the level of patient distress, coping style, and resistance.

The relatively low correspondence between clinician ratings of patient qualities (e.g., on the STS Clinician Rating Form) and patient self-reports (e.g., on the MMPI) is not atypical (Strupp, Horowitz, & Lambert, 1997). Different aspects of patient qualities are captured in external clinician ratings and in self-ratings. It is notable that the correspondence with the MCMI was much higher than with the MMPI, suggesting that the nature of the relationship is measure dependent.

The final step in the process of analysis was to determine whether the clinician-rated dimensions could accurately predict the effectiveness of treatment sufficiently to serve as a basis for basic and optimal guidelines for planning treatment. We turn to this issue in the next two chapters.

APPLICATIONS OF TREATMENT SELECTION
VARIABLES TO CASE EXAMPLES

The value of the descriptive patient dimensions presented in the foregoing discussion of the STS Clinician Rating Form and in the review of literature included in chapter 3 for describing and distinguishing among patients can be illustrated by again referring to the cases of Alice and Harold. Table 5.1 summarizes the findings and compares the standing of Alice and Harold on the serveral dimensions used in treatment planning.

First, we summarize the results of applying the STS Clinician Rating Form and, where applicable, standardized psychological tests to the two cases in question. The results of clinician ratings and of psychological measures are summarized by dimension and then conceptualized by collecting the findings for each patient.

Functional Impairment

The current state of impairment of life functions, work, social activities, and self-care suggested to the clinicians who completed the STS Clinician Rating Forms for the two patients that Alice experienced substantially higher levels of social impairment than did Harold. That is not to say that Harold's level of impairment was inconsequential. Indeed, his life was disrupted substantially by problems in his life, as well. Yet, Alice presented with multiple problems, and these several impairments (e.g., drinking too much, social isolation, physiological complaints, impaired work, failed marriage) were implicated in her seeking treatment. The extent of these problems and the number of areas affected identify her as having been substantially impaired for a considerable period.

Harold is highly distressed but still functional. His life is disrupted, but he is still able to work, he has maintained his marriage, and there are few indications that his problems and symptoms have been widely generalized. While both Harold and Alice have suicidal thoughts, Harold's thoughts have not led to active suicidal efforts, and he has no active suicidal plans.

Although no formal psychological tests purport to tap functional impairment, an approximation of this level is obtained from the multiaxial diagnostic criteria. The GAF scores applied by the intake clinicians who saw Harold and Alice were 70 and 50, respectively, and were similar to the more complex index of impairment derived from the STS Clinician Rating Form. The GAF scores reflect the general impression that Harold was seen as functioning quite well in spite of his symptoms, while Alice's GAF of 50 led the clinicians to judge her to be moderately to seriously impaired.

Subjective Distress

Clinicians using the STS Clinician Rating Form judged both Alice and Harold to be significantly distressed; both had significant suicidal thoughts; both felt helpless; and both felt hopeless about the future. Nonetheless, a quantitative

Table 5.1 Assessment of Alice and Harold

Predictors	Alice	Harold
Diagnosis	Major depression	Major depression
Functional impairment	High	Low
Subjective distress	High	Middle
Social support	Low	Middle
Complexity/chronicity	High	Low
Resistance/reactance	Average	Average
Coping style	External	Internal

difference in clinician ratings was obtained, indicating a higher level of distress for Alice than for Harold. The implication, of course, is that subjective distress is implicated in patient motivation, and while one may question the motivation for treatment for both of these patients, it is apparent that both feel considerable unhappiness and have suffered a loss of self-esteem that may motivate them for change.

These clinician ratings were consistent with scores obtained on the Brief Symptom Inventory (BSI), a self-report measure of symptom severity. Here, Alice produced a Global Severity Index (T score) of 80, and Harold produced a score of 65. While Alice experienced significant elevations on all the symptoms assessed (somatization, obsessive-compulsive patterns, interpersonal sensitivity, depression, anxiety, hostility, phobic anxiety, paranoid ideation, and psychoticism/social isolation), Harold's elevated scores were restricted primarily to three scales—obsessive-compulsive thoughts, anxiety, and depression. As an aside, the relatively more restricted symptoms that characterized Harold's reports confirm his relatively lower level of social impairment compared to Alice's. The scores also confirm Harold's relatively lower level of internal distress.

Social Support

Clinicians were impressed that Harold has more sources of external support and assistance than Alice. He reports family contacts and remains in contact with childhood friends. While he had been uprooted, he is not foundering and isolated, and he continues to find some solace and support in his marriage and from his family. In contrast, Alice is very isolated. She is cut off from her family and has virtually no friends, with the possible exception of a roommate whose own stability is quite uncertain.

The Sarason Social Support Questionnaire, a self-report measure, again confirmed the clinicians' ratings. This measure revealed a substantial difference between Harold and Alice. Harold earned self-reported scores that were in the upper limits of the scale on both number and satisfaction with social supports. On scales whose maximum values are 9, he scored 9 and 6 for the two scales. Alice, in contrast, earned very low scores for both the number of resources and satisfaction level (number and satisfaction scores were 2 and 3, respectively). These scores are not surprising from the descriptions of the patients' histories and confirm the presence of a more supportive environment for Harold than is available for Alice.

Problem Complexity

On the STS Clinician Rating Form, problem complexity is indexed by the history of recurrent problems and of problems of a chronic nature. By these criteria, Alice earned a higher index of problem complexity than did Harold.

Her history reveals the presence of recurrent depression, probably beginning in childhood. Moreover, her problems are associated with a considerable amount of social disruption, vegetative signs, family conflicts, and interpersonal difficulties, all occurring periodically since that time. She has received prior treatment for depression at several points in her life, with at least one previous suicide gesture, and her dysphoria has been relatively continuous over a substantial period of time, all factors that suggest high levels of problem complexity to the clinicians.

Harold, in contrast, is suffering his first bout of depression. His problems are also judged to be situation-specific and transient. The two clinicians who rated Harold's experience saw no evidence of a recurrent pattern of problems, but one of them expressed concern about the uncertain circumstances that surrounded the death of Harold's brother. While the uncertainty about this event must lead us to keep open the possibility of family depressive patterns, the clinicians generally gave Harold the benefit of the doubt and judged his problem to be relatively uncomplicated and associated with normal grieving and to have a relatively good prognosis.

No formal psychological tests were available to reflect directly on the differential level of problem complexity presented by Harold and Alice. Alice earned more scales above clinical levels on the MMPI-2 than Harold did, however. Moreover, as noted in the description of their histories, Alice had a broader-ranging and a more pervasive symptom pattern on other self-report symptom measures like the BSI than did Harold, suggesting a high level of problem complexity. Harold's reported symptoms were relatively confined to a few general clusters, primarily reflecting acute depression.

Resistance Traits

Both Harold and Alice presented with signs and symptoms that led the two clinician-raters to judge them both to be resistant to intervention. Harold was openly reluctant to seek treatment, and Alice has a history of several unsuccessful courses of treatment. Both of these factors suggested to the clinicians that these two patients might be resistant to external intervention. However, it should be noted that Alice described her previous treatment as helpful in spite of the fact that it was not associated with documented change, and Harold has a history of seeking and being receptive to assistance from family and friends, although not from professional therapists.

To clarify the contradictions, we administered Dowd's (Dowd, Milne, & Wise, 1991) Therapeutic Reactance Scale (TRS) to both patients. This instrument yielded some surprising results that were modestly contrary to the judgments made by the external clinicians. The TRS indicated that both Harold and Alice were relatively low in resistant qualities and suggested that both of them might be ready to accept and comply with the therapeutic efforts of the therapist. Surprisingly, Alice's score was somewhat lower than

Harold's. Her score was a full standard deviation below the normative mean, while Harold's score was just slightly above the normative mean. These scores suggested that Alice might be quite responsive to the therapeutic use of directive interventions and that Harold, if anything, would be somewhat more resistant to these interventions than would Alice.

Coping Style

In completing the STS Clinician Rating Form, both Alice and Harold were judged to present predominantly external coping styles. For Alice, this externalized pattern was observed in her active and impulsive suicidal behaviors, her recent history of excessive alcohol use, and the presence of repeated problems with authorities at work. Harold, while less impaired and pathological than Alice, also revealed a history consistent with an external coping style. Notably, he has a history characterized by social gregariousness and assertiveness. However, Harold also has a history that suggests that he might be capable of being reflective and insightful, while Alice's history suggests that she is quite self-critical and guilt-ridden, to the point of being unable to evaluate herself and others objectively. These ambiguities were resolved by the administration of the MMPI-2, a measure of coping styles and personality dispositions.

Alice earned moderately high scores on indices of externalization and of internalization, suggesting a general ambivalence or instability of coping patterns. Her highest scores were on scales reflecting impulsivity, depression, anxiety, unfocused energy, and interpersonal distrust, suggesting the dominance of an externalizing pattern of coping. This pattern is typically described as reflecting the presence of cyclic, unstable, and ambivalent interactions with others.

Psychological tests also confirmed Harold's ambivalence, but his scores were neither as extreme nor as varied as those of Alice. He earned moderately high scores on impulsivity, anxiety, social inhibition, and depression, with the balance favoring the interpretation that an internalizing style of coping dominates his behavior. He is emotionally constricted, seeks to understand his world through self-reflection, and is generally anxious. This interpretation is consistent with the anxiety and obsessive-compulsive scale elevations observed on the BSI.

Implications for Planning Treatments

It is likely that several of the dimensions identified in our review are intercorrelated. Thus, there may be patterns of interest and even of significance to the task of defining categorical or diagnostic groups that are related to treatment assignments. At least conceptually, for example, individuals who are judged to be externalizers are also likely to be resistant. Together with indices of chronicity/complexity, elevations in these areas may identify those with characterological disturbances. The treatment implications suggest that a collaborative (patient-led) focus on symptoms may be indicated and that insight-oriented and authoritative interventions may be contraindicated. Thus, Alice appears to be a candidate for a symptom-focused intervention that emphasizes cognitive and symptomatic change. Her relative receptivity to therapeutic influence suggests that the therapist may take a modestly directive and guiding stance, assigning homework and helping her monitor changes. Involvement in social groups and support systems should be emphasized to provide external support.

In contrast, those with relatively high social impairment but reasonably good levels of social support and generally internalizing coping patterns may be receptive to using available social support systems and to achieving benefit through insight and awareness. Harold may therefore benefit from a search for patterns that govern his life and from the support provided by his family and friends. Both Harold and Alice may require long-term multiperson or socially focused treatments, but, given the greater complexity of Alice's problems, it is likely that work with her will be longer-term than with Harold.

To say that there may be clusters or patterns among the dimensions that are correlated with diagnostic groupings is not to say that conventional diagnoses can be reconstructed to become treatment relevant. Many of the dimensions vary widely within diagnostic groups. As typically applied, for example, it is likely that those diagnosed as having either depressive or anxiety disorders will present with high levels of distress, and either of these designations may draw from the clinician various efforts to reduce discomfort and to provide either structure or support. Patients so diagnosed vary widely in other treatment-relevant dimensions, however. For example, not unless one also knows the relative level of externalization and internalization, the level of symptom specificity versus generality, and the level of resistance can one define a treatment program that will be responsive and meaningful to the particular patient.

The advantage of using a dimensional description rather than a categorical, diagnostic distinction is that dimensions may better capture individual differences and are more likely to be representative and inclusive of relevant patient variations than are nominal classifications. Moreover, dimensions do not convey or necessarily indicate the pejorative judgments associated with diagnoses. Instead, they reflect normal patterns of behavior as well as pathologies and thereby provide a less bias-driven picture of the people involved.

Diagnostic classifications also draw on a wide variety of other dimensions, only some of which have been empirically associated with treatment benefit. By restricting our consideration to a few empirically identified dimensions, it may be possible to clarify and specify needed treatments.

APPLICATION OF BRANCH LOGIC
TO TREATMENT PLANNING

The value of branching logic, described in chapter 4, further illustrates the process of treatment planning.

Branch 1: Causes of the Depression

Did Alice or Harold have co-occuring medical problems or substance abuse that could have contributed to their depressions? Medical conditions are unlikely to account for the depressive symptoms of either Harold or Alice. While alcohol intoxication and medical complications may be more dominant in evoking and maintaining Alice's depressive symptoms than Harold's, the etiological significance is uncertain. Both conditions appear to be reactive, with Alice's being much more chronic and intractable than Harold's. Psychosocial interventions appear to be indicated for both Alice and Harold as primary interventions.

Branch 2 and 3: Extent and Duration of Depressive and Manic Symptoms

Neither Harold nor Alice had experienced prior episodes of mania. The extent and duration of their depressive symptoms were quite different, with Alice's being more recurrent, long-standing, and life threatening than those of Harold. Alice's problems will require longer-term care than those of Harold, and one might expect her to need recurrent, periodic interventions during times of crisis. Alice may even require periods of hospitalization when she becomes very unstable and suicidal, but Harold can be expected to remain ambulatory.

Branch 4: Functional Impairment

The question addressed at the fourth branch pertains to the spread of the problems over the patient's life functioning. Both Harold and Alice have relatively high levels of social impairment, although Harold's level of impairment appears to be associated with many more resources of support and potential assistance than Alice's. While Alice has experienced substantially higher levels of social impairment than Harold, Harold's level of impairment cannot be discounted, since his life has been quite disrupted by the problems he has had to face. Yet, Alice has multiple problems (e.g., drinking too much, social isolation, physiological complaints, impaired work, failed marriage) that result in her being identified as being substantially impaired.

Harold is highly distressed but functional. He is able to work, he has maintained his marriage, and he exhibits no indications that the symptoms have undergone wide generalization. While both he and Alice have suicidal thoughts, his have not been accompanied by any gestures, and he has no active suicidal plans. Decisions at this branch have implications for the length, setting, and intensity of treatment, as well as for the use of external sources of support in the patient's environment.

Branch 5: Coping Style, Resistance, and Subjective Distress

The fifth level of decision directs us to specific interventions that are designed to address the patient's style of coping and ability to accept direction and respond to structure. This is the most refined decisional level, and it requires the therapist to adapt therapeutic techniques and principles to the patient's particular needs and patterns of behavior.

In completing the STS Clinician Rating Forms, clinicians judged both Alice and Harold to present with external coping styles. For Alice, this externalized pattern was observed in her impulsive suicidal behaviors, her recent history of excessive alcohol use, and the presence of repeated problems with authorities at work. Harold, while less impaired and pathological than Alice, also revealed a history that is consistent with an external coping style. Notably, he has a history that suggests that he is assertive and gregarious. However, Harold was also judged to have the capacity to be reflective and insightful, while Alice's history suggests that she is quite self-critical and overcome with guilt. These ambiguities were resolved by the administration of the MMPI-2, a measure of coping styles and personality dispositions.

Alice earned moderately high scores on indices of both externalization and internalization, suggesting a general ambivalence or instability of coping patterns. She earned high scores on scales reflecting impulsivity, depression, anxiety, unfocused energy, and interpersonal distrust. This pattern is typically described as reflecting the presence of cyclic, unstable, and ambivalent coping efforts. Overall, however, externalized tendencies were slightly dominant over internalizing patterns in Alice's profile, while Harold's profile was much more suggestive of self-reflection and self-awareness.

At the same time, both Harold and Alice revealed themselves to be relatively receptive to psychotherapeutic interventions. Thus, both are likely to be responsive to the therapist's suggestions and guidance, homework assignments, and therapist-imposed structure. This is all the better because of the relative levels of distress experienced by these two patients. Alice's high level of distress suggest the need for structure and self-control training to help reduce distress and levels of impulsivity.

Branch 6: Social Support and Self-Esteem

This final level of decision directs our attention to patients' resources for coping and for managing their lives. Clinicians using the STS rating form judged both Alice and Harold to have suffered a loss of self-esteem and a general loss of support from others. These attributes tend to expose a patient to risk of decompensation and to a host of negative consequences of their struggles. The relative differences in levels of social support available to Harold and Alice suggest that Harold may be able to benefit from a much shorter course of treatment than will Alice. Efforts to help Alice enhance her sense of well-being are likely to be time consuming and to require the development of external support systems, friendships, and social contacts.

PART III

Guidelines for Management and Treatment

6 Reasonable and Basic Treatment Guidelines

To this point, we have focused on the identification of probable relationships that can serve as the basis for the development of differential treatment guidelines. Accordingly, in chapter 3, we successfully extracted fifteen suggestions that are provided by contemporary research, all of which are selective in that the principles of recommended treatment are applied selectively to patients who fit different profiles or who present with different predisposing characteristics. However, guidelines extracted from past research can identify only correlations between patient and treatment characteristics. They lack the power to determine cause-and-effect relationships. Cross-validating research is therefore needed to refine and solidify these guidelines. It is to this task that this and the next chapter turn.

This chapter is devoted to defining basic treatment guidelines through a cross-validation of the tenetative suggestions provided earlier. The cross-validation relies on the mixed sample comprising the four samples described in previous chapters. Two of the data sets consisted of individuals who had been carefully and reliably diagnosed with major depressive disorders. Patients in these samples were treated with either group or individual cognitive therapy, group experiential therapy, individual psychodynamic therapy, antidepressant therapy, or a self-directed bibliotherapy.

To broaden the potential for generalization and in order to be consistent with the conclusion that depression is best conceptualized and most relevant to treatment decisions when it is seen as a dimensional quality that is associated with other conditions rather than as a distinct nominal entity in its own right (see chapters 3 and 4; Carson, 1997), we included two other samples in which depression was more broadly distributed. These samples included a general outpatient clinic sample on which was practiced the usual form of general outpatient care and a sample of patients being treated for alcohol abuse in a controlled clinical trial of cognitive therapy and family systems therapy (Beutler, Patterson, et al., 1994).

The combined sample included 284 individuals who ranged in age from seventeen to seventy-nine years, was dominantly female, and was moderately impaired on measures of social impairment. Our interest at this level of analysis, however, was not in what brand of treatment worked but with what types of patients and which families or classes of therapeutic procedures and activities worked best for each type of patient. We obtained measures of relevant patient variables from the STS Clinician Rating Form, described in chapter 5. Trained doctoral clinicians evaluated the presence of these dimensions after reviewing a collection of intake materials and an audio- or videotape of the patient's intake interview. The primary outcome measure was the Beck Depression Inventory (BDI), which was completed by 248 patients, supplemented by the brief version of the STS Clinician Rating Form, which was completed on all 284 patients at the end of treatment by the independent clinicians in order to identify current status and symptoms.

For all patients who entered treatment and completed at least one post-entry assessment period, we obtained audio- or videotapes of therapy sessions. We rated these treatment samples on a series of scales designed and pretested to represent the dimensions of treatment that seemed most consistent with the treatment-matching hypotheses derived from our literature review. This process information was supplemented by coding the intensity (frequency of sessions per week) of treatment and the modality (pharmacotherapy or psychotherapy).

The collective sample allowed us to explore a series of theoretical models used to predict treatment outcomes in our effort to validate the fifteen principles that were extracted from the literature review.

Basic guidelines are principles of treatment that can be applied by a variety of clinicians, from a variety of interventions models, without special training or monitoring to ensure the accuracy of their application. Accordingly, nine of the fifteen principles summarized in chapter 3 pertain to aspects of basic guidelines as we've defined them here (the original numbers are retained in the following list).

1. Level of functional impairment is negatively correlated with prognosis generally.
2. Impairment level may be an indicator for the application of a long-term and intensive treatment, particularly one that focuses on interpersonal relationships.
3. Impairment level may potentiate the effects of pharmacological treatment.
4. Moderate distress may be be important to sustain commitment and participation in treatment. Moderate distress may be be important to sustain commitment and participation in treatment.
6. High distress may be an indicator for interpersonally focused interventions, perhaps including group or family formats.
7. High levels of experienced social support may both improve outcomes in treatment and decrease the likelihood of relapse.

8. Low levels of social support seem to be an indicator for long-term treatment, and conversely, high experienced social support appears to be a contraindicator for long-term treatment.

10. High problem complexity should favor the effects of a broad-band treatment, both of a psychosocial and a medical type.

11. Pharmacotherapy, but not necessarily psychotherapy, achieves its greatest efficacy among patients with complex and chronic depressive symptoms.

These principles represent the bases for two types of guidelines, those related to predicting patient prognosis and those related to assigning levels of care. Of the six predictive models outlined in chapter 4, two apply to the development of basic guidelines. These models are the *prognostic* model and the *health care* model.

Basic guidelines allow us to determine the normal course of a patient's condition and to identify the likelihood that the patient will improve regardless of the specific nature of treatment. These are prognostic considerations and are quite different than those related to assigning levels of care. These latter predictions select those patients who are in need of specialized medical procedures, such as pharmacological interventions, and those who require unusually intensive treatment.

GUIDELINES FOR PREDICTING PROGNOSIS

The use of prognostic indicators is widely accepted in health care fields. Accordingly, the *prognostic* model is probably the most used of the six models presented in chapter 4, both for treatment planning and in effectiveness research. It uses patient predictors of outcomes and simply assesses the interrelationships among our array of patient predisposing variables and outcomes. Among the fifteen preliminary guidelines reviewed in chapter 3, principles 1, 4, and 7 relate to predicting patient prognosis. These preliminary principles suggest that those with high levels of functional impairment, low distress, and low experienced social support are likely to do poorly in all kinds of treatment and, conversely, that those with moderate or low impairment, moderate to high distress, and high levels of social support will do well with virtually any treatment.

In order to allow a complete test of prognostic variables, in our cross-validational analysis of 284 patients, we entered all of the specific variables assessed in the STS Clinician Rating Scale and explored the degree to which their presence corresponded with patient improvement. The variables explored consisted of the six intake variables that we had defined as potential predictors and their several subcomponents. Because of the modest correlations with standardized tests, for measures of coping style and resistance, we relied on standardized self-report measures. Relevant scores from the MMPI, MCMI, and EPI were translated into standard scores (T scores) for this purpose.

The subcomponents included separate measures of both internalization and externalization, along with sixteen problem areas that frequently bring people into treatment (e.g., depression, suicidal risk, anxiety disorders, thought disorder, marital and relationship problems, eating disturbances, chemical abuse, and sexual disturbances), a list of adjunctive problems that may be associated with the primary problems (e.g., problems with nuclear family, problems with significant others, work difficulties, social difficulties, or legal problems), and separate measures that indicate objective signs of distress, estimated subjective distress, and self-esteem.

We sought to determine what balance of these variables best accounted for outcomes, using Structural Equation Modeling (SEM). This procedure allows the determination of latent structures, defined by the intercorrelations among specific measures, that accounted for and accounted for change directly from these patient intake variables. The results are reported in figure 6.1.

We entered and excluded variables selectively in order to find the combination of variables that best predicted ultimate change. The findings provided partial support for our preliminary guidelines. Three consolidating, latent patient constructs emerged that in turn related to positive treatment outcome. Functional impairment did not emerge as a construct separate from felt social support. However, measures of functional impairment, social support, and aspects of social functioning were intercorrelated and defined a common variable that we refer to as "social impairment" in the figure. This construct indicates the level of family problems, the absence of social support from friends and family, and the experience of being socially isolated among friends and work relationships. This construct performed as would be expected of functional impairment.

Patient social impairment loaded at a modest, negative level with beneficial outcome at the end of treatment ($R = -.35$). This finding indicated that the higher level of social impairment, the worse the patient's prognosis. This variable accounted for approximately 10 percent of the variation in outcome among patients.

The second variable to emerge as a prognostic predictor was, also as predicted, patient level of subjective distress. It, too, comprised three specific measures, rated self-esteem, clinician observed distress, and estimated patient self-report. However, it predicted outcomes in a direction opposite to that suggested in our literature review. Patients with high distress were characterized by low levels of self-esteem, by clinical signs of distress and discomfort, and by clinician estimates that they would report themselves to be distressed and dysphoric. In turn, level of subjective distress was positively related to beneficial outcome ($R = .44$), indicating that approximately 17 percent of the variance in outcomes could be attributed to patients with high levels of distress and discomfort.

Patient complexity/chronicity of problems also emerged as a predictor but did not relate directly to outcome. Instead, this variable was related to the

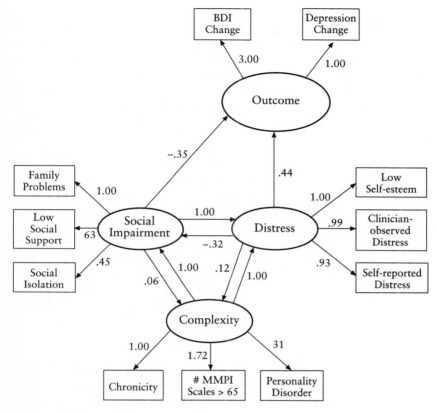

Figure 6.1 Prognosis Model

other two prognostic variables, contributing positive variance indirectly to their predictive power. That is, the effect of complexity/chronicity on outcome was moderated by the other variables in the structural equation. Complex patients required both distress and support to realize treatment benefit, while acute patients were, as could be expected, more resilient and independent of other aspects of environmental context.

These findings suggest that preliminary principles numbers 1, 4, and 7 defined in chapter 3 should be modified (note that we have renumbered the modified principles to keep them in order).

1. The likelihood of improvement (prognosis) is a positive function of social support level and a negative function of functional impairment.
2. Prognosis is facilitated by patient complexity/chronicity and by an absence of patient distress. Facilitating social support enhances likelihood of good outcome among patients with complex/chronic problems.

GUIDELINES FOR ASSIGNING LEVEL OF CARE

Level of assigned care is frequently decided by managed health care on the basis of the severity and the recency of the presenting problem. There are several aspects to this consideration, however. On one hand, level of care implies the assessment of what might be called the context of treatment (Beutler & Clarkin, 1990). Treatment context refers to the intensity, the mode (pharmacological or psychosocial), and the format (multiperson or individual treatment) through which treatment might be offered and is one of the important levels at which health care managers organize and control treatment. Our cross-validation effort was able to explore all of these issues.

At another level, however, the level of care offered is clinically a function of the patient's level of risk for destructive acts. Because risk behaviors, such as suicide and homicide, occur so infrequently but have such tremendous consequences, nomothetic studies are of limited value in the construction of guidelines. Thus, in this presentation, we first consider the cross-validation of principles extracted from our literature review that have to do with treatment intensity, mode, and format. We then, necessarily, depart from our efforts to cross-validate established principles and instead present a research-informed discussion of what is known about treating the patient who is at risk for violence against self or others.

Assigning Treatment Context

In chapter 4, we described the *health care* or *service delivery* model of treatment prediction. This model attempts to assign the patient to varying intensities of treatment as a function of intake characteristics and problem qualities, with the hope that by altering the intensity of treatment, one may be able to reduce costs. As its name implies, this is the general model used by managed health care to reduce costs and to plan treatment. It considers all treatment providers to be equivalent and adjusts the level of care by altering the relative length of treatment, assigning various balances between medication and psychosocial intervention, and treating the patient in individual or multiperson settings (i.e., group or family interventions).

The preliminary principles extracted from our literature review outlined these relationships as follows (original numbering of principles is preserved):

2. Impairment level may be an indicator for the application of a long-term and intensive treatment, particularly one that focuses on interpersonal relationships.
3. Impairment level may potentiate the effects of pharmacological treatment.
6. High distress may be an indicator for interpersonally focused interventions, perhaps including group or family formats.
8. Low levels of social support seem to be an indicator for long-term treat-

ment, and conversely, high experienced social support appears to be a contra-indicator for long-term treatment.

10. High problem complexity should favor the effects of a broad-band treatment, of both a psychosocial and a medical type.
11. Pharmacotherapy, but not necessarily psychotherapy, achieves its greatest efficacy among patients with complex and chronic depressive symptoms.

Our cross-validation sample included a number of different treatments that varied the intensity, format, and modality. For example, manualized forms of cogntive therapy (CT) were applied in groups (weekly ninety-minute sessions), to family couples (weekly ninety-minute sessions), and in individual formats (weekly and biweekly fifty-minute sessions). In addition, there were samples of group experiential therapy (weekly ninety-minute sessions), individual self-directed therapy (weekly twenty-minute sessions), desiprimine plus clinical management (weekly twenty-minute sessions), psychodynamic individual therapy (weekly fifty-minute sessions), family systems therapy for couples (weekly ninety-minute sessions), and a treatment-as-usual condition (weekly fifty-minute sessions). All but the latter treatment were conducted after extensive therapist pretraining to performance criteria and used manual based supervision. Although the specific theoretical model was of little importance to us in this analysis of basic guidelines, the variations of intensity, modality, and format were important to our analyses.

In the application of the health care model in conventional practice, decisions are made about what aspects of intensity, format, and mode of treatment should be offered a patient on the basis of such qualities as patient level of functional impairment and nature of the presenting problem. Thus, to cross-validate the preliminary principles pertaining to level of care, we did not enter into the equation the patient variables alone as had been done in our test of the prognostic model. Instead, we entered scores to indicate matches between aspects of patient predisposing qualities, extracted from the STS Clinician Rating Form, and corresponding aspects of the treatment context (intensity, psychosocial or pharmacological modality, and format [group, couple, or individual therapy]). These matching dimensions were based on the preliminary principles presented in chapter 3. More specifically, we constructed difference scores, the high end of which indicated an expected positive match between (1) high functional impairment and the use of antidepressants, (2) level of social support and treatment intensity (inverse relationship of social support and planned minutes of assigned therapy), (3) level of problem complexity/chronicity and use of psychosocial or pharmacological interventions, and (4) level of social support and the use of multiperson or individual therapy.

We analyzed the data in the same way that we did to test the prognostic model. The results are reported in figure 6.2.

The results indicated that when we systematically extracted and entered

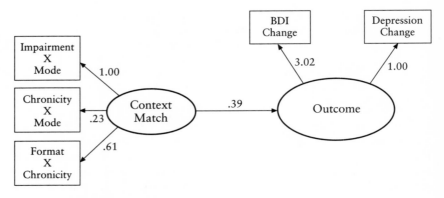

Figure 6.2 Managed Health Care Model

variables to find the combination that made the best prediction, a combination of three matching dimensions emerged as most closely related to the prediction of treatment outcome. These three variables were (1) the level of fit between impairment level and the use of pharmacological interventions, (2) the match between high complexity/chronicity and the use of pharmacotherapy, and (3) the fit between complexity/chronicity and the use of a multiperson therapy (group or couple work).

These variables were intercorrelated with one another and contributed to a general factor of "contextual match." This combined variable was related to positive outcome and accounted for approximately 15 percent of the variance in this dimension.

It should be noted that variability of treatment in the various dimensions represented in our combined samples was limited. Only a single antidepressant (desiprimine) was studied as representative of antidepressants, the pharmacological interventions were applied to only twenty of the 284 patients, most therapies took place in sixty- to ninety-minutes-per-week sessions, and the dimensions of treatment context (intensity, modality, format) were confounded with the site of the study. While significant findings were obtained, we feared that there was simply not enough variation within our data set in type of setting, treatment modality, and intensity to fully understand the implications of the findings. In order to reduce extraneous patient variability associated with the location of the research program, we undertook several analyses of individual samples.

Using sample 4, a group of depressed older adults, we tested the hypotheses that the chronicity and severity of depression would serve as a differential indicator for the use of antidepressant medication versus psychotherapy, using the older adult sample from Palo Alto Veterans Administration Medical Centers (Sandowicz, 1998). Likewise, using sample 3, we sought to test the hypothesis that varying the intensity of treatment would be indicated among patients with high problem severity and chronicity.

In this sample, the sixty patients were administered the BDI before and at the end of a twenty-week course of treatment in which patients were randomly assigned to either psychodynamic therapy, individual cognitive therapy, or antidepressant medication (desiprimine).

In a second test, using sample 3, a group of depressed adults, Albanese (1998) evaluated changes in BDI scores among younger depressed adults who were receiving a varying dose of treatment. Treatment included either professionally run group therapy following one of two treatment models (ninety minutes per week of cognitive therapy and focused expressive psychotherapy [FEP]) or a less intense treatment of twenty-minutes per week conducted by advanced graduate students in clinical psychology. Patients in the latter treatment group were treated via telephone interviews that emphasized support and the supplementation of a self-directed readings program. The results were consistent with the overall structural equation.

We obtained two significant findings: (1) Initial level of patient impairment and problem severity was positively related to benefit if the intensity of treatment was high (longer sessions conducted by a professional), but they were not related to benefit if the treatment was less intense; (2) level of impairment was also a predictor of the effectiveness of desipramine but not of psychotherapy, and the two types of treatment had equivalent effects, overall.

Collectively, these results suggest that level of care can be an effective decision as used by managed health care. While the results do not support the widespread substitution and assumed equivalence of medication and psychotherapy, they do suggest that if medication is to be offered for treating depression, it is best reserved for individuals who have relatively intense and severe problems. Moderate problem levels serve as a contraindicator for the use of antidepressant medication, and in both cases psychotherapy may be an effective intervention.

In addition, high levels of problem impairment suggest the value of intensifying treatment by increasing the frequency or length of sessions. Less severe problems require fewer treatment resources and conceivably can be conducted by clinicians with lesser training and expertise. However, the question of training and expertise is not addressed effectively at this level of analysis. Our consideration of optimal guidelines gives greater consideration to the instance in which specialized skills, procedures, and monitoring are required for effective intervention.

Collectively, we conclude that the preliminary principles pertaining to the use of pharmacotherapy, intensive treatment, and multiperson therapy should be modified as follows:

3. Psychoactive medication exerts its best effects among those patients with high functional impairment and high complexity/chronicity.
4. Likelihood and magnitude of improvement are increased among patients with complexity/chronic problems by the application of multiperson therapy.

5. Benefit corresponds to treatment intensity among functionally impaired patients.

Level of Risk

Suicidal behavior is the most frequently encountered of all mental health emergencies (Schein, 1976), and psychotherapists identify suicidal statements as the most stressful of all client communications (Deutsch, 1984). This is a reflection of the fact that the relationship among psychopathology, suicide attempting, and completed suicide is complex, dynamic, and not yet well understood (Maris, 1981; Peterson & Bongar, 1989; Shneidman, 1989). Recent studies show changes in the identity of high-risk groups (Boyd, 1983; Evans & Farberow, 1988; Maris, 1981, 1989; Roy, 1986; Shneidman, 1989; Weissman, Klerman, Markowitz, & Ouelette, 1989), and follow-up studies demonstrate that risk factors among attempters may be significantly different from those for the general population (Frederick, 1978; Maris, 1981, 1989). Also, studies suggest that the rate of suicide among the mentally ill (Hirschfeld & Davidson, 1988; Maris, 1981; Pokorny, 1964, 1983; Roy, 1986; Simon, 1988) and the physically ill (Abram, Moore, & Westervelt, 1971; Hirschfeld & Davidson, 1988; Maris, 1981; Roy, 1986) far exceeds that of the population as a whole. However, the estimates of the rate of death by suicide due to psychiatric disorders can vary greatly depending on factors such as country of origin (Roy, 1986), regional differences within a single country (Peterson, Bongar, & Netsoki, 1989), and the diagnostic criteria used for the sample; for example, the number of manic depressives who die by suicide ranges from 15 percent to 55 percent (Goldring & Fieve, 1984).

A crucial premise in understanding risk management and the suicidal patient is that clinicians have a duty to take steps to prevent suicide if they can reasonably anticipate the danger. "Therefore, the key issues in determining liability are whether the psychotherapist should have predicted that the patient was likely to attempt suicidal behavior, and (assuming there was an identifiable risk) whether the therapist did enough to protect the patient" (Stromberg et al., 1988, p. 467). In this regard, Pope (1986) stressed the importance of staying within one's area of competence and of knowing one's personal limits, observing "that working with suicidal patients can be demanding, draining, crisis-filled activity. It is literally life or death work" (p. 19). In addition to obtaining adequate training in and knowledge of the literature on suicide, mental health professionals must become familiar with the legal standards involving rights to treatment and to refuse treatment, as well as the rules regarding confidentiality, involuntary hospitalization, and so forth. Pope noted that a standard of care must involve a screening for suicide risk during the initial contact and ongoing alertness to this issue throughout the course of treatment. There also should be frequent consultation and ready access to facilities needed to implement appropriate affirmative precautions (e.g., emergency teams, hospitals, crisis intervention centers, day treatment).

Bongar (1991) noted that the general legal standard for patient care clearly includes a thorough understanding of the complexities of procedures for assessing elevated risk and specific clinical management techniques for the suicidal patient. Mental health professionals have been held liable when they have not taken adequate precautions to manage patients. The courts will not necessarily defer to a clinician's decisional process when they find that "due to a totally unreasonable professional judgment, he or she underestimated the need for special care, or failed to take the usual precautions" (Stromberg et al., 1988, p. 468).

The mental health professional's assessment and treatment efforts represent an opportunity to translate knowledge (albeit incomplete) of elevated risk factors into a plan of action (Bongar, 1991). The management plan for patients who are at an elevated risk for suicide should ameliorate those risk factors that are most likely to result in suicide or self-harm (Brent, Kupfer, Bromet, & Dew, 1988). Although there is a loose fit between diagnosis and suicide, Simon (1988) noted that suicide rarely occurs in the absence of psychiatric illness; the data on adult suicides indicate that more than 90 percent of these suicide victims were mentally ill before their deaths. With both Harold and Alice, the considerations discussed here need to be evaluated (in particular the differentiation between acute versus chronic risk).

With regard to Alice's chronicity of suicidal processes, Litman (1988), Simon (1987, 1988), and Gutheil (1990) noted the special precautions that clinicians must take when assessing and treating patients who present with chronic suicidal ideation and behavior (e.g., where the clinician takes repeated calculated risks in not hospitalizing). Gutheil (1990) noted that here the mental health clinician will feel the tension between short-term solutions (e.g., a protected environment) and long-term solutions (e.g., actual treatment of the chronicity).

For both Harold and Alice, other general principles include family involvement for support and improved compliance; diagnosis and treatment of any comorbid medical and psychiatric condition; the provision of hope, particularly to new-onset patients; the restriction of the availability of lethal agents; and indications for psychiatric hospitalization (Brent et al., 1988). To this list, a risk management perspective would add the critical necessity of assessing personal and professional competencies in order to treat at-risk patients, as well as meticulous documentation and the routine involvement of "a second opinion" through consultation (Bongar, 1991; Bongar, Peterson, Harris, & Aissis, 1989). Simon (1988) noted that suicide results from the complex interplay of a number of diagnostic (psychiatric and medical), constitutional, environmental, occupational, sociocultural, existential, and chance casual elements. It is not simply the result of misdiagnosis or inadequate treatment.

Here, there are several general principles that should guide the treatment of patients at elevated risk for suicide and that apply across broad diagnostic categories:

6. Risk is reduced by a careful assessment of risk situations in the course of establishing a diagnosis and history.

Because most suicide victims take their own lives or harm themselves in the midst of a psychiatric episode (Barraclough et al., 1974; Dorpat & Ripley, 1960; Hirschfeld & Russell, 1997; Murphy, 1988; Robins et al., 1959; Shaffer, 1974; Shaffer et al., 1985; Shaffi, 1986), it is critical to understand that a proper diagnosis and careful management/treatment plan of the acute psychiatric disorder could dramatically alter the risk for suicide (Brent et al., 1988). The data on adult suicides indicate that more than 90 percent of these suicide victims were mentally ill before their deaths.

For acute management, Litman (1988), Simon (1987, 1988), and Gutheil (1990) noted the special precautions that clinicians must take when assessing and treating patients who present with chronic suicidal ideation and behavior (e.g., where the clinician takes repeated calculated risks in not hospitalizing). Gutheil (1990) noted that here the mental health clinician will feel the tension between short-term solutions (e.g., a protected environment) and long-term solutions (e.g., actual treatment of the chronicity).

Another very basic guideline is:

7. Risk is reduced and patient compliance is increased when the treatment includes family intervention.

Not only does family involvement improve compliance and attendance, but it contributes to outcome and long-term maintenance.

Further, as we have emphasized on numerous occassions, diagnosis and treatment of any comorbid medical and psychiatric condition may have little relevance to treatment outcome when applied to psychotherapy, but it is important for recordkeeping, for the application of medical treatment, and for correspondence with other professionals. The diagnosis and treatment of comorbid conditions is of great importance from an immediate treatment standpoint. It alerts the clinician to the presence of comorbid factors and also emphasizes the need to obtain and follow-up with consultation.

One must also remember that, regardless of the treatment, instilling hope is a central and first-line task. This implies keeping patients informed and aware of their own progress. This is particularly important to new patients, especially if they have never before received or sought treatment. But, it cannot be ignored for more established patients, either. The therapist should remind patients periodically of their strengths and assets, the potential for hope and happiness in their futures, and the pleasant things in their current living environments. For facilitating hope, we suggest the following guidelines, which are consistent with general principles of relationship development in psychotherapy:

8. Risk and retention are optimized if the patient is realistically informed about the probable length and effectiveness of the treatment and has a clear understanding of the roles and activities that are expected of him or her during the course of treatment.

An equally important guideline arises when there is a need to restrict the availability of lethal agents and to plan for psychiatric hospitalization (Brent et al., 1988). Suicidal and homicidal patients are very difficult, and these issues must be approached with care to avoid offending. But, approaching these topics is a must. Thus:

9. Risk is reduced if the clinician routinely questions patients about suicidal feelings, intent, and plans.

Any indication of suicidal plans, especially if there is also a history of previous attempts, should invoke an exploration of care options. The question of hospitalization must be broached, and the clinician must be prepared to arrange emergency, involuntary care if the need is present.

To this list, a risk management perspective would add the critical necessity of assessing personal and professional competencies in order to treat at-risk patients. Assessing one's self is extremely difficult. Thus, it helps to seek consultation, even including allowing a respected colleague to view audio- or videotapes. Continuing education and other training opportunities should always be standard, even in states that do not require it for license. These training activities are best if they include both hands-on practice, at least via role playing, and theoretical rationales.

Still another guideline is inserted because of its practicality, beyond the issue of patient risk:

10. Ethical and legal principles suggest that documentation and consultation are advisable.

Meticulous documentation and the routine involvement of "a second opinion" through consultation must always be a consideration (Bongar, 1991; Bongar, Marris, Berman, & Litman, 1992; Bongar et al., 1989). Such consultation is often most important early in treatment, but it becomes equally valuable during difficult periods. It is helpful to obtain consultation, however, even when there is no particular problem or dilemma, as a prophylactic against future problems.

SUMMARY

In summary, the following constitute what we consider to be basic guidelines for planning treatment:

1. The likelihood of improvement (prognosis) is a positive function of social support level and a negative function of functional impairment.
2. Prognosis is attenuated by patient complexity/chronicity, and by an absence of patient distress. Faciliating social support enhances the likelihood of good outcome among patients with complex/chronic problems.
3. Psychoactive medication exerts its best effects among those patients with high functional impairment and high complexity/chronicity.

4. Likelihood and magnitude of improvement are increased among patients with complexity/chronic problems by the application of multi-person therapy.
5. Benefit corresponds to treatment intensity among functionally impaired patients.
6. Risk is reduced by a careful assessment of risk situations in the course of establishing a diagnosis and history.
7. Risk is reduced and patient compliance is increased when the treatment includes family intervention.
8. Risk and retention are optimized if the patient is realistically informed about the probable length and effectiveness of the treatment and has a clear understanding of the roles and activities that are expected of him or her during the course of treatment.
9. Risk is reduced if the clinician routinely questions patients about suicidal feelings, intent, and plans.
10. Ethical and legal principles suggest that documentation and consultation are advisable.
   It should be noted that we do not pretend that these guidelines are arranged in order of importance. Indeed, if we were to prioritize and rank them, a strong case could be made for putting those that relate to the development of a therapeutic relationship and to the reduction of risk at the top of the list.

Going further, the other guidelines cannot be applied without a thorough evaluation of the patient. It goes without saying that all of the assessment and management activities should include a specific evaluation of the patient's capacity, willingness, and competency to participate in management and treatment decisions. These capacities are intimately involved in the ability to and the likelihood of forming a productive therapeutic alliance (Bongar, 1991; Gutheil, 1984, 1990; Kahn, 1990; Luborsky, 1990). Bongar (1991) noted that an essential element in strengthening this alliance is the use of informed consent; patients have the right to participate actively in making decisions about their psychological or psychiatric care. Clinicians need to directly and continuously evaluate the quality of this special relationship, to understand that the quality of this collaborative alliance is inextricably part of any successful treatment/management plan (Bongar, 1991; Bongar et al., 1989; Gutheil, 1984, 1988, 1990; Kahn, 1990; Luborsky, 1990; Shneidman, 1981, 1984; Simon, 1987, 1988).

Beyond the general importance of forming a good working relationship, assessing risk, and providing a thorough evaluation of patient abilities and problems, the guidelines emphasize the importance of certain qualities that relate to treatment planning. Thus, the therapist must immediately make the treatment fit the patient's level of impairment—more impaired patients need more immediate, more frequent, more varied, and longer treatment than less impaired patients. As a rule of thumb, a score of less than 60 on the GAF (DSM-IV) is an index of the need for more than once-per-week treatment. This is especially true when suicidal and homicidal impulses are present. A score of 50 provides a general index for the consideration of a restricted and highly intensive treatment regime. Of course, these intensified treatments may go on for a long or a short time. The decision depends on the continuing level of impairment of the patient. The ultimate objective is for the support provided by the treatment to be subsumed by others in the patient's environment, so the inclusion of family members may also be imperative.

These principles also emphasize the need to seek symptom relief as quickly as possible. That means that as the therapist is developing the relationship, regardless of his or her orientation, he or she should also begin to evaluate problematic symptoms and suggest methods for direct change. This is a general rule and may require that the therapist set aside briefly some favored theoretical positions in favor of empirically established principles. There will be plenty of time to explore dynamic conflicts once the patient is relieved of distressing symptoms and is no longer dangerous.

The flexibility of these principles can be illustrated by considering the variety of ways in which treatment intensity might be increased. Changing the setting to be more or less restrictive, increasing the frequency of sessions, increasing the length of sessions, altering the intensity by using group or individually focused treatments, and supplementing therapy with homework assignments, collateral contact, or supplementary phone call contacts are examples of the latitude available to the therapist.

With these guidelines in hand, committed to memory, incorporated into practice, and automatic to practice, the clinician is well prepared to develop an effective treatment. At this point the therapist is ready to move on to a consideration of optimal guidelines.

7 Guidelines for Optimal and Enhanced Treatment

COMBINATIONS OF MATCHING DIMENSIONS: CONFIRMATORY RESEARCH FINDINGS

Optimal and enhanced treatment attends to parameters that distinguish individual patients beyond the nature of the depression itself. They differ from the basic guidelines described in chapter 6 in that they require some special expertise on the part of the clinician and frequently entail monitoring of actual in-therapy activity in order to ensure that the moment-to-moment interventions are compatible with the needs and reactions of the patient. Unlike basic guidelines that recommend the application of general aspects of treatment and levels of care to patients on the basis of diagnostic conditions, severity, and demographic backgrounds, optimal guidelines help the clinician tailor treatments to the specific strengths and weaknesses of individual patients. Thus, the distinction between basic treatment and enhanced treatment is the degree of individualization of the treatment.

As we have observed from time to time, research has largely studied individual patient-therapy matching dimensions. A smaller body of research has studied two or more matching dimensions in a given study, but because of the limitations of sample sizes, these dimensions are usually studied independently of one another. That is, patients are matched to a given treatment as if each potential patient-therapy matching dimension were independent of the other matching dimensions. While that research has been promising, it does not address the very real likelihood that the several dimensions that have been identified are interrelated. To be useful, research must use large enough samples that it can assess how various of the dimensions that have been identified in literature reviews overlap, enhance, or even suppress one another's effects.

Oliver Williams, Ph.D., provided the data analysis on which this chapter was based and served as a coauthor for this chapter.

The STS Clinician Rating Form is a relatively brief, clinician-based assessment of the treatment-relevant dimensions to which our literature review led us. This instrument was described in chapter 5 and, along with standard ratings of process and outcome, formed the basis for the cross-validation of preliminary principles that underwrites our final rendition of basic and optimal guidelines for systematic treatment selection. In chapter 6, we reviewed our cross-validational findings as they apply to those principles that can be acted on without in-session monitoring or specialized training in treatment models and procedures. In the following pages, we summarize the results of our effort to cross-validate those preliminary principles that relate to the selection of specific treatment models and philosophies or of particular classes and families of techniques. These are the guidelines that seek to apply optimal matches of treatments to patients. As in chapter 6, we rely here on analyses of the combined data set that comprises four separate samples. Here, the focus is on optimal guidelines, those that may require special clinician training and monitoring of in-session treatment.

The pooled data set used for validating the dimensions uncovered in our reviews of differential treatment assignment comprised the same 284 individuals who formed the analysis of basic guidelines. These participants were extracted from the larger pool of 289 patients who served in the development of the STS Clinician Rating Form. These patients were assessed with a common procedure that included an intake evaluation by a trained cadre of experienced clinicians, independent ratings of treatment processes, and formal measures of treatment outcome.

Contextual and relationship aspects of treatment were rated from video- and audiotapes, one each from a randomly selected first and last third of the therapy sessions. Ratings were made by independently trained graduate student trainees using the STS Therapy Rating Scale.

The following treatment dimensions were extracted by rating two treatment samples from all available cases: (1) treatment intensity, (2) frequency of use of procedures designed to increase patient arousal and affect, (3) choice of pharmacotherapy or psychotherapeutic as the treatment mode, (4) choice of individual or multiperson treatment format, (5) amount of focus on symptomatic versus insight-oriented goals, (6) level of therapist directiveness, and (7) quality of the therapeutic alliance (nonspecific therapist effects) and skill. To assess this last dimension, we included among the ratings done by external observers both a rating of the therapist's skill in using therapeutic procedures and the Penn Psychotherapy Alliance Scale.

To capture the complexity of treatment planning, Beutler and Clarkin (1990) proposed that treatment effects could best be understood not as linear relationships among patient, clinician, and treatment models but as cascading effects of four domains of treatment planning. The systematic treatment selection model specified four sequential levels of treatment planning, each with several domains: (1) predisposing variables, (2) context variables, (3) therapist activity and relationship variables, and (4) treatment-matching variables. The basic and distinguishing tenet of what has become the systematic treatment planning (STS) model has been the presence of complex reciprocal interchanges, rather than linear relationships, among these levels as the basis for treatment mix, or matching. Table 7.1 provides a review of the model, similar to the one presented in chapter 4.

The process of treatment planning begins with an assessment of key patient qualities (level 1) that have been related to outcome in the research literature. These qualities are what we have referred as patient predisposing variables—the selection of what to evaluate and its relationship to subsequent levels. The subsequent levels include: (2) context variables (aspects of setting, intensity, modality [e.g., pharmacological, psychological, both], and format [e.g., group, individual, family, couple, drug class]), (3) therapist activity and relationship qualities (e.g., skill, alliance, relationship stance), and (4) matching patient to aspects of treatment (e.g., theoretical goals, strategies for change, specific techniques).

In chapter 6, we described our analysis of two of the models of treatment prediction, one that we called the "prognostic model" and one we called the "health care model" or "service delivery model" of treatment selection and delivery. For the development of optimal guidelines, as described in this chapter, in contrast to the previous chapter, our focus is much more on the activities of treatment. Accordingly, we assess the predictive efficiency of three models from

Table 7.1 Systematic Treatment Selection: A Model of Treatment Planning

Patient Predisposing Qualities
    Problem—symptoms, intensity/severity, complexity/chronicity
    Personality—Coping style, trait defensiveness, subjective distress, readiness/motivation for change, self-esteem
    Environment—functional impairment, social support, breadth of positive functioning

Context of Treatment
    Setting—restrictiveness of care
    Intensity—frequency, spacing
    Mode—pharmacological, psychosocial, or both
    Format—drug class, group/individual/family therapy

Therapist Activity and Relationship
    Personal Fit—therapist-patient matching
    Therapeutic Actions—directiveness, insight vs. symptom focus,
    Cathartic vs affect reduction, skill of therapist
    Alliance/relationship factors

Match of Levels 1 and 3
    Impairment with treatment intensity
    Subjective distress with abreactive vs. affect reduction
    Social support with multi-person vs. individual treatment
    Problem complexity with restrictiveness of setting or multiplicity of treatment modalities
    Resistance traits with directiveness
    Coping style with symptom change vs. insight goals

Table 7.2 Opimal Planning Models Compared

Model	Relationship
Common Factors Model	Between therapist (actions, skill, alliance) and outcomes
Psychotherapy Procedures Model	Between activity/relationship variables and outcomes
Technical-Eclectic Therapy Matching Model	Between matching variables and outcomes, drawn from Beutler (1983)
Systematic Treatment Selection (STS) Model	Joint and interactive, among all levels (excluding context for lack of variability) and outcomes

the psychotherapy research and compare them to that of the more elaborate systematic treatment selection model (Beutler & Clarkin, 1990) (see table 7.2).

1. The *common factors* model explores common relationships among therapist activity, qualities of the relationship, and outcomes. This is a frequently used model for predicting treatment outcomes in psychotherapy and relies on a determination of certain qualities of the treatment relationship that are held in common across treatments.

2. The *psychotherapy procedures* model is the antithesis of the common factors model and is usually expressed as an effort to find some methods, models, or types of interventions that are better than others. As applied to psychotherapy, this model considers therapist activities as trait-like in that a therapist is identified with a point of view that is assumed to be applied to all patients in a similar fashion. Thus, this model identifies cognitive therapists, experiential therapists, dynamic therapists, all evaluated, by means of a manual, to ensure that they are applying the same treatment. The result is a horse-race comparison of psychotherapies in which the identity of the psychotherapist is embedded in the nature of the therapy under study. These horse-race comparisons have been notoriously unsuccessful at finding a superior type of therapy, however. Thus, in the current context, rather than repeating the many efforts to make head-to-head comparisons among whole models or manuals, we have revised the question of patient-to-therapist matching somewhat by reducing the therapy models to classes or families of procedures. This specificity, we believe, provides a better opportunity to address the question of whether some activities are more effective than others, across patient types. This reduces the question of psychotherapy models to a question of psychotherapy procedures, a more manageable question.

3. The *technical-eclectic therapy matching* model extends the foregoing model to the question of fitting the procedure to the patient. There are actually several specific models of this type, all emphasizing the fit between certain types of psychotherapeutic procedures and patient characteristics. All of the available models in the systematic-eclectic movement could not be addressed, so we have selected one with which the current dimensions under investigation were most compatible. The technical-eclectic model studied here is the one originally developed and

defined by Beutler (1983). The test of this model cannot be generalized to other technical eclectic approaches, such as multi-modal therapy (Lazarus, 1976), but it does provide an initial comparison of an earlier rendition of the more comprehensive STS model formulated by Beutler and Clarkin (1990).

4. The *systematic treatment selection* model includes an assessment of the cascading effects of factors at each of the four levels, including predisposing variables, treatment context, therapist activities and relationship qualities, and matching of procedures to patient variables.

As we saw in chapter 6, patient factors and level of care provide some general prediction of likelihood and magnitude of treatment response. Basic guidelines for managing treatment decisions suggest that a constellation of patient and problem features, including patient distress, problem complexity, and level of social impairment, provide guidance for selecting patients who will benefit from treatment. At the same time, level of social impairment and problem severity offer some suggestions regarding the use of antidepressant medication and for intensifying treatment through procedures that increase the time and involvement of the patient in treatment. In contrast to these basic guidelines, optimal guidelines address more specific aspects of treatment, those requiring direct monitoring and observation of treatment and specialized training on the part of the treating clinician. With respect to these optimal guidelines, the STS model anticipates that the effects of patient, context, and relationship variables will exert interdependent and augmenting influences on outcomes.

In chapter 3 we outlined six preliminary principles that bear on the development or definition of optimal guidelines:

5. High initial distress may be an indicator for the use of supportive and self-directed therapy but bears no relationship to the effectiveness of active and therapist-guided interventions.

9. A certain level of experienced or felt support may be necessary to activate the power of interpersonal and relationship therapies.

12. Minimally structured, self-directed interventions, nondirective procedures, or paradoxical directives are effective among patients who are highly prone to interpersonal resistance.

13. Directive treatment interventions and clinician guidance are advantageous to patients who have low resistance tendencies.

14. Extroverted/externalizing/impulsive coping styles indicate the use of interventions designed to directly affect symptoms.

15. Introverted/internalizing/restricted coping styles indicate the use of interventions designed to directly affect insight and awareness.

The various dimensions that are identified in these preliminary principles are reflected, in various ways, in the psychotherapy procedures model, the technical eclectic model, and the systematic treatment selection model. Because of its wide implications and use, we also incorporate tests of the common factors model.

RESULTS

The four models were each tested separately, using structural equation modeling. In applying structural equation methods, we attempted once again to refine the constructs to obtain the highest level of fit. Thus, we withdrew components that were not contributory in order to reduce multicolinearity among the variables within each of the four Beutler and Clarkin domains, consolidating these into the most internally consistent constructs to obtain a final, best-fit model for each test. Space does not permit a complete description of what specific variables were dropped or combined, but suffice it to say that it was noted that when some variables were present in each class, they sometimes suppressed the effects of others and sometimes proved to be redundant concepts. Thus, the specific sets of variables within each domain of the model being tested were ultimately modified, but the framework of each model was kept in tact.

Common Factors Model

The test of the *common factors* model focused on aspects of the relationship. It included ratings of therapist skill, nonverbal ratings of therapist anxiety or arousal level (verbal activity, physical movement), and two scores from the Penn Therapeutic Alliance Inventory. The analysis searched for common aspects of the patient-therapist relationship that contributed to predicting treatment outcome. The three main variables, therapist skill, therapist verbal activity, and total therapeutic alliance score, collectively contributed to a common factor that in turn contributed significantly to treatment outcome.

The results of the analysis of this model are presented in figure 7.1. They indicate that a therapist who is effective not only establishes a collaborative and accepting relationship but remains relatively active and is skillful in presenting therapeutic interventions. This pattern reiterates the importance of some of the principles reported in chapter 6, including the need to provide some structure and direct support to the patient within the context of a collaborative relationship. It also emphasizes the importance of providing a warm, accepting and supportive environment. Such findings are consistent with previous reviews (e.g., Beutler, Machado, & Neufeldt, 1994) and emerging, comparative research (e.g., Stiles, Agnew-Davies, Hardy, Barkham, & Shapiro, 1998).

Psychotherapy Procedures Model

The second optimizing model tested, the *psychotherapy procedures* model, was more complex than the first, therapist-oriented model. It inspected aspects of therapist technique selection, drawn from the STS Therapy Rating Scale, and explored therapist activity level, symptom versus insight focus, use of support versus confrontation, and level of directiveness. This analysis also

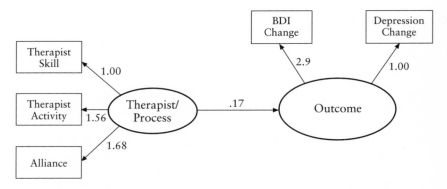

Figure 7.1 Common Factors Model

included the measures of therapist arousal (verbal activity, physical activity) that were incorporated into the test of the common factors model since, it was reasoned, some of these may be related to aspects of the therapists' operational treatment theory. The analysis looked at patterns of therapy activity and treatment outcome. The results are reported in figure 7.2.

None of the therapist activities emerged as meaningful contributors to outcome in their own right. Apparently, to the degree that therapist procedures assert characteristic responses, they are best attributed to their interactions with other variables. That is, our analyses are consistent with the general conclusion that the therapist procedures used are relatively weak, a confirmation of the Do-Do bird verdict at the level of specific intervention classes. Thus, if procedures produce effects, they are absorbed by or confounded with other variables. In fact, this conclusion is consistent with the propositions of STS theory that proposes that interventions must be considered in terms of the cascading and accumulating effects of patient, context, and relationship factors. But, this possibility is not revealed in a direct test of procedures. A more complex analysis is needed to capture these possibilities. Thus, we turn to the consideration of the last two proposed models tested in our analysis.

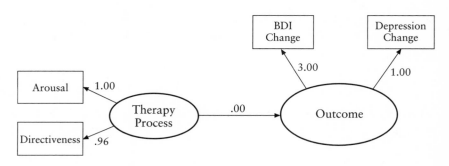

Figure 7.2 Psychotherapy Procedures Model

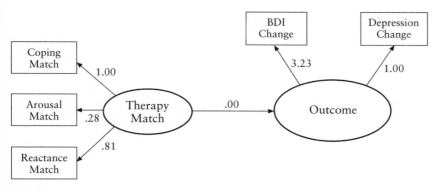

Figure 7.3 Technical-Eclectic Therapy Matching Model

Technical-Eclectic Therapy Matching Model

The third optimal model tested was a simple *technical-eclectic therapy matching* model. This is the early, linear conceptual model of Beutler (1983) in which patient and psychotherapy dimensions are considered. The results are shown in figure 7.3.

As noted in figure 7.3, patient-intervention matching dimensions did not exert direct effects on outcomes. As we tested this model, it became clear that only when patient variables were added independently did a significant fit occur. In this event, the patient variables coalesced around a dimension of subjective distress ($R = .37$), which was the minimal addition that could be added to sustain a data fit. The results of matching patients to treatment insight versus symptomatic focus, abreactive versus supportive interventions, and directive versus nondirective interventions were incidental.

Systematic Treatment Selection (STS) Model

The fourth optimal model tested was the *systematic treatment selection* (STS) model as outlined by Beutler and Clarkin (1990). This was a comprehensive and complex model that included patient predisposing variables, as in the prognostic model; contextual factors, as in the health care model; relationship qualities, as in the common factors model; therapy activities, as in the psychotherapy procedures model; and therapy-patient matching dimensions, as in the technical-eclectic model. The difference between this and the foregoing models is that the STS model allowed for the emergence of complex interactions among the domains of variables. Thus, as noted, the power of matching dimensions became activated only within the presence of therapist actions, notably direct focus on symptoms and facilitation of patient arousal.

The STS model was the most complex of those tested, and its results included the contributing variables from the other models. Indeed, the complexity of this model consumed a large number of the available degrees of free-

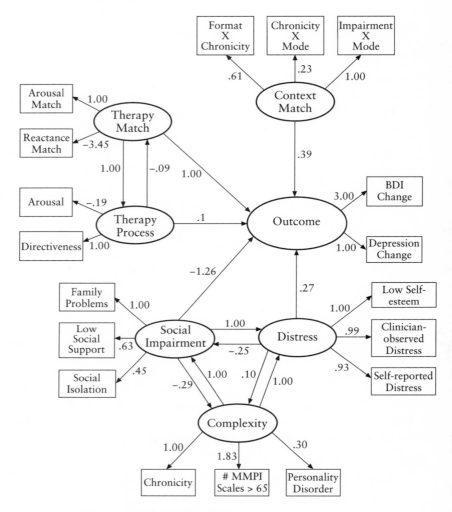

Figure 7.4 Total Systematic Treatment Selection Model

dom. In order to compensate for this problem, we were forced to set tolerance limits on the parameters; if they did not operate within a certain specter,
they were dropped. The best fit was obtained as a complex of functions, as
demonstrated in figure 7.4.

The model presented is clearly consistent with the fundamental premises
of systematic treatment selection. Outcomes of treatment were found to be
a complex function of variables from each domain. As in the test of the
technical-eclectic model, the fit between patient variables and therapy techniques emerged as a single construct. Two dyadic matching variables con-

tributed to the construct of therapy match: (1) the fit between the level of patient distress and the use of abreactive versus supportive techniques, and (2) the fit between the level of patient resistance and the level of therapist directiveness. The variable that defined the fit between patient coping style and the insight versus symptomatic focus of intervention proved to be essentially interchangable with the level of fit between patient resistance and therapist directiveness. One or the other of these matching dimensions allowed a good fit with the data, but adding both did not improve the fit significantly. Including the fit between patient resistance and therapist directiveness yielded a slightly better fit with the data than the variable that described the fit between insight versus symptomatic focus and patient coping style.

The added power of the STS model can be attributed to some interesting relationships that emerged between therapy process factors, extracted from the psychotherapy procedures model, and the dimensions of the technical-eclectic model just described. These relationships were explored in greater depth by testing a model that included only the components of the therapy process/activity dimensions from the psychotherapy procedures model, the therapist and relationship factors from the common factors model, and the matching dimensions from the technical-eclectic model. The results are shown in figure 7.5.

In figure 7.5, one sees some striking differences in the effect of therapy-matching variables on treatment oucome as a function of including the therapist activity and therapist process factors. The insertion of therapy process factors related to therapist skill and verbal activity (note that therapist alliance dropped out as a contributor in this analysis altogether) drained predictive power from therapy-matching variables while increasing the influence of therapist activities/processes (abreactive and directive interventions)

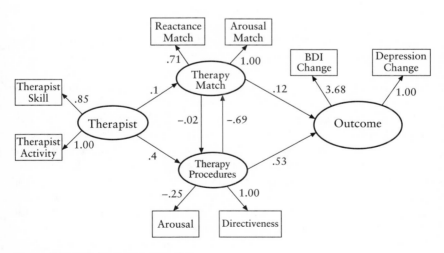

Figure 7.5 STS Component Analysis

and outcomes. While they failed to yield positive relationships with outcomes when studied in isolation, the procedures of psychotherapy, taken within the context of other process and matching factors, were now found to be significantly related to treatment outcomes. Abreactive interventions and directive interventions were both relatively powerful contributors to treatment benefit.

It is notable that when these components were tested in this model, some differences were observed among the interrelationships of contributors to treatment outcome when compared to the more complex STS model tested. For example, while the more complex test had suggested that the therapy-matching dimensions (from the technical-eclectic matching model) had exerted a strong effect on the process/activity utilized by the therapist, this simpler (and more powerful) test suggested that the reverse effect may be more powerful. That is, the activities of the therapist have a stronger effect on the matching dimensions than the matching dimensions have on therapist activity/process. This makes better sense, logically, especially in view of the negative sign attached to the relationship between these clusters of variables. The negative relationship between the use of theory-guided procedures and the power of the matching variables suggests that excessive reliance on procedures, without attention to the patient's receptivity to these interventions, bodes poorly for treatment benefit. On the other hand, the use of abreactive and directive interventions contributes significantly to treatment benefit when the effects of patient receptivity (i.e., the match) are considered. The therapy-matching dimensions of greatest importance are the fit between therapist level of directiveness and patient resistance level and the balancing of abreactive interventions and the level of patient initial level of distress. Collectively, when therapist process factors and therapy activity/process factors are considered, matching dimensions significantly facilitates treatment benefit.

One may note as well that when the analysis is simplified, therapist skill emerged as a contributor to therapy common qualities, even as therapeutic alliance dropped out. Therapist skill made a contribution directly to the effectiveness of matching treatment to patient, but the relationship was not found to exist in the other direction. That is, skill is associated with the development of a treatment that is responsive to fit the interventions to qualities of the patient. Skill, along with level of therapist verbal activity, also contributed to the effective use of abreactive and directive treatment techniques. Thus, skill contributed to benefit of treatment indirectly through two channels: first, by fitting the directiveness and intensity of the intervention to the patient's level of resistance and distress, respectively, and, second, by managing abreactive emotions and offering guidance. Thus, we must conclude that variables such as therapist skill and the selective matching of procedures (from different treatment models) to patient qualities are relevant but complex and exert their effects through their moderating influences on other variables.

Integrating Basic and Optimal Guidelines

To translate these findings into workable guidelines that include both basic and optimal recommendations for care, we separately analyzed the three samples on which structured and controlled treatments were offered. In each of these studies, we assessed several matching dimensions at once and sought to determine their relative and combined effects. One of these studies was a priori in nature and focused on alcohol-dependent individuals. It is reported here as a prototype of prospective matching research and because, in combination with the second study on depressed patients using archival data, it suggests the generality of matching concepts. The third sample comprised older adults. Collectively, analysis of these two samples suggested the degree to which compatibility of treatment-patient match was a significant contributor to outcomes, although the relative contributions of the specific dimensions changed somewhat with the nature of the problem and the sample being presented.

Matching Treatment to Patient
in Alcohol Treatment

Theoretical literature suggests that matching patients to treatments by utilizing a number of dimensions at once may enhance outcome more than the use of any single dimension (Beutler & Clarkin, 1990). However, researchers with Project Match (Project Match Research Group, 1997), the largest investigation of various matching algorithms, found little to recommend the matching dimensions that they studied. Stage of patient readiness, implementation of a AA-based twelve-step program, and the use of motivational interviewing and confrontation were all contributors to patient benefit. Only the last dimension had matching implications, and these were of relatively minor importance.

In spite of these negative findings, our investigations on the dimensions extracted from the STS (Beutler & Clarkin, 1990; Gaw & Beutler, 1995) have produced much stronger yields and have suggested some reasons for the poor showing in Project Match. Specifically, this research demonstrates that the most powerful effects of matching are revealed when one goes beyond general models of treatment and looks at how individual therapists apply individual procedures. This is possible when one views what therapists do at the level of strategy and technique rather than at the level of the theoretical model that defines the nature of treatment. This is possible if one largely sets aside concerns with theoretical orientation and views actual therapist behavior. While more time-intensive than a system that matches patients to therapists' theoretical models, such a system is consistent with an evolving model of training and ongoing supervision that addresses issues of quality control by targeting specific skills and the application of treatment principles rather than theoretical adherence or the acquisition of specific techniques (e.g., Beutler, in press; Caspar, in press; Strupp & Binder, in press).

Matching Dimensions in the Couples
Alcohol Treatment Project

The Couples Alcohol Alcohol Treatment (CAT) Project was designed to test the independent and collective contributions of several of the matching dimensions discussed in this chapter. Both individual and joint effects of various matching dimensions were studied among seventy-nine cohabitating couples, one of whom was a problem drinker (Karno, 1997). The first wave of analyses was based on an assessment of patient attributes contrasted to global, manualized cognitive (CT) (Wakefield, Williams, Yost, & Patterson, 1996) and family systems (FST) (Rohrbaugh, Shoham, Spungen, & Steinglass, 1995) therapies. The therapies were constructed to be representative of specific treatment qualities. A second wave of analyses compared the results of this general analysis with a more precise assessment of therapist-initiated treatment processes, independent of the treatment model. In both cases, outcomes were carefully monitored, and an assessment was made of the mediating roles of patient variables on response to treatments.

On the basis of the STS treatment matching model, the CAT Project focused on the separate and combined effects of correspondence between four client characteristics and corresponding aspects of treatment. Specifically, we assessed the individual and combined effects of the degree of correspondence between (1) level of functional impairment and the number and frequency of treatment sessions; (2) level of patient initial subjective distress and therapist focus on increasing or decreasing level of arousal; (3) level of patient trait-like resistance and level of therapist directiveness; and (4) relative external to internal coping style and relative therapeutic focus on symptom change and insight.

The initial analyses looked at separate matching dimensions, selected for the quality associated with the identity of the therapy model used. For the major analysis, the model of psychotherapy was ignored in favor of a close look at actual in-therapy behaviors of therapists using the various models. We reasoned from prior research that the way particular models are applied results in a considerable amount of overlap in the particular procedures and therapeutic styles represented by different therapists. Thus, we considered the distinctiveness of the model to be less sensitive to differences among therapist behaviors than direct observations (Beutler, Machado, & Neufeldt, 1994). All four matching variables were studied by measuring patient variables before treatment and directly observing the nature of therapy in the sessions.

Patient variables were assessed by using standardized tests (e.g., MMPI, BSI), as suggested in the foregoing sections. Ratio scores reflecting the amount of a given therapeutic activity relative to a corresponding patient quality (e.g., amount of directiveness per patient nondefensiveness; amount of behavioral focus relative to patient externalization; amount of emotional focus relative to patient initial distress level; intensity of treatment relative to level of functional impairment) were used to assess the degree of correspondence between each patient and treatment dimension. Hierarchical linear modeling was used to assess the contributions of each patient and therapy dimension, separately and for the four matching dimensions. Effects were assessed and modeled over time (twenty treatment sessions and one-year follow-up).

To ensure a wide distribution of therapeutic procedures, the two treatments were specifically designed to differ in two dimensions. CT was focused on symptomatic change, while FST was devoted to altering interpersonal and system-wide themes, and CT was therapist directed while FST was patient directed. By chance, the treatments also differed in intensity or concentration (the number of weeks required to complete planned weekly and biweekly sessions), with the twenty sessions of FST taking longer to complete than the twenty sessions of CT. As expected, individual therapists within each treatment also differed in their levels of directiveness, their application of insight-oriented procedures, and their success in raising patient emotions and arousal.

The sample used in this analysis consisted of sixty-two male and twelve female alcoholics. Their partners were included in all treatment conditions, but outcomes were based only on identified patients. The outcome measures reflected the substance abuse status and general psychiatric functioning of the identified alcoholic patients. All identified patients were alcohol dependent, most (85%) were European-American, and they had been partnered for an average of 8.3 years. Nearly half of the patients used illicit drugs in addition to being dependent on alcohol.

The growth curve modeling procedure revealed a relatively steady decline of symptoms throughout treatment, independent of treatment type or level of fit between patient and treatment qualities. Estimated abstinence rates were quite low, but the mean rates were consistent with other research on substance abuse treatment. At termination, abstinence rates were 42.9 percent and 37.5 percent for clients who had received CT and FST, respectively. At follow-up, the rates were 39.3 percent and 29.7 percent. An even lower rate of change was noted in general symptoms, independent of alcoholic symptoms. These low average rates of change, along with wide variations of outcomes within treatments, were not unexpected and precisely underline the need to match patients with those treatments for which they are best suited. Moreover, the initial analyses revealed that resistant patients tended to do poorly in CT, a therapist-guided and -directed treatment. However, these differences were relatively small and were insufficient for making clinical decisions.

In the main analyses, we obtained independent ratings of therapist activities on each of the to-be-matched dimensions, using trained but blind clinical observers. The first step in this analysis was to assess the independent and separate relationships of these patient-assessed (functional impairment, subjective distress, trait-like resistance level, and coping style) and therapist-provided (treatment intensity, relative use of arousal-induction and anxiety reduction procedures, therapist directiveness, and therapist focus on direct behavior change or insight) factors and change in drinking frequency. The results indicated that the level of patient distress and amount of patient impulsivity were inhibitors of treatment benefit, while treatment intensity and level of focus on direct symptom change were associated with the amount of improvement achieved. In all instances, there were wide differences from patient to patient that indicated the presence of patient variables that were selectively determining treatment response.

The next step was to analyze the effects of the level of correspondence between each patient variable and its corresponding therapy quality. In this analysis, standardized difference scores defined level of match. These scores were constructed without respect to the direction of the difference score contributions. Thus, both a therapy relationship consisting of a directive therapist and a nonresistant patient and one comprising a nondirective therapist and a resistant patient were considered good matches.

The analysis of optimal guidelines using the four matching dimensions revealed that by the sixth month after treatment ended, three of the four matching dimensions studied proved to be related to desirable changes in alcohol usage. Specific findings included these:

1. The correspondent match of level of initial severity (functional impairment) and level of care (average time to complete twenty planned sessions) predicted improvement in substance abuse. Patients whose level of care corresponded to the amount of impairment in functioning (high functioning with low-intensive therapies and low functioning with high-intensive procedures) tended to show more alcohol-related improvement than those who did not correspond on this patient-treatment dimension.
2. The match between patient resistance and treatment directiveness predicted change in alcohol use. Resistant patients who received nondirective interventions and nonresistant patients who received directive interventions reduced consumption and abuse more than those patients who were mismatched on level of therapist directiveness.
3. When patients were separated into two groups—abstinent and nonabstinent—the relationship between therapist activation of affect and patient initial distress emerged as a significant predictor. Patients with low levels of distress treated with emotional activating procedures and those whose high levels of distress were treated with emotional reduction procedures were more likely to benefit than their mismatched counterparts.

Collectively, the matching dimensions alone accounted for 76 percent of the variance in alcohol-related changes. Factors associated with basic guidelines and nonmatching qualities of therapy (e.g., social impairment and therapist activities such as directiveness of treatment) independently raised the efficiency of the prediction to 82 percent. These values are of sufficient strength to suggest their value in making clinical decisions.

Admittedly, the leap from studies of substance abuse to depression is a bit long. However, these are related conditions. Nonetheless, it is informative to explore the purer depressive samples to see if these same parameters hold.

Matching Variables in Adult Depression

Analysis of the sixty-three patients from the Arizona Depression Project (sample 3) focused on four matching dimensions of patient and treatment. These included the match of treatment intensity to level of patient social impairment, level of patient subjective distress to the application of procedures that are designed to reduce or increase arousal, patient coping style and the selection of symptomatic versus insight-oriented strategies and goals, and patient resistance levels and therapist level of directiveness. Outcome was evaluated on the BDI and the Hamilton Rating Scale for Depression (HRSD).

While the three treatments did reveal characteristic profiles, there was a good deal of overlap of procedures across the therapeutic procedures, depending on the particular patient. This provides further evidence that formal theoretical models used by therapists are poor descriptors of what is actually done in treatment. The nature of treatment was more a reflection of a particular therapist's proclivities, strengths, and weaknesses than a result of the model the therapist used.

The results indicated that at the end of treatment, using the BDI as an outcome measure, the effects of treatment intensity and induction of arousal accounted for approximately 35 percent of the predicted outcomes. Matching variables added only 17 percent additional predictive efficiency, with the greatest benefit arising from matching the therapist's level of directiveness to patient initial resistance.

When outcome variables were based on clinician ratings of depression rather than on self-reports, the results were somewhat stronger. Patient distress contributed significantly to therapeutic change, and, collectively, the patient qualities contributed approximately 33 percent of the predicted variance. Therapist activities contributed another 36 percent to the predictive efficiency, primarily through the positive role that treatment intensity played in the process. Psychotherapy procedures variables added 39 percent additional predictive efficiency, with the strongest predictor being the relationship between patient coping style and the symptomatic versus insight focus of the therapy.

Measures of the speed of change were also evaluated, with evidence emerging that matching variables significantly contributed to this variable as well. The fit between patient level of distress and the therapist's use of arousal induction and support, as well as the fit between the patient's coping style and behavioral versus insight focus, also added significantly to the 16 percent of variance attributed to matching effects.

Similar predictions were noted at one-year follow-up, with the fit between level of impairment and treatment intensity and between coping style and insight versus symptomatic focus being the strongest predictors of treatment response.

Collectively, treatment effects were most obvious and strongest when basic and optimal guidelines worked together. Specific, treatment benefit was greatest when:

1. The level of patient impairment was adapted to the intensity of treatment
2. The patient's level of distress corresponded with the therapist's emphasis on arousing or lowering discomfort
3. The patient's level of resistance corresponded with the use of nondirective procedures.

Collectively, these findings support the value of matching treatments to patients within the context of varying levels of care and treatment intensity.

Matching Dimensions among Older Depressed Adults

As noted in chapter 5, sample 4 was the basis for the third set of analyses, and these analyses were devoted to understanding the relationship between patient variables and treatment interventions. For this analysis, the samples were confined to sixty individuals, twenty in each of three treatments, who had completed the BDI and HRSD at the beginning and the conclusion of treatment.

Four dimensions of treatment planning were evaluated: (1) the fit between level of impairment and use of psychosocial versus antidepressant treatments, (2) the fit of patient distress to use of arousal induction versus support procedures, (3) the fit of coping style to symptomatic versus insight focus of treatment, and (4) fit of patient resistance to level of therapist directiveness. The strongest predictions supported the distinction between basic and optimal guidelines. The strongest predictive relationships was between level of social impairment and the use of psychoactive versus psychosocial interventions. This level of fit contributed 13 percent to the prediction of treatment outcome.

The findings supported the value of the basic guidelines presented earlier and confirmed the independence of these guidelines from those that we have identified as optimal in treatment planning. The findings indicate that an optimal treatment includes a "fit" between treatment mode and impairment. Functional impairment and the use of medication (a basic guideline) jointly predicted improvement. Medication use was advantaged among those with high levels of functional impairment, although the effects of psychotherapy were relatively less dependent on patient impairment level.

Unlike the other studies, we found that patient resistance and therapist directiveness, patient coping style and therapy focus, and level of patient distress and the use of arousal induction procedures did not make significant and independent contributions of factors that predict outcomes directly.

IMPLICATIONS AND SUMMARY

To summarize our findings, let us revisit the preliminary principles that were extracted from our review of literature.

5. High initial distress may be an indicator for the use of supportive and self-directed therapy but bears no relationship to the effectiveness of active and therapist-guided interventions.

This principle was supported in our analysis of the STS model. The fit between patient intial distress and the use of supportive versus abreactive interventions emerged as one of the predictive factors constituting the therapy match dimension.

9. A certain level of experienced or felt support may be necessary to activate the power of interpersonal and relationship therapies.

We found no direct support for this principle. Social support did not enter into the construction of any of the predictive dimensions as we looked as specific aspects of therapeutic process.

12. Minimally structured, self-directed interventions, nondirective procedures, or paradoxical directives are effective among patients who are highly prone to interpersonal resistance.
13. Directive treatment interventions and clinician guidance are advantageous to patients who have low resistance tendencies.

Both of these principles were supported in the analysis of the STS model. The matching variable used in the analysis considered both low therapist directivenes-high patient resistance and high therapist directiveness-low patient resistance to be good matches, and this variable was a significant contributor to the general factor of therapy match. In turn, this factor contributed to treatment outcome, as predicted.

14. Extroverted/externalizing/impulsive coping styles indicate the use of interventions designed to directly affect symptoms and enhance skills.
15. Introverted/internalizing/restricted coping styles indicate the use of interventions designed to directly affect insight and awareness.

These two principles could be supported, but the dimensions appear to be highly related to the dimension of fit between therapist directiveness and patient resistance. When one of the factors was active, the other added no significant power to the predictions. Thus, we conclude that attention either to trait-like resistance or to coping style be considered in planning a differential treatment response.

There were findings that were not wholly anticipated, indicating that therapist directiveness, and use of emotionally focued interventions tended to be beneficial. There were also inconsistent findings in specific samples relating to the relative role of matching on the dimensions of patient coping style or trait-like resistance. These additions and ambiguities lead us to consolidate all of the optimal guidelines into the following principles.

1. Therapeutic change is greatest when the therapist is skillful and provides trust, acceptance, acknowledgment, collaboration, and respect for the patient within an environment that both supports risk and provides maximal safety.

This principle emphasizes the importance of therapist skill and proficiency in applying psychotherapy and other treatment procedures. In addition to technical proficiency, the ability to establish a trusting and caring relationship is emphasized in this principle.

2. Therapeutic change is most likely when the patient is exposed to the objects or targets of behavioral and emotional avoidance.

This is a principle of exposure and emphasizes that treatment change is a function of contacting avoided experiences.

3. Therapeutic change is greatest when the relative balance of interventions either favors the use of skill building and symptom removal procedures among those who externalize, or favors the use of insight and relationship-focused procedures among internalizers.

This is a principle that defines the relationship between patient coping style and the internal and external focus of treatment. It emphasizes that external change is greatest if the treatment and patient both emphasize active and external behaviors, while internal change is greatest if there is a correspondence between the focus on insight/awareness and patient self-reflective or insight capacities. Principle 3 may be evoked by a relationship therapist by attending to here-and-now issues and by a behavior or cognitive therapist by monitoring and restructuring urges and other cognitions.

4. Therapeutic change is most likely if the initial focus of change efforts is on building skills and altering disruptive symptoms.

This principle emphasizes the importance of symptom change to all of treatment, independent of whether it also holds as relevant the facilitation of insight.

To enact these principles, a behavior therapist may identify external objects of avoidance and use in vivo exposure to activate principle 4, while an interpersonal or relationship-oriented therapist may activate principle 4 by a here-and-now focus on daily problems and relationship and activate principle 5 by identifying a dynamic theme or life narrative as a point of focus. In somewhat similar fashion, a cognitive therapist may focus on identifying automatic thoughts and exposing the patient to feared events in response to principle 4 and monitor and activate schematic injunctions to activate principle 5.

5. Therapeutic change is most likely when the therapeutic procedures do not evoke patient resistance.

This principle emphasizes the value of soliciting patient cooperation.

6. Therapeutic change is greatest when the directiveness of the intervention is either inversely correspondent to the patient's current level of resistance or authoritatively prescribes a continuation of the symptomatic behavior.

This principle corresponds to principle 5 and emphasizes that when cooperation does not occur, it can be facilitated by adapting the therapist's style to minimize confrontation.

Within all theoretical frameworks, there are suggestions for handling and minimizing patient resistance. In a behavioral tradition these may include patient-generated behavioral contracts or behavioral exchange programs, while in a systems framework they may involve prescribing the symptoms and reframing, and in the tradition of relationship therapy they may involve acceptance, approach and retreat, and evocative support.

7. The likelihood of therapeutic change is greatest when the patient's level of emotional stress is moderate, neither excessively high nor excessively low.

This principle emphasizes the motivating properties of distress and acknowledges that some distress is facilitative of movement in treatment. All therapeutic schools identify procedures that confront and procedures that support or structure. Providing structure and support as well as behavioral and cognitive stress management procedures can serve to reduce immediate levels of disruptive emotion, while confrontational, experiential, and open-ended or unstructured procedures tend to increase arousal.

8. Therapeutic change is greatest when a patient is stimulated to emotional arousal in a safe environment until problematic responses diminish or extinguish.

This principle is a correlate of the previous one and emphasizes that when distress is low, confrontation may be necessary in order to facilitate the development of motivation.

While the level of this analysis within treatment settings can become more or less specific, depending on the information available on each patient, the assessment and treatment program that we have proposed allows for a high degree of freedom and flexibility on the part of the therapist. Procedures and techniques have different properties, depending on who is using them and how they are introduced. Thus, while we consider the principles to be sound and relatively inviolate, the selection of specific procedures will depend on the experience and familiarity of the therapist who uses them and the skill level of the therapist with different procedures. It is within this framework that we believe that some hope rests for ensuring flexibility in studies of integrated treatment.

Beyond these specifics, several other conclusions are possible from our analysis of treatment planning guidelines. The most exciting aspect of psychotherapy research is that we may have far underestimated the power of psychotherapy by oversimplifying the ways in which we have studied it. This is truly exciting, since it suggests that the use of skills and procedures, just like the development of artistic skill, is dependent on the quality of the therapist's training and on the supervision the therapist has received. Therapist training and skill are important considerations in effective treatment, but largely for some patients and then only in the context of some relationships.

Of equal importance is the general support these data provide for the systematic treatment selection model (STS) of Beutler and Clarkin (1990). These results point to the fallibility of more simplistic models, including the eclectic-psychotherapy and the common factors psychotherapy models, and the search for specific procedures that are especially effective independent of the contributions of patients.

These findings also have implications for research methodology. They strongly suggest that while marginally predictive, simple treatment matching based on patient self-report and on initial problem and symptom presentations—the most usual type of prognostic model used in managed health care planning (e.g., Butcher, 1990; Lambert, Okiishi, Finch, & Johnson, 1998)—in the absence of direct observation and sequential monitoring of skillfully applied interventions, let alone models based on other myths of treatment simplicity, is doomed to produce unsatisfactory, small, and misleading results. In this, perpetuation of such unidirectional and linear research hypotheses will produce inconsistent and low-power results that reinforce what seem destined to prove to be true myths:

1. That optimal treatment can be planned and conducted without respect to the skill and expertise of those who offer it
2. That specialized training and monitoring within any treatment context are unimportant to distinctive treatment effects
3. That the most efficient avenue to personal and predictable resolution of most of the problems associated with depression is through better biochemistry.

Our findings strongly suggest that optimal use of psychotherapy requires very high levels of technical expertise, experience, and skill, including the ability to interact with and take advantage of computer technology to help the therapist through the morass of cascading influences at the level of complexity needed, and the cognitive flexibility to bridge theories and methods.

As for the issue of empirically based decision making, these findings argue persuasively for the need for empirical guidelines. Linear logic is too simple and fails to add stability. With the exception of the prognostic model, the simple, linear models that we tested produced inconsistent, unstable, or weak findings. The power of patient predisposing factors alone should be clear, and failure to accommodate these factors when planning treatment procedures is destined to result in less than optimal treatment gains.

However, the pattern of relationships that governs the instigation of effective treament decisions is complex. The best application will probably require technical support and knowledge to make use of relevant matching algorithms for a given patient. The use of computer-generated predictions makes sense. We are currently concluding a prospective study of these factors as applied to samples of patients who are comorbid for chemical abuse and depression, comparing an STS-generated treatment protocol with standard CT and manualized relationship/narrative therapy. The results continue to be promising and suggest that statistical predictions based on computer-generated algorithms have some advantages over those based on clinical impressions. The future may offer many opportunities to improve clinician judgment and perception and to enhance clinician training.

PART IV

The Nature of Depression

8 Significance of the Problem of Depression

The reader will note that the guidelines that we have developed are somewhat different from those traditionally presented. They identify principles that can be used to guide any model of treatment rather than list types or models of treatment that have been used in various research programs. This difference is one of the level of specificity that is considered to be most helpful. While our decision to focus on the identification of general principles of treatment derives from both our literature review and our cross-validational study, it also reflects our belief that more is to be gained by looking at the procedures and strategies used to guide treatment than at either the specific therapeutic techniques used or the theory of psychopathology espoused by the therapist. To be fair, however, it is worthwhile to explore what the literature offers in the way of applying various specific packages of intervention to aspects of depression.

Attempts to define treatment models that work for depression rest on two cardinal assumptions: that the condition(s) being treated is (are) in fact a recognizable and distinctive disorder (or set of disorders) and that the treatment offered for it (them) is reasonably specific to that disorder. As we will see, however, both of these assumptions have been seriously questioned as they apply to depression. In this part of this book, we present background material that will allow the reader to explore what is known about the first of these assumptions, that depression is a set of distinctive disorders. Then, in Part V, we explore what is known about the effectiveness of efforts to treat depression as it is conventionally understood. This exploration will allow the reader to consider the evidence that bears on the second assumption, that there is a well-defined, specific treatment for depression. In this way, the reader may be able to decide whether the guidelines that we have presented, based on principles of differential effect, are more or less useful than those based on assumptions about the specificity of depression and its treatment.

211

INCIDENCE AND PREVALENCE OF
DEPRESSIVE CONDITIONS

Among the major mental health problems in North America, depression is arguably the most prevalent and the most costly, in terms of both personal functioning and social productivity. Employee Assistance Program (EAP) managers report that depression ranks with family crisis and stress as the most frequent and costly problems that affect the workplace. Reportedly, the negative impact of depression on society ranks even higher than the more widely recognized workplace problem of alcohol abuse (PRNewswire report, 1996).

Two major stratified probability samples have provided the most ecologically valid survey information on incidence and lifetime prevalence rates for disorders whose definition prominently includes depression (Howard et al., 1996), but these surveys provide widely disparate estimates of the dimensions of the problem. The first, the NIMH Epidemiological Catchment Area (ECA) studies (Regier et al., 1984), gathered structured diagnostic and treatment information from more than twenty thousand adults at five sites between 1980 and 1985. The results indicated that at any given time, approximately 5 percent of the U.S. population, regardless of age, met diagnostic standards for a mood disorder. The findings from the second survey indicate substantially higher rates of depressive disorders. The National Comorbidity Survey (NCS) (Kessler et al., 1994) was drawn from a sample of more than eight thousand adults between 1990 and 1992. The results of this survey revealed that the prevalence rate for recent or current depression was 10 percent, the figure most commonly obtained in small surveys and cited in clinical circles as the prevalence of major depression. The corresponding lifetime prevalence rates were estimated to be 7 percent in the ECA study and 19 percent in the NCS study, the latter figure being, once again, the figure most often cited by other authors (Coyne, in press; Gotlib, 1993).

The discrepancies between the two surveys are probably attributable to the difference in the procedures used to establish diagnoses. The NCS study, for example, employed a more refined, sensitive, and expanded interview procedure than that used in the earlier, ECA study. This refined interview procedure incorporated the judgment of skilled clinicians, rather than rely on the relatively untrained judgments of lay interviewers. Thus, it allowed for the use of a wider range of diagnostic options, even within the domain of depressive spectrum disorders, than the Diagnostic Interview Schedule (DIS) used in the ECA study. High intercorrelations among symptom scales on the DIS and that schedule's limited sensitivity to some symptoms of mild depression and psychological distress are other factors that may have contributed to these differences (Howard et al., 1996).

In an effort to resolve some of the discrepancies between the ECA findings and the figures typically cited as incidence and prevalence rates, Eaton, Dryman, Sorenson, and McCutcheon (1989) reanalyzed data from two of the ECA sites using statistical procedures that were designed to compensate for the effects of symptom interdependence and measurement intercorrelation. Even though the estimates of prevalence were not adjusted for the lack of sensitivity in the DIS assessment procedure, the results still revealed lifetime prevalence rates (14 percent) that were more consistent with the subsequent, NCS survey. Major depressive disorder earned an estimated prevalence rate of 12 percent, with an additional 2 percent of individuals showing more serious depressive signs. Using the Eaton et al. analytic procedure, fully 25 percent of the ECA sample were judged to have experienced at least one symptom of depression in the month prior to the index interview.

One may conclude from these various studies that the prevalence of Major Depression is something over 10 percent. The prevalence of more serious depressive disorders, such as those associated with bipolar disorder and psychotic depressions, are more difficult to estimate but may be approximately 2 percent. If one calculates rates from the available probability samples, the prevalence of minor and transitory (life adjustment) depression is somewhere between 15 percent and 25 percent, and a figure closer to the lower of these values may characterize the lifetime prevalence rate of major depression. Similarly, on the basis of a combined estimate from the two samples, we may speculate that the incidence of double-depression depressive symptoms may be present among as many as one-fifth (20 percent) of the population at any given time, and nearly one-third (30 percent) of the population may experience significant, impairing, but transient dysfunction because of depression sometime in their lives. While these figures must be taken with caution, they paint a sobering picture when one views the importance and social significance of depression in daily life.

More reliable figures based on cross-country surveys suggest that the prevalence of depression is increasing and that the age of first onset is becoming lower with each succeeding generation. It is also clear that women are approximately twice as likely to suffer from depression as men, and whites are more likely to suffer from depression than African Americans. Yet, curiously, black women are the most prone to depression, probably reflecting the impact of economic and educational contributors to depressive conditions. The highest rates of depression are for young females with less than a college degree (Coyne, in press).

COST OF DEPRESSION

The social costs of depression, in terms of lost work days, lost productivity, and treatment costs, are generally estimated to exceed that of coronary heart disease and arthritis and may be as high as $41 billion per year (Coyne, in press). These cost estimates must be viewed cautiously, however. They are based on comparisons of production between those who have been identified as depressed and those who have not. That is, they hinge on the assumption that depression can be recognized. In fact, depressive conditions may lack the degree of specificity that would allow them to be clearly recognized, even by reasonably well-trained primary-care providers.

Detection and Treatment of Depression by Primary-Care Providers

Even in its most severe and obvious form, depression goes undiagnosed by the primary-care providers who are typically identified as the entry points for early treatment and prevention services by managed health care systems. As few as 10 percent of depressed patients may be detected by primary-care providers (Ormel, Koeter, van den Brink, & van de Willige, 1991; Quill, 1985). Some researchers (e.g., Rost, Zhang, Fortney, Smith, & Coyne, 1998) have observed that patients whose depression is undetected may have especially poor outcomes.

However, even when depression is accurately detected, it is uncertain if the treatment provided in primary-care settings is appropriately targeted to depression and can be expected to reduce the symptoms and thereby, presumably, the costs. Several studies suggest that even when their depression is detected, a large percentage of depressed patients receive inadequate treatment (Katon, Von Korff, Lin, Bush, & Ormel, 1992; Regier et al., 1988; Wells, Katon, Rogers, & Camp, 1994).

Moreover, the effectiveness of treatment, even when patients are accurately detected, is uncertain in these settings. Several authors (Dowrick & Buchan, 1995; Schulberg, McClelland, & Gooding, 1987; Tiemens, Ormel, & Simon, 1996) suggest that there are few differences in outcome among those who are recognized as being depressed and those who are not, and at least one study (Coyne, Klinkman, Gallo, & Schwenk, 1997) has found that undetected depressed patients were better off than their detected depressed colleagues after nearly five months of treatment. In a related study, Callahan et al. (1994) found that increasing the proficiency of detection did not lead to increased improvement rates among older adults treated in primary-care settings. These studies raise the question of whether the treatments provided to depressed patients in these settings are appropriate or adequate.

In the large-scale Medical Outcomes Study (MOS), Wells and Sturm (1996) found that an astonishing 39 percent of patients who were known to be depressed and who were being treated in a variety of primary-care settings either received subtherapeutic doses of antidepressant medication or were inappropriately given minor tranquilizers and anxiolytics. The authors note that the level of mistreatment was associated both with a worsening of the patient's condition and with an increase in treatment costs. This finding has been challenged, however. Several studies suggest that there are few differences in outcomes between those treated with antidepressants and those treated with other, "inappropriate" or "inadequate" medications (e.g., Simon, Linn, et al., 1995).

Costs Associated with Depression

Even if one does not consider the possibility that the low percentage of cases of depression that are detected may lead to an underestimate of the social cost of this condition, it is clear that depression is a costly experience to society. Those with diagnosed depression have substantially higher annual medical costs than those without a diagnosed depressive disorder in virtually all categories of service (Simon, Von Korff, & Barlow, 1995). The Medical Outcome Study (Wells & Sturm, 1996) found that the cost of treatment was influenced by the level and type of treating clinician, with nonmedical specialists providing more efficient cost-benefit ratios than medical specialists. The average annual cost of treating a patient who was diagnosed with depression ranged from $2,900 when the treatment was conducted by nonphysicians to $3,900 when it was conducted by psychiatrists. This means that the annual cost of treating depression is between $12 and $20 billion (Zhang, Rost, & Fortney, 1998), depending in part on who provides the services.

Given the problems associated with diagnosing depression, one can be sure that even these high cost estimates for losses linked to depression, including the costs of treatment, are seriously and grossly understated. The estimated costs of $3,000 or more for each identified patient (Simon et al., 1995; Wells & Sturm, 1996) may be as little as 10 percent of the actual cost of treating depression in the United States (Zhang et al., 1998). Given the high probability of misdiagnosis and mismanagement, the indirect cost of additional medical treatment, and lost work productivity, it is difficult to see how the procedure of leaving decisions about treatment in the hands of primary-care physicians and clerks, as is conventional among managed health care programs, can hope to reduce the high costs of treatment.

Even if we could accurately assess the direct costs of treating depression, the figures would not accurately reflect its cost in terms of human suffering and lost social productivity. Not only do EAP managers rank depression as the most significant problem in the workplace (PRNewswire report, 1996), but they identify it as a leading contributor to reduced functioning associated with medical complaints, missed days at work, and accident rates. Moreover, these administrators indicate that they believe that the significance and prevalence of depression have been increasing over the past three to five years.

Myriad secondary problems added to the effects of the primary symptoms themselves place tremendous demands on the health care system to attenuate the impairing effects of depression. Moreover, the typical service that is available through private insurance and managed health care is inadequate to address these needs. Recently, legislators have begun to enact laws designed to ensure that parity between mental and physical health benefits will be achieved at some point. However, to date, coverage and support within the workplace for the treatment of those who are depressed are generally weak. On the basis of a survey that included samples of psychologist providers and health insurance agents, Hunter and Austad (1997) concluded that a disparity between the coverage for mental and for physical health problems continues to exist in spite of legislative mandates for parity. Some surveys indicate that as late as 1996, fewer than 20 percent of workplace-initiated health programs had made changes to accommodate the needs of depressed workers (PRNewswire, 1996).

Many providers and recipients alike believe that neither the recently mandated changes in health care policy nor the unprecedented public outcries against the failures of managed health care policies have, to date, resulted in the establishment of a work environment that offers adequate treatment to those who have emotional and behavioral disorders. The coverage provided to the average worker is barely sufficient to treat mild mental health problems but quite insufficient to treat moderate and severe problems.

The lower levels of mental health coverage relative to coverage for physical disease must be considered within the context of a physical care system that is itself struggling. A plethora of recent mass media reports attest to a medical health care system that is in a major state of crisis and deterioration. Citing three studies conducted under the auspicies of the National Coalition of Health Care, the NBC Nightly News (October 20, 1997) reported that autopsy studies revealed an error rate of 40 percent for major, life-threatening diagnoses across managed health care programs. NBC correspondents estimated that "tens of thousands of individuals" die in the United States each year because of inadequate diagnosis and treatment. If true, this is among the worst mortality rates in the western hemisphere.

The relative weakness of mental health coverage among health care programs means that the $3,000 to $4,000 cost per year (Simon et al., 1995; Wells & Sturm, 1996) for treating each depressed patient in the United States must be absorbed by state, federal, and local governments. With approximately 4 percent (10,000,000 persons) of the population receiving mental health treatment at any given time, the annual tax burden can be extremely high.

Cost Benefits of Treatment

In the final analysis, the benefit of managing health care and of operationalizing the varieties of treatments is the same—to increase the efficiency of interventions. Decreasing the amount of production lost because of depression and reducing the costs and increasing the effectiveness of treatments must all be component parts of the cost-saving equation.

If one assumes that depression is associated with an increase in medical costs, then treatment should logically reduce depression severity or symptomatology and reduce medical costs and medical utilization. However, it should not be expected that reduced costs will be seen in the short term, because, even when treated effectively and well, depression still carries substantial costs. But, a growing body of research demonstrates that a substantial cost savings is sustained by effective treatment, both in long-term medical utilization and in the costs of treatment (Gabbard, Lazar, Hornberger, & Spiegel, 1997; Groth-Marnat & Edkins, 1996). This is especially noticeable when one compares treatment in primary-care settings and treatment in mental health settings.

When the costs of treating patients in primary-care settings and in mental health care settings are compared, the frequently made assumption that primary-care treatment is cheaper is seriously challenged. In a careful longitudinal study of 470 randomly selected individuals, Zhang et al. (1998) concluded that treatment by mental health professionals produced a net annual savings of $877 per patient. In turn, the cost to society was $2,101 per year lower for those treated for depression in mental health settings than for those treated in primary-care settings. These findings suggest a substantial cost offset in the treatment of depression by mental health professionals.

The possibility that there are cost offsets for treatment is particularly intriguing and has broad-ranging implications for service delivery. Support for cost-saving benefits have been particularly strong for professionally delivered, psychotherapeutic interventions among those patients who present with medical and somatic symptoms that are either directly or indirectly associated with depression and anxiety. In the following section, we review some of this evidence.

Costs, Benefits, and Managed Health Care

The low rates at which primary-care providers detect depression raises questions about the reliability of diagnosing depressive conditions. But low reliability alone cannot account for the relatively poor quality and high costs that appear to characterize many of the treatment services provided in the United States. The nature of the health care system itself must be questioned. This system has always been cost-conscious, but it has not traditionally been equally sensitive to issues of benefit.

To much of the managed health care industry, when benefit has been considered, it has been defined as the variety or level of services provided, rather than their effectiveness. As they come to identify benefit in terms that are more akin to those used by the public, it is likely that managed health care (MHC) will begin to look to research findings to help determine what treatments are justified (Aaron, 1996). Already, the evolving health care system in the United States is beginning to consider more than the immediate and direct effects of treatment in assessing treatment costs. To the chagrin of many, it is also coming increasingly to look to empirical research to help it define what treatments will be covered.

It is likely that this shift of focus among the systems that support treatment of depression will eventually lead the field to resolve some of the enduring problems of how depression is identified and defined. If depression were a unitary or even a set of finite disorders, one might expect a higher correspondence to exist between diagnosis and benefit than has been shown to exist. One might also expect that there would be more substantial evidence of a treatment that is specific to depression than currently exist. Kirsh and Sapirstein (1998), as well as Beutler (1998b), for example, have demonstrated that nonantidepressant medications and a variety of psychotherapies are all, on the average, similarly effective among patients diagnosed with Major Depression.

The low correspondence among the specific diagnosis of the non-bipolar depressive disorders, the specific treatment assigned, and the consistency of the experienced benefit all suggest that depression is not a specific and discriminable entity. This point remains in contention, but the very fact that it still stimulates debate among experts in the field (e.g., Coyne, 1994) testifies to our failure to understand the basic nature of depression. At the foundation of the many variations that exist in treatment and the variability of patient functioning that reduces the reliability of diagnosis may be an uncertainty of what symptoms constitute depression itself. It is no consolation that the problems that cloud the definitions of depression are recapitulated in the problems of defining a variety of so-called psychopathologies (Bergner, 1997; Ossorio, 1985; Wakefield, 1992b, 1997). The field has been split as much by varying viewpoints about the nature and etiology of depression as by the diverse values that exist regarding how to treat it.

SPECIFICITY AND NONSPECIFICITY OF DEPRESSION

Theorists argue about whether depression is best considered a unitary or a multifaceted condition, an experience that is continuous with normal sadness or a disorder that is discontinuous with and distinct from normal experience, and about what elements or components of treatment are necessary and sufficient to evoke change. The same body of data has given rise to widely disparate views, even among cadres of highly regarded and objective scientists. At this point, there is no consensus on whether depression is an array of specific disorders or a general indicator of unhappiness that varies mainly in intensity, the so-called common cold of emotional disorders.

The debate over the nature of depression is deeply embedded in a more general and continuing struggle among researchers to define the nature of psychopathology itself. In turn, this struggle is often reduced to values and interpretations, rather than facts.

Social Values in Defining Psychopathology and Depression

Theorists have long debated whether the criteria that define behavioral disorders should include judgments about the social harmfulness or value of a condition or symptom.

As applied to the specific problem of depression, the argument that social judgments must be included in diagnostic decisions suggests that a diagnosis of depression cannot be understood as referring merely to a subjective experience of unhappiness. It must also include judgments about the functional and social value of the symptoms or observed behaviors when it is used for clincial decision making (Coyne, 1994; Gotlib, 1993; Izard, 1977; Kendall & Flannery-Schroeder, 1995; Vredenburg, Flett, & Krames, 1993). If value judgments about what constitutes social harm are included, this suggests that distinctions among pathological conditions can never be made on empirical and statistical clustering procedures alone (c.f. Jason et al., 1997; Ossorio, 1985).

In an effort to integrate various differences between value-based and empirical definitions of psychopathology, Wakefield (1992a, 1992b, 1993, 1997) proposed the concept of "harmful dysfunction" to describe psychopathology. Harmful dysfunction was defined by its low social desirability and its high levels of harmfulness (value-laden variables), but it also included a quantitative description of adaptive functioning and efficiency (an empirical variable). While the concept of harmful dysfunction was designed to blend value-based and empirically based components, Wakefield continued to assume a discontinuous, categorical view of pathological behavior. By so doing, he (perhaps prematurely) closed the door on the question whether depression might be better understood as a normative extreme of typical or nomethetic experience or as a distinctive set of conditions.

It is reasonable to assume that unhappiness and dysphoria are distributed normally throughout the population. The subjective experience of seriously depressed individuals, from this perspective, is distinguished from the experiences of normal people only by degree (Wakefield, 1997). When judgments of depression are made by clinical judges, however, social values are invoked and alter the resulting distribution. Clinical judges intrinsically invoke social values when judging work, relationships, earning power, and family support. In this perspective, the ability to distinguish between behavior that is normal and behavior that is abnormal or disordered invokes a larger view of what is "good" or "socially acceptable" (Ossorio, 1985). As a result, the ratings of depressive intensity is distributed in an idiosyncratic way.

Both of these views of depression involve problems of measurement. One can never be sure that two seemingly equivalent subjective ratings reflect similar experiences. Thus, scaled measures of subjective distress can never guarantee that scores reflect a stable external meaning. Moreover, the external referent on which clinical ratings are made, because it is value laden, is likely to be culture specific and unstable, as well. Societies that are more tolerant of individual expression than ours may find less pathology in clinical symptoms and vegetative signs. Moreover, treatments based on clinical observations run the risk of being used to ensure or enforce social policies rather than to alleviate unhappiness and suffering.

Different ways of viewing depression often characterize different groups of experts. Academic theorists, for example, often are more drawn to a purist view of depression. They are suspicious of attempts to imbue it with social values, and rely on less value-based measures than those used by clinical practitioners. They often conclude that depression is a general and shared experience of people, rather than a unique pathology. Clinicians and clinical theorists, in contrast, more frequently rely on "clinical judgment" and diagnose depression through a lens that is colored by social definitions of "adaptation" and "adjustment." Unsurprisingly, this same group is quite likely to view depression as a set of distinctive conditions whose variations are identified partially by the levels of social harm with which they are associated.

It is notable that these fundamental differences of values may be one reason that academic theorists often have eschewed traditional diagnostic classifications. That is, they tend to favor the view that diagnoses would be more accurate and informative if the social values inherent in assessing "harmfulness" were discarded in favor of statistically defined descriptions and dimensions that represent coexisting continua (e.g., Costa & Widiger, 1994; Follette & Houts, 1996). Accordingly, such academics generally emphasize the similarity of depression and other negative affects.

One may view these disparate viewpoints as incompatible. However, they may be mirror images of each other, and in this there may be a nucleus of some common ground. Specifically, the diagnostic and categorical view of depression favored by clinicians may overemphasize the discontinuity between normal and abnormal experience, but the statistical definition of depression favored by academics may overemphasize the degree of similarity that exists between the experiences of seriously dysfunctional individuals and those whose experiences more closely approximate statistical definitions of "normal" or "average" (see Lilienfeld & Marino, 1995; Widiger, & Trull, 1985). Finding the common ground is not easy, however, and doing so will depend largely on empirical evidence on the question of the continuity-discontinuity of depression.

Definitions of Depression

The continuity-discontinuity debate regarding depression has stimulated a great deal of dialogue and research (e.g., Costello, 1992; Kendall & Flannery-Schroeder, 1995; Tennen, Hall, & Affleck, 1995a, 1995b; Weary, Edwards, & Jacobson, 1995; Widiger & Trull, 1991). The most widely accepted view is that depression is a constellation of separate but related conditions, all distinguished by vegetative signs and patterns of symptoms. The diagnostic system in contemporary use reflects this point of view, and its presence encourages scientist and practitioner alike to find the distinguishing and essential essence of each depressive condition in the constellation. Thus, major and minor depression, bipolar disorder, and dysthymic disorder are all considered to be distinct expressions of different disorders. Some (e.g., Huprich, 1998) even find reason to add depressive personality disorder to the diagnostic nomenclature to further differentiate among the manifestations of dysphoria.

From this discontinuity perspective, and because it relies on the presence of a critical mass of largely interchangeable symptoms, depressive conditions occasionally (especially among older adults) are diagnosed as being present even when there is no evidence of depressed mood or dysphoria. In the conventionally used diagnostic system (American Psychiatric Association, 1994), for example, dysphoria is one of several possible but equally weighted symptoms of an independent depressive disorder (American Psychiatric Association, 1994). The paradox of having a depression without feeling depressed is resolved by considering each of several other symptoms, especially vegetative signs of sleep loss, reduced sexual interest, and loss of social involvement, as being the functional equivalent of dysphoria. To others, the variations that occur among the diagnostic conditions that are identified with depression can be understood as variations in severity. That is, variation among diagnostic labels, all reflecting depression, are thought to vary largely by virtue of the severity of symptoms. In this view, the experience of dysphoria is a necessary feature of the diagnosis.

Within a continuity framework, the presence of vegetative signs may reflect the intensity of depression. A person with vegetative signs has a more severe depression than one who does not; the experience of dysphoria is central to the diagnosis, and other specific symptoms are secondary to this general unhappiness. Among those who take this perspective, an individual who presents with vegetative signs but no dysphoria may experience a diagnosable condition, but it should be either identified as something other than depression or considered to be relatively mild form of depression, one in which the dysphoria is expected to become more obvious if the problem becomes more severe.

Nolen-Hoeksema (1991) suggests that the appearance of categorical disorders in much research may be an artifact of the distinctive styles that people adopt in order to respond or adapt to the depression, rather than a reflection of the inherent nature of depression itself. One's style of coping or responding may be an enduring aspect of one's behavior that transcends the experience of depression. Just and Alloy (1997) found some support for this contention, concluding that individuals whose enduring response styles dispose them to respond to dysphoria by rumination are at escalated risk for developing lasting and more recurrent depressive symptoms than those whose preexisting dispositions reflect other styles of coping.

Even those who assert the discontinuity of depression as a diagnostic entity accept the observation that most symptoms of depression are continuously and normally distributed in the population. Only a few symptoms are demonstrably and qualitatively different from phenomena that exist in the experiences of most people. To scholars who assert the continuity of depression and its lack of diagnostic specificity, depressive conditions are thought to be best defined not by the few qualitative differences that appear in the profiles of some depressed individuals but by the pattern of an individual's performance along multiple continua. Extreme scores on several coexisting dimensions are thought to account for the apparent distinctiveness of depression and lead clinicians to conclude that depression is discontinuous with normal experience.

Flett, Vredenburg, and Krames (1997) explored the evidence for both the continuity and the discontinuity views of depression from the phenomenological, etiological, typological, and psychometric perspectives. They observed that, from most of these perspectives, an assumption of continuity of depressive experiences along a dimension of severity provided the best description of the correlates of depression. Relationships between dysfunctional traits and depression were similar for different subgroups of individuals whose depression varied in clinical severity. Support for a continuity view extends across research domains, from studies of social and interpersonal patterns of behavior among depressives to studies of immune system functioning and of other biological functional correlates of depression.

Flett et al. (1997) observed that the pattern of correlations among formal tests of depression has provided some support for the view of depression as a qualitative and categorical disorder that is separate from normal experiences. However, they assert that the disparity between this research and other sources of evidence can be attributed to problems with the way that tests used are constructed and administered. For example, tests are often developed in order to comply with diagnostic criteria rather than to measure normal variations among people. Thus, Flett et al. conclude that there is "mounting evidence of continuity" in the experience and expression of depression but urge theorists to remain open to the possibility that "there are certain aspects of depression that are indeed discontinuous" (p. 411). Flett et al.'s conclusions are very controversial, limited by the nature of their self-report methodology.

The conflicts between the views of depression would be resolved, at least in part, if one interpreted depression as being both a small collection of specific disorders and a symptom of general distress. Indeed, some authors have suggested such a view and have offered the interpretation that depression includes a variety of related disorders and symptoms, at least some of which are general correlates of distress rather than specific indicators of a given diagnostic entity. Yet, for all its potential for resolving the horns of a diagnostic dilemma, this interpretation is unlikely to resolve conflicts in the field.

Specificity and Sensitivity in the Diagnosis of Depression

The ability to distinguish the presence of subcategories of depression and to differentiate between depression and other forms of psychopathology is critical to determining whether depression is a single disorder, a multitude of related conditions, or a nonspecific response to stress. Research on depression, as we've noted, has been equivocal in its support for either a discontinuous or a continuous view of the relationship between pathological and normal behavior. Our reading of this literature suggests that (1) depressive subjective states are not strongly indicative of the presence of one or more syndromal disorders, and (2) subjective dysphoria is quite highly correlated with a variety of other negative affective states. Together, these findings suggest that subjective dysphoria is a nonspecific or general index of disturbance, rather than a specific one. It is a marker of general distress and unhappiness. Understanding this may provide a clue to why the categorical definitions of depression in traditional diagnoses (American Psychiatric Association, 1994) lack both sensitivity and specificity.

For example, after reviewing extensive literature, Dobson (1985) concluded that anxiety and depression reflect a common dysphoria and that the distinction between them is more clear conceptually than it is empirically. He found that the correlations among measures of *either* anxiety *or* depression were about the same as (sometimes even lower than) the correlations between measures of anxiety and measures of depression. While these latter correlations are stronger when both concepts—dysphoria and anxiety—are measured by self-report measures, clinical raters have been unable to distinguish between the two affective states (e.g., Downing & Rickels, 1974; Gersh & Fowles, 1979). Moreover, clinicians perform only slightly better than chance when they attempt to distinguish between individuals, using the formal diagnostic criteria for anxiety and for depressive disorders. Dobson concluded that individuals within these diagnostic groups were likely to manifest essentially equivalent levels and symptoms of persistent subjective dysphoria. When these studies have successfully distinguished between these diagnostic conditions, the distinguishing variable has virtually always been in the degree of dysphoria present, not in the level of some qualitative attribute or functional level. These findings suggest that anxiety and subjective depression are components of the same dimension, that there is no specific point at which one can identify the presence of a clinical syndrome or entity, and that severity is distributed normally in the population along this dimension of distress.

Drawing from a similar process of reasoning as that later was articulated by Wakefield (1992a, 1992b, 1993), Grove et al. (1987) attempted to resolve the various disparities between conceptualization of continuous and categorical distinctions and to provide a consolidated diagnostic framework by proposing that depressive spectrum disorders comprise both categorical and continuous features that are overlapping and invoked through a hierarchy of response thresholds. Accordingly, they identified two overlapping qualities, one represented as a categorical distinction and the other as a continuous dimension. The categorical features, they reason, reflect what they call "a nuclear depression." This designation is reminiscent of the endogenous or melancholic depression that is described in the diagnostic and clinical literature and that defines a disorder that is a qualitative departure from normal experience and is central to one's personal identity and daily functioning. In the next few paragraphs, we use the terms "nuclear" and "endogenous" interchangeably.

The definition of nuclear or endogenous depression is relatively independent of the level of dysphoria, the second dimension. Dysphoria, in contrast, is a general reflection or marker of distress, rather than a fundamental aspect of the patient's functioning. Thus, dysphoria may range from mild to severe, independent of whether a more fundamental depressive self-identity and life style are present. In the absence of a nuclear or endogenous lifestyle, dysphoria is taken to indicate the reaction of a person to life crises. Depression of this type is reasonably correlated with the presence of external events, with general life changes, and with the presence of stressors. It is a reactive condition, and it may coexist with other disorders. In contrast, when a condition includes both high levels of dysphoria and the presence of an endogenous or nuclear depressive life pattern, the dysphoria may be a secondary reaction to the depression itself or to other disorders.

Because it is a secondary rather than a nuclear aspect of one's functioning and because it reflects a general response to a host of variables, dysphoria may be a marker for the experience of general change in the system, the presence of disruption, and weakened efforts to cope with stressors. It is evoked by a number of environmental events and often is a precursor for the development of other stress-related symptoms and disorders, including nuclear or endogenous depression. Endogenous depression, in contrast to dysphoria, is discontinuously associated with severity, is associated with the presence of vegetative signs, has a high level of heritability, and is associated with a poor prognosis (Grove et al., 1987). The general symptoms of depression and, to a lesser extent, some of the more dysfunctional symptoms that define an endogenous condition are likely to be observable whenever individuals are experiencing long-standing dysphoria.

Dysphoria is thought to define the degree of "neurotic" or unrealistic internal conflict, while nuclear depression represents the degree to which the depression is a central aspect of one's self-definition or character. While the presence and the mean prevalence of vegetative signs are a general index of the presence of a categorical or endogenous depression, on a group basis they are also inexact indicators and do not reliably distinguish among specific individuals with nonendogenous diagnoses (e.g., Haslam & Beck, 1994; Young, Scheftner, Klerman, Andreasen, & Hirschfeld, 1986). Nor do they distinguish depression from other negative affective states. For example, anger and hostility have been found to correlate quite highly with measures of depressed affect (Lemaire & Clopton, 1981) and to coexist with depressive syndrome disorders (Biaggio & Godwin, 1987), extending further the conclusion that the subjective experience of depression may be a stress marker, rather than a specific disorder. Again, the incidence of dysphoria among subjects scoring high for anger is much higher than the incidence of anger among depressed patients (Biaggio & Godwin, 1987; Beutler, Engle, Daldrup, et al., 1991), confirming that depression, not anger, is a reasonable marker of stress. Such findings have led many researchers to conclude that subjective depression reflects a state of negative affectivity (Clark & Watson, 1991) and probably serves as a marker for the presence of threat and fear (Cooke, 1980).

While dysphoria and even vegetative signs (e.g., loss of appetite, low sexual drive, sleep disturbances) are as likely to appear among anxiety-disordered patients as they are among those diagnosed as having major depression, the reverse is not true. Anxiety symptoms are more specific to anxiety disorders than symptoms of depression are to depressive disorders. Ample demonstration of this conclusion is found in the higher overlapping comorbidity rates for depression within anxiety disorders (40 percent) than those for anxiety disorders within groups that have depression diagnoses (25 percent).

While neither subjective dysphoria nor clinical ratings are very specific to the presence of a depressive condition, it should be pointed out that clinical observations (e.g., vegetative signs and qualitative symptoms) are somewhat more specific to a diagnosis of depression. In turn, clinical observations of vegetative signs are rough markers that can grossly distinguish between two subtypes of depression—endogenous and nonendogenous (e.g., Dobson, 1985). Kendall, Hollon, Beck, Hammen, and Ingram (1987) have suggested that a categorical diagnosis of depressive disorder be reserved for those who have both subjective distress and discrete clinical signs of depression. They suggest that those who have dysphoria in the absence of vegetative signs be diagnosed as having a second subtype of depression. This recommendation is roughly consistent with the mixed findings obtained by Flett et al. (1997) and underwrites the belief of Kendall et al. (1987) that depressed groups can be distinguished both by clinical signs and symptoms and by such value-laden projections as differences in prognosis, functional harmfulness, and treatment response.

Research has attempted to compare those who manifest different patterns of relationship between their clinically observed states and their subjective reports. The comparison of greatest interest to research investigators is that between those who have both external and subjective symptoms of depression (true depressives) and those who lack either the subjective dysphoria or the external manifestations of clinical depression. Research comparisons of these groups, however, have not yielded consistent results.

On one side of the continuing debate, Coyne (1994) has concluded that true depressives can be identified and are different from those who lack certain factors in both demographic background and prognosis. He observed that those who have clinical manifestations of depression possess certain background and prognostic factors that are not highly correlated with subjective ratings of distress. For example, clinical signs are more highly correlated with the presence of a chronic course than is the severity of subjective distress, and both family and personal history are more likely to include reference to depression and loss (Coyne & Schwenk, 1997).

On the other hand, Flett et al. (1997) conclude that these clinical signs can be attributed to the interaction of several continuously distributed dimensions. Those with dysphoria differ from one another mainly as a function of two continuously distributed variables—the severity of the problem and its persistence over time. Since both of these dimensions are normally distributed in the general population, the authors conclude that clinical depression does not represent a disease entity that is qualitatively distinct and functionally different from normal experience. Similarly, Gotlib, Lewinsohn, and Seeley (1995) observe that the differences that distinguish those who present with clinical signs from those who present with subjective distress are not sufficient to warrant distinct categorical diagnoses. They point out that there are more similarities than differences in the background factors of both groups that have high levels of both subjective and clinical depression ("true depressives") and groups in which one or another of these qualities is low. The apparent similarities extend to background, presentation, treatment, and functioning.

The similarity between true depressives and those whose external and subjective symptom levels are inconsistent should not be surprising, since most of these comparisons focus exclusively on negative affectivity, cognitions, and expectations. The criteria tend to ignore whatever differential role positive affect plays as a distinguishing element among depressive disorders. The absence, consistency, reactivity, or quality of positive affectivity may distinguish between those with varying levels of depressive severity or those with varying levels of compliance with clinical signs. Nonetheless, it is clear from these debates that the presence of a diagnostic entity of depression or depression subtypes is far from being clearly established, a point to which we return later when we talk about some of the psychological, interpersonal, and biological markers of depression.

Depression and Comorbidity

Setting aside for a moment the debate about whether depression can or does represent a set of specific disorders, depression (and its diagnostic representations) is the most frequently diagnosed co-occurring condition with physical and medical illnesses (Maser, Weise, & Gwirtsman, 1995; Schulberg & McClelland, 1987). One or another depression-related diagnosis has been observed to co-occur among 80 percent of medical patients with certain conditions (Rodin & Voshart, 1986; Stevens, Merikangas, & Merikangas, 1995). Thus, it is no surprise that nearly all physicians identify depression as one of the most frequent problems encountered in their practices (Schulberg & McClelland, 1987).

However, reflecting the difficulty in detecting depression in primary-care settings, there is considerable disparity among the figures offered on the prevalence of depression, as either a clinical entity or a symptom. The inaccuracy with which depression is identified and the variability of depressive symptoms across different medical populations is compounded by the fact that neurovegetative symptoms associated with many physical disorders mirror the vegetative signs that index the presence of depression.

A review of the pattern of depressive symptoms that exist among various medical populations (e.g., Schulberg & McClelland, 1987) suggests the following:

1. Major depressive disorder may be the most common comorbidity seen in general medical practice.
2. The prevalence of major depression is probably higher among hospitalized medical patients than it is in the general population.
   a. Subjective dysphoria is moderate to high among at least one-third of hospitalized patients.
   b. Patients who present with depression along with somatic symptoms are often treated inappropriately and even harmfully.
   c. Estimates of the rate at which depression co-occurs with specified medical problems vary widely, even within any particular medical condition, and range from 9 percent to nearly 50 percent. This disparity suggests, again, the lack of specificity in the concept of depressive disorders.

To further confuse diagnosis, many believe that symptoms of depression can be masked by or represented in symptom patterns in which dysphoria is less obvious and pronounced. Indeed, conditions as diverse and apparently unrelated to each other as alcohol abuse (Winokur & Clayton, 1967) and chronic pain (Beutler, Engle, Oro'-Beutler, Daldrup, & Meredith, 1986) have been viewed as manifestations of underlying or masked depressive conditions. These disorders may be especially subject to inappropriate treatment, and individuals with these conditions are the highest users of medical services, make the most phone calls to physicians, are at highest risk for inappropriate hospitalization, and are candidates for the excessive use of diagnostic tests (Schulberg & McClelland, 1987).

Of course, because depression is frequently a comorbid condition with other psychopathologies, the individual who has a simple or unitary major depression is difficult to find in most clinical practices. Depression is a comorbid condition among 60 percent of general psychiatric patients and among more than 40 percent of those with anxiety disorders (Regier et al., 1988; Regier et al., 1993). Personality disorder is particularly prevalent among those with depression, accounting for from 30 percent to 70 percent of those who warrant Axis I depressive diagnoses (Farmer & Nelson-Gray, 1990).

ALICE AND HAROLD — CASE COMMENT

Viewing the cases only from a diagnostic perspective, and especially within the framework of Axis I, one would conclude that there are more similarities than differences between Alice and Harold in terms of depressive conditions. They both qualify for diagnoses of major depression, both have vegetative signs, and both have suicidal thoughts and impulses. Results of a structured diagnostic interview raise a question about borderline personality disorder for Alice and about a diagnosis of obsessive-compulsive personality disorder for Harold. The two depressive conditions also vary in chronicity, with Alice having a recurrent and long-standing condition and Harold evincing a single episode disorder. Both are similarly impaired, earning scores of "moderate severity" on the Global Assessment of Functioning rating of the DSM-IV. However, within the constraint of these multiaxial diagnostic symptoms, it is clear that categorical diagnoses alone do not capture the rich array of differences that exist in the complexity of their problems and personalities.

To be more specific, while Alice may qualify as having a nuclear or endogenous depression from this perspective, Harold probably does not. Moreover, while both patients are highly dysphoric, the source of Alice's dysphoria is likely to include self-definitions, a depressive lifestyle, and the experience of vegetative signs of the endogenous disorder. Harold, in contrast, is likely to experience dysphoria that is more closely correspondent with the downturn that his life has taken. It reflects an uncomplicated reaction to life stress, rather than a reaction to a depressive lifestyle or chronic interpersonal and social dysfunction. While Alice's depression is certainly affected by events such as losing her job, it also occurs as an overdetermined response to much more minor changes, and sometimes even in the absent of pervasive external events.

Both Alice and Harold exhibit unrealistic and neurotic qualities to which their dysphoria is a reaction. In the case of Alice, these reactive elements may be of less importance to her general functioning than the low level of interpersonal functioning and the central role that depression plays in her interpersonal life experiences. In an endogenous depression like Alices, one's life may become organized around merely controlling, reacting to, avoiding, and managing the depression itself. This is unlike the experience of reactive dysphoria. Harold, for example, may find depression to be a disruptive and intrusive influence, rather than an organizing feature of his daily existence. This lack of precision is observed in the cases of both Harold and Alice.

A more complete picture of the important differences between Alice and Harold can be obtained by looking closely at their distinguishing and separate histories than by studying their diagnoses or vegetative symptoms. We can see a number of dimensions on which they differ, and some of these may be related to how well different treatments work. In their separate histories and patterns, we can also see how value-based judgments of psychopathology might be differentially invoked. Aside from quantitative differences of intensity, there are qualitative differences in the way they relate to other people (e.g., impulsive versus ruminative) and in their prognoses. For example, Alice presented signs, based on the recurrent and long-standing nature of her condition, that may invoke a more value-laden reaction regarding the social destructiveness of her behavior than would be applied to Harold. Harold's condition, in turn, is likely to be more easily represented as dimensional; both the severity of his dysphoria and the likelihood of his being self-destructive may be more easily perceived as representing positions along a continuum than as conditions that are qualitatively different from common experience.

DISCUSSION

If viewed through the lens of cost, distinctiveness, and comorbidity, the failure of primary-care providers to accurately diagnose depression may be less a failure to recognize the presence of dysphoria than a failure to extract the qualitative symptoms that may overlap with the physical symptoms that are often a part of the depressive spectrum. If the depression is both long-standing and acute, as one might believe is true in the case of Alice, a primary-care provider may be distracted by the complexity of the problem and focus on the environmental and historical factors that are present, rather than on the indicators of a nuclear or endogenous depression.

Among people whose depression has many complex features, the indicators that the depression is part of a self-definition and lifestyle may become overshadowed by the intriguing complexity of the concomitant social and interpersonal events that have exacerbated the problem, and a clinician may therefore fail to diagnose the depression as a nuclear condition. To really differentiate endogenous from nonendogenous depression, however, it is likely that the clinician's focus must go beyond the presence of vegetative signs. The clinician must determine the degree to which the patient's life is organized around the act of being depressed. In the case of Alice, we have illustrated how work, family, self-perception, and even sexual activity can all be filtered through one's self-perception of being a depressed person. Depression can become a part of the patient's personal self-definition, seen not simply as a reaction to a threat to one's identity but as an integral part of that identity. Such patients have great difficulty imagining themselves without depression. Indeed, in such cases, the feeling of threat and behaviors of resistance may be most pronounced at the point that the patient considers the possibility of giving up the depressive image.

It should also be recalled that the complexity of depression is increased by the presence of personality patterns and disorders. In our examples, Alice was diagnosed as having a concomitant borderline personality disorder and had psychophysiological and psychological symptoms that had periodically generated separate diagnoses of migraine headache, irritable bowel syndrome, chronic pain, and alcohol abuse. Harold, on the other hand, had a probable Axis II diagnosis of obsessive-compulsive personality disorder to complement his Axis I diagnosis of major depression. However, he had no other complicating comorbidity.

Another indicator that Harold's problem was less fixed and chronic than Alice's is the fact that he had received a variety of previous diagnoses. For example, he had been diagnosed as having a generalized anxiety disorder by his primary physician and treated accordingly. He had also been diagnosed as having a situational disturbance with depression and anxiety. The greater complexity of Alice's dysfunction and disturbance seem to call for treatment decisions different from those applied to Harold. Before we can consider these implications further, however, it will be helpful to have a fuller understanding of the relationship between the experience and diagnosis of depression and other aspects of functioning, prognosis, and etiology. Understanding the influence of social roles and expectations on the evolution of depression, as well as the mechanisms of action that promote and induce depression, if understood, can provide some directions for planning treatment guidelines.

9 Concepts from Basic Research on Depression

The subjective experience of depression almost always includes dysphoria and dejection, feelings of emptiness, loss of hope, and feelings of helplessness. These are the experiences typically identified as depression in common parlance, as well. Within this experience, there are changes in thinking processes, but these are virtually always linked to subjective changes in mood. Thus, persistent negative thoughts, pessimism, sluggish problem solving, and general apathy coincide with depressed mood. Since the introduction of the DSM-III, however, there has been some disparity between these subjective experiences of depression and diagnostic definitions. Clinical depression comprises a range of symptoms, including but not limited to depressed mood. Loss of interest and pleasure in usual activities (anhedonia), weight change, change in sleep patterns, alteration of motor activity, fatigue, low self-regard, loss of concentration, and preoccupation with death and dying are among the symptoms that are used to diagnose the presence of depression.

On its face, the diagnostic spectrum includes a range of depressive disorders extending from various patterns of bipolar conditions, in which the defining features are mania and excitement rather than depression per se, to major depressive disorder, dysthymic disorder, and various "minor" depressions associated with transient environmental and physiological events. Variations along this spectrum are assumed to reflect not only differences in severity and duration but differences of pattern and etiology. Thus, the diagnostic groupings are considered, within the context of the DSM system, to be separate and distinctive diseases or conditions. In this assumption lies a good deal of controversy and disagreement.

A central focus of much of contemporary research on depression is determining how to best categorize and classify it and its many representations. Stated another way, the issue is this: "Is depression best understood as an experience that is qualitatively different from normal experience, or is it simply

231

distinguished from the common experiences of people by its severity and ex-
tremeness of symptoms?"

Over the past two decades, research on the nature of depression has been
focused either on identifying basic mechanisms that account for the development or maintenance of depression or on the development of various treatments and testing their effects and benefits. As a set of guidelines for systematic treatment selection, the concern of this book more heavily relies on the
latter type of research. It is beyond our scope to provide a comprehensive review of the many areas of basic psychopathological research that have occu-
pied the attention of investigators. There are, however, concepts and findings
that have come from basic research that have a direct bearing on questions of
clinical efficacy. It is important that clinicians understand these concepts and
the most salient of these conclusions. Accordingly, we summarize here a number of the findings from basic research that are most closely related to the
treatment models and methods that we discuss in later chapters.

These areas of investigation represent efforts to discover mechanisms of
action in depression and to determine the nature of depression relative to normal or usual experience. They can be roughly clustered into the following
groups: sex role factors, cognitive factors, interpersonal factors, and biological factors. We superficially consider some of the issues in each of these areas,
but our review is not intended to be either a critical or a comprehensive review of the issues and research in these areas.

MECHANISMS OF ACTION IN DEPRESSION

In the following sections, we begin the exploration of the nature of depression by identifying the aspects of depression that have been proposed as
causally related to the depressive experience, with special focus on sociosexual roles, cognitive, interpersonal, and biological contributions to vulnerability.

Sociosexual Role Mechanisms

It is common knowledge that there are sexual differences in the incidence and
manifestation of depression. The risk for depression for women is twice that
for men under even the best of conditions (Gotlib, 1993; Gotlib, Whiffen,
Mount, Milne, & Cordy, 1989; Hammen, 1997). The particular reasons why
women may be susceptible to depression are unclear but have been the focus
of considerable research. One possibility is that women simply are more able
to identify depressive states and are willing to report them, but these artifac-
tual interpretations cannot account for the wide disparity that exists between
men and women (Nolen-Hoeksema, 1987). More likely, cultural and hormonal variables that distinguish women from men may represent specific vulnerabilities for depression, and risk level may be activated by particular stres-

sors. Women, for example, are most susceptible to depression during times when hormonal levels are changing and unstable. Thus, during pregnancy, the prevalence rates of depression range as high as 80 percent in some demographic populations (Gotlib et al., 1989). Depressive states also are activated inordinately during premenstrual periods (Nolen-Hoeksema, 1987), during the second trimester of pregnancy, and during the post-partum period when hormonal changes are particularly great (Hobofoll, Ritter, Lavin, Hulsizer, & Cameron, 1995).

Moreover, analysis of the relative contributions of a number of different variables suggests that different patterns of relationships exist between psychosocial variables and depression at different points in the pregnancy and postpartum periods, indicating that specific causal mechanisms may be at work during these times among women (Gotlib et al., 1989). In spite of these interesting and suggestive correlations, there is a paucity of studies that have systematically controlled hormonal levels independently of depression. Thus, the causal relationship between hormonal levels and depression remains unclear (Nolen-Hoeksema, 1987).

Efforts to understand the role of sex in depression have suggested a number of other interesting possibilities, aside from hormonal balances. For example, some hypotheses suggest that differences in male and female social roles and expected behaviors make men and women differentially susceptible to depression and alcoholism. This hypothesis suggests that women's proclivity toward passivity and emotionality may make them at higher risk for depression than men. Conversely, this view proposes that the active stance of men, along with their intolerance for emotional arousal, accounts for their relative susceptibility to alcohol abuse as a means of insulating themselves against feelings. This viewpoint suggests that alcoholism is a functional equivalent of depression among men (e.g., Nolen-Hoeksema, 1987). Support for this hypothesis is equivocal, however. Instead, some research (e.g., Chevron, Quinlan, & Blatt, 1978) suggests that passivity and emotional access may be less reliable predictors of depression than simply the adoption of nontraditional sex-role behaviors, which may result in depression among both women and men.

An important area of research is the effect of family environments on men and women that differentially predispose them to depression. Early experiences of loss, particularly of parents and close family members, have been suggested as one factor that increases vulnerability to depression (Lloyd, 1980; Nelson, 1982), but this point is disputed in favor of a hypothesis that the quality of care and support during the bereavement period may be the critical variable (Bilfulco, Brown, & Harris, 1987). The quality of such support may indeed be different for boys and girls, thus establishing a differential vulnerability. Overprotecting (Gerlsma, Emmelkamp, & Arrindell, 1990) and controlling (Crook, Raskin, & Eliot, 1981) parental styles, both of which may be more often invoked when raising girls than boys, have been quite consistently related to the development of subsequent depression.

Not infrequently, the stresses of relating to a depressed individual may induce depression in other family members (e.g., Coyne, Kahn, & Gotlib, 1987). In turn, the risk imposed by these factors may be greatest for women because they are most seriously affected by the resultant loss of social support (e.g., Lewinsohn, Hoberman, & Rosenbaum, 1988). The multiple influence of life stressors on women, in particular, has been confirmed in a variety of studies, ranging from research on the the postpartum period among women (e.g., Gotlib, Whiffen, Wallace, & Mount, 1991) to those on the development of depression among unselected community samples of both sexes (e.g., Lewinsohn et al., 1988).

Trait-like variables, in addition to situational stress and past histories, may also moderate the effects of sociosexual roles to increase vulnerability to depression. For example, personality traits such as extroversion and neuroticism (Parker, 1980) or sociotrophy and self-criticism (Coyne & Whiffen, 1995) add to the effects of situational stress to affect the risk of depression among men and women. However, socioenvironmental factors associated with differential sexual responses may tell only part of the story. Warren and McEachren (1983), for example, estimated that sex (and age) contributed only 11 percent of the variance in predicting depression but that nondemographic psychosocial factors contributed an additional 28 percent to the efficiency of prediction. These findings suggest that, for the most part, while differential patterns of response among men and women may be predictors of depression, they must be considered within the context of cognitive, interpersonal, and other factors in establishing a patient's risk for depression.

Cognitive Factors in Depression

Research on correlates of dysphoria suggests that cognitive factors are very important in affecting mood, even beyond the role of life stressors. Lewinsohn et al. (1988), for example, found that depressogenic cognitions and automatic thoughts added even more and relatively independent variance to the prediction of depression level than the variables of sex and social support.

A large amount of research evidence has accumulated on the nature of cognitive mechanisms in determining depression as well as the more limited, subjective state of dysphoria. Because of its central role, even in the diagnosis of most depressive conditions, research on the contributors to persistent dysphoria bears consideration for understanding the nature of depression on a level nearly equal to that accorded to research on samples of those with diagnosed depression.

Studies of cognitive vulnerabilities have gone beyond considerations of dysphoric mood, and many studies have compared individuals with diagnosed depression both to nondepressed individuals and to those with diagnoses other than depression. Distinguishing psychological mechanisms that underlie depression have been sought in the nature of cognitive processes and structures, and in the form of interpersonal relationships established. In this chapter, we provide only a sampling of the type of research done on the nature of cognitive processes and restrict our review to those areas that have the most direct bearing on theories of treatment.

One important area of research has been the development of theories of depression vulnerability. There are several well-developed and clinically relevant theories that have driven cognitive research in its effort to understand the development of dysphoria. Two related theories bear on the broad domain that includes attributional processes. One of these is the theory of learned helplessness (e.g., Abramson, Seligman, & Teasdale, 1978; Hammen, 1987; Miller & Seligman, 1975; Miller & Norman, 1979), and the other is its cousin, the cognitive theory of depression developed by Beck (1967) and colleagues (Beck & Emery, 1985). This latter area of research focuses on the contribution of dysfunctional thoughts and schema to depressive affect and to depressive syndromes. In the first of these lines of theory-based research, attention is directed to how attributions of cause and blame are assigned and to the effects of these attributions both on levels of self-esteem and on problem-solving activities.

The learned helplessness model of depression proposes that self-attributions of weakness and inadequacy are among the consequences of maladaptive ways of perceiving and judging the sudden and radical reduction in the predictability or control of negative life events. These self-attributions are manifest as vulnerabilities both to the onset and to the recurrence of depression (Brewin, 1985; Gotlib, 1993; Miller & Norman, 1979).

The level of perceived helplessness in being able to predict and control negative events—what is typically called learned helplessness—is associated with depressed mood. Individuals who have an active, depressed mood tend to make internal, stable, and global attributions of negative events. They tend to see themselves as the cause and objects of blame for such events, while those who make external, situational, and specific judgments are not as depressed as their counterparts (e.g., Brewin, 1985; Eaves & Rush, 1984; Gong-Guy & Hammen, 1980; Harvey, 1981; Hummer & Hokanson, 1990; Raps, Peterson, Reinhard, Abramson, & Seligman, 1982).

The cognitive patterns that are associated with depressed mood do not always follow this precise pattern of being internal, stable, and global, however. For example, those who make external causal attributions of what are perceived to be global and stable qualities are also vulnerable to depression (e.g., Benassi, Sweeney, & Dufour, 1988; Harvey, 1981). These patterns not only are correlates of depressed mood but may be predictive of future moods, making them indices of depressive vulnerabilities (e.g., Golin, Sweeney, & Shaeffer, 1981; Hammen, Marks, Mayol, & deMayo, 1985). Moreover, these distorted cognitive patterns continue to be in evidence as residuals in both endogenous and nonendogenous depressive syndromes (e.g., Eaves & Rush, 1984; Hedlund & Rude, 1995).

Research findings do not suggest that the cognitive patterns that characterize those who have or who will develop depression are uniformly distorted and negatively biased. Indeed, some of the characteristic attributions associated with depression are more positive than those that characterize nondepressed groups. In some attributions, depressed individuals have a more accurate perception of their performance than nondepressed individuals (Colvin & Block, 1994; Taylor & Brown, 1994). Nondepressed individuals have been observed to overestimate the level of personal control they have in social situations, for example (Taylor & Brown, 1994); they also overestimate the importance of their roles in responding to stressful events (Coyne, Aldwin, & Lazarus, 1981). The greater accuracy demonstrated by depressed populations when assessing personal control compared to their nondepressed counterparts, is surprisingly persistent, even when experimental conditions ensure that personal control is in fact quite absent. This phenomenon has been called the "Illusion of Control" (Golin, Terrell, Weitz, & Drost, 1979, p. 454; Taylor & Brown, 1994, p. 21). The question of why these positive illusions should characterize nondepressed groups more than depressed ones has been hotly debated (Block & Colvin, 1994; Colvin & Block, 1994).

A second major area of research is closely related to the foregoing one but is less global in its objectives. Rather than attempting to develop a comprehensive theory, it focuses on isolated variables that place one at risk for depression or that distinguish those with depression from those who are not depressed. Most of the variables that have been under scrutiny in this line of research bear on aspects of cognitive function or process, rather than on the precise content of cognitions. They address primarily those variables that relate to the processes one uses to deal with stressful events.

A large body of research in this area, for example, has pursued the hypothesis that a negative processing and evaluation bias exists among depressed individuals to complement their tendency to attribute lower levels of personal self-control to themselves than nondepressed individuals do (e.g., Coyne & Gotlib, 1983). More specifically, Beck (1967; Beck, Rush, Shaw, & Emery, 1979) proposed that depression is characterized by generally negative biases in information processes, excessive performance demands, and negative expectations about the future, the present, and the self. This model proposes that depression is distinguishable from other conditions by the intensity of the associated negative evaluations and expectations of events. Unlike those of individuals with anxiety, for example, the negative perceptions of depressed individuals are dominantly self-focused, rather than situational, and reflect the presence of low self-judgments, negative appraisals, and internal attributions. In contrast, anxiety-driven biases are thought to emphasize fear and uncertainty about the outside world.

Research has confirmed that depressed individuals are distinguishable from nondepressed ones by their negative biases in information processing, by the intensity of their negative views, and expectations for future events (Beutler & Guest, 1989; Butler & Mathews, 1983; Kurtzman & Blehar, 1996). However, the proposed roles of negative self-evaluations and excessive expectations of self are less clear.

Negative self-views extend to schematic biases, as well as to attributions about specific events (Carver, LaVoie, Kuhl, & Ganellen, 1988; Ross, Mueller, & De La Torre, 1986; Strauman, 1989). Some evidence (e.g., Lewinsohn et al., 1988) suggests that depressogenic schemas and thoughts are implicated in the prediction of future depression and that negative attributional biases are at least weak predictors of the persistence (Dent & Teasdale, 1988) and the future occurrence (Lewinsohn et al., 1988; Rholes, Riskind, & Neville, 1985) of depression. Caution is still warranted in generalizing these findings, however. The nature of measurements and the structure of research designs leave it still uncertain which and how many of these cognitive patterns are simply additional symptoms of depression, rather than independent risk indicators (Gotlib & Cane, 1987; Silverman, Silverman, & Eardley, 1984).

Several lines of research indicate that studies of isolated variables may be inadequate to understand how depressive affect develops and is maintained. For example, while perfectionism, self-demands for performance and achievement, and exaggerated self-criticism are inconsistently related to level of dysphoric states when evaluated as separate and individual main effects (e.g., Carver & Ganellen, 1983; Carver et al., 1988; Kanfer & Zeiss, 1983; Persons, Miranda, & Perloff, 1991), several lines of research suggest that these variables may interact with one another in complex ways. The individual effects may be less important, therefore, than the interactive and combined effects of multiple risk variables. For example, internal demands for perfection and self-criticism, when coupled with high levels of achievement need, may be associated with depression, whereas the same patterns among those with low achievement drives may not be (Hewitt, Flett, & Ediger, 1996; Kanfer & Zeiss, 1983; Lewinsohn, Steinmetz, Larson, & Franklin, 1981).

Complexities such as the foregoing may also account for why there has been little evidence that levels of achievement drive and socially defined perfectionism, by themselves, consistently distinguish depressed from normal individuals (Carver & Ganellen, 1983; Hewitt et al., 1996). Some evidence indicates that depressogenic cognitions and putative indicators of risk of dysphoria are elevated only if one's level of achievement motive is high and when one is not afforded the opportunity to compensate for failure (Golin, Jarrett, Stewart, & Drayton, 1980). Sex-related roles also interact with achievement drives to account for differences in enduring levels of dysphoria. Among women, but not among men, for example, self-criticism may work to impede or facilitate drives for achievement, depending on levels of dependency (Coyne & Whiffen, 1995).

Still a third line of research involves the search for personality types associated with vulnerability to depression. Both cognitive theory and psychoanalytic theory have proposed that there are distinct, but somewhat similar, personality subtypes or classes of individuals that are particularly vulnerable to depression. Both theories propose that individuals who are socially dependent, including those with a tendency to look to others for self-definition, are more susceptible to depression than are autonomous and self-focused (including perfectionistic and self-critical) individuals (e.g., Coyne & Whiffen, 1995). While research has provided at least partial support for these hypotheses (e.g., Hammen, Ellicott, Gitlin, & Jamison, 1989; Klein, Harding, Taylor, & Dickstein, 1988), most interpretations of these variables is limited by conceptual and methodological shortcomings in the research that preclude causal interpretations. Several methodological issues in this research are raised by Coyne and Whiffen (1995), for example.

These authors point out that the likelihood of obtaining meaningful findings in studies of typologies and then interpretating them are limited by the tendency of investigators to see personality variables as distinct entities rather than dimensions. Likewise, they observe that the difficulty in measuring separately personality types and depressive symptoms themselves results in the emergence of method effects, the interpretation of spurious relationships that are likely to emerge among multicolinear variables. They argue that most of the (assumed) stable patient characteristics that have been studied are probably best described as continuous measures, although they are most often studied as if they were categorical. They further observe that common method variance overshadows and inhibits the emergence of evidence that personality and symptoms are distinctive and uncorrelated dimensions.

A fourth area of cognitive research that has been of interest is that of hopelessness. Hopelessness has been particularly implicated in the prediction of suicidal ideation, intent, and completion (e.g., Beck, Brown, Berchick, Stewart, & Steer, 1990; Beck, Kovacs, & Weissman, 1975; Beck, Steer, Beck, & Newman, 1993). Young, Fogg, Akiskal, and Maser (1996) have attempted to distinguish among various aspects of hopelessness, including baseline levels and characteristic rates of change (i.e., sensitivity). Using archival data from a large multisite study of depression, these authors demonstrated that baseline levels of hopelessness, but not sensitivity to change, were predictors of suicide. This continues to be a promising area of investigation and requires further differentiation among types of cognitive patterns associated with depression and its correlates.

As the foregoing indicates, the negative views and cognitive biases that have been found among depressed samples do not clearly distinguish the dysphoria associated with depressive syndromes from that associated with other psychiatric conditions (Hollon, Kendall, & Lumry, 1986; MacLeod & Byrne, 1996; Persons, Burns, Perloff, & Miranda, 1993). However, they do index and correlate the level of experienced dysphoria and the level of nonspecific stress, as noted earlier. It is the relative levels of positive (as opposed to negative) expectations and perceptions that may be the most important features that differentiate depressive syndromes from anxiety and consequences of general distress. MacLeod and Byrne (1996), for example, found that patients who qualified for various diagnoses could be distinguished from those who did not by the presence of negative biases and attributions. By the same token, they found that these negative biases and attributions distinguished between anxious patients and mixed groups of anxious and depressed patients, although without high levels of precision. That is, depressed and mixed patients all had negative views and expectations. However, groups of patients that had both anxiety and depressive symptoms were distinguished from anxious ones by their reduced expectations of positive events.

Research on positive and negative affectivity also is consistent with this latter view, finding that the distinctiveness of depression, when compared to anxiety-based conditions, is more a function of the absence of positive feelings than of the presence of negative ones (Clark & Watson, 1991). The negative affectivity and even the negative response and evaluation biases that are associated with depression appear to signal the presence of distress, rather than indicate a specific disorder (e.g., Clark & Watson, 1991; Watson, Clark, & Carey, 1988). In turn, this disposition toward negative perception and negative affectivity may constitute a general risk factor for the development of psychiatric disorder. Even more, suggestive evidence on normal samples suggests that the use of affective experience, rather than its codification, in problem solving may be associated with dysphoric symptoms (Anderson & Leitner, 1996).

Collectively, these findings indicate that, to the degree that depression can be seen as a qualitatively distinct disorder, it is what is *lacking* cognitively rather than what is present, that cements the distinction. The absence of positive biases in perceptions of control and expectations, along with the relative absence of positive affectivity, may be specific attributes of depression, while negativity may characterize many different diagnostic groups. Depressed individuals are distinghished from anxious ones by the apparent symptom of anhedonia—the failure to experience positive feelings when engaging in social behavior (Clark & Watson, 1991), at least as much as by the tendency to view themselves and the world negatively.

Interpersonal Mechanisms of Action in Depression

Depression does not occur in a vacuum. It is both a social and an interpersonal phenomenon, a cause and a consequence of interpersonal disturbance. The seeds of depression are often sown in the early attachment between mother and infant (Harlow & Suomi, 1974; Suomi, 1991) and subsequently are manifest both as infant depression and as disturbances of mood at later points in life. Insecurity of attachment during early childhood and even adolescence has been a particularly interesting area of research and one that suggests that qualitatively poor attachment or bonding increases children's vulnerability to later depression and perhaps to other types of psychopathology, as well (Ainsworth, 1989; Main, 1990). For example, comparative studies indicate that impaired attachment between infants and parents, particularly mothers, is manifest as disturbed relationships with parents among both adolescents (Kobak, Sudler, & Gamble, 1991) and adults (Rosenfarb, Becker, & Kahn, 1994). For example, Gaensbauer, Harmon, Cytryn, and McKnew (1984) determined that children of depressed mothers are unusually likely to have insecure attachments, with approximately double the rate expected in the normal population. The level of insecurity was especially high among those whose mothers had bipolar disorder. Insecure attachment further exacerbated the already high general risk of these children, but its impact was on their overall risk of depression, rather than on their specific risk of bipolar disorder.

The nonspecificity of the risk incurred by insecure early attachments is noted in other research. For example, Allen, Hauser, and Borman-Spurrell (1996), in an eleven-year posthospitalization follow-up of sixty-six upper-middle-class adolescents and matched controls, determined that the posthospitalization subjects continued to evidence the insecure attachments developed early. Moreover, level of attachment retrospectively rated as being present in childhood was related to a variety of adult problems, including criminal behavior, drug abuse, and other nondepression-specific pathologies. However, the secondary strategies adopted to cope with the effects of insecure early attachment may have more specific effects. Cole-Detke and Kobak (1996), for example, found that, while both eating disordered and depressed women were rated as having insecure early attachments, these later symptoms were associated with different methods of early coping. Depressed women were distinguished from eating disordered women by the use of hyperactive (vigilance and maximization of attachment behaviors) rather than of deactivating (diversion and minimization of attachment behaviors) coping strategies. In turn, each of these secondary attachment strategies is theoretically related to different types of parent-child relationship patterns (Cowan, Cohn, Cowan, & Pearson, 1996; Lyons-Ruth, 1996; Main & Weston, 1982)

The failure to develop a parental-child bond may be associated with the absence of nurturance, with the transmission of emotional ambivalence by parents, and with a variety of other disruptions to the parenting process (Gaensbauer et al., 1984). But, failing to bond is not the only factor that precipitates depression in children, nor is it the only risk factor for subsequent depression. Depression risk is also associated with interpersonal loss and bereavement (Beardslee, Schultz, & Selman, 1987; Speier, Sherak, Hirsch, & Cantwell, 1995) and with early parental models of depression (Beardslee, Bemporad, Keller, & Klerman, 1983; Hammen, 1988; Hammen, Adrian, & Hiroto, 1987; Zahn-Waxler, McKnew, Cummings, Davenport, & Radke-Yarrow, 1984).

Chaotic environments of all types during childhood may dispose one to adult depression. Parental drinking, mental illness, and violence (Kessler & Magee, 1993) may exacerbate the effects of disturbed parental attachment and may show up as depression among adults. These factors are particularly powerful because they also seem to impair the ability of the child or emerging adult to develop buffering and compensating social support systems to protect them from exacerbating stress (Armsden, McCauley, Greenberg, & Burke, 1990; Daniels & Moos, 1990; Hammen & Rudolph, 1996).

Not only does physical, sexual, or emotional abuse induce a risk for subsequent depression, as one might expect, but those with a history of these conditions are prone to chronic and enduring disturbances when they begin to emerge (Bifulco, Brown, & Adler, 1991; Brown & Anderson, 1991).

Depression not only arises from disruption but may itself create an unstable environment for the patient. As adults, depression impairs both the social functioning and the social competence of the patients (e.g., Gotlib & Lee, 1989; Lewinsohn, Mischel, Chaplin, & Barton, 1980) and negatively impacts the functioning and the feelings of marital partners and significant others (e.g., Gurtman, Martin, & Hintzman, 1990; Schmaling & Jacobson, 1990). Depression is associated with enduring difficulties in relationship skills and in the development of intimacy (Coryell et al., 1993). Marriages in which one partner is depressed are characterized by hostility and negative affectivity (Gotlib & Hammen, 1992; Gotlib & Whiffen, 1989). Withdrawal and rejection by marital partners and other significant figures often follows the onset of depression (Coyne, 1976). However, if one is able to develop a stable marital relationship, it seems to provide a buffer against further depressive episodes (Gotlib & Hammen, 1992; Hooley & Teasdale, 1989).

Depression negatively impacts even the feelings and responses of casual acquaintances toward the depressed patient (Gotlib & Robinson, 1982). Thus, depression affects the way that the depressed person both perceives others and is perceived by them (e.g., Gara et al., 1993; Kowalik & Gotlib, 1987; Lewinsohn et al., 1980). Such individuals don't invite approach responses from others, are difficult for others to relate to, and make demands on the relationship that precipitate depression in others. Moreover, the impaired social functioning of depressed individuals persists, at a reduced level, even after the depression itself dissipates (Gotlib & Lee, 1989).

It is no surprise, considering these factors, that depression is transmitted from generation to generation. Depressed parents are likely to raise depressed children. Infants of depressed mothers are delayed in their emotional and language development (Whiffen & Gotlib, 1989). Young children manifest these disturbances as difficulties in emotional regulation, aggressiveness, difficulties with peers (e.g., Zahn-Waxler, Cummings, Iannoti, & Radke-Yarrow, 1984), and low academic performance (e.g., Anderson & Hammen, 1993). The cycle of depression is complete with the observation that infants and children of depressed mothers have difficulty establishing parental attachment (DeMulder & Radke-Yarrow, 1991) and are then prone to depression themselves (see review by Hammen, 1997).

For all its effects in disposing a child to depression, parental depression (e.g., Cowan et al., 1996) has a stronger effect as a risk factor for all types of emotional disorders. Parental depression clearly increases the risk of receiving any of a number of psychiatric diagnoses in adulthood, for example, as well as of receiving any one of the many depressive spectrum diagnoses (e.g., Beardslee et al., 1983; Goodman, 1987). Moreover, it appears that a chronic pattern of depressive symptoms contributes more to the prediction of future depression than does the emotional stress of repeated acute episodes (Downey & Coyne, 1990).

Beyond the cycle of transgenerational transmission, other disturbances are noted among depressed patients. The positive perceptual and attributional biases that we have noted distinguishes normals from depressed individuals is also noted in interpersonal ratings. Normals tend to exaggerate their level of self-rated social skill and competence relative to the levels they judge to be present among others in their environments. In contrast, the self-ratings of skill and competence made by depressed individuals are much more consistent with the judgments made of them by others (Lewinsohn, Mischel, et al., 1980). This finding may index a particularly insidious and critical issue, since the interpersonally consistent self-judgments that depressed individuals make of themselves come at a time when the ratings of others are likely to be most negative (Belsher & Costello, 1991; Segrin & Dillard, 1992). They also come at a time when patients themselves are at a low ebb of achievement (c.f. Lewinsohn, Mischel, et al., 1980) and are less assertive and less social than they would be in their nondepressed states (Sanchez & Lewinsohn, 1980). Thus, the negative self-perceptions among the depressed may be accurate partly because their social competencies have fallen to a disturbingly low level. That is, depressed patients' competencies may have sunk to a level that coincides with their self-views and therefore mirror the verbal and hopeless judgments made by those who associate with them (Belsher & Costello, 1991). This pattern may, in fact, produce an irrevocable and self-reinforcing cycle of depression in which negative self-views are reinforced by others, perpetuating the condition.

Depression, even among adults, is precipitated or exacerbated by situational stressors (Monroe, Thase, & Simons, 1992) and, in particular, by the responses of others in one's environment. The effect is especially strong when these latter responses replicate early disposing experiences (Coyne, 1976; Hooley & Teasdale, 1989; Keitner et al., 1995). Yet, the nature of the interpersonal transmission and reinforcement of depression, and the nature of the causal relationships between depression and the reactions of others, are more complex than is indicated by the foregoing analysis. Some (e.g., Coyne, 1976), for example, have proposed that depressed individuals may attempt to elicit support and empathy from others by exaggerating their behavior out of desperation, earning, thereby, self-reinforcing, negative interpersonal feedback. They may be perceived as manipulative (Gurtman, Martin, & Hintzman, 1990; Sacco, Milana, & Dunn, 1988) and therefore, may elicit hostility and rejection from others, reinforcing the depression, as a consequence.

While persuasive, the foregoing patterns have been defined largely on the basis of correlational research. While correlational data suggest that depression provokes significant others to respond with overt anger and decreased social support, the causal chain of events has been difficult to confirm, and there have been some contradictory findings (e.g., Belsher & Costello, 1991; McNiel, Arkowitz, & Pritchard, 1987). However, meta-analytic reviews of this literature confirm the correlational patterns (e.g., Segrin & Dillard, 1992). These results have generally supported the presence of increased anger, withdrawal, and negativity associated with depression. Thus, depression may evoke rejection from others and, at least under certain conditions, instill a negative and angry mood in them.

The causal chain of events between disruption in relationships and depression is even less clear among marital and intimate partners. While some research suggests an indirect and complex relationship between marital disruption and depression (Burns, Sayers, & Moras, 1994), longitudinal research on marital couples (e.g., Ulrich-Jakubowski, Russell, & O'Hara, 1988) suggests that the marital disruption noted among couples with a depressed member may be a consequence, rather than a cause, of depressive communication patterns. That is, a majority of those with depression may be provoked to affective disturbance by disruptions or threatened ruptures in intimate relationships.

Biological Mechanisms in Depression

Biological views of depression are based on the assumption that the cyclical and vegetative manifestations of depression are indicative of a true, underlying dysfunction in some aspect of neuroregulatory structures (e.g., Gold, Goodwin, & Ghrousos, 1988a; Mann & Kupfer, 1993a, 1993b; Schatzberg et al., 1989).

Research directed at this possibility has sought to distinguish depression from other disorders by the identification of biological markers (e.g., Heller, Etienne, & Miller, 1995), as well as to identify separate and different biological mechanisms of action in patients with different subtypes of depression. Distinguishing mechanisms of action have been sought within a wide array of physiological systems, including genetic and family background, brain chemistry, hormonal regulation, and diurnal rhythmic patterns associated with sleep and wakefulness. Unfortunately, with the possible exception of some genetic studies, studies in this area are largely correlational, offering little direct evidence of causal links between these variables and depression.

Genetic Mechanisms

Comparisons of monozygotic and dizygotic twins, raised together and apart, are the most direct way of assessing genetic components in psychopathology (e.g., DiLalla, Carey, Gottesman, & Bouchard, 1996; DiLalla & Gottesman, 1995; Gold et al., 1988a). Children of parents who are schizophrenic or alcoholic, for example, are found to be much more likely to develop these same conditions than are other children, even when they have been raised apart from their disturbed parents.

Among the affective disorders, the clearest indication of specific genetic transmission is in the development of manic episodes and bipolar disorder (Kocsis, 1993; Sevy, Mendlewicz, & Mendelbaum, 1995). There is less but suggestive evidence that family background and genetic factors are involved in the development of chronic non-bipolar disorder and depressive temperaments and symptoms, whether or not these develop into formal depressive syndromes and disorders. For most of the depressive spectrum disorders, however, genetic studies reveal that heredity presents more of a general than a specific risk. Even the limited data available from twin studies have found little evidence for specificity in the heredity of depression (Kendler, Neale, Kessler, Heath, & Eaves, 1992). Such data contradict the supposition that depression is a categorically distinct disorder and that it is discontinuous with normal experience.

Discussing the increased vulnerabilities to depression of the children of depressed adults, for example, Downey and Coyne (1990) point out that twin studies fail to reveal consistent evidence of depression-specific risk, although the risk of psychopathology generally appears to be increased. For example, having a bipolar or a unipolar depressed parent fails to predict which specific type of depression the child will ultimately develop. Parental depression contributes to general affectivity and the likelihood of a general affective diagnosis but contributes little to differential predictions of supposedly genetically linked bipolar disorder (Downey & Coyne, 1990). Cadoret and colleagues (Cadoret, 1983; Cadoret, O'Gorman, Heywood, & Troughton, 1985) suggest that if genetic factors offer a specific risk for depression, the link is not observable during childhood and is not manifested directly. Parenting patterns that result in insecure attachments may serve as mediators that activate whatever genetic factors are present to become revealed in adult depression (Beardslee et al., 1983).

Nonetheless, the role of genetic transmission cannot be overlooked. Heritability indices for bipolar disorder average in the neighborhood of .70 (albeit with wide variability from study to study), a figure that is significantly higher than that for non-bipolar depression (Sevy et al., 1995). Taking the prevalence figures discussed earlier in this chapter, this translates to a lifetime probability of about 24 percent for having a diagnosable depressive spectrum disorder if one has a positive history, a figure that is relatively consistent with the estimate of 30 percent provided by Sevy et al. (1995). This figure also means that approximately 70 percent of individuals with a conducive genetic history fail to develop an affective disorder, presumably because they are not exposed to a conducive stress factor in the environment.

Heritability indices are less obvious and more complicated in the case of major depression and chronic dysphoria. In the absence of supportive twin studies, the evidence that non-bipolar depression is correlated with a positive family history of depression suggests only a general familial vulnerability, rather than a specific genetic transmission process. Environmental as well as complex genetic and temperamental factors may account for this correlation. For example, few would argue that being Catholic or owning a bicycle is a genetic trait, but each is probably strongly associated with family history.

Nonetheless, it is notable that incidence rates of chronic non-bipolar depression (dysthymic disorder), which is taken as an index of a depressive temperament, is much higher among those who have a family history of affective disturbance than among those who do not. The presence and the magnitude of this correlation are both (relatively) independent of the type of depression presented by the family and vary as a function of the nature of the depressive condition that is manifested by the patient. Thus, the rates of positive family history are widely variable, ranging from approximately 6 percent to nearly 80 percent. To understand these figures, one must contrast these rates with those that estimate the heritability of dysphoria outside of specific diagnoses. In comparison of monozygotic and dizygotic twins, reared apart and assuming no overlapping environmental forces, DiLalla et al. (1996) found heritability rates for depressive symptoms among monozygotic twins to be from .31 to .48, compared to .60 for anxiety symptoms. The corresponding figures for anxiety symptoms were .13 and .14 for subjective depression and anxiety, respectively, among dizygotic twins. While these figures confirm the heritability of temperaments, when compared to the foregoing, they also suggest that general risk of diagnostic severity is increased by a factor of nearly two by factors other than genetics.

The general heritability of affective disturbance is indicated by the presence of varying levels of relationship between patient diagnosis and the particular disorder that previously characterized his or her family members. Akiskal, King, Rosenthal, Robinson, and Scott-Strauss (1981), for example, demonstrated that those with nondepressive character disorders had the lowest probability of a positive family history of depression (6 percent), while those with subaffective (dysphoric) symptoms of depression (65 percent) and those with chronic unipolar depression (47 percent) had the highest rates of positive family histories of some type of depression. Indeed, among first-order relatives, some investigators maintain that the transmission of both unipolar depression (e.g., Gold et al., 1988a,b) and anxiety disorders (e.g., Kendler et al., 1992) is direct, that is, that major depression begets major depression; dysthymia begets dysthymia, generalized anxiety disorder begets generalized anxiety disorder, and so forth.

The evidence for this degree of specificity in either anxiety or depression is contradictory and generally weak, however, and more so for depressive than for anxiety disorders (Thase & Howland, 1995). For example, Klein, Taylor, Kickstein, and Harding (1988) found that patients with any of a variety of non-bipolar disorders were likely to have a family history that was characterized by any of a variety of depressive conditions. Family histories of major depression (54%) and chronic non-bipolar dysthymia and unipolar depression (78%) were the most likely conditions associated with the subsequent development of chronic dysthymia among non-bipolar patients. Similarly, Kendler et al. (1992) found that both anxiety and depression share a common family risk factor for developing a psychiatric disorder of some kind but not for developing a specific anxiety of depressive condition.

Apparently, depression of any type serves as a risk factor for almost any subsequent depressive diagnosis. While genetic history is relevant, it seems to index a general risk of being dysphoric, rather than a specific risk for a specific subtype of depression.

Neurotransmitter Functioning and Brain Chemistry

The major focus of research on brain chemistry has focused either on the action of monoamines in neurotransmission or on cholinergic-adrenergic balance during neurochemical regulation of nerve impulses. Research has been extensive on monoamine regulation, with special emphasis on disturbances of neurotransmission. The transmitter monoamines, norepinephrine (NE), serotonin (5-HT), and dopamine (DA), have attracted the most attention. Disturbances of neurotransmission may occur because of a process that limits the availability of one or more of these neurotransmitters at the presynaptic site, a reduced or increased transmission rate across the synapses, or an increased or decreased number of receptors either presynaptically or post-synaptically (Thase & Howland, 1995). Studies of neurotransmission have found many correlates of depression in the mechanisms that release transmitter substances and in the reuptake processes that remove and replace these substances at the presynaptic site after neurotransmission.

The catecholamine hypothesis proposes that depression may arise from a functional deficit of NE at key centers of action in the brain. It is thought that these functions reflect an excess (accelerated production or use) of some neurotransmitters at some sites and an insufficient availability (perhaps because of a reduction in the number of available receptor sites) at other sites. Noradrenergic transmitters have received a good deal of attention in biological research because of the role that both deficient and excess NE at the synaptic site seems to play in affect moderation. For example, stimulation of the ventral lateral tegmentum and locus ceruleus activates the release and production of NE and is correlated with the experiences of sadness, anxiety, agitation, loss of concentration, and some of the vegetative signs and intense anguish that are associated with endogenous depression. Conversely, blocking the production of NE is associated with loss of energy, anhedonia, and other vegetative signs (Cooper, Bloom, & Roth, 1991; Thayer, 1989).

Inspecting the products of noradrenergic activity that takes place in the central nervous system (CNS) has been a favorite focus of research because one of the major metabolites of NE, 3-methoxy-4-hydroxyphenyl-glycol (MHPG), is relatively easily extracted from plasma, urine, and cerebral spinal fluid (CSF) samples. Originally, it was thought that MHPG in body fluids was a relatively direct index of brain chemistry, but subsequent research demonstrated that both plasma and urine levels of MHPG were affected by factors other than NE-moderated synaptic transmission in the CNS. Only about 30 percent of MHPG production can be attributed to CNS activity (Potter, Grossman, & Rudorfer, 1993), the remainder coming from sympathetic nervous system (SNS) activity and state-reactive responses in peripheral nerve activity.

In spite of these contaminants to assessing levels, research has demonstrated that the MHPG concentrations in urine, plasma, and cerebral spinal fluid are lower among bipolar patients than among normals, as would be expected (e.g., Schatzberg et al., 1989; Schildkraut, 1982). Moreover, MHPG levels have been shown to correlate longitudinally with the dissipation of depressive symptoms among bipolar patients (Potter, Grossman, & Rudorfer, 1993) and to reverse with the onset of mania (Schildkraut, 1982).

However, the data are much less clear among non-bipolar depressives, with many contradictions among the findings. This point is suggested by the failure to establish a clear causal link between causal NE activity and depressive states and traits. As many as 25 percent of non-bipolar depressed patients have an unusually low level of MHPG output in urine, and these individuals may be particularly responsive to antidepressants that block NE uptake (e.g., Maas et al., 1982; Davis et al., 1988). But, these findings are far from consistent (e.g., Potter et al, 1993), with many studies finding normal levels of MHPG among those diagnosed with major depression. Some studies have even found evidence for hyperactivation of MHPG among non-unipolar endogenous patients compared to normals (e.g., Davis et al., 1988; Maas et al., 1987) and suggest that tricyclic action includes decreasing the firing rate of neurons in the locus ceruleus (Gold et al., 1988a). The relationship of NE transmission and depression is very complex, even bimodal, with either high or low NE activity being associated with somewhat different depressive symptoms.

Serotonin (5-HT) also has received a significant amount of attention in biological research, particularly with the development of SSRIs. Secretion sites for serotonin are in the midbrain, upper brain stem (Cooper et al., 1991), and medulla oblongata (Malone & Mann, 1993). Ascending linkages are extended from these sites to the limbic structures and other mid-brain structures that are implicated in the control of emotion and appetite. These sites include the thalamus, hypothalamus, amygdala, and hippocampus. There are also descending extensions to the spinal cord, and these affect both sensory and motor functions. Dysfunctions of the serotonergic system are involved in many different psychological disturbances in addition to depression, and it is still unclear if reduced function in this type of neuroregulation represents a general or a specific factor in depression (Malone & Mann, 1993).

Serotonin has been particularly implicated in the control of rhythmic activities such as sleep-wake cycles, sleep architecture, and appetite regulation (Depue & Spoont, 1986). Receptor mechanisms for 5-HT are highly differentiated, making the direct assessment of serotonin activity at synaptic sites very complex. Dysfunctions and variations of serotonin levels are indexed by changes in blood platelets, plasma, and CSF, but these indicators often do not allow an easy determination of whether the values arise from inhibited production or excessive use at the CNS sites. Likewise, assays of substrates do not distinguish between trait and state reactions, making it difficult to assign causal meaning to the observed patterns (Malone & Mann, 1993). For example, Amsterdam, Fawcett, Quitkin, et al. (1997) have confirmed an unexpectedly low relationship between blood concentrations of selective serotonin reuptake inhibitors (SSRIs) and changes in mood among those diagnosed with major depression. If selective serotonin uptake is in fact a major factor in inducing changes in mood, then this relationship should be relatively high. The failure to confirm such expected relationships provides further indication of the lack of distinctiveness among non-bipolar disorders as well as evidence of the unreliability of measurement.

Reductions in the net turnover of serotonin at synaptic sites in the brain have been associated with disturbances of appetites related to food and sexual expression, as well as to increases in violent and suicidal impulses (e.g., Malone & Mann, 1993). Most of the support for the serotonin depletion hypothesis in depression, however, arises from treatment studies, rather than from basic psychopathological research. This is a hazardous and conceptually inconsistent way to demonstrate mechanisms of action, given the complex and often contradictory action of synthetically derived pharmacological agents and the difficulty of assessing serotonin depletion directly. Some post-mortem studies have supplemented findings from treatment studies, however, and lend some credence to the findings that reduced 5-HT production and availability are correlated with suicide risk. Again, the failure to find a consistent relationship between SSRI concentrations in the blood and mood changes remains unexplained (e.g., Amsterdam et al., 1997).

Several general, albeit tentative, conclusions, can be extracted from the literature on serotonin (see Delgado et al., 1990; Malone & Mann, 1993; Miller et al., 1992). They include the following points:

1. 5-HT substrates are not directly increased through antidepressant use, suggesting that serotonergic mechanisms of action are more complex than previously thought.
2. Research use of serotonin agonists generally confirms that 5-HT potentiation is increased by antidepressants and is correlated with changes in clinical symptoms; depletion of 5-HT through dietary restriction tends to precipitate recurrence of depressive symptoms.
3. A distinguishable subgroup of patients who are characterized by low levels of presynaptic 5-HT production may be at especially high risk for violent suicide.
4. Both increased cortisol responses and increased availability of serotonergic receptors in the brain stem may be correlated with suicide attempts.

A favored method of studying the role of serotonin has been through measurements of the ingestion and metabolism of tryptophan, a potentiator of 5-HT. The possibility of ingesting synthetic tryptophan and thereby increasing the availability of 5-HT has, from time to time, caught the imagination of the public. Thus, there are popular diets that include the widespread use of L-tryptophan and other preparations as a treatment for sleep problems and mood disorders. There is some support for the value of dietary regulation of this sort. For example, a tryptophan-deficient diet seems to increase vulnerability to relapse among treated patients, but, conversely, the direct effect of tryptophan ingestion on mood and especially depression remains uncertain (Malone & Mann, 1993).

Still a third neurochemical brain activator is dopamine (DA). Like 5-HT and NE, DA has been the focus of many theories about depression. The effect of DA is largely in regulation of involuntary motor behaviors. Its deficiency in Parkinson's Disease is well known, for example, and is the attributed cause for the uncoordinated and shuffling gait and waxy facial expressions that are associated with this condition. DA unavailability (along with serotonin deficiency) is also implicated in diminished goal-directed activity and with compromised efficiency in the performance of higher-order cognitive tasks (Spoont, 1992).

As with other neurotransmitters, a level of DA that is below optimal and usual levels is generally found to be correlated with the severe motoric retardation, loss of appetite and libido, reduced motivation, and lack of concentration (Thase & Howland, 1995). The findings and frequent (but sometimes complex) correlation among DA, NE, and 5-HT levels suggest a coordinated function of these neurotransmitters.

Among the most meaningful and interesting findings related to dopinergic activity, the following stand out:

1. Antidepressant treatment generally increases DA presynaptic receptor sensitivity.
2. Infusion of DA agonists generally is associated with a reduction of depressive symptoms.
3. Decreased DA production accompanies the initiation of a learned helplessness paradigm in animal studies.

Collectively, these findings suggest that a relationship exists between either reduced DA production or increased DA use and vegetative signs and symptoms of depression (Thase & Howland, 1995). Moreover, there is research evidence that in severe depression—whether endogenous, psychotic, or bipolar—there is an associated decrease in the level of activity in those CNS regions that are highly innervated by DA production centers, and this reduction of activity distinguishes these groups from normals (Drevets et al., 1992).

Of particular interest are animal studies that have found that DA activity goes down following the instigation of a learned helplessness paradigm, in which previously reinforced animals are subjected to unpredictable, aversive contingencies (e.g., Healy & Williams, 1988; Wilner, Golembiowski, Klimer, & Muscat, 1991). Particular vegetative signs, notably anhedonia, have been attributed to the interaction of helplessness induction and dopamine depletion.

Ultimately, studies of single-transmitter actions are likely to be inadequate to offer a comprehensive understanding of depression (e.g., Gold et al., 1988a). Studies of cholinergic tone—the balance between systems that produces, inhibits, and restores neurotransmitters—as opposed to studies that focus on isolated activities of single monoamine transmitters, have also lent some understanding to depression. Cholinergic tone reflects the balance between the adrenergic activities of monoamine transmitters and the antagonistic or inhibitory activity of acetylcholine (ACh) and gamma-aminobutyric acid (GABA). That is, it describes the tension and the relative balance that exist between neurotransmitters and their inhibitory agents. Typically, as one may assume, the relationship between these functions is reciprocal (Thase & Howland, 1995). This line of research demonstrates that the *relative* as well as the *absolute* availability of monoamine neurotransmitters is associated with depressive symptom production. The relative availability of neurotransmitters may be facilitated, for example, by increasing the availability of ACh or GABA and is associated with motoric retardation, loss of energy, and other vegetative signs. These signs of depression remain relatively constant, regardless of how the balance is maintained.

Methods of adjusting transmitter availability include (1) reducing production directly by using agonistic agents to suppress production at the synaptic site, (2) inhibiting their neurochemical action by altering the levels of cholinesterase, the substance that removes expended monoamines at the synaptic site, or (3) increasing availability of ACh and GABA through the use of cholinergic agonists (Dube, 1993; Gold et al., 1988a; Thase & Howland, 1995; Thase & Kupfer, 1996). This last method inhibits the influence of monoamines by shifting the balance toward cholinergic activity.

The preponderance of research on cholinergic tone has suggested that depression is associated with an overactive or sensitized cholinergic system, a viewpoint that has been referred to as "cholinergic overdrive" (e.g, Janowsky, Risch, & Gillin, 1983). This hypothesis considers depression and mania to be opposite ends of the same spectrum and assumes that both are responsive to the cholinergic-adrenergic balance. Indeed, research lends some support to this viewpoint, finding that reduced cholinergic activity is associated with a reduction in the severity or a suspension of manic symptoms, as well as reduced depressive symptoms (Janowsky et al., 1983).

Collectively, research on neurotransmitters and brain chemistry confirms that a variety of coordinated mechanisms may be at work in depression. A comprehensive understanding of depression, even at the biological level, must account for both state reactions that stem from acute changes in biology (e.g., Veleber & Templer, 1994) and trait-like bodily functions. At the level of neural biochemistry, the foregoing findings suggest that depressive traits may be associated with:

1. Nonavailability of one or another neurotransmitters, at the point of neural transmission
2. Reduced efficiency of the mechanism that removes the neurotransmitter once it is expended
3. An excess or a deficiency in the number of receptors in the receiving nerve, reducing the ability of the various neurotransmitters to build a bridge.

These relationships are not simple, however. Dube's (1993) summary of research concludes that the available evidence lends further support to the conclusion that the simple dichotomy of depression as either psychological or biological is too simplistic and reaffirms the observation that depression reactions are difficult to distinguish from generalized stress patterns at the level of brain chemistry. Even those who have an ardent commitment to identifying biological disease equivalents for depression (e.g., Gold et al., 1988a) acknowledge that no markers are yet available and that it is still uncertain whether depression is a single pathophysiological process or a group of identifiable and related disorders. Moreover, causal relations among depression, stress, and biological correlates are still uncertain (Thase & Howland, 1995; Thase & Kupfer, 1996).

Hormonal Regulation

The role of the endocrine system in governing mood and affect has long been recognized. The roles of estrogen and progesterone have been of particular concern, given the increased risk experienced by women (e.g., Nolen-Hoeksema, 1987). Other hormones have also received attention, however, especially with respect to the functions of the thyroid, parathyroid, and pituitary glands.

Many hormones that are mediated through the hypothalamus are implicated in sleep, appetite, libido, and other functions that are affected by depression (Gold et al., 1988b). Moreover, regulation of these hormones is governed by the monaminergic and cholinergic neurons that, as we have seen, have also been implicated in depression. Finally, the observed relationship among the administration of either 5-HT potentiator (e.g., tryptophan) or uptake inhibitors (e.g., fenfluramine) and the production of prolactin has further stimulated interest in the role of neuroendocrine functions in depression. One of the most critical and specific findings may be the observation that 5-HT-stimulated prolactin production may be correlated with suicidal impulses and gestures (e.g., Mann, 1991).

The predominance of hypercorticosolism among depressed samples has stimulated the most attention in hormonal research. Cortisol is released in pulsating bursts from the adrenal cortex, following a chain of reactions distally initiated by corticotrophin-releasing hormone (CRH), a hypothalamic peptide, that in turns stimulates the release of adrenocorticotropic hormone (ACTH) from the hypothalamic-pituitary-adrenal (HPA) axis. This chain of events, ending with the development of vegetative symptoms of depression, can be initiated by the intracerebral injection of CRH (Gold et al., 1988b).

Increased levels of cortisol among depressed individuals have long been observed but have often been thought to be a normal response to stress. More recently, the work of Carroll and colleagues (Carroll, 1982, 1991; Carroll, Curtis, & Mendels, 1976) has suggested the possibility that a more specific process is at work. In normal reactions to stress, following the sudden burst-like release of cortisol, the release of ACTH is inhibited for a period of several hours. This process works to reduce the release of more cortisol.

Carroll (1938; 1991) proposed that the integrity of the rapid feedback inhibition process of HPA is compromised in those with depression. That is, he proposed that the process of turning off or preventing the release of ACTH during and following state reactions is impaired. Thus, he reasoned that one should be able to observe continuing release of ACTH and cortisol following a cortisol burst, in depressed people that exceeds that observed among non-depressed individuals. The dexamethasone suppression test (DST) derived from this work and has been the subject of intensive study as a possible specific indicator and marker for diagnosing depression. In this test, a synthetic glucocorticoid is ingested and cortisol levels are monitored over the subsequent twenty-four-hour period. Carroll and others (e.g., Holsboer, 1992) have observed that depressed groups do, indeed, fail to suppress subsequent cortisol secretion. Close to 50 percent of those individuals who present with severe depression and approximately 20 percent of those with mild depression manifest the expected nonsuppression of cortisol.

While promising initially, the DST procedure lacks specificity and sensitivity, and this has cast the procedure into disrepute as a diagnostic test (Gold et al., 1988b). Its interest remains historical, with few groups actively studying it as a marker for depression. While DST may serve as a rough predictor of the patient's responsivity to pharmacotherapy (Corbishley et al., 1990), wide variations and unstable values make this index a poor predictor either of depressogenic psychological patterns (e.g., Zimmerman, Coryell, & Corenthal, 1984) or of treatment response in clinical practice (Thase & Howland, 1993). The state effects of stress on cortisol production, as well as on other functions of the HPA, seem to overshadow trait indicators that might be present and that are required for distinguishing those with depression from those who are only acutely distressed. Once again, we see evidence for depression as a marker of stress and general psychopathology as more persuasive than evidence that non-bipolar depressive symptoms reflect a qualitatively distinct affective disorder.

Diurnal Rhythmic Patterns

One of the facts that has been widely used to support the view that depression is a qualitatively distinct and biologically based disorder, rather than simply a general dysthymia, has been its cyclical nature. The pattern of occurrence and recurrence of depression is reminiscent of the overlapping circadian and ultradian rhythms that characterize all physiological response systems. These cyclical patterns have stimulated considerable research on the relationship between sleep architecture and depressive symptoms (Buysse & Kupfer, 1993).

Sleep research in some ways integrates a number of separate fields of study. For example, the hypercortisolemia observed as a function of impaired HPA activity has been found to be related to disturbances of sleep pattern that, in turn, have been associated with depression (Born, DeKloet, Wenz, Kern, & Fehm, 1991; Jarrett et al., 1987). Likewise, disruptions to normal sleep staging can have profound effects on mood and may induce changes in cognition, loss of social interest, and even disturbances of sexual arousal that are often viewed as depressive signs (Buysse & Kupfer, 1993; Cohen, 1979; Gold et al., 1988b).

In spite of these overlapping areas of functioning and the obvious mediating role of sleep, the relationship between sleep patterns and psychopathology continues to be elusive (Morin & Ware, 1996). Sleep disturbances frequently occur in those with primary psychopathology, and, in turn, psychopathology is a frequent concomitant of sleep disorders. Morin and Ware (1996) observe a 50 to 80 percent incidence of sleep disturbance among general psychiatric patients and more than a 30 percent incidence of psychopathology among those with sleep complaints.

Nocturnal studies of sleep polygraphic recordings (EEG, EMG, eye movement, respiration, and, in men, penile tumescence) reveal sleep to be a complex process. Stages of sleep are defined by EEG amplitude and frequency as well as by arouse ability (Gold et al., 1988b; Morin & Ware, 1996). Typical patterns have been observed in the progression of sleep stages. In most stages, there is a rough but inverse correspondence between increasing amplitude and reducing frequency of electrical patterns, on one hand, and arouse ability, on the other. These stages of sleep, moreover, reflect consistent and sinusoidal patterns of EEG and respiratory activity, collectively earning the descriptor "synchronous sleep." In REM sleep, however, the pattern is dysynchronous. There a relative lack of correspondence between the low arouse ability in this stage and its depth, judged by its similarity to EEG measures of deep sleep. Moreover, the EEG and respiratory patterns are uneven and inconsistent. Relative changes in synchronous and dysynchronous sleep have been of interest to those who search for biological markers and mechanisms of action in depression.

Kupfer and colleagues (Kupfer, Foster, Coble, McPartland, & Ulrich, 1978; Kupfer, Reynolds, Grochocinski, Ulrich, & McEachran, 1986; Kupfer, Targ, & Stack, 1982; Buysse & Kupfer, 1993) have observed that depressed individuals, particularly those with severe and bipolar conditions, are distinguished from normals and those with acute depression by the presence of reduced levels of slow wave (SW) sleep, shortened latency to REM sleep, and increased densities of eye movement during REM activity. Moreover, studies of sleep patterns have been successfully used to define predictors of future depression (Ford & Kamerow, 1990; Reynolds & Kupfer, 1987).

The level of increased risk associated with these sleep and related neurophysiological findings, however, is still quite variable, and establishing a causal connection remains problematic. The degree to which these indices are direct or indirect manifestations of depression is still uncertain. Among the three or four most frequently studied sleep variables in depression, SW sleep appears to be the most stable across time and the most independent of state changes in mood. REM density and latency are both more closely related to diagnoses of depression than SW sleep and more changeable with patient mood. While they are reliable across a few nights of study, there is inconsistent evidence that they change in response to alterations in clinical presentation or that they may be affected by short-term changes in weight and appetite (Buysse & Kupfer, 1993; Thase & Howland, 1995). These findings raise questions about the causal relationship between sleep disturbances and depression (Benca, Obermeyer, Thisted, & Gillin, 1992; Kupfer, 1992).

Sleep patterns, like other biological indicators, appear to be too insensitive as markers of endogenous depression or predictors of treatment response to be useful in clinical practice. While discriminations of endogenous and exogenous conditions are possible in the laboratory (e.g., Healy & Williams, 1988), when comparing selected and relatively pure diagnostic groups, the distinctions are not sufficiently sensitive to allow clear, individual classification (Corbishley et al., 1990; Simons & Thase, 1992; Rush et al., 1989).

Conclusion

Research on the biological bases of depression has produced uncertain and unclear results. Bipolar disorder is the only depressive spectrum condition that is even roughly capable of discrete classification according to psychosocial variables and thus offers the clearest evidence of being a biologically distinctive syndrome. Even this distinction, however, is uncertain. The assumption that there are categorical distinctions among the non-bipolar disorders has received even less consistent support. While there are many correlates of depression at the level of biological processes, few of these processes can be said to be established as causal, and even fewer can be identified as pathological rather than simply variations of normal functioning. In spite of the weak and inconsistent evidence, the belief has persisted that various non-bipolar depressions also represent discrete conditions that are qualitatively and physiologically distinct from normal behavior. This point of view has underwritten a great deal of biological research during "the decade of the brain."

SUMMARY AND CONCLUSIONS

Increasingly, we are forced to come to the recognition that depression is probably not a discrete disorder or even a spectrum of discrete disorders, at least in the same sense that medical conditions and diseases are. It does not have a discrete etiology, an invariate set of symptoms, or a consistent course. Depression is more aptly described as the common cold of emotional disorders or as the fever that indicates the presence of emotional and psychological distress. It is a marker of disturbance and distress and tends to coexist as part of the picture with many other conditions. But, if it is the common cold of emotional disorders, that term is not meant to trivialize its significance (Coyne, in press).

Yet, one can think of dysphoria as a "disorder" in that it is widespread, imposes dysfunction, and is among the most frequent and debilitating symptoms found in community epidemiological samples. The frequency and the level of associated costs and impairments of dysphoria have increased steadily among all sequential birth cohorts studied since the turn of the twentieth century (Kaelber, Moul, & Farmer, 1995). The patterns of symptoms, the prevalence of biological correlates, and the frequent lack of correspondence between depressive symptoms and environmental events have convinced many researchers that factors other than life difficulty are at the basis of serious human unhappiness, the nature of which remains uncertain. However, the evidence we have reviewed in this chapter suggests that it is difficult to define categorical distinctions in how depression is manifested. While bipolar disorder and, to a lesser extent, nuclear depression (endogenous, melancholic depression) can be roughly categorized, the dysphoric symptoms of depression are manifest in a wide variety of both psychological and medical conditions. Symptomatic, psychological, cognitive, and interpersonal variables do not provide clearly distinguishable patterns that identify subclasses of non-bipolar depressive disorders. Depression, at least in the form of dysphoria, appears to be a marker for the presence of psychopathology, rather than a disorder in its own right. For the most part, depression is best described as a set of continuous dimensions, the most prominent of which are reflective of general distress rather than specific disorders.

Research on the mechanisms of depression does not add a lot of clarity to the nature of depression or its specific causes. This research, with the exception of cognitive and genetic studies, is almost exclusively correlational. At best, it can be concluded that there are wide variations in the degree to which different proposed mechanisms are associated with depression onset and maintenance. None of the correlates account for a large amount of the variation in predictions of depression, suggesting that the relationships are very complex and idiosyncratic. The need to move beyond the simplistic models of depression that have dominated genetic and biological research is clear. Thus, contemporary research is increasingly focusing on identifying factors that mediate between these vulnerabilities, or diatheses, and depressive experience. This line of research is often described as being based on a diathesis-stress model of depression.

Diatheses-stress models assume that the supposed mechanisms of depression that exist in the patient—sex roles and cognitive, interpersonal, and biological factors—serve to induce vulnerability but not depression directly. This vulnerability is activated only if person-relevant stressors are presented to the patient. The need to identify specific stressors in addition to specific diatheses is clear in this research. Without such specification, the meaning of increased risk is unclear. However, identification of the mediators of patient response to stress and to separate diatheses from both depression itself and the activating stressors is often difficult, especially when the proposed diatheses are unstable over time, are correlated with dysphoria, or are artificially defined as being dichotomous when they are continuous in natured (e.g., Coyne & Whiffen, 1995). Under any of these conditions, research on the relationship between person variables (diatheses) and situational variables (stressors) is very difficult and often misleading.

The picture is made even more complex because some sources of stress may become diatheses in their own right. One example of this relationship is seen in the transgenerational transmission of a particular vulnerability to depression. Research clearly suggests that children of mothers who are depressed, regardless of the nature of that depression, have a greater than expected risk for some type of depression and for psychiatric disturbances of many types (Goldin & Gerson, 1988; Downey & Coyne, 1990; Klerman et al., 1985; Wrate, Rooney, Thomas, & Cox, 1985). The combined action of diatheses and stressors in the parent may be passed on as an increased vulnerability in the child, increasing susceptibility to subsequent depression.

Lack of independence among diatheses, depressive symptoms, and stressors means that variables that may at one point be treated as diatheses may on other occasions serve as indirect markers of conditions that produce mediating stress. Age, for example, represents a correlate of increased risk of suicide. But, it is not a clear diathesis in its own right. It may, in fact, be a marker for a host of stressors that accumulate at certain life periods. For example, while suicide is one of the most frequent causes of death among all age groups, it is especially so among young and older adults (Robins & Kulbok, 1988). The question remains whether age itself is a factor of vulnerability or whether it is an index of certain stressors that activate the cognitive, interpersonal, and biological diatheses that are present.

To recapitulate, at this point there is no single, clearly defined set of vulnerabilities and stressors that is uniformly implicated in depression. It is clear, however, that a host of possible vulnerabilities are active, including those that derive from sexual roles and biology, as well as a host that come from cognitive, interpersonal, and biological traits. Likewise, the life stressors are inconsistent from person to person, and there is some indication that, at least among unipolar depressed individuals, the factors that activate depression for a particular person likely derive from the personal significance and meaning of those factors in the person's own life (e.g., Hammen, Ellicott, Gitlin, & Jamison, 1989).

We have seen that female sex, certain periods of life, hormonal instability, cognitive misattribution, lack of positive affectivity, lack of social support, inconsistent parenting, and an array of genetic, neurobiological, and environmental variables constitute factors that increase one's risk for affective disorder. The balance and interaction of these factors vary as a function of the particular manifestations of depression (e.g., bipolar, endogenous) and the personal meaning of stressors. These possible diatheses seem to affect how one responds to stress and its subsequent impact. Personality variables, for example, are not direct predictors or causes of depression but may dictate the types of stressors and even the presence of other, mediating diatheses that may determine how depression will be manifest (Coyne & Whiffen, 1995).

Biological dispositions may operate in the same indirect way as other diatheses, requiring that certain stressors be activated before resulting in a depression. Monroe, Thase, and Simons (1992), for example, found that depression was differentially related to stress as a function of degree of biologically defined vulnerability. Among those with normal REM indicators and patterns, depression level was more closely associated with levels of environmental stress, while the depression of those with abnormal REM indicators was less closely associated with environmental factors.

Ultimately, resolution of the remaining questions about the many permutations and patterns of relationships among the potential diatheses described in this chapter will require complex research designs. The ideal studies will be longitudinal in design and will simultaneously track the nature of the activating stressors, dysfunctional cognitive patterns, problematic interpersonal patterns, and biological variations in both symptomatic and nonsymptomatic groups of individuals who are both in and excluded from treatment. These studies will allow the identification of those who differ in risk for depression, using a host of variables, and assess the accumulating activation of these vulnerabilities with the co-occurrence of conducive life events. These will be difficult research designs for which to obtain approval or funding, and there are major problems in implementation. But, such studies are necessary if we are to disentangle the complex relationships and define the very nature of depression itself.

In the examples of Alice and Harold, we may see many of the potential diatheses and stressors at work. Alice and Harold have different patterns and levels of risk, with Alice's risk of depression and suicide being much higher than that of Harold. Alice's high level of risk is noted by a plethora of predisposing variables, including her sex, her history of previous depression, low levels of social support and other dysfunctional interpersonal patterns, vegetative signs, and sundry comorbid conditions. Compared to Harold, Alice is likely to manifest more extreme reactions to stress, to become more hopeless and suicidal, to have more frequent occurrences and relapses, and to experience more biological symptoms and markers when she is depressed.

But, do these differences between Alice and Harold predict different levels of response or benefits from treatment? Or, do they signal different types of treatment needs? While there is some evidence that Alice and Harold may be distinguished by the presence of endogenous and exogenous depression, respectively, even this distinction is inconsistently related to treatment. That is, it is still uncertain that the differences are meaningful at the individual level of predicting patient course or assigning differential treatment. Some evidence exists that various markers of endogenous depression are better predictors of patients' responses to drug treatment than to psychotherapy (Corbishley et al., 1990; Simons & Thase, 1992; Rush et al., 1989).

The weakness of the role of endogenous variables in the prediction and selection of treatment may be even more pronounced among adolescent groups. Using a wide variety of cognitive and social functioning variables ostensibly related to functional ability and to treatment, Gotlib, Lewinsohn, and Seeley (1995), for example, failed to find endogeneity to be a reliable discriminator of depressive pattern and a poor predictor of treatment response. Adolescents who had high levels of subjective distress, regardless of whether they also presented with vegetative signs, were indistinguishable from one another. The authors concluded that different diagnoses for those who did and did not have vegetative signs were not warranted among adolescents.

The relatively clear distinction between bipolar affective disorder, marked as it is by the presence of manic symptoms, and all other varieties of depressive disorder, coupled with the failure of subtypes of non-bipolar depression to be distinguished, has led us to restrict the current volume to a consideration of only non-bipolar conditions. The distinctiveness of bipolar and non-bipolar conditions suggests that the treatments, likewise, will be distinct. Moreover, the lack of definitive distinction among subtypes of nonbipolar depression suggests that treatments for these fictional distinctions may be more often a reflection of treatment intensity and problem severity than of more substantial entities (Coyne, in press).

The major task of this volume is to determine the relationship between the correlates of non-bipolar depression and differential treatment response. We cannot expect to improve treatment unless we can demonstrate that variables that distinguish depressive subtypes and that separate depression from other mental health conditions have relevance for treatment decisions. This volume is devoted to improving our understanding of treatment and its effects as they pertain to the qualitative distinction among depressive conditions; we consider dysphoria and associated symptoms to be reflections of emotional distress rather than as distinct disease or problem entities.

PART V
Contemporary Treatment Models

10 *Treatment Benefit*

Research Issues

Fine diagnostic distinctions among the non-bipolar depressions are difficult to justify. Our reviews have left us convinced that non-bipolar depression may best be described as representing a dimension of general unhappiness. What are defined as diagnostic differences may reflect variations in severity, which, in turn, are associated with symptom changes. This conclusion is controversial in the fields of psychopathology and clinical practice, but, if it is accurate, it would lead one to expect that treatments, too, are largely independent of the specific diagnosis given to a patient. Treatments that are effective for one type of depression should be more or less effective for another, varying as a function more of nondiagnostic qualities of the patient than of the particular diagnosis. A cognitively or interpersonally focused intervention should be of equal benefit for minor depression and for major depression, with the differences being a function of qualities that one might think should change with differences in patient severity (i.e., treatment intensity, use of medication). Likewise, medications that are good for one general condition (e.g., generalized anxiety) of a given severity should be equally effective for depression of the same level of severity. In this section (chapters 10–13), we turn our attention to the issue of whether there are specific treatments for this set of symptoms.

In approaching the tasks of developing effective treatments for non-bipolar depression and of identifying the variables that are implicated in the success and failure of treatments, researchers have employed a wide variety of research methods. The variations among research designs reflect not only an effort to adapt to different external constraints and empirical questions but also differences in the philosophies and beliefs of researchers. Collectively, the methodological and evaluative decisions that a researcher must make when designing a program of investigation fall into two general classes: (1) those related to the research design and methods used to control sources of error in the observations, and (2) those related to the measurement and statistical management of the data. The way that investigators resolve these often highly value-laden issues determines how the findings will be interpreted, as well as both the generality and the practicality of those findings.

Decisions about the design and methods of a research study define what variables are relevant and determine the selection of participating patients and clinicians/therapists and their assignment to treatments, the nature of the treatments themselves, the nature of the control and comparison groups used, and the identification of what outcomes will be measured. These decisions contrast with but are not independent of measurement and statistically driven decisions. These latter decisions determine how those aspects of patients, treatments, and therapists that have been identified as important are measured and how the effects of treatment are identified.

RESEARCH DESIGN

It has become conventional to distinguish between *effectiveness* and *efficacy* research studies. Research methodologists, however, make somewhat finer distinctions, differentiating among three basic designs: randomized clinical trials, quasi-experiments, and naturalistic studies (Kazdin, 1992, 1994, 1998). These three types of design are distinguished by the degree of control exerted over the selection of samples, the level of constancy or control maintained over extraneous factors that may inadvertently affect the results, and the degree to which the integrity of treatment is or can be maintained. Randomized clinical trials (RCT) research is what is referred to as efficacy research. It is tightly controlled and is designed to assess the causal effects of treatment when applied in an optimal way. The other two designs are variations of effectiveness research, or what is sometimes called "cinical utility research." Such studies are designed to approximate clinical practice, and they yield information about the usual or expected effectiveness of treatments.

Randomized clinical trials research uses a methodology that has been borrowed from pharmacological research and that emphasizes maximal control in all aspects of the study. As the name implies, it emphasizes the role of randomizing patients to treatments and embodies the following features:

1. The nature of patient samples is carefully specified, usually by restricting entry to those who comply with certain diagnostic criteria.
2. Patients are asssigned randomly with the expectation that this will balance the presence of unrecognized and idiosyncratic factors.
3. Extraneous variables (e.g., treatment setting, treatment length and frequency, supplementary treatments, stressors) are either held constant at a given level or monitored for subsequent statistical control.
4. Therapists are carefully selected and trained to ensure their competence and skill, usually by defining both entry-to-training criteria and by specifying posttraining performance criteria that must be maintained.

5. Treatments are structured and applied according to a manualized protocol.
6. Outcomes are applied by independent and often masked clinicians and observers.

In each case, the purpose of using these procedures is to ensure that the study's internal (purity and freedom from unmonitored factors) and construct (clarity and accuracy of the theoretical constructs that account for effects) validity are maximized (Kazdin, 1994, 1998). Only this level of control can result in conclusions about what causes the observed changes in patient status.

Over the past decade, RCT methods have come to be considered by many as the "gold standard" of treatment research. However, recently the question has arisen whether this might be "fool's gold." Some researchers question whether knowing the factors that cause change is worth the effort when other methods are more simple and more closely coincide with the way treatment is usually offered. To these skeptics, the critical question is whether treatment works, not what makes it works. They point out that many sacred assumptions of RCT research are often not justified. They point out, for example, that the assumption that randomization results in group equivalence is often a myth that offers no guarantee of group equivalence, as it is designed to do. Additional questions have been raised about the value of the type of control that is used in RCT research for directing clinical decisions. Some investigators point out that such controls make generalization of results to the world of practice impractical (e.g., Howard, Moras, Brill, Zoran, & Lutz, 1996). Seligman (1995, 1996) has suggested that the value of research designs that are appropriate for assessing the efficacy of treatments under optimal conditions cannot tell us much about the effectiveness of the treatment under usual conditions. Hollon (1996) adds that RCT designs are optimal for assessing causal relationships between treatments and outcomes, while quasi-experimental and naturalistic studies are optimal for determining whether the expected outcomes translate to practice.

In truth, both highly controlled efficacy research and naturalistic effectiveness research are needed to advance the field. Experimental RCT studies can help us understand the probable effects of treatment when the treatment is specific to the problem, is conducted by skilled and trained individuals, and extraneous factors are minimal. However, the careful patient selection procedures invariably result in groups of individuals who are quite dissimilar from those actually treated by most clinicians, the careful selection and training of therapists makes them quite unlike most of those who actually apply the treatments, the manualized treatment protocols requires a level of expertise and rigidity of adherence that is quite unlike the type of nonspecific and general treatment that takes place in the real clinical world, and the emphasis on structure minimizes the importance of clinician judgment. These controls threaten the external or ecological validity of the study—its generalization to the real clinical world (Kazdin, 1998). Thus, findings obtained in this way should be cross-validated in more naturalistic designs.

Some researchers (e.g., Beutler, 1989; Garfield, 1998; Howard et al., 1996) argue that naturalistic, effectiveness studies circumvent many of the problems of RCT designs. Naturalistic research, for example, avoids some of the problems of selecting diagnostically pure samples. Such homogenizing of the samples fails to acknowledge the complexity and the multidimensionality of most problems presented by real patients and does not deal with the fact that random assignment to treatment falsely suggests that treatments can be applied randomly. Some (e.g., Beutler & Baker, 1998) even argue that the dimensions of patients and treatments implied by selecting diagnostic groups and applying theory-based manuals misrepresent the ways in which treatments are adapted to patient needs in the real world.

Quasi-experiments and naturalistic studies are variations of what have been called effectiveness studies and can counterbalance some of the weaknesses of efficacy (i.e., RCT) methodologies. While manualization of treatment and random assignment distinguish RCT designs from experimental research, quasi-experiments do not often employ control groups of patients that are similar in some ways to those receiving treatment. However, both efficacy and effectiveness designs can and often do apply statistical corrections to tease out relationships among variables.

In quasi-experimental and other effectiveness research designs, investigators select from among the usual types of patients seen in practice, work in typical practice settings, and utilize clinicians who are representative of those providing service in the community (e.g., Wells & Sturm, 1996). In contrast, efficacy methodologies study ideal treatments, exemplary clinicians, and uncomplicated patients. The strength of effectiveness studies is in the degree to which they suggest that more or less specified treatments can be effective among the type of mixed and comorbid patients who are typically seen in practice. One is handicapped in using these methodologies, however, when the internal processes of treatment must be specified or when the causal direction of effects must be specified. When the treatment is well understood or can be expected to produce a reasonably specific effect among those with a given disorder, and when the treatment is specifiable, as may be the case when the treatment entails giving the patient a particular medication, this problem is not serious. It becomes more serious, however, when the treatment available and practiced in the community is very heterogeneous, when the nature of the treatment is not commonly accepted or widely understood, or when the treatment does not have a specific effect that is restricted to the condition being treated. This is often the case for psychotherapy, for example, where the nature of treatment varies widely among professionals even within a community and among those who share a common theory and where similar treatments are offered to those with a variety of quite different conditions and symptoms.

The quasi-experimental methods of effectiveness studies are not well suited to disaggregating and inspecting the effects of the many techniques and procedures that are included under the terms "psychotherapy" and "counseling."

To the degree that this is done, it involves an assessment of processes that are either common to different treatments (in different amounts), or performing an analysis that is independent of the theoretical labels and constructs that characterize psychotherapy approaches. One must be careful to avoid making ratings of processes that are tied to a theory that is different from the one(s) being evaluated.

Because "psychotherapy" is not a treatment that is uniform either in meaning or in practice, particular caution is indicated when comparing treatments given under this general label to other, more specific interventions. Comparing a specific medication, such as Prozac, to "psychotherapy" in the treatment of depression, for example, is likely to be decidedly uninformative without specifying the nature of the psychotherapy. Consider, for example, what we could conclude if we were to compare a group of anxious patients who were treated with a highly specified and manualized cognitive-behavioral skill training protocol to a similar group of patients who received any of several different types of medication, ranging in type from aspirin to neuroleptics, that were not identified by the researcher. If the cognitive therapy proved to be superior, what knowing scientist would dare conclude that cognitive therapy is superior to "medication"? Yet, when the reverse of this is done—when a specific medication is compared to a general and unspecified psychotherapy—such a conclusion is frequently drawn.

One must know the types, classes, and doses of medication, as well as the nature of the sample, to draw conclusions about medication. In the same vein, however, one must know the attributes of the psychotherapy and both the therapist and the patient characteristics to draw a conclusion about the benefits of psychotherapy. This logic is frequently forgotten, however, when scientists are evaluating the relative effectiveness of medical and nonmedical treatments.

For example, Wells and Sturm (1996) compared the cost-effectiveness of treating depressed patients with antidepressant medication (a moderately well-specified treatment), nonantidepressant medication (a poorly specified medication), and counseling/psychotherapy (an unspecified treatment). Conclusions based on such comparisons, in the absence of a common level of specificity in the identification of the treatments, confounds differences in effects with differences in variability of application. They do not tell us much about what would and could happen if the unspecified and most heterogeneous treatments were made more focused and consistent.

Wells and Sturm conclude that while counseling/psychotherapy has a more favorable cost-benefit ratio than medication, little additional benefit to outcome would be realized by additional therapist training in psychotherapy. They assume that counseling/psychotherapy is near the peak of efficiency possible. In contrast, they conclude that, since medication variability was so great, training physicians to recognize and apply a specific and appropriate class of medication would pay off with reduced costs. This conclusion assumes a degree of similarity and commonality that probably does not exist in the practice of counseling and psychotherapy. In truth, quasi-experimental studies of this type provide little information on how costs might be affected by the use of a specified and consistently applied variety of psychotherapy.

Some scholars (e.g., Jacobson & Christensen, 1996) suggest that the randomization of samples and the treatment structuring that characterize efficacy (i.e., RCT) studies can be applied to the questions raised by clinically relevant quasi-experimental methods. They argue that as long as treatment is controlled and patient randomization is maintained, internal validity is preserved, and one need not sacrifice external validity. For this to be true, investigators must implement procedures to ensure equivalence between treatment groups and to identify and monitor the ingredients that constitute the treatments themselves. Randomization provides such assurance only if very large samples are involved, and then it doesn't matter too much to the assumptions of randomization whether the research design is a tightly controlled experiment or a lesser controlled effectiveness (e.g., group contrast) design. Probably, with sufficiently large samples, such levels of control could be preserved in quasi-experimental designs by using random treatment assignment and systematic treatment monitoring. Even therapist training and manual adherence could be a part of such quasi-experimental effectiveness studies to ensure at least minimal levels of internal and construct validity and to more clearly allow these studies to address questions of effectiveness.

Jacobson and Christensen (1996) introduced the term "clinical utility" to supplement or supplant the description of effectiveness research. This term emphasizes the importance of research that includes an assessment of the meaningfulness of the results in clinical terms. A study may possess clinical utility if it can be applied in the real world and with representative clinical populations. Howard et al. (1996) have suggested a domain of research questions that supplements those that can be answered by efficacy and effectiveness research. These questions require that one assess the degree to which a given treatment is appropriate and is working for a given patient in a given situation. Addressing questions related to this domain of understanding requires both that the treatment be considered in terms of its limitations and strengths and that its effects be noticeable at the level of the individual.

While efficacy and effectiveness studies rely on aggregated mean effects, often of large groups, studies that address this domain of questions focus on individual changes. Moreover, rather than focusing on whether one treatment is better than another, this domain of questions addresses the patient factors that might serve as indicators and contraindicators for the treatment. It addresses the need for change that is sufficiently large or important as to be noticed by all of those groups that have a vested interest in the outcomes. While clinical researchers may be interested in the mean effects of different treatments as reported in efficacy and effectiveness research, most vested groups have interests that incorporate a more refined and individual analysis of change. These vested groups include patients themselves, the clients, those (e.g., patients, parents, schools) whose interests are served by the treatment, the clinicians who provide the treatment, the managers who allocate resources for treatment, and the sponsors who pay for those services (Howard et al., 1996).

Some (e.g., Russell, Bryant, & Estrada, 1996) have advocated the increased use of $N = 1$ studies—systematic and planned investigations of the treatment of individual patients. Unlike traditional case study methods, these designs, when used and modified in sequentially studied cases, allow fairly concise determinations of cause-and-effect relationships and permit the investigator to inspect clinically relevant and utilitarian changes. Innovative statistical procedures have been developed to assist the interpretation of findings from such studies (Kazdin, 1992, 1994; Russell, Bryant, & Estrada, 1996). The sophistication of these procedures increases the detection of important aspects of change.

The downside of $N = 1$ research, as is true of RCT designs, is its uncertain level of generalization. While some procedures, such as linking multiple participants (multiple baseline studies) to one another, allow for replication and rule out effects of time and extraneous events, generalizability of most findings is still dependent on the use of larger and representative groups.

Jacobson and Christensen (1996) point out that ensuring clinical utility requires a number of decisions, all based on certain valued positions and assumptions made by the investigators. Some of the types of decisions that affect conclusions about the generalization and utility of research include:

- The methods used for selecting patient samples
- The strategy for assigning patients to treatments
- The criteria for selecting, training, and assigning therapists to treatments
- The structure lent to specifying the nature of the treatments themselves
- The nature of the control and comparison groups used
- The identity of the outcomes and outcome measurements that are used.

Selecting Patient Samples

Methodologically, when clinical scientists establish criteria that define how and which patients will be selected for a study, they must balance two competing considerations.

First, the selection criteria should ensure that the patients selected for study are appropriate for the treatment(s) being investigated or compared and are reasonably similar across the various treatments to be studied. If selection attends to treatment-relevant patient characteristics, the outcomes of each of the investigated treatments will be relatively uniform. Such selection, if relevant to the nature of treatment, will respond relatively similarly to the particular treatment(s) provided. If there is reason to believe that the treatments provided might be effective for different patients, then subsets of patients should be selected or stratified. A resulting differential hypothesis would specify which patients within the group would respond to one treatment and not the other. The treatment-relevant patients in each treatment group could be expected to respond quite uniformly to one of the treatments but to have either a lower rate of response or a more heterogeneous response to the other treatment(s). If the selection criteria fail to reduce the variability of response to treatment, this is an indication that the selected dimension(s) for identifying patients is not relevant for determining the patient's suitability for this (these) treatment(s). In chapter 3 we applied this type of reasoning to the understanding of patient subgroups that are differentially responsive to different treatments.

The second consideration is that the research criteria should establish the limits of the study's generalizability. This function requires decisions that may conflict with the function of ensuring a patient sample's optimal suitability for a treatment. While optimal suitability is served by reducing patient heterogeneity, generalizability is best served by having a patient sample that is widely heterogeneous. As previously noted, homogenized patient samples are characteristic of efficacy research, and heterogeneous samples are characteristic of effectiveness research. The distinguishing feature of studies that have clinical utility is the representative nature of the samples of both patients and treatment. An optimal treated sample is one that is very similar to the usual patient groups that seek treatment; an optimal therapist sample is representative of therapists who typically provide this service. Thus, for optimal generalizability, samples of depressed patients studied in research protocols should include a large proportion of patients with comorbid Axis II diagnostic conditions and others with comorbid Axis I conditions. Unfortunately, current applications of efficacy methodologies do not include samples that have these features, and, if they did, one might expect that the response rate to different treatments would be lower than it currently is.

For example, the favored procedure for restricting patient variability in RCT studies is the use of diagnostically pure patient samples. This is the procedure initiated by the NIMH Collaborative Study of the Psychobiology of Depression and extrapolated to the study of psychotherapy in the NIMH Treatment of Depression Collaborative Research Program (TDCRP) (Elkin, 1994). Its procedure assumes that diagnosis is, in fact, an important differential contributor to treatment response. Furthermore, the method assumes that diagnostic compliance is an indicator that the treatments are relevant and appropriate and that it will limit, in a meaningful way, the wide variability of benefits that typically occur among different patients for any given treatment. But these assumptions have seldom been tested. To the degree that they have, they have not proven to be accurate. With the exception of some classes of medication, diagnosis (of itself) has never been found to be either an indicator of a treatment's appropriateness or a major differential determiner of a treatment's effects.

It may be fair to say that the usual practice of selecting groups that are similar by virtue of only a single, common diagnosis is ill suited to either of the major intentions and purposes of sample selection procedures in depression research. Selecting depressed patients to ensure diagnostic homogeneity does not ordinarily limit the amount of variability among patient responses to treatment or allow treatment differences to emerge. That is, diagnostic homogeneity alone does not appear to limit the variability of patient responses to treatments or indicate the appropriateness of a specific treatment (Howard, Krause, & Lyons, 1993). Neither does it ensure sample generalizability. In the case of depression, for example, diagnostic homogeneity tells us very little about the nature of the sample, as far as differentiating treatment-relevant characteristics are concerned.

We have already pointed out that for most of the diagnostic conditions, depressive affect, even when accompanied by vegetative signs, is a relatively nonspecific attribute. It is a marker for psychological distress and frequently accompanies one or more other and more specific diagnostic conditions. Even to the degree that endogenous and bipolar disorders represent specific entities, and they appear to represent reasonably identifiable conditions, they tend to overlap enough with a variety of other conditions to make the identification of their specific signs and symptoms relatively weak. While it is important to homogenize patient groups for research purposes, and while it is important to include depressive symptoms in this selection process, limiting the sample to those who have depressive symptoms and no other conditions is misleading and provides a less than optimal dimension on which to assess treatment effects.

Selecting research patients on the basis of the presence of depressive symptoms does not accomplish the intended purposes of restricting the range of treatment response and treatment options in the research sample. The disparity that exists within depressed groups along such dimensions as problem complexity, defensiveness, comorbidity, coping style, and interpersonal expectations, among others, is likely to introduce so much variance in the outcomes as to occlude any differences that exist because of different treatments. Indeed, this is exactly what has happened in most comparative research. The variations of outcome that are attributable to different treatments are overshadowed by the variation of outcomes within any one treatment (Beutler, 1991; Howard et al., 1993). Only when one can account for or eliminate sources of this intradiagnostic variation does one begin to see treatment differences.

Assigning Patients to Treatments

A second distinguishing characteristic of efficacy research methodology, such as that used in RCT studies, is the use of random assignment to distribute the sample of patients across treatments or experimental conditions. This procedure assumes that random assignment will result in a balance of extraneous factors among groups. That is, it assumes that the resulting groups will be comparable and equivalent in all respects except for the treatment to which they are exposed.

There are three major problems with the assumptions that underlie random assignment as applied to treatment studies. First, random assignment works only in the long run and only with large samples. Such procedures seldom result in groups of equivalent size (Howard et al., 1993; Howard et al., 1996). It takes a very large sample of patients to justify the expectation that the many ways in which people differ will be equally distributed among two or more groups through randomization. Most samples (e.g., Kazdin & Bass, 1989) are far too small to justify such an expectation. Thus, some studies resort to stratification on one or more patient characteristics, but this procedure introduces a systematic bias into the groups. It may systematically distribute to one or another group unrecognized but important additional variables that are correlated at a low level with the variable according to which stratification takes place. Since it is unlikely that the investigator will be aware of the many variables that correlate with the stratification variable, there is virtually no way to ensure that these differences will be acknowledged and addressed in comparisons of pretreatment status. Thus, statistical corrections and controls are usually inadequate to correct the effects of this source of bias.

A second problem is that random assignment is never really random in RCT studies. Howard and colleagues (Howard, Cox, & Saunders, 1990; Howard, Krause, & Orlinsky, 1986) have pointed out that only a small percentage of patients who have a given condition ever reach the point of being randomized. Many sources of interference result in a high degree of attrition before one ever reaches the point of randomization. In most studies, this pretreatment attrition is ignored even though it disrupts the assumptions on which randomized assignment hinge. Attention is paid only to the attrition that takes place after treatment is initiated. However, Howard et al. have observed that such a small percentage of qualified patients ever reach the point of assignment to treatment, even in the most liberal of RCT studies, as to severely challenge the assumption that the treatment sample is representative even of patients who meet the exclusion and inclusion criteria. The more severe these inclusion and exclusion criteria, however, the higher the attrition rate and the more seriously the assumption of representativeness is violated.

The third problem with randomization is that even if the ideal of equivalence through random assignment could be achieved, it is based on an indefensible assumption about how patients are distributed among practitioners in the real world. In clinical practice, patients are never paired with a treatment or a clinician randomly. The nature of their treatment is confounded with the route to treatment used, the severity of their problem, and sexual and location preferences, as well as with many other variables, thereby presenting very difficult statistical issues for the researcher (e.g., Kahneman, 1963). The variables that affect treatment and therapist preferences are not just random noise or error in the assessment of outcomes, although they are assumed to be so by random assignment procedures. Treating them that way assumes that they are uncorrelated with the effects of specific treatments, acting the same way across all treatments. However, expectations of particular activities and roles on the part of the therapist or clinician are likely to have different effects in the presence of different treatment components. This means that they cannot be controlled by randomizing patients to treatments. Indeed, their effects may be masked by such procedures, and it is even possible that randomizing neutralizes the potential benefits that may occur with self-initiated matching.

This is not to say that we should abandon random assignment research. But, it does say that we must not overvalue it. It also suggests that efficacy and effectiveness studies have more in common than is usually assumed. Often the findings from effectiveness studies are rejected by academics in the same way that the results of efficacy studies are rejected by practitioners. Yet, neither method is pure, and both may exist on a common dimension represented by the level of external validity warranted. Finding ways to treat depression effectively will probably require the acceptance of findings from both methodologies as equal partners.

Selection and Assignment of Therapists

In the RCT design, therapists are selected either because of their general competence or because of their prior experience with the treatments to be studied. Three problems are introduced as a result of the method of selecting and assigning therapists to treatments. The most obvious problem is that therapist samples are usually even smaller than patient samples and are usually too small to assume representativeness with respect to the therapists in the community. All of the problems of generalization that apply to small patient samples are magnified when applied to even smaller samples of therapists. Particularly good or poor therapists, especially if they see an unusually high proportion of patients, may overly affect the results.

An even more serious concern arises in analyzing the data. Statistical procedures assume that each outcome is independent of every other outcome. But, this is true only when each patient is treated by a different therapist. When the number of therapists is smaller than the number of patients (i.e., when one or more therapists treats more than one patient), the power of of the statistical tests used should be computed on the number of therapists used. That is, the effective size of the sample is best represented by the number of therapists, not the number of patients as is usually done (Beutler, Johnson, Neville, & Workman, 1973; Chinsky & Rappaport, 1970; Cicchetti & Ryan, 1976; Crits-Christoph & Mintz, 1991). Crits-Christoph and Mintz point out that as little as a 5 percent disparity in outcomes among patients treated by different therapists may result in dramatically altered and misleading conclusions. Unless one can be certain that therapist effects are negligible, therefore, one is not justified in using statistics that are based on a sample size that equals the number of patients. But most studies employ fewer than a dozen therapists distributed among all treatments. Applying the most conservative statistical rules would reduce the sample sizes (and the degrees of freedom in statistical procedures) in most analyses to such a small number that treatment effects would be virtually impossible to detect.

Still another problem arises indirectly from the size of the therapist sample and applies to the method of assigning therapists to treatments. If therapists are randomly assigned to the various therapies under study, all of the problems of randomization discussed with regard to patients are equally relevant for therapists and are exacerbated by the use of an even smaller number of therapists than of patients. However, therapists are seldom assigned to treatments randomly; they are assigned to those treatments with which they are most familiar and compatible. This selective assignment heightens the possibility that therapist contributions will confound the effects of the particular treatments and ensures that therapist effects will be confounded with the effects of treatments. It also increases the amount of variability of treatment effects and reduces the probability of observing actual treatment differences. For example, even in the large-scale NIMH Treatment of Depression Collaborative Research Program (TDCRP) (Elkin et al., 1989), the numbers of therapists used was insufficient to conclude with confidence that the effects of treatments were adequately teased apart from the effects of different therapists.

The most direct way of circumventing this problem is to select a large group of therapists, train them in all of the treatment formats to be used, and then have them treat some patients who are assigned to each of these modalities. Yet, training therapists in two or more different procedures also introduces problems into the method and runs the risk that systematic biases in therapists' preferences for one or another treatment will cause them to lose motivation for conducting the less interesting treatment. If a preponderance of therapists favor one or another of the treatments, the effects of these treatments may be magnified, not because the procedures are better but because they are more interesting to therapists than the others used. This is not a farfetched possibility. It is clear that even the particular preferences and beliefs of the investigator affect research results, probably because these preferences are communicated to the therapists. Several investigations (e.g., Elliott, 1996; Luborsky, Diguer, Schweizer, & Johnson, 1996; Robinson, Berman, & Neimeyer, 1990) have found that, even in studies that do not cross treatments and clinicians, the treatment allegiances of the principal investigator exert a significant effect on the outcomes reported.

The problem of investigator allegiance is not unique to studies of psychotherapy. Pharmacotherapy also appears to be subject to investigator bias, as shown by evidence that the treatment effect of a given drug, when used as a comparison standard for a more recently developed drug and with both then compared to a placebo control group, is approximately one-third as great (and usually nonsignificant) as it is when it is the new drug that is the target of the investigation (Greenberg, Bornstein, Greenberg, & Fisher, 1992). Moreover, if a placebo is used, it is difficult to ensure that the commitment of those who provide the placebo and those who administer the other treatments is equivalent. Unfortunately, few studies have the resources to ensure that a large enough sample of therapists in each condition can be selected to balance the effects of therapist preferences and biases across treatments or to ensure that the investigator remains uninvolved in the development or application of the treatments. The use of nested and mixed-effects designs offers some hope for extracting these variables, as does the practice of sharing and combining research data from several sites and laboratories.

Manualization of Treatments

The use of structured treatment manuals to guide the interventions used in making research comparisons was introduced as a methodological innovation in the TDCRP, funded by NIMH (Elkin, Parloff, Hadley, & Autry, 1985). In this study, manualized versions of cognitive therapy (Beck, Rush, Shaw, & Emery, 1979), interpersonal psychotherapy (IPT) (Klerman, Weissman, Rounsaville, & Chevron, 1984), and pharmacotherapy plus clinical management (either placebo or imiprimine) (Fawcett, Epstein, Fiester, Elkin, & Autry, 1987) were compared. It had become apparent through prior research that mental health treatment, particularly psychotherapy, was being applied in widely varying ways by psychotherapists within any and all of the established theoretical traditions (Elkin et al., 1985; Fiedler, 1950; Meltzoff & Kornreich, 1970). Manualization offered a way of identifying the active ingredients of treatment and separating them from the general therapeutic qualities of those individuals who offered the treatment. Because spontaneous recovery and placebo responses are so high among depressed patients, without systematizing the interventions in this way outcomes could not be attributed to the mechanisms postulated by various approaches to be effective.

The introduction of manuals was heralded as a revolution in psychotherapy research (Luborsky & DeRubeis, 1984; p. 5). Indeed, the introduction of manualized forms of treatment in research spawned a proliferation of uses for such manuals. Not only have a very large number of manuals been created (Lambert, & Ogles, 1988), but they have been used for training and supervision as well as for treatment (Neufeldt, Iversen, & Juntunen, 1995) and for the determination of third-party payments for services (Chambless et al., 1996).

While the use of manuals in research has facilitated efforts to evaluate which treatments make a difference, recent research has exposed a number of problems with this approach. One problem arises from the fact that most comparisons of treatments based on different manuals have failed to find meaningful differences between them. These ambiguous findings have stimulated widely varying opinions among investigators. While many researchers assert that the nonsignificant differences found indicate that all treatments invoke common or similar mechanisms of change (Lambert & Bergin, 1994), others observe that the large variations in outcomes within treatments argue for the need to disaggregate patients and to determine which treatments are working for different (previously unidentified) subgroups of patients (Howard et al., 1993). The number of patient variables and treatment variables that

274 Contemporary Treatment Models

fruitfully might be disaggregated to discover differential responses and effects number in the millions, however (Beutler, 1991).

A second problem with manuals arises from evidence that, at least within some psychodynamic therapies, the therapists who can most easily be trained in the use of manuals tend to be among the least empathic and most angry, and that training further reduces important, human, and nonspecific contributors to treatment benefit still further (Henry, Schacht, Strupp, Butler, & Binder, 1993; Henry, Strupp, Butler, Schact, & Binder, 1993). In other words, the therapist factors that cut across treatments but that account for a substantial portion of the benefits noted for treatment of any type tend to be trained out of people who use some psychodynamic manuals. A related finding is that these nonspecific effects function differently and with different degrees of impact in different types of psychotherapy (Rounsaville et al., 1987). This finding underlines the importance of considering the effect of different types of training on therapists' ability to understand and empathize with patients. If the foregoing findings are ultimately replicated for a wide range of treatments, it may be concluded that the structure that must be imposed to follow a manual may inhibit the strength of variables that are even more important in facilitating change than the specific model of treatment selected. Such knowledge would surely point us in new and beneficial directions for training and monitoring training.

Control and Comparison Groups

Ordinarily, treatment research seeks to answer one or more of three basic comparative questions:

1. Is this treatment safe and effective?
2. Are the effects of this treatment a function of its specific and unique qualities?
3. How do the effects of this treatment compare to the usual treatments provided?

Each of these questions requires a different standard of comparison. The safety and efficacy of a treatment requires a comparison with an untreated condition; assessment of the unique effects of treatment requires a comparison of the treatment that includes the unique qualities that are assumed to produce benefit with a treatment that is composed largely of qualities that are common to most or all other treatments; determination of the relative effects of a treatment requires comparison to treatments that have been established in use by prior research or tradition.

RCT methodologies and other efficacy studies ordinarily employ a no-treatment control group, a placebo control group, and/or an alternative-treatment group, depending on which of the foregoing questions is being addressed.

In contrast, quasi-experimental research uses natural groupings of individuals to serve as controls and supplements these comparisons with statistical methods that partial out the effects of certain concomitant or confounded treatments. To answer the three questions just listed, these studies ordinarily compare the posttreatment response of a group that has received the treatment to the group's pretreatment condition, would statistically partial out the effects of common or nonspecific aspects of the treatment of these individuals, and would compare responses to nonequivalent groups selected from convenience samples, respectively.

Naturalistic research designs are forced to rely almost entirely on statistical methods to arrive at answers to the same three research questions. Correlational procedures, covariate procedures, and statistical modeling are examples of the methods typically employed.

In determining the safety and the efficacy of depression medications, the U.S. Food and Drug Administration (FDA) requires that a placebo control group be included in the comparisons as a means of teasing out the specific effects of the drug from the patient's expectancies and hopes resulting from contact with the prescribing physician. Depression is very responsive to suggestion, minor life changes, and other factors associated with spontaneous (nontreatment) recovery rates; for medication trials, these factors must be ruled out as the sources of improvement. Placebo controls are designed to activate positive expectations, attitudes, and other psychological factors, but without applying the active ingredients of treatment.

In experimental tests of pharmacological interventions, these factors are considered to be noise and are factored out by the use of control groups that are maintained on medication placebos. The FDA has required the use of such groups before determining whether a medication is either safe or effective. Klein (1996) argues that the pill placebo control has been so useful in drug research that the principle of placebo should be a requirement in any study of psychotherapy as well, whether or not an active medication treatment is considered.

Others are more skeptical about the information obtained by comparing a treatment to an inert pill placebo. Kirsch and Sapirstein (1998), for example, in what has become an infamous paper, calculated that the average response to a placebo is 75 percent of the total mean response to antidepressants (no substantial differences were noted among class of antidepressants). They concluded that only one-fourth of a patient's response is the direct result of the active medication and urge the use of an active placebo condition as a better standard against which to assess the effectiveness of antidepressant medications.

Kirsh and Sapirstein's conclusion that an active placebo is necessary in order to adequately evaluate medication effects is hotly debated. In fact, the several issues raised by these authors have elicited a wide variety of response, including open hostility. However, at least some of their suggestions, notably that pertaining to the relative size of placebo and active treatment effects, have been confirmed by others, utilizing data from several separate studies (e.g., Beutler, 1998b).

Klein, however, goes beyond simply arguing for the inclusion of a placebo group in all standard comparisons of treatment. He also argues that all psychotherapy studies should include a comparison with a purified medication treatment condition. Participants in this group would be those who had independently been determined to be "medication responders." Thus, both placebo responders and those who are intractable to medication would be excluded from this group. This suggestion requires that assignment to this condition not be random but be specifically biased in a way that would ensure a favorable response to the medication used. Such a procedure would violate certain cardinal assumptions about the value of randomization and its use as a standard against which alternative treatments must be considered and would ignore the possibility that there may also be undisclosed subgroups of depressed patients who are more or less responsive to the psychotherapy used in the comparison studies. A comparison of drug responders with psychotherapy responders, using this methodology, would reveal little, unless the factors that determine this differential response were known and incorporated into the design.

For three decades, there has been a great deal of dispute as to whether a suitable placebo group can be ethically used in psychotherapy studies, and most psychotherapy studies do not include either a psychological or a medical placebo group for ethical or methodological reasons (Clum & Bowers, 1990; Garfield & Bergin, 1994; Lambert & Bergin, 1994). One argument holds that the use of placebo controls is unacceptable because of the potential ethical problems that would arise if treatment were withheld for the time necessary to evaluate the presence of posttreatment prophalactic effects (a factor that is given little attention in drug studies). Another argument emphasizes that placebos activate what are important active qualities of most psychotherapies and that eliminating these qualities from the targeted treatment would be akin to using a medication that lacked a central ingredient. It is reasoned that, while activating expectations and hope is central to all psychotherapies, each theory accomplishes this task in different ways and with differing impact on those factors that distinguish the treatments. Many investigators believe that to study treatments while canceling out such central and necessary precursors to their effectiveness is to render the findings uninterpretable (Bergin, 1971; Bergin & Strupp, 1972; Kazdin, 1994). This assumption underwrites the decision to exclude a placebo comparison.

What seems to us to be a reasonably balanced view of these viewpoints was reached by Jacobson and Hollon (1996a, 1996b), after scholarly debate on the merits of various design features of the NIMH TDCRP. They agreed that use of a medication placebo control group in psychotherapy studies may be a desirable (but not a required) methodology, depending in part on the nature of the questions being asked. We add the suggestion, however, that drug studies also include an active placebo condition by which the effects of placebo can be extracted from the placebo and drug responses (e.g., Beutler, 1998b; Kirsch & Sapirstein, 1998).[1]

Alternatives to a placebo control condition include the use of a no-treatment, delayed treatment, or minimal treatment condition for comparison. Each of these options has different interpretative implications. The ethics of using placebo or no-treatment conditions require that a traditional or demonstrably effective treatment be offered to patients who do not respond to the no-treatment condition. However, some of the more important questions about the effects of treatments and the differences among treatments concern the degree to which they reduce relapse or maintain their effects over time (e.g., Willis, Faitler, & Snyder, 1987), and these procedures limit the usefulness of the studies by making it impossible to detect these differences.

When different manualized treatments are compared, investigators need to employ three checks on fidelity and integrity. First, they must demonstrate that each of the therapists is complying with each treatment manual to a satisfactory extent. Second, they must determine that the competency or proficiency of the therapists in applying the procedures is equivalent across the compared treatments. And third, they must show that the treatments themselves are distinguishable in theoretically important ways. If any of these comparisons fails, the validity and the interpretability of the treatment differences or lack of differences will be compromised.

Identifying Outcome Measures

Different theoretical conceptualizations of depression identify different causes and correlates of the clinical presentation. Investigators must decide what aspect of depression to use as the major determiners of change. Minimally, measures of depression must include assessment of severity, social functioning, and symptomatic patterns (e.g., Katz, Shaw, Vallis, & Kaiser, 1995). The most common measures of change are the number of individuals, who continue to meet categorical, diagnostic criteria following treatment and how many evidence a change in dysphoria over the course of treatment, While these two symptomatic criteria appear to be reasonable indices of benefit on the surface, changes in functional and adaptive capacity are frequently ignored, as are changes in theory-relevant constructs. Assessment of patterns of change in these dimensions may yield quite different results from measures based on symptoms alone.

Because of the wide differences that exist in how different investigators measure change, there have been several efforts to develop guidelines and

1. We acknowledge that Kirsch and Sapirstein are widely criticized for this suggestion and that there are some good arguments against it, but we believe that our recommendation errs in favor of conservatism, as does Klein's argument in favor of including placebos in psychotherapy research.

standards for the measures used. Waskow and Parloff (1975) initially developed a list of standard instruments that they recommended for inclusion in treatment research. However, these recommendations were clearly not followed, and a later review (Lambert, 1991) revealed that most studies still relied on measures that were specifically developed for each individual project. Thus, the comparability of findings across studies was suspect. Other efforts were initiated to identify standards that were applicable in the field. Lambert, Christensen, and DeJulio (1983) and Maruish (1994) initiated further reviews of available tests and their use but were unable to arrive at a specific recommendation for particular measures.

Horowitz, Lambert, and Strupp (1997), after confronting these differences, abandoned the effort to identify a common battery of tests. Instead, they identified domains of experience that should be assessed and the standards that tests should meet for assessing these domains. They emphasized the importance of using change measures; in the area of depression, for example, they concluded that several different domains of change should be included as outcomes. Outcome domains should include changes in levels of compliance with diagnostic criteria, subjective dysphoria, and functional impairment. They also acknowledged that other dimensions might be included to help determine the theory-relevant mechanisms of change and outcomes of particular theoretical note to supplement and complement the central domains of change.

Horowitz et al. (1997) proposed that measures of dysphoria, severity, diagnostic compliance, and functional impairment be included in the assessment of change. They also urged the use of measures that ensure reliability appropriate to the construct measured and to construct validity. Finally, they emphasized the importance of assessing change from a variety of perspectives and across dimensions that are both shared with other conditions and unique to the problem to which treatment is addressed.

Reconciling Differences in Research Designs

In recent years, a number of investigators have become concerned with how results and interpretation of research may differ as a function of whether they derive from controlled or quasi-experimental studies (Beutler, Kim, Davison, Karno, & Fisher, 1996; Goldfried & Wolfe, 1998; Lipsey & Wilson, 1993; Smith, Glass, & Miller, 1980; Shadish & Ragsdale, 1996). Using a statistical comparison of many different meta-analytic comparisons, Lipsey and Wilson (1993) concluded that there was no definable pattern that distinguished findings of studies in which samples were randomized to treatments and those that were naturalistically defined. These conclusions were echoed by Beutler et al. (1996) on the basis of a qualitative review and support our earlier recommendation that efficacy and effectiveness studies be seen as places along a continuum that addresses external validity, rather than as two distinct types of research.

However, Shadish and Ragsdale (1996) cast some doubts on these conclusions, faulting the methods used in meta-analytic studies. They point out that different investigators use different procedures for identifying whether randomization has occurred, make different decisions about the affect of attrition on random assignment, and compute the effects of treatments differently. Applying a stringent and consistent definition across studies within the domain of family therapy, they determined that some significant and consistent differences in the strength of findings do appear between studies that rely on randomized (RCT) research designs and those that do not. More highly controlled, efficacy experiments obtained larger mean effect sizes than nonrandomized effectiveness studies (ds of .60 and .03, respectively). Rather than confirming the importance of one type of research over the other, however, these findings, we think, if generalizable to other types of treatment, underline the importance of integrating and consolidating these different types of research. It would be useful to bring more control, in the form of manualized treatment and quasi-random assignment, into effectiveness paradigms and more representative sample selection into efficacy research methods.

As we've stated, there is nothing inherent in controlled experimental designs that precludes making adjustments to all of the design features that we have identified as potentially problematic (Jacobson & Christensen, 1996). Quasi-experiments may also exert varying levels of experimental control without completely adopting the methodology of the RCT procedures. Controlled research can be conducted on samples that are selected on bases that are more treatment-relevant than diagnosis, sample selection and assignment procedures can be used that incorporate and study pretreatment attrition rates, and controlled research can be conducted with flexible manuals as well as with procedures that allow one systematically to study the effect of patient self-selection and preferences. However, as usually conducted, these variations of design are not incorporated into the variations of controlled research that most people equate with the "true" experiment.

The difficulty of making such methodological adjustments within controlled laboratory studies is confounded by the absence of external funding to support research on long-term treatments, as would be required to ensure that the treatments themselves are representative of those used in clinical practice. Only coordinated studies within a program of research that incorporates the use of both experimental and quasi-experimental, if not naturalistic, designs can come to grips with these many problems (Beutler & Clarkin, 1991; Seligman, 1995, 1996; Howard et al., 1996).

Contemporary methods of funding the large-scale studies needed emphasize individual projects rather than programmatic ones. To keep a program of research going, an investigator must propose a second study before the findings from the first are known and understood. It is important that this focus on individual studies and findings, which has characterized most of treatment research, be adjusted to give greater emphasis to supporting systematic programs of coordinated studies that use a variety of methods to sharpen the focus on relevant variables. This would allow investigators to build progressively on results as they are obtained in order to implement the next study phase.

<u>STATISTICAL MEASUREMENT AND MANAGEMENT OF DATA</u>

Investigators must attend to a number of statistical issues, aside from the design of the research study. They must ensure that the study has sufficient power to detect differences, make decisions about how to assess change, determine the priority to be assigned to different types of outcomes, resolve concerns with interdependence among sets or classes of variables, manage missing data and attrition, and select the analytic procedure that will yield the most valid results. These decisions have implications not only for how data will be interpreted but for what results will emerge from the analysis.

Statistical Power

Kazdin and Bass (1989) have clearly demonstrated that most research studies do not include enough participants to ensure that the predicted differences can be detected. The power to detect a difference is directly proportional both to the complexity of the research design (i.e, the number of variables studied) and to the number of participants used as subjects. Even a relatively large difference (effect size) between treatments cannot be detected in a study that includes more than two independent variables (treatment and patient characteristics) when the treatments include no more than the average number of participants per treatment (about twenty). As the field has moved from the simple notion of attempting to demonstrate that one treatment is superior to another to using designs that include patient factors, the ability to statistically detect what differences actually exist among treatments has declined.

There is a limit to the number of patient participants that any setting and study can produce. Each observation (subject/participant) contributes degrees of freedom to the analysis and each variable targeted for assessment (independent variable) uses up some of these degrees of freedom. As the number of degrees of freedom decreases, the power of the comparison to detect differences also is reduced. To resolve inadequate statistical power, researchers must rely on alternatives such as simplifying the designs, combining data across sites, developing collaborative studies, and coordinating among sequential research projects within a research program. Coincidentally, the development of multisite studies also helps address some concerns about the effects of researcher alliance and sample representativeness that introduce variability or consume degrees of freedom (Klein, 1996).

A related concern raised by Kazdin and Bass (1989) is that when clinical experience leads to the prediction of a significant interaction effect, the demands on the sample become almost unwieldy and impractical. Yet, there must be some way to bring research to bear on the complex questions that are raised in clinical practice. If the bridge between the questions of relevance to clinical practice and those that can be practically answered by research cannot be navigated, then research has little to offer practitioners. Thus, it has been necessary to develop statistical procedures that are both powerful and complex.

Some procedures for conserving statistical power require focusing the analyses only on the comparisons of greatest interest. Thus, if the investigator does not expect the treatments to differ in outcome except when their effects are moderated by some characteristic of the patient or the environment, it is possible to analyze just the specific interaction term of interest, preserving the degrees of freedom that would otherwise be used by analyzing the main effects that are expected to be of little importance.

Similarly, if an investigator expects that certain combinations of patient and treatment characteristics may be too complex to analyze separately in a single analysis, the design can be altered to preserve statistical power by a simple comparison of well-matched and poorly matched groups. If such global findings are significant, then one is both logically and statistically justified in analyzing the specific effects of the different contributors to the successful matching algorithm.

A more reasonable strategy, in the long run is to build up larger samples by combining similarly designed data sets to provide a larger sample than can be assembled for a single study. This procedure allows the use of more complex statistics and permits more refined interpretations. Increasing the sample size can be accomplished by using similar measures and populations in sequential studies, allowing the accumulation of data to then be used to answer some of the questions that require the larger samples. Another procedure is to use archival data from other, similar research projects. Sharing data among investigators is a good way of increasing the sample sizes but may be limited unless researchers can extract the same constructs and a common set of measures from the various samples (Beutler & Clarkin, 1991). There are statistical procedures, such as the transformation of different scales to standardized scores and the use of latent structure analyses, that may assist in the development of common metrics and measures when different methods are used. However, coordinated projects involving several sites and longitudinal accumulation of similar data from sequential projects are more reliable methods for accomplishing these purposes.

Assessing Change

On its face, assessment of change should be simple—give the patient a test of depression and subtract the pretreatment score from the posttreatment score. The differences should indicate how much improvement has occurred. However, aside from the thorny problem of deciding what domains of behavior have to be assessed in order to accurately capture the phenomenon of depression (a procedural and design consideration), there are also statistical problems that alter and complicate the use of different procedures for computing changes (Beutler & Hamblin, 1986; Beutler & McNabb, 1981; Sechrest, McKnight, & McKnight, 1996). Tests of any abstract concept, including depression, vary over time because of two general factors. If the test is valid, most of the variation reflects actual change in depression (true variance). A smaller portion of the change, however, may be random and occur because the test itself is an imperfect measure. Score variations that occur because of these factors are called error variance. Sources of error variance include misunderstandings of vocabulary or about the nature of the response form, distractions in the environment that reduce concentration, simple mistakes in marking the answer sheet, and regional differences in the meanings of words.

Sometimes these sources of error overestimate the patient's depression, and, at other times, they may underestimate depression. When the scores obtained before and after treatment are subtracted, much of the true variance is deducted and the remainder is heavily weighted toward error variance. This is because much of the true variance, in a reliable test, is the same on the two occasions. Thus, a raw difference score is likely to be unreliable, because contributors to error variance are random, and of questionable validity. There is an exception, however. If there is reason to think that the error variability in scores arises from the same factors on the two occasions—that they are correlated—then a difference score may be appropriate. When the source of the rating (e.g., patient self-report or clinician rating) is a major contributor to score variations, for example, the errors of measurement may be correlated and the use of a raw difference score may be justified statistically (Rogosa, 1988).

Computing residual gain scores or regressing pretreatment scores on post-treatment scores are the usual ways of assessing outcomes in order to adjust for the error variances that are present. The specific method used for assessing change, however, depends on a variety of factors to which the investigator must be sensitive. Whichever method is selected, it is necessary to ensure that both the measure itself and the estimate of change are reliable and that the measure meets at least minimal criteria of construct validity. More extensive descriptions of the psychometric properties that should characterize tests are presented by Anastasi (1988), Beutler and Berren (1995), Groth-Marnat (1997), among others.

Beyond the issue of how to construct a change measure is the issue of its meaning. The conventional method, calculating and reporting the effects of treatments in terms only of the probability that the results could have occurred by chance, leads to misleading conclusions. Obtaining a statistically significant finding is directly related to the size of the sample used and provides little real information about how meaningful the finding may be for clinical practice.

As a precursor to employing any statistical comparison, it is necessary to ensure that the scores obtained are referenced to some actual clinical value and behavior. Sechrest, McKnight, and McKnight (1996) have pointed out that ratings have largely replaced the often more difficult method of directly observing problematic behaviors as means of assessing change in mental health status. They emphasize the importance of calibrating scores on clinician and patient-based rating forms to external behaviors in order to ensure that the metrics that are used to express a given phenomena have a meaning in the real world.

A related alternative is to address the question of clinical significance by reference to the internal norms of the measure used. Beginning with a provocative analysis of the problem by Jacobson, Follette, and Revenstorf (1984), a variety of procedures and modifications have been suggested and debated (Jacobson, Follette, Revenstorf, Baucom, et al., 1984; Jacobson & Truax, 1991; Kendall & Grove, 1988; Tingy, Lambert, Burlingame, & Hansen, 1996a, 1996b). At present, procedures proposed by Jacobson and Truax (1991) for estimating the clinical meaningfulness of change are relatively well established. These procedures use the norms of nonpathological samples and the standard errors of measurement of the instruments used to determine the degree to which a given change brings the patient within the limits expected for normal functioning. Unfortunately, to date, few research studies have addressed this critical issue as applied to depression; when it is addressed, it is done only through an assessment of depressive or dysphoric symptoms. These procedures lack the precision and generalizability that are necessary to accurately reflect the power of treatments, as suggested by these many authors.

Coincidental with the movements toward assessing clinical meaning of findings, there has been a concerted movement among scientists to abandon the usual methods of estimating probability levels associated with findings. Many scientists (e.g., Goodman & Royall, 1988) favor replacing the conventional methods with tests of exact probability or likelihood ratios, which require more precise tests of hypotheses and offer more information about the amount of change obtained.

Prioritizing Dependent Variables

Typically, outcome is assessed by a number of separate measures, and these outcomes reflect different aspects of the problem being treated. These different measures are usually correlated with one another, at least at a relatively low level, but they cannot be considered to be equivalent to one another from the standpoint of clinical meaningfulness. Hence, one of the tasks of the investigator is to select a variable that best represents the type of change that is the focus in the study and then to prioritize the order in which this and other dependent variables will be analyzed. In a study of depression, for example, outcomes may include dropout, comorbidity, dysphoria, diagnostic symptoms, clinician ratings of functional impairment, and ratings of functioning by a collateral or significant other. Even if we assume that these various indicators are measured reliably, they may not be highly correlated. And, if they all reflect aspects of the common problem of depression, then the researcher must select from among them the measures that will be used to draw a conclusion about treatment and then decide how to use them to that end.

One method recommended for selecting the most representative variable is to create a statistical composite to represent the common variance among the measures (Beutler & Hamblin, 1986). More often, however, one of the targeted dependent variables is selected, usually on the basis of pragmatic reasoning and without clear guiding rules. Given the nature of and the relationship between depression as a diagnostic entity and dysphoria, it makes some sense to consider these two variables as the primary indicators of change in the equation.

Interdependence among Variables

Research typically evaluates the effects of treatments on several different aspects of patient behavior or dependent variables. Additionally, research sometimes considers, through the use of separate analyses, the roles of several different patient variables on the effects of treatments. Whenever different constructs are evaluated by the use of separate analyses, there is the possibility of drawing misleading conclusions. These misinterpretations arise because different measures, whether of outcomes or of patient characteristics, may be correlated or interdependent. Lack of independence among dependent variables in treatment studies of depression is a particular problem. If, for example, investigators attempt to assess changes both in depressive mood and in general psychiatric-status self-report, they are likely to find similar effects of treatment on both variables. They may conclude that the treatment alleviated both depression and general psychiatric disturbance. However, because self-report measures of dysphoria and general well-being are highly interrelated, both measures may be assessing the same dimension; the tests may merely embody different labels and alternative ways of assessing the same thing.

To avoid misleading conclusions in depression research, it is advisable to ensure that the measures come from different sources (patient, therapist, clinician, significant others) and that they have no more than a modest degreee of correlation with each other. Specifically, outcomes should be assessed both as they are reflected in subjective distress and as changes in the levels of compliance with categorical diagnostic criteria (Coyne & Schwenk, 1997).

Intercorrelations among patient variables and among treatment process variables pose similar problems. At times, various patient qualities are labeled as if they represented distinctive aspects of a person or problem when in reality, they are indicative of the same characteristic or construct. Many of the labels that are applied to define patient characteristics are derived from particular theories, are identified by different names, and are measured by different instruments, but in fundamental ways and effects, they represent the same quality. A construct such as patient coping style may be highly correlated with distress, flexibility, oppositional traits, or other qualities that are reflective of one or another particular theoretical framework. An investigator must ensure that the various constructs measured are in fact statistically independent and maintain construct validity in order to reach the most justified conclusion about the roles of these variables on treatments.

Finally, particular statistical problems arise when various processes of treatment are assessed as a means of defining the contributors to change. Process dimensions, the assessment of which is undertaken in order to determine the mechanisms of change mechanisms, even more than patient characteristics, are governed and defined by theories. The labels or names of the dimensions to which change is attributed may sound more distinctive than they really are. Again, it is necessary that the researcher ensure that the measures used are independent of other constructs and that they have construct validity.

Attrition and Missing Data

Attrition in treatment research occurs at a number of points during the process of conducting the study. Some attrition is initiated by the investigator, prior to treatment assignment, a particular characteristic of RCT research designs in which patients are carefully selected and screened before inclusion. Clinician-initiated attrition also occurs during the study when a patient participant ceases to be eligible because of decompensation or failure to comply with the treatment protocol. In many RCT studies, for example, if a patient fails to respond to treatment and in fact, begins deteriorating, a special process is implemented on ethical grounds in order to explore options to the experimental treatments used in the study.

In some studies, patients are kept blind to certain aspects of the treatment, and if this masking is violated, either by accident or by clinician error, they may be dropped from treatment and referred to another type of intervention. This is done in order to preserve the integrity of data that may be influenced by patient expectations and knowledge. This is especially true of medical treatments, where patient knowledge that they are receiving an inert or placebo medication may be expected to affect their response.

At other times, the patient may initiate the conditions of attrition, either by refusing to enter the study or by dropping out once treatment has begun. In random-assignment studies, patients who are not randomized to the treatment that they prefer may experience a reduction of motivation and commitment to the project. These patients frequently leave prior to receiving any actual treatment. In other cases, the failure to respond or even the presence of a rapid positive response after treatment has been initiated may lessen the patient's motivation to continue.

Among the various points at which attrition may occur, only a few are typically reported in research reports. Howard et al. (1990) have illustrated the effect that this might have in a typical RCT study. They report that in one large-scale study of treatments for alcoholism, more than six thousand patients were screened for participation. Seventy-six percent were excluded from participation by the researcher because they failed to meet one or another preestablished criterion. More than 1,600 patients were judged to be eligible for participation, but of these, 1,006 refused participation. The final sample consisted of 594 people. Thus, of the original pool, only 9 percent were both eligible and willing to be assigned to treatment. This low figure does not include those who were either terminated during treatment by the researcher because of failure to respond or those who subsequently dropped out of treatment on their own. In many studies, dropouts of the latter types may result in fewer than 50 percent of the original treatment sample being available for assessment at the end of treatment. Issues of representativeness and generalizability are critical in such cases.

A number of statistical and methodological procedures have been advocated as ways of increasing confidence in the results that are derived from attritted samples (e.g., Flick, 1988; Howard et al., 1990; Howard et al., 1986; Welch, Frank, & Costello, 1983). These solutions include using mathematical simulations of missing data points (e.g., using averages based on other patients' responses or previous scores) and developing creative ways of incrasing patient motivation, compliance, and participation (e.g., payment, follow-up, contracting). Each of these decisions carries implications for how representative the resulting samples might be. Howard et al. (1986), in summarizing some of the available avenues of correction, emphasize the importance of tracking patient attrition from the point of initial contact through screening and treatment assignment, through the duration of the project, to follow-up in order to ensure that some estimate of response can be obtained from those who leave the program at these different points. Most contemporary RCT studies use an intent-to-treat methodology, including data on all patient participants who are initially assigned to treatment as part of the study sample, whether or not any treatment is actually warranted. While this procedure may improve the generalizability of the findings to those who seek treatment, Howard et al. emphasize that only when monitoring and follow-up includes preassignment attrition can one get a full perspective on how representative the sample is and how generalizable the results might be.

Selecting Analytic Procedures

Much depends on the selection of analytic procedures. In part, the specific statistical analyses are set by the methods and design of the research. Small sample research, including $N = 1$ research designs, are particularly problematic for the definition of statistical procedures. No statistical procedures approach perfection, and all have limitations in their use and on the interpretations warranted by their results. The selection of statistical procedures influences the power of the comparison, the number of dependent or independent variables that can be assessed siumultaneously, and how well the underlying statistical assumptions are met by the sample selected and their response (Kazdin, 1994).

Large sample studies, those that use pre-posttest designs, and those that select homogeneous patient samples and use structured (manualized) treatments to reduce variability of treatment response (assuming that the patient qualities do in fact reduce the variability of response) all improve their power to detect differences in outcomes (Kazdin, 1994; Howard et al., 1993). For example, multivariate procedures have advantages over univariate ones because, they increase the number of independent variables or dependent variables that can be managed in one statistical procedure. Alternatively, researchers can use some form of statistical correction to adjust the levels of probability accepted in order to ensure that error rates throughout the study are kept within acceptable limits as the process of conducting multiple analyses on the same data set continues. Deciding how to do this is not simple nor is any decision likely to be uncontested. Researchers reviewing even the careful analyses and multiple levels of statistical expertise applied to the TDCRP data have questioned the use of the conservative Bonferroni correction to adjust for multiple analyses in that study (e.g., Klein, 1996; Klein & Ross, 1993).

Likewise, methodological decisions have a direct bearing on which statistical procedures are appropriate. For example, perhaps the greatest benefit attendant on selecting patients in terms of diagnostic homogeneity is that doing so ensures a degree of equivalence in the measures used for assessing outcome that would not be present if different dependent variables were measured on each individual. While patients may produce widely different scores on many variables, ensuring, for example, that they all have depression also ensures that a measure of this construct will be relevant for assessing change among all subjects. This is not to say that a depressive symptom measure is or will be the most relevant or useful outcome measure; such decisions are ultimately ones of value and theory. Nonetheless, the type of measure chosen will bring some degree of comparability to bear from which to draw conclusions about a treatment's effects. All treatments, directly or indirectly, are intended to produce a reduction in symptoms. If the symptoms are widely different from patient to patient, with no common features, measurement of outcomes is hampered. Symptoms of thought disorder and dysphoria, for example, may respond at different rates and be more and less responsive to treatment. This is why a general measure of distress, such as depression or anxiety, that represents patient status across a number of different conditions has been suggested as a common measure of outcome by Strupp, Horowitz, and Lambert (1997). Unless the outcomes can be assessed on some commonly present index such as this, these measurement factors may preclude observations of treatment-related changes. It may be necessary to select and monitor other aspects of patient characteristics in order both to ensure their similarity to the

288 Contemporary Treatment Models

patient groups to which one desires to generalize and to determine which patients are most likely to benefit from the different treatments (Beutler, 1991, 1998a; Horowitz et al., 1997).

Of course, the importance of all of these statistical analyses is to be able to improve prediction and control of the outcomes of treatment. Here, a persistently curious paradox is noted. While statistical prediction has consistently been found to be more accurate than predictions based on clinical impression and judgment, clinicians remain doubtful and rejecting of statistical procedures that supplant or replace the clinician's judgment. The very biases and perceptual distortions that make clinical judgment a poor predictor of patient prognosis and an unreliable measure of patient diagnosis and that distort measures of outcome also lead to the rejection of statistical prediction. The challenge to the scientist who hopes to influence clinical practice is to combine the sense of clinical wisdom with the accuracy of statistical predictive methods (see Clement, 1996; Fonagy & Target, 1996; Nathan, 1996; Nelson-Gray, 1996; Roth & Fonagy, 1996). It is the burden of the scientist to ensure that constructs, concepts, and measures that are used in the process of statistical prediction are meaningful to clinicians. It is also imperative that the researcher communicate with practitioners to ensure that the findings of research make sense and are implemented in practice. In the final analysis, for example, the usefulness of the suggestions and recommendations provided in this volume depend both on their scientific accuracy and, even more important, on their clinical sensibility and sensitivity.

SUMMARY AND CONCLUSIONS

In this chapter, we have identified some of the major attributes of treatment research, along with some of the threats that the methodologies selected pose to the validity of findings. The decisions made in designing research programs fall into two general classes: (1) those related to the research design and methods used to control sources of error in the observations, and (2) those related to the measurement and statistical management of the data. Collectively, decisions made within these two domains all pose certain threats to the validity of research. Typically, one must balance the desirability for internal control, what is called "internal validity," against the desirability of generalizing findings to representative samples and treatment conditions in the real world.

To allow treatment effects to emerge, one must control the variability that arises from extraneous factors. Unfortunately, we do not always know whether a factor is extraneous or central to the effects of treatment. As one establishes more control over the nature of treatment, the nature of the samples, and the outcomes addressed, the generalizability of the findings suffers. This means that it is unlikely that any given study, regardless of how large or expensive, will yield results that are immediately either believable or universally generalizable. It is only through the collection of research findings in a given area that a clinician or researcher can come to identify patterns of response and effects. Thus, a combination of tightly controlled, randomized clinical trials studies and naturalistic studies may do more to point to conclusions that are transferable to practice than a consideration of tightly controlled studies alone.

With this in mind, it is important that we now turn our attention to a consideration of which research findings provide enough of a pattern that they will be able to inform our practices in sufficient detail as to begin to point toward principles that will form treatment guidelines. It should be noted that while research findings are given priority in our search for guidelines, there are many areas in which research has been neither forthcoming nor informative. That is, there are decisions that must be made in the absence of empirically valid knowledge. In these instances, we are left with our best educated judgment and the wisdom derived from clinical experience.

The value of clinical decisions and treatment guidelines cannot be captured by a simple determination of whether a decisional dimension is valid or invalid. Making clinical decisions requires weighing multiple dimensions, constructing a multifaceted treatment, and assessing complex outcomes. The validity of treatment guidelines depends not on these individual dimensions but on the efficiency of their gestalt. Thus, the development of valid treatment guidelines is always a work in process as variables are combined in new ways, as new treatments and research methods evolve, and as more comprehensive criteria of benefit are developed. At best, the various outcomes that we extract from controlled research are interpretations and generalizations. Each one's predictive validity depends on its conceptual relevance, our ability to measure its presence, with what other decisions it is grouped, and the limits of its generalizability. While systematic observation and controlled research offer the hope of more reliable and demonstrably valid guidelines, clinical judgment is deeply and extrinsically embedded in all empirical interpretations and definitions. Thus, there is only a quantitative distinction between the validity of decisions based on research and the validity of decisions based solely on experience.

Treatment guidelines incorporate a variety of sources of information that varies in validity and precision. This point must be kept in mind as we review the disparate sources of information that provide the foundation for our cohesive set of practice guidelines.

11 *Benefits of Treatment*

What Works

As we've noted, knowledge about treatment benefits and practices derives from numerous sources of information. Methods and criteria used to conclude that a given proposition is factual vary in objectivity and replicability. Idiosyncratic experience, personal and private beliefs, and strong feelings exert substantial influences on what we accept as factual. Among mental health practitioners, clinical theory and personal observations are probably more often accepted as true than are the more objective and reliable facts that derive from systematic scientific research. Rational theory and idiosyncratic belief are insufficient as bases for treatment guidelines, however.

Of the various sources of information that can usefully guide clinical practice, it is our belief that findings from systematic research are by far the most important. Controlled research represents the most efficient way to sort wheat from chaff among clinical judgments. From controlled research, we can determine if treatment works and, to some degree, test the limits of differential effectiveness of treatments.

However, as we've noted, clinical judgment cannot and should not be eliminated as a source of information about treatment. Clinical judgment is critical in extrapolating the relevant and meaningful patient dimensions that should be considered in evaluating the limits of treatment. Thus, clinical judgment is deeply embedded in any interpretation of research results. Indeed, some problems are more reliant on these clinical impressions and judgments than others. Suicide risk is a case in point. The nature of suicide and suicidal behavior is such that empirical research on the effects of different treatments is difficult to do, and the samples from which one can draw conclusions are invariably selective.

Various guidelines of practice exist for working with those who are at risk for suicide. However, compared to the research that underlies other treatment decisions, the body of research from which suicide guidelines are derived is less cohesive and is subject to greater misinterpretation. It is here, in the area of identifying and treating those who are at risk for suicide, that one sees that we have most closely blended research findings and clinical impressions (see chapter 6).

This chapter addresses the questions of whether treatments are specific to the experience of depression and whether they work. An affirmative answer to these questions is necessary as foundation knowledge if one is to fully implement the treatment guidelines we have recommended. This foundation knowledge includes the status of empirically derived standards for treating patients who are judged to be at risk for self-harm. One must know what treatments have predictable effects before one can begin to adapt and blend these treatments to fit the needs of different patients.

STATUS OF RESERCH-BASED KNOWLEDGE

Contemporary research on the treatment of depressive spectrum disorders allows a number of general conclusions.[1] These conclusions generally reflect on questions within two general domains of outcome: effectiveness—how effective is treatment for alleviating symptoms? and durability—how well do treatment effects endure? The answers to these questions in turn raise subquestions and invoke consideration of special issues related to generalization, relative effects, and the suitability of different treatments to special populations. In this chapter, we consider the general issues of effectiveness and durability of treatment and also begin to answer the more specific question of the limits of generalizability. This latter consideration lays the groundwork for later explorations of the outcomes and limits of specific treatment models and differential guidelines.

Treatment Effectiveness

The question of treatment effectiveness must be addressed within two general domains. One of these is the direct effects of treatment on depression, and the second is the indirect or ancillary effects of treatment on patient general functioning, well-being, and health. Explorations of both of these domains provide us with information about the overall effectiveness of treatment and also pro-

---

1. Specific research findings on depression have been reviewed at length in the AHCPR guidedlines documents and by numerous other authors. Rather than repeat an analysis of these reviews, we have accepted and summarized these analyses in this review. In the review of the treatment of depression that we have initiated, in contrast to these earlier ones, we have placed the greatest emphasis on factors that differentially predict outcome. In this chapter, we base our summaries on collections of findings from meta-analytic studies and research summaries. Thus, our interest is in cross-validation and differential outcomes, areas in which this book breaks new ground. Our focus throughout this volume is on cross-validated findings, particularly those that allow a determination of the indicators and contraindicators for various treatments.

vide information that bears on the even more important questions of the relative effects of different treatments and the limits of their influence. While the weaknesses of the research methods used, as presented in chapter 9, doom many questions relating to relative efficacy—especially those comparisons made within psychosocial and pharmacological classes of treatment—to remain unclear, contemporary research methods allow us to reach relatively stable and valid conclusions regarding the question of overall efficacy. The more general the question, the more valid the conclusion we can derive. Thus, we believe that current research methods are compatible with reaching quite valid conclusions about how effectively depression can be treated and, to a lesser degree, about the relative value of pharmacotherapy and psychosocial intervention. However, traditional research paradigms allow us to reach only tentative conclusions regarding the differential effectiveness of one class of psychosocial intervention against another or about one class of medication against another. A different type of research paradigm altogether, such as that we have described in chapters 6 and 7, is required to address the even more interesting question of which patients are likely to respond to each of the various treatments.

Direct Effects of Treatment

Efficacy of Treatment.   Looking across studies, it is common to reduce the symptoms of depression to subclinical levels among 65 percent to 70 percent of patients with major depression, at least by the time treatment is ended (e.g., Blackburn, Bishop, Glen, Whalley, & Christie, 1981; Hollon et al., 1992; Hollon, Shelton, & Loosen, 1991; Imber et al., 1990; Klerman, DiMascio, Weissman, Prusoff, & Paykel, 1974; Kovacs, Rush, Beck, & Hollon, 1981; McLean & Hakstian, 1979; Murphy, Simons, Wetzel, & Lustman, 1984; Raskin, Schulterbrandt, Reatig, & McKeon, 1970; Rush, Beck, Kovacs, & Hollon, 1977; Weissman et al., 1979; Wilson, 1982). Meta-analytic studies of the treatment of depression (e.g., Nietzel, Russell, Hemmings, & Gretter, 1987; Robinson, Berman, & Neimeyer, 1990; Steinbrueck, Maxwell, & Howard, 1983) generally conclude that a variety of treatments are effective and that the probability of receiving benefit during a relatively brief treatment course is about 70 percent.

Efficacy research, however, is usually conducted on short-term treatments and is conducted with relatively noncomplex depressive disorders. As we've noted, clinical utility studies may give a more accurate and generalizable estimate of effects in the type of clinical practices in which most patients will seek treatment. However, the figures from efficacy research correspond reasonably well to those from effectiveness studies, using a broader definition of symptomatic distress (Howard, Cornille, et al., 1996; Howard, Kopta, Krause, & Orlinsky, 1986; Kopta, Howard, Lowry, & Beutler, 1995; Seligman, 1995). A general conclusion from such studies suggests that approximately 80 percent of anxious and depressed patients admitted to an outpatient service become asymptomatic within a period of one year.

Comparative and Differential Efficacy. Current evidence suggests few major differences in the overall efficacy of pharmacotherapy and psychosocial approaches to treatment, although the former may produce more rapid effects and the latter may produce more lasting effects (e.g., Hollon et al., 1992; Hollon, Shelton, & Loosen, 1991). The second conclusion is less certain when pharmacotherapy is compared to interpersonal psychotherapy than when it is compared to cognitive therapy, however (see Nezu, Nezu, Trunzo, & McClure, 1998; Reynolds, Frank, et al., 1994). Psychosocial treatments have proven to be at least as effective as medical ones in most studies, and there is little current justification for combining the two (Antonuccio, Thomas, & Danton, 1997).

The best overall estimates of the effectiveness of treatment are derived from meta-analytic findings. In meta-analyses, the effects of many studies are translated into a common metric, collapsed, and evaluated for statistical significance. The power of a treatment subsequently is expressed as an "effect size," or E.S. An effect size is expressed either as a correlation, in cases where one is assessing the influence of some continuously distributed variable such as therapist experience or patient distress, or as an expression of the number of standard deviations that separate the outcomes derived from two or more observations. Typically, the latter metric derives from research in which scores at the end of a standard treatment are compared either to pretest scores or, more commonly, to scores obtained from a comparison group. The comparison group may have received no treatment, or it may have received an alternative treatment. Comparisons of treatment and pretreatment are not equivalent to comparisons of treatment and some other treatment or to a nontreatment condition. The effect size is much larger when it is expresesd as an index of how much change one group has experienced since receiving treatment than when it is expressed as a comparison of the treatment group and a seperate group that received no treatment. It is smaller still when the treatment group is compared to a group that has received an alternative type of treatment.

When assessed against a no-treatment control, for example, a given treatment package may earn an effect size of 1.0. This value indicates that the average patient in the treated group was better off at the end of treatment than 84 percent of the untreated patients. Sixteen percent might have improved to a similar degree with or without treatment. An E.S. of 1.0 is not nearly as impressive, however, if it is used to describe the treated group's end-of-treatment scores compared to their intake scores. When the patients in the treatment group are assessed against their own pretest scores, an E.S. of 1.0 indicates that 84 percent of patients were better off at the end of treatment than they were at the beginning, and 16 percent failed to improve.

Effect sizes cannot be automatically translated into an estimate of meaningfulness, although this is often done. Effect sizes are affected by the size of samples in the studies that are included, by the sensitivity of the measures, by the number of variables or outcomes used, and by many other things (e.g.,

Cappelleri et al., 1996; Smith, Glass, & Miller, 1980; Strube, Gardner, & Hartmann, 1985). All of these things may influence the interpretation and meaningfulness of the findings. Even if the E.S.s are quite large, they do not give a precise indication of either the degree to which the change made is clinically significant or how closely the treated group approximates normal functioning.

Generally, nonetheless, an effect size of 0.25 is considered to be of moderate magnitude when two different treatments are compared or when a treatment is compared to notreatment, and it is usually statistically significant for the sample sizes that are typical in treatment research (Cohen, 1977). Many of the effects of treatments and programs that support major decision in medicine, education, and social programs are within this range (e.g., Lipsey & Wilson, 1993). In contrast, comparisons of pre- and posttest scores for one treatment generate E.S.s that conceivably may range from 1.0 to 3.0.

In addressing the question of whether particular treatments for depression are effective, the appropriate E.S.s are reflections of comparisons between a treated and an untreated group. Additional and subsequent comparisons between groups receiving different types of treatment are informative (e.g., pharmacotherapy versus psychotherapy) but offer information on differential effectiveness only if the initial comparisons of each treatment with a no-treatment condition are favorable.

Inspections of most meta-analyses of mental health treatment reveal that treatments normally produce effect sizes in the range of 0.60 to 0.90, regardless of the wide variations that are present in levels of patient severity, the heterogeneity of the disorders included, and the types of treatments offered (c.f., Kirsch & Sapirstein, 1998; Linde et al., 1996; Matt & Navarro, 1997; Shapiro & Shapiro, 1982; Smith et al., 1980; Wampold et al., 1997). For reference, it should be noted that an effect size of .68 marks the point at which the mean improvement of the treated samples exceeds the seventy-fifth percentile of patients in the comparison samples. This is a convenient reference point by which to compare the effect sizes obtained in studies that are specifically aimed at assessing the effects of treating depression.

Several published meta-analyses (e.g., Dobson, 1989; Neitzel et al., 1987; Robinson et al., 1990; Rush et al., 1993b; Steinbrueck, Maxwell, & Howard, 1983; Wampold et al., 1997) address the specific question of the effectiveness of treatments for depression. These reviews are overlapping and include many of the same studies, although they have employed somewhat different criteria both for selecting studies and for defining the outcomes of treatment. Not surprising, their findings are very similar, and their interpretations differ mainly in the way that different aspects of the findings are emphasized. In a representative review that was more comprehensive than earlier ones, for example, Robinson et al. (1990) summarized the results of fifty-eight studies of major depression and concluded that the effectiveness of psychotherapeutic treatments is well established. Among studies in which some form of psychotherapy for depression was compared to a no-treatment control group, the average effect size was 0.73. When compared to results for a waiting-list control group, the effect size was somewhat higher (0.84), but it was substantially lower when the treatment group was compared to a group that had received medical or psychological placebo treatment (0.28). By comparison, the average effect size for a variety of medications appears to be more variable. One meta-analysis of nineteen studies that allowed comparisons of tricyclics, tetracyclics, and SSRIs has provided one of the most liberal estimates of effects, noting that all treatments produced effect sizes that clustered close to 0.75 (Kirsch & Sapirstein, 1998). Notably, the effect size for St. John's wort, an herbal treatment that has been most frequently studied as an intervention for mild depressive symptoms, has been estimated to range from 0.51 to 1.00 (Linde et al., 1996). .

Meta-analyses that have addressed specific differences among different types or models of treatment for depression (e.g., Linde et al., 1996; Smith et al., 1981; Kirsch & Sapirstein, 1998) generally find few indications of significant mean outcome differences. Most treatments produce, on the average, similar magnitudes of effects across a wide range of patient factors. This conclusion is most apparent among the psychotherapies. However, whether one looks at the level of specific studies or across meta-analyses, there are wide differences in the size of the effects obtained for all treatments (Howard, Krause, Saunders, & Kopta, 1997). All treatments are associated with substantial and positive effects among some patients and with poor effects among others.

Robinson et al. (1990) have provided a sophisticated comparison of the relative effects of different psychotherapeutic treatments. They found the range of effect sizes to vary from 0.49 for general, relationship-focused treatment to 1.02 for behavior therapy. Individual and group therapy for depression were equally effective on the average (effect sizes of 0.83 and 0.84, respectively). Moreover, the durability of effects of psychotherapy over the follow-up periods studied was also generally very good, with an effect size of 0.69 being obtained at the end of a mean of thirteen weeks posttreatment. This figure is consistent with that reported by others during slightly longer follow-up periods (e.g., Nietzel et al., 1987).

By comparison with the relatively strong, if general, effects of psychotherapy, the most noted meta-analysis has estimated the overall effects of pharmacotherapy among a variety of outpatient conditions to be 0.37 (Smith et al., 1980). But, one might argue that this figure is misleading because the effects of medication may be more specific than those of the psychotherapies to which it is compared. That is, medications may be more selective in the nature of the patient for which they work, and this may dilute the overall effect size. If this is so, one might expect that across symptom and diagnostic groups, estimates of efficacy attendant on psychoactive medication treatment would be quite variable. Indeed, this appears to be the case. Effect size estimates for antidepressant medications have ranged from 0.31 to 0.75 in various meta-analyses, depending on the restrictiveness of the selection criteria used (see the variations among Kirsch & Sapirstein, 1998; Greenberg, Bornstein, Greenberg, & Fisher, 1992; Steinbrueck et al., 1983). Interestingly, comparisons of the effects associated with the highly touted selective serotonin reuptake inhibitors (SSRIs) and those associated with older tricyclic and tetracyclic medications have found no reliable mean differences in effect sizes (Greenberg et al., 1992; Kirsch & Sapirstein, 1998). An exception to this generalization is to be found in the literature on post traumatic stress disorder (PTSD). Van Etten and Taylor (1998), for example, conducted a meta-analysis of patients treated with various psychosocial and pharmacological interventions. They separately compared the use of monamine oxidase Inhibitors (MAOIs), SSRIs, and benzodiazapines (BDZs). They found that among anxious patients, those with concomitant depression tended to respond somewhat better to SSRIs than to psychosocial interventions.

In contrast, few significant differences have been observed in comparisons of the relative effects of psychotherapeutic and pharmacological interventions for depression, but when they do occur, they uniformily favor psychotherapeutic interventions. The general difference between an effect size of 0.37 obtained for general psychopharmacological treatment and an effect size of 1.09 for equally nonspecifiable psychotherapy reported by Smith et al. (1980) among mixed groups of patients exceeds estimates based on more specific disorders and treatments. The largest differences between medication and psychotherapy effects have been reported by Steinbrueck et al. (1983). These authors report a mean effect size for tricyclic antidepressants (TCA) of 0.67, compared with a mean effect size of 1.22 for a variety of psychotherapies, when both were compared to an untreated or a placebo control group.

In still another comparison that employed even more rigorous criteria, Robinson et al. (1990) inspected studies in which direct comparisons were made between TCA and psychotherapeutic treatments. They found a mean effect size difference of only 0.12 between the two classes of treatment. While this difference was statistically significant, interpretation of this finding is limited because of the relatively few studies that directly compared psychotherapy and medication and because the theoretical allegiances of the investigators affected the findings in significant ways.

The role of investigator allegiance is a mitigating variable in estimating the effects of all treatments in this area. While it has been observed to occur in a modest but significant amount in psychotherapeutic treatments (Luborsky, Diguer, Schweizer, & Johnson, 1996; Robinson et al., 1990), its most important and unrecognized influence is likely to emerge in pharmacological studies. Greenberg et al. (1992), for example, found that when a given TCA was first contrasted with a placebo control group, the effect size averaged 0.31. However, when a newer TCA was introduced and the original one was now used as a comparison treatment, the effect size attributed to the (now) old TCA was reduced to an average of 0.25 in comparison to a placebo condition.

Noting the consistency with which meta-analytic comparisons have revealed the relative value of psychotherapy over drug therapy in the treatment of depression, several authors (e.g., Barlow, 1994; Wexler & Cicchetti, 1992) have questioned why the practice guidelines established both by the American Psychiatric Association and the Agency for Health Care Policy and Research (AHCPR) have relied so heavily on medication therapy as a front-line treatment for depression (Rush et al., 1993a, 1993b). Using the AHCPR data themselves, Barlow (1994) called into question the conclusion that pharmacotherapy has a higher probability of producing success if offered as a first-line treatment than psychotherapy. To illustrate his point, he translated outcomes into estimates of the percentage of patients who experienced a clinically meaningful change in each condition. Thus, rather than the usual procedure of simply looking at the magnitude of the difference between treatments, he employed a measure of clinically meaningful change, a much more stringent criterion of improvement than a purely statistical definition of significance. He then observed that the average response rates uniformly favored the psychotherapies.

Psychodynamic therapies had the least favorable outcome among the psychotherapies but still produced an 8.4 percent more favorable probability of inducing a clinically positive change than TCAs. In similar comparisons with TCAs, cognitive therapy was determined to have a 15.3 percent more favorable probability of response for depression. Interpersonal psychotherapy (IPT) earned a probability of success that was 12.3 percent greater than that for TCAs, and behavior therapy earned a positive outcome likelihood that was 23.9 percent higher than that for medication.

Another popular perception among clinicians is that treatment outcome is benefited by the combined use of psychotherapy and antidepressant medication (e.g., Feldman & Feldman, 1997; Rivas-Vazquez & Blais, 1997). This perception is also called into question by comparative reviews of both depression (Antonuccio, Danton, & DeNelsky, 1995; Wexler & Cicchetti, 1992) and anxiety disorders (Westra & Stewart, 1998). Meta-analyses of comparisons uniformly fail to support a superior effect for a combination of psychotherapy and medication compared to the result achieved by either one used alone (Robinson et al., 1990; Steinbrueck et al., 1983). Antonuccio et al., (1995) suggest that the major studies on which this popular conclusion is based are all relatively old and predated the use of structured and specific psychotherapies, and Wexler and Cicchetti (1992) found no advantage for combined treatment when outcomes were categorized into classes reflecting success, failure, and dropout rates. In a hypothetical cohort of one hundred patients with major depression, the authors estimate that twenty-nine would recover with pharmacotherapy alone, and forty-seven would improve with psychotherapy alone; the numbers would not change if patients were given both pharmacotherapy and psychotherapy.

While there continue to be many difficulties in any effort to reduce treatment effectiveness arguements to issues of proportional or comparative cost, it bears mentioning that cost-benefit analyses generally yield findings that are consistent with the foregoing analysis. Recall, for example, the results we have previously reported from the large-scale Medical Outcomes Study (Wells & Sturm, 1996), using naturalistic methods. Anonuccio et al. (1997) found even stronger effects when randomized trial studies were compared. They determined that on a cost-benefit basis, SSRIs when used alone cost 33 percent more per unit of benefit than cognitive-behavior therapy (CBT) used alone, and the combination of SSRIs and CBT cost 23 percent more per unit of benefit than CBT alone. Thus, one must conclude that, at this time, little evidence can be mustered to suggest that pharmacotherapy enhances the effects of psychotherapy.

Indirect Health Benefits

It is difficult and hazardous to assess outcomes of treatment purely or even primarily on the basis of costs. The cheapest treatments may be those in which people die or leave treatment early, for example. Yet, cost-benefit analysis should not be ignored. Therefore, it is helpful to look at the indirect effects of treatment for depression on health and health care costs.

While treatment of depression is effective, its cost benefit is highly variable, probably reflecting some of the problems with cost-benefit analysis to which we have alluded. For example, it is difficult to document that treatment for depression has an indirect or offsetting effect on medical well-being. For example, Wells and Sturm (1996) failed to find significant evidence of cost offset for treating depression during a two-year follow-up period, but others (e.g., Schlesinger, Mumford, Glass, Patrick, & Sharfstein, 1983; Shemo, 1985) suggest that these cost offsets begin to be quite noticeable in the third to fifth years of follow-up. This pattern has led some (e.g., Yates, 1995) to suggest that long follow-up periods are necessary if cost-effectiveness research is to report accurately the nature of medical cost offsets. This recommendation is especially important in the treatment of complex, characterological, or recurrent depression.

The picture is clearer among those individuals whose depression is associated with real-life events, such as facing life-threatening medical procedures, or whose depression is manifested in somatic and medical symptoms. Among these groups, a large body of accumulating research demonstrates that successful psychosocial treatment is followed by a substantial cost savings both in long-term medical utilization and in medical cost. For example, in a comprehensive review of meta-analytic and well-controlled primary investigations of the effects of supportive psychotherapy on physical health and costs, Groth-Marnat and Edkins (1996) conclude that cost offset is an important outcome among individuals who initially present for treatment with diffuse physical symptoms associated with depression and other mental health conditions. Patients who present with unusual allergies, tension headaches, abdominal pains, urination urgency, malaise, and hypertension are the ones who most frequently fit this profile. Patients with such complaints and symptoms consume up to nine times more resources than the average medical patient

(Fink, 1992; Smith, 1994); they are the ones who are most likely to have their treatment delayed while their providers seek medical explanations and refer them to expensive laboratory tests; and they are often then denied mental health treatment by the managed-care system.

In the same vein, Gabbard, Lazar, Hornberger, and Spiegel (1997) found that 80 percent of the randomized clinical-trials studies they found on this topic and 100 percent of the nonrandomized clinical trials revealed that the application of psychotherapy was accompanied by a reduction in subsequent medical-care costs.

In one comparison reviewed by Groth-Marnat and Edkins (1996), groups receiving psychosocial interventions were estimated to experience nearly a 10 percent decline in subsequent medical costs, while the nontreated group experienced an estimated 10 percent increase in costs—a total 20 percent differential in costs (Groth-Marnat & Edkins, 1996). Groth-Marnat and Edkins (1996) also conclude that substantial cost offset accrues with the use of presurgical psychotherapy, with the use of supportive therapy among those with general somatic complaints, and with the application of behavioral therapies and biofeedback among patients after myocardial infarction and brain injury. Postdischarge psychotherapy has been found to substantially reduce risk of reinfarction (Frasure-Smith, 1991), and survival rates have been shown to improve among cancer patients with the application of group psychotherapy interventions during the postdiagnostic period (Spiegel, Bloom, Kraemer, & Gottheil, 1989).

It should be noted that Groth-Marnat and Edkins's review is not restricted to individuals with diagnoses of depression. Imposing such a limitation may lead to somewhat different results. Nonetheless, one may conclude from what research is available that support for cost savings has been particularly strong for psychotherapeutic interventions among patients with primary mental health disorders associated with somatic symptoms and among medical patients who receive treatment in order to help them prepare for or adapt to medical treatment and recovery. For example, in a meta-analysis of forty-nine surgical preparation studies, Devine and Cook (1983) found that preoperative psychological interventions resulted in a savings of approximately 1.5 postoperative hospital days among patients with a variety of surgically treated conditions. Savings of more than 50 percent have been documented in both postoperative hospital days and outpatient visits and at least a 30 percent reduction in side effects has been noted for some conditions when patients receive pre-operative behavioral and psychotherapy (e.g., Anderson, 1987; Jacobs, 1987; Olbrisch, 1981).

Because medical practitioners fail to recognize the presence of emotional problems when they are presented along with physical symptoms, the figures for the cost of providing medical services to those with emotional problems presented in the foregoing paragraphs may be understated. Thus, in studies such as that described by Simon, Von Korff, and Barlow (1995), the selected samples of supposedly nondepressed individuals may include a great many whose depression goes unrecognized. Wells and Sturm (1996) suggest that the greatest increase in cost savings for treatments of depressed individuals may well come from increasing the efficiency of prescription practices, rather than from increasing the availability or efficiency of psychotherapy. Their conclusion arises from the assumption that the effectiveness of psychotherapy is near its maximal value in current practice, an assumption that contrasts with the observation that contemporary medical treatment is extremely inefficient.

More specifically, Wells and Sturm observed that (1) a majority of depressed patients seen in primary-care settings were inaccurately diagnosed and provided with treatment that was considered to be insufficient or inappropriate for ameliorating their problem, and (2) psychotherapy had a more favorable cost-benefit ratio than medication in these settings. They concluded that a ceiling effect in psychotherapy would prevent a substantial increase in the efficiency of psychotherapeutic treatment. On the other hand, they reasoned that the inefficiency with which medication is typically applied allowed substantial room for improvement. The assumption that the effectiveness of psychotherapy had reached the upper limits of its potential efficacy deserves to be questioned, however. There is evidence that the favorable effects of psychotherapy are more than just a product of poor diagnosis and mismanagement of medical treatment. For example, as we've seen, when medication and psychotherapeutic treatments are offered by equally well trained practitioners to equally well-diagnosed patient groups, the results continue to strongly favor psychotherapy over pharmacotherapy (Antonuccio et al., 1997). These findings suggest that at its best, even general psychosocial interventions hold some advantage over very specific psychopharmacological ones and warrant consideration as front-line treatments among depressed patients.

It has not been our intention to provide a comprehensive argument regarding and review of medical cost offset studies in this chapter. The few studies cited do illustrate the findings in the available literature, however. In our review, we failed to find a coherent body of studies that does not provide some evidence for the cost offset of psychotherapy. This being the case, the results of cost-offset studies have broad-ranging implications for service delivery. Interestingly, however, they are all but completely ignored by federal legislation, health care administrators, and the medical utilization panels that approve treatments.

Durability of Effects

Barlow (1994) observes that one of the strongest arguments in favor of psychotherapeutic treatment is its ability to maintain improvement at a much higher rate than pharmacotherapy. He concluded, on the basis of one-year follow-up data, that psychotherapy maintains a response rate of approximately 30 percent, compared to 20 percent for those receiving TCAs. The relative durability of psychotherapeutic effects has also been noted by others (e.g., Hollon et al., 1992; Hollon et al., 1991). Across studies, while differences are often not statistically significant, whenever they are present, they favor psychotherapeutic interventions.

It should be noted, however, that maintenance of treatment effects is very difficult. Two-thirds of those who have had a major depressive episode are likely to develop another one within a three- to five-year period; the more frequent the prior episodes, the more likely the recurrence (Kupfer et al., 1992; Frank et al., 1990). While psychotherapeutic interventions tend to reduce relapse rates, these rates are still unacceptably high for all treatments that are currently used. Nonetheless, it remains unclear why prior treatment guidelines have favored front-line psychopharmacological interventions over psychotherapy in view of the disparities noted even in the data produced by those who develop the guidelines. It is likely that at least some of this disparity can be attributed to the relative ease and consistency that are possible with pharmacological treatment as compared to the application of specific psychotherapies. Another factor is that medication produces a more immediate and noticeable effect than psychotherapeutic interventions (Watkins et al., 1993). Certainly, these considerations make sense when making recommendations to primary-care providers who are especially unlikely to be trained and skilled in using such procedures as cognitive therapy, interpersonal psychotherapy, and other demonstrably effective treatments for depression.

As we've noted previously, Wells and Sturm (1996) argue for the potential cost savings of improving medication delivery for depression compared to the cost of psychotherapy. They observe that the initial and short-term costs of psychotherapy are somewhat higher than those for medication and argue that, unlike with psychotherapy, increased efficacy of medication can be instituted at relatively little increase in cost, to a point where the benefit surpasses that of psychotherapy. But, such an analysis assumes that patients will seek out and comply with medical treatments over long periods of time. This may not be so, and this in itself may be one of the reasons that both amount of benefit and long-term cost benefits tend to increase the degree to which psychotherapy surpasses medication's cost benefit, reaching substantial differences when one views two-year follow-up data (Antonuccio et al., 1997).

Meta-analyses findings also raise question about the economic and social benefit of combining these modes of treatment. Only if the clinician values relatively immediate effects and initial costs over maintainance or cost per unit of benefit in the long run can a convincing case be made for the relative value of pharmacotherapy for most depressed conditions. The balance does seem to tip at least modestly toward pharmacotherapy in the case of the most severe depressive conditons. Medication side effects, patient preferences, and third-party payer policies are more elusive variables to consider in making a final treatment decision.

In the preceding paragraphs, we have addressed generally the questions of effectiveness and durability of treatment effects. In chapter 12, we explore some of the more common treatments offered to depressed patients. This chapter complements the information we provided in chapter 3 on the important issue of the differential effectiveness of treatments—are there types of patients for whom different treatments are particularly or uniquely helpful? Before moving on to the more specific nature of treatments used in the contemporary mental health care, however, let us shed some light on what is known about the extremely important issue of the patient who poses significant risk of self-injury.

TREATING POPULATIONS AT RISK: INFORMED CLINICAL KNOWLEDGE

Suicide is the major life-threatening complication of depression that most mental health professionals must face, and it is the most common clinical emergency encountered in mental health practice (Shein, 1976). Greaney (1995) found that the average practicing psychologist treats an average of five suicidal patients per month, and one in three of these psychologists has lost a patient to suicide. Other empirical studies have shown that the average clinical psychologist involved in direct patient care has greater than a one-in-five chance of losing a patient to suicide during his or her professional career (Chemtob, Hamada, Bauer, Torigoe, et al., 1988).

The risk of experiencing a patient's sucide is even higher among physicians. Fifty percent of psychiatrists face this outcome (Chemtob, Hamada, Bauer, Kinney, et al., 1988). While they face a lower risk of treating suicidal patients, inexperienced clinicians whose lack of seasoning makes them especially vulnerable are a particular concern. One in seven clinicians-in-training experiences a patient's suicide (Brown, 1987). In any of these instances, the effect on the professional is profound, usually being as strong as one might expect had the professional lost a family member (Chemtob, Hamada, Bauer, Torigoe, et al., 1988).

In spite of the prevalence of suicidal behaviors and the degree to which they may impede a clinician's effectiveness, we know little from the empirical literature about how to treat those with suicidal thoughts, impulses, and behaviors. Most treatment research systematically excludes groups who are or who appear to be suicidal for fear that the stress of research added to the usual stress of treatment itself may place them at accelerated risk. Yet, because of the seriousness of the threat of suicide, those who treat depression often must address suicidal potential and must therefore know the nature of suicidal risk and the forces that increase this risk. Conventional, clinical wisdom and research on the nature of suicidal behavior must guide us in this process. The question of the likelihood of suicidal and self-destructive behavior as well as the question of how treatment should or might be adapted to the needs of these individuals must be considered in our search to define treatment guidelines. It behooves us, therefore, to define what is known about identifying patients who are at risk and to use this information in an effort to identify how such individuals may be treated.

Risk and Comorbidity

Psychiatric disorder and suicidal risk are related, although the relationship is difficult to tease out. For example, research reveals that people who commit suicide are likely to have suffered from one or more psychiatric disorders (Henriksson et al., 1993; Robins et al., 1959; Runeson, 1989). In a review of the literature, researchers found that at least 88 percent of the subjects from the studies they reviewed qualified for a psychiatric diagnosis at the time of suicide (Barraclough, Bunch, Nelson & Sainsbury, 1974). Psychological autopsies suggest that as many as 93 percent of patients who commit suicide may have qualified for a psychiatric disorder immediately before the suicide (Clark & Fawcett, 1992).

While the causal relationship of psychiatric disorder and suicide cannot be extrapolated directly from these ratings, the figures are sobering and certainly suggest that psychiatric disorder may be considered a risk factor for suicide. Moreover, some diagnoses are more closely related to this risk than are others. The two diagnoses whose presence is most strongly related to completed suicide are depressive disorders and alcohol abuse (Cheng, 1995; Clark, 1992; Isometsä, Henriksson, Hillevi, Kuoppasalmi, & Lönnqvist, 1994; Keller, 1994; Montano, 1994; Pokorny, 1964). Of the two, depressive disorder has consistently been the more common indicator and the stronger predictor of suicide (Isometsä et al., 1994; Keller, 1994; Murphy, 1983; Rihmer, Barsi, Arató, & Demeter, 1990; Zweig & Hinrichsen, 1993). However, it should be pointed out that, knowing what we know about the nonspecific nature of major depression, moderate and severe depressive feelings themselves may be a more important contributor to this relationship than the qualitative determination of diagnostic eligibility. This point should be kept in mind as we consider the relationship between the diagnosis of depression and suicidal behavior.

Black, Warrack, and Winokur (1985) found that nearly one-third of patients who went on to complete suicide had a present, diagnosable affective disorder. The lifetime risk of suicide among patients who have an untreated depressive disorder is nearly 20 percent (Guze & Robins, 1970; Miles, 1977; Montano, 1994; see also Isometsä et al., 1994). The increased risk of suicide that is associated with comorbid depression is summarized in the observation that while the base rate risk of suicide in the United States is 11.2 per 100,000 population (Hirschfeld & Russell, 1997), it is estimated to be between 230 and 566 per 100,000 population among patients who have a current depression, a fifty-fold increase (Clark, Young, Scheftner, Fawcett, & Fogg, 1987; Fremouw, de Perczel, & Ellis (1990).

Similar concerns about comorbidity as a correlate of suicide risk has arisen with older and younger age groups (Callahan, 1993; Morgan, 1989). In a psychological autopsy study, for example, researchers found that two-thirds of the adolescents studied were positive for one of the following three risk factors before their deaths: a history of a prior suicide attempt, the presence of a mood disorder, or a history of alcohol or substance abuse (Shaffer et al., 1996).

Likewise, depressive disorder has been found to predominate in the psychopathological backgrounds of children and youth who are suicidal (Runeson & Rich, 1992). In five published studies of successive adolescents and young adults who suicided, the average reported rate of major depression was 41 percent, and comorbidity of suicide and substance abuse was 48 percent.

Brent et al. (1993a) found that the most significant psychological risk factors associated with adolescent suicide were major depression, bipolar mixed state, substance abuse, and conduct disorder. Eighty-two percent of depressed adolescent suicide victims had a primary affective disorder, and 31 percent had been depressed less than three months prior to committing suicide (Brent et al., 1993a).

Windle, Miller-Tutzauer, & Domenica (1992) conducted a study on 11,400 eighth- and tenth-grade students. Researchers found that higher levels of alcohol use and participation in risky activities were interrelated and were associated with increases in suicidal ideation and attempts across age groups and sexes. Substance abuse as a risk factor for youth suicide has been found to be even more significant when it is comorbid with an affective illness than to when it occurs alone (Brent et al., 1993a). King et al. (1993) examined alcohol consumption in relation to depression in a study of fifty-four psychiatrically disturbed inpatient females between the ages of thirteen to eighteen. They found alcohol consumption to be associated with the severity of recent suicidal behaviors in a subsample of subjects with major depression (King et al., 1993).

Brent at al. (1993b) found that the rates of major depression, posttraumatic stress disorders, and suicidal ideation beginning after exposure to peer suicide were elevated in their exposure group compared to their control group. Almost all of the exposed subjects who developed new-onset suicidality did so in the context of a new-onset depressive episode beginning within one month of their suicide exposure (Brent et al., 1993b).

Lewinsohn, Gotlib, & Seeley (1995) have identified adolescents who are at risk for major depression. They found risk factors specific to major depressive disorder to be: stress (minor and major events), emotional reliance, physical symptoms and disease, history of suicide attempt, and a past episode of depression or anxiety disorder. Garland & Zigler (1993) suggest that intervention efforts have not benefited from current research findings since communication between the two areas of research and clinical practice is lacking. Slap et al. (1992) suggest that suicide attempters are common among adolescent clinic patients and that physicians may not recognize them and thus may not treat them.

Likewise, comorbidity among older adults constitutes an apparent risk factor. McIntosh (1988), Morgan (1989), and Osgood (1985) have noted that diagnostically, depression, alcoholism, and organic brain syndrome are the most common mental disorders of the suicidal elderly, in a way that is similar to younger persons. However, Achte (1988), McIntosh (1988), and Morgan (1989) point out that while it is convenient to speak epidemiologically about the elderly as a homogeneous group, the correct assessment of risk must always evaluate the elderly from an individualized perspective. This recommendation extends to all age groups, primarily because the influence of diagnosis, while significant, is sufficiently small as to preclude any individual identification of risk.

Diagnosis-Specific Risk Profiles

In an effort to define who is at risk for suicide in a more specific and precise fashion than what can be predicted from diagnosis alone, Clark and Fawcett (1992) advocate the formulation of diagnosis-specific suicide risk-profiles. In justifying this approach, Clark (1990) suggests that there may be different types of suicide, "defined in terms of demographic situation, psychodynamic motives, or diagnostic features, and that it would be better to tailor risk prediction equations to different *types* of high-risk patients" (p. 104). Although profiles of suicide completers can generally be created from epidemiological data, a more specific focus (a subcategorization) of individuals is needed to enhance the specificity of risk profiles. Many have assumed that one's diagnosis provides such a subcategorization. The creation of diagnosis-specific (or perhaps, symptom-specific) profiles uses the diagnosis (or symptom) as the initial and most general point at which patients who are at risk for suicide are defined. Pokorny (1983) articulates the rationale for this decision, pointing out that psychiatric disorders may be funneling points that help narrow and delineate patients who are at risk. This position is consistent with the research demonstrating that the accuracy of suicide predictions is enhanced by a knowledge of whether the patient qualifies for one or more psychiatric disorders (Martin, Cloninger, Guze, & Clayton, 1985). If depression is better described by the severity of affect, hopelessness, or some other correlate of mood than by the presence of a certain number of qualitative symptoms, however, the power of the proposed profiles would be better fit to this dimension. Which of these approaches will be of most value is yet to be determined.

Clark (1990) summarizes his four-point rationale for making diagnosis-specific profiles. First, the positive relationship between mental illness and suicide may lead one to believe that mental illness itself may be a risk factor. Second, the elevated rate of death by suicide among patients with specific disorders, particularly major affective disorders, alcoholism, and schizophrenia, leads one to infer that suicide risk is more specific to some disorders than to others. Third, since these predictive disorders have quite distinct (although overlapping) clinical presentations, courses, prognoses, and treatments, it is logical to infer that there are distinguishing profiles that are associated with suicide risk. Fourth, according to Clark, the advent of structured interviews and well-delineated diagnostic categories provides the means to define reliable distinctions among patients.

In the development of diagnosis-specific profiles, an effort is made to enhance predictive accuracy by developing predictive algorithms within each diagnosis. These algorithms are based on patterns of demographic and family history, originally drawn from an analysis of patterns that are present among successful suicides.

In a program that bears on the effort to define diagnosis specific groups, the National Institute of Mental Health Collaborative Program on the Psychobiology of Depression sought to derive from a review of current clinical status and family history a comprehensive description of both the biological and the psychological characteristics of some one thousand affective-disordered patients (Katz, Secunda, Hirschfeld, & Koslow, 1979). Fawcett (1988) and Fawcett and colleagues (Fawcett et al., 1987, 1990) participated by assessing a comprehensive range of demographic, clinical, and family variables collected from patients at risk for suicide, by use of standardized methods, with a focus on evaluating the impact of major affective disorder. Unfortunately, the complicated multidimensional nature of suicide made it difficult to formulate a set of generalizable risk profiles that had predicitive validity beyond the sample from which they were created (Clark et al., 1987; Murphy, 1983).

To date, these and other efforts to define profiles that are associated with suicide risk have been inconsistent and overlapping. While overlap itself may not be a constraining factor, the greater the overlap, the less meaningful and specific the resulting predictions. When the overlap is so complete as to prevent the identification of clear patterns, the results do not allow enhanced prediction of risk. Clark and Fawcett (1992) assert that the inevitable overlap that exists among diagnosis-specific profiles is a small price to pay if one can in fact extract a specific profile that yields efficient prediction rather than an all-purpose or general risk profile. However, to date, clear profiles based on diagnosis have not emerged. No pathognomic sign for suicide has been identified, and research has failed to create generalized risk profiles that have any predictive validity beyond the sample from which they were created (Clark et al., 1987; Murphy, 1983). This, once again, may be reflective of the poor fit between categorical diagnoses and other quantitative variables that may be reflected in one's mood in the case of depressive disorders.

Murphy (1983) suggests another possibility to account for the failure. He suggests that the difficulty, to date, in defining diagnosis-specific predictions resides in the tendency to use broad, demographic dimensions rather than specific aspects of behavior or presentation. He suggests that these features and background factors are far too general to be of practical use. However, he continues to be optimistic about the possibility that diagnosis-specific profiles can eventually provide usable data if investigators will work to identify more specific characteristics and patterns that identify recognizable subgroupings of suicidal patients.

Ultimately, the value of diagnosis-specific groupings will hinge on the validity and specificity of diagnosis-specific patient qualities that are associated with suicide. Fawcett (1988) emphasizes this point: "The more complete and valid the clinical profile of the patient on the verge of suicide, the more successful the clinician may be in recognizing the imminent suicide in time to take preventive action" (p. 7). It is still uncertain if diagnostic criteria can be applied with sufficient reliability and specificity to serve this purpose. Thus, current efforts to predict suicide have turned to more specific aspects of depression, such as age, severity, and specific aspects of family history.

Age

In the general population, the expectation of suicide is 11.2 completions per 100,000 population (Hirschfeld & Russell, 1997). These rates are especially high among the young and the old. Youth suicide is a mental and health problem of epidemic proportions (Felner, Adan, & Silverman, 1992). Evidence indicates that over the past three decades the rate of suicide has increased among fifteen- to twenty-four-year-olds and is currently the third leading cause of death for this age group after accidents and homicide (Garland & Zigler, 1993; Henry, Stephenson, Hanson, & Hargett, 1993; National Center for Health Statistics, 1991; Sokol & Pfeffer, 1992).

Worldwide, suicide is usually the second or third leading cause of death, after accidents and homicides, for adolescents, depending on the country in which they reside (Jeanneret, 1992). Data show that suicide rates for males are regularly higher than for females (Jeanneret, 1992). Data for 1987 show that nearly five thousand officially recorded suicides were logged for adolescents between the ages of fifteen and twenty-four in the United States during that year, which works out to a rate of 12.9 per 100,000 (Berman & Jobes, 1992; National Center for Health Statistics, 1989). Between the years 1957 and 1987, completed suicide among fifteen- to twenty-four-year-olds more than tripled, from 4.0 per 100,000 to 12.9 per 100,000. Rates for fifteen- to nineteen-year-olds have quadrupled, from 2.5 per 100,000 to 10.3 per 100,000 (Berman & Jobes, 1992).

A typical United States high school with two thousand students can expect to lose one student or former student to suicide every five years (Davis & Sandoval, 1991). The vast majority of adolescents who commit suicide seem to have long histories of disturbed behavior, such as depression and substance abuse, and have experienced situational stressors involving feelings of humiliation, anger, or futility (Rich, Sherman, & Fowler, 1990).

The problem reveals itself to be only slightly less significant as research focuses on younger age groups. Suicide has been ranked as the sixth leading cause of death among prepubertal children aged five to fourteen according to the 1989 National Center for Health Statistics census (Greene, 1994). Greene (1994) suggested that mental health professionals regard this as an underestimate, since suicide may in fact be the third leading cause of death for children of this age. Signs of depression in children may manifest differently from how they appear in adults. The DSM-IV (American Psychiatric Association, 1994) allows for irritability as a sign of depressed mood in children.

Depressed children may not verbalize their feelings; depressed mood can be observed during play by observing the child's demeanor (Sokol & Pfeffer, 1992). However, somatic signs may be present as well as anhedonia, poor academic performance, feelings of hopelessness, guilt, worthlessness, and a withdrawn quality (Sokol & Pfeffer; 1992). Asarnow (1992) found that suicidal children had more depressive symptoms than were noted in a control group. In terms of interventions, Sokol and Pfeffer (1992) suggests informing the child's guardians, performing a psychiatric evaluation, and hospitalizing the child if necessary.

Similarly, the emergence of old age appears to place an individual at risk. One of the most basic facts about suicide in the United States is that its risk increases as a function of age (Vaillant & Blumenthal, 1990), and although in the past thirty years we have seen a great increase in the rate of suicide in youth, "80-year-olds are still twice as likely to commit suicide as 20-year-olds" (Vaillant & Blumenthal, 1990, p. 1). Achte (1988) noted that although the frequency of attempted suicide decreases as people get older, the number of successful suicides increases. Elderly people are in fact more likely to succeed in taking their own lives than are younger persons. Results of a survey of crisis prevention centers that examined the training, knowledge, and current practices relating to elder suicide criticized the insufficient training, the lack of familiarity with recent suicide trends, and the limited outreach to older adults (Adamek & Kaplan; 1996).

Achte (1988) stated that risk factors for suicide in the elderly include losses and loneliness, injuries to self-esteem in old age, aging and poor body image, and depression and depressive disorders. In confirmation of Achte's observation on the relative importance of social isolation as a risk factor in the elderly, Maris reports that, in one study of the general population, suicide completers generally scored higher in social isolation than did nonfatal attempters or those who died by natural causes (Maris, 1981, 1989). Also, Osgood and Thielman (1990) point out that early recognition of depression and other underlying mental disoders is essential for suicide prevention among the elderly.

Severity of Depression

Traditional clinician-based measures of depression severity, such as the Hamilton Rating Scale for Depression (Hamilton, 1967) and clinician ratings of functional impairment, do not relate strongly to suicide risk (Goodwin & Guze, 1989). Even some self-report instruments (e.g., Beck Depression Inventory; Beck & Steer, 1987; Beck Hopelessness Scale, Beck & Steer, 1988) have been shown to fluctuate widely or even to show improvement immediately prior to suicide gestures on measures of depression and helplessness (e.g., Beck & Steer, 1989). In an effort to explain this finding as it pertains to the Beck Depression Inventory, Beck, Steer, Kovacs, & Garrison (1985) conclude that suicide is a direct reflection not of the severity of depression alone but of the related experiences of hope and hopelessness. Thus, they assert that the patient's experience of hopelessness is the overriding factor of importance in predicting suicide. If this is true, then a profiling system built around the pattern of responses associated with increasing levels of helplessness would be a better approach to suicide prevention than a diagnostic-based one.

Family History

Shaffer (1988; Shaffer et al., 1985) compared the family histories of depressed patients who completed suicide to the histories of those who did not. The authors found no appreciable difference in suicide completion rates for first- and second-degree relatives of either group of patients. This is not an unusual finding and has led Clark and Fawcett (1992) to conclude that there is no empirical support for the suggestion that suicidal family history may be a risk factor in current suicide risk. Clark and Fawcett suggest that whatever added risk may be incurred by a positive family history is subsumed by the stronger relationship between family history and psychopathology. Family history does not appear to add predictive power beyond that available from a knowledge of a family history of major affective disorder.

Other Correlates of Suicide Risk

Virtually the only historical indicator of suicide beyond the general contribution of affective disorder is a history of previous suicide gestures. Fawcett and colleagues (Fawcett et al., 1987, 1990) found that a history of suicide attempts was significantly associated with completed suicide over the subsequent two- to ten-year period. However, the medical seriousness of these attempts did not differentiate completers from those who did not ultimately kill themselves, and such personality features as loss of self-esteem, guilt, and weight loss were not significantly associated with suicide completion in either the short or the long run. Finally, neither endogenous nor reactive depression placed subjects at increased risk of suicide, beyond the general contribution of depression itself (Fawcett et al., 1987, 1990).

Treatment and Modifiable Risk Factors

In spite of the failure to find clear suicide profiles, Fawcett et al. (1990) point out that the correlation between suicide rate and affective state provides enough of a reason to implement preventive care. They suggest that factors such as alcohol abuse, anxiety, depressive disorder, and other correlates constitute modifiable risk factors. For example, among severely depressed patients, both severe anxiety and panic attacks, identified as important risk factors, can be treated with a combination of pharmacological intervention (such as benzodiazepines or neuroleptics in the presence of psychotic anxiety or depressive turmoil), ego-supportive therapy, and environmental manipulation. Similarly, hopelessness and anhedonia, the two specific cognitive-affective dimensions that are most highly correlated with suicide, can be managed with intensive pharmacotherapy, cognitive therapy, or interpersonal therapy (Fawcett, 1988, p. 8).

Beck et al. (1985) agree with Fawcett et al.'s insights into the treatment of hopelessness and recommend that cognitive therapy, perhaps supplemented with pharmacotherapy, be utilized as initial interventions to reduce levels of hopelessness and therefore suicidal risk.

Much of what constitutes treatment for suicidal risk relies on the use of clinical wisdom and experience to treat such patients. Unfortunately, there are few general guidelines available, and even if there were more, few mental health professionals (i.e., psychiatrists, psychologists, social workers, and marriage and family therapists) undergo the training that one would suppose may be required to learn to treat such people. Indeed, Bongar and Harmatz (1991) have reported that an average of only approximately 40 percent of graduate-level university-based and professional clinical psychology programs offer formal training in the study of suicide. Similarly, Kubin (1994) found that 41 percent of marriage and family training curricula offer a formal suicidology course, and only 29 percent of accredited social work programs in the United States offered formal training in the study of suicide (Levin, 1994). These figures raise the question of whether clinicians working with suicidal patients are adequately trained to deal with their patients' suicidal crises. However, the failure of research to identify those who are at risk of suicide has also limited the development of empirically based treatments for those patients.

Because the identification of risk is difficult, some researchers have turned their attention away from making predictions of patient risk to examination of the behaviors of clinicians who are interacting with suicidal patients (e.g., Bruno, 1995; Greaney, 1995; Mahrer, 1993). The resulting efforts to develop standards of care blend the little empirical evidence available on risk identification with a great deal of clinical impression and wisdom. This approach also seeks to join studies of patient characteristics with the field of clinician training in hopes of describing reasonable and prudent practitioner behaviors. A profile of reasonable clinician strategies for addressing the patient who is felt to be at risk not only is useful in identifying the standard of care but also can form the basis for practice guidelines and provide a direction for training professionals to work with these patients.

CONCLUSIONS

We find little support for the assumption that there are specific treatments that affect depression but not related conditions, such as substance abuse and anxiety. Indeed, there are a wide variety of effective treatments for depression and dysphoria, suggesting that guidelines for treating depression should be of broad use and appeal.

In spite of the generally positive findings regarding the rate of success in treating depression, there are large omissions in the data. This is particularly true for those patients who are at risk for suicide. Perhaps because the predictors of suicide have been so hard to identify, the treatment of suicidal patients lacks a strong empirical base. Indeed, it is not unusual for the predictors of sucidal risk to be essentially unrelated to treatment. For example, while age is a correlate of increased suicidal risk, it does not contribute to the development of a specific treatment.

Practice guidelines are becoming more and more prominent, and are being presented to the average practitioner for use in many situations and with numerous disorders (e.g., American Psychiatric Association, 1994; Depression Guideline Panel, 1993). However, such guidelines typically are not empirically based, especially as they apply to suicide, but blend a little empirical knowledge with available clinical wisdom. Nonetheless, as Furrow (1993) has pointed out, regardless of their intended use, practice guidelines are likely to be used by both plaintiff and defense attorneys in malpractice litigations. Although Black (1979) describes a standard of care as "that degree of care which a reasonable prudent professional should exercise in same or similar circumstances" (p. 1260; see also Bongar, 1991; Bongar, Maris, Berman, & Litman, 1992), when a case of negligence is brought against a practitioner, the "reasonableness" of the practitioner's behavior is more often determined by expert witness testimony than by empirically established evidence (VandeCreek, Knapp, & Herzog, 1987). Treatment of the suicidal patient, therefore, is guided by practicality, experience, and concerns with legal liability (Clark & Fawcett, 1992; Simon, 1992).

A more sound and empirically defined base of treatment is needed. Since the predictors of suicidal risk are essentially unrelated to the development of specific treatments, it may be possible to extract principles of treatment from the results of research on the effectiveness of different treatment models and approaches for those with depression and related disorders. In chapter 12, we review what is known about the treatment of specific problems and the use of specific treatment approaches.

12 *Structuring Treatment*

From Managed Care to Treatment Manuals

As research has evaluated the hundreds of treatment modalities that have evolved to ameliorate depression and other disorders, it has become apparent that many different views and models of treatment produce good results. Treatments for depression and anxiety are quite successful, at least for the initial alleviation of symptoms. Moreover, the average benefits and effectiveness of treatment seem to be quite similar across a variety of treatments, and the average value of any given intervention appears to be quite independent of the accuracy of the theory on which it is based (e.g., Barlow, 1994; Clarkin, Pilkonis, & Magruder, 1996; Thase & Kupfer, 1996). Even more, it seems to matter little whether the treatment is medical or psychological, or even whether it is delivered by a highly trained professional or by a specially trained lay person (Berman & Norton, 1985; Christensen & Jacobson, 1994; Holloway & Neufeldt, 1995; Stein & Lambert, 1995).

In spite of the generally good short-term results of treatment, the long-term performance of many treatments is less than remarkable. Relapse rates are unacceptably high, and the unabated and increasing prevalence and pervasiveness of depressive spectrum conditions underscore how weak even our most effective interventions are. While some studies conclude that treatment improvements are well maintained (e.g., McLean & Hakstian, 1990; Robinson, Berman, & Neimeyer, 1990), other research suggests that relapse rates are high. For example, Jacobson and Hollon (1996b) report that relapse rates may be from 60 percent to 80 percent during the two years following treatment termination. The failure to find one or more treatments whose effects are uniquely strong and specific as well as the limited success of current treatments in reducing relapse rates, has presented a special dilemma for a health care system whose avowed objectives are the reduction of costs and of long-term care.

These facts about the treatment of depressive disorders suggest the two

312

important conclusions that we have iterated on several occasions: that non-bipolar depression is less a set of finite and discrete disorders than a marker for unhappiness and stress and that, because depression is nonspecific, it is difficult to generate much faith in the existence of one or more treatments whose effects are unique and specific. If depression were a specific and delineated condition, one would expect there to be quite specific treatments for it. The fact that the average effects of virtually all treatments are nearly equal suggests that depression is not a specific symptom or condition but a general one. Not even the presence of vegetative signs, which are most frequently used to support the belief that depressive spectrum disorders are coherent entities (Grove et al., 1987), serves as a marker to identify who will respond better and specifically to treatments designed for depression than to general and nonspecific treatments.

If neither diagnosis of depression nor its treatment is specific, then we must look for aspects beyond the diagnostic symptoms and the treatment qualities to decide for whom a variety of methods are best suited. In this instance, depressive symptoms, and probably other diagnostic criteria as well, would serve better as criteria of change than as differential indicators for prescribing and proscribing treatments.

Reconfiguring the spectrum of depression as we suggested would be warranted if it could be demonstrated that some patients respond to certain treatments and not to others. As we have already noted, it is in fact reasonably clear that, in spite of the generally good average level of effectiveness among treatments, within all treatments there are wide variations of response that include many individuals who get better, some who do not change, and some who get worse. In comparisons of pharmacotherapy and psychotherapy, there is some conceptual agreement that severity of impairment may be an indicator for determining which patients will respond better to a particular treatment (Elkin, 1994), but identification of indicators of the relative responsivity of patients to different psychotherapies has been longer in coming. Evidence is now emerging that certain characteristics, either hidden within or masked by diagnostic criteria, may predetermine a patient's positive response to one treatment and a negative or nonresponse to another (Beutler & Clarkin, 1990). These characteristics, for the most part, are not captured by diagnostic criteria. It is this possibility that directs the focus of this book.

Ultimately, treatment guidelines must help clinicians make two decisions: Who will and who will not respond to treatment? To what specific treatment or treatments is a given patient most likely to respond? The answers to these questions are central to identifying both what we think of as the basic or common qualities of treatment—those that must be present to ensure that most patients will respond favorably—and the specific qualities to which patients will respond discriminatively, in an optimal and escalated way.

PACKAGING TREATMENT: SEPARATING
THE TREATMENT FROM THE TREATER

Applying effective treatments and avoiding ineffective ones require that the relevant components of treatments be identified separately from the clinician who applies the treatment. However, this is no mean task. All treatment is at least partially guided by a set of assumptions, and these assumptions arise both from the formal theory underlying the treatment and from the clinician who uses it. These assumptions constitute a theory or model that explains, rightly or wrongly, the nature of the problem and identifies what is expected to alleviate the problem and why.

There are literally hundreds of formal theories (Herink, 1980), each of which is given a slightly different twist by each clinician who applies it. Some of these formal theories are very abstract, and it is often difficult either to specify the component activities that constitute a given treatment or to identify which of these components accounts for the observed effects of treatment. One of the greatest difficulties in identifying effective components of treatment arises because the aspects of the environment that make up the treatment context are assigned different weights and meanings by different theoretical perspectives. Even constructs that are acknowledged and defined by many or all theories (e.g., patient expectancy, support, remoralization), may be treated as integral and active parts of one model of treatment but be considered incidental and nonspecific by another.

The fact that each clinician gives her own twist to these formal theories further complicates the effort to understand the effective components of treatment. There is often only a weak relationship between clinical theory and clinical practice. Even clinicians who share a common theoretical perspective vary widely in how they apply their treatment, and these variations are compounded by wide differences in the effects that follow the use of identical or similar procedures.

Such variations of application both within and across ostensibly distinct treatments, as well as in the excessive power often attributed to very abstract and unmeasurable variables by various theories, make it necessary to determine empirically the nature of the components of treatment that effect and inhibit change. The uncertain nature of these variables has been among the forces that have both encouraged the development of clinical guidelines in practice and augured the development of treatment manuals in outcomes research.

Identifying the factors that actually constitute effective treatment would probably have remained an exercise to be reserved for academic discussions and esoteric research had it not been for a number of social developments that forced clinical practice to become relatively less concerned with theoretical models of treatment and more concerned with the actual methods of clinical practice. There are two ways in which this renewed emphasis on objective aspects of practice have been manifest. One way is the development of managed-care programs that can be translated across clinicians and environments. The second is the increasing reliance on treatment manuals to guide the training and practice of service delivery.

The clinician, in structuring treatment, must always seek some balance between the desirability of individualizing patient care and the economics of one-size-fits-all standardized care. Individual clinicians value individualization of treatment, while third-party payors usually favor some form of standardization. An inspection of managed-care programs provides a laboratory in which we can see the nature and consequence of replacing individually tailored treatments and clinical judgment with standard, structured treatments and cost-based decisions. In this chapter, we inspect some of the efforts to structure treatments, which is necessary both for well-managed clinical care and for research that tries to identify the effective and ineffective components of treatment. We believe that it will be informative to review the historical trends that have led up to the standardization of treatment programs and to evaluate the effects of these movements on the psychosocial context of treatment, especially as represented in the practice of psychotherapy.

Standardization of Clinical Treatment

A variety of factors have led to the introduction of increasing structure into clinical decision making and treatment monitoring. The fee-for-service tradition of the U.S. health care system has been decidedly individualistic in nature. Treatment, in this tradition, has been a matter to be decided between a patient and a provider. The foci of the treatments advocated from this perspective invariably emphasize the uniqueness of each patient and the importance of individual treatment tailored by an experienced and highly trained clinician. The language of this perspective is reflected in such goals as personal well-being, quality of life, emotional health, and personal growth. The advocates of theoretical models that are compatible with this clinical approach eschew what they perceive as the impersonal or cold factuality that is inherent in a system that is driven by cost rather than service and criticize the shortsightedness of programs that arise from efforts to reduce treatment to a matter of cost. However, the structure and components of individualized treatment plans differ widely across clinicians, and the accuracy of individualized assignment of attributes and predictions of outcomes is significantly affected by incidental experiences and by the background of the clinician (Brooks, 1981; Garb, 1989; Houts & Graham, 1986; Langer & Abelson, 1974; Wierzbicki, 1993; Wilson, 1996).

Practitioners from numerous different theoretical backgrounds are included among those who adopt and advocate an ideographic tradition; they emphasize the value of clinical impressions and the development of uniquely individualized treatments based on these impressions (e.g., Davison & Lazarus, 1995; Malatesta, 1995; Persons, 1991). Such practitioners disparage the lack of flexibility and specificity that is necessarily inherent in formulations based on treatment restricted by mean group values and statistical algorithms. Yet, for forty years, it has been apparent empirically that such clinical judgments are far more fallible and expensive than those based on statistical formulas. Meehl's (1960) now old conclusion that diagnostic accuracy and behavioral predictions based on simple statistical formula are more accurate than even the most complex clinical judgment has never been refuted empirically (Dawes, Faust, & Meehl, 1989).

Clinicians' faith in their own perceptions and opinions far surpasses either the accuracy or efficiency of these opinions and viewpoints (Houts & Graham, 1986), and clinicians frequently are persuaded by illusory relationships between observations, even when these relationships have no foundation in fact (Chapman & Chapman, 1969). Clinicians' opinions are unduly influenced by unusual but interesting events, personal beliefs and biases, and emotionally charged events (Houts & Graham, 1986; Nisbett & Ross, 1980). These are not unlike the factors that stimulate belief in astrology and fortune telling. Jeanne Dixon, for example, became famous as a psychic because of one prophecy—the prediction that President John F. Kennedy would die in office, a prediction that had such an emotional impact that her reputation as a psychic became cemented without regard to whether this or any of her other predictions exceeded chance levels of accuracy. Clinicians, too, may be more likely to remember successful predictions than unsuccessful ones, particularly if there are strong emotions associated with these successes. This leads them to exaggerate the frequency of successful clinical judgments. Clinicians come to believe firmly in the validity of their own clinical judgments, even though their formulations often are incorrect and their predictions are of no greater than chance significance. Often, clinician perceptions and judgments are no more accurate than observations made by untrained lay persons, and the strength of clinicians' beliefs bears no relationship to the accuracy of their judgments (Wierzbicki, 1993). Clinical experience, if anything, increases one's reliance on illusory correlations—relationships that are perceived and accepted but that are not factual. This reliance impedes both the flexibility and the accuracy of judgments.

Given these factors and sources of interference in judgment, it should be no surprise that reliance on the illusory accuracy of clinical judgments is costly, especially among those who are not specifically trained in methods of anchoring their own perceptions and judgments to external observations. For example, the rate of accurate detection of depression among primary-care providers hovers under 10 percent in spite of the high level of confidence that these clinicians have in their judgments (Quill, 1985). The fallibility and the inaccuracy of clinical judgments have been major factors in the increased cost of treatment and prevention programs and are partly behind the movement by managed health care programs to standardize care. The failure of front-line providers to recognize the role of emotional factors in health care and concomitantly to accurately identify mental health conditions that accompany physical symptoms contributes to the high medical costs of treating those with depression.

The large-scale Medical Outcomes Study (MOS) (Wells & Sturm, 1996) revealed that the mean annual per-patient cost of mental health treatment can reach $3,900 for depressed, primary-care patients. Other evidence suggests that the annual cost for depressed patients are at least 1.5 times as high as those for nondepressed individuals (Johnson, Weissman, & Klerman, 1992; Manning & Wells, 1992).

On another level, the traditional clinician-centered system of health care placed the responsibility for defining patients' needs for treatment in the fallible hands of the same group of individuals who provided, and financially benefited from, the care recommended. Usually, in fact, the same individual was responsible for both assigning the level of treatment and providing it, an invariable conflict of interest. Regardless of the good intentions of well-meaning practitioners, such a system was both highly susceptible to bias and notoriously unreliable. It proved to be a costly, often self-serving, and easily abused system of care. It should be no surprise, therefore, that, in this environment, the estimated needs for service in any community came to be a direct function of the number of mental health providers who practiced in that community. The epidemiology of disorders changed to fit the availability of services, rather than vice versa. The result was an unworkable system, and the United States saw dramatically escalating and unsustainable increases in health care costs during the 1970s and 1980s.

In an effort to rectify this provider-centered and costly system, state and federal legislation was initiated to develop structured systems of care that could monitor and control costs. But, invariably, standardization came at the expense of individualization of treatment. The resulting managed health care programs were and are designed to reduce the symptoms and increase the functioning of the average, rather than either the unique or even the representative, patient. But, this nomothetic approach has also proven to be problematic. The average patient is a statistical anomaly, not a reality. No patient fits a given multidimensional average, and, inevitably, treatment that is designed for this average patient will fit no one very well. Regardless of their professional training, the keepers and advocates of this nomothetic perspective are more easily identified as pragmatists and agents of the political system than they are as clinicians, idealists, and theorists. Indeed, the tasks of such keepers have often been relegated to clerks whose language is filled with terms such as cost-effectiveness, efficiency, functional adaptability, and normality. Accordingly, their prescribed interventions are more easily described as systems of care than as treatments. Those who advocate such programmatic approaches to treatment have tended to perceive traditional practitioners as lacking business sense and as softheaded and opportunistic.

A continuing obstacle to realizing the promise of a truly cost-effective and integrated treatment has been that, within a politicized managed-care system, cost and access of services have become more important criteria of a treatment's worth than the effects of the services provided or the amount of benefit actually achieved. In chapter 2, we described the phases through which managed care has evolved. The initial movement, predictably, identified effects in economic terms, and the second phase added ease of access and utilization rates to the criteria of effectiveness. Only quite recently have we begun to add clinical outcomes to the cost-based criteria of benefit by which programs are evaluated.

Advent and Development of Managed Care

Managed care arose as a response to escalating medical costs. It has rapidly become the dominant method of providing medical coverage to U.S. citizens and is a major and omnipresent element in the United States today (Appelbaum, 1993). Health care is estimated to be a $100 billion industry with more than 80 percent of working people enrolled in HMOs (Newman, 1996). But, managed-care procedures have increasingly received criticism from both the public and health professionals. Rabasca (1998), for example, reports that, whereas affected employees were generally as well satisfied with managed health care programs in 1991 as they had been with indemnity programs, by 1998, 77 percent of consumers believed that changes were needed. It is likely that health care programs will undergo significant changes in the next few years to accommodate the accumulating dissatisfaction.

It is apparently true that managed health care has been successful in reducing health care costs and that people are more satisfied with the care they receive than they are with the system of managed care in general. Nonetheless, as we consider the effectiveness of current treatments, it will be useful for us to describe some of the current problems that have been identified with these programs.

The central focus of managed care has been cost containment. Success in this endeavor has largely been dependent on establishing a prospective or concurrent review of care provided to individual patients with payment denied for care thought to be unnecessary or not cost-effective (Appelbaum, 1993). Short-term care and, increasingly, demonstrably efficient psychotherapy have been prioritized (e.g., Cummings, Budman, & Thomas, 1998). Thus, managed care impacts both the provider and the patient at every level of the treatment process. This is demonstrated by the requirement that preauthorization be obtained before treatment begins (Kerr, 1986; Knopp, 1986; Lazarus, 1993, 1995; Olfson, 1989; Professional Liability, 1991; Rissmiller et al., 1994), by the creation of evaluation criteria (Garnick, Hendricks, Dulski, & Thorpe, 1994; Flynn and Henisz, 1975; Sederer, 1987; Sederer and Summergrad, 1983), by the reliance on paraprofessionals (Westermeyer, 1991), by the indirect rationing of treatment (Miller, 1996), and by the premature discharge of patients or discharge direct from the emergency room (Bradbury, Golec, and Stearns, 1991; Forster and King, 1994; Hymowitz, 1995; Olfson, 1989; Professional Liability, 1991).

Kerr (1986) reported that rigorous regulations by managed-care organizations are employed to reduce the usage of emergency medical treatment by patients. Kerr (1986) reported that seven managed-care companies he surveyed, instructed patients to go to the emergency room (ER) only when their "life is threatened" or there is "danger of permanent damage or disability" (p. 727). Further, if a patient is in need of "immediate attention" but his or life life is not threatened, the patient is told to call a phone number provided or the primary-care physician. In short, managed-care patients are told that if their illness is not life threatening, then the company will not pay for emergency room treatment received (Kerr, 1986, citing policies of Compcare Health Services Insurance Corporation, Family Health Plan, Health Plus, Inc., HealthReach, Primecare Health Plan of Wisconsin, Inc., Samaritan Health Plan, and Total Care Health Plan, Inc.).

The managed-care procedures cited place the patient in the "nearly impossible situation of having to decide whether he is dying" (Kerr, 1986, p. 727). Patients are not trained to determine whether their symptoms are serious enough to be considered life threatening. As a result, the cost-conscious patient will try to contact his physician or use the managed-care hotline first, rather than risk having an emergency room visit not covered. This action may waste valuable time in situations that are life threatening by postponing the arrival of emergency services (Kerr, 1986; Knopp, 1986; Lazarus, 1993).

Additionally, the role of managed care in the treatment decision process is of marked significance when crises arise for patients and their physicians (Kerr, 1986; Knopp, 1986; Lazarus, 1993, 1995; Olfson, 1989; Professional Liability, 1991; Rissmiller, Steer, Ranieri et al., 1994; Schuster et al., 1995; Wise, 1989). Preauthorization for treatment is processed by outside reviewers, often completely removed from contact with the patient (Olsen, Rickles, and Travlik, 1995; Sharfstein, 1989). Additional concerns arise for the ER provider. Dr. T. A. Mitchell reported that federal law obligates him to provide care, but there is no standard that obligates an HMO to pay for treatment (Pear, 1995). This point is seconded by Dr. Stephen G. Lynn, of St. Luke's-Roosevelt Hospital in New York City. He reported that HMOs are increasingly refusing to pay for emergency room treatment (Pear, 1995).

Kerr's (1986) concern for the role of managed care in the treatment decision process is echoed by Lazarus (1993), who documented how managed care affects the use of resources in intensive-care units. Lazarus (1993) proposed that in situations where illness is considered life threatening, care should not wait for a decision by managed-care personnel. Such decisions often result in decreased quality of care delivery and can lead to protracted treatment made necessary by treatment delays (Knopp, 1986).

Garnick, Hendricks, Dulski, and Thorpe (1994) investigated utilization management programs for mental health and alcohol and drug abuse treatment. They surveyed thirty-one companies with agreements with a large corporation that furnished decision support software to aid in evaluations of employees' health care costs and usage. The questionnaire was administered to employee benefits managers or managed-care representatives. Areas covered included qualifications of case management personnel, admissions criteria and length-of-stay criteria, carve-out programs for mental health and drug/ alcohol benefits; penalties for not following procedures; and review of outpatient services. Also, the investigators asked questions that targeted the following: penalties for not receiving preadmission certification, operating proprietary standards, and case managers' training. Findings of the Garnick et al. (1994) survey included the observation that, although most companies stated they had a range of personnel for reviewing claims, it was unclear from the data what percentage of mental health and substance abuse cases actually were reviewed by an employee who had specialized training in those areas.

With respect to admissions and length of stay, only three companies stated that they followed publicly available standards. More than two-thirds of the companies surveyed reported that utilization review for mental health and substance abuse was the same as for other services. However, the majority of the companies also stated that there were particular nurse reviewers for mental health and substance abuse. With regard to following protocol, all companies required preauthorization; failure to gain preadmission certification resulted in penalties. These penalties reportedly ranged from a 10 percent reduction in benefits to complete denial of payment.

The Garnick et al. (1994) study lends support to previous statements that patients must undergo a process of preauthorization prior to receiving emergency care (Kerr, 1986; Knopp, 1986; Lazarus, 1993; Olsen et al., 1995). Garnick et al. (1994) also demonstrated that failure to do so may result in a decrease in benefits.

Other research into managed care continues to demonstrate the growth of an industry that impedes the delivery of high-quality patient care (Levine, 1995; National Association of Private Psychiatric Hospitals, 1991). In a survey by the National Association of Private Psychiatric Hospitals (NAPPH) (1991), respondents reported that quality care was hampered by managed care. The NAPPH (1991) surveyed 134 utilization review coordinators at 134 private hospitals. It found that 78 percent of patients needed outside preadmission for the year 1991, compared to only 70 percent the year before. Also, the rate of concurrent review went from 70 percent for patients hospitalized in 1990 to 74 percent for those hospitalized in 1991. With respect to preadmission, only 6 percent of the hospitals reported that outside reviewers were always clinicians. Ninety-three percent of the respondents saw outside utilization management as a hindrance to delivering care. Furthermore, 96 percent reported that reviewers required "discharge too soon for the good of the patient" (p. 965). Sixty-two percent of the hospitals reported that patients leave when their request for additional care is turned down by managed care (even if it's against the physician's advice), and 60 percent reported that the need for preadmission authorization stops patients from seeking hospital care. The NAPPH (1991) study also noted the apparent failure of managed-care companies to provide specific review criteria to hospitals. In fact, 45 percent of those hospitals surveyed reported they were rarely or never given specific criteria.

It may be concluded from the Garnick et al. (1994) and the NAPPH (1991) research that managed care has a direct impact on the treatment decision process through preauthorization requirements. Thus, concerns reflecting the influence of managed care on the treatment decision process are not unfounded (Kerr, 1986; Knopp, 1986; Lazarus, 1993, 1995; Olfson, 1989; Rissmiller et al., 1994; Schuster et al., 1995; Wise, 1989). Furthermore, managed care may go beyond influencing preadmission. Managed-care companies' concern with costs may actively discourage patients from seeking medical care or encourage patients to leave treatment by rejecting their benefit claims (NAPPH, 1991).

Are there differences in admitting rates for managed-care patients and traditional insurance patients? Olfson (1989) conducted a comparison that reviewed the charts of patients attending the Yale-New Haven Hospital psychiatric emergency room. He compared patients who participated in the Connecticut Health Care Plan (CHCP), a managed health organization, to persons enrolled in Blue Cross/Blue Shield (BC/BS), a fee-for-service provider. The study included a review of 109 charts, from September 1986 through August 1987, for each group. Olfson (1989) reported that approximately one-third of the patients in each group presented at the emergency room with suicidal ideation; 22 percent had made an overt suicidal gesture before coming to the ER. However, 71 percent of the BC/BS patients who had made a suicide gesture were admitted to the psychiatric unit, whereas only 29 percent of the CHCP patients were admitted. There were no significant differences between the groups in diagnosis, level of symptoms, or agitation.

The Olfson (1989) study also found the BC/BS patients significantly more likely to be admitted voluntarily; there was no difference in the admission rate for nonvoluntary admissions. The CHCP patients were more often given a referral and a follow-up appointment within forty-eight hours. Also, there was a high correlation between payment method and admitting disposition. Those patients with BC/BS were 1.9 times more likely to be admitted. Because CHCP required preadmission approval by a CHCP staff psychiatrist or psychologist, it exerted significant control over who was admitted.

The criterion that is being utilized to authorize treatment remains unclear. There is a lack of consensus among company managers to enable companies to follow their own policies regarding reimbursement. This has led to benefit capitation, subjective payments, and the questioning of providers' treatment plans. Furthermore, as the demand from managed care for predictable outcome increases, the ability of the medical profession to generate diagnoses and treatment regimens is being replaced by objective criteria and defined treatment plans. Rodriguez (1985) calls this "cookbook medicine" (p. 345).

Preadmission approval by managed-care companies has presented both patients and providers with important considerations at all levels of the treatment decision process. First, the patient is placed in the position of deciding whether or not his or her illness warrants immediate attention or whether a call to a managed-care hotline would be more appropriate (Kerr, 1986; Knopp, 1986; Lazarus, 1993). Second, when treatment is provided in the ER, the provider often needs to seek authorization for admission and treatment reimbursement from a managed-care agent (Garnick et al., 1994; NAPPH, 1991; Olfson, 1989; Olsen et al., 1995; Pear, 1995; Rodriguez, 1985; Sharfstein, 1989). Finally, when treatment is furnished in the ER, there is no guarantee that a managed-care company will provide reimbursement unless the treatment has previously been authorized (Kerr, 1986; Garnick et al., 1994; NAPPH, 1991; Pear, 1995; Rodriguez, 1985).

In spite of their low popularity and in view of the lack of evidence that they improve clinical outcomes, the jury remains out on the question of whether managed-care programs actually reduce mental health care costs in the long run. However, even if they are successful in this endeavor, the success of managed-care programs must be judged on a broader set of criteria than cost and access alone. Both immediate and long-term clinical outcomes, as well as subscriber satisfaction and changes in functional ability, must be included in the definition of benefits. Moreover, research and health care systems must collaborate in order to identify which components of the many that constitute comprehensive mental health treatments in contemporary society actually affect both immediate and future treatment costs and benefits (Barrow, 1994; Hunter & Austad, 1997; Showstack, Luri, Leatherman, Fisher, & Inui, 1996).

Standardization of Psychosocial Interventions

While arising from a quite different set of environmental pressures and needs—the desire to implement experimental control conditions for research, rather than pressures to control costs—the movement to standardize psychotherapies and other psychosocial interventions has something in common with the movement to standardize health care programs. In both cases, the result has been to minimize clinical judgment and to use statistical algorithms and objective criteria to guide decisions.

Psychotherapy research has always been the component of mental health treatment that most lacked standardization. Psychotheapists, it might be said, are fiercely committed to maintaining treatment individuation and preserving clinician choice. There are well over four hundred different psychotherapy theories (Corsini, 1981; Herink, 1980) that guide practice, even though, at the level of intervention, these are difficult to distinguish from one another. Unlike pharmacotherapy, where the doses and regimens are easily specified, in the domain of psychotherapy it has been difficult to identify the active ingredients of treatment and to know what one means by "dose" and "effect." A given model or type of psychotherapy may be offered according to different schedules, may owe its effects to different qualities as a function of the context in which it is offered, and has effects that are highly dependent on the

peculiarities and strengths of different clinicians. This distinction is oversim-
plified, however, and overstates the simplicity of using pharmacological intervention in mental health. Medication effects, like psychotherapy effects,
are clinician dependent and respond to a variety of nonspecific and often un-
specifiable variables unrelated to the chemical compositon of the drugs being
used. Not only do practitioners offer quite different medications to patients
with similar presentations (e.g., Wells & Sturm, 1996), for example, but both
the way that the medications are presented and the effects expected by the
clinician make substantial differences in the level of medication efficacy
(Fawcett, Epstein, Fiester, Elkin, & Autry, 1987; Greenberg, Bornstein, Greenberg, & Fisher, 1992). The view that the administration of medication is objective and consistent may be largely based on myth or illusion. Nonetheless,
this illusion was sufficiently strong until recently that it fell to psychotherapy
research to highlight the need for treatment standardization.

It became apparent two decades ago that intertherapist variability in both
the process and the outcome of psychosocial treatments was so great that it
limited clinicians' understanding of what treatment was actually doing.
Ultimately, psychotherapy outcome research elected to address this problem
by the development of treatment manuals. This is a somewhat different and
more specific approach than that used in managed-care programs, both because psychotherapy outcome research addressed clinical change rather than
costs and access and because the manuals' application was much more clearly
specified and monitored.

Until the mid-1970s, the nature of psychosocial treatments was defined by
the preferences expressed by the clinician for one theory over another, ignoring the fact that what therapists did often was far removed both from what
their theories dictated and from what they said they did. It became apparent
that without being able to accurately measure the ingredients and distinctiveness of the treatment, it was impossible to subject the treatments to fair
scientific tests. Thus, it became apparent that only if it were possible to distinguish between the subjective theory held by the individual clinician and the
procedures or practices that were implemented (Beutler, 1983; Beutler,
Machado, & Neufeldt, 1994) could we hope to advance the goal of improving treatments and training clinicians. The development of treatment manuals offered the possibility of distinguishing among the contributors to outcomes in a way that eventually might improve the training and practices of
clinicians.

In the mid-1970s, the National Institute of Mental Health (NIMH) initiated several programs designed to standardize methods of intervention and
methods of evaluating treatment outcome. The first of these standardization
efforts was the publication of a recommended set of assessment devices to be
used to standardize the assessment of patient status and benefit (Waskow &
Parloff, 1975). But, it was apparent from the outset of this effort that without controlling what went into the treatment, standardized outcome assess-

ment would not be able to add much to clinicians' understanding of what constituted effective and ineffective treatments. Thus, toward the end of the 1970s, the NIMH instituted a second program, the Treatment of Depression Collaborative Research Program (TDCRP) (Elkin, 1994). The TDCRP was a multisite study of three treatment modalities used with depression, tested against a combined treatment consisting of a medication placebo and a baseline program of clinical management. The targeted treatments included two structured models of psychotherapy and a standard regimen of imipramine. This complex and ambitious program was the first to utilize manuals to guide the application of both psychotherapy and pharmacotherapy as a method of ensuring that the treatments comprised known ingredients (Elkin et al., 1989). This introduction of randomized clinical trials (RCT) methodology taken from pharmacological research forever changed the face of psychotherapy research, for better and for worse. Indeed, it may have had even more profound effects on the clinical training of psychotherapists. Specific manualized descriptions of cognitive therapy (CT) (Beck, Rush, Shaw, & Emery, 1979), interpersonal psychotherapy (IPT) (Klerman, Weissman, Rounsaville, & Chevron, 1984), and pharmacotherapy (Fawcett et al., 1987) were developed, clinicians were trained to predetermined levels of compliance, and outcomes were evaluated on 239 depressed outpatients at three different treatment sites.

Treatments were monitored, therapist compliance was ensured, and common patient selection procedures were implemented across the sites. The manualized treatments employed a standard length and format, along with theory-consistent protocols for intervention and methods for monitoring both the active and placebo medications. In spite of these many controls and innovations, the results were less than impressive, but the lack of clear superiority for any of the treatments has been far overshadowed in subsequent years by the level of controversy generated by the findings (Elkin, Gibbons, Shea, & Shaw, 1996; Jacobson & Hollon, 1996a, 1996b; Klein, 1990, 1996).

None of the active treatments surpassed the minimal treatment or placebo control condition combined with clinical management. While the substantial equivalence of the putative treatments should not have been unexpected and was consistent with research previously reviewed in this volume, the lack of superiority of the expensive and time-intensive treatments over the minimal treatment condition was surprising and often disconcerting. However, in the long term, it is likely that the greatest contribution of this research program will prove to be methodological rather than informational. Among other methodological developments, perhaps the most important was that the TDCRP demonstrated that manuals could be successfully developed and used in controlled research programs.

We have considered findings from various reanalyses of the TDCRP data from time to time throughout this book. We have seen that the initial findings of this and of most comparative studies are unnecessarily simplistic and that the expectation of finding a single treatment that is uniformly effective within a diagnostic group of patients is inordinately optimistic, for many reasons that we have come to understand only after the fact. However, something is to be learned by the failure of this study to find a clear-cut and uniform difference in outcomes among treatments and by the furor that this failure initiated. The persistent hope of finding a treatment nirvana, in spite of repeated demonstrations that head-to-head comparisons yield low payoffs (e.g., Shapiro & Shapiro, 1982; Smith, Glass, & Miller, 1980; Steinbruek, Maxwell, & Howard, 1983), underscores the strong tendency of clinicians to (1) overestimate the level of clinical change initiated by treatment, (2) underestimate the degree of relapse associated with treatment, and (3) overestimate the amount of difference that exists among different treatments.

In the years since the initiation of the TDCRP, the use of RCT designs and treatment manuals has been a virtual requirement for obtaining federal research support. As the use of manuals was successful in research, it was extended to clinical work. In 1995 the Task Force on Promotion and Dissemination of Psychological Procedures, a body commissioned by the Division of Clinical Psychology of the American Psychological Association, identified nearly two dozen manualized treatments that it said met certain minimal standards of empirical validation. The task force defined these criteria as consisting of two independently conducted, controlled clinical trial studies in which a manualized treatment was found to be superior to a no-treatment or wait-list control group. The task force allowed some variance in these criteria (e.g., if a critical mass of systematic $N = 1$ studies had accumulated results that pointed in a consistent direction).

The release of the task force report was met with much controversey and angry criticism (e. g., Garfield, 1996; Kazdin, 1996; Silverman, 1996; Smith, 1995; Wilson, 1996). The annual updates and revisions planned for the task force listings (e.g., Chambless et al., 1996, 1998) have not ameliorated these problems (e.g., Beutler, 1998a; Chambless, 1996). Criticsm has been especially loud in pointing to the potential problems of using manuals that are inherently inflexible, and the belief has been expressed that, whatever their advantages, manual-driven treatments have not been sufficiently tested on the types of complex problems that typically are seen in clinical practice. The listing and supposedly "proven" treatments provoked the fear among practitioners that the report would be used by managed health care entities to make reimbursement decisions. Beneath this expressed concern was the threat that the favored psychodynamic theories that were adopted by many practitioners would be denied insurance coverage because they were not well represented in the task force listings. We can see in this controversy one more example of the strains that exist between ideographic and nomothetic forces whenever the importance of clinician intuition and judgment is pitted against the power of statistics and science.

DIMENSIONS OF STRUCTURING: IMPLICATIONS
AND APPLICATIONS

Many treatments are selected, organized, and applied within the context of complex iterations of abstract explanatory theories of patient pathology, while others are the products of loosely structured clinical opinions and lore. Those that rely on informal theory and impression often lack a detailed and specific method of application, while those that are based on elaborate clinical theories are often supported by the shallowest of scientific evidence.

Some theories that guide treatment are more practical and realistic than others. Pharmacotherapeutic and behavioral models, for example, are often closely related to clinician behavior and are not highly reliant on a particular view of the etiology of pathology or of the dynamics of behavior. An SSRI might be prescribed and efficaciously used regardless of whether the prescribing clinician believes that serotonin re-uptake is the principle etiological force in depression, for example.

It is impossible to determine from the label that identifies any given theory or model of psychotherapy just how comprehensive and broad-ranging the treatment guidelines might be. The presence of different brand names (e.g., behavioral, interpersonal, cognitive) may mask certain similarities, while similar-sounding labels may conceal the widely different applications, levels of specificity, and levels of comprehensiveness.

For the most part, psychotherapy treatment manuals suffer from being based on one single theory. Each manual represents an underlying theoretical model that provides guidance for and sets limits on the types of interventions that will be used in treatment. Necessarily, these manualized renditions of psychotherapy limit the variety and types of interventions that will be practiced. All patients are treated from the same perspective, regardless of differences in their presentation and makeup. This unitheoretical approach to treatment is unduly inflexible and misrepresents the multitheoretical perspective that characterizes most clinicians and their practices (Norcross & Prochaska, 1982, 1988).

Inflexibility is not a necessary correlate of manualized psychotherapy, although it does appear to be a frequent one. Neither is it the only criticism against forces that would subject complex psychotherapeutic processes to such structuring. Treatment manualization has also been criticized for failing to incorporate complex aspects of theoretical models, for ignoring individual differences and ideographic formulations, for discounting the artistry of psychotherapeutic practice, and for being inappropriate for the complex populations that are characteristic of clinical work as opposed to research samples (Beutler, Kim, Davison, Karno, & Fisher, 1996; Silverman, 1996; Wilson 1996). Most of these criticisms can be understood in terms of the general concern of clinicians that professional judgment is being abrogated by attempts to structure treatment. These fears are not well founded in fact. Other criticisms, such as those regarding the lack of generalizability to representative samples, are subject to empirical test. At least some evidence exists, however, to indicate that the findings of research on manualized treatments are not remarkably different from those of research that involves less specific treatment guidelines and that assumes that manuals may generalize across populations (e.g., Beutler, Kim, et al., 1996).

CONSEQUENCES OF MANUALIZATION AND STRUCTURING

At least for inpatient psychiatric services, large-scale structuring through the development of managed health care programs has been associated with a reduction in the rate at which treatment costs are increasing. Robinson (1996) reported that, over a ten-year period, inpatient care costs in California grew 44 percent less rapidly when managed health care penetration was high in a service area than in locations in which managed health care penetration was low. While some studies of select medical disorders have failed to find any substantial reduction in the nature of the services provided by managed health care programs (Yelin, Criswell, & Feigenbaum, 1996), there is still some question as to whether the reductions of service noted by many (e.g., Ware, Bayliss, Roger, Kosinski, & Tarlov, 1996) reflect an actual reduction in the use of duplicate and unnecessary services or are simply a side effect of the reduced quality of services available. Indeed, there is some suggestion that at least some of the reductions in cost that are noted in such analyses may be an artifact of an alteration in the nature of the population of patients who are covered and recruited for these programs (Angus et al., 1996).

Indeed, some of the largest and best-controlled studies indicate that the costs associated with treating depression in managed-care systems are at least as high as those in fee-for-service systems. Wells and Sturm (1996) found no relationship between cost and type of coverage in the MOS. Similarly, Simon, Von Korff, and Barrow (1995) inspected the computerized records of a large staff-model health maintenance organization for a sample ($N = 12,514$) of consecutively admitted primary-care patients with or without an admitting diagnosis that included depression. Those with recognized depression had substantially higher annual medical costs than those without depression in all categories assessed (e.g., outpatient visits, inpatient days, pharmaceuticals, laboratory tests, facilities utilization, overhead costs), with a mean annual cost of $4,246, then did those who were not depressed (mean annual cost = $2,371). The increased cost among depressed patients is at least equal to that attributed to depression in nonmanaged-care settings (Johnson, Weissman, & Klerman, 1992; Manning & Wells, 1992).

Beyond the issue of reduced costs, the question of whether managed health care represents an improved level of service is a more complex matter. Some evidence suggests that the effects of managed health care structuring have been negative. In a direct comparison of patients (ranging in age from young adult to elderly) who were being treated for a variety of medical and mental conditions in either a fee-for-service (FFS) or a managed health care (MHC) environment, Ware, Bayliss, Roger, Kosinski, and Tarlov (1996) found a general decline in health status among managed-care patients. Older adults and the poor were at particular risk of decline in MHC programs, compared to those in FFS ones. This decline in well-being was not noticeable among mental health patients, as a general rule, but wide variations in the quality of service was noted from site to site among the MHC programs.

Similar concerns with MHC programs are noted in studies of patient satisfaction. Few managed-care programs have managed to overcome the public's fear of "one treatment fits all" and to garner substantial public support. Subscribers are dissatisfied with the restrictions, with the structure, and with the lack of choice that they see as being part of such systems (Seligman, 1995). A plethora of recent lawsuits has alleged that the care provided in managed-care systems is inadequate, and a spate of stories in the mass media (Raab, 1996) have reported that managed-care systems have become prey for organized crime, which finds in them means of laundering money and gathering data that can be used to blackmail both patients and health care providers. Even if these factors were inconsequential, managed-care programs would still be judged as having failed in their bid to earn the regard and satisfaction of enrollees. The 1995 Care Data Annual Health Plan Member Survey of more than ten thousand enrollees, sponsored by Eli Lilly (PRNewswire, 1996), reported that 35 percent of those surveyed rated the mental health coverage of their managed-care plans as inadequate. Only 15 percent viewed their plans very positively. These viewpoints apparently are consistent with those held by providers and insurance agents, alike, particularly with regard to the ability of MHC programs effectively to treat those with serious problems (Hunter & Austad, 1997). It is no wonder, then, that the PRN report also observed that nearly half of enrollees (42 percent) did not intend to re-enroll.

Even if the costs of treatment in managed-care programs are somewhat lower than those incurred by indemnity programs (Robinson, 1996), the public has not been convinced that treatment quality has been adequately maintained by managed-care programs. The general opinion has been that reduced costs are reflected in reduced services. These concerns are reflected not only in low satisfaction rates when patients and former patients are surveyed about their opinions about managed care but in contemporary humor as well.

One listserve e-mail (Barach, 1996), for example, contained a tongue-in-cheek suggestion of how a managed-care reviewer would respond if allowed to apply his health care reasoning to a performance of Shubert's *Unfinished Symphony.*

> For a considerable period, the oboe players had nothing to do. Their number should be reduced, and their work spread over the whole orchestra, thus avoiding peaks of inactivity.
>
> All twelve violins were playing identical notes. This seems unnecessary duplication, and the staff of this section should be drastically cut. If a large

volume of sound is really required, this could be obtained through the use of an amplifier.

Much effort was involved in playing the sixteenth notes. This seems an excessive refinement, and it is recommended that all notes should be rounded up to the nearest eighth note. If this were done, it would be possible to use paraprofessionals instead of experienced musicians.

No useful purpose is served by repeating with horns the passage that has already been handled by the strings. If all such redundant passages were eliminated, the concert could be reduced from two hours to twenty minutes.

This symphony had two movements. If Schubert didn't achieve his musical goals by the end of the first movement, then he should have stopped there. The second movement is unnecessary and should be cut. In light of the above, one can only conclude that had Schubert given attention to these matters, he probably would have had the time to finish his symphony.

The humor in this story should not be taken as a rejection on our part of a health care system that attends to cost-based value of treatment. Indeed, the focus on costs among managed health care providers is warranted in view of the widespread influence of depression on health status and rising health care costs. In chapter 11, we recommended that the criteria of clinical utility or effectiveness used by managed care should supplement the focus on immediate cost and benefit with an assessment of long-term costs, gains, and medical offsets. Even more criteria can now be added to the list of things that should be incorporated in an assessment of the value and utility of service. After all, if only the ratio of cost to quality is considered in efficiency data, regardless of the time frame, services can decline in quality and still show increasing efficiency. The critical challenge in improving the efficiency of services, therefore, is not simply ensuring that the gradient of costs declines more steeply than the gradient of quality. Both the quality and the effectiveness of services must actually increase over time.

Improving efficiency requires that treatments be assigned in a discriminatory fashion, on the basis of an analysis of what particular treatment may best fit a particular patient or need (Clarkin, Pilkonis, & Magruder, 1996). At first blush, such a proposal seems logical and uncontroversial. It is consistent with conventional clinical wisdom and practice, but, unfortunately, contemporary programs are so embroiled in political fears and agendas that the simplicity of such decisions is lost. The managed health care field continues to persist in seeking a solution by improving cost-benefit ratios, seeking to find cheap treatments, to reduce the use of ineffective treatments, or to increase the accessibility of treatments, rather than to find better and more powerful interventions.

For example, after finding little cost benefit in favor of particular providers or types of treatment, Wells and Sturm (1996) proposed that the greatest opportunity to reduce cost was to eliminate the use of subtherapeutic and inappropriate doses of medication. Statistical estimates convinced them that simply increasing the dosage of medication and eliminating the use of anxiolytic medications to individuals diagnosed as having major depression would produce a substantial savings. Their recommendation was based solely on fitting patient diagnosis to medication. But diagnosis, as we've seen, is not sufficiently specific or reliable to serve as an indicator of any specific treatment (e.g., Carson, 1997). If left at this, such a recommendation ignores the possibility of improving the effectiveness of clinicians and developing better services. Might it be logical to attempt to increase the quality of nonpharmacological treatments in a roughly similar fashion by assigning both a therapist and a treatment that are selected for their appropriateness for a particular patient's problems?

The limited structure imposed by manuals that guide psychotherapy and pharmacotherapy has been somewhat more successful than the large-scale structuring of comprehensive health care. Manualization has had a major influence on the establishment and refining of research methodology (Luborsky & DeRubeis, 1984), and it is beginning to have a significant impact on practice and training, as well (Dobson & Shaw, 1988; Holloway & Neufeldt, 1995; Neufeldt, Iverson, & Juntunen, 1995; Rounsaville, O'Malley, Foley, & Weissman, 1988).

There is an emerging body of evidence to suggest that specialized and structured training and experience in the use of a manualized form of psychotherapy enhance treatment effectiveness (Burns & Nolen-Hoeksema, 1992; Henry, Schacht, Strupp, Butler, & Binder, 1993; Schulte, Kunzel, Pepping, & Schulte-Bahrenberg, 1992). In fact, a moderately high relationship appears to exist between the degree of compliance with a manual and the effectiveness of the treatment, regardless of the particular manual used (Dobson & Shaw, 1988; Shaw, 1983). The use of manuals in treatment also reduces therapist variability and increases therapist consistency (Crits-Christoph et al., 1991).

Perhaps of greatest interest is the evidence that using a highly structured and inflexible manual is more effective than using the same therapy in a modified form that allows the therapist to adapt the manual to particular patients and needs (Emmelkamp, Bouman, & Blaaw, 1994; Schulte et al., 1992). Interestingly, Schulte et al. (1992) found that clinicians tended to prefer and rate the benefits of the ideographic and individualized treatment more highly than those of the structured, nomothetic one in spite of clear, empirical evidence to the contrary. Clinicians misidentified which treatment was most effective, demonstrating again the fallibility of clinical judgment in these matters.

Two interesting side notes must be added to these positive results. First, finding of a positive relationship between use of a structured manual and clinical benefit is not entirely consistent over studies. In a study that compared a standard, highly structured, and inflexible combination of treatment components with a treatment that allowed the therapist to rearrange the order but not the nature of the components, the more flexible treatment proved to be more effective than the inflexible one by the six-month posttreatment follow-up (Jacobson et al., 1989).

Second, being trained in and following some structured treatment manuals appear to have some negative side effects. These effects are most clearly seen in the attitudes and functioning of the therapist, however, rather than in the patient's well-being. For example, some research (Henry, Schacht, et al., 1993; Henry, Strupp, Butler, Schacht, & Binder, 1993) found that, while therapists who were trained in a manual-guided psychodynamic psychotherapy became more proficient technically, they were less empathic and understanding than they had been prior to training. Those who were most proficient in applying the psychodynamic manual had fewer of the nonspecific qualities that have come to be expected as a part of effective psychotherapy (Henry, Schacht, et al., 1993). Technically proficient therapists who found it easiest to follow a guided and structured treatment were more hostile, less empathic, less personal, and less caring than those who found it difficult to employ such manuals.

SUMMARY AND CONCLUSIONS

We have noted that several forces, including the need for research standardization and increasing health care costs, have augured the development of structured and systematic treatments. While the success of these programs has not been uniform, standardized treatment, at least as applied to depression, seems to enhance the mean effects of treatment, reduce variability of outcomes, reduce errors of clinical judgment, and even reduce at least short-term treatment costs.

For example, in the middle and late 1970s, research scientists found that standardizing psychotherapeutic treatment methods was necessary in order to control for the widely different methods, means, and outcomes that characterized different clinicians, even within a given theoretical model. More recently, clinical teachers and educators have come to look at treatment standardization as a means of improving the instruction and supervision of trainees (Neufeldt, Iversen, & Juntunen, 1995).

The most profound effects of standardization are seen in the development of managed health care programs, in the use of manuals in randomized clinical trials research, and in the development of training standards and procedures. Whether these procedures increase efficiency in the long run is still to be determined. At present, there is emerging evidence that, at least in the short run, manualization of treatment is one way of improving clinical benefit. Impediments to this benefit arise both from the failure of these structured approaches to generate the support and enthusiasm of therapists and from the loss of empathic ability and interpersonal warmth that accompanies structured training.

An adequate test of the effectiveness of structuring treatment must balance external structure with procedures that offer clinicians choice and flexibility. Given that unbridled flexibility may impede the effectiveness of treatment, a careful balance must be struck between flexibility and structure. One possibility is the development of structured choice points at which empirically derived patient indicators are used to set limited choices for therapists in the selection and use of different procedures (e.g., Beutler & Clarkin, 1990). Procedures may be needed that will optimize the clinician's level of choice.

The ultimate success of structured treatments may depend on their ability to be comprehensive and to extend to a variety of treatment modalities. Theories that unduly restrict the nature of the interventions used, without the benefit of empirically derived guidelines for doing so, are doomed to reduce treatment value. Optimal treatments probably will be those that operationalize flexibility, rather than treat clinical judgment as if it does not or cannot follow rules and guidelines. Optimal treatments will also allow the use of many different interventions and will be guided by empirical knowledge.

It seems clear that treatment guidelines and manualization are here to stay. Fortunately, many different treatment models and manuals have been found to be effective, although not all, especially when compared to other treatments. It is to our advantage to outline some of these specific treatment guidelines and methods. We now turn to a description of these structured treatments and to the presentation of some of those that have generated at least a modicum amount of empirical support.

13 *Models of Treatment in Clinical Practice*

The variety of mental health treatments must be understood, at least partially, as a reflection of evolving sets of values and assumptions, sharing certain common theoretical roots along with some distinctive perspectives. Each new treatment development introduces new assumptions about what causes change, and these assumptions, in turn, contribute to the evolution of a society's philosophy about the nature of the people who live within the society itself. Biological models, psychodynamic models, and behavioral models of change all reflect different assumptions, and all come from slightly different branches on the evolutionary tree of knowledge. Each has been built on models that went before, but the evolution of each was accepted only because it occurred within a nurturing culture or subculture and at a time when those views were ecologically compatible with the particular social groups who gave them recognition.

Biological and psychodynamic models are branches from the same tree. Freud was forced to explain hysteria in terms of the neurological constructs of the time; it is unlikely that behavioral and cognitive models could have developed within the social values and philosophies of that time. Psychodynamic thought was born in a European society that placed a high value on external control and personal constraint and as the world recovered from one world war and moved toward another. In the evolutionary course of an expanding economy and the industrial revolution that was taking place in North America, however, the societal values placed on self-expansion and freedom were conducive to the development of experiential, interpersonal, behavioral, and cognitive models (Cushman, 1992).

Thus, modern models of treatment only partially reflect the accumulation of new scientific findings. They are amalgamations of earlier theories, supported and fostered by convenient social philosophies and values. While Freud's view of the world was not a large step away from a biological view of psychopathology, more recent modifications of Freud's views have accommodated new social philosophies and have taken them further from biological models. Thus, the modern split between biological and psychological views of psychopathology and treatment is ever widening at the same time that many (if not most) researchers are calling for a merging of these viewpoints. Each theoretical models is partially bound by its evolutionary history and the cultural values that were present at the time of its birth. To one degree or another, these values and their accompanying assumptions exist independent of the evolution of research evidence. They represent beliefs and organizing philosophies that become less and less reliant on research as they become more and more established. Thus, older models and views are more difficult to change and are less responsive to new and contradicting research than new and less established models. Survival begets survival.

The assumptions that organize the offerings of any treatment not only identify a viewpoint about the development of psychopathology but also make certain determinations about who can provide treatment and what settings are appropriate for its implementation. Thus, these assumptions can have a significant impact on the costs of treatment for a society. As mental health care (MHC) systems have modified and adapted their initial assumptions, under the pressure of political and social systems, the nature of treatment has also changed. Thus, there are many treatment models or theories and a host of concomitant treatment procedures employed in contemporary practice. Many of these treatments may be effective and efficient (Beckham, 1990), but most are at variance with those that have been used in systematic research programs on treatment efficacy and effectiveness. Moreover, contemporary treatments invariably represent not only the needs of patients but also the political and social agendas of the organizations that sponsor the particular treatment modalities and the society that gave rise to them. That is, treatments are not determined solely by a society's accumulation of scientific knowledge.

Some health care organizations, for example, reimburse treatments independent of their scientific status, while others require at least nominal supportive empirical evidence. That is, some organizations value nomethetic observations, while others place greater value on ideographic ones. These differences in the value placed on different types of observations only magnify differences that often exist between health care systems and clinicians. There is some inherent tension between the nomothetic values that often characterize health care management systems and the ideographic values that more often characterize the values of individual clinicians. But this tension captures only some of the intensity of the value conflicts that are present at any point in time. Conflicts exist among various viewpoints within groups who share ideopathic values just as they do among those who share nomethetic value systems.

There are many different ways in which a nomothetic value system may be expressed. While these views may share a common belief in the desirability of standaridizing treatment, they differ in how they view other criteria of knowledge. For example, the nomothetic approach often favored by managed health care programs is to control costs by controlling variables that correlate with costs. Thus, they restrict, standardize, and limit coverage for chronic problems and restrict the length of treatment primarily by reference to cost. In contrast, research applications of nomethetic value systems are likely to emphasize the use of improved functioning and also place value on methodological aspects of the supporting evidence such as the use of randomized selection and assignment of patients during the validation of the treatment. In these applications, an effort is often made to improve treatment by refining algorithms for predicting changes in symptomatic severity, functional impairment, and relapse from initial measures of patient and treatment characteristics. This may be in contrast to a focus on short-term costs, cost offsets, and ease of access as criteria of effectiveness. Not only do these various nomothetic perspectives reflect different value systems, but they each place different limitations on their use in the prediction of outcomes for individual cases. While more statistically based assessments rely on procedures that have been developed for the prediction of individual change, the identification of suitable providers, and the assessment of clinical utility, large-scale managed health care programs have seldom relied on such sophisticated predictions. The failure to access statistical technology in applying health care programs reflects the tendency of service-oriented programs to value outcomes other than the symptomatic and functional ones valued by most research endeavors.

An additional problem occurs when one attempts to apply research findings obtained in one system to the clinical care provided in another. Integrating treatment components is often difficult. While the treatment guidelines that are used by management systems identify various components of treatments that are helpful, they seldom assign these components in any way that takes into account their interaction and differential weighting. Each treatment component is subject to inclusion in a treatment package without extensive or explicit consideration being given either to the internal integrity of the separate treatments or to the compatibility of the components. While this method of developing treatments endeavors to remain atheoretical, research applications of treatment guidelines and manuals have typically been constructed within a fairly precise and explicit theory that is used to guide the internal structure of the various components, and these applications routinely include the imposition of control in the very nature of how the treatment, largely psychotherapy, is conducted. In contrast to the guidelines that direct health management systems, the treatment manuals that guide the training and practice of psychotherapy are closely tied to a specific underlying theories of psychopathology and change. The guiding manuals, therefore, ordinarily include methods for monitoring the integrity or fidelity of the treatment, as assessed against criteria that are determined by the guiding theory, and sometimes for evaluating the skill and competence of the provider. These aspects of care are either missing or conducted nonsystematically in the application of treatments in clinical settings.

At a still more refined level, treatment manuals themselves vary in specificity and flexibility (Lambert & Ogles, 1988; Wilson, 1996). Anderson and Strupp (1996), for example, observe that the most effective clinicians find it necessary to depart from structured manuals from time to time. This flexibility can be very difficult to implement. Some guidelines offer a detailed description of session-to-session interventions, while others are more flexible, suggesting choices among interventions and defining decision points that might maximize clinician judgment and input.

Because of their distal relationships to empirical research, the power and influence of the beliefs and values that underlie the variations among therapy manuals and treatment guidelines carry at least as much weight as do specific empirical findings regarding the efficacy of a particular treatment. And, it should be noted that the importance played by personal values is not restricted to mental health treatment, as can be observed by noting the variability in the coverage allowed for controversial birth control and abortion procedures within different health care programs. The treatment guidelines that have been developed by consensus panels cannot help but reflect the social and political viewpoints of those professional groups that sponsor and select the various panels. While consensus panels are guided by scientific findings, the weighting of evidence and treatment priorities are far from a direct reflection of these empirical results. As we noted earlier, Barlow (1994) has illustrated the role played by extrascientific values by pointing out the relatively weak evidence that exists to support the Primary-Care Treatment Guidelines' preference for psychopharmacological treatments for depression and anxiety over psychotherapeutic ones.

The infusion of nonempirical, anecdotal evidence and political popularity into the decisional bases for determining whether a belief is factual is replete with dangers. One outgrowth of a society that values nonempirical sources of evidence more than empirical ones is the infusion of political processes and legalistic, adversarial systems into the process of deciding matters of malpractice. In the legal system, such questions have been decided by the application of the standard of "customary and usual practice." This standard has assumed a place of importance beyond the question of the validity and effectiveness of a procedure or treatment. The standard of "customary and usual" places the burden of proof for determining the ethical and practical value of a given treatment directly on a majority vote of practitioners within a community. This standard of acceptability is often far removed from those that are constrained by scientific evidence of safety, efficacy, and effectiveness.

If using different criteria for answering questions about the effectiveness (empirical criteria) and appropriateness ("customary and usual" criteria) of treatment were not sufficiently problematic, the infusion of political values into decisions of efficacy, safety, and effectiveness has resulted in the evolution of legal instances in which even a vocal minority can move to have a dangerous treatment accepted by the court as appropriate. This is made possible through legal protections afforded to those with unusual views and is embodied in the legal principle of the "respectable minority." When a given practice is unusual within a community, it can be held to constitute inappropriate treatment or malpractice only if there is not an organized group of individuals who accept its use. Case law has established that as long as there is both a written theoretical argument in favor of the treatment and a set of guidelines to govern its ethical practice, as few as six individuals constitute a respectable minority and place the procedure beyond the reach of malpractice claims. Malpractice cannot be held to be present, in such a case, even if the treatment has proven to be dangerous to patients (see Beutler, Bongar, & Shurkin, 1998).

As one can see from the foregoing, in the realm of mental health treatment, there is an inordinately large number of philosophies and theories that guide treatment. As we have repeatedly observed, there are hundreds of theories of psychotherapy (Beutler, 1991; Corsini, 1981; Herink, 1980) and only slightly fewer theories of psychopharmacological action (Mann & Kupfer, 1993a; Thase & Howland, 1995). To these are added numerous theories of depression, in which the proposed mechanisms of development run the gamut from genetic to traumatic and situational factors. Most of these theories, whether of psychotherapy, psychopharmacy, or psychopathology, have failed to generate solid research support. Moreover, it is statistically unlikely that all of the treatments generated by the thousands of permutations of theories and practitioners are observably different from one another. Nonetheless, some of these theories have been translated into testable assumptions and operationalized in sufficient detail to allow empirical study. It is to these approaches for treating depression that we now turn.

CONTEMPORARY MODELS OF INDIVIDUAL TREATMENT

In developing and presenting our basic and optimal treatment guidelines, we elected to abandon reliance on techniques and procedures that derive from specific theories of psychopathology. To put this decision in perspective, it will be useful to obtain a brief overview of what models of treatment, based on such theories, are in conventional use for applying the major treatment components. It will also be useful to provide a brief assessment of the level of scientific support available for those treatment models. At this point, we are less concerned with identifying treatments that have been identified as being empirically supported than with identifying those that are in popular use. However, these issues are not entirely unrelated, and, in providing some brief commentary on the level of empirical support that exists for models of treatment in current use, we have relied on the several reports of the Task Force

338 Contemporary Treatment Models

on the Dissemination of Empirically Validated Psychological Treatments (1995; Chambless et al., 1996; Chambless et al., 1998) and on the critical reviews by Nathan and Gorman (1998) and by Roth and Fonagy (1996) on effective treatments.

Since the labels used by different authors to identify the underlying theory of a given approach are often inexact, we have applied our own labels to identify the nature of the treatment models in common use. We have identified eight general models of intervention that guides the individual care and treatment of patients: diagnostic models, psychodynamic models, interpersonal models, behavioral models, cognitive models, experiential models, biological models, and mixed or pragmatic models.

These treatment models are often considered to be relatively comprehensive, although we must remember that they are applied within a larger treatment network of values and decisions. They are, nonetheless, characterized by distinguishing assumptions about the nature, cause, course, and treatment of conditions that are usually considered to be relatively pure examples of depressive spectrum disorders. While we find little empirical reason to accept the assumption of the diagnostic specificity of depression that underwrites many of these models, we will set aside this concern for the purposes of accurately describing the nature of how these models are applied in conventional practice.

Similarly, for purposes of these descriptions, we will set aside our concern that jargon and theoretical constructs leave one with the misleading impression that there are more differences among those who adhere to different ones of these models than there are similarities. This assumption is inconsistent not only with the systematic treatment selection model that has guided the development of the guidelines previously presented here but with a good deal of empirical evidence as well (e.g., Goldfried, Radin, & Rachlin, 1997). Yet, obtaining the maximal help from the research in this area requires that we work closely within the broad perspectives that have been incorporated in this research.

From the descriptions of the various models, presented in their relatively pure and general form, clinicians may find ways to implement the principles that we have presented as guidelines for treatment development.

Diagnostic Models

Diagnostic models of treatment assume that some inherent aspects of the criteria used to assign a diagnosis are usefully related to the nature of the treatment provided. The development and implementation of diagnoses in classical medicine was designed to accomplish the tripartite goals of determining a differential etiology, predicting a prognosis, and defining a discriminating and distinctive treatment. The foundation of diagnosis, indeed, has always been to distinguish among conditions with similar symptoms in regard to one or more of these goals. Their utility as applied to mental health conditions has always been suspect, however. In mental health, the nature of diagnoses and their uses is inseparable from political processes. Political forces have included and then excluded (and, sometimes, then re-included) diagnoses among the list of recognized "diseases." Sociopolitical agendas as much as symptom clusters have been incorporated into decisions about whether those who adopt homosexual lifestyles, those with self-defeating personalities, and those with neuroses will be defined as having mental illness.

One sees the political forces at work not only in the processes themselves but in the exponential growth that has taken place over the past thirty years in the varieties of labels that have been applied to behavioral disorders. Not only do the labels, as we have seen with depression, fail to adequately represent what is known about the symptoms themselves, but they come and go as an apparent function of contemporary political exigencies (Beutler, 1989; Carson, 1997; Follette & Houts, 1996). Follette and Houts have observed the conflict of interest that is inherent in the process of placing the vote on whether to add a new diagnosis in the hands of those who will then be responsible for and benefit from using that diagnosis for the treatment of those who newly qualify as being ill.

In spite of the potential problems, however, Barlow (1994) has articulately argued for the value of diagnostic symptoms in treatment planning for anxiety disordered individuals. Unfortunately, as we have seen, the symptoms of depression are neither as reliably applied nor as distinctive as those of anxiety disorders, making the generalization to this more general condition difficult to justify.

Indeed, in the case of non-bipolar depressive symptoms, we have been unable to establish the presence of treatments whose value is specific and restricted to those who meet the diagnostic criteria. Cognitive therapy works for depression, but also for those with chronic pain, anxiety, and bulimia; interpersonal psychotherapy is effective among depressed patients, but also with those who are diagnosed as having eating disorders or substance abuse disorders (e.g., Chambless et al., 1996; Chambless et. al., 1998); tricyclic antidepressants are effective in treating symptoms of depression but apparently equally effective in treating symptoms of chronic pain, anxiety, and panic (Beutler, 1998b; Kirsh & Sapirstein, 1998; Lydiard, Brawman-Mintzer, & Ballenger, 1996; Thase & Kupfer, 1996). While there are relationships between patient background and both current and recurrent depression, these correlations are often low and fail to provide assurance of the specificity of depression for either etiological identification or prognostic prediction. Overall, there is little evidence that a diagnosis of a major depression results in a viable and discriminating treatment plan (e.g., Carson, 1997). That is not to say that diagnostic criteria are irrelevant. Indeed, Wells and Sturm (1996) observe that a failure to prescribe antidepressant medication for symptoms associated with moderate severity of depressive affect (i.e., a diagnosis of major depression) contributes to the low rate of effectiveness for psychoactive medication and increases health care costs.

Contemporary treatment guidelines based on such unreliable evidence of diagnostic specificity have tended to rely heavily on the use of psychoactive medication (e.g., Depression Guidelines Panel, 1993; Fawcett, Epstein, Feister, Elkin, & Autry, 1987; Wells & Sturm, 1996). This decision is understandable from a perspective of expediency but is not reflective of the status of outcome research. But, in a similar way, the many psychotherapy manuals that have been developed are equally lacking in evidence that their effects are specific to depression nor even that depression is a necessary element for the treatment's being effective.

Working from a diagnostic model, some of these points might be illustrated in the cases of Alice and Harold, the examples presented in earlier chapters. According to contemporary treatment guidelines and diagnostic procedures, it is likely that Alice and Harold would receive similar treatments because they carry similar diagnoses. While the nature of the treatment would differ widely depending upon which clinician was able to initiate an acceptable treatment, from a purely diagnostic perspective these differences probably would be more reflective of clinician differences than of patient differences. Following the suggestions of Wells and Sturm (1996), both Alice and Harold would be treated pharmacologically with the same class of medication. This decision would reflect the assumed cost reduction attendant on pharmacological rather than nonspecified psychosocial interventions. However, several models of psychotherapeutic intervention might also be suggested as supplemental. A clinician could conceivably find justification for recommending cognitive therapy (Beck, Rush, Shaw, & Emery, 1979), interpersonal psychotherapy (IPT) (Klerman, Weissman, Rounsaville, & Chevron, 1984), or experiential therapy (Greenberg & Watson, 1996), depending on the clinician's own preferences and familiarity with the research literature.

It may be reasonable to assume that Alice would accept any of these suggestions, depending more on whether she liked the therapist than on her understanding of the procedures involved. In contrast, Harold would probably be more interested in the medication and might even reject the use of psychotherapy. While diverse, in each case, the recommended treatments are reasonable and are supported by empirical evidence that the particular models of treatment are more effective than a no-treatment condition among people who share the diagnosis of major depression.

However, Alice and Harold are very different people with very different depression histories, coping patterns, and expectations. Treatment from a diagnostic model would only partially comply with the basic guidelines that we have provided and would not address the issues raised in our rendition of optimal guidelines. Such a model is too nondiscriminating to allow a refined and patient-specific treatment to evolve. To us, such a model appears somewhat lacking.

Psychodynamic Models

Psychoanalysis was the earliest and is still the most comprehensive model of personality designed both to understand human difference and to guide treatment for mental illnesses. Classical psychoanalysis has given way to brief-therapy models, some of which share little of the original theory and few of the concepts that characterized Freud's psychoanalysis. These models are collectively referred to as psychodynamic models.

While varied, contemporary psychodynamic approaches to psychotherapy share three basic assumptions. These assumptions are preserved from Freud's original theory:

1. Unresolved conflict results in patterns of behavior and feelings that become rigid and, unless resolved, are reenacted in subsequent relationships, including the psychotherapeutic relationship.
2. Effective treatment consists of a "corrective emotional experience" in which whatever was missing from an earlier relationship or a process that interrupted earlier healthy growth is incorporated into the current treatment in order to correct or resolve the conflict.
3. Change comes from insight into the nature of one's conflicts.

These central assumptions of contemporary psychodynamic theories bind a collection of varied theoretical frameworks based on the role of inner conflict and derived, in one way or another, from the psychoanalytic viewpoint of Sigmund Freud. To understand the progression and growth of these conflict models, we recommend three thoughtful reviews that place psychoanalytic theory within the context of contemporary models. These include a chapter by Cushman (1992) that is a historical review of the evolution of psychotherapy generally and review chapters by Eagle and Wolitzky (1992) and by Karon and Widener (1995) that offer historical perspectives that are more specific to the psychoanalytic tradition.

The concepts of classical psychoanalytic theory are well known but do not serve as the basis for the most-used theories and models that have been the subject of outcome research to date. While Freud's original theory does not bear substantial review here, we do need to describe briefly some of the modern renditions of this tradition, particularly those that have been subject to empirical test. This review will provide a foundation for describing contemporary research that bears on the question of which treatments are or are not effective for treating those with depressive conditions.

Classical psychoanalytic thought identified important constructs within three specific theoretical domains. The first domain included the structures of personality (id, ego, superego); the second constituted stages of development (oral, anal, phallic, latency, and genital); and the third included the mechanisms that either transfer and conserve energy (ego defenses) or reveal its hidden content (psychic determinism and repetition compulsion). Interactions among these domains of function have traditionally been used to define how both normal and pathological patterns of behavior develop.

In Freud's original conception, motivation was postulated to arise from the structures, specifically from the id; the stages of development defined the physical systems through which this energy would be discharged or gratified; and the dynamic process of conserving and channeling energy was assumed to be responsible for the initiation, maintenance, and cessation of behavior. Within this framework, depression is either a masked representation of anger and of frustrated libidinal energy (Newman & Hirt, 1983) or, in a more modern conceptualization, an expression of one's needs for autonomy and control (Dauber, 1984).

Treatment implications can be understood if one knows the interplay among the conscious and interpersonal domains of functioning. Interpretation of unconscious motives, identification of gratification behaviors, and confrontation of defenses became the forces of treatment, and achieving insight into these processes was the assumed mechanism of change.

In the years since Freud, and especially within the past decade, as the efficacy and effectiveness of psychodynamic therapies have been studied in research settings, the constructs that were so important within Freud's model have changed. At least one reason for this change has been the difficulty of measuring and observing these constructs in a reliable way. Original notions of intrapsychic structure as the means of channeling motivational energy have been replaced by a focus on the motivating power of interpersonal desires and needs. Concomitantly, the length and intensity of treatment have been substantially altered to place more emphasis on short-term than on long-term changes. Deficit motives and anxiety reduction have received correspondingly less attention than the roles of interpersonal power, influence, status, confirmation, approval, achievement, and self-esteem. In modern object relations and self-psychology theories, for example, an emphasis on drives such as attachment striving, social needs, and interpersonal differentiation has replaced Freud's focus on deficit motives and anxiety reduction. The introduction of ideas about such general drives and conflicts has brought psychoanalytic viewpoints into alliance with theories of psychological change that are more general than the older, psychoanalytic ones (Kolden, 1996).

Along with these changes in theories about the nature pathological development and of conflict resolution, there have been a variety of changes to the way in which treatment is conducted within psychodynamic psychotherapies. For example, modern approaches have largely done away with the tradition of the couch, have adopted a short-term or time-limited treatment framework, and have encouraged the development of a more active and focused role on the part of therapists.

Modern treatment thus represents an amalgamation of both traditional and modified procedures. Horowitz (1988, 1991) provides an example of contemporary time-limited (twelve session), evocative treatment for individuals with a variety of stress-related symptoms, including reactive depression, that illustrates many of the principles of contemporary treatment within this framework.

From the perspective offered by Horowitz, psychotherapy is designed for and applied to the treatment of patients with depression associated with loss, those with acute situational anxiety, and those with other disorders resulting from traumatic or sudden loss. Its application extrapolates principles and predictions from three component theories. The first theoretical component derives from state theory and emphasizes patient variability in determining reactions to serious life events. Reactions may include overcontrol of anxiety, increased impulsivity and anger, and depression, as well as well-modulated arousal.

The second theoretical component in Horowitz's perspective derives from personal schema theory and suggests that when a traumatic event occurs, there may not be appropriate schemas available for guiding a person's response in adapting to the event. In this case, adaptability is lost as the person reverts to ineffective and primitive strategies developed earlier in life.

The third component of stress responses described by Horowitz derives from control process theory. This component suggests that patient variability exists because people use different control procedures to either facilitate (exaggerate) or inhibit (minimize) their recognition of conflicts. These three contributing theories are clinically combined and applied within a framework of selecting therapeutic techniques.

Like most contemporary models, Horowitz's (1991) model of psychodynamic treatment assumes that one of the central tasks of the therapist is to stimulate the patient to focus on the implicit meanings of loss and crisis. The therapist assumes the role of a benign authority whose caring support provides the opportunity for the patient both to evaluate personal motives and to achieve some self-understanding. Because this treatment, like most contemporary psychodynamic therapies, is time limited, the therapist gives relatively little attention to unconscious material. It is assumed that, by focusing on adolescent struggles with self-definition and control, the patient may gain some knowledge of the internal forces that guide and direct his or her responses. The therapist encourages self-expression, is accepting and supportive of emotional conflict, and provides confrontation and interpretation of defenses. While some attention is paid to classical transference material, the preponderance of the therapist's effort goes to assessing the historical significance of patterns of variability in the patient's reactions, and to exploring the historical significance of loss in these experiences.

Initial evaluation is designed to establish the nature of the traumatic event to which the patient is responding and to evaluate the significance and severity of the symptoms. The therapist establishes the patient's level of motivation and ability to develop a therapeutic bond and a working relationship. The twelve sessions of therapy vary in focus and content according to individual circumstances, characteristics, and responses. The early sessions, however, are designed to provide a focus that is agreeable to both patient and therapist. The patient is also encouraged to explore and outline the story of the traumatic event and its assumed consequences. In subsequent sessions, the therapist explores at greater length the patient's psychiatric history and provides what he or she believes represents a realistic appraisal of the syndrome. Throughout, the therapist realigns the focus of treatment and begins the process of interpreting the patient's resistance to efforts to force confrontation with stress-related events. This realignment of focus involves outlining the patient's problems in a broader conceptualization and an interpretation of the relationship between previous events and current symptom development. The therapist's interpretations encourages the development of linkages between stress events and responses through the medium of the patient's early history and schematic structure. The patient is asked to contemplate the implications of the provoking event for the present situation. Indeed, linking past and present becomes a salient issue in this and later sessions.

By mid-treatment, the therapist begins to actively confront feared topics and encourages reengagement of the patient in a process of confronting feared activities. The therapist encourages the patient to explore any themes that seem to suggest a pattern of avoidance. In the sessions immediately preceding the termination session, the therapist devotes effort to clarifying and interpreting what has emerged as the central conflicts. The subjects of termination, unfinished issues between the therapist and the patient, and future plans are also introduced at this point. Termination events are also interpreted as repetitions of responses to previous life and crisis events.

Horowitz's model of psychodynamic treatment has many procedures in common with other contemporary applications of this model of treatment (e.g., Luborsky, 1984; Messer & Warren, 1995; Strupp & Binder, 1984). One may find methods for implementing some of the principles we described as optimal in treatment planning and that emphasize the use of insight interventions and exposure to sources of avoidance in the following list of psychodynamic principles:

1. Emphasis on the development of a theme that characterizes a set of relationships and that serves to focus the therapy. These themes are derived from a review of early and current experience and result in a formulation that directs the therapist's interventions.
2. More focus on the types of conflicts that one might expect to emerge in adolescence and postadolescence than on conflicts that arise from very early experience.
3. Techniques that center on interpretations and that direct attention to patient defense and transference reactions, rather than the traditional techniques of free association, dream analysis, and analysis of unconscious material.
4. A great deal of attention to the role of the therapist; therapists directly outline and suggest the presence of an integrated, conflictual themes and directly offer suggestions and recommendations to the patient for resolution.
5. Direct interpretation of the significance of how the patient defends against threatening information and discussion of how these behaviors may be reenactments of earlier relationships.

6. Consideration of the effects of psychotherapy as a reflection of the degree to which the patient is able to establish a sense of collaborative involvement and a positive attachment.

One can understand some of the varieties of psychodynamic approaches by inspecting their treatment implications for Harold and Alice. Alice presents with long-standing difficulties and many losses. Rather than stemming from a single traumatic loss, as would be suggested by early theorists, Alice's behavior is consistent with patterns proposed in contemporary approaches (e.g., Horowitz, 1991; Strupp & Binder, 1984; Luborsky, 1984), such as a long-standing effort to achieve self-validation and approval, a choice to avoid anticipated abandonment and abuse, or a response to introjects of worthlessness and sinfulness.

Harold, in contrast, presents with a more reactive condition of recent onset. The treatment outlined by Horowitz may fit Harold's sense of loss and grief associated with his career and the more remote loss of his brother. If this is so, the central themes developed for Harold and Alice probably would differ, as would the course of treatment. Alice could be expected to be offered a longer-term treatment than that offered to Harold. Both short-term dynamic psychotherapy (STDP) (Strupp & Binder, 1984) and supportive expressive psychotherapy (Luborsky, 1984), for example, are designed to work within a format of twenty to forty sessions. Harold's initial course of twelve structured sessions may need to be lengthened because of concern about the emerging chronicity of the condition. In both cases, however, the focus would be on interpersonal aspects of his needs and wants, expectations, and subjective states. Understanding principles of attachment might be especially valuable for Alice as part of treatment within a psychodynamic perspective, given her past failure to develop a stable bonding pattern. In contrast, the work of grieving probably would be emphasized more strongly for Harold.

Some of the general distinctions we have made between the treatment provided to Harold and that given to Alice are consistent with the principles that we outlined in chapters 6 and 7. However, our guidelines would go a bit further. Our guidelines suggest that the thematic and insight focus advocated by psychodynamic theory would be more appropriate for Harold than for Alice, given the internalizing nature of his coping style (see table 5.1). Alice may need more of a symptomatic focus than Harold. Our guidelines also suggest that the planned length and frequency of treatment would be much longer for Alice than for Harold, given the level of functional impairment she presents. It is entirely possible that a brief psychodynamic treatment model would be inappropriate for Alice but quite appropriate for Harold.

Interpersonal Models

A variety of interpersonal psychotherapy models have gained prominence in recent years as guides to treatment. Although diverse, the views represented in this set of models have in common their adherence to two basic premises:

(1) Symptoms and problems arise within a social context and cannot be understood without knowing that context, and (2) change in interpersonal needs, expectations, or direct functioning is necessary as part of the process of ameliorating symptoms and problems (Clarkin & Carpenter, 1995). These approaches reflect the belief of Sullivan (1953) that human behavior must be understood within its social and interpersonal context.

Most contemporary interpersonal models are either short term or time limited, most are directed to relatively specific problems, and all accept the importance of the interpersonal context in which problems occur. Accordingly, they emphasize the role of altering cross-situational interpersonal themes and social expectations in the course of treatment. Following the lead articulated by Klerman et al. (1984), theorists suggest that symptoms such as anxiety and depression involve three component processes: symptom formation, social and interpersonal relations, and personality.

Interpersonal psychotherapy (Klerman et al., 1984) is the most widely researched model within this group (Frank & Spanier, 1995; Klerman & Weissman, 1993) and can serve as one example of how interventions are developed for depression and related problems. In this model of treatment, a therapist and a patient work to identify which of four common interpersonal problems or themes lends the most understanding to the patient's own depression or anxiety. These themes include grief over loss, role disputes, role transitions, and interpersonal deficits. The type of problem identified then serves as a focus of the intervention, with different types of interventions being constructed to reflect these different interpersonal problems. IPT endeavors to facilitate the development of new interpersonal skills, to encourage the grieving process, to anticipate and accommodate to change, or to support the adoption of coping strategies that are needed for dealing with interpersonal disputes. Usually, therapy remains focused on one or two of the conflicts that represent dominant themes in the patient's problems.

IPT is a time-limited, evocative intervention for ambulatory, non-bipolar, nonpsychotic depressed individuals. It has especially been useful as a maintenance treatment for those with recurrent depression (Frank, 1991; Frank & Spanier, 1995). With minor modifications, it has also been successfully applied to patients with eating disorders, substance abuse disorders, and anxiety disorders (Klerman & Weissman, 1993). IPT is based on the assumption that clinical problems related to depression occur and must be understood within an interpersonal context. Accordingly, it emphasizes the role of altering cross-situational interpersonal themes and social expectations in the course of treatment.

Depression is thought to involve three component processes: symptom formation, social and interpersonal relations, and personality. The first two areas are addressed in treatment. Symptoms—the first component process—are alleviated by the development of productive strategies for dealing with social and interpersonal difficulties—the second component process—associated with the onset of the depressive symptoms. In turn, social and interpersonal relationships are altered through understanding and insight. Specifically, patients are encouraged to identify which of the four common problems or themes already mentioned lends the most understanding to their own depression. The therapy endeavors to foster skills or effective coping strategies for dealing with the identified conflicts.

An aspect of IPT that distinguishes it from most other psychotherapy models is the emphasis given to the patient's willingness to assume a "sick role." Correspondingly, the therapist assumes the role of "doctor" and expert. However, this is not to say that the therapy itself is directive. The therapist's role, in fact, varies between being evocative and supportive, on one hand, and leading the patient to a new understanding, on the other. The therapy time is spent discussing the identified theme or problem and its manifestation in the patient's current life experiences.

In accepting the role of "doctor," the clinician must first evaluate the suitability of the patient for treatment and establish a diagnosis. This is accomplished through a structured or semistructured diagnostic interview and mental status examination. Patients who have major thought disorders, substance abuse problems, endogenous depression, or bipolar disorder are referred for an alternative treatment. Potentially suitable patients are queried in order to obtain a clear picture of their interpersonal histories and interpersonal problems. Evidence is also sought to ensure that the patient is able to establish supportive interpersonal relationships sufficient to support the therapy process.

The treatment takes place in three phases over a total of from twelve to sixteen weekly sessions. The first phase, usually lasting for three or four sessions, includes the establishment of a working relationship and the development of an understanding by the patient of his or her problem. The therapist first reviews the client's symptoms and gives the symptoms a name in standard diagnostic nomenclature. The therapist then gives a description of depression and its epidemiology, assures the patient that its course is self-limiting, outlines its prognosis, and provides an overview of the intended treatment. The client is asked to accept a "sick role" in order to be exempt from certain social obligations and from felt responsibility for his or her state of depression. The therapist then reviews with the patient the interpersonal problem areas to be worked on in therapy, using the patient's experience to illustrate the salience of the identified problem areas.

The middle stage of treatment applies interventions to the task of resolving the particular problems that have been identified for the patient. The patient's tasks in therapy include identifying the disputed issues, choosing a plan of action, and modifying unrealistic expectations or faulty communication to bring about a resolution.

Techniques used in IPT are similar to those used in dynamic psychotherapy and are used in a specific sequence and with varying frequency, depending on the characteristics of the client and his or her particular interpersonal problem. Specific techniques are not emphasized, but some of the techniques most frequently used include reassurance, clarification of internal emotional states, improvement of communication skills, and reality testing of perceptions and performance.

The final few sessions of the time-limited treatment are devoted to planning for termination. This means planning responses to the recurrence of depression, anticipating problems, and identifying sources of support and help. The patient is encouraged to let a brief period of time pass before returning to therapy. Supplementary sources of support are also identified as avenues for future help.

While the several approaches that adopt this interpersonal model are clearly related in their fundamental views to that of Klerman et al. (1984), they also differ in substantial ways. Some approaches (e.g., Klerman et al., 1984; Luborsky, 1984) are closely tied to psychodynamic theory and technique. Other approaches, however, adopt a systems view that, at least on its surface, owes more to theories derived from the disciplines of sociology and anthropology than they do to social psychiatry. For example, in some applications of systems theory, family and other natural groupings of people are thought to operate according to rules that serve to maintain and advance the needs of the system over the needs and motives of its individual members (Rohrbaugh, Shoham, Spungen, & Steinglass, 1995; Steinglass, 1987).

What if Harold and Alice were to encounter a clinician who views depression through an interpersonal framework? Consider the probable applications of the IPT model of individual psychotherapy, one in which specific tailoring of treament to the patient theme or problem is a central concern. First, one would rightly expect that, because of the medical emphasis of the model, the therapist would make some decisions on the basis of the common diagnosis of Alice and Harold. This commonality would be evidenced in the transmission of a common set of expectations about the prognosis, recurrence, and symptoms of depression, the "disease." Beyond this, the clinician would likely offer more tailored interpretations and interventions for these two patients. Alice would be seen as struggling with problems of role transition and skill deficits. She has transitioned across religious belief systems and, more recently, from wife and mother to single person and then back to single parent. Expectations, losses, and adjustments to these various roles have taken their toll. Concomitantly, she would be seen as lacking certain interpersonal skills in her work and parenting roles. Thus, treatment would focus largely on helping her grieve her role changes, explore positive aspects of the new roles in which she finds herself, and develop new skills for handling these transitions. The therapist would work to help her establish role stability and might provide instruction on the development of key skills that might help her acclimate to work and single parenthood. Placing her in a "sick role" might also mean putting her on medication, probably an SSRI, to help her mood stabilize while she developed interpersonal skills and higher levels of self-confidence.

Harold, in contrast, does not have the intensity of vegetative signs that suggests the need for medication to an IPT therapist. He, too, might be seen as struggling with role transition difficulties and associated grief, but his treatment would probably concentrate on both short-term gains and the issue of loss. It is likely that, compared to Alice, Harold would require less attention to the development of specific skills. While Alice's treatment might at times be led and guided by the therapist, particularly as she worked on developing skills, Harold's treatment would probably be more patient-led and evocative in nature.

One may also see the variations in how more broad-ranging systems interventions could be applied in work with Alice and Harold. While traditional interpersonal models, such as IPT (Klerman et al. 1984), usually are applied to individuals, systems approaches often include entire families, sometimes extending to more than one generation. Whereas individual interpersonal theories are usually used in short, time-limited treatment frameworks, therapy based on systems theories varies in length and in the degree to which time constraints are set in advance of treatment (Guerin & Chabot, 1992; Rohrbaugh et al., 1995). Given the immediate impact of Harold's depression on his family, for example, it is likely that a systems approach would include his wife and other family members. Harold might be asked to review his early relationships with his parents and his living siblings and also with his deceased brother. The goal of these interventions might be to uncover his implicit expectations and to relieve him of the role of "model" for the family, as well as to explore the nature of family role demands.

From the perspective of the guiding principles that we provided in chapters 6 and 7, the greater complexity and the chronic nature of Alice's problem relative to Harold's (see table 5.1) would suggest the desirability of assuming an interpersonal focus such as that proposed by IPT. Moreover, the skill focus of some IPT work would fit with Alice's reliance on external coping strategies, while the focus on grief and insight might be compatible with Harold's internalizing coping style.

Finally, the low level of social support available to Alice suggests the desirability of family interventions and other efforts to raise her level of social support. The use of a family-based intervention might not be possible in work with Alice because of her more isolated state, but even within an individual context, the nature of the interactions would be a primary focus, reflecting the therapist's beliefs about the nature of what motivates, maintains, and changes behavior within the interpersonal and the systems models.

The guidelines presented in this volume suggest that interventions that focus on systemic changes may be useful for working with patients who have low social support and whose problems are complex. One should note that there are many differences between IPT and the larger individual or systems variations of the interpersonal model that might inform such treatments. Strategic systems theories, for example, emphasize the processes that families use to maintain system structures and to keep the system intact. In contrast, structural variations emphasize the nature of the family organization itself, with special emphasis given to identifying the alliances that govern the distribution of power and influence. One might be drawn to the strategic implications of the communications within Alice's family, for example, while these would be less important in work with Harold.

The strategic implications of one's interactions can be drawn into focus by a variety of specific techniques that have become identified with systems theory. One popular intervention, for example, is to encourage patients who manifest certain symptomatic behaviors to continue or even to increase the level of that behavior—"prescribing the symptom" and then observing the effect on others. Even though Alice might be treated individually, such a "symptom prescription" might be informative if Alice could observe some changes in the level of contact with her former husband and her children that corresponded with her increase or decrease in depression and withdrawal.

Alternatively, structural variations of the systems view place relative emphasis on how attachments are formed and power is maintained in the system. In these views (e.g., Bowen, 1966; Minuchin, 1974; Minuchin & Fishman, 1981), the functions of symptoms derive in part from their historical meanings and the myths or assumptions attached to them by previous generations of family members. Thus, members of the family are encouraged to identify the values, wants, and needs that have passed from prior generations as well as the assumptions and reputations that derive from these stories. Such a viewpoint might be useful in work with Harold and help to clarify how the role of "model" had been passed through the generations and to identify the consequences of the associated rites of passage. A therapist might work to identify the role these family traditions have played in Harold's own symptom development and maintenance. Information would be gathered about how family traditions are maintained and about intergenerational transmission of alcoholism and abuse—how the family identifies and attempts to prevent or solve problems and what expectations govern the development of certain behaviors. Unlike in strategic approaches, insight plays a significant role in the theory of therapeutic change within structural conceptualizations.

Behavioral Models

Behavioral models emphasize the role of learning and experience over biological endowments in the development of problems and view problems as deriving from both enduring and situational factors (Craighead, Craighead, & Hardi, 1995; Dilk & Bond, 1996; Fishman & Franks, 1992). Typically, this means that they attribute the cause of feelings and behavior to outside circumstances rather than to characteristics of the person or patient. Behavior therapy is particularly noted for its individualization of treatment, its attention to life situations and circumstances as well as to the individual patient, and its close tie to empirical research (Goldfried & Castonguay, 1993). In this view, feelings and behaviors occur because of how others in one's environment have responded in the past, the likelihood of evoking a similar response in the present and the future, and habit. Behavior that is reinforced by the environment is developed and maintained; that which is not reinforced is not developed or maintained.

Reinforcement refers to two consequences of performing a targeted or observed behavior (see Mueser & Liberman, 1995): (1) a desirable and wanted (positive reinforcement) event, and (2) cessation of discomfort (negative reinforcement). Any behavior that has consistently been followed by a desirable event or by the termination of an undesirable one tends to persist—it is reinforced. The longer the period of time over which a behavior or feeling has been reinforced, the stronger the tendency to repeat that behavior or to have that feeling.

There are some peculiarities to this concept of reinforcement, however. It is assumed that a behavior will develop most rapidly if the positive or negative reinforcement is immediate, consistent, and predictable. But, behaviors are maintained longer and are less tractable if the reinforcement—positive or negative—has become unpredictable and inconsistent. This is especially true for behaviors that arise from negative reinforcement, as is the case for most problematic and destructive feelings and behaviors.

There are three particularly noteworthy variations in the values and assumptions that guide behavioral models—social learning theory, radical behaviorism, and behavior therapy (Fishman & Franks, 1992; Wilson & Franks, 1982). The first (Bandura, 1977) emphasizes the power of imitation, social reward, and the experience of self-efficacy in changing behavior, the second emphasizes the role of environmental contingencies and overt behavior, and the third emphasizes the way that subjective states of anxiety and fear evolve and their mediating role in behavior.

Treatment according to a social learning paradigm includes an analysis of events and social activities that are or once were gratifying and desirable. It is assumed that troubled people do things that reduce their access to positive reinforcements, and treatment focuses both on psychoeducation (Brown & Lewinsohn, 1984) and on creating situations in which patients can again enjoy the rewards that are maintained in social and intimate relationships (Lewinsohn, Munoz, Youngren, & Zeiss, 1986; Lewinsohn, Sullivan, & Grosscup, 1980). Thus, patients may be encouraged to do more of the things that once produced pleasure, to seek out more social enjoyments, and to benefit from watching how others cope and achieve. Keeping records and carrying out homework assignments are important characteristics of this treatment.

Treatment of Alice and Harold from a radical behaviorist viewpoint would involve identifying the ways in which these individuals' unhappy feelings are manifested in their overt behavior (Nelson & Hayes, 1986). This includes determining how certain behaviors can interrupt one's ability to work or to carry on desired life activities. Harold's withdrawal from family and friends, for example, may reduce his access to the important social rewards that inoculate against depressive moods. Sometimes, a focus on these behaviors may mean identifying anticipated negative consequences that keep one from behaving in desirable ways. Such an interpretation may especially apply to Alice's interactions with her children and her inappropriate behaviors at work and in intimate relationships. At other times, explorations of consequences means simply identifying the consequences that accrue from either positive or negative behavior. This is usually done by graphing either the frequency of positive and negative events or the consequences of these reinforcers. Such an analysis can be applied to the interactions of Alice and her children, with an emphasis on finding and developing reinforcement contingencies that she could implement to reduce the level of conflict in the family. Disturbed behavior in both cases would be seen as more likely a reflection of efforts to avoid discomfort or pain than either a reflection of the low probability of achieving a positive reinforcement (as suggested by social learning theory) or of having achieved a desirable consequence by one's disturbed behavior. It may be assumed that many events that originally provoked fear and avoidance are no longer likely to occur. Thus, Alice's fear of parental abuse or dismissal would be seen as inappropriately generalized. The therapist might concentrate on finding ways to expose Alice to feared situations in order for her to learn that the feared consequence of rejection and abandonment no longer occur.

A behavior therapist does much the same thing as a radical behaviorist but may give relatively more attention to altering subjective fears and anxiety. These, rather than overt behaviors, are the primary targets of change. Both social learning theorists and radical behavior theorists would emphasize that levels of fear and anxiety may change as a result of changes in one's behavior, while a behavior therapist would probably take the tack of changing first the anxiety and then the accompanying behavior.

Fundamentally, the task of behavior therapy is to increase the number of positive reinforcements for desirable behaviors and to reduce the number of negative reinforcements for undesirable ones that the patient experiences. This requires, first, a simple increase in activity level, both because it allows exposure to pleasant events and because activity and exercise have some direct antidepressant effects (Simons, Epstein, McGowan, Kupfer, & Robertson, 1985). Second, the patient is encouraged to expose him- or herself to things that are feared and to seek out events and circumstances that produce pleasure and comfort. The therapeutic relationship is intended and used, but, unlike the case of relationship therapies, in behavior therapy its significance is the role it plays as a reinforcer for coming to sessions and carrying out homework tasks. Harold may be encouraged to confront feared social situations and Alice may be encouraged to risk moving toward intimacy and accepting external control.

An example of a manualized treatment that relies on behavioral principles is that of Becker, Heimberg, and Bellack (1987). Social skills training treatment for depression combines procedures that teach patients specific skills and knowledge. These skills include those that are involved in achieving meaningful relationships and those necessary for accurately and clearly communicating with others, evaluating oneself, and rewarding one's own behaviors. The specific skills may include learning how to meet people, speaking in public, seeking out pleasurable activities, identifying and entering support groups, and becoming self-assertive. The treatment uses instruction, demonstration, role playing, coaching and practicing as direct training methods for improving interpersonal behaviors and skills.

Social skills training has been shown to be effective in the treatment of both adolescent (Fine, Forth, Gilbert, & Haley, 1991; Reed, 1994) and adult (Hersen, Bellack, Himmelhoch, & Thase, 1984) patients with major depressive and dysthymic disorders (Becker, Heimberg, & Bellack, 1987). It has also been used successfully in work with socially dysfunctional schizophrenics and other severely disturbed individuals (Bellack, Turner, Hersen, & Luber, 1984; Hogarty et al., 1986). It could be used with Harold to increase his exposure to feared friends and new job opportunities and with Alice to encourage greater control in working with employers and relating to her children.

The treatment begins with a systematic assessment of the patient's depression, using any of several standardized, reliable, and widely used measures. Social skills evaluation covers six key areas. The first area to be assessed is the molecular components of social skill deficits, which consists of such aspects as loudness, latency to response, duration of response, smiles, speech disturbances, affect, and eye contact. The second area assessed is dynamic control of social behavior. This area includes such things as topic changes, clarification of others' communications, persistence, and the ability to detect one's partner's emotions.

The third focus of assessment is the patient's situational control of social behavior. These include demographic characteristics (e.g., sex, age) and the settings in which social skills are lacking (e.g., work, home, public places). There follows an assessment of the patient's response quality and cognitions, with particular emphasis on two related aspects of behavior: the actual social performance displayed by the patient, and the particular aspects of performance to which the patient gives attention. Attention is also given to how these facets of behavior are judged and what self-generated consequences are assigned to the performance.

Assessment then focuses on the frequency and location of positive assertions, negative assertions, and conversational skills. This assessment is specific to the settings and problems that characterize the patient. The nature of the assessed responses would be very different for Harold and for Alice, for example. Indeed, among the psychosocial treatments, behavioral models are clearly the most tailored.

The therapist assesses the consequences of these identified responses and the availability of natural reinforcers and sources of punishment. From this point on, the nature of the treatments for Harold and for Alice would be roughly similar, differing primarily in the target and context of change and in the reinforcements used to establish and maintain prosocial behaviors. After completion of assessments, the treatment for both would begin with direct behavior training in the identified deficits. The therapist would first lay the groundwork for treatment and provide a rationale and description of the forthcoming sessions. Many of the skills are taught by the use of role playing, so a response class would be chosen and would form the target of work-related change until a criterion level of performance was achieved. The therapist then would work to "overtrain" the improved performance by role-playing many repetitions and would ensure the transfer of new skills to other situations by both varying the situational context and setting the stage for social perception training by training the client to be aware of dynamic variables. Homework assignments would be given throughout the training, and Harold and Alice would be asked to keep a diary in which they would record situations where interactions occurred, persons with whom these interactions occurred, and topics of conversations during the interactions.

In social skills training, each session is planned to include certain elements of the training according to a time line. During the first ten minutes, the therapist reviews previous homework and incorporates the patient's new data into the day's session. During the next forty minutes, the therapist selects particular situations for role plays and carries out the following training sequence:

1. The therapist provides information about components of the new performance being taught.
2. The therapist demonstrates the new performance in a reverse role play in which the therapist plays the client and the client plays the other partner.
3. The therapist checks to see that the client has attended to the relevant aspects of the demonstrated performance and understands what is expected of him or her.
4. The patient engages in prescribed role plays, with the intent of imitating the demonstration just provided by the therapist.
5. The therapist provides response-specific praise and feedback to the client and encourages the client to try some more role plays. The therapist provides praise for the patient when the instructions are followed.
6. The patient completes several repetitions of the role plays until a criterion level of performance is achieved.
7. The therapist trains the client in techniques for handling similar situations or in a different set of component behaviors.

Once the techniques have been taught, the therapeutic focus shifts to practicing and generalizing these skills. In this stage of therapy, the client learns to recognize the meaning and the dynamic nature of social skills. Recognizing social norms and learning to carry out several alternative responses to social cues, while monitoring social expectations and modifying responses to improve interactions, constitute the next tasks to be learned.

The final task of treatment is learning to engage in accurate self-evaluation and self-reinforcement. This should be incorporated into the process of direct behavioral training. Four goals characterize this process. The first is to improve the client's ability to attend to important details and to not overlook critical information. The second goal is to help the client base his or her self-evaluations on the technical adequacy of her or his behavior, rather than on others' responses to these behaviors. A third goal is to help the client develop more rational and lenient standards for self-evaluation. The fourth goal is to increase the range and frequency of positive self-reinforcers.

From the perspective of the principles outlined in this volume, behaviorally focused interventions are most appropriate under two conditions: when the patient manifests a preponderance of externalizing coping or acting-out strategies, and when the focus is on specific symptom change, especially early in treatment. Alice, for example, presents with many external symptoms (impulsivity, suicidal ideation, vegetative signs) that could be altered by altering behavioral contingencies. She also lacks socially reinforcing and pleasurable contacts with others that could be fostered through skills training and through an increase in pleasurable activities. These treatments could legitimately form much of Alice's therapy. Because Harold's symptoms are less external, he may be less of a candidate for these procedures except as they can be applied to the alteration of specific behaviors and symptoms early in treatment.

Cognitive Models

Cognitive therapy represents one of the most recent models of behavior change to have been incorporated into treatment on a large scale. There are a number of different specific approaches to cognitive therapy, but all hold in common the belief that one's feelings and behaviors are reflections of one's failure to check and correct one's beliefs (Dobson & Shaw, 1995; Mahoney, 1995; Meichenbaum, 1995). Cognitive models emphasize that patients' beliefs and assumptions, not the situations to which they are exposed, are at the root of depression and disruptive behavior. This belief is often expressed this way: If a situation or antecedent (A) is given a characteristic and negative mental interpretation or is associated with a belief (B) that is automatic, unrealistic, and persistent, it is likely to result in problematic consequences (C) and behavior. As originally formulated, the A-B-Cs were seen as sequentially linked—A causes B causes C. While ample evidence exists to support the efficacy of treatments based on CT principles (e.g., Chambless et al., 1996; Chambless et al., 1998; Dobson, 1989), many questions have been raised about the validity of many of the inherent assumptions (Addis & Jacobson, 1996; Beutler & Guest, 1989; Hollon, Shelton, & Davis, 1993; Jacobson et al., 1996). Most contemporary critics suggest that the three cardinal A-B-C elements are not directly or causally linked—change in any one may reciprocally evoke changes in the others, and much of the benefit of the treatment may derive from its provision of structure, goals, and a compatible explanatory framework for the patient, rather than from the specific interventions proposed by the theory (e.g., Addis & Jacobson, 1996).

Nonetheless, within the CT framework, the causes of distress and behavioral disturbance are attributed to thoughts and beliefs that vary in the locus of attribution and the degree to which they are seen as changeable or unchangeable. Some beliefs are viewed as being personally controlled (i.e., they are internally attributed and considered to be unstable or changeable). These include some that are judged to be situationally induced (sometimes called "automatic thoughts") and some that are viewed as enduring traits (sometimes called "schema"). The latter causes of distress may be residual effects of one's genetic and learning history and frequently are distorted perceptions of self and others (especially when events are negative). Those who use cognitive models of behavior change tend to focus on (1) the methods that one uses to solve problems and gather information, (2) the assumptions that one tends to make when bad and good events occur (Beck et al., 1979; Dobson & Shaw, 1995; Hollon & Beck, 1994), and (3) methods of self-monitoring and establishing self-control (Fuchs & Rehm, 1977).

The various cognitive models of psychotherapy share two fundamental beliefs about what is needed to correct problems and symptoms. They assume that patients will benefit from learning (1) to accurately appraise and evaluate the truth of their beliefs and (2) to employ a systematic method of evaluating experience and processing new information. In application, therapists who adopt different specific cognitive theories of behavior place different amounts of emphasis on learning new problem-solving strategies and correcting the accuracy of one's assumptions, but both aspects are usually involved. There are also many variations among practitioners in how the responsibilities for initiating topics and developing ideas for such things as home-practice assignments are distributed between therapist and patient. And finally, different therapists may assign different weights to the situational or temporary aspects of one's mental life (automatic thoughts) and to the enduring aspects of one's beliefs (schema). Nonetheless, the therapist in most of these approaches is relatively active, is goal- and task-oriented, and relies on homework assignments to encourage transfer of learning. These assignments include monitoring patients' thoughts, their reactions to selective and troublesome situations, and any identifying feelings that are related to particular situations and thoughts. In vegetative depression, the therapy also includes a number of behavioral interventions to encourage the patient to become active, increase social involvement, and practice new thoughts and behaviors.

The best-known manualized version of cognitive therapy (CT) for depression (Beck et al., 1979) describes an active, time-limited and therapist-led approach to correcting symptoms. Using both in-session and home-based activities to effect and support change, CT assumes that an individual's affect and behavior are largely determined by the way in which he or she structures the world—that these are not isomorphic reflections of situations alone. These cognititions become automatic and unquestioned, frequently presenting themselves in the form of verbal or pictorial cues that persist in the individual's stream of consciousness. These thought patterns become ritualized, persistent, and predisposed to occur whenever stressful events occur.

Automatic thoughts are assumed to be an indirect reflection of more firmly held, entrenched attitudes and assumptions (schemas) that are developed from early experiences and that subsequently go unquestioned because of these assumptions. These automatic thoughts, in turn, are usually distorted and reflect negatively on the person's view of him- or herself, of the future, and of current events. These distorted beliefs (dysfunctional beliefs) are the nucleus of depression and most other emotional and behavioral disorders and, in turn, result in errors of logic (i.e., cognitive errors) and a fault-ridden method of processing information. Beck et al. identify six basic dysfunctional thoughts or logical errors that characterize those who are depressed: (1) arbitrary inference—the tendency to draw conclusions without considering external evidence; (2) selective abstraction—the habit of weighing differentially the importance of positive and negative events, usually with priority given to negative events; (3) overgeneralization—the tendency to draw a general conclusion from a single event (usually a negative one) or happening; (4) magnification and minimization—the tendency to exaggerate the importance or frequency of negative events while at the same time underestimating and devaluing the importance or frequency of positive ones; (5) personalization— the tendency to see events as being personally directed, in the absence of independent, supporting evidence; and (6) absolutistic (i.e., dichotomous) thinking—the tendency to view events as existing in polar opposites (e.g., as either all good or all bad or as always or never happening). It is the nature of these automatically invoked errors of logic to both reinforce previous beliefs and to prevent close inspection of their truth or logic.

If Harold and Alice were to be treated with cognitive therapy, the processes of intervening would likely be similar, differing primarily in the nature of the thought processes identified as problematic and perhaps in the length of treatment. In both cases, the first goal of the therapist would be to establish a collaborative and supportive relationship. Alice and Harold would be encouraged to view their problems through the perspective of a scientist. That is, by stepping back and assessing the situation as if they were outsiders, they would seek an objective perspective. In the course of evaluating their personal problems from an objective distance, the therapist would raise questions and encourage Alice or Harold to reflect on and explore their underlying assumptions, suggest alternative interpretations and viewpoints, and engage in collaborative problem solving. The patient's tendency to filter new information through distorted thoughts and beliefs is often highlighted by these questions, and the patient and therapist together can then embark on a collaborative task of testing the assumptions and constructing more rational and supportable belief systems and assumptions.

Cognitive therapy for depression is designed as a twenty-session intervention that usually is applied over a sixteen-week period. However, concerns have been raised about such a short-term model when the depression is complicated by other symptoms and conditions (e.g., Hollon et al., 1993; Laberge, Gauthier, Côté, Plamondon, & Cormier, 1993). Given the evidence that Alice may qualify as having a personality disorder, some models would suggest a longer course of treatment in her case, extending over as much as two or more years (Linehan, 1993).

At each session, after reviewing the homework assignments, the therapist would likely inspect instances of depression for both Harold and Alice, evaluating these instances within a cognitive perspective (e.g., "What thoughts or feelings occurred when you had difficulty beginning the homework?"). The remainder of the session would be committed to exploring the agenda that has been set, with a focus on identifying specific problematic situations, evaluating automatic thoughts, exploring dysfunctional aspects of these beliefs, and applying a correction. The end of each session typically is devoted to outlining and constructing a homework assignment that addresses the issues raised in the session.

In the early phase of CT treatment, patients are instructed in how to identify and then to evaluate the validity of their automatic thoughts. They then identify and evaluate the dysfunctional nature of the thoughts that accompany disruptive feelings and behavior. They do this by examining evidence from their experience and environment that supports or negates the validity of these thoughts. Through a process of questioning, the therapist would encourage both Alice and Harold to consider alternative thoughts and interpretations to replace the problematic ones and to observe events that contradict their preferred views and assumptions. Experiments within the session and homework assignments are often suggested in order to gather evidence that can be used either to support or to refute old and new assumptions or to allow the patient to practice new responses (behaviors) that are more consistent with external evidence. Harold's fear of being criticized and Alice's fear of being discounted can be checked and evaluated for validity by encouraging them to seek feedback from others, to tabulate instances of both positive and negative consequences of self-exposure, or by observing the consequences of "acting from" a different assumption.

The question of whether cognitive therapy is more effective when combined with medication is also critical with respect to treating Alice and Harold. Early research (e.g., Rush, Beck, Kovacs, & Hollon, 1977; Rush, Khatami, & Beck, 1975) suggested that the use of medication may interfere with CT effects. This observation has raised concern among many theorists that incompatible assumptions and theories are represented in cognitive and pharmacological models of change (Beutler, Machado, & Neufeldt, 1994). More recent comparisons have failed to replicate the early results (e.g., Elkin, 1994), but there continues to be virtually no evidence that combining medical interventions with CT improves the benefits that can be expected from either alone (Antonuccio, Danton, & DeNelsky, 1995). Empirical evidence, therefore, does not support the concomitant use of antidepressants with either Harold or Alice, even though clinical conjecture and medical guidelines might argue that at least Alice is a candidate for pharmacotherapy.

The final sessions of the usual sequence of CT are devoted to issues of termination. The patient may be assured that symptom recurrence is expected but is not permanent. The possibility that such symptom recurrence may provide opportunities for practicing newly established coping and information-processing skills is raised, and this perspective is encouraged and reinforced. The patient's social support systems are also reviewed in this stage of treatment, and alternative ways of coping in times of disstress are outlined. Social support systems may be identified and their development encouraged. In the cases of Alice and Harold, the differential availability of social support systems would again indicate that terminating and transitioning treatment to environmental resources would be easier in Harold's case than in Alice's.

In addition to the adjustments of length and intensity of treatment, variations in CT to accommodate patients such as Alice include the use of follow-up and booster sessions. Among those with recurrent depression, for example, follow-up meetings are scheduled to provide maintenance or "booster sessions." The recurrence of Alice's depression and its potential lethality, as well as the absence of a supportive environment, for example, suggest that she may be a candidate for maintenance treatment.

The guidelines presented in chapters 6 and 7 of this book emphasize that Alice may be a better candidate for cognitive therapy than Harold. The reliance on external coping styles and the plethora of external symptoms all lead us to this conclusion. While the focus on internal life may make cognitive therapy a bit more appropriate than behavior therapy for the treatment of Harold, this is not a demonstrable point at this time. Overall, the same principles that guide the selection of behaviorally focused interventions would apply equally well for the selection of a cognitive intervention: (1) an external coping style, and (2) planned use in the early stages of treatment for purposes of altering disruptive symptoms.

Experiential Models

There are a variety of experiential models of psychotherapy. These models include variations of client-centered therapy, gestalt therapy, and humanistic therapy (Beutler, Booker, & Peerson, 1998). Of all the theories considered in this chapter, existential theories are the most similar to the psychodynamic ones, at least in practice and form, but they are also the ones whose base of empirical support is the least known or available (Elliott & Greenberg, 1995; Greenberg, Elliott, & Lietaer, 1994). The client-centered tradition of Carl Rogers emphasized therapist acceptance and passive support and was among the first to receive independent scientific support of its efficacy (Truax & Carkhuff, 1967). The importance of empathy and other relationship qualities of the therapist is accepted among psychotherapy researchers (Beutler, Machado, & Neufeldt, 1994), so much so that the relationship and therapist qualities considered by Rogers (1951) as so central to patient improvement and growth have largely been incorporated into the body of mental health treatment more generally. Concomitantly, therapies that are active, therapist guided, and focused, usually within the gestalt therapy tradition, have come to the fore. These therapies are receiving increased research attention and have been adapted to a number of particular problem areas, including depression (Daldrup, Beutler, Engle, & Greenberg, 1988; Greenberg, Rice, & Elliott, 1991), relationship problems (Johnson & Greenberg, 1985; Elliott, 1996), and general distress (Greenberg & Watson, 1996; Paivio & Greenberg, 1995).

Experiential models of therapy are built on assumptions that bear a number of similarities to those found in psychodynamic models of behavior. Like them, experiential awareness models assume that problematic behaviors and symptoms are internally caused and that these events reflect enduring characteristics of the individuals who produce them. They also assume that these symptoms represent compromises between internal experience and external demands, a compromise that is paid for by ignoring, suppressing, or denying certain experiences (Bugental & McBeath, 1995; Elliott & Greenberg, 1995).

To the psychodynamic theorist, it is the impulse and the resulting conflict that are disowned, usually by repression (pushing it out of consciousness); to the experiential theorist, it is the emotion that is attached to the impulse, rather than the impulse itself, that is disowned. Psychodynamic models adhere to the assumption that self-knowledge, particularly about one's impulses, motives, and wants, is ignored in order to accommodate to pressing social demands. In contrast, experiential models of treatment emphasize that it is sensory and emotional processes, rather than knowledge, that are restrained by social forces.

Fundamentally, however, the difference between psychodynamic and experiential models can be seen in the degree to which each sees one's innate or basic drives as inherently adaptive or destructive. In psychodynamic conceptualizations, the valence of impulses is at best neutral and often is frankly destructive. The goal of socialization and dynamic growth is to bring these impulses under control. In contrast, experiential theory sees such externally derived control as contrary to full functioning. It views social forces, not impulses, as the destructive elements in the equation. Instead of viewing social forces as desirable for its role in keeping destructive impulses in check, experiential models conceptualize socialization forces as preventing the free and growth-producing expression of natural feelings. Indeed, these models assume an inherent growth force that, if left to grow free of social inhibition, will be expressed in positive ways. Thus, the principle goals of treatment are not only insight or understanding, both of which are mental experiences, but awareness and growth. These experiences arise from enhanced sensory and perceptual experiences. Sensitivity to and interpretation of sensory experience are the type of awareness that is sought and encouraged.

The several research-based models in the experiential domain have in common three assumptions: (1) There is an inherent growth-oriented process, often referred to as "self-actualization"; (2) emotional and sensory experiences are inherently good but are suppressed by a restrictive environment; and (3) the growth forces are activated by unencumbered emotional expression

(Elliott & Greenberg, 1995; Greenberg, Elliott, & Lietner, 1994). Methods of facilitating or activating the actualizing or growth process vary from patient-directed explorations to active exercises. In client-centered therapy, the therapist typically is quite passive, tending to respond only in a way designed to keep the patient focused on internal, emotionally laden experiences. In contrast, gestalt therapists tend to see themselves as guides whose job it is to direct attention, overcome constraints against expression, and construct exercises and experiments that encourage the patient to focus on and magnify the nature of those experiences that have been blocked from awareness.

The variations among experiential models of therapy are probably more a function of the particular theory selected and adopted than of the unique characteristics of the patient. There is likely to be a good deal of similarity in the treatments offered to most patients; the treatments given to Alice and Harold are likely to be quite similar, regardless of the patient's distinguishing problem presentations, at least if they are treated within the same model of experiential treatment. Those in client-centered therapy are likely to be treated in a relatively passive and reflective way, while those in gestalt therapy may be treated actively and with considerable therapist direction. In client-centered therapy, passive interventions will be applied, while in gestalt therapy, more active interventions will be used.

There are few systematic efforts to adapt experiential approaches to the patient. An exception is the attention given to whichever emotion is seen to be primary. Therapeutic work is directed at whatever emotion—sadness, joy, anger, fear—is seen as the principal focus of denial. In gestalt therapy, moreover, the patient's particular defensive strategy is also a consideration in tailoring the treatment to the patient, but it is uncertain how effectively or consistently this is done in practice. If Harold and Alice were to enter one of the more active, contemporary gestalt therapies, they could expect to engage in intensive sessions designed to exaggerate or intensify their emotional reactions to a host of events to which they are exposed. The therapist would focus on emotionally charged events, particularly those that seemed to evoke efforts by the patient to avoid emotional expression or those that seemed to create considerable ambivalence in the patient. The therapist might use directed imagery to encourage Harold and Alice to practice self-expression and self-exploration, or they might be asked to enact prescribed roles and otherwise to try and confront events, memories, and thoughts that evoke fear. Many therapists in these traditions use homework assignments that are designed to help patients identify the types of emotions that are most uncomfortable for them and the environments that provoke these fears.

Referring back to the guiding principles outlined for optimal treatment in chapter 7, one might expect experiential interventions to be most helpful for patients who exercise internal coping styles, who are low resistant, and who are not unduly impaired or chronic in their presentations. Harold, therefore, might be a better candidate for this type of intervention than Alice. Harold's internalizing coping style, relative resilience, and availability to social support are all indicators for a treatment that embodies many of the qualities described as part of experiential therapy work.

Biological Models

Biological and diagnostic models of depression have many overlapping features. Both rely on a concept of "illness" to explain behavior, and both are largely derived from a medical tradition. However, diagnostic models are somewhat broader and do not necessarily accept the view that depression is a fundamentally biological condition. The biological models, in contrast, specifically make this assumption of biological causality and disease. Evidence for the biological underpinnings for depressive "disorders" is seen by many researchers to exist in the presence of commonalities in the pattern and nature of depression (e.g., Rivas-Vazquez & Blais, 1997). These commonalities include: (1) the phasic and cyclic nature of depression, (2) the presence of disturbances in physiological patterns of functioning among individuals with dysphoria (e.g., vegetative signs), (3) the existence of a relationship between individual and family depressive histories, and (4) the responsiveness of dysphoria and vegetative signs to somatic treatments (Thase & Howland, 1995). Yet, it has always been difficult for biological theorists to explain why depression is not more uniform in its manifestation and why it is represented by so many idiosyncratic patterns and variations, many of which do not fit into the commonalities just noted. Many have considered it improbable that a single array of biological factors and disorders could account for these diverse presentations.

With the third edition of the *Diagnostic and Statistical Manual*, the American Psychiatric Association (1987) adopted the position that depression comprised a variety of different disorders, with distinct etiologies, that share a common syndromal manifestation. Subsequent biological models of depression have assumed that causes of the behaviors that are thought to coincide with depression exist in either (1) one's genetic history, (2) neurochemical processes within the central nervous system, (3) alterations in hormonal secretions, or (4) structural changes in the brain and nervous system.

In their strictest rendition, biological theories provide true "illness" models of disordered behavior, fitting the assumptions of the diagnostic models of treatment discussed earlier. Thus, conditions that can be diagnosed are assumed to reflect not extreme (but normal) variability in biological understructures but actual defects, loss, or breakdown of normal biological processes. Concomitantly, the biological perspective assumes that the causes of behavior exist within the individual but are frequently not substantially under the person's control (Kravitz & Newman, 1995; Sevy, Mendlewicz, & Mendelbaum, 1995). By extrapolation, the patient bears little responsibility either for symptom development or for change.

While biological explanations often sound very logical and authoritative, it must be kept in mind that they are usually quite speculative and are far from uniform. There is not one biological model of depression, but many, and these models pose extremely diverse explanations for depression. On the basis of that observation, we have accorded them the same status as other theories of symptom development and their treatment.

Various views of the relationship between biological events and behavior or feelings give different weightings to the various biological processes that are assumed to underlie the condition. Likewise, different models place varying amounts of emphasis on the role of environment and psychotherapeutic work in facilitating change (e.g., Mann & Kupfer, 1993a; McNeal & Cimbolic, 1996). Thus, to those who focus on genetic factors, the limits on and the proclivity to develop some behaviors are seen as established by heritability, but activation of the behavior typically depends on environmental and behavioral factors. Genetic endowment is not considered to be an inalterable cause of behavior but instead constitutes a level of "risk." The risk is realized when the environment is conducive to the development of the behavior; risk is not an infallible indicator of the presence of the disorder. A heritability index, based on studies of individuals who vary in their degree of relationship to one another, defines the probability of having a condition.

Theories that attribute depression to disturbances in the monoamine neurotransmitters, serotonin, norepinephrine, and dopamine have drawn particular attention in recent years. These theories have stimulated extensive research aimed at developing medications that can treat the symptoms of depression. Theories about cholinergic transmission, particularly involving acetylcholine, have been promising and have underwritten the development of many of the most used antidepressants, especially monoamine oxidase inhibitors (MAOIs). The role of acetylcholine in modulating vegetative symptoms through descending parasympathetic tracts has proven to be a productive line of research. Affective regulation through these parasympathetic pathways is complex and involves maintaining a reciprocal balance between cholinergic tone and monoaminergic activity.

Many other theories involving widely diverse neurochemical balances, outside of comparatively simple neurotransmitter actions, have also drawn attention. Thase and Howland (1995), for example, briefly summarize theories that involve GABA (gama-aminobutyric acid) and tyramine, intracellular concentrations of substances used in bridging membrane activity—what are called, membrane-second messenger interactions. Changes in the body's ability to process glucose or carbohydrates and accompanying changes in blood and oxygen flow to the brain, the production of toxins, or the overproduction of brain stimulants are also among the biological events that sometimes are thought to be causes of disordered behavior. In this domain, as in research on neurotransmitters, it has been difficult to establish the difference between normal variation and actual defects, as well as to move research beyond the correlational stage to establishing causal relationships between biological conditions and depressive spectrum conditions.

Usually, when a clinician talks about "chemical imbalance," he or she is

364 Contemporary Treatment Models

pressing the point of view that there are disruptions to either neurotransmitter systems or other neurochemical systems in the brain. The dominant chemical treatments for depression, the use of tricyclic antidepressants (TCAs) and selective serotonin reuptake inhibitors (SSRIs), are both assumed to exert their effects by altering the action of specific neurotransmitters. Less frequently, clinicians who refer to "chemical imbalance" as an explanatory principle in depression are referring to damage or alteration that they think has occured to specific structures in the brain. When they do refer to changes in neurophysiology and structure, most theories postulate the presence of effects from unknown trauma or exposure to environmental toxins to account for many forms of disrupted behaviors. The nature of these structural alterations is difficult to document, and even when one is able to do so prior to autopsy, identifying the point at which the alteration slips into the murky realm of the abnormal or diseased is even more difficult.

Therapists who accept biological defect models as the primary explanation for problems in living are likely to urge the use of medications and sometimes even medical procedures such as surgery to correct the problems. Both Alice and Harold, for example, would be candidates for the use of antidepressants. The usual signal for this decision are vegetative signs of motoric retardation and loss of activation, and these signs are present in both Alice and Harold. However, if we consider these factors within the constraints posed by the guidelines presented in chapters 6 and 7, treatment becomes more discriminating.

Alice's condition is clearly more chronic, and the vegetative signs are more clearly defined and entrenched as aspects of the depression. Thus, within the framework of our basic guidelines, she is a more likely candidate for the use of psychopharmacological treatment than is Harold. Our guidelines emphasize that the indicators for biological interventions include: (1) high functional impairment, and (2) high complexity/chronicity. As noted in table 5.1, Alice more clearly meets these criteria than Harold.

Beyond their common reliance on biological explanations and medication, clinicians vary widely in the ways they think about and interpret the biological foundations of behavior. There are few specific treatment guidelines available, aside from those recently developed by the American Psychiatric Association and others. Moreover, there continues to be poor evidence that antidepressant medications in fact exert a specific effect on the symptoms of depression. Anxiolytics and minor tranquilizers, those whose effects are not expected to be depression-specific, appear to be as effective as drugs that have been specifically developed from a biological model of depression, a most disconcerting observation (Beutler, 1998b; Kirsh & Sapirstein, 1998).

Mixed or Pragmatic Models

Each of the foregoing theoretical models prescribes a limited number of interventions, prioritizes goals somewhat differently, and defines both mental health and mental illness differently. As we've seen, some of these treatments may offer more discriminating decisions than others. To accommodate to the varying utility of different models, some clinicians operate from two or more models at once, usually integrating them according to some implicit guidelines. The guidelines that we have presented, and the STS model itself, is of this tradition. It is aimed at identifying what particular interventions work with a given patient, regardless of the theory that gave birth to those interventions.

As a result of the sheer diversity of human problems, we, like many clinicians (some surveys even suggest most of them), find that a single theoretical model fails to provide the breadth of therapeutic techniques that we think is needed to help people deal with difficult problems. This belief has become more widespread over the past two decades and results from the frustrations inherent in trying to fit every person and his or her life problems into a single conceptual framework. The resulting eclecticism and its many derivative names (integrationism, prescriptive therapy, differential therapeutics, among others) emphasize that the model that guides treatment should be selected to fit the patient and the patient's problems, rather than trying to make one method fit the needs of all (Norcross & Goldfried, 1992; Striker & Gold, 1993).

Three basic approaches have been developed to help address the need to fit the model to the patient. The first method is to select a model from among those represented in this chapter that fits a particular patient and problem. For example, many clinicians hold to both a biological model and some variant of one of the other models. They may employ one model with one patient and another with a different patient, depending usually on some vague, implicit guidelines. Psychodynamic, cognitive, and interpersonal models are the most compatible with a biological viewpoint and may be variously employed by different theorists, some of whom adhere to three or even four models at one time. Those who adopt these mixed models may recommend both biological interpretations and treatments, on one hand, and psychosocial explanations, on the other. Other clinicians accept only portions of the biological model. Some of these clinicians think that biological causes explain only certain behaviors and not others; thus, they prescribe medication for some symptoms and psychotherapy for others.

This type of integration also applies when a clinician shifts between different psychological models. Thus, patients whose behavior is disruptive might be treated from a behavioral model, while a person whose thinking is distorted and depressive may be treated using a cognitive model, and one with marital or family problems may be treated with an interpersonal-systems model. Others argue that this method does little to address the complexity of people, any one of whom may have a variety of problems. Thus, within this framework, one may be in danger of receiving rather fragmented treatment, with components operating from different and sometimes contradictory sets of assumptions and none addressing the interrelationships among the various problematic domains of one's life.

The second method of integrating treatment models is to maintain a commitment to one model but attempt to vary its use as a function of certain patient characteristics. Usually this involves having a perspective that incorporates aspects of the patient and the patient's experience beyond the information used for diagnosis. Clinicians who use this method tend to separate their beliefs about causation from those related to treatment. They view the treatments that derive from biological research as useful even if the assumptions of biological causation are inaccurate. Thus, these clinicians may recommend the use of medications as ways of reducing symptomatic presentations but often deny belief in biological variables as the major explanations of behavior and feelings. Such clinicians are likely to recommend multiple treatments for both Harold and Alice, emphasizing some form of insight or behavioral therapy along with the use of psychoactive medication.

A third approach to integrating models of treatment is the construction of a new or superordinate model that includes the various approaches endorsed by the separate individual theoretical models. Those who adopt this approach emphasize that the procedures and goals of treatment can be applied independent of any particular theory about how problems develop. Thus, they combine components of several models within the treatment of a given individual. One can offer homework assignments and use procedures designed to help people develop new skills whether or not one believes that problems evolve from faulty learning or internal conflicts. The effort among those who take this "prescriptive" or "technical" approach is to construct a list of interventions and strategies that are useful for relieving distress or changing behavior for different people, regardless of how the particular problems developed. The deciding feature, then, is pragmatism—if something has been scientifically demonstrated to be effective for a certain type of person or type of problem, it can be justified and should be used.

The critical feature in these approaches is the presence of evidence of the beneficial effects of a given strategy for a given person, but evidence is not always available. To address this lack of evidence, the pragmatic, eclectic clinician develops a systematic method for selecting interventions that most closely approximate those that have been demonstrated to be effective in similar conditions or with similar people. The use of extradiagnostic information is usually required to make differential treatment decisions for people like Alice and Harold. For example, Bellack, Hersen, and Himmelhoch (1980) attend to level of social support as a moderating factor in determining the appropriateness of social skills training. They may be particularly likely to recommend social skills training to Alice, who has few support systems, but less inclined to implement social support treatment for Harold. A number of authors within the prescriptive or eclectic tradition may use this and other patient characteristics to develop and offer distinctive recommendations for different patients (e.g., Norcross & Goldfried, 1992; Striker & Gold, 1993).

There are three major variations of these integrated, prescriptive models in contemporary practice: multimodel methods, stages-of-change methods, and systematic treatment selection methods.

Multimodal methods (Lazarus, 1976) identify the range of functioning areas in which one has a problem (e.g., emotions, behaviors, interpersonal) and determines a "firing order" or pattern of interrelationship. Then, interventions are defined and integrated, drawing on procedures used in a wide range of different models, and applied in a structured and systematic manner. The method hinges on a careful analysis of the pattern of disturbing and dysfunctional behaviors and on the clinician's ability to use a wide range of methods in an integrated fashion.

Treated from this model, Alice and Harold would go through an intensive initial evaluation in which various domains of response would be assessed and a determination made about the priority and relative importance of these areas for their separate problems. Treatment would then be planned as a set of interventions designed to affect and alter these prioritized domains of experience. Both Alice and Harold, for example, might be seen as having significant problems in the interpersonal area. But, Harold's problem is manifested in social withdrawal, while Alice's presents as impulsivity. Concomitantly, cognitive patterns that characterize Harold are likely to be ruminative and indecisive, while Alice's are angry and bear a hint of victimhood. Although other dimensions would also go into the equation, it is evident that the variations presented by these patients on just these two dimensions would result in different therapeutic interventions. While Harold might benefit from anxiety management and training in how to initiate social contact, Alice would probably receive treatment focused on establishing impulse control and increasing tolerance for anxiety and distress.

The stages-of-change model of integration (Prochaska, 1984) suggests that there is a patterned sequence to how people attempt to solve problems. Further, it assumes that each stage leads naturally to the next and that at each stage there is a range of interventions to which one is likely to be receptive. Thus, the application of interventions requires finding a match between the type of interventions and the stage of change that characterizes the patient's efforts to solve and resolve problems. Within each stage, the interventions address a variety of levels of performance, and their effects are judged both by how well they relieve the problems and how well they move the patient to the next stage of problem resolution.

Treated from this model, one of the first steps in treating Harold and Alice would be to see what stage of readiness they were at. It's likely that one would conclude that Harold is a bit further along in the self-help process than is Alice. Harold may be at the stage of contemplation or even beyond, but Alice is likely to be found to be only barely entering such a thoughtful and ruminative stage. Thus, treatment for Alice would emphasize relationship building to encourage movement along the dimension of readiness. Active listening, reflection, support, and evocation of exploration are likely to be the treatments selected.

Treating Harold, on the other hand, might involve more activity and more work on problem solution and action than does treatment for Alice. While

Alice might be asked to think about and contemplate her course of action, Harold might be asked to begin testing new actions and behaviors.

Systematic treatment selection (STS) (Beutler & Clarkin, 1990), the guiding framework within which the current guidelines were developed, represents a structured procedure for selecting therapeutic strategies and techniques on the basis of both the characteristics of the problem presented (e.g., symptoms, complexity, severity) and the characteristics of the unique way that a given patient organizes his or her interpersonal experiences. These qualities entail matching the treatment to patient demographic qualities (e.g., age, sex), expectations for treatment (goals, therapist-patient roles, prior experience in treatment), and personality qualities (e.g., level of social gregariousness and impulsivity, sensitivity to other's opinions, level of trust). Notably, by including among the dimensions to be matched to treatment aspects of behavior that are not tied to the presence of problems and symptoms, the clinician attempts to address the role of normal behavior variations in how the patient adapts to life stresses and disruptions. This model therefore provides a summary of how the principles of both basic and optimal treatment, outlined in earlier chapters, would and could be implemented differentially for Harold and Alice.

The STS model emphasizes that the first step in treatment planning is for the patient and the problem dimensions to be assessed and used to determine the optimal setting and intensity of treatment, the type of therapist who is likely to get the best results, the type of theoretical model that best fits the patient's views of behavior, and the intervention strategies that fit the patient's expectations and needs. The nature of the interventions are unrestricted by theoretical view, and, like other of the pragmatic models, interventions that have been found to be effective in scientific research are applied as a function of how well they tend to accomplish the aims of symptom removal and conflict resolution.

A formal assessment of Alice, for example (see table 5.1), reveals her to have high functional impairment, chronic problems, an unsteady and inconsistent style of coping with stress, and moderate levels of resistance, high subjective distress, and impaired social support systems. These factors may indicate the value of a long-term treatment that is behaviorally and cognitively focused, perhaps including pharmacological interventions. Treatment would ideally address both behavior change and insight and would seek to provide skills to control and reduce levels of distress. A group therapy model and a model that includes other family members might also be indicated to increase the level of social support and interpersonal stability.

In contrast, Harold is much more self-reflective and internalizing than Alice. His level of social impairment is lower and his level of available social support is higher than those of Alice. This pattern suggests the value of a time-limited treatment that emphasizes insight or awareness more than simple behavior change. Treatment would seek to activate available support systems through homework assignments rather than attempt to seek new friendships and avenues of social interaction. Harold, interestingly, also exhibits more indicators of being resistant and oppositional than does Alice, indicating that the treatment should be less directive and might include more emphasis on developing self-directed control rather than relying on the authority of the therapist. Specific procedures may include the use of interpretation and reframing, nondirective encouragement toward self-exploration, and homework assignments that include bibliotherapy as a means of facilitating insight and behavior change.

SUMMARY AND CONCLUSIONS

Depressive disorders are highly characteristic of Western societies. Depression may have a lifetime incidence rate of nearly 20 percent, for example. While many effective treatments have been established, evidence suggests that the magnitude of the problem is increasing in Western societies, and recurrence or relapse rates are unacceptably high. It is unclear how frequently the empirically based treatments for this disorder are actually being implemented in the day-to-day world of managed health care. More significant, the preponderance of patients with depression either fail to be recognized by primary-care providers or, if identified, frequently are treated inadequately with sub-therapeutic doses of medication, and probably other treatments as well. Some researchers have suggested that there has been an overreliance on medication beyond what can be justified by contemporary research, especially of medications (e.g., minor tranquilizers) that appear to actually impede long-term improvement.

At the same time, there are many effective psychoactive medications and an equally large array of psychological and psychosocial interventions that have shown promise in the treatment of depression. Again, some researchers have argued that the importance of psychosocial treatments has been underemphasized and their role in relapse prevention and medical offset ignored by a health care system that looks only for immediate cost savings. In recent years, a large number of psychosocial interventions have been standardized, and ample evidence has emerged to suggest that some or all of them reduce medical utilization, long-term health care costs, and even mortality rates for medical conditions. In view of these considerations, the role of these treatments as both adjunctive and primary treatments deserves further consideration.

In preparation for considering the status of the many treatments that have been applied to depressive spectrum conditions, we have briefly outlined some of the major theories and associated manuals that have been in conventional use among practitioners for altering depression and for increasing social functioning. Eight general theoretical models have been identified in outcome research and will serve as a basis for further consideration of what treatments work for which patients, throughout the remainder of this volume. These models include diagnostic models, psychodynamic models, interpersonal models, behavioral models, cognitive models, experiential models, biological models, and mixed or pragmatic models. We have seen that, predictably, most of these models are quite rigid. They ignore the differences in presentation and background that characterize Alice and Harold. Some models, particularly interpersonal psychotherapy, behavioral interventions, and pragmatic models, systematically build variations of treatment into the assessment and implementation of treatment. While IPT and behavioral interventions make these adjustments without stepping outside the beliefs, assumptions, and values that characterize these particular theories, pragmatic models cut across theoretical schools and may apply procedures from several different models at any given point, depending upon the availability of empirical evidence to direct the way.

We have seen how the principles of treatment outlined both by the STS model and by our cross-validating research might be applied to Alice and Harold. It is our expectation that use of these principles in clinical practice would significantly reduce patient dropout while improving both treatment efficiency and effectiveness.

Part VI

Implications for Education and Training

14 *Issues in the Continuing Development of Treatment Guidelines*

The application of psychotherapy to the many problems that affect people's lives is largely a post–World War II phenomenon. The late 1940s and 1950s saw an expansion of the role of psychotherapy and the development of a climate that fostered an increase in the number of psychotherapists as the federal government attempted to address the vocational and mental health needs of returning veterans. Psychologists and social workers, and, eventually, marital, behavioral, alcohol, and family counselors, came to be recognized, along with psychiatrists, as experts in the treatment of various mental and emotional problems.

As the number of available and practiced theories grew, so did disillusion with the original hope that one of them might hold the truth about how problems occurred and could be eliminated. By 1970, 50 percent of practicing psychologists had come to identify themselves as eclectic (Garfield & Kurtz, 1977), indicating, by this choice, that they had given up the effort to find a single-theory viewpoint that was consistently valid as a way of viewing psychological problems. In subsequent years, more and more professionals came to forsake single-theory frameworks and adopted a poorly defined eclecticism as their preferred model of practice (e.g., Norcross & Prochaska, 1988). As many as 70 percent of members of some groups of mental health professionals now identify themselves as eclectic in orientation and practice (Jensen, Bergin, & Greaves, 1990). These psychotherapists have sought to add interventions drawn from several different treatment models to their array of available procedures in order to increase their ability to address the widely different needs of those who seek their services.

Inevitable results of the introduction of new theories included a decline in the consistency of treatment processes and an increase in the variety of techniques and procedures used. Theories and methods came to be applied according to varying standards and theories and were applied to equally vague groups of patients and problems. While psychotherapists came to acknowledge the importance of integrating interventions across theoretical lines, this was usually accomplished in the absence of an organizing, integrative theory.

By the mid 1970s, it became apparent that the diversity of psychotherapy practices, even within a given theoretical model, was too great to allow researchers to disentangle the effects of the different interventions used. Psychotherapy research in the late 1970s and 1980s emphasized the need to identify reliably the components of psychotherapeutic treatments, to homogenize patient groups to which treatments were applied, and to compare models that were founded on different theoretical premises. Accordingly, the Treatment of Depression Collaborative Research Project (TDCRP) (Elkin, 1994) introduced the use and comparison of treatments that were conducted via standardized manuals, each reflecting a different theoretical conceptualization and a different array of interventions. These manuals were applied on a diagnostically homogeneous sample of patients, with diagnosis as the basis for grouping and identifying patients.

The use of manuals in supportive research is now accepted as a major criterion for determining a proposal's acceptance for federal funding, for identifying those treatments that have received sufficient empirical support to warrant transfer to practice (Chambless et al., 1996; Chambless et al., 1998), and for determining what treatments should be included in the curricula of major graduate training programs (Maki & Syman, 1997).

In spite of the several advantages of manuals, three problems have not been resolved. One major problem is that manuals do not allow sufficiently for the therapist to adapt treatments to the multitude of important nondiagnostic states and needs of particular patients. This point was emphasized by Anderson and Strupp (1996), who found that the most effective therapists departed from the manualized rules when particular situations arose. From such findings, it is clear that structured treatment manuals create a needed degree of technical consistency, but they do so by sacrificing therapist flexibility.

A second problem is that manual-based training may actually increase the presence of countertherapeutic attitudes on the part of therapists. Henry, Strupp, Butler, Schacht, & Binder (1993) found that the therapists who were most compliant with manualized demands were more rigid, angry, insensitive, and rejecting than those who were less compliant. Indeed, while therapists' increasing technical proficiency, manual-based training also reduced their empathic attunement and attitudinal readiness.

Finally, and perhaps because of these other counteractive factors, comparisons of manualized therapies have failed to demonstrate that their distinguishing methods and theories translate to differences in outcomes for any of a wide variety of patient problems. The selection of diagnosis as the criterion on which to group patients and the use of single-theory manuals as the basis for structuring treatment have clearly resulted in a lack of sensitivity to the specific and selective demand characteristics that distinguish different psychotherapies and to the different patients for whom these treatments may be best suited. Indeed, the relatively weak evidence that experience, training, theoretical model, or type of intervention makes a substantial difference in outcomes among patients has led some researchers to suggest that we abandon altogether advanced psychotherapy training in techniques, procedures, and theories (e.g., Christensen & Jacobson, 1994).

The perpetuation of the statistically correct, albeit suspect on clinical grounds, conclusion that experience and training are irrelevant may well rest in the failure of research to disaggregate patients in logical ways in order to reveal their distinguishing responses to the things that a therapist might do (Howard, Krause, & Lyons, 1993). In contrast to the broad diagnostic symptoms and criteria to which research looks for differential response indicators, clinicians tend to look to patterns of interpersonal styles and emotional response states as guides by which to make treatment decisions. These patient qualities, most of which are not inherent and often not even captured in the diagnostic nomenclature, are used by clinicians to proscribe some strategies and intervention styles and to prescribe others. An effective manual would guide the therapist to adapt to patient differences and would demonstrate that doing so improves the level of treatment effects beyond that achieved by single-theory models and associated manuals.

GUIDING OBJECTIVES OF PRESCRIPTIVE PSYCHOTHERAPY

Keys to Success

Systematic Treatment Selection (STS) (Beutler & Clarkin, 1990), like the principles of effective treatment defined in this volume, is based on a prescriptive model of intervention that cuts across specific theoretical frameworks. The principles of treatment that we have identified have been articulated in a way that both reflects the results of our scientific explorations and is not bound to any given theoretical framework. That is, they reflect what we think are the scientific bases of the assumptions that are inherent in mental health practice. STS, as a model of treatment planning, provides a framework for selecting interventions differentially to selectively accommodate a variety of patient qualities and characteristics. In this process, the STS model advocates using multicomponent methods of intervention derived from a variety of systematic approaches to treatment. Like all available prescriptive treatment models, the STS model eschews comprehensive clinical theories of either psychopathology or psychotherapy as guides to intervention. Instead, it focuses on identifying specific and individual patient characteristics that suggest the use of equally specific treatment strategies. The principles of treatment espoused in this book are designed to lead logically to the application of differential treatment strategies. These strategies can be implemented through a wide variety of techniques and procedures that vary in their particular use and reflect the particular strengths of individual clinicians.

The first author and his research colleagues at the University of California at Santa Barbara are currently in the last year of a four-year treatment development study of a prescriptive therapy (PT) based on the principles articulated in this volume. This treatment is being applied to and tested on a sample of individuals who are characterized by comorbid chemical abuse and depressive disorders. Two sets of principles are at the core of this treatment development. The first set applies to principles of training, and the second set to principles of therapeutic change.

Principles of Training

In our research, we have completed a pilot test of a training program in PT that emphasizes cue recognition, an understanding of the principles of change, and the flexible application of strategies and techniques that are consistent with these principles. Training of this type centers on the development of six keys to being an effective psychotherapist: attitude, knowledge, tools, techniques, time, and creative imagination.

Attitude

Effective therapy begins with attitudes of respect, optimism about the patient's potential for growth and change, empathic sensitivity, curiosity, and self-awareness. These attitudes are the foundation for the interpersonal and listening skills that are the nucleus of the powerful healing forces that contribute to the benefits of all forms of effective psychotherapy.

Knowledge

To maximize the power of psychotherapy, the therapist must have a sound understanding or knowledge of the fundamental principles of change, in addition to appropriate therapeutic attitudes. Knowledge of the principles that guide clinical change is important but never subsumes or replaces therapeutic attitudes such as respect and caring.

Tools

The tools of psychotherapy include procedures for assessing patient state and functioning, environment, personality, and personal resources. Standardized psychological assessment procedures and materials are invaluable for these purposes. Moreover, the act of providing such assessment often begins the process of creating the environment in which the therapist will work and ensures that it is a place of safety and predictability for the patient.

Techniques

In the PT model, not a great deal of emphasis is placed on the development of specific and theoretically defined techniques. The techniques of psychotherapy are allowed to vary as a function of the explanatory theory and past training of each particular therapist. However, techniques are not irrelevant, and we do attempt to help therapists expand their armametarium of procedures through examples and training in technique expansion. We also emphasize those techniques that can be used to implement the changes defined by the working principles. We view tools and techniques as the basis of any therapist's skill, but skill also includes the therapist's willingness to modify and alter the interventions applied in a flexible fashion.

From the perspective of our model of prescriptive therapy, it is assumed that techniques are flexible, depending on who uses them and how skilled and experienced that individual is. Thus, most techniques can be used for multiple purposes and in many different ways. While this makes them a poor focus for training, especially for experienced therapists, it does allow the therapist creative license.

Time

As the fifth key to success, time is inherently related to therapist skill. Skillful therapists are able to time interventions and allow patients the time necessary to change. They seem to intuitively understand that things that take more time now will save time later.

The consideration of time is many faceted. It implies not only the need for patience but the therapist's willingness and even eagerness to let the patient be correct or feel affirmed. Time is spent not debating whose theory of the patient's problem is correct but looking for understanding and mechanisms for change. But, time also refers to the timing of interventions. Therapists who are time-sensitive know when to respond, where to respond, and what to respond with. They know when to become active, when to revert to inaction, when to assert their opinion, and when to withdraw. Timing approaches and retreats is a skill that can be honed to attract the patient as the therapist sorts his or her way through the process of relationship tear and repair.

Imagination

The therapist's attitudes, knowledge, skills, and timing come together through the use of creative imagination. Imagination is the basis of creativity and works in tandem with flexibility. It is what sets technicians and artists apart. The application of established principles to new and novel environments is the essence of therapeutic art and flexibility.

As in any art, the prize goes to the one who has the new and attractive idea, not to the one who enacts procedures, one after the other, by rote. Any artist must abide by rules of physics—the basic principles of change, if you will. It is the artist who applies these principles in ways that address the particular needs of this patient and draws forth this patient's response who is the master therapist.

Structure of Training

The principles of PT are taught through a three-tier system designed to ensure that clinicians learn to identify the patient cues that reliably identify the presence of treatment-relevant traits and states, assess the levels at which these qualities occur, and then select and fit therapeutic interventions appropriate to these qualities and levels.

At the first level, therapists are taught basic relationship skills and the principles of change that are derived from empirically established relationships across a variety of theories. At the second level, therapists are taught differential strategies of influence that derive from these principles and that distinguish among the treatments that are effective with different groups of patients. At the third level, therapists are taught some representative but nonexhaustive techniques and procedures for carrying out the strategies.

What distinguishes our approach from traditional manual-based training is the focus on principles and strategies, not techniques. The first principle stressed is the need to develop accepting and acknowledging attitudes. Beyond those required for relationship enhancement and alliance development, techniques are considered virtually interchangeable. Thus, unlike most approaches that emphasize the techniques of intervention—techniques of interpretation, two-chair work, reinforcement—the prescriptive therapy that arises from STS urges therapists to learn the principles and strategies and to select techniques that will advance these goals. They use their own arrays of techniques and their own imaginations to develop treatment plans that are consistent with these principles.

Principles of Therapeutic Change

The second set of principles applies to the mechanisms of therapeutic change. In the first year and a half of the current study, we conducted a thorough literature search to identify a set of hypothetical but general principles that could govern treatment selection without sacrificing therapist flexibility in the selection of explanatory frameworks and techniques. From this review, we identified several principles that direct the development of the treatment relationship and other principles of change that can be used to guide the application of treatments in a selective manner. These principles facilitate the therapist's efforts to adopt a treatment plan that fits the unique pattern of characteristics of a particular patient. We will use some of these principles to illustrate the flexibility that may be possible while practicing within the cross-theory guidelines they represent.

In our current research program, we have selected and identified ten of the principles (sometimes in slightly modified form) that were articulated in chapters 6 and 7 for the limited purposes of our investigation. These principles fall into three groups, depending on their focus: relationship principles, principles related to level of care, and principles that relate to the selection and discriminating use of therapeutic strategies and procedures. The principles we use are selected from the lists of basic and optimal guidelines. The principles, as modified for the purposes of the specific study, are as follows (Beutler & Harwood, in press):

1. Therapeutic change is greatest when the therapist is skillful and provides trust, acceptance, acknowledgment, collaboration, and respect for the patient and to do so in an environment that both supports risk and provides maximal safety (Optimal Guideline 1).
2. Risk and retention are optimized if the patient is realistically informed about the probable length and effectiveness of the treatment and if the patient has a clear understanding of the roles and activities that are expected during the course of treatment (Basic Guideline 8).

These two principles define the nature of a treatment and psychotherapeutic relationship. They are relatively self-explanatory, and the way they are enacted varies more according to the personality of the therapist than according to the nature of the theoretical model to which the therapist adheres. Thus, illustrations of flexibility are more easily and better made by inspecting other principles that apply to specific treatment selection.

3. Therapeutic change is most likely if the initial focus of change efforts is on building skills and altering disruptive symptoms (Optimal Guideline 4).

This principle relates to level of care, as well as to the selectively ordering of psychotherapeutic interventions. It is an optimal tenet of psychotherapy but can also be conceived as a basic principle of treatment guidelines. Compliance with this principle can be evidenced by a relationship therapist who attends to here-and-now issues and by a behavior or cognitive therapist who monitors and restructures urges and other cognitions. Even relationship therapists tend to respond to the pull of symptoms early in treatment and do so by maintaining a here-and-now focus. Research informs us that the therapist who ignores this pull will be less effective than one who responds to the patient's felt need and immediate pressures, even providing suggestions and options to enhance change.

4. Benefit corresponds to treatment intensity among functionally impaired patients (Basic Guideline 5).

This principle addresses concerns with level of care. The flexibility of this principle can be illustrated by considering the variety of ways in which treatment intensity might be increased. Changing the setting to be more or less restrictive, increasing the frequency of sessions, increasing the length of sessions, altering the intensity by using group or individually focused treatments, and supplementing therapy with homework assignments, collateral contact, or supplementary phone calls are examples of the latitude available to the therapist.

5. Therapeutic change is most likely when the patient is exposed to the objects or targets of behavioral and emotional avoidance (Optimal Guideline 2).
6. Therapeutic change is greatest when the relative balance of interventions either favors the use of skill building and symptom removal procedures among those who externalize or favors the use of insight and relationship-focused procedures among internalizing patients (Optimal Guideline 3).

These two principles begin to narrow the therapeutic approach to the specific presentation of the patient, beyond the nature of the symptoms themselves. To enact these principles, a behavior therapist may identify external objects of avoidance and use in vivo exposure to activate principle 5, while an interpersonal or relationship-oriented therapist may activate principle 5 by a here-and-now focus on daily problems and relationships and may activate principle 6 by identifying a dynamic theme or life narrative as a point of focus. In somewhat similar fashion, a cognitive therapist might focus on identifying automatic thoughts and exposing the patient to feared events in response to principle 5 and might monitor and activate schematic injunctions to activate principle 6.

7. Therapeutic change is most likely when the therapeutic procedures do not evoke patient resistance (Optimal Guideline 5).
8. Therapeutic change is greatest when the directiveness of the intervention is either inversely correspondent to the patient's current level of resistance or authoritatively prescribes a continuation of the symptomatic behavior (Optimal Guideline 6).

These are companion principles that address methods for dealing with patient resistance. The first line of effort is to avoid resistance altogether, but, failing this, the principle emphasizes that nondirectiveness is a suitable response. Within all theoretical frameworks, there are suggestions for handling and minimizing patient resistance and for minimizing conflict. In a behavioral tradition, these may include patient-generated behavioral contracts or behavioral exchange programs, while in a systems framework they may involve prescribing the symptoms and reframing. In the tradition of relationship therapy, they may involve acceptance, approach and retreat, and evocative support.

9. The likelihood of therapeutic change is greatest when the patient's level of emotional stress is moderate, neither excessively high nor excessively low (Optimal Guideline 7).

All therapeutic schools identify procedures that confront and procedures that support or provide structure. Providing structure and support, as well as behavioral and cognitive stress management procedures, can serve to reduce immediate levels of disruptive emotion, while employing confrontational, experiential, open-ended, and unstructured procedures tends to increase arousal. Thus, sensitivity to the differential outcomes of these interventions can direct the therapist of any persuasion to a suitable intervention.

10. Therapeutic change is greatest when a patient is confronted with avoided behaviors and experiences to the point of raising emotional distress until problematic responses diminish or extinguish (Optimal Guideline 8).

This is a restatement of the simple behavioral principle of exposure and extinction. Its activation can be through repeated interpretation of a consistent dynamic theme or through in vivo exposure training, again depending on a therapist's proclivities. The central ingredients are continual or repeated exposure (returning to important topics) and maintenance until the patient sorts through the issues and experiences some sense of relief by these efforts.

COMPARISON OF OUR GUIDELINES WITH OTHERS

The practicing clinician is and will continue to be besieged with treatment guidelines issued by various interest groups. To highlight the thinking in this book, it is useful to compare our treatment guidelines for depression with those that have been articulated by others (see chapter 2). The AHCPR guidelines, while articulated not for mental health clinicians but for primary-care doctors, are the most complete in their directives and are backed by a thorough literature review (table 14.1).

Depression, as we have emphasized before, is not a precise diagnosis, nor does it indicate the pathway to the current condition. Rather, depression is a symptom state with multiple pathways. Second, the manner in which the individual deals and copes with the depression is quite variable across individuals and contributes to the variance in prognosis and outcome. Taking these two factors into account, we have articulated treatment guidelines that incorporate (1) the stressors that have led to the depressed state, and (2) the elements of the individual's coping that contribute to treatment efforts and other efforts to overcome the symptom state. In contrast, the AHCPR guidelines emphasize the symptom state and its target for medication.

Guidelines for Individual Practitioners or Systems of Care

Mental health practitioners who work alone, in their private offices, receive clients from various referral sources and operate their own businesses, gener-

Table 14.1 Summary of AHCPR Guidelines

Aims of Treatment

1. The objective of treatment is to reduce and remove symptoms of depression, restore occupational and psychosocial functioning, and reduce the likelihood of relapse and recurrence.
2. Patients' adherence to treatment is improved by education for patients and their families.
3. If the patient shows only a partial response to treatment (whether medication or psychotherapy) by twelve weeks, other treatment options should be considered.

Planning for Acute-Phase Treatment

4. Treatment is indicated for those with major depression but not for those with normal sadness or distress.
5. Patients with moderate to severe major depressive disorder are appropriately treated with medication.
6. Patients with mild to moderate major depression who prefer psychotherapy without medication as the initial acute treatment may be treated with this option.
7. Combined treatment may have an advantage for patients with partial responses to either treatment alone, and for those with a chronic history or poor interepisode recovery.

Acute-Phase Management with Medication and ECT

8. Medications are first-line treatments for major depression when depression is moderate to severe; psychotic, or melancholic or shows atypical symptoms; when the patient requests medication; when psychotherapy not available; when patient has a history of positive response to medication; or when maintenance treatment is planned.
9. Medication is recommended as the first-line treatment in patients with melancholic (endogenous) symptom features.
10. Indications for ECT for acute-phase depression include severe depression associated with severe vegetative symptoms and/or marked functional impairment; presence of psychotic symptoms; or failure to respond fully to several adequate trials of medication.
11. By six weeks of medication treatment, those patients with continued impairment may find psychotherapy beneficial.

Acute-Phase Management with Psychotherapy

12. Psychotherapy alone as a first-line treatment may be considered if the major depressive episode is mild to moderate, the depression is not chronic, psychotic, or melancholic, and the patient desires psychotherapy.
13. If psychotherapy alone is ineffective by six weeks or does not result in nearly a full symptomatic remission within twelve weeks, a switch to medication may be appropriate.
14. Psychotherapies that target depressive symptoms such as cognitive or behavioral therapy, or specific interpersonal problems, such as interpersonal psychotherapy are more similar than different in efficacy. Long-term therapies are not indicated as first-line acute-phase treatments.

Acute-Phase Management with Medication and Psychotherapy

15. Combined treatment is reasonable if the depression has been chronic or characterized by poor interepisode recovery, if either treatment alone has been only partially effective, or if the patient has a history of chronic psychosocial problems or of treatment adherence difficulties.

(continued)

Table 14.1 (*Continued*)

16. Psychotherapy can be combined with medication to address problems related to depression, such as pessimism, low self-esteem, or marital difficulties.

Special Situations

17. When major depressive disorder is comorbid with another psychiatric disorder, there are three options: (1) treat the major depression first, (2) treat the associated condition as the initial focus, or (3) decide which condition is primary, and select it as the initial treatment target.
18. Suicide.

Continuation and Maintenance Phase

19. The objective of continuation treatment is to decrease the likelihood of relapse. If the patient responds to acute-phase medication, it is usually continued.
20. Continuation phase psychotherapy is advisable if there are residual symptoms, psychosocial problems, or a history of psychological functioning between episodes.
21. Patients with a history of three or more episodes of major depression are potential candidates for long-term maintenance medication.
22. Maintenance psychotherapy does not appear to be effective in preventing recurrence, although it may delay the onset of the next episode.

ating their own incomes. In contrast, there are mental health practitioners who work as part of a health care delivery system, whether in a clinic or in a group practice. In this regard, it is interesting to compare the orientation in the United States to that in Britain. The model in the United States is the private practitioner who evaluates and treats clients. In the United Kingdom care is traditionally provide by the National Health Service in local communities.

The details and the orientation of the treatment guidelines reflect the anticipated users of the guidelines and the overall orientation of the country in which the guidelines are to be used. For example, the AHCPR guidelines (Rush et al., 1993a, 1993b) are directed to primary-care physicians who have approximately five minutes to spend with any particular patient. It is assumed that the physician will assess and rapidly treat or refer the patient. This context colors the very fabric of the resulting treatment guidelines. The guidelines are as simple and brief as possible so that a busy primary-care physician who knows little about "psychiatric" patients can act with dispatch. The focus of the guidelines is on symptoms, congruent with the medical training of the primary-care physician. Treatment focuses primarily on medications, since the primary-care physician is not trained in psychotherapy and knows little about it. If the primary-care physician is to treat the patient when depression is mild and nonsuicidal and to satisfy concerns for efficiency and cost-effectiveness, the only practical choice is the use of medication or referral.

In contrast, the treatment guidelines envisioned for the system of mental health care in the United Kingdom (Roth and Fonagy, 1997) recommend a

384 Implications for Education and Training

much more thorough evaluation of the client, with an emphasis on the context and stressors on the individual with depression. A combination of treatments that should be available in the system of care are envisioned for patients. This system does not assume that every therapist can deliver every treatment, but it does assume that triage is available after a careful evaluation and matching of patient needs with treatment needs.

Our own orientation in this book is somewhere between those articulated by the AHCPR and those identified in the United Kingdom, but much closer to the latter. One difficulty faced by anyone who is trying to articulate treatment guidelines for use in the United States is the difficulty of predicting what will happen to the delivery of mental health services in the United States. At the present time, we have no system of care. Rather, there is a predominance of private practitioners who deal directly with the clients. With the advent of managed-care companies, private practitioners spend many hours talking with managed-care reviewers to get approval for a few sessions to treat patients. The "treatment guidelines" used by the managed-care companies are very simple: a few sessions of anything for everyone.

There is currently a public backlash against the managed-care system, with its focus on denying care and limiting costs. How the provision of mental health services will evolve is difficult to predict, impairing our ability to articulate a consistent and clear set of treatment guidelines that are adapted to the care environment. Thus, we focus our treatment guidelines on the individual practitioner and the client who comes for assistance.

Like Roth and Fonagy (1997) and unlike the AHCPR, we exert much effort on a thorough evaluation of the client in order to tailor the treatment to the individual client. We assume not that depression is a single entity to be treatment in a uniform way but rather that depression is a heterogeneous construct and only a beginning marker of treatment planning.

Of course, whatever system of care evolves, there will be limits on the amount and the quality of care available. Aware of these inherent limitations, we have articulated treatment guidelines for both typical care and optimal care. This is in contrast to the AHCPR guidelines, which seem to be focused on the basic, just minimally acceptable care.

Role of Symptom Course

Both the APA and the AHCPR anchor their treatment guidelines in the course of depressive symptoms across time. They relate treatment to the so-called acute, continuation, and maintenance phases of symptoms and treatment. This way of thinking is probably best suited to managing medications, both types and dosage, as the symptoms of depression progress over time. In contrast, our view of treatment planning focuses less on the symptoms of depression than on the context in which the depression arises.

Table 14.1 identifies the AHCPR guidelines in terms of these stages of change. We differ from these guidelines in that we do not find empirical justification for considering medication as the first-line treatment in any of the stages, except perhaps as a maintenance treatment, even for moderately severe patients, and even among primary-care providers. Wexler and Cicchetti's (1992) observation summarizes our rationale. They observed that among a sample of one hundred patients with moderate depression, only twenty-nine could be expected to benefit from pharmacotherapy, whereas forty-seven would be likely to benefit from psychotherapy. Moreover, the high relapse rates among those who are treated with pharmacotherapy (e.g., Hollon et al., 1992), and the large effect of placebo alone (Beutler, 1998b; Carson, 1997; Greenberg, Bornstein, Greenberg, & Fisher, 1992; Kirsch & Sapirstein, 1998) suggest that psychotherapy is a more likely first-line choice for treatment than an active course of medication. We suggest that it is the level of the patient's functional impairment and the complexity and chronicity (prior episodes, comorbidity) of the depression, rather than vegetative signs, that indicate the use of medication as a frontline treatment.

We also disagree with the AHCPR's suggestion that medication should be implemented even for patients in psychotherapy who have mild and moderate depression if changes are not noted by six weeks. Again, the absence of convincing evidence for the superiority of pharmacotherapy over psychotherapy, in either speed or magnitude of improvement, among such patients and the risk of relapse suggest that a more convincing tactic is to allow approximately three months for the effects of psychotherapy to be manifest. The focus of our guidelines is on modifying the nature of the treatment, especially in terms of handling resistance (high and low directiveness), intensity of intervention, and subjective distress (support versus abreaction) to make the treatment better fit the patient's needs, rather than switching to another treatment modality such as antidepressants.

Finally, our review of the literature and our own research lead us to disagree with the AHCPR guidelines' conclusion that all psychotherapies are of essentially equal effectiveness. Instead, we emphasize the tailoring of psychotherapy to fit patient qualities. The findings reported in this volume and the resulting principles emphasize modifying the interpersonal or individual focus of treatment, the symptomatic and insight objectives, and the directiveness of interventions to fit presenting patient factors. Our principles emphasize that interpersonally focused treatments, especially when they enhance social support and facilitate interpersonal attachments, appear to be of some specific use among patients with chronic and complex problems; cognitively and behaviorally oriented interventions may be most effective among those with externalizing coping styles or those with high levels of defensiveness; nondirective and self-directed interventions are of most value with those with high resistance traits. Our principles also address the need to facilitate patient emotional processing and, concomitantly, the value of supportive treatments (including anxiety management) among those with very high distress levels. Those with low levels of distress have relatively poor prognoses, and our findings suggest that these patients may benefit from interventions that enhance emotional arousal through confrontation and experiential learning.

On the other hand, our guidelines are defined with less reliance on specific models and theories of treatment than those offered by Roth and Fonagy (1997). Their guidelines, while more compatible with our own than those presented by the AHCPR, are nonetheless bound to comparisons of different theoretical models. They are not framed in a way that allows therapists from different models to extend the range of their interventions. The U.K. guidelines suggest that treatments should be selected from an array of manuals and theories. Thus, therapists should become more or less specialists, working with patients whose problems are compatible with the therapist's theoretical model.

Collectively, the guidelines presented in this volume offer more specific and tailored treatments than either those offered by the AHCPR guidelines or those offered by Roth and Fornagy (1997). Of course, these are not the final words, and the issues raised by these different models can be empirically tested and verified. Guidelines, at this stage of the development of the field, are only guides. They are not rules, and they should be used not for dictating treatment but for guiding and enhancing it. Clinicians should be trained in principles and values, then set to using these principles to explicitly address the problems and the unique qualities of patients who come to their doors.

We do not see it as a concession to the obvious to emphasize that further research is needed. Indeed, we think that research is always needed and that all guidelines should be responsive to the information that evolves from this research. However, we do not think that the application of the current guiding principles for basic and optimal care need or even should await this research. This would be a never-ending wait, since more research is always needed.

One major disadvantage of treatments that are embedded within theories of psychopathology and change is that they are themselves resistant to change. They are selective in their acceptance of research findings. It is our intention that the guidelines presented here be responsive to research and seek to change as research uncovers more powerful predictors, indicators, and contraindicators. Both basic and optimal guiding principles must be subject to these changes, irrespective of the theories that stimulate this research.

Bibliography

Aaron, H. (1996). End of an era. *Brookings Review, 14 (1)*, 35–37.

Abram, H. S., Moore, G. I., & Westervelt, F. B. (1971). Suicidal behavior in chronic dialysis patients. *American Journal of Psychiatry, 127*, 1199.

Abramson, L. Y., Seligman, M. E. P., & Teasdale, J. (1978). Learned helplessness in humans: Critique and reformulation. *Journal of Abnormal Psychology, 87*, 49–74.

Achte, K. (1988). Suicidal tendencies in the elderly. *Suicide and Life-Threatening Behavior, 18*, 55–65.

Ackerman, D. L., Greenland, S., & Bystritsky, A. (1994). Predictors of treatment response in obsessive-compulsive disorder: Multivariate analyses from a multicenter trial of comipramine. *Journal of Clinical Psychopharmacology, 14*, 247–253.

Adamek, M. E., & Kaplan, M. S. (1996). Managing elder suicide: A profile of American and Canadian crisis prevention centers. *Suicide and Life-Threatening Behavior, 26*(2), 122–131.

Addis, M. E., & Jacobson, N. S. (1996). Reasons for depression and the process and outcome of Cognitive-Behavioral psychotherapies. *Journal of Consulting and Clinical Psychology, 64*, 1417–1424.

Ainsworth, M. D. S. (1989). Attachments beyond infancy. *American Psychologist, 44*, 709–716.

Akiskal, H. S., King, D., Rosenthal, T. L., Robinson, D., & Scott-Strauss, A. (1983). Chronic depressions: Clinical and familial characteristics in 137 probands. *Journal of Affective Disorders, 3*, 297–315.

Albanese, A. L. (1998). *Identifying predictors of differential treatment effects in the treatment of adults diagnosed with depression.* Unpublished doctoral dissertation, University of California, Santa Barbara.

Allen, J. P., Hauser, S. T., & Borman-Spurrell, E. (1996). Attachment theory as a framework for understanding sequelae of severe adolescent psychopathology: An 11-year follow-up study. *Journal of Consulting and Clinical Psychology, 64*, 254–263.

American Psychiatric Association (1987). *Diagnostic and statistical manual of mental disorders* (3rd ed., rev.). Washington, DC: Author.

American Psychiatric Association (1993). Practice guidelines for major depressive disorder in adults. *American Journal of Psychiatry, 150* (Supplement 4), 1–26.

American Psychiatric Association (1994). *Diagnostic and statistical manual of mental disorders* (4th ed.). Washington, DC: Author.

American Psychiatric Association Task Force on Electroconvulsive Therapy (1990). *The practice of electroconvulsive therapy.* Washington, DC: Author.

American Psychological Association (1994). *Template for developing guidelines: Interventions for mental disorders and psychosocial aspects of physical disorders.* Washington, DC: Author.

Amsterdam, J. D., Fawcett, J., Quitkin, F. M., Reimherr, F. W., Rosenbaum, J. F., Michelson, D., Hornig-Rohan, M., & Beasley, C. M. (1997). Fluoxetine and norluoxetine plasma concentrataions in major depression: A multicenter study. *American Journal of Psychiatry, 154,* 963–969.

Anastasi, A. (1988). *Psychological testing* (6th ed.). New York: Macmillan.

Anderson, C. A., & Hammen, C. L. (1993). Psychosocial outcomes of children of unipolar depressed, bipolar, medically ill, and normal women: A longitudinal study. *Journal of Consulting and Clinical Psychology, 61,* 448–454.

Anderson, E. A. (1987). Preoperative preparation for cardiac surgery facilitates recovery, reduces psychological distress, and reduces the incidence of acute postoperative hypertension. *Journal of Consulting and Clinical Psychology, 55,* 513–520.

Anderson, K. W. (1998). Utility of the five-factor model of personality in psychotherapy aptitude-treatment interaction research. *Psychotherapy Research, 8,* 54–70.

Anderson, T., & Leitner, L. M. (1996). Symptomatology and the use of affect constructs to influence value and behavior constructs. *Journal of Counseling Psychology, 43,* 77–83.

Anderson, T., & Strupp, H. H. (1996). The ecology of psychotherapy research. *Journal of Consulting and Clinical Psychology, 64,* 776–782.

Andrew, B., Hawton, K., Fagg, J., & Westbrook, D. (1993). Do psychosocial factors influence outcome in severely depressed female psychiatric in-patients? *British Journal of Psychiatry, 163,* 747–754.

Angus, D. C., Linde-Zwirble, W. T., Sirio, C. A., Rotondi, A. J., Chelluri, L., Newbold, R. C., III, Lave, J. R., & Pinsky, M. R. (1996). The effect of managed care on ICU length of stay: Implications for medicare. *Journal of the American Medical Association, 276,* 1075–1082.

Antonuccio, D. (1995). Psychotherapy for depression: No stronger medicine. *American Psychologist, 50(6),* 450–451.

Antonuccio, D. O., Danton, W. G., & DeNelsky, G. Y. (1995). Psychotherapy versus medication for depression: Challanging the conventional wisdom with data. *Professional Psychology: Research and Practice, 26,* 574–585.

Antonuccio, D. O., Thomas, M., & Danton, W. G. (1997). A cost-effectiveness analysis of Cognitive Behavior Therapy and fluoxetine (Prozac) in the treatment of depression. *Behavior Therapy, 28,* 187–210.

Appelbaum, P. S. (1993). Legal liability and managed care. *American Psychologist, 48,* 251–257.

Armsden, G. C., McCauley, E., Greenberg, M. T., & Burke, P. M. (1990). Parent and peer attachment in early adolescent depression. *Journal of Abnormal Child Psychology, 18,* 683–697.

Arntz, A., & Van den Hout, M. (1995). Psychological treatments of panic disorder without agoaphobia: Cognitive therapy versus applied relaxation. *Behavioral Research and Therapy, 34,* 113–121.

Asarnow, J. R. (1992). Suicidal ideation and attempts during middle childhood: Associations with perceived family stress and depression among child psychiatric inpatients. *Journal of Clinical Child Psychology, 21(1),* 35–40

Avery, D., & Winokur, G. (1977). The efficacy of electroconvulsive therapy and antidepressants in depression. *Biological Psychiatry, 12,* 507–523.

Azrin, N. H., Sisson, R. W., Meyers, R., et al. (1982). Alcoholism treatment by disulfiram and community reinforcement therapy. *Journal of Behavioral Therapy and Experimental Psychiatry, 13,* 105–112.

Bandura, A. (1977). *Social learning theory.* Englewood Cliffs, NJ: Prentice-Hall.

Barach, P. M. (1996, Oct. 17). *Managed care meets Schubert.* Personal communication.

Barber, J. P., Morse, J. Q., Krakauer, I. D., Chittams, J., & Crits-Christoph, K. (1997). Change in obsessive-compulsive and avoidant personality disorders following time-limited supportive-expressive therapy. *Psychotherapy, 34,* 133–143.

Barber, J. P., & Muenz, L. R. (1996). The role of avoidance and obsessiveness in matching patients to cognitive and interpersonal psychotherapy: Empirical findings from the treatment for depression collaborative research program. *Journal of Consulting and Clinical Psychology, 64,* 951–958.

Barlow, D. H. (1994). Psychological interventions in the era of managed competition. *Clinical Psychology: Science and Practice, 1,* 109–122.

Barraclough, B., Bunch, J., Nelson, B., & Sainsbury, P. (1974). A hundred cases of suicide: Clinical aspects. *British Journal of Psychiatry, 125,* 355–373.

Basoglu, M., Marks, I. M., & Swinson, R. P. (1994). Pre-treatment predictors of treatment outcome in panic disorder and agoraphobia treated with alprazolam and exposure. *Journal of Affective Disorders, 30,* 123–132.

Baxter, L. R., Schwartz, J. M., Phelps, M. E., Mazziotta, J. C., Guze, B. H., Selin, C. E., Gerner, R. H., & Sumida, R. M. (1989). Reduction of prefrontal cortex glucose metabolism common to three types of depression. *Archives of General Psychiatry, 46,* 243–250.

Beach, S. R., Winters, K. C., & Weintraub, S. (1983). *The link between marital distress and depression: A prospective design.* Paper presented at the World Congress of Behavior Therapy.

Beardslee, W., Bemporad, J., Keller, M. B., & Klerman, G. L. (1983). Children of parents with a major affective disorder: A review. *American Journal of Psychiatry, 140,* 825–832.

Beardslee, W. R., Schultz, L. H., & Selman, R. L. (1987). Level of social cognitive development, adaptive functioning, and DSM-III diagnoses in adolescent offspring of parents with affective disorders. *Developmental Psychology, 23,* 807–815.

Beck, A. T. (1967). *Depression: Clinical, experimental, and theoretical aspects.* New York: Harper & Row.

Beck, A. T., Brown, G., Berchick, R. J., Stewart, B. L., & Steer, R. A. (1990). Relationship between hopelessness and ultimate suicide: A replication with psychiatric outpatients. *American Journal of Psychiatry, 147,* 190–195.

Beck, A. T., & Emery, G. (1985). *Anxiety disorders and phobias: A cognitive perspective.* New York: Basic Books.

Beck, A. T., Kovacs, M., & Weissman, A. (1975). Hopelessness and suicidal behavior. *Journal of the American Medical Association, 234,* 1146–1149.

Beck, A. T., Rush, A. J., Shaw, B. F., & Emery, G. (1979). *Cognitive therapy of depression: A treatment manual.* New York: Guilford Press.

Beck, A. T., & Steer, R. A. (1987). *Beck Depression Inventory: Manual.* San Antonio, TX: Psychological Corporation.

Beck, A. T., & Steer, R. A. (1988). *Beck Hopelessness Scale: Manual.* San Antonio, TX: Psychological Corporation.

Beck, A. T., & Steer, R. A. (1989). Clinical predictors of eventual suicide: A 5- to

10-year prospective study of suicide attempters. *Journal of Affective Disorders, 17,* 203–209.

Beck, A. T., Steer, R. A., Beck, J. S., & Newman, C. F. (1993). Hopelessness, depression, suidical ideation, and clinical diagnosis of depression. *Suicide and Life-Threatening Behavior, 23,* 139–145.

Beck, A. T., Steer, R. A., Kovacs, M., & Garrison, B. (1985). Hopelessness and eventual suicide: A 10-year prospective study of patients hospitalized with suicidal ideation. *American Journal of Psychiatry, 142,* 559–563.

Beck, A. T., Ward, C. H., Mendelson, M., Mock, J., & Erbaugh, J. (1961). An inventory for measuring depression. *Archives of General Psychiatry, 4,* 561–569.

Beck, R. W., Morris, J. B., & Beck, A. T. (1974). Cross-validation of the Suicidal Intent Scale. *Psychological Reports, 34,* 445–446.

Becker, R. E., Heimberg, R. G., & Bellack, A. S. (1987). *Social skills training for depression.* New York: Pergamon Press.

Beckham, E. E. (1990). Psychotherapy of depression research at a crossroads: Directions for the 1990s. *Clinical Psychology Review, 10,* 207–228.

Bellack, A. S., Hersen, M., & Himmelhoch, J. M. (1980). Social skills training for depression: A treatment manual. *JSHS Catalog of Selected Documents in Psychology, 10,* 92 (MS 2156).

Bellack, A. S., Turner, S. M., Hersen, M., & Luber, R. F. (1984). An examination of the efficacy of social skills training for chronic schizophrenic patients. *Hospital and Community Psychiatry, 35,* 1023–1028.

Belsher, G., & Costello, C. G. (1991). Do confidants of depressed women provide less social support than confidants of nondepressed women? *Journal of Abnormal Psychology, 100,* 516–525.

Benassi, V. A., Sweeney, P. D., & Dufour, C. L. (1988). Is there a relation between locus of control orientation and depression? *Journal of Abnormal Psychology, 97,* 357–367.

Benca, R. M., Obermeyer, W. H., Thisted, R. A., & Gillin, J. C. (1992). Sleep and psychiatric disorders: A meta-analysis. *Archives of General Psychiatry, 49,* 651–668.

Bergin, A. E. (1971). The evaluation of therapeutic outcomes. In A. E. Bergin & S. L. Garfield (Eds.), *Handbook of psychotherapy and behavior change* (pp. 217–270). New York: Wiley.

Bergin, A. E., & Strupp, H. H. (1972). *Changing frontiers in the science of psychotherapy.* Chicago: Aldine-Atherton.

Bergner, R. M. (1997). What is psychopathology? And so what? *Clinical Psychology: Science and Practice, 4,* 235–248.

Berman, A. L., & Jobes, D. A. (1992). Suicidal behavior of adolescents. In B. Bongar (Ed.), *Suicide: Guidelines for assessment, management and treatment* (pp. 84–105). New York: Oxford University Press.

Berman, J. S., & Norton, N. C. (1985). Does professional training make a therapist more effective? *Psychological Bulletin, 98,* 401–407.

Beutler, L. E. (1979). Toward specific psychological therapies for specific conditions. *Journal of Consulting and Clinical Psychology, 47,* 882–897.

Beutler, L. E. (1983). *Eclectic psychotherapy: A systematic approach.* New York: Pergamon Press.

Beutler, L. E. (1989). Differential treatment selection: The role of diagnosis in psychotherapy. *Psychotherapy, 26,* 271–281.

Beutler, L. E. (1991). Have all won and must all have prizes? Revisiting Luborsky et. al.'s verdict. *Journal of Consulting and Clinical Psychology, 59,* 226–232.

Beutler, L. E. (1997). Measuring changes in patients following psychological and pharmacological interventions: Depression. In L. J. Horowitz, M. J. Lambert,

& H. H. Strupp (Eds.), *Measuring patient change after treatment for mood, anxiety, and personality disorders: Toward a core battery* (pp. 247–262). Washington, DC: American Psychological Association Press.

Beutler, L. E. (1998a). Identifying empirically supported treatments: What if we didn't? *Journal of Consulting and Clinical Psychology, 66,* 113–120.

Beutler, L. E. (1998b). Prozac and placebo: There's a pony in there somewhere. *Treatment and Prevention, 1*(1), 15–20.

Beutler, L. E. (in press). Training in systematic treatment selection: Information processing in prescriptive psychotherapies. In F. Caspar (Ed.), *The inner processes of psychotherapists: Innovations in clinical training.* New York: Oxford University Press.

Beutler, L. E., & Baker, M. (1998). The movement towards empirical validation: At what level should we analyze and who are the consumers? In K. S. Dobson & D. Craig (Eds.), *Best practice: Developing and promoting empirically supported interventions* (pp. 43–65). Newbury Park, CA: Sage Press.

Beutler, L. E., & Berren, M. R. (1995). *Integrative assessment of adult personality.* New York: Guilford Press.

Beutler, L. E., Bongar, B., & Shurkin, J. C. (1998). *Am I crazy or is it my shrink?* New York: Oxford University Press.

Beutler, L. E., Booker, K., & Peerson, S. (in press). Experiential treatments: Humanistic, client-centered, and gestalt approaches. In P. Salkovskis (Ed.), *Comprehensive clinical psychology* (Vol. 6). Oxford: Pergamon Press.

Beutler, L. E., & Clarkin, J. (1990). *Systematic treatment selection: Toward targeted therapeutic interventions.* New York: Brunner/Mazel.

Beutler, L. E., & Clarkin, J. (1991). Future research directions. In L. E. Beutler & M. Crago (Eds.), *Psychotherapy research: International programmatic studies* (pp. 329–334). Washington, DC: American Psychological Association.

Beutler, L. E., & Consoli, A. J. (1992). Systematic eclectic psychotherapy. In J. C. Norcross & M. R. Goldfried (Eds.), *Handbook of psychotherapy integration* (pp. 264–299). New York: Basic Books.

Beutler, L. E., Consoli, A. J., & Williams, R. E. (1995). Integrative and eclectic therapies in practice. In B.Bongar & L. E. Beutler (Eds.), *Comprehensive textbook of psychotherapy: Theory and practice* (pp. 274–292). New York: Oxford University Press.

Beutler, L. E., Dunbar, P. W. & Baer, P. E. (1980). Individual variation among therapists' perceptions of patients, therapy process and outcome. *Psychiatry, 43,* 205–210.

Beutler, L. E., Engle, D., Mohr, D., Daldrup, R. J., Bergan, J., Meredith, K., & Merry, W. (1991). Predictors of differential and selfdirected psychotherapeutic procedures. *Journal of Consulting and Clinical Psychology, 59,* 333–340.

Beutler, L. E., Engle, D., Oro'-Beutler, M. E., Daldrup, R., & Meredith, K. (1986). Inability to express intense affect: A common link between depression and pain? *Journal of Consulting and Clinical Psychology, 54,* 752–759.

Beutler, L. E., Engle, D., Shoham-Salomon, V., Mohr, D. C., Dean, J. C., & Bernat, E. M. (1991). University of Arizona Psychotherapy Research Program. In L. E. Beutler & M. Crago (Eds.), *Psychotherapy research: International programatic studies* (pp. 90–97). Washington, DC: American Psychological Association.

Beutler, L. E., Frank, M., Scheiber, S. C., Calvert, S., & Gaines, J. (1984). Comparative effects of group psychotherapies in a short-term inpatient setting: An experience with deterioration effects. *Psychiatry, 47,* 66–76.

Beutler, L. E., Goodrich, G., Fisher, D., & Williams, O. B. (1999). Use of psychological tests/instruments for treatment planning. In M. E. Maruish (Ed.), *The*

use of psychological tests for treatment planning and outcome assessment
(2nd ed.) (pp. 81–113). Hillsdale, NJ: Lawrence Erlbaum.

Beutler, L. E., & Guest, P. D. (1989). The role of cognitive change in psychotherapy. In A. Freeman, K. M. Simon, L. E. Beutler, & H. Arkowitz (Eds.), *Comprehensive handbook of cognitive therapy* (pp. 123–142). New York: Plenum.

Beutler, L. E., & Hamblin, D. L. (1986). Individual outcome measures of internal change: Methodological considerations. *Journal of Consulting and Clinical Psychology* (special edition), *54*, 48–53.

Beutler, L. E., & Harwood, T. M. (in press). *Prescriptive psychotherapy: The treatment of co-morbid depression and substance abuse.* New York: Guilford Press.

Beutler, L. E., Johnson, D. T., Neville, C. W., Jr., & Workman, S. N. (1973). Some sources of variance in "Accurate Empathy" ratings. *Journal of Consulting and Clinical Psychology, 40,* 167–169.

Beutler, L. E., Kim, E. J., Davison, E., Karno, M., & Fisher, D. (1996). Research contributions to improving managed health care outcomes. *Psychotherapy, 33,* 197–206.

Beutler, L. E., Machado, P. P. P., Engle, D., & Mohr, D. (1993). Differential patient X treatment maintenance of treatment effects among cognitive, experiential, and self-directed psychotherapies. *Journal of Psychotherapy Integration, 3,* 15–32.

Beutler, L. E., Machado, P. P. P., & Neufeldt, S. (1994). Therapist variables. In S. L. Garfield & A. E. Bergin (Eds.), *Handbook of psychotherapy and behavior change* (4th ed.) (pp. 259–269). New York: Wiley.

Beutler, L. E., & McNabb, C. (1981). Self-evaluation of the psychotherapist. In C. E. Walker (Ed.), *Clinical practice of psychology* (pp. 397–440). New York: Pergamon Press.

Beutler, L. E., & Mitchell, R. (1981). Psychotherapy outcome in depressed and impulsive patients as a function of analytic and experiential treatment procedures. *Psychiatry, 44,* 297–306.

Beutler, L. E., Mohr, D. C., Grawe, K., Engle, D., & MacDonald, R. (1991). Looking for differential effects: Cross-cultural predictors of differential psychotherapy efficacy. *Journal of Psychotherapy Integration, 1,* 121–142.

Beutler, L. E., Patterson, K. M., Jacob, T., Shoham, V., Yost, E., & Rohrbaugh, M. (1994). Matching treatment to alcoholism subtypes. *Psychotherapy, 30,* 463–472.

Beutler, L. E., Sandowicz, M., Fisher, D., & Albanese, A. L. (1996). Resistance in psychotherapy: Conclusions that are supported by research. *In Session: Psychotherapy and Practice, 1,* 77–86.

Beutler, L. E., Wakefield, P., & Williams, R. E. (1994). Use of psychological tests/instruments for treatment planning. In M. Maruish (Ed.), *Use of psychological testing for treatment planning and outcome assessment* (pp. 55–74). Chicago: Lawrence Erlbaum.

Beutler, L. E., & Williams, O. B. (1995, July/Aug.). Computer applications for the selection of optimal psychosocial therapeutic interventions. *Behavioral Healthcare Tomorrow, 66–68.*

Beutler, L. E., Williams, R. E., Wakefield, P. J. & Entwistle, S. R. (1995). Bridging scientist and practitioner perspectives in clinical psychology. *American Psychologist, 50*(12), 984–994.

Biaggio, M. K., & Godwin, W. H. (1987). Relation of depression to anger and hostility constructs. *Psychological Reports, 61,* 87–90.

Bifulco, A. T., Brown, G. W., & Adler, Z. (1991). Early sexual abuse and clinical depression in adult life. *British Journal of Psychiatry, 159,* 115–122.

Bilfulco, A. T., Brown, G. W., & Harris, T. O. (1987). Childhood loss of parent, lack of adequate parental care and adult depression: A replication. *Journal of Affective Disorders, 12,* 115–128.

Billings, A. G., Cronkite, R. C., & Moos, R. H. (1985). Difficulty of follow-up and posttreatment functioning among depressed patients. *Journal of Nervous and Mental Disease, 8,* 9–16.

Billings, A. G., & Moos, R. H. (1984). Chronic and nonchronic unipolar depression: The differential role of environmental stressors and resources. *Journal of Nervous and Mental Disease, 172,* 65–75.

Billings, A. G., & Moos, R. H. (1985). Life stressors and social resources affect posttreatment outcomes among depressed patients. *Journal of Abnormal Psychology, 94,* 140–153.

Bischoff, M. M., & Tracey, T. J. G. (1995). Client resistance as predicted by therapist behavior: A study of sequential dependence. *Journal of Counseling Psychology, 42,* 487–495.

Black, D. W., Warrack, G., & Winokur, G. (1985). The Iowa record-linkage study: I. Suicides and accidental deaths among psychiatric patients. *Archives of General Psychiatry, 42,* 71–75.

Black, H. C. (1979). *Black's law dictionary.* St. Paul, MN: West.

Black, H. C. (1990). *Black's law dictionary* (6th ed.). St. Paul, MN: West.

Blackburn, I. M., Bishop, S., Glen, A. I. M., Whalley, L. J., & Christie, J. E. (1981). The efficacy of cognitive therapy in depression: A treatment trial using cognitive therapy and pharmacotherapy, each alone and in combination. *British Journal of Psychiatry, 139,* 181–189.

Blackburn, I. M., Eunson, K. M., & Bishop, S. (1986). A two-year naturalistic follow-up of depressed patients treated with cognitive therapy, pharmacotherapy, and a combination of both. *Journal of Affective Disorder, 10,* 67–75.

Blanchard, E. B., Schwarz, S. P., Neff, D. F., & Gerardi, M. A. (1988). Prediction of outcome from the self-regulatory treatment of irritable bowel syndrome. *Behavior, Research and Therapy, 26,* 187–190.

Blatt, S. J., Zuroff, D. C., Quinlan, D. M., & Pilkonis, P. A. (1996). Interpersonal factors in brief treatment of depression: Further analyses of the National Institute of Mental Health Treatment of Depression Collaborative Research Program. *Journal of Consulting and Clinical Psychology, 64,* 162–171.

Block, J., & Colvin, C. R. (1994). Positive illusions and well-being revisited: Separating fiction from fact. *Psychological Bulletin, 116,* 28.

Bongar, B. (1991). *The suicidal patient: Clinical and legal standards of care.* Washington, DC: American Psychological Association.

Bongar, B., Berman, A.L, Litman, R.E., & Maris, R. (1992). Outpatient standards of care in the assessment, management and treatment of suicidal persons. *Suicide and Life-Threatening Behavior, 22,* 453–478.

Bongar, B., & Harmatz, M. (1991). Clinical psychology graduate education in the study of suicide: Availability, resources, and importance. *Suicide and Life-Threatening Behavior, 21*(3), 231–244.

Bongar, B., Maris, R. W., Berman, A. L., & Litman, R. E. (1992). Outpatient standards of care and the suicidal patient. *Suicide and Life-Threatening Behavior, 22*(4), 453–477.

Bongar, B., Peterson, L. G., Harris, E. A., & Aissis, J. (1989). Clinical and legal considerations in the management of suicidal patients: An integrative overview. *Journal of Integrative and Eclectic Psychotherapy, 8,* 53–67.

Born, J., DeKloet, E. R., Wenz, H., Kern, W., & Fehm, H. L. (1991). Gluco- and antimineralocorticocoid effects on human sleep: A role of central corticosteriod receptors. *American Journal of Physiology, 22,* 183–186.

Bowen, M. (1966). The use of family theory in clinical practice. *Comprehensive Psychiatry, 7*, 345–374.

Boyd, J. (1983). The increasing rate of suicide by firearms. *New England Journal of Medicine, 308*, 872–898.

Bradbury, R. C., Golec, J. H., & Stearns, F. E. (1991). Research notes and data trends: Comparing hospital length of stay in independent practice association HMOs and traditional programs. *Inquiry, 28*, 87–93.

Brehm, J. W. (1966). *A theory of psychological reactance.* New York: Academic Press.

Brehm, S. S. (1976). *The application of social psychology to clinical practice.* New York: Halstead Press.

Brehm, S. S., & Brehm, J. W. (1981). *Psychological reactance: A theory of freedom and control.* New York: Academic Press.

Brent, D. A., Kupfer, D. J., Bromet, E. J., & Dew, M. A. (1988). The assessment and treatment of patients at risk for suicide. In A. J. Frances & R. E. Hales (Eds.), *American Psychiatric Press review of psychiatry* (vol. 7, pp. 353–385). Washington, DC: American Psychiatric Press.

Brent, D. A., Perper, J. A., Moritz, G., Allman, C., et al. (1993a). Psychiatric risk factors for adolescent suicide: A case control study. *Journal of the American Academy of Child and Adolescent Psychiatry, 32*(3), 521–529.

Brent, D. A., Perper, J.A., Moritz, G., Allman, C., et al. (1993b). Psychiatric sequelae to the loss of an adolescent peer to suicide. *Journal of the American Academy of Child and Adolescent Psychiatry, 32*(3), 509–517.

Brewin, C. R. (1985). Depression and causal attributions: What is their relation? *Psychological Bulletin, 98*, 297–309.

Brooks, V. R. (1981). Sex and sexual orientation as variables in therapists' biases and therapy outcomes. *Clinical Social Work Journal, 9*, 198–210.

Brown, G. R., & Anderson, B. (1991). Psychiatric morbidity in adult inpatients with childhood histories of sexual and physical abuse. *American Journal of Psychiatry, 148*, 55–61.

Brown, H. N. (1987). Patient suicide and therapists in training. *Comprehensive Psychiatry, 28*(2), 101–112.

Brown, R. A., & Lewinsohn, P. M. (1984). A psychoeducational approach to the treatment of depression: Comparison of group, individual, and minimal contact procedures. *Journal of Consulting and Clinical Psychology, 52*, 774–783.

Brown, T. A., & Barlow, D. H. (1995). Long-term outcome in cognitive-behavioral treatment of panic disorder: Clinical predictors and alternative strategies for assessment. *Journal of Consulting and Clinical Psychology, 63*, 754–765.

Bruder-Mattson, S. F., & Hovanitz, C. A. (1990). Coping and attributional styles as predictors of depression. *Journal of Clinical Psychology, 46*, 557–565.

Bruno, G. (1995). *Suicide assessment practices among psychologists.* Unpublished doctoral dissertation, Pacific Graduate School of Psychology.

Bugental, J. F. T., & McBeath, B. (1995). Depth existential therapy: Evolution since World War II. In B. Bongar & L. E. Beutler (Eds.), *Comprehensive textbook of psychotherapy: Theory and practice* (pp. 111–122). New York: Oxford University Press.

Burns, D. D., & Nolen-Hoeksema, S. (1992). Therapeutic empathy and recovery and recovery from depression in cognitive-behavioral therapy: A structural euation model. *Journal of Consulting and Clinical Psychology, 60*, 441–449.

Burns, D. D., Sayers, S. L., & Moras, K. (1994). Intimate relationships and depression: Is there a causal connection? *Journal of Consulting and Clinical Psychology, 62*, 1033–1043.

Burns, D. D., Shaw, B. F., & Croker, W. (1987). Case histories and shorter communications. *Behavior Therapy and Research, 25,* 223–225.

Burvill, P. W., Hall, W. D., Stampfer, H. G., & Emmerson, J. P. (1991). The prognosis of depression in old age. *British Journal of Psychiatry, 158,* 64–71.

Buss, A. H., & Durkee, A. (1957). An inventory for assessing different kinds of hostility. *Journal of Consulting Psychology, 21,* 343–349.

Butcher, J. N. (1990). *The MMPI-2 in psychological treatment.* New York: Oxford University Press.

Butcher, J. N. (1995). Interpretation of the MMPI-2. In L. E. Beutler & M. R. Berren (Eds.), *Integrative assessment of adult personality* (pp. 206–239). New York: Guilford Press.

Butcher, J. N., Dahlstrom, W. G., Graham, J. R., Tellegen, A. M., & Kaemmer, B. (1989). *Minnesota Multiphasic Personality Inventory-2 (MMPI-2): Manual for administration and scoring.* Minneapolis: University of Minnesota Press.

Butler, G., & Mathews, A. (1983). Cognitive processes in anxiety. *Advances in Behavior Research and Therapy, 5,* 51–62.

Buysse, D. J., & Kupfer, D. J. (1993). Sleep disorders in depressive disorders. In J. J. Mann & D. J. Kupfer (Eds.), *Biology of depressive disorders. Part A: A systems perspective* (pp. 123–154). New York: Plenum.

Cadoret, R. (1983). Discussion. In S. B. Guze, F. J. Earls, & J. E. Varrett (Eds.), *Child psychopathology and development* (p. 65). New York: Raven Press.

Cadoret, R., O'Gorman, T., Heywood, E., & Troughton, E. (1985). Genetic and environmental factors in major depression. *Journal of Affective Disorders, 9,* 155–164.

Callahan, C. M., Hendrie, H. C., Dittus, R. S., Brater, D. C., Hui, S. L., & Tierney, W. M. (1994). Improving treatment of late-life depression in primary care: A randomized clinical trial. *American Geriatric Society, 42,* 839–846.

Callahan, J. (1993). Blueprint for an adolescent suicidal crisis. *Psychiatric Annals, 23*(5), 263–270.

Calvert, S. J., Beutler, L.E., & Crago, M. (1988). Psychotherapy outcome as a function of therapist-patient matching on selected variables. *Journal of Social and Clinical Psychology, 6,* 104–117.

Capelleri, J. C., Ioannidis, J. P. A., Schmid, C. H., de Ferranti, S. D., Aubert, M., Chalmers, T. C., & Lau, J. (1996). Large trials vs meta-Analysis or smaller trials: How do their results compare? *Journal of the American Medical Association, 276,* 1332–1338.

Carroll, B. J. (1982). The dexamethasone suppression test for melancholia. *British Journal of Psychiatry, 140,* 292–304.

Carroll, B. J. (1991). Psychopathology and neurobiology of manic-depressive disorders. In B. J. Carroll & J. E. Barrett (Eds.), *Psychopathology and the brain* (pp. 265–286). New York: Raven Press.

Carroll, B. J., Curtis, G. C., & Mendels, J. (1976). Neuroendocrine regulation in depression. I: Limbic system-adrenocortical dysfunction. *Archives of General Psychiatry, 33,* 1039–1044.

Carroll, K. M., Rounsaville, B. J., Gordon, L. T., Bruce, J., & Nick, C. (1994). Psychotherapy and pharmacotherapy for ambulatory cocaine abusers. *Archives of General Psychiatry, 51,* 177–187.

Carson, R. C. (1997). Costly compromises: A critique of the diagnostic and statistical manual of mental disorders. In S. Fisher & R. P. Greenberg (Eds.), *From placebo to pancea: Putting psychiatric drugs to the test* (pp. 98–112). New York: Wiley.

Carver, C. S., & Ganellen, R. J. (1983). Depression and components of self-punitiveness: High standards, self-criticism, and overgeneralization. *Journal of Abnormal Psychology, 92,* 330–337.

Carver, C. S., LaVoie, L., Kuhl, J., Ganellen, R. J. (1988). Cognitive concomitants of depression: A further examination of the roles of generalization, high standards, and self-criticism. *Journal of Social and Clinical Psychology, 7,* 350–365.

Caspar, F. (1995). *Plan analysis: Toward optimizing psychotherapy.* Seattle: Hogrefe & Huber.

Caspar, F. (in press). Introduction to the issue of therapist inner processes and their training. In F. Caspar (Ed.), *The inner processes of psychotherapists: Innovations in clinical training.* New York: Oxford University Press.

Cattell, R. B., Eber, H. W., & Tatsuoka, M. M. (1970). *Handbook for the Sixteen Personality Factor Questionnaire.* Champaign, IL: Institute for Personality and Ability Testing.

Chambless, D. L. (1996). In defense of dissemination of empirically supported psychological interventions. *Clinical Psychology: Science and Practice, 3,* 230–235.

Chambless, D. L., Baker, M. J., Baucom, D. H., Beutler, L. E., Calhoun, K. S., Crits-Christoph, P., Daiuto, A., DeRubeis, R., Detweiler, J., Haaga, D. A. F., Johnson, S. B., McCurry, S., Mueser, K. T., Pope, K. S., Sanderson, W. C., Shoham, V., Stickle, T., Williams, D. A., & Woody, S. R. (1998). Update on empirically validated therapies, II. *Clinical Psychologist, 51,* 3–16.

Chambless, D. L., Sanderson, W. C., Shoham, V., Johnson, S. B., Pope, K. S., Crits-Christoph, P., Baker, M., Johnson, B., Woody, S. R., Sue, S., Beutler, L. E., Williams, D. A., & McCurry, S. (1996). An update on empirically validated therapies. *Clinical Psychologist, 49(2),* 5–14.

Chapman, L. J., & Chapman, J. P. (1969). Illusory correlation {a an} obstacle to the use of valid psychodiagnostic signs. *Journal of Abnormal Psychology, 74,* 193–204.

Chemtob, C. M., Hamada, R. S., Bauer, G. B., Kinney, B., & Torigoe, R. Y. (1988). Patient suicide: Frequency and impact on psychiatrists. *American Journal of Psychiatry, 145,* 224–228.

Chemtob, C. M., Hamada, R. S., Bauer, G. B., Torigoe, R. Y., & Kinney, B. (1988). Patient suicide: Frequency and impact on psychologists. *Professional Psychology: Research and Practice, 19(4),* 421–425.

Cheng, A. T. A. (1995). Mental illness and suicide: A case-control study in Taiwan. *Archives of General Psychiatry, 52,* 594–603.

Chevron, E. S., Quinlan, D. M., & Blatt, S. J. (1978). Sex roles and gender differences in the experience of depression. *Journal of Abnormal Psychology, 87,* 680–683.

Chinsky, J. M., & Rappaport, J. (1970). A brief critique of the meaning and reliability of accurate empathy ratings. *Psychological Bulletin, 73,* 379–382.

Christensen, A., & Jacobson, N. S. (1994). Who (or what) can do psychotherapy: The status and challenge of nonprofessional therapies. *Psychological Science, 5,* 8–14.

Cicchetti, D. V., & Ryan, E. R. (1976). A reply to Beutler et al.'s study: Some sources of variance in accurate empathy ratings. *Journal of Consulting and Clinical Psychology, 44,* 858–859.

Clark, D. C. (1990). Suicide risk assessment and prediction in the 1990s. *Crisis, 11(2),* 104–112.

Clark, D. C. (1992). "Rational" suicide and people with terminal conditions or disabilities. *Issues in Law and Medicine, 8(2),* 147–166.

Clark, D. C., & Fawcett, J. (1992). Review of empirical risk factors for evaluation of the suicidal patient. In B. Bongar (Ed.), *Suicide: Guidelines for assessment, management and treatment.* New York: Oxford University Press.

Clark, D. C., Young, M. A., Scheftner, W. A., Fawcett, J., & Fogg, L. (1987). A field test of Motto's risk estimator for suicide. *American Journal of Psychiatry, 144,* 923–926.

Clark, L. A., & Watson, D. (1991). Tripartite model of anxiety and depression: Psychometric evidence and taxonomic implications. *Journal of Abnormal Psychology, 100,* 316–336.

Clarkin, J. F., & Carpenter, D. (1995). Family therapy in historical perspective. In B. Bongar & L. E. Beutler (Eds.), *Comprehensive textbook of psychotherapy: Theory and practice* (pp. 205–227). New York: Oxford University Press.

Clarkin, J. F., Pilkonis, P. A., & Magruder, K. M. (1996). Psychotherapy of depression: Implications for the reform of the health care system. *Archives of General Psychiatry, 53,* 717–723.

Clement, P. W. (1996). Evaluation in private practice. *Clinical Psychology: Science and Practice, 3,* 146–159.

Clinton, J. J., McCormick, K., & Besteman, J. (1994). Enhancing clinical practice: The role of practice guidelines. *American Psychologist, 49(1),* 30–33.

Clum, G. A., & Bowers, T. G. (1990). Behavior therapy better than placebo treatments: Fact or artifact? *Physchological Bulletin, 107,* 110–113.

Cohen, D. B. (1979). Dyphoric affect and REM sleep. *Journal of Abnormal Psychology, 88,* 73–77.

Cohen, J. (1977). *Statistical power analysis for the behavioral sciences* (rev. ed.). New York: Academic Press.

Cole-Detke, H., & Kobak, R. (1996). Attachment processes in eating disorder and depression. *Journal of Consulting and Clinical Psychology, 64,* 282–290.

Colvin, C. R., & Block, J. (1994). Do positive illusions foster mental health? An examination of the Taylor and Brown formulation. *Psychological Bulletin, 116,* 3–20.

Compcare Health Services Insurance Corporation (1985). *Employee benefits brochure.*

Connors, G. J., Carroll, K. M., & DiClemente, C. C. (1997). The therapeutic alliance and its relationship to alcoholism treatment participation and outcome. *Journal of Consulting and Clinical Psychology, 65,* 588–598.

Cooke, D. J. (1980). Conceptual and methodological considerations of the problems inherent in the specification of the simple event-syndrome link. In I. G. Sarason & C. D. Spielberger (Eds.), *Stress and anxiety* (Vol. 7). Washington, DC: Hemisphere.

Cooney, N. L., Kadden, R. M., Litt, M. D., & Getter, H. (1991). Matching alcoholics to coping skills or interactional therapies: Two-year follow-up results. *Journal of Consulting and Clinical Psychology, 59,* 598–601.

Cooper, J. R., Bloom, F. E., & Roth, R. H. (1991). *The biochemical basis of neuropharmacology* (6th ed.). New York: Oxford University Press.

Corbishley, M. A., Beutler, L. E., Quan, S., Bamford, C., Meredith, K., & Scogin, F. (1990). Rapid eye movement density and latency and dexamethosone suppression as predictors of treatment response in depressed older adults. *Current Therapeutic Research, 47,* 856–859.

Corney, R. H. (1987). Marital problems and treatment outcome in depressed women: A clinical trial of social work intervention. *British Journal of Psychiatry, 151,* 652–659.

Corsini, R. J. (1981). *Handbook of innovative psychotherapies.* New York: Wiley.

Coryell, W., Scheftner, W., Keller, M. B., Endicott, J., Maser, J. D., & Klerman, G. L. (1993). The enduring psychological consequences of mania and depression. *American Journal of Psychiatry, 150,* 720–727.

Costa, P. T., & Widiger, T. A. (1994). *Personality disorders: And the five factor model of personality.* Washington, DC: American Psychological Association.

Costello, C. G. (1992). Research on symptoms versus research on syndromes:

Arguments in favour of allocating more research time to the study of symptoms. *British Journal of Psychiatry, 160,* 304–308.

Cowan, P. A., Cohn, D. A., Cowan, C. P., & Pearson, J. L. (1996). Parents' attachment histories and children's externalizing and internalizing behaviors: Exploring family systems models of linkage. *Journal of Consulting and Clinical Psychology, 64,* 53–63.

Coyne, J. C. (1976). Toward an interactional description of depression. *Psychiatry, 39,* 28–40.

Coyne, J. C. (1994). Self-reported distress: Analog or ersatz depression? *Psychological Bulletin, 116,* 29–45.

Coyne, J. C. (in press). Mood disorders. In Kazdin (Ed.), *Encyclopedia of psychology.* Washington, DC: Oxford University/American Psychological Association.

Coyne, J. C., Aldwin, C., & Lazarus, R. S. (1981). Depression and coping in stressful episodes. *Journal of Abnormal Psychology, 90,* 439–447.

Coyne, J. C., & Gotlib, I. H. (1983). The role of cognition in depression: A critical appraisal. *Psychological Bulletin, 94,* 472–505.

Coyne, J. C., Kahn, J., & Gotlib, I. H. (1987). Depression. In T. Jacob (Ed.), *Family interaction and psychopathology: Theories, methods, and findings* (pp. 509–533). New York: Plenum.

Coyne, J. C., Klinkman, M. S., Gallo, S. M,. & Schwenk, T. L. (1997). Short-term outcomes of detected and undetected depressed primary care patients and depressed psychiatric outpatients. *General Hospital Psychiatry, 19,* 333–343.

Coyne, J. C., & Schwenk, T. L. (1995). AHCPR depression guidelines: Countering misconceptions with more misconceptions? *American Psychologist, 50(6),* 452–453.

Coyne, J. C., & Schwenk, T. L. (1997). The relationship of distress to mood disturbance in primary care and psychiatric populations. *Journal of Consulting and Clinical Psychology, 65,* 161–177.

Coyne, J. C., & Whiffen, V. E. (1995). Issues in personality as diathesis for depression: The case of sociotropy-dependency and autonomy-self-criticism. *Psychological Bulletin, 118,* 358–378.

Craighead, W. E., Craighead, L. W., & Hardi, S. S. (1995). Behavior therapies in historical perspective. In B. Bongar & L. E. Beutler (Eds.), *Comprehensive textbook of psychotherapy: Theory and practice* (pp. 64–83). New York: Oxford University Press.

Cramer, P., Blatt, S. J., & Ford, R. Q. (1988). Defense mechanisms in the anaclitic and introjective personality configuration. *Journal of Consulting and Clinical Psychology, 56,* 610–616.

Crits-Christoph, P., Baranackie, K., Durcias, J. S., Beck, A. T., Carroll, K., Perry, K., Luborsky, L., McLellan, A. T., Woody, G. E., Thompson, L., Gallagher, D., & Zitrin, C. (1991). Meta-analysis of therapist effects in psychotherapy outcome studies. *Psychotherapy Research, 1,* 81–91.

Crits-Christoph, P., & Mintz, J. (1991). Implication of therapist effects for the design and analysis of comparative studies of psychotherapies. *Journal of Consulting and Clinical Psychology, 59,* 20–26.

Crook, T., Raskin, A., & Eliot, J. (1981). Parent-child relationships and adult depression. *Child Development, 52,* 950–957.

Cull, J. G., & Gill, W. S. (1982). *Suicide Probability Scale (SPS) manual.* Los Angeles: Western Psychological Services.

Cummings, N. A., Budman, S. H., & Thomas, J. L. (1998). Efficient psychotherapy as a viable response to scarce resources and rationing of treatment. *Professional Psychology: Research and Practice, 29,* 460–469.

Cushman, P. (1992). Psychotherapy to 1992: A historically situated interpretation. In D. K. Freedheim (Ed.), *History of psychotherapy: A century of change* (pp. 21–64). Washington, DC: American Psychological Association.

Dadds, M. R., & McHugh, T. A. (1992). Social support and treatment outcome in behavioral family therapy for child conduct problems. *Journal of Consulting and Clinical Psychology, 60,* 252–259.

Daldrup, R. J., Beutler, L. E., Engle, D., & Greenberg, L. S. (1988). *Focused expressive psychotherapy: Freeing the overcontrolled patient.* New York: Guilford Press.

Daniels, D., & Moos, R. H. (1990). Assessing life stressors and social resources among adolescents: Applications to depressed youth. *Journal of Adolescent Research, 5,* 268–289.

Dauber, R. B. (1984). Subliminal psychodynamic activation in depression: On the role of autonomy issues in depressed college women. *Journal of Abnormal Psychology, 93,* 9–18.

Davis, J. M., Koslow, S. H., Gibbons, R. D., Maas, J. W., Bowden, C. L., Casper, R. Hanin, I., Javaid, J. L., Chang, S. S., & Stokes, P. E. (1988). Cerebrospinal fluid and urinary biogenic amines in depressed patients with healthy controls. *Archives of General Psychiatry, 45,* 705–717.

Davis, J. M., & Sandoval, J. (1991). *Suicidal youth: School-based intervention and prevention.* San Francisco: Jossey-Bass.

Davison, G. C., & Lazarus, A. A. (1995). The dialetics of science and practice. In S. C. Hayes, V. M., Follette, R. M. Dawes, & K. E. Grady (Eds.), *Scientific standards of psychological practice: Issues and recommendations* (pp. 95–120). Reno, NV: Context Press.

Dawes, R. M., Faust, D., & Meehl, P. E. (1989). Clinical versus actuarial judgment. *Science, 243,* 1668–1674.

Delgado, P. L., Charney, D. S., Price, L. H., Aghajanian, G. K., Landis, H., & Henninger, G. R. (1990). Serotonin function and the mechanism of antidepressant action reversal of antidepressant-induced remission by rapid depletion of plasma tryptophan. *Archives of General Psychiatry, 47,* 411–418.

DeMulder, E. K., & Radke-Yarrow, M. (1991). Attachment with affectively ill and well mothers: Concurrent behavioral correlates. *Development and Psychopathology, 3,* 227–242.

Dent, J., & Teasdale, J. D. (1988). Negative cognition and persistence of depression. *Journal of Abnormal Psychology, 97,* 29–34.

Depression Guideline Panel (1993). *Depression in primary care: Vol. 2. Treatment of major depression* (Clinical practice guideline, No. 5, AHCPR Publication No. 93-0551). Rockville, MD: US Department of Health and Human Services, Public Health Service, Agency for Health Care Policy and Research. AHCPR Publication No. 93–0551.

Depue, R. A., & Spoont, M. R. (1986). Conceptualizing a serotonin trait as a behavioral dimension of constraint. In J. J. Mann & M. Stanley (Eds.), *Psychobiology of suicidal behavior* (pp. 47–62). New York: New York Academy of Sciences.

Derogatis, L. R. (1974). The Hopkins Symptom Checklist (HSCL): A measure of primary symptom dimensions. In P. Pichot & R. Olivier-Martin (Eds.), *Psychological measurements in psychopharmacology.* Basel, Switzerland: S. Karger.

Derogatis, L. R. (1977). *The SCL-90 manual I: Scoring, administration and procedures.* Baltimore: Johns Hopkins University School of Medicine, Clinical Psychometrics Unit.

Derogatis, L. R. (1992). *BSI: Administration, scoring, and procedures manual-II* (2nd ed.). Baltimore: Clinical Psychometric Research.

Derogatis, L. R. (1994). *SCL-90: Administration, scoring, and procedures manual* (3rd ed.). Minneapolis, MN: National Computer Systems.

DeRubeis, R. J., Evans, M. D., Hollon, S. D., Garvey, M. J., Grove, W. M., & Tuason, V. B. (1990). How does cognitive therapy work? Cognitive change and symptom change in cognitive therapy and pharmacotherapy for depression. *Journal of Consulting and Clinical Psychology, 58,* 862–869.

Devine, E. L., & Cook, T. D. (1983). A meta-analytic analysis of effects of psychoeducational intervention on length of post-surgical hospital stay. *Nursing Research, 32,* 267–274.

DiLalla, D. L., Carey, G., Gottesman, I. I., & Bouchard, T. J., Jr. (1996). Heritability of MMPI personality indicators of psychopathology in twins reared apart. *Journal of Abnormal Psychology, 105,* 491–499.

DiLalla, D. L., & Gottesman, I. I. (1995). Normal personality characteristics in identical twins discordant for schizophrenia. *Journal of Abnormal Psychology, 104,* 490–499.

Dilk, M. N., & Bond, G. R. (1996). Meta-analytic evaluation of skills training research for individuals with severe mental illness. *Journal of Consulting and Clinical Psychology, 64,* 1337–1346.

DiMascio, A., Weissman, M. M., Prusoff, B. A., Neu, C., Zwilling, M., & Klerman, G. L. (1979). Differential symptom reduction by drugs and psychotherapy in acute depression. *Archives of General Psychiatry, 36,* 1450–1456.

Dobson, K. S. (1985). The relationship between anxiety and depression. *Clinical Psychology Review, 5,* 307–324.

Dobson, K. S. (1989). A meta-analysis of the efficacy of cognitive therapy for depression. *Journal of Consulting and Clinical Psychology, 57,* 414–419.

Dobson, K. S., & Shaw, B. F. (1988). The use of treatment manuals in cognitive therapy: Experience and issues. *Journal of Consulting and Clinical Psychology, 56,* 673–680.

Dobson, K. S., & Shaw, B. F. (1995). Cognitive therapies in practice. In B. Bongar & L. E. Beutler (Eds.), *Comprehensive textbook of psychotherapy: Theory and practice* (pp. 159–172). New York: Oxford University Press.

Dorpat, T. L., & Ripley, H. S. (1960). A study of suicide in the Seattle area. *Comprehensive Psychiatry, 1,* 349–359.

Dowd, E. T., Milne, C.R., & Wise, S. L. (1991). The Therapeutic Reactance Scale: A measure of psychological reactance. *Journal of Counseling and Development, 69,* 541–545.

Dowd, E. T., Wallbrown, F., Sanders, D., & Yesenosky, Y. (1994). Psychological reactance and its relationship to normal personality variables. *Cognitive Therapy and Research, 18,* 601–613.

Downey, G., & Coyne, J. C. (1990). Children of depressed parents: An integrative review. *Psychological Bulletin, 108,* 50–76.

Downing, R. W., & Rickels, K. (1974). Mixed anxiety depression: Fact or myth? *Archives of General Psychiatry, 30,* 312–317.

Dowrick, C., & Buchan, I. (1995). Twelve-month outcome of depression in general practice: Does detection or disclosure make a difference? *British Medical Journal, 311,* 1274–1276.

Drevets, W. C., Videen, T. O., Price, J. L., Preskorn, S. H., Carmichael, S. T., & Raichle, M. E. (1992). A functional anatomical study of unipolar depression. *Journal of Neuroscience, 12,* 3628–3641.

Dube, S. (1993). Cholinergic supersensitivity in affective disorders. In J. J. Mann & D. J. Kupfer (Eds.), *Biology of depressive disorders: Part A. A systems perspective* (pp. 51–78). New York: Plenum.

Eagle, M. N. & Wolitzky, D. L. (1992). Psychoanalytic theories of psychotherapy.

In D. K. Freedheim (Ed.), *History of psychotherapy: A century of change* (pp. 109–158). Washington, DC: American Psychological Association.

Eaton, W. W., Dryman, A., Sorenson, A., & McCutcheon, A. (1989). DSM-III Major Depressive Disorder in the community: A latent class analysis of data from the NIMH Epidemiologic Catchment Area Programme. *British Journal of Psychiatry, 155,* 48–54.

Eaves, G., & Rush, A. J. (1984). Cognitive patterns in symptomatic and remitted unipolar major depression. *Journal of Abnormal Psychology, 93,* 31–40.

Edelman, R. E., & Chambless, D. L. (1993). Compliance during sessions and homework in exposure-based treatment of agoraphobia. *Behavioral Research and Therapy, 31,* 767–773.

Edwin, D., Andersen, A. E., & Rosell, F. (1988). Outcome prediction of MMPI in subtypes of anorexia nervosa. *Psychosomatics, 29,* 273–282.

Elkin, I. (1994). The NIMH treatment of depression colloboative research program: Where we began and where we are. In A. E. Bergin & S. L. Garfield (Eds.), *Handbook of psychotherapy and behavior change* (4th ed., pp. 114–139). New York: Wiley.

Elkin, I., Gibbons, R. D., Shea, M. T., & Shaw, B. F. (1996). Science is not a trial (but it can sometimes be a tribulation). *Journal of Consulting and Clinical Psychology, 64,* 92–103.

Elkin, I., Parloff, M. B., Hadley, S. W., & Autry, J. H. (1985). NIMH Treatment of Depression Collaborative Research Program: Background and research plan. *Archives of General Psychiatry, 42,* 305–316.

Elkin, I., Shea, T., Watkins, J. T., Imber, S. D., Sotsky, S. M., Collins, J. F., Glass, D. R., Pilkonis, P. A., Leber, W. R., Docherty, J. P., Feister, S. J., & Parloff, M. B. (1989). National Institute of Mental Health treatment of depression collaborative research program. *Archives of General Psychiatry, 46,* 971–982.

Ellicott, A., Hammen, C., Gitlin, M., Brown, G., & Jamison, K. (1990). Life events and the course of bipolar disorder. *American Journal of Psychiatry, 147,* 1194–1198.

Elliott, R. (1996, June). *Are client-centered/experiential therapies effective?* Paper presented at the annual meeting of the Society for Psychotherapy Research, Amelia Island, FL.

Elliott, R., & Greenberg, L. S. (1995). Experiential therapy in practice: The process-experiential approach. In B. Bongar & L. E. Beutler (Eds.), *Comprehensive textbook of psychotherapy: Theory and practice* (pp. 123–139). New York: Oxford University Press.

Emmelkamp, P. M., Bouman, T. K., & Blaaw, E. (1994). Individualized versus standardized therapy: A comparative evaluation with obsessive-compulsive patients. *Clinical Psychology and Psychotherapy, 1,* 95–100.

Endicott, J., Cohen, J., & Nee, J. (1979). Brief vs standard hospitalization: For whom? *Archives of General Psychiatry, 36,* 706–712.

Endicott, J., Cohen, J., Nee, J., Fleiss, J., & Sarantakos, S. (1981). Hamilton Depression Rating Scale. *Archives of General Psychiatry, 38,* 98–103.

Endler, N. S., Hunt, J. McV., & Rosentein, A. J. (1962). An S-R inventory of anxiousness. *Psychological Monographs, 76* (Whole No. 536).

Evans, G., & Farberow, N. L. (1988). *The encyclopedia of suicide.* New York: Facts on File.

Eysenck, H. J., & Eysenck, S. B. G. (1969). *Personality structure and measurement.* San Diego: Knapp.

Fahy, T. A., & Russell, G. F. M. (1993). Outcome and prognostic variables in bulimia nervosa. *International Journal of Eating Disorders, 14,* 135–145.

Fairburn, C. G., Jones, R., Peveler, R. C., & Hope, R. A. (1993). Psychotherapy and bulimia nervosa. *Archives of General Psychiatry, 50*, 419–428.

Farmer, R., & Nelson-Gray, R. O. (1990). Personality disorders and depression: Hypothetical relations, empirical findings, and methodological considerations. *Clinical Psychology Review, 10*, 453–476.

Fawcett, J. (1988). Predictors of early suicide: Identification and appropriate intervention. *Journal of Clinical Psychiatry, 49*(suppl.), 7–8.

Fawcett, J., Clark, D. C., & Busch, K. A. (1993). Assessing and treating the patient at risk for suicide. *Psychiatric Annals, 23*(5), 244–255.

Fawcett, J., Epstein, P., Fiester, S. J., Elkin, I., & Autry, J. H. (1987). Clinical Management: Imiprimine/Placebo Administration Manual: NIMH Treatment of Depression Collaborative Research Program. *Psychopharmacology Bulletin, 23*, 309–324.

Fawcett, J., Scheftner, W. A., Clark, D. C., Hedeker, D., Gibbons, R. D., & Coryell, W. (1987). Clinical predictors of suicide in patients with major affective disorders: A controlled prospective study. *American Journal of Psychiatry, 144*, 35–40.

Fawcett, J., Scheftner, W. A., Fogg, L., Clark, D. C., Young, M. A., Hedeker, D., & Gibbons, R. D. (1990). Time related predictors of suicide in major affective disorder. *American Journal of Psychiatry, 147*, 1189–1194.

Feldman, L. B., & Feldman, S. L. (1997). Integrating psychotherapy and pharmacotherapy in the treatment of depression. *In Session: Psychotherapy in Practice, 3*, 23{endash}38.

Felner, R. D., Adan, A. M., & Silverman, M. M. (1992). Risk assessment and prevention of youth suicide in schools and educational contexts. In R. W. Maris, A. L. Berman, J. T. Maltsberger, & R. I. Yufit (Eds.), *Assessment and prediction of suicide* (pp. 420–447). New York: Guilford Press.

Fiedler, F. E. (1950). A comparison of therapeutic relationships in psychoanalytic, nondirective and Adlerian therapy. *Journal of Consulting Psychology, 14*, 436–445.

Field, M. J., and Lohr, K. N. (Eds.). (1990). *Clinical practice guidelines: Directions for a new program.* Washington, DC: National Academy Press.

Fine, S., Forth, A., Gilbert, M., & Haley, G. (1991). Group therapy for adolescent depressive disorder: A comparison of social skills and therapeutic support. *Journal of the American Academy of Child and Adolescent Psychiatry, 30*, 79–84.

Fink, P. (1992). The use of hospitilization by persistent somatizing patients. *Psychological Medicine, 22*, 173–180.

First, M. B., Gibbon, M., Williams, J. B., & Spitzer, R. L. (1995). *Users manual for the Mini-SCID (for DSM-IV-version 2).* North Tonewanda, NY: Multi-Health Systems/American Psychiatric Association.

First, M. B., Spitzer, R. L., Gibbon, M., Williams, J. B. W. (1995). The structured clinical interview for DSM-III-R personality disorders (SCID-II): I. Description. *Journal of Personality Disorders, 9*, 83–91.

Fisher, D., Beutler, L. E., & Williams, O. B. (in press). STS clinician rating form: Patient assessment and treatment planning. *Journal of Clinical Psychology.*

Fisher, S., & Greenberg, R. P. (Eds.). (1997). *From placebo to pancea: Putting psychiatric drugs to the test.* New York: Wiley.

Fishman, D. B., & Franks, C. M. (1992). Evolution and differentiation within behavior therapy: A theoretical and episemological review. In D. K. Freedheim (Ed.), *History of psychotherapy: A century of change* (pp. 159–196). Washington, DC: American Psychological Association.

Flett, G. L., Vredenburg, K., & Krames, L. (1997). The continuity of depression in clinical and nonclinical samples. *Psychological Bulletin, 121*, 395–416.

Flick, S. N. (1988). Managing attrition in clinical research. *Clinical Psychology Review, 8,* 499–515.

Flynn, H. R., & Henisz, J. E. (1975). Criteria for psychiatric hospitalization: Experience with a checklist for chart review. *American Journal of Psychiatry, 132*(8), 847–850.

Folkman, S., Lazarus, R. S., & Dunkel-Schetter, C. (1986). Dynamics of a stressful encounter: Cognitive appraisal, coping, and encounter outcomes. *Journal of Personality and Social Psychology, 50,* 992–1003.

Follette, W. C., & Houts, A. C. (1996). Models of scientific progress and the role of theory in taxonomy development: A case study of the DSM. *Journal of Consulting and Clinical Psychology, 64,* 1120–1132.

Fonagy, P., & Target, M. (1996). Should we allow psychotherapy research to determine clinical practice? *Clinical Psychology: Science and Practice, 3,* 245–250.

Ford, D. E., & Kamerow, D. B. (1990). Epidemiologic study of sleep disturbances and psychiatric disorders: An opportunity for prevention? *Journal of the American Medical Association, 262,* 1479–1484.

Ford, J. D., Fisher, P., & Larson, L. (1997). Object relations as a predictor of treatment outcome with chronic posttraumatic stress disorder. *Journal of Consulting and Clinical Psychology, 65,* 547–559.

Forster, P., & King, I. (1994). Definitive treatment of patients with serious mental disorders in an emergency service, part II. *Hospital and Community Psychiatry, 45*(12), 1177–1178.

Frances, A., Clarkin, J., & Perry, S. (1984). *Differential therapeutics in psychiatry.* New York: Brunner/Mazel.

Frances, A. F., Docherty, J. P., & Kahn, D. A. (1996). The expert consensus guideline series: Treatment of bipolar disorder. *Journal of Clinical Psychiatry, 57*(Supplement 12A), 5–88.

Frances, A., Kahn, D. A., Carpenter, D., Ross, R., & Docherty, J. P. (1996). The expert consensus practice guideline project: A new method of establishing best practice. *Journal of Practical Psychiatry and Behavioral Health, 5,* 295–306.

Frank, E. (1991). Interpersonal psychotherapy as a maintenance treatment for patients with recurrent depression. *Psychotherapy, 28,* 259–266.

Frank, E., Kupfer, D. J., Perel, J. M., Corenes, C., Jarrett, D. B., Mallinger, A. G., Thase, M. E. McEachran, A. B., & Grochocinski, V. J. (1990). Three-year outcomes for maintenance therapies in recurrent depression. *Archives of General Psychiatry, 47,* 1093–1099.

Frank, E., & Spanier, C. (1995). Interpersonal psychotherapy for depression: Overview, clinical efficacy, and future directions. *Clinical Psychology: Science and Practice, 2,* 349–369.

Frank, J. D., & Frank, J. B. (1991). *Persuasion and healing* (3rd ed.). Baltimore: Johns Hopkins University Press.

Frasure-Smith, N. (1991). In-hospital symptoms of psychological stress as predictors of long-term outcome after acute myocardial infarction in men. *American Journal of Cardiology, 67,* 121–127.

Frederick, C. J. (1978). Current trends in suicidal behavior. *American Journal of Psychotherapy, 32,* 172–200.

Fremouw, W. J., de Perczel, M., & Ellis, T. E. (1990). *Suicide risk: Assessment and response guidelines.* New York: Pergamon Press.

Fremouw, W. J., & Zitter, R. E. (1978). A comparison of skills training and cognitive restructuring-relaxation for the treatment of speech anxiety. *Behavior Therapy, 9,* 248–259.

Friedman, A. S. (1975). Interaction of drug therapy with marital therapy in depressive patients. *Archives of General Psychiatry, 32,* 619–637.

Fromme, K., & Rivet, K. (1994). Young adults' coping style as a predictor of their alcohol use and response to daily events. *Journal of Youth and Adolescence, 23*, 85–97.

Fuchs, C. Z., & Rehm, L. P. (1977). A self-control behavior therapy program for depression. *Journal of Consulting and Clinical Psychology, 45*, 206–215.

Furrow, B., Johnson, S., Jost, T., & Schwartz, R. (1985). *Health law: Cases, materials, and problems.* St. Paul, MN: West.

Furrow, B. R. (1993). Quality control in health care: Developments in the law of medical malpractice. *Journal of Law, Medicine and Ethics, 21*(2), 173–192.

Gabbard, G. O., Lazar, S. G., Hornberger, J., & Spiegel, D. (1997). The economic impact of psychotherapy: A review. *American Journal of Psychiatry, 154*, 147–155.

Gaensbauer, J. J., Harmon, R. J., Cytryn, L., & McKnew, D. H. (1984). Social and affective development in infants with a manic-depressive parent. *American Journal of Psychiatry, 141*, 223–229.

Gangadhar, B. N., Kapur, R. L., & Kalyanasundaram, S. (1982). Comparison of electroconvulsive therapy with imipramine in endogenous depression: A double blind study. *British Journal of Psychiatry, 141*, 367–371.

Gara, M. A., Woolfolk, R. L., Cohen, B. D., Goldston, R. B., Allen, L. A., & Novalany, J. (1993). Perception of self and other in major depression. *Journal of Abnormal Psychology, 102*, 93–100.

Garb, H. N. (1989). Clinical judgment, clinical training, and professional experience. *Psychological Bulletin, 105*, 387–396.

Garfield, S. L. (1996). Some problems associated with "avalidated" forms of psychotherapy. *Clinical Psychology: Science and Practice, 3*, 218–229.

Garfield, S. L. (1998). Some comments on empirically supported treatments. *Journal of Consulting and Clinical Psychology, 66*, 121–125.

Garfield, S. L., & Bergin, A. E. (1994). Introduction and historical overview. In A. E. Bergin & S. L. Garfield (Eds.), *Handbook of psychotherapy and behavior change* (4th ed., pp. 3–18). New York: Wiley.

Garfield, S. L., & Kurtz, R. (1977). A study of eclectic views. *Journal of Consulting and Clinical Psychology, 45*, 75–83.

Garland, A. F., & Zigler, E. (1993). Adolescent suicide prevention: Current research and social policy implications. *American Psychologist, 48*(2), 169–182.

Garnick, D. W., Hendricks, A. M., Dulski, J. D., & Thorpe, K. E. (1994). Characteristics of private-sector managed care for mental health and substance abuse treatment. *Hospital and Community Psychiatry, 45*, 1201–1205.

Garvey, M. J., Hollon, S. D., & DeRubeis, R. J. (1994). Do depressed patients with higher pretreatment stress levels respond better to cognitive therapy than to imipramine? *Journal of Affective Disorders, 32*, 45–50.

Gaw, K. F., & Beutler, L. E. (1995). Integrating treatment recommendations. In L. E. Beutler and M. Berren (Eds.), *Integrative assessment of adult personality* (pp. 280–319). New York: Guilford Press.

George, L. K., Blazer, D. G., & Hughes, D. C. (1989). Social support and the outcome of major depression. *British Journal of Psychiatry, 154*, 478–485.

Gerlsma, C., Emmelkamp, P. M. G., & Arrindell, W. A. (1990). Anxiety, depression, and perception of early parenting: A meta-analysis. *Clinical Psychology Review, 10*, 251–277.

Gersh, F. S., & Fowles, D. C. (1979). Neurotic depression: The concept of anxious depression. In R. A. Depue (Ed.), *The psychobiology of the depressive disorders.* New York: Academic Press.

Gitlin, M. J., Swendsen, J., & Heller, T. L. (1995). Relapse and impairment in bipolar disorder. *American Journal of Psychiatry, 152*, 1635–1640.

Gold, P. W., Goodwin, F. K., & Ghrousos, G. P. (1988a). Clinical and biochemical manifestations of depression: First of two parts. *New England Journal of Medicine, 319,* 348–353.

Gold, P. W., Goodwin, F. K., & Ghrousos, G. P. (1988b). Clinical and biochemical manifestations of depression: Second of two parts. *New England Journal of Medicine, 319,* 413–420.

Goldberg, L. R. (1992). The development of markers for the big-five factor structure. *Psychological Assessment, 4,* 26–42.

Goldfried, M. R., & Castonguay, L. G. (1993). Behavior therapy: Redefining strengths and limitations. *Behavior Therapy, 24,* 505–526.

Goldfried, M. R., Radin, L. B., & Rachlin, H. (1997). Theoretical jargon and the dynamics of behaviorism. *Clinical Psychologist, 50(4),* 5–12.

Goldfried, M. R., & Wolfe, B. E. (1998). Toward a more clinically valid approach to therapy research. *Journal of Consulting and Clinical Psychology, 66,* 143–150.

Goldin, L. R., & Gerson, E. S. (1988). The genetic epidemiology of major depressive illness. In A. J. Frances and R. E. Hales (Eds.), *Psychiatric update* (Vol. 7, pp. 149–168). Washington, DC: American Psychiatric Press.

Golin, S., Jarrett, S., Stewart, M., & Drayton, W. (1980). Cognitive theory and the generality of pessimism among depressed persons. *Journal of Abnormal Psychology, 89,* 101–104.

Golin, S., Sweeney, P. D., & Shaeffer, D. E. (1981). The causality of causal attributions in depression: A cross-lagged panel correlational analysis. *Journal of Abnormal Psychology, 90,* 14–22.

Golin, S., Terrell, F., Weitz, J., & Drost, P. L. (1979). The illusion of control among depressed patients. *Journal of Abnormal Psychology, 88,* 454–457.

Gong-Guy, E., & Hammen, C. (1980). Causal perceptions of stressful events in depressed and nondepressed outpatients. *Journal of Abnormal Psychology, 89,* 662–669.

Gonzales, L. R., Lewinsohn, P. M., & Clark, G. N. (1985). Longitudinal follow-up of unipolar depressives: An investigation of predictors of relapse. *Journal of Consulting and Clinical Psychology, 53,* 401–469.

Goodman, S. (1987). Emory University Project on children of disturbed parents. *Schizophrenia Bulletin, 13,* 412–423.

Goodman, S. N., & Royall, R. (1988). Evidence and scientific research. *American Journal of Public Health, 78,* 1568–1574.

Gotlib, I. H. (1993). Depressive disorders. In A. A. Bellack and M. Hersen (Eds.), *Psychopathology in adulthood* (pp. 179–194). Boston: Allyn & Bacon.

Gotlib, I. H., & Cane, D. B. (1987). Construct accessibility and clinical depression: A longitudinal investigation. *Journal of Abnormal Psychology, 96,* 199–204.

Gotlib, I. H., & Hammen, C. L. (1992). *Psychological aspects of depression: Toward a cognitive-interpersonal integration.* Chichester, UK: Wiley.

Gotlib, I. H., & Lee, C. M. (1989). The social functioning of depressed patients: A longitudinal assessment. *Journal of Social and Clinical Psychology, 8,* 223–237.

Gotlib, I. H., Lewinsohn, P. M., & Seeley, J. R. (1995). Symptoms versus a diagnosis of depression: Differences in psychosocial functioning. *Journal of Consulting and Clinical Psychology, 63,* 90–100.

Gotlib, I. H., & Robinson, L. A. (1982). Responses to depressed individuals: Discrepancies between self-report and observer-rated behavior. *Journal of Abnormal Psychology, 91,* 231–240.

Gotlib, I. H., & Whiffen, V. E. (1989). Depression and marital functioning: An examination of specificity and gender differences. *Journal of Abnormal Psychology, 98,* 23–30.

Gotlib, I. H., Whiffen, V. E., Mount, J. H., Milne, K., & Cordy, N. I. (1989). Prevalence rates and demographic characteristics associated with depression in pregnancy and the postpartum. *Journal of Consulting and Clinical Psychology, 57,* 269–274.

Gotlib, I. H., Whiffen, V. E., Wallace, P. M., & Mount, J. H. (1991). Prospective investigation of postpartum depression: Factors involved in onset and recovery. *Journal of Abnormal Psychology, 100,* 122–132.

Graham, J. R. (1993). *MMPI-2: Assessing personality and psychopathology* (2nd ed). New York: Oxford University Press.

Greaney, S. (1995). *Psychologists' behaviors and attitudes when working with the nonhospitalized suicidal patient.* Unpublished doctoral dissertation, Pacific Graduate School of Psychology, Palo Alto, California.

Greenberg, L. S., Elliott, R. K., & Lietaer, G. (1994). Research on experiential psychotherapies. In A. E. Bergin & S. L. Garfield (Eds.), *Handbook of psychotherapy and behavior change* (4th ed., pp. 509–542). New York: Wiley.

Greenberg, L. S., Rice, L. N., & Elliott, R. (1991). *Facilitating emotional change: The moment-by-moment process.* New York: Guilford Press.

Greenberg, L. S., & Watson, J. (1996). Experiential therapy of depression: Differential effects of client-centered conditions and active experiential interventions. *Journal of Consulting and Clinical Psychology, 64,* 459–464.

Greenberg, R. P., Bornstein, R. F., Greenberg, M. D., & Fisher, S. (1992). A meta-analysis of antidepressant outcome under "blinder" conditions. *Journal of Consulting and Clinical Psychology, 60,* 664–669.

Greene, D. B. (1994). Childhood suicide and myths surrounding it. *Social Work, 39*(2), 230–232.

Greene, R. L. (1991). *The MMPI-2/MMPI: An interpretive manual.* Boston: Allyn & Bacon.

Greene, R. L., & Banken, J. A. (1995). Assessing alcohol/drug abuse problems. In J. N. Butcher (Ed.), *Clinical personality assessment: Practical approaches* (pp. 460–474). New York: Oxford University Press.

Groth-Marnat, G. (1997). *Handbook of psychological assessment* (3rd ed.). New York: Wiley.

Groth-Marnat, G., & Edkins, G. (1996). Professional psychologists in general health care settings: A review of the financial efficacy of direct treatment interventions. *Professional Psychology, 27,* 161–174.

Grove, W. M., Andreasen, N. C., Young, M., Endicott, J., Keller, M. B., Hirschfeld, R. M. A., & Reich, T. (1987). Isolation and characterization of a nuclear depressive syndrome. *Psychological Medicine, 17,* 471–484.

Guerin, P. J., Jr., & Chabot, D. R. (1992). Development of family systems theory. In D. K. Freedheim (Ed.), *History of psychotherapy: A century of change* (pp. 225–260). Washington, DC: American Psychological Association.

Gurtman, M. B., Martin, K. M., & Hintzman, N. M. (1990). Interpersonal reactions to displays of depression and anxiety. *Journal of Social and Clinical Psychology, 9,* 256–267.

Gutheil, T. G. (1984). Malpractice liability in suicide. *Legal Aspects of Psychiatric Practice, 1,* 479–482.

Gutheil, T. G. (1988). *Suicide and suit: Liability and self-destruction.* Paper presented at a symposium of the Suicide Education Institute of Boston, in collaboration with the Center for Suicide Research and Prevention, at the annual meeting of the American Psychiatric Association, Montreal, Quebec, Canada.

Gutheil, T.G. (1990). Argument for the defendant-Expert opinion: Death in hindsight. In R. I. Simon (Ed.), *Review of clinical psychiatry and the law* (pp. 335–339). Washington, DC: American Psychiatric Association.

Guze, S. B., & Robins, E. (1970). Suicide and primary affective disorders. *British Journal of Psychiatry, 117,* 437–438.

Haley, J. (1973). *Uncommon therapy.* New York: Norton.

Hall v. Hilbun, 455 So. 2d 856 (Miss. 1985).

Hamilton, M. (1959). A rating scale for depression. *Journal of Neurology and Neurosurgical Psychiatry, 23,* 56–62.

Hamilton, M. (1967). Development of a rating scale for primary depressive illness. *British Journal of Social and Clinical Psychology, 6,* 278–296.

Hammen, C. (1987). The causes and consequences of attribution research on depression. *Journal of Social and Clinical Psychology, 5,* 485–500.

Hammen, C. (1988). Self-cognitions, stressful events, and the prediction of depression in children of depressed mothers. *Journal of Abnormal Child Psychology, 16,* 347–360.

Hammen, C., Adrian, C., & Hiroto, D. (1987). Children of depressed mothers: Maternal strain and symptom predictors of dysfunction. *Journal of Abnormal Psychology, 96,* 37–46.

Hammen, C., Ellicott, A., Gitlin, M., & Jamison, K. R. (1989). Sociotropy/autonomy and vulnerability to specific life events in patients with unipolar depression and bipolar disorders. *Journal of Abnormal Psychology, 98,* 154–160.

Hammen, C., Marks, C., Mayol, A., & deMayo, R. (1985). Depressive self-schemas, life stress, and vulnerability to depression. *Journal of Abnormal Psychology, 94,* 308–319.

Hammen, C. L. (1997). *Depression.* East Sussex, UK: Psychology Press.

Hammen, C. L., & Rudolph, K. D. (1996). Childhood depression. In E. J. Mash & R. A. Barkley (Eds.), *Child psychopathology* (pp. 153–195). New York: Guilford Press.

Harlow, H. F., & Suomi, S. J. (1974). Induced depression in monkeys. *Behavioral Biology, 12,* 173–296.

Harris, M. (1973). Tort: Liability of the psychotherapist. *University of San Francisco Law Review, 8,* 405–436.

Harrison, P. A., Hoffmann, N. G., Hollister, C. D., & Gibbs, L. (1988). Determinants of chemical dependency treatment placement: Clinical economic and logistic factors. *Psychotherapy, 25,* 356–364

Harvey, D. M. (1981). Depression and attributional style: Interpretations of important personal events. *Journal of Abnormal Psychology, 90,* 134–142.

Haslam, N., & Beck, A. T. (1994). Subtyping major depression: A taxometric analysis. *Journal of Abnormal Psychology, 103,* 686–692.

Hathaway, S. R., & McKinley, J. C. (1943). *Manual for the Minnesota Multiphasic Personality Inventory.* New York: Psychological Corporation.

Hayes, S. C., Nelson, R. O., & Jarrett, R. (1987). Treatment utility of assessment: A functional approach to evaluating the quality of assessment. *American Psychologist, 42,* 963–974.

Healy, D., & Williams, J. M. G. (1988). Dysrhythmia, dysphoria, and depression: The interaction of learned helplessness and circadian dysrhythmia in the pathogenesis of depression. *Psychological Bulletin, 103,* 163–178.

Hedlund, S., & Rude, S. S. (1995). Evidence of latent depressive schemas in formerly depressed individuals. *Journal of Abnormal Psychology, 104,* 517–525.

Heimberg, R. G., & Becker, R. E. (1981). Cognitive and behavioral models of assertive behavior: Review, analysis, and integration. *Clinical Psychology Review, 1,* 353–373.

Heller, W., Etienne, M. A., & Miller, G. A. (1995). Patterns of perceptual asymmetry in depression and anxiety: Implications for neuropsychological models of emotion and psychopathology. *Journal of Abnormal Psychology, 104,* 327–333.

Henriksson, M. M., Aro, H. M., Marttuner, M. S., Heikkinen, M. E., Isometsä, E. T., Kuoppasalm, K. I., & Lönnqvist, J. K. (1993). Mental disorders and comorbidity in suicide. *American Journal of Psychiatry, 150,* 935–940.

Henry, C. S., Stephenson, A. L., Hanson, M. F., & Hargett, W. (1993). Adolescent suicide and families: An ecological approach. *Adolescence, 28*(110), 291–308.

Henry, W. P., Schacht, T. E., Strupp, H. H., Butler, S. F., & Binder, J. L. (1993). Effects of training in time-limited dynamic psychotherapy: Mediators of therapists' responses to training. *Journal of Consulting and Clinical Psychology, 61,* 441–447.

Henry, W. P., Strupp, H. H., Butler, S. F., Schacht, T. E., & Binder, J. L. (1993). Effects of training in yime-limited dynamic psychotherapy: Changes in therapist behavior. *Journal of Consulting and Clinical Psychology, 61,* 434–440.

Herink, R. (1980). *The psychotherapy handbook: The A to Z guide to more than 250 different therapies in use today.* New York: New American Library.

Hersen, M., Bellack, A. S., Himmelhoch, J. M., & Thase, M. E. (1984). Effects of social skill training, amitriptyline, and psychotherapy in unipolar depressed women. *Behavior Therapy, 15,* 21–40.

Hewitt, P. L., Flett, G. L., & Ediger, E. (1996). Perfectionism and deprssion: Longitudinal assessment of a specific vulnerability hypothesis. *Journal of Abnormal Psychology, 105,* 276–280.

Hilsenroth, M. J., Holdwick, D. J., Castlebury, F. D., & Blais, M. A. (1998). The effects of DSM-IV Cluster B personality disorder symptoms on the termination and continuation of psychotherapy. *Psychotherapy: Theory/Research/ Practice/Training, 35,* 163–176.

Hirschfeld, R., & Davidson, L. (1988). Risk factors for suicide. In A. J. Fraces and R. E. Hales (Eds.), *American Psychiatric Press review of psychiatry* (vol. 7, pp. 307–333). Washington, DC: American Psychiatric Press.

Hirschfeld, R. M. A., & Russell, J. M. (1997). Assessment and treatment of suicidal patients. *New England Journal of Medicine, 337*(13), 910–915.

Hobofoll, S. E., Ritter, C., Lavin, J., Hulsizer, M. R., & Cameron, R. P. (1995). Depression prevalence and incidence among inner-city pregnant and postpartum women. *Journal of Consulting and Clinical Psychology, 63,* 445–452.

Hoencamp, E., Haffmans, P. M. J., Duivenvoorden, H., Knegtering, H., & Dijken, W. A. (1994). Predictors of (non-)response in depressed outpatients treated with a three-phase sequential medication strategy. *Journal of Affective Disorders, 31,* 235–246.

Hoffart, A., & Martinsen, E. W. (1991). Cognition and copin in agoraphobia and depression: A multivariate approach. *Journal of Clinical Psychology, 47,* 9–17.

Hoffman, H., Loper, R. G., & Kammeier, M. L. (1974). Identifying future alcoholics with MMPI alcoholism scales. *Quarterly Journal of Studies on Alcohol, 35,* 490–498.

Hogarty, G. E., Anderson, C. M., Reiss, D. J., Kornblith, S. J., Greenwald, D. P., Javna, C. D., & Madonia, M. J. (1986). Family psychoeducation, social skills training, and maintenance chemotherapy in the aftercare treatment of schizophrenia. *Archives of General Psychiatry, 43,* 633–642.

Hollon, S. D. (1990). Cognitive therapy and pharmacotherapy for depression. *Psychiatric Annals, 20,* 249–258.

Hollon, S. D. (1996). The efficacy and effectiveness of psychotherapy relative to medications. *American Psychologist, 51,* 1025–1030.

Hollon, S. D., & Beck, A. T. (1986). Research on cognitive therapies. In S. L. Garfield & A. E. Bergin (Eds.). *Handbook of psychotherapy and behavior change* (3rd ed., pp. 443–482), New York: Wiley.

Hollon, S. D., & Beck, A. T. (1994). Cognitive and cognitive-behavioral therapies. In A. E. Bergin & S. L. Garfield (Eds.), *Handbook of psychotherapy and behavior change* (4th ed., pp. 428–466). New York: Wiley.

Hollon, S. D., DeRubeis, R. J., Evans, M. D., Wiemer, M. J., Garvey, M. J., Grove, W. M., & Tuason, V. B. (1992). Cognitive therapy and pharmacotherapy for depression: Singly and in combination. *Archives of General Psychiatry, 49,* 774–781.

Hollon, S. D., Kendall, P. C., & Lumry, A. (1986). Specificity of depressotypic cognitions in clinical depression. *Journal of Abnormal Psychology, 95,* 52–59.

Hollon, S. D., Shelton, R. C., & Davis, D. D. (1993). Cognitive therapy for depression: Conceptual issues and clinical efficacy. *Journal of Consulting and Clinical Psychology, 61,* 1028–1037.

Hollon, S. D., Shelton, R. C., & Loosen, P. T. (1991). Cognitive therapy and pharmacotherapy for depression. *Journal of Consulting and Clinical Psychology, 59,* 88–99.

Holloway, E. L. & Neufeldt, S. A. (1995). Supervision: Its Contributions to treatment efficacy. *Journal of Consulting and Clinical Psychology, 63,* 207–213.

Holsboer, F. (1992). The hypothalamic-pituitary-adrenocortical system. In E. S. Paykel (Ed.), *Handbook of affective disorders* (2nd ed., pp. 267–287). New York: Guilford Press.

Hood v. Phillips, 537 s.w.2d 291 (Tex. Civ. App. 1976).

Hooley, J. M., Orley, J., & Teasdale, J. D. (1986). Levels of expressed emotion and relapse in depressed patients. *British Journal of Psychiatry, 148,* 642–647.

Hooley, J. M., & Teasdale, J. D. (1989). Predictors of relapse in unipolar depressives: Expressed emotion, marital distress, and perceived criticism. *Journal of Abnormal Psychology, 98,* 229–235.

Horn, J. L., Wanberg, K. W., Foster, F. M. (1974). *The alcohol use inventory.* Denver: Center for Alcohol Abuse Research and Evaluation.

Horowitz, L. J., Lambert, M. J., & Strupp, H. H. (Eds.). (1997). *Measuring patient change after treatment for mood, anxiety, and personality disorders: Toward a core battery.* Washington, DC: American Psychological Association Press.

Horowitz, M. J. (1988). *Introduction to psychodynamics: A new synthesis.* New York: Basic Books.

Horowitz, M. J. (1991). Short-term dynamic therapy of stress response syndromes. In P. Crits-Christoph & J. P. Barber (Eds.), *Handbook of short-term dynamic psychotherapy.* New York: Basic Books.

Horvath, A. O., & Goheen, M. D. (1990). Factors mediating the success of defiance- and compliance-based interventions. *Journal of Counseling Psychology, 37,* 363–371.

Houts, A. C., & Graham, K. (1986). Can religion make you crazy? Impact of client and therapist religious values on clinical judgments. *Journal of Consulting and Clinical Psychology, 54,* 267–271.

Hovanitz, C. A. (1986). Life event stress and coping style as contributors to psychopathology. *Journal of Clinical Psychology, 42,* 34–41.

Howard, K. I., Cornille, T. A., Lyons, J. S., Vessey, J. T., Lueger, R. J., & Saunders, S. M. (1996). Patterns of mental health service utilization. *Archives of General Psychiatry, 53,* 696–703.

Howard, K. I., Cox, W. M., & Saunders, S. M. (1990). Attrition in substance abuse comparative treatment research: The illusion of randomization. In

L. Onken & J. Blaine (Eds.), *Psychotherapy and counseling in the treatment of drug abuse*. (DHHS Publication No. [ADM] 90-1722, pp. 66–79). Washington, DC: National Institute of Drug Abuse.

Howard, K. I., Kopta, S. M., Krause, M. S., & Orlinsky, D. E. (1986). The dose-effect relationship in psychotherapy. *American Psychologist, 41*, 159–164.

Howard, K. I., Krause, M. S., & Lyons, J. (1993). When clinical trials fail: A guide for disaggregation. In L. S. Onken & J. D. Blaine (Eds.), *Behavioral treatments for drug abuse and dependence* (NIDA Research Monograph No. 137, pp. 291–302. Washington, DC: National Institute of Drug Abuse.

Howard, K. I., Krause, M. S., & Orlinsky, D. E. (1986). The attrition dilemma: Toward a new strategy for psychotherapy research. *Journal of Consulting and Clinical Psychology, 54*, 106–110.

Howard, K. I., Krause, M. S., Saunders, S. M., & Kopta, S. M. (1997). Trials and tribulations in the meta-analysis of treatment differences: Comment on Wampold et al. (1997). *Psychological Bulletin, 122*, 221–225.

Howard, K. I., Moras, K., Brill, P. L., Zoran, M., & Lutz, W. (1996). Evaluation of psychotherapy: Efficacy, effectiveness, and patient progress. *American Psychologist, 51*, 1059–1064.

Hummer, J. T., & Hokanson, J. E. (1990). The causal relations of attributions for interpersonal events to depression: A prospective longitudinal study. *Journal of Social and Clinical Psychology, 9*, 511–528.

Hunsley, J. (1993). Treatment acceptability of symptom prescription techniques. *Journal of Counseling Psychology, 40*, 139–143.

Hunter, R. D. A., & Austad, C. S. (1997). Mental health care benefits and perceptions of health insurance agents and clinical psychologists. *Professional Psychology: Research and Practice, 28*, 365–367.

Huprich, S. K. (1998). Depressive personality disorder: Theoretical issues, clinical findings, and future research questions. *Clinical Psychology Review, 18*, 477–500.

Hymowitz, C. (1995). *High anxiety: In the name of Freud, why are psychiatrists complaining so much?* Unpublished manuscript. Dec. 21.

Imber, S. D., Pilkonis, P. A., Sotsky, S. M., Elkin, I., Watkins, J. T., Collins, J. F., Shea, M. T., Leber, W. R., & Glass, D. R. (1990). Mode-specific effects among three treatments for depression. *Journal of Consulting and Clinical Psychology, 58*, 352–359.

Isometsä, E. T., Henriksson, M. M., Hillevi, M. E., Kuoppasalmi, K. I., Lönnqvist, J. K. (1994) Suicide in major depression. *American Journal of Psychiatry, 151*, 530–536.

Izard, C. E. (1977). *Emotions in personality and psychopathology*. New York: Plenum.

Jacob, R. G., Turner, S. M., Szekely, B. C., & Eidelman, B. H. (1983). Predicting outcome of relaxation therapy in headaches: The role of "depression." *Behavior Therapy, 14*, 457–465.

Jacobs, D. F. (1987). Cost-effectiveness of specialized psychological programs for reducing hospital stays and outpatient visits. *Journal of Clinical Psychology, 43*, 729–735.

Jacobson, N. S., & Christensen, A. (1996). Studying the effectiveness of psychotherapy: How well can clinical trials do the job? *American Psychologist, 51*, 1031–1039.

Jacobson, N. S., Dobson, D. S., Truax, P. A., Addis, M. E. Koerner, K., Gollan, J. K., Gortner, E., & Prince, S. E. (1996). *Journal of Consulting and Clinical Psychology, 64*, 295–304.

Jacobson, N. S., Follette, W. C., & Revenstorf, D. (1984). Psychotherapy outcome research: Methods for reporting variability and evaluating clinical significance. *Behavior Therapy, 15,* 336–352.

Jacobson, N. S., Follette, W. C., Revenstorf, D., Baucom, D. H., Hahlweg, K., & Margolin, G. (1984). Variability in outcome and clinical significance of behavioral marital therapy: A reanalysis of outcome data. *Journal of Consulting and Clinical Psychology, 52,* 497–504.

Jacobson, N. S., & Hollon, S. D. (1996a). Cognitive-Behavior Therapy versus pharmacotherapy: Now that the jury's returned its verdict, it's time to present the rest of the evidence. *Journal of Consulting and Clinical Psychology, 64,* 74–80.

Jacobson, N. S., & Hollon, S. D. (1996b). Prospects for future comparisons between drugs and psychotherapy: Lessons from the CBT-versus-pharmacotherapy exchange. *Journal of Consulting and Clinical Psychology, 64,* 104–108.

Jacobson, N. S., Schmaling, K. B., Holzworth-Munroe, A., Katt, J. L., Wood, L. F., & Follette, V. M. (1989). Research structured vs clinically flexible versions of social learning-based marital therapy. *Behaviour Research and Therapy, 27,* 173–180.

Jacobson, N. S., & Truax, P. (1991). Clinical significance: A statistical approach to defining meaningful change in psychotherapy research. *Journal of Consulting and Clinical Psychology, 59,* 12–19.

Janowsky, D. S., Risch, S. C., & Gillin, J. C. (1983). Adrenergic-cholinergic balance and the treatment of affective disorders. *Progress in Neuropsychopharmacology and Biological Psychiatry, 7,* 297–307.

Jarrett, D. B., Miewald, J. M., Fedorka, I. B., Coble, P., Kupfer, D. J., & Greenhouse, J. B. (1987). Prolactin secretion during sleep: A comparison between depressed patients and healthy control subjects. *Biological Psychiatry, 22,* 1216–1226.

Jason, L. A., Richman, J. A., Friedberg, F., Wagner, L., Taylor, R., & Jordan, K. M. (1997). Politics, science, and the emergence of a new disease: The case of chronic fatigue syndrome. *American Psychologist, 52,* 973–983.

Jeanneret, O. (1992). A tentative epidemiological approach to suicide prevention in adolescence. 5th Congress of the International Association for Adolescent Health (1991, Montreux, Switzerland). *Journal of Adolescent Health, 13(5),* 409–414.

Jensen, J. P., Bergin, A. E., & Greaves, D. W. (1990). The meaning of eclecticism: New survey and analysis of components. *Professional Psychology: Research and Practice, 21,* 124–130.

Jobes, D. A., Eyman, J. R., & Yufit, R. I. (1990, May). *Suicide risk assessment survey.* Paper presented at the annual meeting of the American Association of Suicidology, New Orleans, LA.

Johnson, J., Weissman, M., & Klerman, G. (1992). Service utilization and social morbidity associated with depressive symptoms in the community. *Journal of the American Medical Association, 267,* 1478–1483.

Johnson, S. M., & Greenberg, L. S. (1985). Emotionally focused marital therapy: An outcome study. *Journal of Marital and Family Therapy, 11,* 313–317.

Jones, E. E., Cummings, J. D., & Horowitz, M. J. (1988). Another look at the nonspecific hypothesis of therapeutic effectiveness. *Journal of Consulting and Clinical Psychology, 56,* 48–55.

Joyce, A. S., & Piper, W. E. (1996). Interpretive work in short-term individual psychotherapy: An analysis using hierarchical linear modeling. *Journal of Consulting and Clinical Psychology, 64,* 505–512.

Just, N., & Alloy, L. B. (1997). The response styles theory of depression: Tests and extension of the theory. *Journal of Abnormal Psychology, 106,* 221–229.

Kadden, R. M., Cooney, N. L., Getter, H., & Litt, M. D. (1989). Matching alcoholics to coping skills or interactional therapies: Posttreatment results. *Journal of Consulting and Clinical Psychology, 57,* 698–704.

Kaelber, C. T., Moul, D. E., & Farmer, M. E. (1995). Epidemiology of depression. In E. E. Beckham & W. R. Leber (Eds.), *Handbook of depression* (2nd ed., pp. 3–35). New York: Guilford Press.

Kahn, A. (1990). Principles of psychotherapy with suicidal patients. In S. J. Blumenthal & D. J. Kupfer (Eds.), *Suicide over the life cycle: Risk factors, assessment, and treatment of suicidal patients* (pp. 441–468). Washington, DC: American Psychiatric Press.

Kahneman, D. (1963). Control of the spurious association and the reliability of the controlled variable. *Psychological Bulletin, 64,* 326–329.

Kanfer, R., & Zeiss, A. M. (1983). Depression, interpersonal standard setting, and judgments of self-efficacy. *Journal of Abnormal Psychology, 92,* 319–329.

Karasu, T. B., Merriam, A. E., Glassman, A. H., Gelenberg, A. J., & Kupfer, D. (1994). Dr. Karasu and colleagues respond. *American Journal of Psychiatry, 151*(4), 625–626.

Karno, M. (1997). *Identifying patient attributes and elements of psychotherapy that impact the effectiveness of alcoholism treatment.* Unpublished doctoral dissertation, University of California at Santa Barbara.

Karon, B. P., & Teixeira, M. A. (1995). "Guidelines for the treatment of depression in primary care" and the APA response. *American Psychologist, 50*(6), 453–455.

Karon, B. P., & Widener, A. J. (1995). Psychodynamic therapies in historical perspective. In B. Bongar & L. E. Beutler (Eds.), *Comprehensive textbook of psychotherapy: Theory and practice* (pp. 24–47). New York: Oxford University Press.

Katon, W., Von Korff, M., Lin, E., Bushe, T., & Ormel, J. (1992). Adequacy and duration of antidepressant treatment in primary care. *Medical Care, 30,* 67–76.

Katz, M. M., Secunda, S. K., Hirshfeld, R. M. A., & Koslow, S. H. (1979). NIMH clinical research branch collaborative program on the psychobiology of depression. *Archives of General Psychiatry, 36,* 765–771.

Katz, R., Shaw, B. F., Vallis, T. M., & Kaiser, A. S. (1995). The assessment of severity and symptom patterns in depression. In E. E. Beckham & W. R. Leber (Eds.), *Handbook of depression* (2nd ed., pp. 61–85). New York: Guilford Press.

Kazdin, A. E. (1992). *Research design in clinical psychology* (2nd ed.). Needham Heights, MA: Allyn & Bacon.

Kazdin, A. E. (1994). Methodology, design, and evaluation in psychotherapy research. In A. E. Bergin & S. L. Garfield (Eds.), *Handbook of psychotherapy and behavior change* (4th ed., pp. 19–71). New York: Wiley.

Kazdin, A. E. (1996). Validated treatments: Multiple perspective and issues: Introduction to the series. *Clinical Psychology: Science and Practice, 3,* 216–217.

Kazdin, A. E. (1998). *Research design in clinical psychology* (3rd ed.). Boston: Allyn & Bacon.

Kazdin, A. E., & Bass, D. (1989). Power to detect differences between alternative treatments in comparative psychotherapy outcome research. *Journal of Consulting and Clinical Psychology, 57,* 138–147.

Keeton, W. P., Dobbs, D. B., Keeton, R. E., & Owen, D. G. (1984). *Prosser and Keeton on the law of torts.* St. Paul, MN: West.

Keijsers, G. P. J., Hoogduin, C. A. L., & Schaap, C. P. D. R. (1994). Predictors of treatment outcome in the behavioural treatment of obsessive-compulsive disorder. *British Journal of Psychiatry, 165,* 781–786.

Keithly, L. J., Samples, S. J., & Strupp, H. H. (1980). Patient motivation as a predictor of process and outcome in psychotherapy. *Psychotherapy and Psychosomatics, 33,* 87–97.

Keitner, G. I., Ryan, C. E., Miller, I. W., Kohn, R., Bishop, D. s., & Epstein, N. B. (1995). Role of the family in recovery and major depression. *American Journal of Psychiatry, 152,* 1002–1008.

Keller, M. (1994). Depression: A long-term illness. *British Journal of Psychiatry, 165,* 9–15.

Kendall, P. C., & Flannery-Schroeder, E. C. (1995). Rigor, but not rigor mortis, in depression research. *Journal of Personality and Social Psychology, 68,* 892–894.

Kendall, P. C., & Grove, W. (1988). Normative comparisons in therapy outcome research. *Behavioral Assessment, 10,* 147–158.

Kendall, P. C., Hollon, S. D., Beck, A. T., Hammen, C. L., & Ingram, R. E. (1987). Issues and recommendations regarding the use of the Beck Depression Inventory. *Cognitive Therapy and Research, 11,* 289–299.

Kendler, K. S., Neale, M. C., Kessler, R. C., Heath, A. C., & Eaves, L. J. (1992). Major depression and generalized anxiety disorder: Same genes, (partly) different environments? *Archives of General Psychiatry, 49,* 716–722.

Kerr, H. D. (1986). Prehospital emergency services and health maintenance organizations. *Annals of Emergency Medicine, 15,* 727–729.

Kessler, R. C., & Magee, W. J. (1993). Childhood adversities and adult depression: Basic patterns of association in a US national survey. *Psychological Medicine, 23,* 679–690.

Kessler, R. C., McGonagle, K. A., Zhao, S., Nelson, C. B., Hughes, M., Eshleman, S., Wittchen, H., & Kendler, K. S. (1994). Lifetime and 12-month prevalence of DSM-III-R psychiatric disorders in the US: Results from the National Comorbidity Survey. *Archives of General Psychiatry, 51,* 8–19.

Kiesler, C. A. (1992). US mental health policy: Doomed to fail. *American Psychologist, 47,* 1077–1082.

King, C. A., Hill, E. M., Naylor, M., Evans, T., et al. (1993). Alcohol consumption in relation to other predictors of suicidality among adolescent inpatient girls. *Journal of the American Academy of Child and Adolescent Psychiatry, 32(1),* 82–88.

King, H. E. (1987, Aug.). *Pragmatic factors in dealing with families of suicidal clients: Issues for clinicians.* Paper presentedd at a symposium on suicide in the family conducted at the convention of the American Psychological Association, New York City.

Kirsch, I., & Sapirstein, G. (1998). Listening to Prozac by hearing placebo: A meta-analysis of antidepressant medications. *Treatment and Prevention, 1(1).* Article 0001c, at http://journals.apa.org/prevention/volume 1/pre 0010001c.html.

Klein, D. F. (1990). NIMH collaborative research on treatment of depression. *Archives of General Psychiatry, 47,* 682–684.

Klein, D. F. (1996). Preventing hung juries about therapy studies. *Journal of Consulting and Clinical Psychology, 64,* 81–87.

Klein, D. F., & Ross, D. C. (1993). Reanalysis of the National Institute of Mental Health Treatment of Depression Collaborative Research Program general effectiveness report. *Neuropsychopharmacology, 8,* 241–251.

Klein, D. N., Harding, K., Taylor, E. B., & Dickstein, S. (1988). Dependency and self-criticism in depression: Evaluation in a clinical population. *Journal of Abnormal Psychology, 97,* 399–404.

Klein, D. N., Taylor, E. B., Kickstein, S., & Harding, K. (1988). Primary, early-onset dysthymia: Comparison with primary nonbipolar nonchronic major depression od demographic, clinical, familial, personality, and socioenvironmental characteristics and short-term outcome. *Journal of Abnormal Psychology, 97,* 387–398.

Klerman, G. L. (1983). The efficacy of psychotherapy as the basis for public policy. *American Psychologist, 38,* 929–934.

Klerman, G. L. (1986). Drugs and psychotherapy. In S. L. Garfield & A. E. Bergin (Eds.), *Handbook of psychotherapy and behavior change* (3rd ed., pp. 777–818). New York: Wiley.

Klerman, G. L. (1990). The psychiatric patient's right to effective treatment: Implications of *Osheroff v. Chestnut Lodge. American Journal of Psychiatry, 147*(4), 409–418.

Klerman, G. L., DiMascio, A., Weissman, M., Prusoff, B., & Paykel, E. S. (1974). Treatment of depression by drugs and psychotherapy. *American Journal of Psychiatry, 131,* 186–191.

Klerman, G. L., Lavori, P. W., Rice, J., et al. (1985). Birth cohort trends in rates of major depressive disorder among relatives of patients with affective disorder. *Archives of General Psychiatry, 42,* 689–693.

Klerman, G. L., & Weissman, M. M. (1993). *New applications of interpersonal psychotherapy.* Washington, DC: American Psychiatric Association.

Klerman, G. L., Weissman, M. M., Rounsaville, B. J., & Chevron, E. S. (1984). *Interpersonal psychotherapy of depression.* New York: Basic Books.

Knight-Law, A., Sugarman, A. A., & Pettinati, H. M. (1988). An application of an MMPI classification system for predicting outcome in a small clinical sample of alcoholics. *American Journal of Drug and Alcohol Abuse, 14,* 325–334.

Knopp, R. K. (1986). Impact of HMOs on emergency medical services. *Annals of Emergency Medicine, 15,* 730.

Kobak, R. R., Sudler, N., & Gamble, W. (1991). Attachment and depressive symptoms during adolescence: A developmental pathways analysis. *Development and Psychopathology, 3,* 461–474.

Kocsis, J. H. (1993). The biology of chronic depression. In J. J. Mann, & D. J. Kupfer (Eds.), *Biology of depressive disorders: Part B: Subtypes of depression and comorbid disorders* (pp. 75–88). New York: Plenum.

Kocsis, J. H., Frances, A. J., Voss, C., et al. (1988). Imipramine treatment for chronic depression. *Archives of General Psychiatry, 45,* 253–257.

Kocsis, J. H., Mason, B. J., Frances, A. J., et al., (1989). Prediction of response of chronic depression to imipramine. *Journal of Affective Disorders, 17,* 255–260.

Kolden, G. G. (1996). Change in early sessions of dynamic therapy: Universal processes and the generic model of psychotherapy. *Journal of Consulting and Clinical Psychology, 64,* 489–496.

Kopta, S. M., Howard, K. I., Lowry, J. L., & Beutler, L. E. (1994). Patterns of symptomatic recovery in time-unlimited psychotherapy. *Journal of Consulting and Clinical Psychology, 62,* 1009–1016.

Korchin, S. J., & Schuldberg, D. (1981). David the future of clinical assessment. *American Psychologist, 36,* 1174–1158.

Kovacs, M., Rush, A. J., Beck, A. T., & Hollon, S. D. (1981). Depressed outpatients treated with cognitive therapy or pharmacotherapy: A one-year follow-up. *Archives of General Psychiatry, 38,* 33–39.

Kowalik, D. L., & Gotlib, I. H. (1987). Depression and marital interaction: Concordance between intent and perception of communication. *Journal of Abnormal Psychology, 96,* 127–134.

Kravitz, H. M., & Newman, A. J. (1995). Medical diagnostic procedures for depression: An update from a decade of promise. In E. E. Beckham & Leber, W. R. (Eds.), *Handbook of depression* (2nd ed., pp. 302–328). New York: Guilford Press.

Kubin, M. (1994). *The study of suicide in the marriage and family therapist training curriculum.* Unpublished doctoral dissertation, Pacific Graduate School of Psychology, Palo Alto, California.

Kupfer, D. J. (1992). Comment. *Archives of General Psychiatry, 49,* 669–670.

Kupfer, D. J., Foster, G., Coble, P. A., McPartland, R. J., & Ulrich, R. F. (1978). The application of EEG sleep for the differential diagnosis of affective disorders. *American Journal of Psychiatry, 135,* 69–74.

Kupfer, D. J., Frank, E., Perel, J. M., Corenes, C., Jarrett, D. B., Mallinger, A. G., Thase, M. E. McEachran, A. B., & Grochocinski, V. J. (1992). Five-year outcome for maintenance therapies in recurrent depression. *Archives of General Psychiatry, 49,* 769–773.

Kupfer, D. J., Reynolds, C. F., Grochocinski, J. J., Ulrich, R. F., & McEachran, A. (1986). Aspects of short REM latency in affective states: A revisit. *Psychiatric Research, 17,* 49–59.

Kupfer, D. J., & Spiker, D. G. (1981). Refractory depression: Prediction of nonresponse by clinical indicators. *Journal of Clinical Psychiatry, 42,* 307–312.

Kupfer, D. J., Targ, E., & Stack, J. (1982). Electroencephalographic sleep in unipolar depressive subtypes: Support for a biological and familial classification. *Journal of Nervous and Mental Disease, 170,* 494–498.

Kurtzman, H. S., & Blehar, M. C. (1996, Fall). New research on cognition and depression. *Psychotherapy and Rehabilitation Research Bulletin,* (3), 11–13.

Laberge, B., Gauthier, J. G., Côté, Plamondon, J., & Cormier, H. J. (1993). Cognitive-behavioral therapy of panic disorder with secondary major depression: A preliminary investigation. *Journal of Consulting and Clinical Psychology, 61,* 270–275.

LaCroix, J. M., Clarke, M. A., Bock, J. C., & Doxey, N. (1986). Physiological changes after biofeedback and relaxation training for multiple-pain tension-headache patients. *Perceptual and Motor Skills, 63,* 139–153.

Lafferty, P., Beutler, L.E., & Crago, M. (1989). Differences between more and less effective psychotherapists: A study of select therapist variables. *Journal of Consulting and Clinical Psychology, 57,* 76–80.

Lambert, M. J. (1991) An introduction to psychotherapy research. In L. E. Beutler & M. Crago (Eds.), *Psychotherapy research: An international review of programatic studies* (pp. 1–11). Washington, DC: American Psychological Association.

Lambert, M. J. (1994). Use of psychological tests for outcome assessment. In. M. E. Maruish (Ed.), *The use of psychological testing for treatment planning and outcome assessment* (pp. 75–97). Hillsdale, NJ: Lawrence Erlbaum.

Lambert, M. J., & Bergin, A. E. (1983). Therapist characteristics and their contribution to psychotherapy outcome. In C. E. Walker (Ed.), *The handbook of clinical psychology* (Vol. 1, pp. 205–241). Homewood, IL: Dow Jones-Irwin.

Lambert, M. J., & Bergin, A. E. (1994). The effectiveness of psychotherapy. In A. E. Bergin & S. L. Garfield (Eds.), *Handbook of psychotherapy and behavior change* (4th ed., pp. 143–189). New York: Wiley.

Lambert, M. J., Christensen, E. R., & DeJulio, S. S. (Eds.) (1983). *The assessment of psychotherapy outcome.* New York: Wiley.

Lambert, M. J., & Ogles, B. M. (1988). Treatment manuals: Problems and promise. *Journal of Integrative and Eclectic Psychotherapy, 7,* 187–204.

Lambert, M. J., Okiishi, J. C., Finch, A. E., & Johnson, L. D. (1998). Outcome assessment: From conceptualization to implementation. *Professional Psychology: Research and Practice, 29,* 63–70.

Langer, E. J., & Abelson, R. P. (1974). A patient by any other name . . . : Clinician group difference in labeling bias. *Journal of Consulting and Clinical Psychology, 42,* 4–9.

Lantz, A. E., Carlberg, C. G., & Wilson, N. Z. (1983). Mental health treatment outcome by sex, diagnosis, and treatment. *Professional Psychology: Research and Practice, 14,* 293–309.

Last, C. G., Thase, M. E., & Hersen, M. (1985). Patterns of attrition for psychosocial and pharmacologic treatment of depression. *Journal of Clinical Psychiatry, 46,* 361–366.

Lazarus, A. (1993). Managed competition and access to emergency psychiatric care. *Hospital and Community Psychiatry, 44,* 1134–1136.

Lazarus, A. (1995). The role of primary-care physicians in managed mental health care. *Psychiatric Services, 46,* 345–330.

Lazarus, A. A. (1976). *Multimodal behavior therapy.* New York: Springer.

Leach v. Braillar, 275 F. Supp. 897, 537 s.w.2d (D. Ariz. 1967).

Lemaire, T. E., & Clopton, J. R. (1981). Expressions of hostility in mild deprssion. *Psychological Reports, 48,* 259–262.

Leung, A. W., & Heimberg, R. G. (1996). Homework compliance, perceptions of control, and outcome of cognitive-behavioral treatment of social phobias. *Behavioral Research and Therapy, 34,* 423–432.

Levin, C. (1994). *Graduate training in clinical social work and suicide.* Unpublished doctoral dissertation, Pacific Graduate School of Psychology, Palo Alto, California.

Levine, C. (1995). A view from the front lines of bioethics. *Bulletin of the New York Academy of Medicine, 72*(1)(Summer Supplement), 187–201.

Lewinsohn, P. M., Gotlib, I. H., & Seeley, J. R. (1995). Adolescent psychopathology: IV. Specificity of psychosocial risk factors for depression and substance abuse in older adolescents. *Journal of the American Academy of Child and Adolescent Psychiatry, 34*(9), 1221–1229.

Lewinsohn, P. M., Hoberman, H. M., & Rosenbaum, M. (1988). A prospective study of risk factors for unipolar depression. *Journal of Abnormal Psychology, 97,* 251–264.

Lewinsohn, P. M., Mischel, W., Chaplin, & Barton, R. (1980). Social competence and depression: The role of illusory self-perceptions. *Journal of Abnormal Psychology, 89,* 203–212.

Lewinsohn, P. M., Munoz, R. F., Youngren, M. A., & Zeiss, A. M. (1986). *Control your depression.* New York: Prentice-Hall.

Lewinsohn, P. M., Steinmetz, J. L., Larson, D. W., & Franklin, J. K. (1981). Depression-related cognitions: Antecedent or consequence? *Journal of Abnormal Psychology, 90,* 213–219.

Lewinsohn, P. M., Sullivan, J. M., & Grosscup, S. J. (1980). Changing reinforcing events: An approach to the treatment of depression. *Psychotherapy: Theory, Research and Practice, 17,* 322–334.

Lilienfeld, S. O., & Marino, L. (1995). Mental disorder as a Roschian concept: A critique of Wakefield's "A Harmful Dysfunction analysis." *Journal of Abnormal Psychology, 104,* 411–420.

Linde, K., Ramirez, G., Mulrow, C. D., Pauls, A., Weidenhammer, W., & Melchart, D. (1996). St John's wort for depression: An overview and meta-analysis of randomised clinical trials. *British Medical Journal, 313,* 253–258.

Linehan, M. M. (1993). *Cognitive-behavioral treatment for borderline personality disorder.* New York: Guilford Press.

Linehan, M. M., Goodstein, J. L., Nielsen, S. L., & Chiles, J. A. (1983). Reasons for staying alive when you are thinking of killing yourself: The Reasons for Living Inventory. *Journal of Consulting and Clinical Psychology, 51,* 276–286.

Lipsey, M. W., & Wilson, D. B. (1993). The efficacy of psychological, educational, and behavioral treatment: Confirmation from meta-educational and behavioral treatment: Confirmation from meta-analyses. *American Psychologist, 48,* 1181–1209.

Litman, R. E. (1988, May). *Treating high-risk chronically suicidal patients.* Paper presented at a symposium of the Suicide Education Institute of Boston, in collaboration with the Center for Suicide Research and Prevention, at the annual meeting of the American Psychiatric Association, Montreal, Quebec, Canada.

Litt, M. D., Babor, T. F., DelBoca, F. K., Kadden, R. M., & Cooney, N. L. (1992). Types of alcoholics: II. Application of an empirically derived typology to treatment matching. *Archives of General Psychiatry, 49,* 609–614.

Lloyd, C. (1980). Life events and depressive disorder reviewed: 1. Events as predisposing factors. *Archives of General Psychiatry, 37,* 529–535.

Longabaugh, R., Beattie, M., Noel, N., Stout, R., & Malloy, P. (1993). The effect of social investment on treatment outcome. *Journal of Studies on Alcohol, 54,* 465–478.

Longabaugh, R., Rubin, A., Malloy, P., Beattie, M., Clifford, P. R., & Noel, N. (1994). Drinking outcomes of alcohol abusers diagnosed as antisocial personality disorder. *Alcoholism: Clinical and Experimental Research, 18,* 778–785.

Lowman, R. L. (1991). Mental health claims experience: Analysis and benefit redesign. *Professional Psychology: Research and Practice, 22,* 36–44.

Luborsky, L. (1984). *Principles of psychoanalytic psychotherapy: A manual for supportive-expressive treatment.* New York: Basic Books.

Luborsky, L. (1990). Who is helped by psychotherapy? *Harvard Mental Health Letter, 7*(2), 4–5.

Luborsky, L. (1996). *The symptom-context method.* Washington, DC: American Psychological Association.

Luborsky, L, & DeRubeis, R. J. (1984). The use of psychotherapy treatment manuals: A small revolution in psychotherapy research style. *Clinical Psychology Review, 4,* 5–14.

Luborsky, L., Diguer, L., Schweizer, E., & Johnson, S. (1996, June). *The researcher's therapeutic allegiance as a "wildcard" in studies comparing the outcomes of treatments.* Paper presented at the annual meeting of the Society for Psychotherapy Research, Amelia Island, FL.

Luborsky, L., Mintz, J., Auerbach, A., Crits-Christoph, P., Bachrach, H., Todd, T., Johnson, M., Cohen, M., & O'Brien, C. P. (1980). Predicting the outcome of psychotherapy: Findings of the Penn Psychotherapy Project. *Archives of General Psychiatry, 37,* 471–481.

Lueger, R. J. (1996). Using feedback on patient progress to predict the outcome of psychotherapy. *Journal of Clinical Psychology, 55,* 1–27.

Lundgren v. Eusterman, 356 NW2nd 762 (Minn Ct. App. 1984), rev'd *Lundgren v. Eusterman,* 370 NW2nd 877 (Minn 1985).

Lydiard, R. B., Brawman-Mintzer, O., & Ballenger, J. C. (1996). Recent developments in the psychopharmacology of anxiety disorders. *Journal of Consulting and Clinical Psychology, 64,* 660–668.

Lykouras, E., Malliaaras, D., Christodoulou, G. N., Malliaras, D., & Papkostas, Y. (1986). Delusional depression: Phenomenology and response to treatment. A prospective study. *Acta Psychiatrica Scandanavica, 73,* 324–329.

Lyons, J. P., Welte, J. W., & Brown, J. (1982). Variation in alcoholism treatment orientation: Differential impact upon specific subpopulations. *Alcoholism: Clinical and Experimental Research, 6,* 333–343.

Lyons-Ruth, K. (1996). Attachment relationships among children with aggressive behavior problems: The role of disorganized early attachment patterns. *Journal of Consulting and Clinical Psychology, 64,* 64–73.

Maas, J. W., Kocsis, J. H., Bowden, C. L., Davis, J. M., Redmond, D. E., Hanen, I., & Robins, E. (1982). Pretreatment on neurotransmitter metabolites and response to imipramine or amitriptyline treatment. *Psychological Medicine, 12,* 37–43.

Maas, J. W., Koslow, S. H., Davis, J., Katz, M., Frazer, A., Bowden, C. L., Berman, N., Gibbons, R., Stokes, P., & Landis, D. H. (1987). Catecholamine metabolism and disposition in health and depressed subjects. *Archives of General Psychiatry, 44,* 337–344.

MacAndrew, C. (1965). The differentiation of male alcoholic outpatients from nonalcoholic psychiatric outpatients by means of the MMPI. *Quarterly Journal of Studies on Alcohol, 26,* 238–246.

MacLeod, A. K., & Byrne, A. (1996). Anxiety, depression, and the anticipation of future positive and negative experiences. *Journal of Abnormal Psychology, 105,* 286–289.

Mahoney, M. J. (1995). *Cognitive and constructive psychotherapies: Theory, research, and practice.* New York: Springer.

Mahrer, J. (1993) The use of "no-suicide contracts" and agreements with suicidal patients (doctoral dissertation, Pacific Graduate School of Psychology). *Dissertation Abstracts International, 54*(6B), 3345.

Main, M. (1990). Cross-cultural studies of attachment organization: Recent studies, changing methodologies, and the concept of conditional strategies. *Human Development, 33,* 48–61.

Main, M., & Weston, D. R. (1982). Avoidance of the attachment figure in infancy: Descriptions and interpretations. In C. Parkes & J. Stevenson-Hinde (Eds.), *The place of attachment in human behavior* (pp. 31–59). New York: Basic Books.

Maisto, S. A., O'Farrell, T. J., & Mckay, J. R. (1988). Alcoholic and spouse concordance on attributions about relapse to drinking. *Journal of Substance Abuse Treatment, 5,* 179–181.

Maki, R. H., & Syman, E. M. (1997). Teaching of controversial and empirically validated treatments in APA-accredited clinical and counseling psychology programs. *Psychotherapy, 34,* 44–57.

Malatesta, V. J. (1995, May). Technological behavior therapy for obsessive-compulsive disorder: The need for adequate case formulation. *Behavior Therapist,* (2) 88–89.

Malcolm, J. G. (1986). Treatment choices and informed consent in psychiatry: Implications of the Osheroff case for the profession. *Journal of Psychiatry and Law, 14,* 9–107.

Maling, M. S., Gurtman, M. B., & Howard, K. I. (1995). The response of interpersonal problems to varying doses of psychotherapy. *Psychotherapy Research, 5,* 63–75.

Malone, K., & Mann, J. J. (1993). Serotonin and major depression. In J. J. Mann & D. J. Kupfer (Eds.), *Biology of depressive disorders: Part A: A systems perspective* (pp. 29–50). New York: Plenum.

Mann, J. J. (1991). Integration of neurobiology and psychopathology in a unified model of suicidal behavior. *Exerpta Medica, 968,* 114–117.

Mann, J. J., & Kupfer, D. J. (1993a). *Biology of depressive disorders: Part A. A systems perspective.* New York: Plenum.

Mann, J. J., & Kupfer, D. J. (1993b). *Biology of depressive disorders: Part B. Subtypes of depression and comorbid disorders.* New York: Plenum

Manning, W., & Wells, K. B. (1992). The effects of psychological distress and psychological well-being on use of medical services. *Medical Care, 30,* 541–553.

Maris, R. W. (1981). *Pathways to suicide: A survey of self-desctructive behaviors.* Baltimore: Johns Hopkins University Press.

Maris, R. W. (1989). The social relations of suicide. In D. G. Jacobs & H. N. Brown (Eds), *Suicide: Understanding and responding* (Harvard Medical School perspectives on suicide, pp. 87–125). Madison, CT: International Universities Press.

Maris, R. W. (Ed) (1988). *Understanding and preventing suicide: Plenary papers of the first combined meeting of the AAS and IASP.* New York: Guilford.

Martin, R. L., Cloninger, C. R., Guze, S. B., & Clayton, P. J. (1985). Mortality in a follow-up of 500 psychiatric outpatients: II. Cause specific mortality. *Archives of General Psychiatry, 42,* 58–66.

Maruish, M. (Ed.). (1994). *Use of psychological testing for treatment planning and outcome assessment.* Chicago: Lawrence Erlbaum.

Maruish, M. (Ed.). (in press). *Use of psychological testing for treatment planning and outcome assessment* (2nd ed.). Chicago: Lawrence Erlbaum.

Maser, J. D., Weise, R., & Gwirtsman, H. (1995). Depression and its boundaries with selected Axis I disorders. In E. E. Beckham & W. R. Leber (Eds.), *Handbook of depression* (2nd ed., pp. 86–106). New York: Guilford Press.

Matt, G. E., & Navarro, A. M. (1997). What meta-analyses have and have not taught us about psychotherapy effects: A review and future directions. *Clinical Psychology Review, 17,* 1–32.

Mazure, C. M., Nelson, J. C., & Jatlow, P. I. (1990). Predictors of hospital outcome without antidepressants in major depression. *Psychiatry Research, 33,* 51–58.

McCullough, L., Farber, B. A., & Porter, F. (1991). The relationship of patient-therapist interaction to outcome in brief psychotherapy. *Psychotherapy, 28,* 525–533.

McIntosh, J. L. (1988). Official US elderly suicide data bases: Levels, availability, omissions. *Omega: Journal of Death and Dying, 19,* 337–350.

McLean, P. D., & Hakstian, A. R. (1979). Clinical depression: Comparative efficacy of outpatient treatments. *Journal of Consulting and Clinical Psychology, 47,* 818–836.

McLean, P. D., & Hakstian, A. R. (1990). Relative endurance of unipolar depression treatment effects: Longitudinal follow-up. *Journal of Consulting and Clinical Psychology, 58,* 482–488.

McLean, P. D., & Taylor, S. (1992). Severity of unipolar depression and choice of treatment. *Behavior Research and Therapy, 30,* 443–451.

McLellan, A. T., Woody, G. E., Luborsky, L., O'Brien, C. P., & Druley, K. A. (1983). Increased effectiveness of substance abuse treatment: A prospective study of patient-treatment "matching." *Journal of Nervous and Mental Disease, 171,* 597–605.

McNeal, E. T., & Cimbolic, P. (1996). Antidepressants and biochemical theories of depression. *Psychological Bulletin, 99,* 361–374.

McNiel, D. E., Arkowitz, H. S., & Pritchard, B. E. (1987). The response of others to face-to-face interaction with depressed patients. *Journal of Abnormal Psychology, 96,* 341–344.

Meehl, P. E. (1960). The cognitive activity of the clinician. *American Psychologist, 15,* 19–27.

Megargee, E. I., Cook, P. E., & Mendelsohn, G. A. (1967). Development and validation of an MMPI scale of assaultiveness of overcontrolled individuals. *Journal of Abnormal Psychology, 72,* 519–528.

Meichenbaum, D. (1995). Changing conceptions of cognitive behavior modification: Retrospect and prospect. In M. J. Mahoney (Ed.), *Cognitive and con-*

structive psychotherapies: Theory, research, and practice (pp. 20–26). New York: Springer.

Meltzoff, J., & Kornreich, M. (1970). *Research in psychotherapy.* New York: Atherton Press.

Mersch, P. P. A., Emmelkamp, P. M. G., & Lips, C. (1991). Social phobia: Individual response patterns and cognitive interventions. A follow-up study. *Behavioral Research and Therapy, 29,* 357–362.

Messer, S. B., & Warren, C. S. (1995). *Models of brief psychodynamic therapy: A comparative approach.* New York: Guilford Press..

Miles, C. P. (1977). Conditions predisposing to suicide: A review. *Journal of Nervous and Mental Disease, 164,* 213–242.

Miller, H. L., Delgado, P. L., Salomon, R. M., Licinio, J., Barr, L. C., & Charney, D. S. (1992). Acute tryptophan depletion: A method of studying antidepressant action. *Journal of Clinical Psychiatry, 53,* 28–35.

Miller, W. R., Benefield, G., & Tonigan, J. S. (1993). Enhancing motivation for change in problem drinking: A controlled comparison of two therapist styles. *Journal of Consulting and Clinical Psychology, 61,* 455–461.

Miller, W. R., & Joyce, M. A. (1979). Prediction of abstinence, controlled drinking, and heavy drinking outcomes following behavioral self-control training. *Journal of Consulting and Clinical Psychology, 47,* 773–775.

Miller, W. R., & Norman, W. H. (1979). Learned helplessness in humans: A review and attribution-theory model. *Psychological Bulletin, 86,* 93–118.

Miller, W. R., & Seligman, M. E. P. (1975). Depression and learned helplessness in man. *Journal of Abnormal Psychology, 84,* 228–238.

Millon, T., & Davis, R. (1995). Putting Humpty Dumpty together again: Using the MCMI in psychological assessment. In L. E. Beutler & M. R. Berren (Eds.), *Integrative assessment of adult personality* (pp. 240–279). New York: Guilford Press.

Minuchin, S. (1974). *Families and family therapy.* Cambridge, MA: Harvard University Press.

Minuchin, S., & Fishman, H.C. (1981). *Family therapy techniques.* Cambridge, MA: Harvard University Press.

Miranda, J. (Ed.). (1996). Special section on recruiting and retaining minorities in psychotherapy research. *Journal of Consulting and Clinical Psychology, 64,* 848–908.

Mohr, D. C., Beutler, L. E., Engle, D. Shoham-Salomon, V., Bergan, J., Kaszniak, A. W., & Yost, E. (1990). Identification of patients at risk for non-response and negative outcome in psychotherapy. *Journal of Consulting and Clinical Psychology, 58,* 622–628.

Monroe, S. M., Thase, M. E., & Simons, A. D. (1992). Social factors and the psychobiology of depression: Relations between life stress and rapid eye movement sleep latency. *Journal of Abnormal Psychology, 101,* 528–537.

Montano, C. B. (1994). Recognition and treatment of depression in a primary care setting. *Journal of Clinical Psychiatry, 55*(12), 18–34.

Moos, R., & Moos, B. (1981). *The process of recovery from alcoholism: III. Comparing family functioning in alcohol and matched control families.* Palo Alto, CA: Social Ecology Laboratory, Stanford University and Veterans Administration Medical Center.

Moos, R. H. (1990). Depressed outpatients' life contexts, amount of treatment and treatment outcome. *Journal of Nervous and Mental Disease, 178,* 105–112.

Morey, L. C. (1991). Classification of mental disorder as a collection of hypothetical constructs. Special issue: Diagnoses, dimensions, and DSM-IV: The Science of Classification. *Journal of Abnormal Psychology, 100,* 289–293.

Morgan, A. C. (1989). Special issues of assessment and treatment of suicide risk in the elderly. In D. Jacobs & H. N. Brown (Eds.), *Suicide: Understanding and responding* (Harvard Medical School perspectives, pp. 505–524). Madison, CT: International Universities Press.

Morgan, R., Luborsky, L., & Crits-Christoph, P. (1982). Predicting the outcomes of psychotherapy by the Penn helping alliance rating method. *Archives of General Psychiatry, 39*, 397–401.

Morin, C. M., & Ware, J. C. (1996). Sleep and psychopathology. *Applied and Preventive Psychology, 5*, 211–224.

Moses-Zirkes, S. (1993, June). Flaws seen in guidelines for detecting depression. *APA Monitor,* 17.

Mueser, K. T., & Liberman, R. P. (1995). Behavior therapy in practice. In B. Bongar & L. E. Beutler (Eds.), *Comprehensive textbook of psychotherapy: Theory and Practice* (pp. 84–110). New York: Oxford University Press.

Munoz, R. F., Hollon, D., McGrath, E., Rehm, L. P., & VandenBos, G. R. (1994). On the AHCPR depression in primary care guidelines. *American Psychologist, 49*, 42–61.

Murphy, G. E. (1983). On suicide prediction and prevention. *Archives of General Psychiatry, 40*, 343–344.

Murphy, G. E., Simons, A. D., Wetzel, R. D., & Lustman, P., J. (1984). Cognitive therapy and pharmacotherapy: Singly and together in the treatment of depression. *Archives of General Psychiatry, 41*, 33–41.

Nathan, P. E. (1996). Validated forms of psychotherapy may lead to better-validated psychotherapy. *Clinical Psychology: Science and Practice, 3*, 251–255.

Nathan, P. E. (1998). Practice guidelines: Not yet ideal. *American Psychologist, 53*, 290–299.

Nathan, P. E., & Gorman, J. M. (Eds.). (1998). *A guide to treatments that work.* New York: Oxford University Press.

National Association of Private Psychiatric Hospitals (NAPPH). (1991). Managed Care survey finds improvements, but problems remain. *Hospital and Community Psychiatry, 42*, 964–965.

National Center for Health Statistics (1989). *Monthly vital statistics report.* Washington, DC: US Public Health Service.

National Center for Health Statistics (1991). *Monthly vital statistics report.* Washington, DC: US Public Health Service.

Nelson, G. (1982). Parental death during childhood and adult depression: Some additional data. *Social Psychiatry, 17*, 37–42.

Nelson, R. O., & Hayes, S. C. (Eds.). (1986). *Conceptual foundations of behavioral assessment.* New York: Guilford Press.

Nelson-Gray, R. O. (1996). Treatment outcome measures: Nomothetic or idiographic? *Clinical Psychology: Science and Practice, 3*, 164–167.

Neufeldt, S. N., Iversen, J. N., & Juntunen, C. L. (1995). *Supervision strategies for the first practicum.* Alexandria, VA: American Counseling Association.

New federal guidelines seek to help primary care providers recognize and treat depression (1993). *Hospital and Community Psychiatry, 44*, 598.

Newman, D. L., Moffitt, T. E., Silva, P. A., Avshalom, C., & Magdol, L. (1996). Psychiatric disorder in a birth cohort of young adults: Prevalence, comorbidity, clinical significance, and new case incidence from ages 11 to 21. *Journal of Consulting and Clinical Psychology, 64*, 552–562.

Newman, R. (1993, June). Debate on guidelines: Quality vs. autonomy. *APA Monitor,* 22. {vol. #?}

Newman, R. (1999, Feb.). A tumutous 10 years. *APA Monitor, 30*(2), 30.

Newman, R. S., & Hirt, M. (1983). The psychoanalytic theory of depression:

Symptoms as a function of aggressive wishes and level of field articulation. *Journal of Abnormal Psychology, 92,* 42–48.

Nezu, A. M., Nezu, C. M., Trunzo, J. J., & McClure, K. S. (1998). Treatment maintenance for unipolar depression: Relevant issues, literature review, and recommendations for research and clinical practice. *Clinical Psychology; Science and Practice, 5,* 496–512.

Nietzel, M. T., Russell, R. L., Hemmings, K. A., & Gretter, M. L. (1987). Clinical significance of psychotherapy for unipolar depression: A meta-analytic approach to social comparison. *Journal of Consulting and Clinical Psychology, 55,* 156–161.

NIMH Consensus Development Conference Statement (1985). Electroconvulsive therapy. *Journal of the American Medical Association, 254,* 2103–2108.

Nisbett, R., & Ross, L. (1980). *Human inference.* Englewood Cliffs, NJ: Prentice-Hall.

Nolen-Hoeksema, S. (1987). Sex differences in unipolar depression: Evidence and theory. *Psychological Bulletin, 101,* 259–282.

Nolen-Hoeksema, S. (1991). Responses to depression and their effects on the duration of the depressive episode. *Journal of Abnormal Psychology, 100,* 569–582.

Norcross, J. C. (1986). *Handbook of eclectic psychotherapy.* New York: Brunner/Mazel.

Norcross, J. C. (1994). *Prescriptive eclectic psychotherapy.* Videotape in the APA Psychotherapy Videotape Series. Washington, DC: American Psychological Association Press.

Norcross, J. C., & Goldfried, M. R. (Eds.). (1992). *Psychotherapy integration.* New York: Basic Books.

Norcross, J. C., & Prochaska, J. O. (1982). A national survey of clinical psychologists: Views on training, career choice, and APA. *Clinical Psychologist, 35*(4), 1-6.

Norcross, J. C., & Prochaska, J. O. (1988). A study of eclectic (and integrative) views revisited. *Professional Psychology: Research and Practice, 19,* 170–174.

Ogles, B. M., Sawyer, J. D., & Lambert, M. J. (1995). Clinical significance of the national institute of mental health treatment of depression collaborative research program data. *Journal of Consulting and Clinical Psychology, 63,* 321–326.

Olbrisch, M. (1981). Evaluation of stress management program. *Medical Care, 19,* 153–159.

Olfson, M. (1989). Psychiatric emergency room dispositions of HMO enrollees. *Hospital and Community Psychiatry, 40,* 639–641.

Olsen, D. P., Rickles, J., & Travlik, K. (1995). A treatment-team model of managed mental health care. *Psychiatric Services, 46,* 252–256.

Orlinsky, D. E., Grawe, K., & Parks, B. K. (1994). Process and outcome in psychotherapy—Noch Einmal. In A. E. Bergin & S. L. Garfield (Eds.), *Handbook of psychotherapy and behavior change* (4th ed., pp. 270–376). New York: Wiley.

Ormel, J., Koeter, M. W., van den Brink, W., & van de Willige, G. (1991). Recognition, management and course of anxiety and depression in general practice. *Archives of General Psychiatry, 48,* 700–706.

Ormel, J., Van Den Brink, W., Koeter, M. W. J., et al. (1990). Recognition, management and outcome of psychological disorders in primary care: A naturalistic follow-up study. *Psychological Medicine, 20,* 909–923.

Osgood, N. J. (1985). *Suicide in the elderly: A practitioner's guide to diagnosis and mental health intervention.* Rockville, MD: Aspen Press.

Osgood, N. J., & Thielman, S. (1990). Geriatric suicidal behavior: Assessment and treatment. In S. J. Blumenthal & D. J. Kupfer (Eds.), *Suicide over the life cycle: Risk factors, assessment, and treatment of suicidal patients* (pp. 341–380). Washington, DC: American Psychiatric Press.

Ossorio, P. (1985). Pathology. In K. Davis & T. Mitchell (Eds.), *Advances in descriptive psychology* (Vol. 4, pp. 151–202). Greenwich, CT: JAI Press.

Overall, J. E., & Gorham, D. R. (1962). The Brief Psychiatric Rating Scale. *Psychological Reports, 10,* 799–812.

Paivio, S. C., & Greenberg, L. S. (1995). Resolving "unfinished business": Efficacy of experiential therapy using empty-chair dialogue. *Journal of Consulting and Clinical Psychology, 63*(3), 419–425.

Parker, G. (1980). Vulnerability factors to normal depression. *Journal of Psychosomatic Research, 24,* 67–74.

Parker, G., Brown, L., & Blignault, I. (1986). Coping behaviors as predictors of the course of clinical depression. *Archives of General Psychiatry, 53,* 561–565.

Parker, G., Holmes, S., & Manicavasagar, V. (1986). Depression in general practice attenders—"caneness," natural history and predictors of outcomes. *Journal of Affective Disorders, 10,* 27–35.

Patterson, G. R., & Forgatch, M. S. (1985). Therapist behavior as a determinant for client noncompliance: A paradox for the behavior modifier. *Journal of Consulting and Clinical Psychology, 53,* 846–851.

Pear, R. (1995, July). HMO's refusing emergency claims, hospitals assert; Two missions in conflict; managed care groups insist they must limit costs—doctors are frustrated. *New York Times, 144,* July 9.

Pearlman, T. (1994). Practice guideline for adult major depressive disorder. *American Journal of Psychiatry, 151,* 625.

Persons, J. B. (1991). Psychotherapy outcome studies don't accurately represent current models of psychotherapy: A proposed remedy. *American Psychologist, 46,* 99–106.

Persons, J. B., Burns, D. D., & Perloff, J. M. (1988). Predictors of dropout and outcome in cognitive therapy for depression in a private practice setting. *Cognitive Therapy and Research, 12,* 557–575.

Persons, J. B., Burns, D. D., Perloff, J. M., & Miranda, J. (1993). Relationships between symptoms of depression and anxiety and dysfunctional beliefs about achievement and attachment. *Journal of Abnormal Psychology, 102,* 518–524.

Persons, J. B., Miranda, J., & Perloff, J. M. (1991). Relationships between depressive symptoms and cognitive vulnerabilities of achievement and dependency. *Cognitive Therapy and Research, 15,* 221–235.

Persons, J. B., & Silberschatz, G. (1998). Are results of randomized controlled trials useful to psychotherapists? *Journal of Consulting and Clinical Psychology, 66,* 126–135.

Peterson, L. G., & Bongar, B. (1989). The suicidal patient. In A. Lazare (Ed.), *Outpatient psychiatry: diagnosis and treatment* (2nd ed., pp. 569–584). Baltimore: Williams & Wilkins.

Pfohl, B., Stangl, D., & Zimmerman, M. (1984). The implications of DSM-III personality disorders for patients with major depression. *Journal of Affective Disorders, 7,* 309–318.

Pokorny, A. D. (1983). Prediction of suicide in psychiatric patients: Report of a prospective study. *Archives of General Psychiatry, 40,* 249–257.

Pokorny, I. N. (1964). Suicide rates in various psychiatric disorders. *Journal of Nervous and Mental Disease, 139,* 499–506.

Pope, K. (1986, January). Assessment and mangement of suicidal risks: Clinical and legal standards of care. *Independent Practitioner,* 17–23.

Potter, W. Z., Grossman, F., & Rudorfer, M. V. (1993). Noradrenergic function in depressive disorders. In J. J. Mann & D. J. Kupfer (Eds.), *Biology of depressive disorder: Part A. A systems perspective* (pp. 1–28). New York: Plenum.

PRNewswire (1996, Oct. 7). *Study finds adequacy of care for mental illness perceived as low.* New York.

Prochaska, J. O. (1984). *Systems of psychotherapy: A transtheoretical analysis* (2nd ed.). Homewood, IL: Dorsey Press.

Professional liability (1991). *New Jersey Medicine, 88,* 387.

Project Match Research Group (1997). Matching alcoholism treatments to client heterogeneity: Project Match posttreatment drinking outcomes. *Journal of Studies in Alcoholism, 58,* 7–29.

Prudic, J., Sackeim, H. A., Davanand, D. P., & Kiersky, J. E. (1993). The efficacy of ECT in double depression. *Depression, 1,* 38–44.

Quill, T. E. (1985). Somatization disorder: One of medicine's blind spots. *Journal of the American Medical Association, 254,* 3075–3079.

Raab, S. (1996, Aug. 21). NJ officials say mob ring infiltrated health care. *New York Times.*

Rabasca, L. (1998, Oct.). Putting the quality back in health care. *APA Monitor, 29*(10), 34–35.

Raps, C. S., Peterson, C., Reinhard, K. E., Abramson, L. Y. & Seligman, M. E. P. (1982). Attributional style among depressed patients. *Journal of Abnormal Psychology, 91,* 102–108.

Raskin, A., Schulterbrandt, J. G., Reatig, N., & McKeon, J. J. (1970). Differential response to chlorpromazine, imipramine, and placebo. *Archives of General Psychiatry, 23,* 164–173.

Reckase, M. D. (1996). Test construction in the 1990s: Recent approaches every psychologist should know. *Psychological Assessment, 8,* 354–359.

Reed, M. K. (1994). Social skills training to reduce depression in adolescents. *Adolescence, 29,* 293–302.

Regier, D. A., Boyd, J. H., Burke, J. D., Jr., Rae, D. S., Myers, J. K., Kramer, M., Robins, L. N., George, L. K., Karno, M., & Locke, B. Z. (1988). One-month prevalence of mental disorders in the United States based on five Epidemiologic Catchment Area sites. *Archives of General Psychiatry, 45,* 977–986.

Regier, D. A., Myers, J. K., Kramer, M., Robins, L. N., Blazer, D. G., Hough, R. L., Eaton, W. W., & Locke, B. Z. (1984). The NIMH Epidemiologic Catchment Area program. *Archives of General Psychiatry, 41,* 934–941.

Regier, D. A., Narrow, W. E., Rae, D. S., Manderscheid, R. W., Locke, B. Z., & Goodwin, F. (1993). The de facto US mental and addictive disorders service system: Epidemiologic Catchment Area prospective 1-year prevalence rates of disorders and services. *Archives of General Psychiatry, 50,* 85–94.

Rehm, L. P., Fuchs, C. Z., & Roth, D. M. (1979). A comparison of self-control and assertion skills treatments of depression. *Behavior Therapy, 10,* 429–442.

Reynolds, C. F., Frank, E., Perel, J. M., Imber, S., & Kupfer, D. J. (1994). Maintenance therapies in late-life depression. *Neuropsychopharmacology, 10,* 615.

Reynolds, C. F., & Kupfer, D. J. (1987). Sleep research in affective illness: State of the art circa 1987. *Sleep, 10,* 199–215.

Rholes, W., Riskind, J. H., & Neville, B. (1985). The relationship of cognitions and hopelessness to depression and anxiety. *Cosial Cognition, 3,* 36–50.

Rich, C. L., Sherman, M., & Fowler, R. C. (1990). San Diego suicide study: The adolescents. *Adolescence, 25*(100), 855–865.

Rihmer, Z., Barsi, J., Arató, M., Demeter, E. (1990). Suicide in subtypes of primary major depression. *Journal of Affective Disorders, 18,* 221–225.

Rismiller, D. J., Steer, R., Ranierei, W. F., Rissmiller, F., & Hogate, P. (1994). Factors complicating cost containment in the treatment of suicidal patients. *Hospital and Community Psychiatry, 45,* 782-788.

Rivas-Vasquez, R. A., & Blais, M. A. (1997). Selective serotonin reuptake inhibitors and atypical antidepressants: A review and update for psychologists. *Professional Psychology: Research and Practice, 28,* 526–536.

Robertson, J. D. (1988). *Psychiatric malpractice: Liability of mental health professionals.* New York: Wiley.

Robins, E., Gassner, S., Kayes, J., Wilkenson, R. H. Jr., Murphy, G. E. (1989). The communication of suicidal intent: A study of 134 consecutive cases of successful (completed) suicide. *American Journal of Psychiatry, 115,* 724–733.

Robins, E., Murphy, G. E., Wilkinson, R. M., Gassner, S., & Kays, J. (1959). Some clinical considerations in the prevention of suicide based on a study of 134 successful suicides. *American Journal of Public Health, 49,* 888–898.

Robins, L. N., & Kulbok, P. A. (1988). Epidemiologic studies in suicide. *Review of Psychiatry* (Vol. 7, pp. 289–306). Washington, DC: American Psychiatric Press.

Robinson, J. C. (1996). Decline in hospital utilization and cost inflation under managed care in California. *Journal of the American Medical Association, 276,* 1060–1064.

Robinson, L. A., Berman, J. S., & Neimeyer, R. A. (1990). Psychotherapy for the treatment of depression: A comprehensive review of controlled outcome research. *Psychological Bulletin, 108,* 30–49.

Rodin, G., & Voshart, K. (1986). Depression in the medically ill: An overview. *American Journal of Psychiatry, 143,* 696–705.

Rogers, C. R. (1951). *Client-centered therapy.* Boston: Houghton-Mifflin.

Rogers, J. L., Howard, K. I., & Vessey, J. T. (1993). Using significance tests to evaluate equivalence between two experimental groups. *Psychological Bulletin, 113,* 553–565.

Rogosa, D. (1988). Myths about longitudinal research. In D. W. Schaie, R. T. Campbell, W. Meredith, & S. C. Rawlings (Eds.), *Methodological issues in aging research* (pp. 171–210). New York: Springer.

Rohrbaugh, M., Shoham, V., Spungen, C., & Steinglass, P. (1995). Family systems therapy in practice: A systemic couples therapy for problem drinking. In B. Bongar & L. E. Beutler (Eds.), *Comprehensive textbook of psychotherapy: Theory and practice* (pp. 228–253). New York: Oxford University Press.

Rosenfarb, I. S., Becker, J., & Kahn, A. (1994). Perceptions of parental and peer attachments with mood disorders. *Journal of Abnormal Psychology, 103,* 637–644.

Ross, M. J., Mueller, J. H., & De La Torre, M. (1986). Depression and trait distinctiveness in the self-schema. *Journal of Social and Clinical Psychology, 4,* 46–59.

Rost, K., Zhang, M., Fortney, J., Smith, & Coyne, J. (1998). Persistently poor outcomes of undetected major depression in primary care: Implications for intervention. *General Hospital Psychiatry, 20,* 12–20.

Roth, A., & Fonagy, P. (1996). *What works for whom? A critical review of psychotherapy research.* New York: Guilford Press.

Rounsaville, B. J., Chevron, E. S., Prusoff, B. A., Elkin, I., Imber, S., Sotsky, S., & Watkins, J. (1987). The relation between specific and general dimensions of the psychotherapy process in interpersonal psychotherapy of depression. *Journal of Consulting and Clinical Psychology, 55,* 379–384.

Rounsaville, B. J., O'Malley, S., Foley, S., & Weissman, M. M. (1988). The role of manual guided training in the conduct and efficiency of interpersonal psychotherapy for depression. *Journal of Consulting and Clinical Psychology, 56*, 681–688.

Roy, A. (Ed) (1986). *Suicide.* Baltimore: Williams and Wilkins.

Runeson, B. (1989). Mental disorders in youth suicide: DSM-III-R axis I and II. *Acta Psychiatrica Scandinavica, 79*, 490–497.

Runeson, B. S., & Rich, C. L. (1992). Diagnostic comorbidty of mental disorders among young suicides. *International Review of Psychiatry, 4*, 197–203.

Rush, A. J. (1993). Clinical practice guidelines: Good news, bad news or no news? *Archives of General Psychiatry, 50*, 483–490.

Rush, A. J., Beck, A. T., Kovacs, M., & Hollon, S. D. (1977). Comparative efficacy of cognitive therapy and pharmacotherapy in the treatment of depressed outpatients. *Cognitive Therapy and Research, 1*, 17–38.

Rush, A. J., Beck, A. T., Kovacs, M., Weissenberger, J., & Hollon, S. D. (1982). Comparison of the effects of cognitive therapy on hopelessness and self-concept. *American Journal of Psychiatry, 139*, 862–866.

Rush, A. J., Giles, D., Jarrett, R., Feldman-Koffler, E., Debus, F., Weisenburger, J., Orsulak, P., & Roffward, H. (1989). Reduced REM latency predicts response to tricyclic medication in depressed outpatients in depressed outpatients. *Biological Psychiatry, 26*, 61–72.

Rush, A. J, Golden, W. E., Hall, G. W., Herrera, M., Houston, A., Kathol, R. G., Katon, W., Matchett, C. L., Petty, F., Schulberg, H. C., Smith, G. R. & Stuart, G. W. (1993a). *Depression in primary care: Vol 1. Detection and Diagnosis* (Clinical Practice Guideline No. 5, AHCPR Publication No. 93-0550). Rockville, MD: US Department of Health and Human Services, Agency for Health Care Policy and Research.

Rush, A. J, Golden, W. E., Hall, G. W., Herrera, M., Houston, A., Kathol, R. G., Katon, W., Matchett, C. L., Petty, F., Schulberg, H. C., Smith, G. R. & Stuart, G. W. (1993b). *Depression in primary care: Vol. 2. Treatment of Major Depression* (Clinical Practice Guidelines No. 5, AHCPR Publication No. 93-0551). Rockville, MD: US Department of Health and Human Services, Agency for Health Care Policy and Research.

Rush, A. J., Khatami, M., & Beck, A. T. (1975). Cognitive and behavior therapy in chronic depression. *Behavior Therapy, 6*, 398–404.

Russell, R. L., Bryant, F. B., & Estrada, A. U. (1996). Confirmatory P-technique analyses of therapist discourse: High- versus low-quality child therapy sessions. *Journal of Consulting and Clinical Psychology, 64*, 1366–1376.

Sacco, W. P., Milana, S., & Dunn, V. K. (1988). The effect of duration of depressive episode on the response of others. *Journal of Social and Clinical Psychology, 7*, 297–311.

Sanchez, V., & Lewinsohn, P. M. (1980). Assertive behavior and depression. *Journal of Consulting and Clinical Psychology, 48*, 119–120.

Sandowicz, M. M. (1998). *Identifying predictors of differential effects in the treatment of depressed older adults.* Unpublished doctoral dissertation, University of California, Santa Barbara.

Sarason, I. G., Levine, H. M., Basham, R. B., & Sarason, B. R. (1983). Assessing social support: The Social Support Questionnaire. *Journal of Personality and Social Psychology, 44*, 127–139.

Sargeant, J. K., Bruce, M. L., & Florio, L. P., & Weissman, M. M. (1990). Factors associated with 1-year outcome of major depression in the community. *Archives of General Psychiatry, 47*, 519–526.

Schatzberg, A. F., Samson, J. A., Bloomingdale, K. L., Orsulak, P. J., Gerson, B., Kizuka, P. P. , Cole, J. O., & Schildkraut, J. J. (1989). Toward a biochemical classification of depressive disorders. *Archives of General Psychiatry, 46,* 260–268.

Schildkraut, J. J. (1982). The biochemical discrimination of subtypes of depressive disorders: an outline of our studies on noreprinephrine metabolism and psychoactive drugs in the endogenous depression since 1967. *Pharmacopsychiatry, 15,* 121–127.

Schlesinger, H. J., Mumford, E., Glass, G. V., Patrick, C., & Sharfstein, S. (1983). Mental health treatment and medical care utilization in a fee-for-service system: Outpatient mental health treatment following the onset of chronic disease. *American Journal of Mental Health, 73,* 422–429.

Schmaling, K. B., & Jacobson, N. S. (1990). Marital interaction and depression. *Journal of Abnormal Psychology, 99,* 229–236.

Schulberg, H. C., & McClelland, M. (1987). Depression and physical illness: The prevalence, causation, and diagnosis of comorbidity. *Clinical Psychology Review, 7,* 145–167.

Schulberg, H. C., McClelland, M., & Gooding, W. (1987). Six-month outcomes for medical patients with major depressive disorders. *Journal of General Internal Medicine, 2,* 312–317.

Schulberg, H. C., & Rush, J. A. (1994). Clinical practice guidelines for managing major depression in primary care practice: Implications for psychologists. *American Psychologist, 49,* 34–41.

Schulte, D., Kunzel, R., Pepping, G., & Schulte-Bahrenberg, T. (1992). Tailor-made versus standardized therapy of phobic patients. *Advances in Behaviour Research and Therapy, 14,* 67–92.

Schuster, J., Thienhaus, O., Fogel, B., Restak, R., et al. (1995). Cost-effective inpatient care of neuropsychiatric patients. *Journal of Neurosciences, 7,* 1–5.

Scogin, F., Bowman, D., Jamison, C., Beutler, L. E., & Machado, P. P. (1994). Effects of initial severity of dysfunctional thinking on the outcome of cognitive therapy. *Clinical Psychology and Psychotherapy, 1,* 179–184.

Sechrest, L., McKnight, P., & McKnight, K. (1996). Calibration of measures for psychotherapy outcome studies. *American Psychologist, 51,* 1065–1071.

Sederer, L. I. (1987). Utilization review and quality assurance: Staying in the black and working with the blues. *General Hospital Psychiatry, 9,* 210–219.

Sederer, L. I., & Summergrad, P. (1983). Criteria for hospital admission. *Hospital and Community Psychiatry, 44,* 116–118.

Segrin, C., & Dillard, J. P. (1992). The interactional theory of depression: A meta-analysis of the research literature. *Journal of Social and Clinical Psychology, 11,* 43–70.

Seligman, M. E. P. (1995). The effectiveness of psychotherapy: The *Consumer Reports* study. *American Psychologist, 50,* 965–974.

Seligman, M. E. P. (1996). Science as an ally of practice. *American Psychologist, 51,* 1072–1079.

Sevy, S., Mendlewicz, J., & Mendelbaum, K. (1995). Genetic research in bipolar illness. In E. E. Beckham & W. R. Leber (Eds.), *Handbook of depression* (2nd ed., pp. 203–212). New York: Guilford Press.

Shadish, W. R., & Ragsdale, K. (1996). Random versus nonrandom assignment in controlled experiments: Do you get the same answer? *Journal of Consulting and Clinical Psychology, 64,* 1290–1305.

Shaffer, D. (1988). The epidemiology of teen suicide: An examination of risk factors. *Journal of Clinical Psychiatry, 49* (Suppl.), 36–41.

Shaffer, D., Gould, M. S., Fisher, P., & Trautman, P. (1996). Psychiatric diagnosis in child and adolescent suicide. *Archives of General Psychiatry, 53,* 339–348.

Shaffer, D., Gould, M., & Trautman, P. (1985, Sept.). *Suicidal behavior in chil-*

dren and young adults. Paper presented at the Psychobiology of Suicidal Behavior Conference, New York, NY.

Shaffi, M. (1986, Oct.). *Psychological autopsy study of suicide in adolescents.* Paper presented at the Child Depression Consortium, St. Louis, MO.

Shapiro, D. A., Barkham, M., Rees, A., Hardy, G. E., Reynolds, S., & Startup, M. (1994). Effects of treatment duration and severity of depression on the effectiveness of cognitive-behavioral and psychodynamic-interpersonal psychotherapy. *Journal of Consulting and Clinical Psychology, 62,* 522–534.

Shapiro, D. A., Rees, A., Barkham, M., Hardy, G., Reynolds, S., & Startup, M. (1995). Effects of treatment duration and severity of depression on the maintenance of gains after cognitive-behavioral and psychodynamic-interpersonal therapy. *Journal of Consulting and Clinical Psychology, 63,* 378–387.

Shapiro, D. A., & Shapiro, D. (1982). Meta-analysis of comparative therapy outcome studies: A replication and refinement. *Psychological Bulletin, 92,* 581–604.

Sharfstein, S. S. (1989). The catastrophic case: A special problem for general hospital psychiatry in the era of managed care. *General Hospital Psychiatry, 11,* 268–270.

Shaw, B. F. (1983, July). *Training therapists for the treatment of depression: Collaborative study.* Paper presented at the meeting of the Society for Psychotherapy Research, Sheffield, England.

Shea, M. T., Elkin, I., Imber, S. D., Sotsky, S. M., Watkins, J. T., Collins, J. F., Pilkonis, P. A., Beckham, E., Glass, D. R., Dolan, R. T., & Parloff, M. B. (1992). Course of depressive symptoms over followup: Findings from the National Institute of Mental Health Treatment of Depression Collaborative Research Program. *Archives of General Psychiatry, 49,* 782–787.

Shein, H. M. (1976). Suicide care: Obstacles in the education of psychiatric residents. *Omega: Journal of Death and Dying, 7*(1), 75–81.

Shemo, J. P. D. (1985). Cost-effectiveness of providing mental health services: The offset effect. *International Journal of Psychiatry in Medicine, 15,* 295–307.

Sheppard, D., Smith, G. T., & Rosenbaum, G. (1988). Use of MMPI subtypes in predicting completion of a residential alcoholism treatment program. *Journal of Consulting and Clinical Psychology, 56,* 590–596.

Sherbourne, C. D., Hays, R. D., & Wells, K. B. (1995). Personal and psychosocial risk factors for physical and mental health outcomes and course of depression among depressed patients. *Journal of Consulting and Clinical Psychology, 63,* 345–355.

Shneidman, E. S. (1989). Overview: A multidimensional approach to suicide. In D. G. Jacobs & H. N. Brown (Eds.), *Suicide: Understanding and responding* (Harvard Medical School perspectives on suicide, pp. 1–30). Madison, CT: International Universities Press.

Shoham-Salomon, V. (1991). Introduction to special section on client-therapy interaction research. *Journal of Consulting and Clinical Psychology, 59,* 203–204.

Shoham-Salomon, V., Avner, R., & Neeman, K. (1989). "You are changed if you do and changed if you don't": Mechanisms underlying paradoxical interventions. *Journal of Consulting and Clinical Psychology, 57,* 590–598.

Shoham-Salomon, V., & Hannah, M. T. (1991). Client-treatment interactions in the study of differential change processes. *Journal of Consulting and Clinical Psychology, 59,* 217–225.

Shoham-Salomon, V., & Jancourt, A. (1985). Differential effectiveness of paradoxical interventions for more versus less stress-prone individuals. *Journal of Counseling Psychology, 32,* 443–447.

Shoham-Salomon, V., & Rosenthal, R. (1987). Paradoxical interventions: A meta-analysis. *Journal of Consulting and Clinical Psychology, 55,* 22–28.

Showstack, J., Luri, N., Leatherman, S., Fisher, E., & Inui, T. (1996). Health of the public: The private-sector challenge. *Journal of the American Medical Association, 276,* 1071–1074.

Silverman, J. S., Silverman, J. A., & Eardley, D. A. (1984). Do maladaptive attitudes cause depression? *Archives of General Psychiatry, 41,* 28–30.

Silverman, W. H. (1996). Cookbooks, manuals, and paint-by-numbers: Psychotherapy in the 90's. *Psychotherapy, 33,* 207–215.

Simon, G. E., Lin, E. H. B., Katon, W., et al. (1995). Outcomes of "inadequate" antidepressant treatment. *Journal of General Internal Medicine, 10,* 663–670.

Simon, G. E., Von Korff, M., & Barlow, W. (1995). Health care costs of primary care patients with recognized depression. *Archives of General Psychiatry, 52,* 850–856.

Simon, R. I. (1987). *Clinical psychiatry and the law.* Washington, DC: American Psychiatric Press.

Simon, R. I. (1988). *Concise guide to clinical psychiatry and the law.* Washington, DC: American Psychiatric Press.

Simon, R. I. (1992). *Concise guide to clinical psychiatry and the law for clinicians.* Washington, DC: American Psychiatric Press.

Simons, A. D., Epstein, L. H., McGowan, C. R., Kupfer, D. J., & Robertson, R. J. (1985). Exercise as a treatment for depression: An update. *Clinical Psychology Review, 5,* 553–568.

Simons, A. D., Garfield, S. L., & Murphy, G. E. (1984). The process of change in cognitive therapy and pharmacotherapy for depression. *Archives of General Psychiatry, 41,* 45.

Simons, A. D., Gordon, J. S., Thase, M. E., & Monroe, S. M. (1995). Toward an integration of psychologic, social, and biologic factors in depression: Effects on outcome and course of cognitive therapy. *Journal of Consulting and Clinical Psychology, 63,* 369–377.

Simons, A. D., & Thase, M. E. (1992). Biological markers, treatment outcome, and 1-year follow-up in endogenous depression: Electroencephalographic sleep studies and response to cognitive therapy. *Journal of Consulting and Clinical Psychology, 60,* 392–401.

Skinner, H. A. (1981). Comparison of client assigned to in-patient treatment for alcoholism and drug abuse. *British Journal of Psychiatry, 138,* 312–320.

Slap, G. B., Vorters, D. F., Khalid, N., Margulies, S. R., et al. (1992). Adolescent suicide attempters: Do physicians recognize them? *Journal of Adolescent Health, 13*(4), 286–292.

Smith, E. W. L. (1995). A passionate, rational response to the "manualization" of psychotherapy. *Psychotherapy Bulletin, 30*(2), 36–40.

Smith, G. R. (1994). The course of somatization and its effects on utilization of health care resources. *Psychosomatics, 35,* 263–267.

Smith, M. L., Glass, G. V., & Miller, T. I. (1980). *The benefits of psychotherapy.* Baltimore: Johns Hopkins University Press.

Snow, R. E. (1991). Aptitude-treatment interaction as a framework for research on individual differences in psychotherapy. *Journal of Consulting and Clinical Psychology, 59,* 205–216.

Sokol, M. S., & Pfeffer, C. R. (1992). Suicidal behavior of children. In B. Bongar (Ed.), *Suicide: Guidelines for assessment, management and treatment* (pp. 69–83). New York: Oxford University Press.

Sotsky, S. M., Glass, D. R., Shea, T. M., Pilkonis, P. A., Collins, J. F., Elkin, I., Watkins, J. T., Imber, S. D., Leber, W. R., Moyer, J., & Oliveri, M. E. (1991).

Patient predictors of response to psychotherapy and pharmacotherapy: Findings in the NIMH Treatment of Depression Collaborative Research Program. *American Journal of Psychiatry, 148,* 997–1008.

Spangler, D. L., Simons, A. D., Thase, M. E., & Monroe, S. M. (1997). Response to cognitive-behavioral therapy in depression: Effects of pretreatment cognitive dysfunction and life stress. *Journal of Consulting and Clinical Psychology, 65,* 568–575.

Speier, P. L., Sherak, D. L., Hirsch, S., & Cantwell, D. P. (1995). Depression in children and adolescents. In E. E. Beckham & W. R. Leber (Eds.), *Handbook of depression* (2nd ed., pp. 467–493). New York: Guilford Press.

Sperry, L., Brill, P. L., Howard, K. I., & Grissom, G. R. (1996). *Treatment outcomes in psychotherapy and psychiatric interventions.* New York: Brunner/ Mazel.

Spiegel, D., Bloom, J. R., Kraemer, H. C., & Gottheil, E. (1989, Oct., 14). Effect of psychosocial treatment on survival of patients with metastatic breast cancer. *Lancet,* 888–891.

Spielberger, C. D. (1988). *Manual for the State-Trait Anger Expression Inventory (STAXI).* Odessa, FL: Psychological Assessment Resources.

Spielberger, C. D., Gorsuch, R. L., & Lushene, R. E. (1970). *The State-Trait Anxiety Inventory (STAI) test manual for form X.* Palo Alto, CA: Consulting Psychologists Press.

Spielberger, C. D., Gorsuch, R. L., Lushene, R., Vagg, P. R., & Jacobs, G. A. (1983). *Manual for the State-Trait Anxiety Inventory.* Palo Alto, CA: Consulting Psychologists Press.

Spielberger, C. D., Johnson, E. H., Russell, S. F., Crane, R. J., Jacobs, G. A., & Worden, T. J. (1985). The experience and expression of anger: Construction and validation of an anger expression scale. In M. A. Chesney & R. H. Rosenman (Eds.), *Anger and hostility in cardiovascular and behavioral disorders* (pp. 5–30). New York: Hemisphere/McGraw-Hill.

Spitzer, R. L., Williams, J. B. W., & Gibbon, M. (1986). *The structured clinical interview for DSM III-R—Patient version.* New York: Biometrics Research Department, New York State Psychiatric Institute.

Spoont, M. R. (1992). Modulatory role of serotonin in neural information processing: Implications for human psychopathology. *Psychological Bulletin, 112,* 330–350.

Stein, D. M., & Lambert, M. J. (1995). Graduate training in psychotherapy: Are therapy outcomes enhanced? *Journal of Consulting and Clinical Psychology, 63,* 182–196.

Steinbrueck, S. M., Maxwell, S. E., & Howard, G. S. (1983). A meta-analysis of psychotherapy and drug therapy in the treatment of unipolar depression with adults. *Journal of Consulting and Clinical Psychology, 51,* 856–862.

Steinglass, P. (1987). *The alcoholic family.* New York: Basic Books.

Steinmetz, J. L., Lewinsohn, P. M., & Antonuccio, D. O. (1983). Prediction of individual outcome in a group intervention for depression. *Journal of Consulting and Clinical Psychology, 51,* 331–337.

Stevens, D. E., Merikangas, K. R., & Merikangas, J. R. (1995). Comorbidity of depression and other medical conditions. In E. E. Beckham & W. R. Leber (Eds.), *Handbook of depression* (2nd ed., pp. 147–199). New York: Guilford Press.

Stiles, W. B., Agnew-Davies, R., Hardy, G. E., Barkham, M., & Shapiro, D.A. (1998). Relations of the alliance with psychotherapy outcome: Findings in the second Sheffield Psychotherapy project. *Journal of Consulting and Clinical Psychology, 66,* 791–802.

Stone, A. A. (1990). Law, science and psychiatric malpractice: A response to

Klerman's indictment of psychoanalytic psychiatry. *American Journal of Psychiatry, 147,* 419- 427.

Stoolmiller, M., Duncan, T., Bank, L., & Patterson, G. R. (1993). Some problems and solutions in the study of change: Significant patterns in client resistance. *Journal of Consulting and Clinical Psychology, 61,* 920–928.

Strauman, T. J. (1989). Self-discrepancies in clinical depression and social phobia: Cognitive structures that underlie emotional disorders? *Journal of Abnormal Psychology, 98,* 14–22.

Striker, G., & Gold, J. R. (Eds.). (1993). *Comprehensive handbook of psychotherapy integration.* New York: Plenum.

Strombert, C. D., Haggarty, D. J., Leibenluft, R. F., McMillan, M. H., Mishkin, B. R., Rubin, B. L., & Trilling, H. R. (1988). *The psychologist's legal handbook.* Washington, DC: Council for the National Register of Health Service Providers in Psychology.

Strube, M. J., Gardner, W., & Hartmann, D. P. (1985). Limitations, liabilities, and obstacles in reviews of the literature: The current status of meta-analysis. *Clinical Psychology Review, 5,* 63–78.

Strupp, H. H., & Binder, J. L. (1984). *Psychotherapy in a new key.* New York: Basic Books.

Strupp, H. H., & Binder, J. (in press). Therapist inner processes in the Vanderbilt project, and conclusions for future training. In F. Caspar (Ed.), *The inner processes of psychotherapists: Innovations in clinical training.* New York: Oxford University Press.

Strupp, H. H., Horowitz, L. M., & Lambert, M. J. (1997). *Measuring patient changes in mood, anxiety, and personality disorders: Toward a core battery.* Washington, DC: American Psychological Association.

Sullivan, H. S. (1953). *The interpersonal theory of psychiatry.* New York: Norton.

Suomi, S. J. (1991). Primate separation models of affective disorders. In J. Madden IV (Ed.), *Neurobiology of learning, emotion, and affect* (pp. 195–213). New York: Raven Press.

Swindle, R. W., Cronkite, R. C., & Moos, R. H. (1989). Life stressors, social resources, coping, and the 4-year course of unipolar depression. *Journal of Abnormal Psychology, 98,* 468–477.

Swoboda, J. S., Dowd, E. T., & Wise, S. L. (1990). Reframing and restraining directives in the treatment of clinical depression. *Journal of Counseling Psychology, 37,* 254–260.

Tasca, G. A., Russell, V., & Busby, K. (1994). Characteristics of patients who choose between two types of group psychotherapy. *International Journal of Group Psychotherapy, 44,* 499–508

Task Force on Promotion and Dissemination of Psychological Procedures (1995). Training in and dissemination of empirically validated psychological treatments: Report and recommendations. *Clinical Psychologist, 48*(1), 3–23.

Taylor, J. A. (1953). A personality scale of manifest anxiety. *Journal of Abnormal and Social Psychology, 48,* 285.

Taylor, S. E., & Brown, J. D. (1994). Positive illusions and well-being revisited: Separating fact from fiction. *Psychological Bulletin, 116,* 21–27.

Tennen, H., Hall, J. A., & Affleck, G. (1995a). Depression research methodologies in the *Journal of Personality and Social Psychology*: A review and critique. *Journal of Personality and Social Psychology, 68,* 870–884.

Tennen, H. Hall, J. A., & Affleck, G. (1995b). Rigor, rigor mortis, and conspiratorial views of depression research. *Journal of Personality and Social Psychology, 68,* 895–900.

Teri, L., & Lewinsohn, P. M. (1986). Individual and group treatment of unipolar depression: Comparison of treatment outcome and identification of predictors of successful treatment outcome. *Behavior Therapy, 17,* 215–228.

Thase, M. E., & Howland, R. H. (1995). Biological processes in depression: An updated review and integration. In E. E. Beckham & W. R. Leber (Eds.), *Handbook of depression* (2nd ed., pp. 213–279). New York: Guilford Press.

Thase, M. E., & Kupfer, D. J. (1996). Recent developments in the pharmacotherapy of mood disorders. *Journal of Consulting and Clinical Psychology, 64,* 646–659.

Thase, M. E., Simons, A. D., Cahalane, J., McGeary, J., & Harden, T. (1991). Severity of depression and response to cognitive behavior therapy. *American Journal of Psychiatry, 148,* 784–789.

Thayer, R. E. (1989). *The biopsychology of mood and arousal.* New York: Oxford University Press.

Thompson, L. W., Gallagher, D., & Breckenridge, J. S. (1987). Comparative effectiveness of psychotherapies for depressed older adults. *Journal of Consulting and Clinical Psychology, 55,* 385–390.

Thompson, L. W., Gallagher-Thompson, D., Hanser, S., Gantz, F., & Steffen, A. (1991, Aug.). *Comparison of desipramine and cognitive-behavioral therapy for the treatment of depression in the elderly.* Paper presented at the American Psychological Association Meetings, San Francisco, CA.

Tiemens, B. G., Ormel, J., & Simon, G. E. (1996). Occurrence, recognition, and outcome of psychological disorders in primary care. *American Journal of Psychiatry, 153,* 636–644.

Tingey, R. C., Lambert, M. J., Burlingame, G. M., & Hansen, N. B. (1996a). Clinically significant change: Practical indicators for evaluating psychotherapy outcome. *Psychotherapy Research, 6,* 144–153.

Tingey, R. C., Lambert, M. J., Burlingame, G. M., & Hansen, N. B. (1996b). Assessing clinical significance: Proposed extensions to method. *Psychotherapy Research, 6,* 109–123.

Tracey, T. J., Ellickson, J. L., & Sherry P. (1989). Reactance in relation to different supervisory environments and counselor development. *Journal of Counseling Psychology, 36,* 336–344.

Trief, P. M., & Yuan, H. A. (1983). The use of the MMPI in a chronic back pain rehabilitation program. *Journal of Clinical Psychology, 39,* 46–53.

Truax, C. B., & Carkhuff, R. R. (1967). *Toward effective counseling and psychotherapy: Training and practice.* Chicago: Aldine.

Ulrich-Jakubowski, D., Russell, D. W., & O'Hara, M. W. (1988). Marital adjustment difficulties: Cause or consequence of depressive symptomatology? *Journal of Social and Clinical Psychology, 7,* 312–318.

Vaillant, G. E., & Blumenthal, S. J. (1990). Introduction: Suicide over the life cycle: Risk factors and life-span development. In S. J. Blumenthal & D. J. Kupfer (Eds.), *Suicide over the life cycle: Risk factors, assessment, and treatment of suicidal patients* (pp. 1–16). Washington, DC: American Psychiatric Association Press.

Vallejo, J., Gasto, C., Catalan, R., Bulbena, A., & Menchon, J. M. (1991). Predictors of antidepressant treatment outcome in melancholia: Psychosocial, clinical, and biological indicators. *Journal of Affective Disorders, 21,* 151–162.

VandeCreek, L., Knapp, S., & Herzog, C. (1987). Malpractice risks in the treatment of dangerous patients. *Psychotherapy: Theory, Research, and Practice, 24,* 145–153.

Van Etten, M. L., & Taylor, S. (1998). Comparative efficacy of treatment for Post-Traumatic Stress Disorder: A meta analysis. *Clinical Psychology and Psychotherapy, 5,* 126–144.

Vaughn, C. E., & Leff, J. P. (1976). The influence of family and social support factors on the course of psychiatric illness. *British Journal of Psychiatry, 129,* 125–137.

Veiel, H. O., Kuhner, C., Brill, G., & Ihle, W. (1992). Psychosocial correlates of clinical depression after psychiatric in-patient treatment: Methodological issues and baseline differences between recovered and non-recovered patients. *Psychological Medicine, 22,* 415–427.

Veleber, D. M., & Templer, D. I. (1984). Effects of caffeine on anxiety and depression. *Journal of Abnormal Psychology, 93,* 120–122.

Vissides, D. N., & Jenner, F. A. (1982). The response of endogenously and reactively depressed patients to electroconvulsive therapy. *British Journal of Psychiatry, 141,* 239–242.

Vredenburg, K., Flett, G. L., & Krames, L. (1993). Analogue versus clinical depression: A critical reappraisal. *Psychological Bulletin, 113,* 327–344.

Wakefield, J. C. (1992a). Disorder as harmful dysfunction: A conceptual critique of DSM-III-R's definition of mental disorder. *Psychological Review, 99,* 232–247.

Wakefield, J. C. (1992b). The concept of mental disorder: On the boundary between biological facts and social values. *American Psychologist, 47,* 373–388.

Wakefield, J. C. (1993). Limits of operationalization: A critique of Spitzer and Endicott (1978) proposed operational criteria for mental disorder. *Journal of Abnormal Psychology, 102,* 160–172.

Wakefield, J. C. (1997). Normal inability versus pathological disapbility: Why Ossorio's definition of mental disorder is not sufficient. *Clinical Psychology: Science and Practice, 4,* 249–258.

Wakefield, P. J., Williams, R. E., Yost, E. B., & Patterson, K. M. (1996). *Couple therapy for alcoholism: A cognitive-behavioral treatment manual.* New York: Guilford Press.

Wampold, B. E., Mondin, G. W., Moody, M., Stich, F., Benson, K., & Ahn, H. (1997). A meta-analysis of outcome studies comparing bona fide psychotherapies: Empirically, "All must have prizes." *Psychological Bulletin, 122,* 203–215.

Ware, J. E., Bayliss, M. S., Rogers, W. H., Kosinski, M., & Tarlov, A. R. (1996). Differences in 4-year health outcomes for elderly and poor, chronically ill patients treated in HMO and fee-for-service system: Results from the Medical Outcomes Study. *Journal of the American Medical Association 276,* 1039–1047.

Warren, L. W., & McEachren, L. (1983). Psycholsocial correlates of depressive symptomatology in adult women. *Journal of Abnormal Psychology, 92,* 151–160.

Waskow, I. E., & Parloff, M.B. (Eds.). (1975). *Psychotherapy change measures* (Publication No. 74-120). Rockville, MD: National Institute of Mental Health.

Watkins, J. T., Leber, W. R., Imber, S. D., Collins, J. F., Elkin, I., Pilkonis, P. A., Sotsky, S. M., Shea, M. T., & Glass, D. R. (1993). Temporal course of change of depression. *Journal of Consulting and Clinical Psychology, 61,* 858–864.

Watson, D., Clark, L. A., & Carey, G. (1988). Positive and negative affectivity and their relation to anxiety and depressive disorders. *Journal of Abnormal Psychology, 97,* 346–353.

Weary, G., Edwards, J. A., & Jacobson, J. A. (1995). Depression research methodologies in the *Journal of Personality and Social Psychology*: A reply. *Journal of Personality and Social Psychology, 68,* 885–891.

Weed, N. C., Butcher, J. N., Ben-Porath, Y. S., & McKenna, T. (1992). New measures for assessing alcohol and drug abuse with the MMPI-2: The APA and AAS. *Journal of Personality Assessment, 58.*

Weissman, M. M., & Bothwell, S. (1976). Assessment of social adjustment by patient self-report. *Archives of General Psychiatry, 33,* 111–115.

Weissman, M. M., Klerman, G. L., Markowitz, J. S., & Ouelette, R. (1989). Suicidal ideation and suicide attempts in panic disorder and attacks. *New England Journal of Medicine, 321,* 1209–1214.

Weissman, M. M., Prusoff, B. A., DiMascio, A., Neu, C., Goklaney, M., & Klerman, G. L. (1979). The efficacy of drugs and psychotherapy in the treatment of acute depressive episodes. *American Journal of Psychiatry, 136,* 555–558.

Welch, W. P., Frank, R. G., & Costello, A. J. (1983). Missing data in psychiatric research: A solution. *Psychological Bulletin, 94,* 177–180.

Wells, K. B., Burman, M. A., Rogers, W., & Hays, R. (1992). The course of depression in adult outpatients: Results from the Medical Outcomes Study. *Archives of General Psychiatry, 49,* 788–794.

Wells, K. B., Katon, W., Rogers, W. H., & Camp, P. (1994). Use of minor tranquilizers and antidepressant medications by depressed outpatients: Results from the Medical Outcomes Study. *American Journal of Psychiatry, 151,* 694–700.

Wells, K. B., & Sturm, R. (1996). Informing the policy process: From efficacy to effectiveness data on pharmacotherapy. *Journal of Consulting and Clinical Psychology, 64,* 638–645.

Welsh, G. S. (1952). An anxiety index and an internalization ratio for the MMPI. *Journal of Consulting Psychology, 16,* 65–72.

Westermeyer, J. (1991). Problems with managed psychiatric care without a psychiatrist-manager. *Hospital and Community Psychiatry, 42,* 1221–1224.

Westra, H. A., & Stewart, S. H. (1998). Cognitive-behavioural therapy and pharmacotherapy: Complementary or contradictory approaches to the treatment of anxiety? *Clinical Psychology Review, 18,* 307–340.

Wexler, B. E., & Cicchetti, D. V. (1992). The outpatient treatment of depression: Implications of outcome research for clinical practice. *Journal of Nervous and Mental Disease, 180,* 27–286.

Whiffen, V. E., & Gotlib, I. H. (1989). Infants of postpartum depressed mothers: Temperament and cognitive status. *Journal of Abnormal Psychology, 98,* 274–279.

Widiger, T. A., & Trull, T. J. (1985). The empty debate over the existence of mental illness: Comments on Gorenstein. *American Psychologist, 40,* 468–471.

Widiger, T. A., & Trull, T. J. (1991). Diagnosis and clinical assessment. *Annual Review of Psychology, 42,* 109–133.

Wierzbicki, M. (1993). *Issues in clinical psychology.* Boston: Allyn & Bacon.

Wiggins, J. G. (1992, Dec.). Practice guidelines: We sorely need them. *APA Monitor, 3.*

Wills, R., Faitler, S., & Snyder, D. (1987). Distinctiveness of behavioral versus insight-oriented marital therapy: An empirical analysis. *Journal of Consulting and Clinical Psychology, 55,* 685–690.

Wilner, P., Golembiowski, K., Kilmer, V., & Muscat, R. (1991). Changes in mesolimbic dopamine may explain stress-induced anhedonia. *Psychobiology, 19,* 79–84.

Wilson, G. T. (1996). Manual-based treatments: The clinical application of research findings. *Behavior Research and Therapy, 34,* 295–314.

Wilson, G. T., & Franks, C. M. (Eds.). (1982). *Contemporary behavior therapy: Conceptual and empirical foundations.* New York: Guilford Press.

Wilson, P. H. (1982). Combined pharmacological and behavioral treatment of depression. *Behavior Research and Therapy, 20,* 173–184.

Windle, M., Miller-Tutzauer, C., & Domenica, D. (1992). Alcohol use, suicidal behavior, and risky activities among adolescents. *Journal of Research on Adolescence, 2*(4), 317–330.

Winokur, G., & Clayton, P. J. (1967). Family history studies: II. Sex differences and alcoholism in primary affective illness. *British Journal of Psychiatry, 113,* 973–979.

Woody, G. E., McLellan, A. T., Luborsky, L., O'Brien, C. P., Blaine, J., Fox, S., Herman, I., & Beck, A. T. (1984). Severity of psychiatric symptoms as a predictor of benefits from psychotherapy: The Veterans Administration–Penn Study. *American Journal of Psychiatry, 141,* 1172–1177.

Wrate, R. M., Rooney, A. C., Thomas, P. F., & Cox, J. L. (1985). Postnatal depression and child development: A three-year follow-up study. *British Journal of Psychiatry, 146,* 622–627.

Yates, B. T. (1995). Cost-effectiveness analysis, cost-benefit analysis, and beyond: Evolving models for the scientist-manager-practitioner. *Clinical Psychology: Science and Practice, 2,* 385–398.

Yelin, E. H., Criswell, L. A., & Feigenbaum, P. G. (1996). Health care utilization and outcomes among persons with rheumatoid arthritis in fee-for-service and prepaid group practice settings. *Journal of the American Medical Association, 276,* 1048–1053.

Yost, E. B., Beutler, L. E., Corbishley, M. A., & Allender, J. R. (1986). *Group cognitive therapy.* New York: Pergamon Press.

Young, M. A., Fogg, L. F., Akiskal, H., & Maser, J. (1996). Stable trait components of hopelessness: Baseline and sensitivity to depression. *Journal of Abnormal Psychology, 105,* 155–165.

Young, M. A., Scheftner, W. A., Klerman, G. L., Andreasen, N. C., & Hirschfeld, R. M. A. (1986). The endogenous sub-type of depression: A study of its internal construct validity. *British Journal of Psychiatry, 148,* 257–267.

Zahn-Waxler, C., Cummings, E. M., Iannotti, R. J., & Radke-Yarrow, M. (1984). Young children of depressed parents: A population at risk for affective problems. In D. Cicchetti (Ed.), *Childhood depression.* (New directions for child development, no. 26, pp 81–105). San Francisco: Jossey-Bass.

Zahn-Waxler, C., McKnew, D., Cummings, E. M., Davenport, Y. B., & Radke-Yarrow, M. (1984). Problem behaviors in peer interaction of young children with manic-depressive parent. *American Journal of Psychiatry, 141,* 236–240.

Zhang, M., Rost, K. M., & Fortney, J. C. (in press). Earnings changes for depressed individual treated by mental health specialists. *American Journal of Psychiatry.*

Zhang, M., Rost, K. M., Fortney, J. C., Smith, J., & Smith, G. R., Jr. (1998) Earnings changes for depressed individuals treated by mental health specialists. *American Journal of Psychiatry, 155,* 883–888.

Zimmerman, M., Coryell, W., & Corenthal, C. (1984). Attribution style, the dexamethasone suppression test, and the diagnosis of melancholia in depressed inpatients. *Journal of Abnormal Psychology, 93,* 373–377.

Zlotnick, C., Shea, M. T., Pilkonis, P., Elkin, I., & Ryan, C. (1996). Gender dysfunctional attitudes, social support, life events, and depressive symptoms over naturalistic follow-up. *American Journal of Psychiatry, 153,* 1021–1027.

Zuckerman, D. M., Prusoff, B. A., & Weissman, M. M. (1980). Personality as a predictor of psychotherapy and pharmacotherapy outcome for depressed outpatients. *Journal of Consulting and Clinical Psychology, 48,* 730–735.

Zung, W. W. (1971). A rating instrument for anxiety disorders. *Psychosomatics, 12,* 371–379.

Zung, W. W. (1974). Measurement of affects: Depression and anxiety. In P. Pichot & R. Olivier-Martin (Eds.), *Psychological measurements in psychopharmacology* (pp 267–289). Basel, Switzerland: S. Karger.

Zweig, R. A., & Hinrichsen, G. A. (1993). Factors associated with suicide attempts by depressed older adults: A prospective study. *American Journal of Psychiatry, 150,* 1687–1692.

Index